KEY WEAPONS
OF THE WORLD

W9-AOX-282

KEY WEAPONS
OF THE WORLD

Tanks, Small Arms, Aircraft & Warships from 1860 to the Present

GENERAL EDITOR: CHRIS McNAB

amber
BOOKS

First published in 2019

Copyright © Amber Books Ltd 2019

All rights reserved. With the exception of quoting brief passages for the purpose of review no part of this publication may be reproduced without prior written permission from the publisher. The information in this book is true and complete to the best of our knowledge. All recommendations are made without any guarantee on the part of the authoror publisher, who also disclaim any liability incurred in connection with the use of this data or specific details.

Published by
Amber Books Ltd
United House
North Road
London N7 NDP
United Kingdom
www.amberbooks.co.uk
Instagram: www.instagram.com/amberbooksltd
Facebook: www.facebook.com/amberbooks
Twitter: @amberbooks

Editor: Michael Spilling
Designer: Brian Rust
Picture researcher: Terry Forshaw

ISBN 978-1-78274-760-4

Printed in China

4 6 8 10 9 7 5 3 2

Contents

Introduction	8	M48 Patton (1952)	57	BMP-3 (1990)	104
		PT-76 (1952)	58	Type 89 (1991)	105
TANKS and AFVs	10	M60 Patton (1960)	59	IAV Stryker (2002)	106
		T-62 (1961)	60	BTR-90 (2004)	107
Tanks		Chieftain Mk 5 (1963)	61	BVS 10 Viking (2005)	108
Mark V Male (1917)	12	Leopard 1 (1965)	62	FV430 Bulldog Mk 3 (2006)	109
Whippet (1917)	13	M551 Sheridan (1967)	63		
Renault FT-17 (1917)	14	Stridsvagn 103B (1967)	64	**ARTILLERY and MORTARS**	110
Sturmpanzerwagen A7V (1918)	15	T-72 (1971)	65		
Vickers 6-ton Light Tank (1932)	16	Merkava (1977)	66	**Field and Heavy Artillery**	
BT-5 (1932)	17	Leopard 2 (1979)	67	Canone de 75 Mle (1897)	112
Type 95 Kyugo Light Tank (1934)	18	Challenger 1 (1982)	68	Ordnance QF 13pdr (1904)	113
T-35 (1935)	19	M1A1 Abrams (1985)	69	Ordnance BL 60pdr (1905)	114
Panzer II Ausf F (1936)	20	Stingray (1989)	70	7.7cm FK 96 n.A. (1905)	115
Somua S-35 (1936)	21	AMX-56 Leclerc (1991)	71	Ordnance QF 4.5in Howitzer (1908)	116
Char B1 bis (1937)	22	T-90 (1992)	72	Skoda 30.5cm Howitzer (1911)	117
Type 97 Chi-Ha (1938)	23	M1A2 Abrams (1996)	73	Canon de 105mm mle Schneider (1913)	118
Panzer 38(t) (1938)	24	Type 99 (1998)	74	'Big Bertha' (1914)	119
Mk III Valentine Infantry Tank (1939)	25	Challenger 2 (1998)	75	Paris Gun (1918)	120
Panzer III Ausf F (1940)	26	Arjun Mk 2 (2014)	76	10.5cm leFH 18 Light Field Howitzer	
Sturmgeschütz III (1940)	27	K2 Black Panther (2014)	77	(1927)	121
KV-1A Heavy Tank (1940)	28	T-14 Armata (2015)	78	15cm sIG 33 Heavy Infantry Gun (1927)	122
Panzer IV Ausf F1 (1941)	29			15cm sFH 18 Medium Field Howitzer	
Mk VI Crusader I Cruiser Tank (1941)	30	**Armoured Personnel Carriers and**		(1934)	123
Churchill Mk IV (1941)	31	**Infantry Fighting Vehicles**		Katyusha Rocket Launcher (1939)	124
M3A3 Stuart (1941)	32	Autoblinde Peugeot (1914)	79	122mm Howitzer M1938 (M-30) (1939)	125
M3A3 General Lee (1941)	33	Panhard et Levassor Type 178 (1937)	80	Ordnance QF 25 pdr Mk 2 (1940)	126
T-70 (1942)	34	SdKfz 232 (1938)	81	Wurfgranate 41 (1941)	127
T-34/76 Model 1943 (1942)	35	SdKfz 251 (1939)	82	105mm Howitzer M2A1 (1941)	128
Panzer VI Tiger Ausf E (1942)	36	SdKfz 234/2 (1943)	83	152mm Howitzer M1943 (D-1) (1943)	129
M4A4 Sherman (1942)	37	AEC Mk III Armoured Car (1943)	84	105mm Howitzer M3 (1945)	130
Semovente DA 75/18 (1942)	38	LVT-4 'Water Buffalo' (1943)	85	OTO-Melara 105mm Mod 56 (1956)	131
Panzer V Panther Ausf D (1943)	39	T17E1 Staghound I (1944)	86	BM-21 Rocket Launcher (1963)	132
KV-85 Heavy Tank (1943)	40	Panhard EBR/FL-11 (1951)	87	122mm Howitzer D-30 (1963)	133
M26 Pershing (1943)	41	M50 Ontos (1955)	88	M109 Howitzer (1963)	134
Churchill AVRE (1943)	42	FV601 Saladin (1958)	89	Soltam M68 (1968)	135
Churchill Crocodile (1943)	43	M113 (1960)	90	2S3 (1971)	136
Sturmmörser Tiger (1943)	44	BTR-60PA (1963)	91	FH-70 155mm Howitzer (1974)	137
Sherman Crab Mine-Clearing Tank (1944)	45	BMP-1 (1965)	92	L118 105mm Light Gun (1976)	138
Sherman VC Firefly (1944)	46	Scimitar (1970)	93	M198 155mm Howitzer (1978)	139
Cromwell Mk VIII (1944)	47	Marder (1971)	94	M270 MLRS (1983)	140
Tiger II 'King Tiger' (1944)	48	AAV-7 (1972)	95	2S19 Msta (1989)	141
Jagdpanzer VI Jagdtiger (1944)	49	Ratel (1976)	96	M777 155mm Howitzer (2005)	142
M24 Chaffee (1944)	50	BTR-70 (1976)	97		
T-34/85 (1944)	51	M2 Bradley (1981)	98	**Anti-Aircraft Artillery**	
IS-3 (1945)	52	LAV-25 (1983)	99	40mm Bofors L/60 (1929)	143
Centurion (1945)	53	Pandur (1986)	100	8.8cm Flak 18 (1933)	144
T-54/55 (1947)	54	BTR-80 (1986)	101	3.7in QF Gun Mk 1 (1937)	145
M41 Walker Bulldog (1951)	55	Warrior (1987)	102	3.7cm Flak 36 (1937)	146
AMX-13 (1952)	56	B1 Centauro (1988)	103	2cm Flak 38 L/65 (1939)	147

Oerlikon 20mm (1939)	148
90mm Gun M2 (1940)	149
M163 Vulcan Air Defense System (1961)	150
ZSU-23-4 (1962)	151
Flakpanzer Gepard (1970)	152

Anti-Armour Guns

5cm Pak 38 L/60 (1940)	153
7.5cm Pak 40 L/46 (1940)	154
3in Gun M5 (1940)	155
Ordnance QF 17pdr Gun (1942)	156
76.2mm Divisional Gun 1942 (ZiS-3) (1943)	157

Mortars

Ordnance ML 3in Mortar (1932)	158
sGrW 34 8cm Mortar (1934)	159
M1938 120mm Mortar (1938)	160
60mm Mortar M2 (1941)	161
M120 Mortar System (1991)	162
M224A1 Mortar (2011)	163

AIRCRAFT, HELICOPTERS and DRONES — **164**

Fighters

Fokker E series (1915)	166
Sopwith Camel (1916)	167
Nieuport 17 (1916)	168
S.E.5a (1916)	169
Fokker Dr.1 (1917)	170
SPAD XIII (1917)	171
Polikarpov I-16 (1933)	172
Messerschmitt Bf 109 (1935)	173
Hawker Hurricane (1935)	174
Mitsubishi A5M 'Claude' (1936)	175
Supermarine Spitfire (1936)	176
Lockheed P-38 Lightning (1939)	177
Mitsubishi A6M Zero (1939)	178
Focke-Wulf Fw 190 (1939)	179
North American P-51 Mustang (1940)	180
Yakovlev Yak-1/3/7/9 (1940)	181
Vought F4U Corsair (1940)	182
Republic P-47 Thunderbolt (1941)	183
Grumman F6F Hellcat (1942)	184
Messerschmitt Me 262 (1942)	185
Northrop P-61 Black Widow (1942)	186
Lockheed F-80 Shooting Star (1944)	187
Mikoyan-Gurevich MiG 15 (1947)	188
North American F-86 Sabre (1949)	189
Mikoyan-Gurevich MiG-17 (1950)	190
Dassault Mirage III (1956)	191
McDonnell Douglas F-4 Phantom II (1958)	192
Mikoyan-Gurevich MiG-21 (1959)	193

Grumman F-14 Tomcat (1970)	194
Lockheed Martin F-16 Fighting Falcon (1974)	195
Panavia Tornado (1974)	196
Sukhoi Su-27 'Flanker' (1977)	197
Mikoyan MiG-29 'Fulcrum' (1977)	198
Dassault Mirage 2000 (1978)	199
McDonnell Douglas F/A-18 Hornet (1978)	200
Boeing F-15E Strike Eagle (1986)	201
Dassault Rafale (1986)	202
Lockheed Martin F-22 Raptor (1990)	203
Eurofighter Typhoon (1994)	204
Lockheed Martin F-35 Lightning II (2006)	205

Ground-Attack Aircraft

Breguet XIX (1922)	206
Junkers Ju 87 Stuka (1935)	207
Junkers Ju 88 (1936)	208
Messerschmitt Bf 110 (1936)	209
Ilyushin Il-2 Shturmovik (1939)	210
De Havilland Mosquito (1940)	211
SBD-3 Dauntless (1940)	212
Hawker Typhoon (1941)	213
General Dynamics F-111 (1964)	214
Fairchild A-10 Thunderbolt II (1972)	215
AV-8B Harrier II (1978)	216
Lockheed F-117 Nighthawk (1981)	217

Bombers

Gotha bombers (1917)	218
Boeing B-17 Flying Fortress (1935)	219
North American B-25 Mitchell (1939)	220
B-24 Liberator (1939)	221
Handley Page Halifax (1940)	222
Avro Lancaster (1941)	223
Boeing B-29 Superfortress (1944)	224
English Electric Canberra (1949)	225
Boeing B-52 Stratofortress (1952)	226
Avro Vulcan (1952)	227
Tupolev TU-95 (1952)	228
Tupolev Tu-22M (1969)	229
Northrop B-2 Spirit (1989)	230

Logistic and Specialist

Douglas C-47 Skytrain (1935)	231
Consolidated PBY Catalina (1935)	232
Lockheed C-130 Hercules (1954)	233
Lockheed SR-71 'Blackbird' (1962)	234
Lockheed C-5 Galaxy (1968)	235
E-3 Sentry (1976)	236

Helicopters

UH-1 Iroquois (1956)	237
MiL Mi-24 'Hind' (1969)	238

Lynx (1971)	239
AH-64 Apache (1975)	240
UH-60A Black Hawk (1979)	241

Unmanned Aerial Vehicles

MQ-1 Predator (1994)	242
RQ-4 Global Hawk (1998)	243
MQ-9 Reaper (2001)	244
MQ-8B Fire Scout (2009)	245

WARSHIPS — **246**

Submarines

CSS Hunley (1863)	248
Intelligent Whale (1866)	249
Gustav Zede (1893)	250
USS Holland (1897)	251
B-Class (1904)	252
U-9 (1910)	253
HMS E-11 (1914)	254
Deutschland (1916)	255
UC-25 (1916)	256
Surcouf (1929)	257
USS Nautilus (V-6) (1930)	258
U-47 (Type VIIB) (1938)	259
U-459 (Type XIV) (1941)	260
Type XXI (1943)	261
I-400 (1943)	262
USS Tench (1944)	263
USS Nautilus (1954)	264
Sturgeon Class (1966)	265
HMS Resolution (1966)	266
USS Los Angeles (1974)	267
Project 705 Lira (Alfa Class) (1977)	268
USS Ohio (1979)	269
Le Triomphant (1994)	270
Kursk (1994)	271
USS Seawolf (1995)	272
Type 039 (Song) (1999)	273
USS Virginia (2003)	274
Astute Class (2007)	275
Type 094 (Jin Class) (2007)	276
Soryu (2009)	277
INS Arihant (2015)	278

Aircraft Carriers

HMS Furious (1917)	279
HMS Eagle (1924)	280
Akagi (1927)	281
USS Lexington (CV-2) (1927)	282
Hiryu (1937)	283
USS Yorktown (CV-5) (1937)	284
USS Enterprise (CV-6) (1938)	285
HMS Ark Royal (1938)	286
USS Lexington (CV-16) (1938)	287

Jun'yo (1942)	288	Sovremennyy Class (1980)	341	SA80 (1985)	391
USS *Intrepid* (1943)	289	Ticonderoga Class (1983)	342	Barrett M82A1 (1989)	392
Shinano (1944)	290	Type 23 Frigate (1987)	343	M4 Carbine (1994)	393
USS *Midway* (1945)	291	Arleigh Burke Destroyer (1991)	344	Heckler & Koch G36 (1995)	394
HMS *Eagle* (1951)	292	*Visby* (2002)	345	OICW/XM29 (1996)	395
USS *Forrestal* (1955)	293	Type 45 Destroyer (2009)	346	AK-101 & AK-103 (2001)	396
HMS *Hermes*/INS *Viraat* (1959)	294	DDX (Zumwalt Class) (2016)	347	QBZ-03 (2003)	397
Clemenceau (1960)	295			M27 IAR (2008)	398
USS *Enterprise* (CVN-65) (1961)	296	**SMALL ARMS**	**348**	M110 Semi-Automatic Sniper System	
HMS *Fearless* (1965)	297			(2008)	399
Moskva (1967)	298	**Handguns**		FN SCAR (2009)	400
USS *Nimitz* (1975)	299	Adams Revolver (c. 1851)		AK-12 (2011)	401
Kiev (1975)	300	Colt M1851 Navy & M1860 Army	350		
USS *Tarawa* (1976)	301	(1851/1860)	351	**Submachine Guns and Personal**	
HMS *Invincible* (1980)	302	Borchardt C/93 (1893)	352	**Defence Weapons**	
Admiral Kuznetsov (1995)	303	Mauser C/96 (1896)	353	Bergmann MP 18 (1918)	402
HMS *Ocean* (1998)	304	Pistole Parabellum P-08 (1908)	354	Thompson M1928 (1928)	403
Charles de Gaulle (2001)	305	Colt M1911 (1911)	355	MP 38/MP 40 (1938)	404
USS *Ronald R. Reagan* (2003)	306	Webley Mk V & Mk VI (1913 & 1915)	356	MAS 38 (1939)	405
Liaoning (2012)	307	Colt Detective Special (1927)	357	Sten Mk 2 (1941)	406
HMAS *Canberra* (2014)	308	Browning GP35 HP (1935)	358	PPSh-41 (1941)	407
Izumo (2015)	309	Walther P38 (1938)	359	Austen (1942)	408
HMS *Queen Elizabeth* (2017)	310	Beretta 92 & 93R (1976)	360	M3A1 'Grease Gun' (1942)	409
USS *Gerald R. Ford* (2017)	311	IMI Desert Eagle (1979)	361	Sterling L2A1 (1953)	410
INS *Vikrant* (2018)	312	Glock 17 (1982)	362	Uzi (1954)	411
		SiG P320 (2014)	363	Heckler & Koch MP5 (1966)	412
Surface Warships				FN P90 (1980)	413
USS *Monadnock* (1864)	313	**Rifles**		BXP (1984)	414
HMS *Devastation* (1873)	314	Dreyse Needle Gun (1841)	364	Calico M950 (1990)	415
Imperator Alexander II (1891)	315	Chassepot Carbine (1866)	365		
USS *Maine* (1895)	316	Martini-Henry (1871)	366	**Machine Guns**	
Mikasa (1902)	317	Mosin-Nagant M1891/30 (1891/1930)	367	Gatling Gun (1878)	416
HMS *Dreadnought* (1906)	318	SMLE (1903)	368	Madsen Light Machine Gun	417
Vittorio Emanuele (1908)	319	M1903 Springfield (1903)	369	Maxim Gun/MG 08 (1908)	418
HMS *Indomitable* (1908)	320	Kar 98k (1935)	370	Lewis Gun (1911)	419
USS *South Carolina* (1910)	321	M1 Garand (1936)	371	Vickers Machine Gun (1912)	420
USS *Utah* (1911)	322	M1 Carbine (1942)	372	Hotchkiss Modèle 1914 (1914)	421
Derfflinger (1913)	323	FG 42 (1942)	373	BAR (1918)	422
HMS *Royal Oak* (1914)	324	MP44/StG44 (1943)	374	M1919 Browning (1919)	423
USS *Texas* (1914)	325	AK-47/AKM (1949)	375	M2 Browning .50-cal (1933)	424
Fuso (1915)	326	EM2 (1951)	376	MG 34 (1934)	425
HMS *Hood* (1920)	327	FN FAL/L1A1 SLR (1954)	377	Bren Gun (1938)	426
HMS *Rodney* (1927)	328	CETME Model 58 (1957)	378	MG 42 (1942)	427
Deutschland/*Lützow* (1933)	329	M14 (1959)	379	RPD (1953)	428
De Ruyter (1936)	330	Heckler & Koch G3 (1959)	380	M60 (1957)	429
Scharnhorst (1939)	331	M16 (1963)	381	FN MAG (1958)	430
Richelieu (1940)	332	SVD Dragunov (1963)	382	RPK (1961)	431
Bismarck (1940)	333	M21 (1969)	383	PK (1961)	432
Vittorio Veneto (1940)	334	Galil (1973)	384	FN Minimi/M249 SAW (1974)	433
Yamato (1941)	335	AK-74 (1974)	385	CETME Ameli (1982)	434
Tirpitz (1941)	336	Steyr AUG (1977)	386	L86 Light Support Weapon (1985)	435
USS *Indiana* (1942)	337	FAMAS (1978)	387		
USS *Iowa* (1943)	338	Vektor R4 (1980)	388	**Glossary**	**436**
Kirov Class (1977)	339	M16A2 (1982)	389	**Index**	**438**
Type 22 (1979)	340	PSG-1 (1985)	390	**Picture Credits**	**448**

Introduction

The pace of change in weapons development over the past 150 years has been nothing short of revolutionary. Above all, technology has been the key driver, creating ever more sophisticated and lethal types of weapon systems, from small arms through to aircraft carriers.

ABOVE:
The Panzer IV was the workhorse of German and Axis forces during World War II, serving on every front in large numbers. More than 8000 were built of all variants.

By 1900, many landmarks in weapon design had already been reached. In small arms, the nineteenth century saw the demise of the muzzle-loader, replaced by breech-loading multi-shot cartridge firearms. Artillery went through a similar breechloading journey: developments in breech and shell technology, and in fire control, had dramatically increased range, accuracy and explosive power, giving artillery the status as the battlefield's biggest killer. Naval history had been reshaped by the switch from sail to steam, and from wooden hulls to steel, these heavy and fast warships now fitted with turreted firepower. Yet alongside change there was also a persistent traditionalism. The decisive tools in war remained the field artillery piece, the bolt-action rifle and the naval gun.

TRANSFORMATION

If we were to define the true historical moments of transition between the ways of nineteenth-century warfare and the technology-dominated present, we must surely look to the world wars (1914–18 and 1939–45). At the level of weaponry alone, World War I saw numerous inventions or refinements, including the near-perfection of the bolt-action rifle and the machine gun (light, medium and heavy types), the introduction of the submachine gun and more effective artillery (guns, shells and fire control). Yet we can point to three genuine revolutions, ones that changed the face of warfare forever: the birth and ascent of combat aircraft; the emergence of strategic submarine warfare; and the militarization of the internal combustion engine, in the form of trucks, armoured cars and history's first tanks.

The 1920s, 1930s and the years of World War II took the innovations of World War I and either magnified them exponentially with industrial rapidity, or added to them with futuristic new weapons, allied to great strides forward in electronic communications and surveillance technologies. Explaining those achievements would take a book in itself. They include the true rise of airpower – high-performance monoplane fighters and bombers becoming central to both strategic and tactical warfare – aircraft carriers, turreted main battle tanks, multiple-launch rocket systems, early guided and ballistic missiles, more lethal oceanic submarines (and the weapons designed to destroy them) and the first atomic weapons. The latter above all, despite having been used in anger only twice in history, not only altered the conditions of warfare, but also the nature of international politics forever.

COMPUTER AGE

Although World War II saw ground-breaking leaps in long-range weaponry, much of the conflict remained a direct-fire business. The post-war era also relied on direct-fire technologies, but increasing computerization of the battlefield from the 1960s onwards brought weaponry into the space age. Guided missiles of every size, range and purpose became primary instruments of destruction. Powerplants were revolutionized; jet aircraft, nuclear-powered naval vessels and gas-turbine tanks now have capabilities of speed, power and endurance that would have been the stuff of fantasy in 1939. Even the humble infantryman possesses weapon systems capable of destroying the fastest jets and most potent armour.

This book collects some of the most important weapons in this 100-plus-year evolution, illustrating how far we have come in perfecting lethality.

LEFT:
An AH-64D Apache Longbow from the US 3rd Armored Cavalry Regiment hovers on the flight line at Forward Operating Base Sykes, Nineveh Province, Iraq, before a flight mission.

BELOW:
Two F-15C Eagle fighters and an F-16C Falcon fly in formation over the Gulf of Mexico after routine training missions while deployed to Tyndall Air Force Base, Florida.

Tanks and AFVs

The design and development of armoured vehicles has historically been the attempt to strike a balance between three factors: weight of armour, mobility and firepower. It is possible to prioritize one, or perhaps two, of these factors, but rarely all three. For example, the more armour protection you add, the heavier the vehicle becomes, reducing its speed and manoeuvrability. Conversely, reduce the armour and focus on speed, then the less protection the crew has from heavy weaponry. Nevertheless, since the first crude experiments in tanks and armoured cars during World War I, heavy armoured vehicles are still one of the decisive battlefield instruments, albeit one under an ever-more sophisticated range of missile threats.

AUSTRALIAN LEOPARD
A German-designed Leopard AS1 tank from the 1st Armored Regiment participates in a simulated battle during the Talisman Saber 2005 exercise at the Shoalwater Bay Training Area, Queensland, Australia.

Mark V Male (1917)

SPECIFICATIONS

DIMENSIONS:	Length: 8.5m (27ft); Width: 4.11m (13ft 6in); Height: 2.64m (8ft 7in)
WEIGHT:	29.5 tonnes (29 tons)
ENGINE:	1 x Ricardo six-cylinder petrol engine delivering 110kW (150hp)
SPEED:	7.4km/h (5mph)
ARMAMENT:	Main: 2 x 6pdr (57mm/2.34in) QF guns; Secondary: 4 x Hotchkiss 7.7mm (0.303in) machine guns
ARMOUR:	6–14mm (0.24–0.55in)
RANGE:	72km (45 miles)
CREW:	8

Entering production in late 1917, the British Mark V Male tank was a significant improvement over prior models, particularly the Mark I that had made history at the Somme in 1916. The service life of the Mark V Male spanned the inter-war years.

Right: The rear view of the Mark V Male tank reveals the extended sponsons for the 6pdr guns, the characteristic all-around tracks of British tanks and the innovative unditching beam that assisted with movement through difficult terrain.

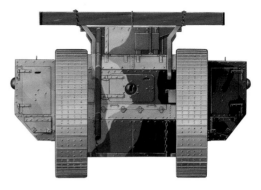

6PDR GUNS
Although their traverse was limited, the pair of 6pdr sponson-mounted guns of the British Mark V Male tank provided formidable firepower, while the improved hull design facilitated movement across the uneven terrain of the battlefield. The enhanced mobility fostered cooperation between armour and infantry formations.

DRIVER COMPARTMENT
The Mark V was the world's first tank that required only a single driver. The Wilson epicyclic gearbox eliminated the need for the second. A machine-gunner was seated on the driver's right in the forward section of the tank.

UNDITCHING BEAM
Similar to a railway sleeper, an unditching beam was carried at the rear of the Mark V, secured to the superstructure with chains. The beam assisted with extricating the tank from muddy terrain.

ARMOUR
The armour protection of the Mark V tank varied from 6–14mm (0.24–0.55in) and was adequate against small-arms fire. However, the tank remained vulnerable to German artillery and mortar rounds.

ENGINE
The lone Ricardo petrol engine of the Mark V generated 110kW (150hp) and delivered greater speed than the older Mark IV. It was the first purpose-built powerplant installed in a tank.

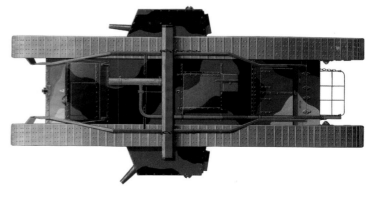

TOP VIEW
This top view of the Mk V shows the 6pdr sponsons to good effect. Like the other British tanks of similar layout, the Mk V had 'male' and 'female' versions, the latter armed purely with machine guns.

Whippet (1917)

SPECIFICATIONS

DIMENSIONS:	Length: 6.1m (20ft), Width: 2.62m (8ft 7in); Height: 2.74m (9ft)
WEIGHT:	12.7 tonnes (14 tons)
ENGINE:	Two Tylor JB4 petrol engines
SPEED:	12.9km/h (8mph)
ARMAMENT:	4 x Hotchkiss 7.7mm (0.3in) machine guns
ARMOUR:	14mm (0.55in)
RANGE:	129km (80 miles)
CREW:	3

Designed at a time when tanks were for the most part lumbering monstrosities, the Medium A – or Whippet – was built instead for speed and mobility. It carried only machine guns but was capable of penetrating a defensive line and causing mayhem in the enemy's rear area, pioneering the concept of armoured exploitation.

Right: The Whippet's exhaust was positioned in front of the crew compartment, resulting in fumes sometimes being vented back into the crew space.

DOCTRINAL ADVANCE

The Whippet's major contribution to warfare was in the field of armoured doctrine. The idea of tanks bursting through the enemy line and going on to destroy supply and command centres in an 'expanding torrent' was shown as workable in 1918, although it was not until World War II that it became a reality. In the meantime, Whippets were sent to Russia, where experiments took place with a 37mm (1.4in) gun. The Whippet also served in Ireland, and a very small number were exported to Japan.

CREW
The Whippet had a crew of three, all concentrated in the fighting compartment at the rear of the tank.

MEDIUM MK A WHIPPET
The Whippet mounted four Hotchkiss machine guns, one on each side of its blocky fixed superstructure. Only one gunner was carried, but the commander could also man a gun.

DRIVER
The Whippet was the first tank that could be driven by one man.

A321

JAPANESE WHIPPETS
Japanese Army Whippet tanks halt during a road march. Although primitive, the Whippet demonstrated that tanks could do more than break a defensive line. Armoured exploitation restored mobility to a battlefield previously dominated by trenches and artillery.

FT-17 (1917)

SPECIFICATIONS

DIMENSIONS:	Length: 5m (16ft 5in); Width: 1.71m (5ft 7.33in); Height: 2.13m (7ft)
WEIGHT:	6 tonnes (6.7 tons)
ENGINE:	Renault 4-cylinder petrol engine
SPEED:	7.7km/h (4.8mph)
ARMAMENT:	37mm (1.4in) gun or Hotchkiss 8mm (0.31in) machine gun
ARMOUR:	8–22 mm (0.31–0.87in)
RANGE:	60km (37 miles)
CREW:	2

PATTON IN THE FT-17
In World War I, General George S. Patton commanded a force of FT-17s that were supplied by the French as an interim measure until American-made M1917 tanks (which were a licence-built version of the FT-17) became available. The US M1917 did not become available before the war's end, but saw service in the inter-war years. As late as 1940, ex-US M1917s were used as training vehicles by the Canadian army, and many were in service around the world. France still had large numbers, some stationed in the colonies. FT-17s saw action in defence of France, Belgium, Yugoslavia and Greece.

The French FT-17 was a highly successful design, remaining in service from 1917 until the end of World War II. It influenced both US and Russian tank design, and was exported to several nations including Finland, Japan and Brazil. It was designed from the outset to be fielded in massed formations.

Above: The FT-17 entered service at a time when camouflage was in its infancy. Nevertheless, measures were taken to conceal tanks from enemy view where possible.

MAIN GUN
The FT-17 carried a single weapon, either a machine gun or a 37mm (1.4in) gun.

ARMOUR
Although relatively light, the FT-17 was armoured against machine-gun and small-arms fire.

'TAIL'
The 'tail' effectively lengthened the hull to enable the tank to cross wide trenches.

AMERICAN TRANSPORT
American soldiers ride on the back of FT-17 tanks. The FT-17 was provided to the US tank forces as an interim measure until the US-built version was available.

Sturmpanzerwagen A7V (1918)

SPECIFICATIONS

DIMENSIONS:	Length: 8m (26ft 3in) Width: 3.2m (10ft 6in) Overall Height: 3.5m (11ft 6in)
WEIGHT:	32.5 tonnes (31.9 tons)
ENGINE:	2 x Daimler-Benz 4-cylinder inline 165204 petrol engines each developing 74.6kW (100hp) @ 1800rpm
SPEED:	8km/h (5mph)
ARMAMENT:	Main: 1 x 57mm (2.24in) L/12 Maxim-Nordenfelt short recoil gun with 500 rounds Secondary: 6+ x 7.92mm (0.31in) MG08/15 machine guns in flexible mounts with 18,000 rounds
ARMOUR:	20–30mm (0.78–1.1in)
RANGE:	Road: 80km (50 miles) Cross-country: 30km (18 miles)
CREW:	18

LIMITED NUMBERS

Only 20 of the A7V are known to have been deployed prior to the end of World War I. Coupled with its operational shortcomings, its feeble numbers made the tank an inadequate response to British production that reached more than 7700. Although several improved German tank designs were in development by late 1918, none were fielded before the Armistice.

When British tanks reached the World War I battlefields in 1916, Germany rushed to keep pace with the technology that threatened the deadlock of trench warfare. The A7V, however, did not deploy until 1918 and then only in small numbers.

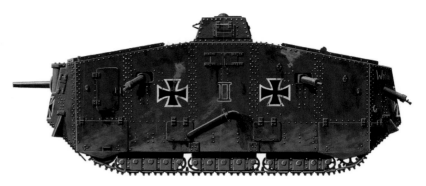

Above: Although the multiple machine guns and single heavy gun mounted aboard the German A7V tank were deadly to enemy infantry, the vehicle was an unstable platform for accurate gunnery and its high silhouette attracted hostile artillery fire.

ARMAMENT
The main weapon aboard the A7V was a single 57mm (2.24in) L/12 Maxim-Nordenfelt short-recoil gun. The tank carried 500 rounds of 57mm ammunition, stored inside the crew compartment.

COMMAND
The commander and two drivers were housed in a raised compartment centred on the vehicle and increasing its overall height to 3.5m (11ft 6in).

ARMOUR
The thick armour of the A7V, 20–30mm (0.78–1.1in), protected the 18 crewmembers, but added considerably to the ponderous weight of the tank and impeded its progress across the battlefields of the Western Front.

ENGINE
A pair of Daimler-Benz four-cylinder inline petrol engines were mounted in the centre of the A7V and each was capable of producing 74.6kW (100hp) at 1800rpm.

RUSHED DESIGN
Smoke and dust billow around this German A7V tank engaged near an abandoned farmhouse somewhere in France during the final major German offensive of World War I. The A7V was hurriedly designed and produced and only 20 were actually to become operational from the spring of 1918 to the Armistice in November of that year.

Vickers 6-ton Light Tank (1932)

SPECIFICATIONS

DIMENSIONS:	Length: 4.57m (15ft); Width: 2.42m (7ft 11in); Height: 2.08m (6ft 10in)
WEIGHT:	6.3 tonnes (7 tons)
ENGINE:	Armstrong-Siddeley 4-cylinder petrol engine
SPEED:	Speed: 32km/h (20mph)
ARMAMENT:	Type A: 2 x 7.7mm (0.3in) machine guns, Type B: 47mm (1.8in) gun with co-axial 7.7mm (0.303in) machine gun
ARMOUR:	19–25mm (0.75 –0.98 in)
RANGE:	160km (99 miles)
CREW:	3

The Vickers 6-ton light tanks was produced in two versions, defined by the armament. The Type A variant had two .303in Vickers machine guns, each fitted in an individual turret, while the Type B featured a single 47mm (1.8in) gun.

Right: Vickers 6-ton tanks of the Type A design. The twin turret configuration was inefficient but reasonably effective in an infantry support role.

ARMOUR
The armour of the Vickers 6-ton was 19–25mm (0.75–0.98in), sufficient to small-arms fire and shell fragments.

MACHINE GUN
The Vickers Type A was fitted with two individual turrets, each mounting a Vickers-brand 7.7mm (0.3in) machine gun.

OUTMATCHED

Based on the Vickers 6-ton, the T-26 was produced in vast numbers and was the main Russian tank at the time of the German invasion in 1941. By then it was outmatched by heavier and better-protected tanks, and suffered enormous losses. Similarly, the Polish 7TP was outmatched against German tanks, but still gave a good account of itself. Many were lost for lack of fuel rather than to enemy action.

POLISH 7TP LIGHT TANK
Based on the Vickers Mk E, the 7TP was fitted with a Saurer diesel engine and thicker armour. It was armed with two 7.92mm (0.3in) machine guns.

BT-5 (1932)

SPECIFICATIONS

DIMENSIONS:	Length: 5.58m (18ft 4in); Width: 2.23m (7ft 4in); Height: 2.25m (7ft 5in)
WEIGHT:	11.5 tonnes (11.3 tons)
ENGINE:	1 x Model M5 12-cylinder petrol powerplant based on the American Liberty aircraft engine delivering 298kW (400hp)
SPEED:	72km/h (45mph)
ARMAMENT:	Primary: 1 x 45mm (1.8in) Model 32 gun; Secondary: 1 x 7.62mm (0.3in) DT machine gun
ARMOUR:	6–13mm (0.24–0.51in)
RANGE:	Road: 200km (120 miles); off-road: 90km (56 miles)
CREW:	3

An upgunned transitional variant of the Soviet BT series of light or cavalry tanks, the BT-5 entered production in late 1932. It proved superior to the contemporary tanks of other world powers through to the end of the decade.

Right: A variant of the original light tank design, the BT-7A mounted a 76.2mm (3in) howitzer. Only a relative few of these were adapted for field service. Note the coaxial machine gun atop the turret, which includes a prominent bustle.

SLOPED ARMOUR
During the 1930s, the Soviets began developing tanks with sloped armour, maximizing the protection afforded with such designs. The BT-5 had a design influence over the later T-34 medium tank.

MAIN ARMAMENT
The main weapon on the BT-5 light tank was improved to a 45mm (1.8in) gun from the 37mm (1.45in) gun of the earlier BT-2. The weapon was heavier than those of most opposing light tanks.

TURRET
The BT-5 incorporated a major improvement in turret design compared to its predecessor, the BT-2. A larger, conical turret allowed easier movement along with better ammunition storage and visibility.

CHRISTIE SUSPENSION
The innovative Christie suspension allowed the BT-5 light tank to reach impressive road and cross-country speeds. J. Walter Christie was an American designer whose work had been rejected in the United States.

REMOVABLE TRACKS
An early version of the BT-5 light tank allowed crewmen to remove the tracks rapidly and operate the tank as a wheeled vehicle on improved roadways.

COMBAT RECORD

The most notable combat service of the BT-5 occurred during the series of Soviet–Japanese clashes at Nomonhan, or Khalkhin Gol as it was known in Russia, in 1939. During the Spanish Civil War of 1936–39, a battalion of BT-5s fought with Republican forces and fared well against the German and Italian tanks deployed by the Nationalists. The Chinese Nationalist Army fielded four BT-5s against the Japanese during the Second Sino-Japanese War and the Soviets used the BT-5 during the Winter War with Finland. With the outbreak of World War II, the BT-5 deployed during the Soviet offensive against Poland and in defence of the Motherland against the invading Nazis in 1941. Some BT-5s remained in service through to the end of the war.

BT-7 TANKS ON MANOUEVRES
BT-7 tanks on manoeuvre in the late 1930s. The BT-7 variant was introduced in 1935, with thicker armour and a new Mikulin M-17T engine, which was a licensed copy of a BMW engine.

Type 95 Kyugo Light Tank (1934)

SPECIFICATIONS

DIMENSIONS:	Length: 4.38m (14ft 4in); Width: 2.06m (6ft 9in); Height: 2.18m (7ft 2in)
WEIGHT:	7.4 tonnes (7.2 tons)
ENGINE:	1 x six-cylinder air-cooled Mitsubishi NVD 6120 diesel powerplant generating 89kW (120hp)
SPEED:	Road: 45km/h (28mph)
ARMAMENT:	Main: 1 x 37mm (1.45in) Type 98 gun Secondary: 2 x 7.7mm (0.303in) Type 97 machine guns
ARMOUR:	6–14mm (0.24–0.55in)
RANGE:	250km (156 miles)
CREW:	3

DISAPPOINTING DAYS

When the Kwantung Army clashed with the Soviets in Manchuria in 1939, the Type 95 achieved limited success. Yet it was soon discovered that the heavier 45mm (1.8in) main guns of the Red Army's BT-5 and BT-7 tanks were capable of destroying Japanese armour at a standoff range. In contrast, the Type 95's 37mm (1.45in) gun could penetrate the Soviet armour, but required closer combat. Frankly, the Type 95 was functionally obsolescent with the outbreak of World War II. Improved Soviet tanks, the American M3 Stuart light tank and M4 Sherman medium tank and the British Matilda each easily outclassed the Type 95.

When the Japanese Army called for a light or cavalry tank to support its infantry operations, the resulting Type 95 performed capably until confronted with the superior firepower and armour protection of Soviet, American and British tanks.

Right: This forward view of the Japanese Type 95 light tank shows the small size of the turret and its offset to the left, as well as the driver's view port to the lower right in the hull.

ARMOUR
The thin armour of the Type 95, only 6–14mm (0.24–0.55in) thick, offered little protection against the standard main weapons of opposing tanks. This weakness was discovered in battle against Soviet tanks in Manchuria and remained throughout World War II.

TURRET
Characteristic of Japanese tank designs of the 1930s, the Type 95 turret was irregularly shaped and quite cramped, requiring the commander to direct the crew in combat and operate the main 37mm (1.45in) gun.

MAIN ARMAMENT
The Type 95 light tank initially mounted the Type 94 37mm (1.45in) gun; its disappointing penetrating power resulted in a transition to the Type 98 37mm gun, which supplied greater muzzle velocity.

ENGINE
A six-cylinder air-cooled Mitsubishi NVD 6120 diesel engine powered the Type 95 light tank, producing 89kW (120hp). It was mounted at the rear of the hull.

SUSPENSION
The Type 95 employed a bell crank suspension with four rubber-edged road wheels on each side. The drive sprocket was at the front and the idler at the rear with two return rollers.

CHINA THEATRE
Japanese crewmen service a Type 95 light tank during a lull in the fighting somewhere in China. Introduced in 1936, the Type 95 was intended as an infantry support weapon and ultimately failed in confrontations with enemy armour and artillery.

T-35 (1935)

SPECIFICATIONS

DIMENSIONS:	Length: 9.72m (31ft 10in); Width: 3.2m (10ft 6in); Height: 3.43m (11ft 3in)
WEIGHT:	45 tonnes (42.2 tons)
ENGINE:	Mikulin M-17M V-12 petrol engine, genrating 500hp (370kW)
SPEED:	30km/h (18.64mph)
ARMAMENT:	1 x 76.2mm (3in) KT-28 gun Secondary: 2 x 45mm (1.8in) 20K guns; 5 or 6 x 7.62mm (0.3in) DT machine guns
ARMOUR:	11–30mm (0.43–1.2in)
RANGE:	150km (93.21 miles)
CREW:	11 or 12

The Soviet T-35 was the only tank with five turrets that reached deployment with the armed forces of any country. Its operational issues were numerous and the majority of the T-35's service life consisted of parade duties in Moscow.

Above: An overhead view of the Soviet T-35 heavy tank indicates a crowded configuration of five turrets. Although the T-35 presented a formidable façade, in truth the tank was lightly armed.

Above: The T-35's main forward-firing 76.2mm (3in) gun was insufficient for tank-versus-tank combat.

MAIN TURRET
The main turret of the T-35 heavy tank was identical to that of the T-28 medium tank, as was the 76.2mm (3in) main gun. Later production models included a main turret with armour protection increased to 25mm (0.98in).

ARMAMENT
The main weapon of the T-35 was a 76.2mm (3in) gun housed in the largest of five turrets (right). Two small turrets contained 45mm (1.8in) cannon and 7.62mm (0.3in) machine guns, while two still smaller ones mounted single 7.62mm (0.3in) machine guns.

ENGINE
The mammoth T-35 heavy tank was powered by a 12-cylinder petrol Mikulin M-17M engine generating 500hp (370kW). Critics assert that the tank was underpowered for its prodigious 45-tonne (42.2-ton) weight.

ARMOUR
Armour protection for the T-35 heavy tank generally varied from 11–30mm (0.43–1.2in) and changed at times during production. Typically, the thickest armour was to the vehicle's front.

IMPROVISED ARMOUR
Side skirts of 10mm (0.39in) plating were added to protect the T-35's tracks, wheels and coil-spring suspension from anti-tank fire. Destruction of any of these parts would result in what is known as a 'mobility kill', in which the tank's hull, turrets and armaments are intact but the vehicle is unable to move.

EXCESSIVE WEIGHT
At 45 tonnes (42.2 tons) in weight, the mammoth Soviet T-35 heavy tank was difficult to steer, while its five turrets and lengthy chassis presented inviting targets for enemy gunners.

Panzer II Ausf F (1936)

SPECIFICATIONS

DIMENSIONS:	Length: 4.64m (15ft 3in); Width: 2.30m (7ft 6.5in); Height: 2.02m (6ft 7.5in)
WEIGHT:	9.5 tonnes (9.3 tons)
ENGINE:	1 x Maybach six-cylinder petrol powerplant delivering 104kW (140hp)
SPEED:	55km/h (34mph)
ARMAMENT:	Main: 1 x 20mm (0.79in) KWK 30 cannon; Secondary: 1 x 7.92mm (0.31in) MG 34 machine gun
ARMOUR:	35mm (1.37in) front; 20mm (0.79in) side; 14.5mm (0.57in) rear; 5mm (0.19in) underside
RANGE:	200km (125 miles)
CREW:	3

Originally intended to bridge a gap in German tank design as heavier, more powerful machines were developed, the Panzerkampfwagen II became a mainstay of the German armoured force during campaigns in Poland and France.

Right: This frontal view of the PzKpfw II reveals the degree of the two-man turret's offset atop the chassis. The placement of the engine to the rear of the chassis afforded even distribution of weight throughout the tank.

MAIN ARMAMENT
The main armament of the PzKpfw II was a light 20mm (0.79in) cannon. Experiments with heavier weapons were abandoned and the tank performed more in a reconnaissance role as World War II progressed.

ARMOUR PROTECTION
The armour protection of the PzKpfw II was initially 11–30mm (0.43–1.2in) thick. Combat experience in the Spanish Civil War, however, and the heavy guns of Allied tanks prompted progressive increases in armour as later variants were developed.

ENGINE
The original powerplant of the PzKpfw II was a 130hp (97kW) petrol engine. When this was deemed inadequate it was replaced by a six-cylinder Maybach petrol engine generating 140hp (104kW).

COMBAT CHARACTER
During the opening months of World War II, the PzKpfw II delivered the ideal combination of speed and firepower to execute the rapid ground advance of the German Blitzkrieg. Although its main gun was lighter than those of opposing armoured forces, particularly the French Char B1-bis, Somua S-35 and Renault R35, which mounted 75mm (2.95in), 47mm (1.85in) and 37mm (1.45in) weapons respectively, the PzKpfw II was fast and quite manoeuvrable in a cross-country advance.

SUSPENSION
The D and E variants of the PzKpfw II utilized a torsion bar suspension. However, the Ausf F, the final production model of the series, was reconfigured with a leaf spring suspension.

FINDING COVER
Here a formation of PzKpfw II and Panzer 38(t) tanks advances cautiously through an open field and into a treeline during the opening weeks of World War II in Poland.

Somua S-35 (1936)

SPECIFICATIONS

DIMENSIONS:	Length: 5.38m (17ft 7.8in); Width: 2.12m (6ft 11.5in); Height: 2.62m (8ft 7in)
WEIGHT:	17.4 tonnes (19.2 tons)
ENGINE:	V8 petrol engine
SPEED:	40.7km/h (25.3mpH)
ARMAMENT:	Main gun: 47mm (1.8in) gun; Co-axial: 7.5mm (0.29in) machine gun
ARMOUR:	20–47mm (0.79–1.85in)
RANGE:	Road 230km (143 miles); off-road 130km (80 miles)
CREW:	3

The Somua S-35 was an advanced inter-war design. It was superior in many ways to the German Panzers, mounting a powerful gun by the standards of the time. It was not any deficiency in its design that prevented the Somua S-35 from achieving its potential – it was simply overtaken by events.

Right: The front view of the tank illustrates its very slender profile, although it had a relatively high silhouette.

FAST CAVALRY TANK

The Somua S-35, entering service in 1935, was a new departure for the French Army. Up until its introduction, the cavalry were required to refer to their armoured vehicles as *automitrailleuse*, or armoured cars, whether they had tracks or not. The S-35 was explicitly a cavalry tank, intended to do what cavalry did best. It was fast and had a good operating radius, enabling it to undertake mobile operations. Its 47mm (1.8in) gun was powerful enough to take on any other tank with a good prospect of success.

MAIN GUN
The S-35's 47mm (1.8in) gun was relatively large for a medium tank of its era.

TURRET
The S-35 used a two-man turret design, increasing efficiency over earlier models.

SIDE HATCH
Lack of turret hatches forced the commander to exit the tank and position himself on the upper surface when not 'buttoned up'.

ARMOUR
Cast armour sections were fitted over much of the tank, giving good protection but making the vehicle expensive to produce.

BULKHEAD
Crew protection was increased by a bulkhead between the engine and crew compartments.

CAMOUFLAGE
This S-35 fought in the May 1940 campaign. It is painted in a three-tone, green and brown disruptive-pattern camouflage that was popular with French armoured forces at the time.

Char B1 bis (1937)

SPECIFICATIONS

DIMENSIONS:	Length: 6.63m (21ft 9in); Width: 2.52m (8ft 3in); Height: 2.84m (9ft 4in)
WEIGHT:	31.5 tonnes (31 tons)
ENGINE:	1 x Renault six-cylinder inline petrol powerplant delivering 229kW (307hp)
SPEED:	Road: 28km/h (17.5mph) Off-road: 21km/h (13mph)
ARMAMENT:	Main: 1 x 75mm (2.95in) ABS SA35 L/17 fixed in azimuth in hull front; Secondary: 1 x 47mm (1.85in) SA35 L/32 in fully traversing turret; 1 x coaxially mounted 7.5mm (0.3in) Chatellerault Mle. 31 MG; 1 x flexible mount 7.5mm (0.3in) Chatellerault Mle. 31 MG
ARMOUR:	14–60mm (0.55–2.36in)
RANGE:	Road: 135km (85 miles); off road: 100km (60 miles)
CREW:	4

Several major French factories, including Renault, produced the Char B1 bis heavy tank for the French Army. The Char B1 bis was the final production version of the Char B1, entering service in 1937 as one of the most powerful tanks in the world.

Right: The frontal view of the French Char B1 bis heavy tank presents a formidable array of firepower. The Char B1 bis was capable of destroying the best German armour in the field during the early months of World War II, but it was not available in sufficient numbers.

COMMUNICATIONS
The four crewmen of the Char B1 bis were dispersed throughout the tank, with the commander occupying the small turret. Communications, particularly in combat, were difficult at best.

ARMOUR
French engineers combined welded and riveted construction along with some cast components in the Char B1 bis. Armour ranged from 14–60mm (0.55–2.36in) and was thickest toward the front of the hull.

ENGINE
The production powerplant of the Char B1 bis was a single six-cylinder inline Renault petrol engine, delivering superior performance to the engine installed in the earlier Char B1.

AIR INTAKE
The air-cooled engine of the Char B1 bis required a substantial intake on the hull's flank. However, the 55mm (2.16in) side armour was considered adequate despite this potential weakness.

ARMAMENT
The Char B1 bis heavy tank fielded greater firepower than any other contemporary armoured vehicle in 1940. A turret-mounted 47mm (1.85in) gun was serviced by the tank commander, while a 75mm (2.95in) howitzer was located in the hull. Highly-responsive steering compensated for the heavy weapon's lack of traversing capability.

ABANDONED TANK
An apparently disabled Char B1 bis with a section of armour plating removed lies by the side of the road following the German invasion of France in May 1940.

Type 97 Chi-Ha (1938)

SPECIFICATIONS

DIMENSIONS:	Length: 5.5m (18ft); Width: 2.33m (7ft 8in); Height: 2.23m (7ft 4in)
WEIGHT:	14.3 tonnes (140.7 tons)
ENGINE:	127kW (170hp) Mitsubishi Type 97 V-12 diesel engine
SPEED:	The Type 97 had a maximum road speed of 39km/h (24mph) and a road range of 240km (149 miles)
ARMAMENT:	Main: 57mm (2.24in) gun; Secondary: 2 × 7.7mm (0.303in) Type 97 machine guns
ARMOUR:	8–33mm (0.31–1.2in)
RANGE:	210km (130 miles)
CREW:	4

The Type 97 Medium Chi-Ha was as good as any contemporary light tank, but remained in production long after it had been surpassed by Allied designs.

ARMOUR
The thickest armour was on the vertical parts of the turret and was 33mm (1.2in) steel. Elsewhere, the armour was mainly 25mm (0.9in) thickness.

MAIN GUN
The Chi-Ha's main armament was a 57mm (2.24in) Type 97 cannon, backed up by two 7.7mm (0.3in) Type 97 machine guns, one in the bow and one in the rear of the turret.

HE SHELLS
The Chi-Ha was mainly used in the infantry support role and was supplied with high explosive (HE) shells. These were largely useless against heavier Allied tanks.

SUSPENSION
The Chi-Ha's suspension was refined compared to previous Japanese tanks, but still gave the crew an uncomfortable ride over uneven terrain.

VARIANTS
A successful development of the Type 97 was the *Shinhoto* ('modified turret') Chi-Ha, which had the turret of the Type 1 medium tank and a 47mm (1.85in) high-velocity gun. This more effective version was produced until the war's end, along with specialist versions, such as bridgelayers, mine flail tanks and command tanks. The command version, the Shi-Ki, had extra radio equipment in place of armament and a dummy gun to avoid this being singled out by enemy gunners.

CAPTURED
An Allied soldier tries out a captured Chi-Ha for size. These tanks suffered heavy losses later in the Pacific War, when they were confronted by superior US armour.

Panzer 38(t) (1938)

SPECIFICATIONS

DIMENSIONS:	Length: 4.61m (15ft 1in); Width: 2.135m (7ft); Height: 2.252m (7ft 5in)
WEIGHT:	9.85 tonnes (9.7 tons)
ENGINE:	1 x Praga EPA six-cylinder water-cooled inline petrol powerplant delivering 112kW (150hp)
SPEED:	Road: 42km/h (26.1mph); Off-road: 15km/h (9.32mph)
ARMAMENT:	Main: 1 x Czech 37mm (1.45in) Skoda A7 gun; Secondary: 2 x 7.92mm (0.31in) ZB-53 machine guns
ARMOUR:	8–50mm (0.31–1.97in)
RANGE:	Road: 250km (160 miles) Cross-country: 100km (62.14 miles)
CREW:	4

After occupying Czechoslovakia, the German Army ordered production of the LT vz 38, the standard Czechoslovakian light tank, to continue. Redesignated the Panzer 38(t), the design proved one of the world's best in German service early in the war.

Right: While the armour protection of the Panzer 38(t) exhibited some degree of slope, as seen in this frontal view, later production Axis and Allied tanks incorporated armour with a more pronounced slope in both chassis and turret designs.

MAIN ARMAMENT
The Czech 37mm (1.45in) Skoda A7 gun turret mounted atop the Panzer 38(t) was heavier than the primary weaponry of other light tanks early in World War II, providing a definite edge in combat situations.

RIVETED CONSTRUCTION
The turret and hull of the Panzer 38(t) were of riveted construction rather than welded and some ancillary components of the tank were bolted to the superstructure.

ARMOUR
On early versions of the Panzer 38(t), armour protection varied from 8mm (0.31in) in less vulnerable areas to 30mm (1.18in) of frontal thickness. Later production models provided increased crew protection with armour up to 50mm (1.97in).

ENGINE
The Praga EPA six-cylinder water-cooled inline petrol engine delivered 112kW (150hp) and the Panzer 38(t) reached a top road speed of 42km/h (26.1mph).

STOLEN PROPERTY
One of the most notable weapons to emerge from the Czech arsenal emblazoned with the German cross was the LT vz 38 light tank, the standard armoured fighting vehicle of the Czech Army. The Germans redesignated the tank the Panzer 38(t), with the 't' designating *tschechnisch*, the German word for Czechoslovakian. An efficient design, the Panzer 38(t) was originally conceived following specifications issued by the Czech military in 1935 for a new light tank.

MARDER III
As shells explode in their path and thick smoke obscures their vision, Red Army soldiers rush past an abandoned Marder III tank destroyer on the Eastern Front. The Marder III was an adaptation of the Czech-designed chassis that was utilized with the Panzer 38(t) light tank.

Mk III Valentine Infantry Tank (1939)

SPECIFICATIONS

DIMENSIONS:	Length: 5.41m (17ft 9in); Width: 2.63m (8ft 7.5in); Height: 2.273m (7ft 5.5in)
WEIGHT:	16.96 tonnes (16.6 tons)
ENGINE:	1 x AEC A190 six-cylinder diesel generating 98kW (131hp)
SPEED:	Road: 24km/h (15mph); Off road: 12.9km/h (8mph)
ARMAMENT:	Main: 1 x 2pdr (40mm/1.57in) QF gun; Secondary: 1 x 7.92mm (0.31in) BESA machine gun
ARMOUR:	8–65mm (0.31–2.55in)
RANGE:	145km (90 miles)
CREW:	3

Derived from a previous Vickers design, the A10, the Mk III Valentine Infantry Tank was available in large numbers at a critical time for Great Britain and the Commonwealth nations as a potential Nazi invasion of Britain loomed.

Right: The Mk III Valentine Infantry Tank, the most prominent in the series, benefited greatly from the Vickers experience with the A10. The numerous shortcomings discovered in the A10 were corrected in the Mk III.

SECONDARY ARMAMENT
The BESA machine gun was a British version of the Czech-made ZB-53 air-cooled machine gun and was utilized extensively by the British military during World War II.

MAIN ARMAMENT
The 2pdr (40mm/1.57in) QF main gun of the Mk III Valentine Infantry Tank lost its effectiveness with the advent of heavier Axis tanks and was replaced in later variants with the 6pdr (57mm) gun.

ARMOUR PROTECTION
The armour protection of the Mk III Valentine Infantry Tank varied from 8–65mm (0.31–2.55in), heavier than the A10 Cruiser Tank from which the Valentine was derived.

ENGINE
The AEC A190 six-cylinder diesel engine of the Mk III Valentine Infantry Tank generated 103kW (131hp). It was replaced in later variants with an American GMC diesel engine.

VALENTINES FORWARD

In total, 11 different marks of the original Valentine were produced during World War II. One of the tank's greatest virtues was in fact its ability to accept substantially heavier weaponry. While I–VII mounted the 2pdr gun, the 57mm (2.24in) 6pdr QF was introduced with the VIII and continued up to the X. With the XI, a 75mm (2.95in) QF gun was mounted. The Valentine tank saw extensive service with Commonwealth forces in the Mediterranean, the North African desert and in Burma, where it was superior to most Japanese tanks. It was, however, relatively slow and inferior to newer tank designs entering service by 1943.

TURRET
The two-man turret of the Mk III Valentine Infantry Tank required the commander to serve as a loader for the 2pdr gun.

THE GLOBAL VALENTINE

The Mk III Valentine Infantry Tank was deployed with British and Commonwealth troops around the globe during World War II. In this photo, tank crewmen allow a group of children to climb aboard and inspect their Valentine on the Mediterranean island of Malta during the local celebration of the birthday of King George VI.

Panzer III Ausf F (1940)

SPECIFICATIONS

DIMENSIONS:	Length: 5.38m (17ft 8in); Width: 2.91m (9ft 7in); Height: 2.44m (8ft)
WEIGHT:	23 tonnes (22.6 tons)
ENGINE:	1 x 12-cylinder inline water-cooled Maybach HL 120 TRM petrol engine developing 224kW (300hp)
SPEED:	Road: 40km/h (25mph); Off-road: 20km/h (12mph)
ARMAMENT:	Main: Initially 1 x 37mm (1.45in) KwK L/46.5; later 50mm (1.97in) KwK 38 L/42 gun; Secondary: 2 x 7.92mm (0.31in) MG 34 machine guns
ARMOUR:	15–50mm (0.59–1.97in)
RANGE:	155km (96 miles)
CREW:	5

The most numerous tank in the German arsenal at the time of the Soviet invasion, the PzKpfw III was developed as a lighter medium tank, equipping three companies of each armoured battalion, while a fourth was outfitted with the heavier PzKpfw IV.

Above: The PzKpfw III served with the German Army on all fronts during World War II. Its chassis was also used for assault guns, recovery and observation vehicles.

ARMAMENT
The main armament of the PzKpfw III was initially the 37mm (1.45in) KwK 36 L/46.5 gun, later supplanted by the 50mm (1.97in) KwK 38 L/42 gun. Secondary armament consisted of a pair of 7.92mm (0.31in) MG 34 machine guns, one in the turret and the other in the hull.

TURRET
The three-man turret of the PzKpfw III included a gunner and loader, freeing the commander to direct the tank in combat, whereas numerous Allied tanks required the commander to operate the main gun as well.

ENGINE
The 12-cylinder inline water-cooled Maybach HL 120 TRM petrol engine was positioned in the rear of the PzKpfw III hull. It developed 224kW (300hp).

TANK DEVELOPMENT

Development of the durable Panzerkampfwagen III began in 1935 with an order from the German arms ministry for a medium tank that could complement the medium PzKpfw IV. During a four-year production run from 1939 to 1943, more than 5800 were produced and the role of the PzKpfw III evolved with the changing conditions of the battlefield. During the course of World War II, no fewer than 11 variants of the original PzKpfw III production model, Ausf E, were built. Variants A to D were prototype models constructed in 1937 and 1938.

ARMOUR
The armour protection of the PzKpfw III was upgraded with successive variants of the basic tank. Structural armour and bolted plating varied from 15–50mm (0.59–1.97in).

EVOLVING COMBAT ROLE

Buildings blaze in the background as German soldiers, supported by a PzKpfw III, clear a war-torn street somewhere on the Eastern Front. The PzKpfw III was continually modified during World War II and evolved from a main battle tank to an infantry support vehicle as its firepower and armour protection were eclipsed by subsequent generations of Allied tanks.

Sturmgeschütz III (1940)

SPECIFICATIONS

DIMENSIONS:	Length (gun forward): 5.4m (17.7ft); Width: 2.9m (9.5 ft); Height: 1.98m (6.5ft)
WEIGHT:	23.9 tonnes (23.5 tons)
ENGINE:	Powerplant: 1 x Maybach HL120TRM 6-cylinder in-line water-cooled petrol engine
SPEED:	40km/h (25mph)
ARMAMENT:	Manual
ARMOUR:	1 x 75mm (2.95in) StuK 37 L/24 1 x 7.92mm (0.31in) MG34 machine gun (unmounted)
RANGE:	Road: 155km (96 miles)
CREW:	4

UPGUNNED

The short-barrelled 75mm (2.95in) StuK 37 L/24 gun mounted on the StuG III Ausf A was effective against fixed fortifications such as pillboxes and bunkers, which could slow the progress of German infantry. However, as World War II progressed, the Sturmgeschütz's low muzzle velocity proved problematic against Allied armour. As the role of the StuG III evolved to one of tank destroyer and at times a main battle tank, its armament was upgunned to higher-velocity, long-barrelled 75mm (2.95in) L/43 and L/48 cannon. The StuG III was not well suited to the tank role, primarily because of the lack of a turret, which restricted the traverse of the weapon.

During the course of World War I, a glaring deficiency in German infantry tactics grew apparent. The ponderous weight of artillery prevented it from supporting advancing infantry once the foot soldiers had moved beyond effective range. However, a mobile assault gun would remedy the situation.

Right: Sturmgeschütz crews were considered to be the elite of the artillery units of the German army and were issued special grey field uniforms. Overall, the Sturmgeschütz series proved highly successful and served on all fronts as assault guns and tank destroyers.

MAIN ARMAMENT
The Sturmgeschütz III (StuG III) was initially armed with a short-barrelled 75mm (2.95in) StuK 37 L/24 cannon as shown. However, as its role expanded to include that of tank hunter, the vehicle was increasingly upgunned.

MANTLET
The *Topfblende* gun mantlet of the StuG III Ausf G was effective at deflecting Allied shells and was an improvement over previous box-like mantlets nicknamed *Saukopf*, or sow's heads.

ENGINE
The V-12, 221-kW (296-hp) Maybach HL 120 TRM engine powered the StuG III Ausf G at a top speed of 40 m/h (25mph) with a range of 155km (96 miles).

CREW COMPARTMENT
The four-man crew of the StuG III was situated primarily along the left side of the vehicle with later variants carrying a hull-mounted 7.92mm (0.31in) MG 34 machine gun. The Ausf G was armed with a shielded coaxial MG 34 as well.

SILHOUETTE
The low profile of the StuG III made the vehicle easy to conceal, while the addition of armour plating was effective against hollow charge shells.

INFANTRY TRANSPORT
Weary German infantrymen pause for a moment as they hitch a ride aboard an early variant of the Sturmgeschütz III self-propelled assault gun. This Sturmgeschütz III is armed with the short-barrelled 75mm (2.95-in) StuK 37 L/24 gun.

KV-1A Heavy Tank (1940)

SPECIFICATIONS

DIMENSIONS:	Length: 6.25m (20ft 6in); Width: 3.25m (10ft 9in); Height: 2.75m (9ft)
WEIGHT:	46 tonnes (45.2 tons)
ENGINE:	1 x V-2K Series V-12 water-cooled diesel engine generating 410kW (550hp)
SPEED:	35km/h (22mph)
ARMAMENT:	Main: 1 x 76.2mm (3in) long-barrelled F32 gun; Secondary: 3 x 7.62mm (0.3in) DT machine guns
ARMOUR:	37–78mm (1.45–3.07in)
RANGE:	225km (140 miles)
CREW:	5

SOLID FOUNDATION

Although the KV tanks were prone to mechanical failure and some critics maintained that their main armament lacked the firepower of opposing heavy tanks, they were the product of sound design concepts and rendered vital service with the Red Army during the bleakest period following the German invasion. They also established a basis for the improved Stalin tanks that were to come.

The KV series was often used in offensive operations, spearheading breakthroughs of defensive lines. Named for Klimenti Voroshilov, Soviet Commissar for Defence, the KV tanks were the foundation of Soviet heavy tank design for decades to come.

Right: The KV-1A heavy tank entered production along with the KV-2, an ill-conceived self-propelled assault gun with a tremendously oversized turret that mounted a 152mm (6in) howitzer. The KV-1A played a pivotal role in turning the tide of on the Eastern Front.

MAIN ARMAMENT
The long-barrelled 76.2mm (3in) F32 main gun of the KV-1A replaced the shorter L-11 76.2mm weapon that had been mounted on the early KV-1 and seen action during the Winter War with Finland.

TURRET
The original KV-1A turret was fashioned of steel plating; with the KV-1C a cast hull, offering better structural integrity, was introduced.

ENGINE
The V-2K Series V-12 water-cooled diesel engine generating 550hp (410kW) was overtaxed, as the KV tanks were fitted with additional armour plating and could not deliver the power needed for efficient operation over great distances.

ARMOUR PROTECTION
The armour protection of the KV-1A heavy tank varied from 37–78mm (1.45–3.07in) and was increased steadily during the production of KV Series variants as the firepower of German tanks grew steadily more lethal.

KV-1 HALT
Red Army soldiers, their banner whipping in the wind, have halted during a counteroffensive. Tank crewmen have joined infantrymen atop the hulls of KV-1 Model 1942 heavy tanks that were instrumental in stopping the Germans and seizing the initiative in the East.

Panzer IV Ausf F1 (1941)

SPECIFICATIONS

DIMENSIONS:	Length: 5.91m (19ft 5in); Width: 2.88m (9ft 5in); Height: 2.68m (8ft 10in)
WEIGHT:	22 tonnes (21.6 tons)
ENGINE:	1 x 12-cylinder inline Maybach HL 120 TRM water-cooled petrol engine generating 220kW (296hp)
SPEED:	42km/h (26mph)
ARMAMENT:	Main: 1 x short-barrelled 75mm (2.95in) L/24 gun; Secondary: 2 x 7.92mm (0.31in) MG 34 machine guns
ARMOUR:	15–50mm (0.59–1.97in)
RANGE:	Road: 240km (150 miles); cross-country: 120km (75 miles)
CREW:	5

The workhorse of the German armoured forces during the war, the Panzer IV Ausf F1 was originally intended as an infantry support tank; however, it later assumed a tank-fighting combat role as Allied armoured vehicles became more powerful.

Right: A front view of the Panzer IV Ausf F1. The frontal hull armour was 50mm (1.97in) in thickness.

ENGINE
The 12-cylinder inline Maybach HL 120 TRM water-cooled petrol engine of the PzKpfw IV generated 296hp (220kW) and a top road speed of 42km/h (26mph).

TURRET
The asymmetrical construction of the PzKpfw IV included a turret that was offset 66.5mm (2.6in) for the tank's centre to allow the torque shaft to clear the rotary base junction.

MAIN ARMAMENT
The main armament of the PzKpfw IV Ausf F included two sub-variants, the F1 and F2. The F1 mounted the short-barrelled 75mm (2.95in) L/24 gun and the F2 the long-barrelled 75mm L/43 gun (shown here).

PRODUCTION FIGURES

The most widely manufactured and deployed German tank of World War II, the PzKpfw IV was the mainstay of the German army's forces. The first rolled off the Krupp assembly line in the mid-1930s and from that date through 1945 more than 8800 were built. It was the only German tank in production throughout the war.

MOBILITY
Wider tracks and modified front sprockets and rear idler wheels assisted with handling the PzKpfw IV in difficult terrain. Ice springs were added for manoeuvrability in winter weather.

ARMOUR PROTECTION
Throughout its service life, the armour protection of the PzKpfw IV was improved. Armour thickness ranged from 15–50mm (0.59–1.97in) and was of homogeneous rolled and welded nickel steel.

GUN BARREL
The long barrel of the 75mm (2.95in) L/43 cannon of PzKpfw IV Ausf F2 was an imposing sight on the battlefield, here deployed for the Kursk offensive in July 1943.

Mk VI Crusader I Cruiser Tank (1941)

SPECIFICATIONS

DIMENSIONS:	Length: 5.99m (19ft 8in); Width: 2.64m (8ft 8in); Height: 2.23m (7ft 4in)
WEIGHT:	19.73 tonnes (19.4 tons)
ENGINE:	Nuffield 12-cylinder Liberty L-12 water-cooled petrol engine generating 254kW (340hp)
SPEED:	Road: 43.4km/h (27mph); off-road: 24km/h (15mph)
ARMAMENT:	Main: 1 x 6pdr (57mm/2.24in) QF gun Secondary: 1 x 7.92mm (0.31in) BESA machine gun
ARMOUR:	Up to 51mm (2in) in Mk III
RANGE:	204km (127 miles)
CREW:	3

The British Crusader tanks were conceived between the world wars as rapid exploitation armoured vehicles that would exploit breaches in enemy defensive lines created by heavier weapons and then slash into rear areas to create havoc.

Right: The angular design of the turret sides could create an unfortunate 'shot trap' between the turret and the top of the hull.

ENGINE
The Nuffield 12-cylinder Liberty L-12 water-cooled petrol engine of the Crusader series was prone to overheating, while its Nuffield constant mesh transmission often broke down as well.

ARMOUR PROTECTION
The essence of the cruiser tank lay in its speed, which was achieved by the sacrifice of armour. Early Crusaders were thinly protected with up to 40mm (1.57in) of armour, while later variants were slightly improved to 50mm (1.97in).

TURRET
The Mk VI Crusader III Cruiser Tank was equipped with a larger turret than earlier variants. However, its heavier 6pdr main weapon actually reduced the space available for the crew.

MAIN ARMAMENT
The Mk VI Crusader I Cruiser Tank was armed with a weak 2pdr (40mm/1.57in) QF gun, which was ineffective against a new generation of German tanks. The Crusader III introduced the more powerful 6pdr (57mm/2.24in) QF gun.

CRUSADER III
The Crusader III, which became the definitive fighting variant of the series, made its combat debut at the pivotal battle of El Alamein in October 1942 and during the 1770km (1100-mile) pursuit of the German *Panzerarmee Afrika* into Tunisia. About 100 of the Crusader III participated in the great El Alamein victory and the introduction of the 6pdr QF gun with 65 rounds of ammunition at long last gave the Crusader the ability to destroy the German PzKpfw III and IV tanks then deployed by the Germans in North Africa.

OUTRANGED
With their 2pdr (40mm/1.57in) QF main guns, the first Crusader tanks deployed in North Africa were capable of taking on the German PzKpfw III with its short-barrelled 50mm (1.97in) gun. The short-barrelled 75mm (2.95in) gun of the PzKpfw IV was another story. The heavier German gun outranged the Crusader, a decided disadvantage in the desert.

Churchill Mk IV (1941)

SPECIFICATIONS

DIMENSIONS:	Length: 7.44m (24ft 5in); Width: 2.44m (8ft) Height: 3.45m (11ft 4in)
WEIGHT:	39 tonnes (38.4 tons)
ENGINE:	Bedford Twin-Six Petrol developing 350bhp (261kW)
SPEED:	Road: 25km/h (15.5mph); Off-road: 13km/h (8 mph)
ARMAMENT:	Main: One OQF 6 pdr L/43 Mk. V Gun; Secondary: 2 × 7.92mm (0.31in) BESA machine guns; 1 × 7.7mm (0.303in) Bren machine gun
ARMOUR:	19–89mm (0.75–3.5in)
RANGE:	259km (161 miles)
CREW:	5

Conceived as an infantry support tank that would take on obstacles on a battlefield reminiscent of World War I trench warfare, the Churchill Mk IV evolved into a versatile fighting vehicle that fulfilled a variety of combat and support roles.

Right: The box-like shape of the Churchill Mk IV hull and turret were unmistakable on the battlefield. As the tank's main armament was upgraded, it became more proficient indealing with Axis armour.

MAIN ARMAMENT
The Mark IV turret mounted a variety of main weapons, including the 2pdr (40mm/1.57in) and 6pdr (57mm/2.24in) QF, the American 75mm (2.95in) (shown), the 76.2mm (3in) and the 25pdr (95mm/3.7in) howitzer.

TURRET
The Churchill turret was of both welded and cast construction. When the 75mm (2.95in) gun was installed, it required a 90° rotation for loading from the left side due to the configuration of the crew inside the turret.

VERSATILITY
During the course of World War II, nearly 7400 Churchill infantry tanks of all marks were produced. The specialized vehicles derived from the original included several that were instrumental during the Allied landings in Normandy on 6 June 1944 and the ensuing campaign in Western Europe, including the AVRE (Armoured Vehicle Royal Engineers), which carried a 290mm (11.4in) spigot mortar, the flamethrower-equipped Crocodile, the Kangaroo personnel carrier, the AVRE/CIRD mine clearing vehicle, the ARV (Armoured Recovery Vehicle) and the ARK (Armoured Ramp Carrier) bridging tank. Production of the Churchill Mk IV infantry tank continued throughout World War II and the various specialized vehicles spawned by the design remained in service with the British Army until 1952.

SECONDARY ARMAMENT
A single hull mounted 7.92mm (0.31in) BESA machine gun was sometimes complemented with a 7.7mm (0.303in) Bren light machine gun in the Churchill Mk IV.

SUSPENSION
The coiled spring suspension of the Churchill Mk IV included 11 bogeys covered by panniers and each mounting a pair of 254mm (10in) wheels. It proved most effective in providing traction on various surfaces.

ENGINE
A horizontally opposed Bedford Twin-Six 12-cylinder petrol engine generated 261kW (350hp) and remained with the Churchill Mk IV throughout its service life despite the tank's increasing weight.

SUSPENSION SYSTEM
The unique suspension of the Churchill with its covering panniers is easily distinguishable from other contemporary tank suspension systems. The suspension was ideal for infantry support across broken ground and relatively steep gradients.

M3A3 Stuart (1941)

SPECIFICATIONS

DIMENSIONS:	Length: 4.53m (14ft 10in); Width: 2.23m (7ft 4in) Height: 2.52m (8ft 3in)
WEIGHT:	14.7 tonnes (14.4 tons)
ENGINE:	1 x Continental W-670-9A air-cooled, seven-cylinder radial engine generating 186kW (250hp)
SPEED:	58km/h (35mph)
ARMAMENT:	Main: 1 x 37mm (1.45in) M6 gun; Secondary: 2 x 7.62mm (0.3in) M1919A4 air-cooled Browning machine guns
ARMOUR:	10–65mm (0.39–2.6in)
RANGE:	Road: 120km (75 miles) Off-road: 60km (40 miles)
CREW:	4

The American Light Tank M3 was developed as an infantry support vehicle with excellent speed and effective armament, and served with the US, British and Soviet armies in both the European and Pacific theatres during World War II.

Right: The relatively high silhouette of the M3 Light Tank made concealment difficult; speed was the primary advantage the tank possessed in the face of superior enemy forces. Thicker sloped armour increased the survivability of the M3A3.

MULTIPLE THEATRES

British crews in North Africa grew fond of the diminutive 14.7-tonne (14.4-ton) tank and nicknamed it the 'Honey'. Along with the M3 Grant and M4 Sherman tanks supplied by the United States, the M3 light tank helped the British and later American forces to win the North African campaign. In the Pacific, the M3 light tank was effective as an infantry support vehicle, penetrating thick jungle and negotiating terrain that heavier tanks could not. Japanese armour development was significantly behind that of the United States and the M3 was powerful enough to neutralize Japanese tanks, machine-gun nests, bunkers and troop concentrations as American troops fought their way, island by island, across the Pacific.

MAIN ARMAMENT
Throughout the service life of the Light Tank M3, the 37mm (1.45in) M6 gun was its main armament, unsuitable for tank versus tank combat, but adequate against other targets in infantry support.

SECONDARY ARMAMENT
The M3A3 Stuart mounted at least a pair of 7.62mm (0.3in) M1919A4 Browning air cooled machine guns, one coaxially in the turret and a second ball-mounted in the hull. Some models included an anti-aircraft machine gun at the turret hatch.

ENGINE
The Continental W-670-9A air-cooled, seven-cylinder radial engine generated 250hp (186kW) in the M3A3. Other M3 powerplants included a pair of Cadillac V8 engines and a Guiberson diesel.

SUSPENSION
The vertical volute spring suspension was characteristic of American armoured vehicles of the World War II era. It featured rear idlers that were on the ground, reducing pressure and providing better support for the rear of the M3A3.

RIVETED HULL
The riveted construction of the hull of this early M3 series light tank is clearly visible as this M3 negotiates a steep hill during training exercises. Note the hull-mounted 7.62mm (0.3in) Browning machine gun.

M3A3 General Lee (1941)

SPECIFICATIONS

DIMENSIONS:	Length: 5.64m (18ft 6in); Width: 2.72m (8ft 10in); Height: 3m (10ft)
WEIGHT:	27 tonnes (26.5 tons)
ENGINE:	1 x General Motors 6046 12-cylinder diesel combining two GM 6-71 engines and generating 313kW (420hp)
SPEED:	40km/h (25mph)
ARMAMENT:	Main: 1 x 75mm (2.95in) M2 L/31 cannon in sponson hull mount Secondary: 1 x 37mm (1.45in) M6 turret-mounted cannon; up to 3 x 7.62mm (0.3in) Browning M1919A4 machine guns
ARMOUR:	12.5–76mm (0.49–3in)
RANGE:	Road: 240km (160 miles) Off-road: 150km (90 miles)
CREW:	6 or 7

In the rush to provide additional armoured firepower to counter German tanks in North Africa, American designers adapted an existing hull to carry a sponson-mounted 75mm (2.95in) gun.

Right: The M3 turret was offset to the left, shifting the weight for balance with the installation of the 75mm (2.95in) gun in the tank's hull.

COMBAT DEBUT

The combat debut of the M3 medium tank occurred at Gazala in North Africa in 1943. The Germans had no warning that a heavier Allied tank mounting a 75mm (2.95in) gun was in the field and were startled at the appearance of the M3. The Grant tanks at Gazala quickly added substantial firepower and actually engaged German tanks while remaining safely out of range of the towed 50mm (1.97in) anti-tank guns.

MAIN ARMAMENT
The M3 medium tank carried a 75mm (2.95in) gun mounted in a sponson in the hull and a 37mm (1.45in) cannon in the turret. The configuration was expedient for US factories during a time when new tanks were badly needed to replace British losses in the North African desert.

TURRET
The small turret of the M3 could not accommodate a gun heavier than 37mm (1.45in). The British made some modifications, eliminating the commander's cupola and lengthening the turret to hold radio equipment.

ENGINE
Early M3 medium tanks were powered by the Wright Continental R975 EC2 engine, originally an aircraft powerplant. Later M3s introduced the General Motors 6046 diesel that combined two GM 6-71 engines and the Chrysler A57 engine.

SUSPENSION
The vertical volute suspension, common among American tanks, was improved in later M3 models with the addition of heavy bogeys rather than springs.

NEED FOR FIREPOWER
The unorthodox appearance of the American M3 light tank was largely due to the urgency with which the tank was produced. The need for firepower was addressed with a 75mm (2.95in) sponson-mounted gun in the tank's hull.

T-70 (1942)

SPECIFICATIONS

DIMENSIONS:	Length: 4.29m (14ft 1in); Width: 2.32m (7ft 7in); Height: 2.04m (6ft 8in)
WEIGHT:	9.2 tonnes (9 tons)
ENGINE:	2 x tandem six-cylinder GAZ 202 petrol car engines generating 104kW (140hp)
SPEED:	45km/h (28mph)
ARMAMENT:	Main: 1 x 45mm (1.8in) L/46 Model 38 cannon Secondary: 1 x 7.62mm (0.3in) DT machine gun
ARMOUR:	10–60mm (0.3–2.3in)
RANGE:	360km (220 miles)
CREW:	2

Although the Soviets largely abandoned light tanks as World War II progressed, the T-70 was manufactured by small factories and combined the reconnaissance and infantry support functions.

Right: The T-70 light tank entered production in March 1941, at a time when the importance of such vehicles was obviously declining in the Soviet military and attention was focusing on the T-34 medium and KV-1 heavy tanks.

SELF-PROPELLED GUN SUCCESSOR

The remaining inventory of T-70 chassis was earmarked for production of the SU-76 self-propelled gun. The SU-76 mounted a highly effective 76mm (3in) gun that was well suited for infantry support and more than 14,000 were completed between 1942 and the end of the war, more than any other armoured vehicle deployed with the Red Army, except the legendary T-34 medium tank. It was open-turreted and was unpopular with its crews due to a lack of armour protection and exposure to the elements. Another self-propelled weapon that utilized the light tank chassis was the open turreted T-90, the first mobile anti-aircraft vehicle fielded by the Red Army, mounting a pair of 12.7mm (0.5in) DShK machine guns. The ZSU-37 followed in 1945 with a 37mm (1.45in) anti-aircraft gun and was manufactured until 1948.

MAIN ARMAMENT
The 45mm (1.8in) L/46 Model 38 gun of the T-70 light tank was more powerful than the 37mm (1.45in) weapon of the preceding T-60. Along with heavier armour protection, the tank increased in weight to 9.2 tonnes (9 tons).

TURRET
The multi-sided angular turret of the T-70 light tank was offset substantially to the left, while heavier components and ammunition storage compensated with even weight distribution and stability.

ENGINE
A pair of tandem six-cylinder GAZ 202 petrol car engines delivered 104kW (140hp) and drove the T-70 at a maximum speed of 45km/h (28mph).

SUSPENSION
Later T-60 and T-70 light tanks utilized solid rather than spoked wheels in the durable torsion bar suspension.

WINTER WARFARE
In this photo, snow covered T-70s pause in a forest on the Eastern Front as soldiers clad in winter camouflage gear trudge forward.

T-34/76 Model 1943 (1942)

SPECIFICATIONS

DIMENSIONS: Length: 6.68m (21ft 11in; Width: 3.0m (9ft 10in); Height: 2.45m (8ft)

WEIGHT: 26.5 tonnes (26 tons)

ENGINE: 1 x V-2-34 V-12 38.8-litre (8.5-gallon) diesel engine delivering 375kW (500hp)

SPEED: 53km/h (33mph)

ARMAMENT: Main: 1 x 76.2mm (3in) ZIS5 F 34 gun; Secondary: 2 x 7.62mm (0.3in) DT machine guns

ARMOUR: 15–60mm (0.59in–2.24in)

RANGE: 400km (250 miles)

CREW: 4

The T-34 medium tank is one of a few weapons that may be partially credited with winning World War II. The T-34 reached the battlefield in large numbers in 1941 and quickly evened the odds for the Red Army against German tanks.

Right: The high ground clearance and proven Christie suspension of the T-34 medium tank made it ideal for mobile warfare across the vast Russian steppes as the Red Army pursued the Germans westwards towards Berlin in 1944 and 1945.

TURRET
Earlier model T-34s had a very cramped turret, but the Model 1943 had an enlarged cast hexagonal turret, which gave welcome extra space for the crew.

ENGINE
The T-34 incorporated a V-2-34 V-12 38.8-litre diesel engine that generated 500hp (375kW).

MAIN ARMAMENT
The main weapon of the T-34 Model 1943 was the 76mm (3in) M1940 F-34 gun.

SUSPENSION
The coil-spring suspension developed by American Walter Christie and utilized with the T-34 was carried over from the earlier BT series of tanks.

PANZERS SURPRISED

When the T-34 reached the frontlines in the East, the Germans were amazed at the tank's performance, with its powerful 76.2mm (3in) gun its speed and its cross-country mobility. After German tanks of Panzergruppe II under the command of General Heinz Guderian met the T-34 in battle for the first time, the general wrote: 'Numerous Russian T-34s went into action and inflicted heavy losses on the German tanks at Mzensk in 1941. Up to this time, we had enjoyed tank superiority, but from now on the situation was reversed. The prospect of rapid, decisive victories was fading in consequence. I made a report on this situation, which for us was a new one … I described in plain terms the marked superiority of the T-34 to our PzKpfw IV….'

MASS WEAPON
Silhouetted against a barren landscape, three Soviet T-34 medium tanks pause, their hatches open, before moving forward to the frontlines. The overwhelming numbers and performance of the T-34 doomed the German Army to defeat on the Eastern Front.

Panzer VI Tiger Ausf E (1942)

SPECIFICATIONS

DIMENSIONS:	Length: 8.45m (27ft 8in); Width: 3.7m (12ft 1in); Height: 2.93m (9ft 7in)
WEIGHT:	56.9 tonnes (56 tons)
ENGINE:	1 x Maybach V-12 HL 230 P45 engine, generating 700hp (522kW)
SPEED:	45.4km/h (28.2mph)
ARMAMENT:	Main: 1 x 88m (3.5in) KwK 36 L/56 high-velocity gun; Secondary: 2 x 7.92mm (0.31in) MG 34 machine guns
ARMOUR:	25–120mm (0.98–4.7in)
RANGE:	Road: 195km (121 miles); Off-road: 110km (68 miles)
CREW:	5

The most feared and respected tank of World War II, the formidable Panzerkampfwagen VI Tiger was in production for two years, but only slightly more than 1300 were ever completed. For all its drawbacks and difficulties in the field, the basic design of the Tiger was outstanding. The tank struck fear into the hearts of Allied soldiers who encountered it, becoming one of the iconic weapons of World War II.

The tracks of the PzKpfw VI Tiger tank were changed depending on whether the vehicle was operating on roadways or cross-country. Wider cross-country tracks resulted in lower ground pressure and better mobility.

TURRET
The three-man turret of the Tiger I weighed 9.9 tonnes (9.7 tons) with the gunner forward on the left, the loader seated on the right facing the rear and the commander placed behind the gunner.

ENGINE
After 250 Tigers were produced, the early 12-cylinder Maybach HL 210 P45 engine was replaced by the Maybach V-12 HL 230 P45 engine, generating 700hp (522kW).

MAIN ARMAMENT
The high-velocity 88m (3.5in) KwK 36 L/56 mounted in the Tiger turret was adapted from a successful anti-aircraft gun that had already been used in an improvised anti-tank role.

VICTOR AT VILLERS-BOCAGE
During World War II, the PzKpfw VI Tiger tank was reported to have achieved a six-to-one kill ratio against Allied tanks. Its overwhelming firepower and heavy armour protection allowed the Tiger to dispatch enemy vehicles from safe distances and ward off shells from most Allied anti-tank weapons. Despite several drawbacks, it was a formidable weapon in combat – as demonstrated by SS Hauptsturmführer Michael Wittman at the French village of Villers-Bocage on 13 July 1944. In minutes, Wittman's single Tiger of SS Heavy Panzer Battalion 101 destroyed 13 British tanks, two anti-tank guns and up to 15 troop carriers.

ARMOUR PROTECTION
At 100mm (3.9in) and 120mm (4.7in) respectively, the heavy armour of the Tiger I frontal hull and turret were substantially thicker than that of any other German tank, and the Tiger was impervious to many of the anti-tank weapons in the Allied arsenal.

EASTERN FRONT TIGER
SS-manned Tiger I Ausf E tanks advance through snow-covered forest somewhere on the Eastern Front, 1943.

M4A4 Sherman (1942)

SPECIFICATIONS

DIMENSIONS:	Length: 6.06m (19ft 1in); Width: 2.9m (9ft 6in); Height: 2.84m (9ft 4in)
WEIGHT:	31.62 tonnes (31.1 tons)
ENGINE:	1 x Chrysler A57 30-cylinder multibank petrol engine generating 317kW (425hp)
SPEED:	47km/h (29mph)
ARMAMENT:	1 x 75mm (2.95in) M3 L/40 gun Secondary: 2 x 7.62mm (0.3in) Browning M1919A4 machine guns; 1 x 12.7mm (0.5in) Browning M2HB machine gun
ARMOUR:	9–85mm (0.35–3.35in)
RANGE:	Road: 160km (100 miles); Off-road: 100km (60 miles)
CREW:	5

The American Medium Tank M4, popularly known as the Sherman, reached the battlefield in great numbers during World War II and essentially overwhelmed the technologically superior German tanks in North Africa and Western Europe. The Sherman sacrificed armour protection for speed. Although it was vulnerable to the fire of German tanks and anti-tank weapons, the Sherman was available in large numbers and contributed significantly to victory in World War II.

Above: The M4A4 Sherman tank incorporated the Chrysler A57 engine along with greater separation of the road wheels for better traction. The hull of the M4A4 was 280mm longer than other Sherman variants.

MAIN ARMAMENT
Originally, the M4 Sherman medium tank was armed with a 75mm (2.95in) gun that produced insufficient muzzle velocity to penetrate the armour of some German tanks. It was later upgunned with a high-velocity 76mm (2.9in) and with the British 17pdr (76.2mm/3in) QF.

SECONDARY ARMAMENT
The M4 Sherman was armed with a 12.7mm (0.5in) Browning machine gun for defence against enemy aircraft, and a pair of 7.62mm (0.3in) Browning M1919A4 machine guns, one mounted coaxially in the turret and the other forward in the hull.

ARMOUR PROTECTION
The armour protection of the Sherman generally could not stand up to the 75mm (2.95in) and 88mm (3.5in) high-velocity shells of the German Panther and Tiger. Armour ranged from 9mm (0.35in) on the turret top to 50mm (1.97in) on the frontal hull and 85mm (3.35in) on the turret front.

MASS PRODUCTION
The story of the Sherman, conceived, manufactured and deployed in a matter of months, demonstrates the capability of American industry to produce war materiel on a scale that not only equipped the US armed forces, but allowed the nation to serve as the great 'arsenal of democracy', sending thousands to Great Britain and other allies through Lend-Lease. More than 49,000 were produced in total.

ENGINE
Several powerplants were installed in Sherman tanks. The hull of the M4A4 (shown) was lengthened to accommodate the 30-cylinder multibank petrol Chrysler A57 engine, generating 317kW (425hp).

AMMUNITION STORAGE
Up to 90 rounds of 75mm (2.95in) ammunition were carried aboard the M4A4 Sherman in wet storage, reducing the potential of a catastrophic explosion if the tank took a serious hit.

SHERMAN IN FRANCE
In the photo here, American infantrymen hug the flank of a Sherman tank as they proceed cautiously through a small French village. Note the plough-like appendages on the front hull of the Sherman used to negotiate the French bocage (hedgerows).

Semovente DA 75/18 (1942)

SPECIFICATIONS

DIMENSIONS:	Length: 5.04m (16ft 6in); Width 2.23m (7ft 4in); Height: 1.85m (6ft 1in)
WEIGHT:	13.1 tonnes (12.9 tons)
ENGINE:	SPA 15-TM-41 V-8 petrol engine, developing 145hp (108kW)
SPEED:	38km/h (24mph)
ARMAMENT:	Main: 1 × 75mm (2.95in) obice da 75/18 mod. 34; Secondary: 1 × 8mm (0.31in) Breda mod. 38 or 6.5mm (0.25in) Breda mod. 30 machine gun
ARMOUR:	6–50mm (0.24–2in)
RANGE:	Road: 230km (143 miles)
CREW:	3

The DA 75, also known as the M41 self-propelled gun, was intended as a counter to the Soviet T-34, but was never in fact sent to serve on the Eastern Front. Most of the vehicles were used in Sicily against US and British forces.

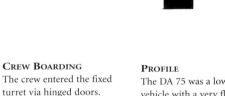

Right: The low profile of the DA 75 is apparent here in this front-view image. The basic purpose of these vehicles was to provide mobile assault artillery and also anti-tank fire. One of their biggest issues was the limited number of shells they carried – 44 in total.

GERMAN SERVICE

About 262 of the DA 75/18 were built during the war years. The improved M43 105/25 was completed in smaller numbers – only about 90 – but sported a much more effective 105mm (4.1in) gun. In German service, the Semovente was renamed Sturmgeschütz M42 mit 75/18 850(i), or StuG M42. Including vehicles built by the Germans, 294 were issued to Wehrmacht divisions in Italy and the Balkans in 1943 and 1944. By the end of 1944, 200 had been destroyed, captured or abandoned.

CREW BOARDING
The crew entered the fixed turret via hinged doors. Simple fixed steps aided boarding.

PROFILE
The DA 75 was a low profile vehicle with a very flat roof. There were few fittings for attaching ancilliary equipment, such as tools or crew bedding.

STRUCTURE
The Semoventes dispensed with the high turret and the superstructure of the M15/42 and replaced them with a box-like fixed riveted structure with no commander's cupola. Turret access was through a large hinged hatch cover, which opened to the rear.

OFFSET GUN
The gun was offset slightly to make room for the driver/gunner, who had only an armoured slit for vision.

DESERT OPERATIONS

The DA 75/18 proved itself in the desert battles in North Africa in 1942–43. They were reliable and their low profile was ideal for improving survivability in the very flat desert hinterlands. The vehicle did not have a coaxial weapon, however, so could be weak against infantry assaults.

Panzer V Panther Ausf D (1943)

SPECIFICATIONS

DIMENSIONS:	Length: 8.86m (29ft); Width: 3.4m (11ft 2in); Height: 2.95m (9ft 8in)
WEIGHT:	47.4 tonnes (46.6 tons)
ENGINE:	1 x V-12 Maybach HL 230 P30 petrol engine generating 514.5kW (690hp)
SPEED:	46km/h (28.6mph)
ARMAMENT:	Main: 1 x long-barrelled high-velocity 75mm KwK 42 L/70 gun Secondary: 2 x 7.92mm (0.31in) MG 34 machine guns
ARMOUR:	15–80mm (0.59–3.14in)
RANGE:	200km (124 miles)
CREW:	5

After overcoming early mechanical problems, the Panzerkampfwagen V Panther, with its high-velocity 75mm (2.95in) gun, became in the opinion of some, the best all-around tank of World War II.

Right: The wide tracks and double torsion bar suspension with interwoven road wheels allowed the PzKpfw V Panther to handle varied types of terrain with relative ease.

TURRET
A three-man turret had already been developed when the Panther was being evaluated, and several modifications were introduced. Among these were the addition of a cast commander's cupola and a bracket for an MG 34 anti-aircraft machine gun in later models.

AMMUNITION STORAGE
Up to 48 rounds of 75mm (2.95in) ammunition were stored in sponsons on either side of the Panther medium tank's hull. No ammunition was routinely stored in the turret.

ARMOUR PROTECTION
Armour thickness in the Panther Ausf D was up to 80mm (3.14in) thick and sloped at 55° to improve its effectiveness in protecting the five-man crew. Side armour generally varied in thickness from 40mm to 50mm (1.57in to 1.97in).

PROWLING PANTHER
The leading Panther tank ace of World War II was SS Oberscharführer Ernst Barkmann. Barkmann halted his Panther in a thick stand of oak trees near the French village of Le Lorey one day in late July 1944. A column of 15 American M4 Sherman tanks and auxiliary vehicles approached; Barkmann waited for the appropriate moment and opened fire. In quick succession, Barkmann destroyed nine Shermans, a fuel truck and several support vehicles. Barkmann was able to withdraw to safety at Neufbourg.

ENGINE
The primary engine of the production Panther tank was the V-12 Maybach HL 230 P30 petrol engine generating 690hp (514.5kW) and a top speed of 46km/h (28.6mph).

ANTI-MINE PASTE
Anticipating a review by senior officers, the commander and driver of a PzKpfw V Panther emerge from the hull and turret of their tank. Note the Zimmerit anti-magnetic mine paste on the tank's exterior, the black Panzerwaffe uniforms and the anti-aircraft machine gun bracketed to the commander's cupola.

KV-85 Heavy Tank (1943)

SPECIFICATIONS

DIMENSIONS:	Length: 8.6m (28ft 2in); Width: 3.25m (10ft 8in); Height: 2.8m (9ft 2in)
WEIGHT:	43 tonnes (42.3 tons)
ENGINE:	1 x V-2K V-12 diesel engine generating 448kW (600hp)
SPEED:	42km/h (26mph)
ARMAMENT:	Main: 1 x 85mm (3.35in) DT5 gun; Secondary: 2 x 7.62mm (0.3in) DT machine guns
ARMOUR:	40–90mm (1.57–3.54in)
RANGE:	330km (205 miles)
CREW:	4–5

Although it was few in number, the KV-85 heavy tank entered service in 1943 as a bridge from the older KV series of Red Army tanks to the Josef Stalin series that spearheaded the Soviet victory in the Great Patriotic War.

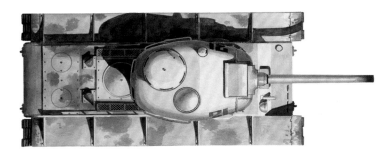

Above: The turret and main gun of the new IS-85 tank were paired with the chassis of the existing KV-1S heavy tank to create the stopgap KV-85, deployed in small numbers during the autumn of 1944 to battle German tanks on the Eastern Front.

MAIN ARMAMENT
The KV-85 featured the 85mm (3.35in) DT5 cannon, a significantly more powerful weapon than the original 76.2mm (3in) weapon mounted on the KV-1 heavy tank.

TURRET
The KV-85 turret was actually a new tank component, originally designed and manufactured for the IS-85, one of a new generation of Soviet heavy tanks in the IS series.

ENGINE
The 12-cylinder V-2K diesel engine generated adequate power for the 43-tonne (42.3-ton) KV-85. The tank's top speed, in turn, was 42km/h (26mph).

KV-85 IN COMBAT

The combat record of the KV-85 is mixed. While the tank offered comparable firepower to German armoured fighting vehicles, its armour was susceptible to the high-velocity rounds of enemy tanks and anti-tank weapons. During one engagement in the Ukraine in November 1943, the 34th Guards Heavy Tank Regiment lost seven of its 20 KV-85s to fire from German PzKpfw IV tanks and Marder tank destroyers. The following day, a German attack was repulsed with no losses to the remaining KV-85s.

ARMOUR
The armour of the KV-85 was characteristically sloped to enhance its effectiveness and ranged from 40–90mm (1.57–3.54in). Later Soviet tanks of the Josef Stalin series were more heavily armoured.

MUSEUM VEHICLE
A KV-85 tank sits silently today, a monument to the service of its crews during World War II.

M26 Pershing (1943)

SPECIFICATIONS

DIMENSIONS:	Length: 8.61m (28ft 3in); Width: 3.51m (11ft 6in); Height: 2.77m (9ft 1in)
WEIGHT:	37.3 tonnes (41.2 tons)
ENGINE:	Ford GAF 8-cylinder petrol engine, 450–500hp (340–370kW)
SPEED:	48km/h (30mph)
ARMAMENT:	Main gun: 90mm (3.5in) M3 gun Co-axial: 7.62mm (0.3in) Browning M1919 machine gun Turret top: 12.7mm (0.5in) M2 machine gun; Bow: 7.62mm Browning M1919 machine gun
ARMOUR:	50–102mm (2–4in)
RANGE:	160km (100 miles)
CREW:	5

The M26 was developed as a counter to heavy German tanks in World War II, but arrived only in the closing stages of the conflict. Its 90mm (3.5in) gun could easily penetrate a T-34, which might have been useful if the Cold War had turned hot in the early 1950s.

Above: The weight of the M26 meant that lighter tanks spearheaded the drive across the Rhine in 1945. The Pershings followed once the far bank was secure.

MACHINE GUN
A .50-calibre M2H2 machine gun was mounted on the top of the turret, for both anti-aircraft and anti-personnel purposes.

CREW
The M26 had a crew of five: commander, driver, assistant driver, gunner and gun loader.

MAIN GUN
The Pershing was armed with the powerful 90mm (3.5in) M3 gun.

ARMOUR
The hull front included sloped armour of 102mm (4in) thickness.

ALWAYS TOO LATE

The M26 Pershing has acquired a reputation of always being just too late to make a difference. Even in the Korea War (1950–53), by the time it was deployed in significant numbers there were few enemy tanks left for it to fight. It stood ready in Europe to repel a Soviet invasion that never came, passing into Belgian service after being phased out by the US military. However, the Pershing marked a maturing of US tank design, which led to the M48 Patton.

KOREAN WAR PERSHINGS

By the end of 1950, more than 300 M26 Pershings had been deployed in Korea. By that time, the majority of North Korean tank forces had been eliminated.

Churchill AVRE (1943)

SPECIFICATIONS

DIMENSIONS:	Length: 7.44m (24ft 5in); Width: 2.44m (8ft); Height: 3.45m (11ft 4in) with log carpet mounted above tank
WEIGHT:	40.72 tonnes (40.07 tons)
ENGINE:	1 x Bedford Twin-Six petrol engine developing 261kW (350hp)
SPEED:	Road: 20km/h (12.5mph)Cross-country: 12.8km/h (8mph)
ARMAMENT:	Main: 1 x Petard 290mm (11.41in) spigot mortar; Secondary: 1 x 7.92mm (0.31in) BESA machine gun
ARMOUR:	16–102mm (0.62–4in)
RANGE:	144.8km (90 miles)
CREW:	5

APPLICATIONS

Apart from the log-carpet application seen here, the Churchill AVRE could be put to a broad spectrum of other uses. Its 'Mortar, Recoiling Spigot, Mark II' was ideal for close-range assault operations, blasting reinforced enemy positions. On its front it could carry a Small Box Girder bridge, which could be laid across ditches or rivers up to 9m (30ft) wide. For laying tracks over soft terrain, it could also carry and deploy large rolls of canvas in drums, known as 'Bobbbins'.

The Churchill AVRE (Assault Vehicle Royal Engineers) was developed in 1943 for a variety of uses by combat engineers, who had to overcome natural and man-made obstacles across the beaches of Normandy and into the Third Reich.

Right: The AVRE with its log carpet in the elevated position. The vehicle could also carry fascines, large bundles of logs dropped into trenches or ditches to create a crossing surface.

MAIN ARMAMENT
The main armament of the Churchill AVRE was a 290mm (11.4in) spigot mortar that used a powerful spring to hurl an 18.1kg (40lb) projectile at enemy fixed emplacements more than 73m (239ft) away.

LOG CARPET
The AVRE Log Carpet variant carried 100 logs measuring 152mm (6in) in diameter and 4.26m (14ft) in length. The logs were tied together with wire and carried on an overhead frame. When deployed they fashioned a temporary road across difficult terrain.

ENGINE
The Churchill AVRE engine was a single Bedford Twin-Six petrol powerplant that produced 261kW (350hp).

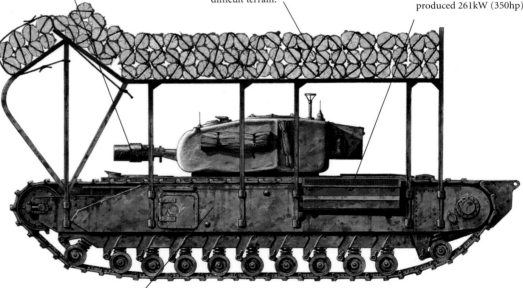

CREW COMPARTMENT
The interior of the Churchill AVRE was modified to allow room for Royal Engineers and their array of gear, including tools, equipment and explosives used to clear obstacles, deploy bridging and other tasks.

OBSTACLE CROSSING
This Churchill AVRE demonstrates its ability to traverse challenging obstacles during field testing. Note the large bundles of fascines that have been dropped at the foot of the obstacle to assist in negotiating its formidable height.

Churchill Mk VII Crocodile (1943)

SPECIFICATIONS

DIMENSIONS:	Length: (without trailer) 7.44m (24ft 5in); Width: 2.74m (9ft 0in); Height: 3.45m (11ft 4in)
WEIGHT:	40.6 tonnes (40 tons)
ENGINE:	Bedford 12-cylinder patrol, 261kW (350hp)
SPEED:	maximum road speed of 20km/h (12.5mph)
ARMAMENT:	1 x 75mm Ordnance QF main gun; 1 x Flame Projector Unit
ARMOUR:	51–152mm (2–6in)
RANGE:	Road range of 144km (90 miles)
CREW:	5

The Churchill Crocodile was a conversion of the Churchill Mk VII adapted for the beach assault role and used in the Normandy invasion as a flamethrower and assault tank.

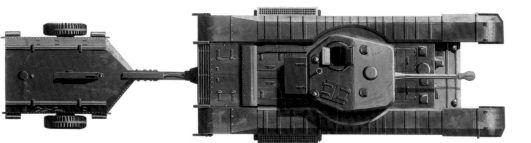

Above: The Crocodile got its name because it came on to the beach with a motion suggestive of a crocodile crawling out of the water.

HULL
Although superficially similar to earlier models, the Churchill VII was of completely new construction. It had no hull frame, but was constructed from frameless armour plate that was joined to form a rigid structure.

TURRET
The Churchill VII had a new heavy cast and welded turret with a commander's cupola.

ARMAMENT
Unlike some other flamethrower tanks, the Crocodile could use its main gun at the same time as its projector and retained its coaxial machine gun.

CANNON
The main difference from earlier marks was the 75mm (17pdr) MV (Medium Velocity) cannon, which replaced the outdated 57mm (6pdr) of earlier versions.

TRAILER
The trailer could be jettisoned when empty or hit and had enough fuel for 80 one-second bursts of fire.

FLAME UNIT
The Crocodile, of which 800 were made, replaced the hull machine gun with a projector that emitted a jet of flame 73–110m (80–120yd) long. This was fed under pressure by a pipe from the 6.5-tonnes (6.3-ton) armoured trailer. On D-Day, the Crocodiles were used against bunkers and machine gun positions on the beach, and later as flamethrowers or conventional tanks, as the situation dictated.

CAMP LIBERATION
A Crocodile tank from the 79th Armoured Division helps in the destruction of the Bergen-Belsen concentration camp, in May 1945.

Sturmmörser Tiger (1943)

SPECIFICATIONS

DIMENSIONS:	Length: 6.28m (20ft 7in); Width: 3.57m (11ft 4in); Height: 2.85m (9ft 4in)
WEIGHT:	65 tonnes (64 tons)
ENGINE:	Maybach HL210P45 V-12 petrol engine, generating 700hp (522kW)
SPEED:	40km/h (25mph)
ARMAMENT:	Main: 380mm (14.9in) RW 61 rocket launcher L/5.4; Secondary: 100mm (3.94 in) grenade launcher; 7.92 mm (0.31in) MG 34
ARMOUR:	28–150 mm (1.1–5.9in)
RANGE:	Road range of 120km (75 miles)
CREW:	5–7

The Sturmmörserwagen 606/4 mit 38 cm RW 61, or also known as the Sturmmörser Tiger or Sturmtiger, was created by converting the Tiger E battle tank to fire huge rocket-assisted projectiles in the assault role. Very few were actually built.

ROCKET PROJECTOR
The ball-mounted *Raketenwerfer* (rocket projector) was mounted slightly off-centre and had a series of holes around its rim for venting rocket gases.

LOW PRODUCTION
Estimates for the number produced vary between 10 and 81, but a likely figure is 18. They were issued to three different Sturmmörser companies and their giant mortars played a role in the defence of Germany rather than being used for their intended purpose of blowing apart enemy strongpoints with a single shot.

MAIN WEAPON
The main weapon of the Sturmtiger was the 380mm (14.9in) StuM RW61 rocket

CREW COMPARTMENT
A crew of seven operated the Sturmtiger in action, although most travelled

WINCH SYSTEM
Handling the shells, which weighed 345kg (761lb) each, was a delicate and dangerous

WEIGHT
The weight of the Sturmtiger was 65 tonnes (66 tons) compared to the 57 tonnes (57.9 tons) of a standard Tiger.

DEFENSIVE WEAPON
A Sturmmörser lies wrecked in a village in Germany, 1945. The vehicles was ineffective in the defensive role and most were destroyed or captured in early 1945.

Sherman Crab Mine-Clearing Tank (1944)

SPECIFICATIONS

DIMENSIONS:	Length: 6.35m (20ft 10in); Width: 2.81m (9ft 3in); Height: 3.96m (13ft)
WEIGHT:	32.28 tonnes (31.7 tons)
ENGINE:	1 x Ford GAA V-8 petrol powerplant generating 373kW (500hp)
SPEED:	46km/h (28.75mph)
ARMAMENT:	Main: 1 x 75mm (2.95in) gun Secondary: 1 x 7.62mm (0.3in) Browning machine gun (removed from some tanks)
ARMOUR:	15–76mm (0.59–2.9in)
RANGE:	62km (100 miles)
CREW:	5

The Medium Tank M4, popularly known as the Sherman, has been adapted for specialized service more than any other tank. The Sherman Crab Mine-Clearing Tank utilized a flail to detonate land mines, clearing a path for troops that followed.

Right: Using a rotating bobbin and 43 lengths of chain, the Sherman Crab detonated land mines in its path and marked the passage through a minefield with coloured chalk, smoke or luminous poles periodically fired into the ground automatically.

CHAIN LINKS
Replacement chains were carried aboard the tank in a rack attached to the hull. Cutter disks were added to the flail to destroy barbed-wire entanglements.

MAIN ARMAMENT
The Sherman Crab mining tank mounted the standard 75mm (2.95in) gun and was sometimes employed in the infantry support or tank versus tank role. When the flail was in use, the gun faced to the rear.

ENGINE
The Sherman Crab's Ford GAA V-8 petrol engine was modified to accept the drive shaft that powered the flail. Operating the flail off the main tank engine was a decided advantage over an external engine that was prone to breakdowns.

CRABS AT WAR
During the Normandy landings on 6 June 1944, the Sherman Crabs of the Westminster Dragoons, 22nd Dragoons and 1st Lothians and Border Yeomanry were with the first wave of British and Canadian troops to land on Gold, Juno and Sword Beaches, clearing mines and engaging German machine-gun nests and bunkers. The Crabs saw service throughout the rest of World War II.

HYDRAULIC APPARATUS
The right arm of the Sherman Crab flail was hydraulically powered, raising and lowering the apparatus as needed. The Mk II variant included a jib that was weighted and balanced to follow the contour of the terrain.

FLAIL TESTING
The flail of a Sherman Crab kicks up a cloud of dust and dirt while undergoing extensive testing in April 1944. British designers and engineers used the American M4 medium tank as the basis for the most effective Allied mine clearing tank of World War II.

Sherman VC Firefly (1944)

SPECIFICATIONS

DIMENSIONS:	Length: 7.85m (25ft 9in); Width: 2.67m (8ft 9in); Height: 2.74m (8ft 11in)
WEIGHT:	33 tonnes (32.4 tons)
ENGINE:	1 x Chrysler A57 30-cylinder petrol powerplant generating 350kW (470hp)
SPEED:	40km/h (25mph)
ARMAMENT:	Main: 1 x 17pdr (76.2mm/3in) QF gun; Secondary: 1 x 7.62mm (0.3in) Browning machine gun
ARMOUR:	15–100mm (0.59–3.9in)
RANGE:	Road: 201km (125 miles); Cross-country: 145km (90.1 miles)
CREW:	4

Intended as a short-term solution to the need for additional firepower, British designers replaced the main gun of the M4 Sherman with the heavier 17pdr QF and produced a tank that was effective against German Tigers and Panthers. By D-Day, 6 June 1944, nearly 350 Sherman Firefly tanks were in service with British forces. As the campaign in Normandy came to an end, the number of Fireflies in service topped 400.

ARMOUR
The armour protection of the Firefly varied from the basic M4 Sherman tank only in the greater thickness of the turret mantlet, which was 13mm (0.5in) thicker.

MAIN ARMAMENT
The 17pdr (76.2mm/3in) QF anti-tank gun was the most powerful weapon of its kind built by the British during World War II. Modified to fit the M4 Sherman turret, it proved an equalizer in combat against German Tiger and Panther tanks.

RADIO BUSTLE
To accommodate the large 17pdr QF gun, the turret of the M4 Sherman tank was modified. Among the changes was the removal of the radio to a bustle at the rear of the turret.

ENGINE
The Firefly powerplant varied with the version of M4 Sherman that was being modified. Those that were M4A4 conversions were powered by the Chrysler A57 30-cylinder petrol engine.

STINGING FIREFLY
When the Sherman VC Firefly entered service with the British 21st Army Group in the spring of 1944, the Germans quickly grew to respect the new Allied tank mounting the QF 17pdr gun. In several documented actions, the Firefly got the best of the heavy German Tiger and medium Panther tanks, particularly when firing from concealed positions. One such event occurred on 8 August 1944, near the French village of Saint-Aignan-de-Cramesnil. Fireflies of the Northamptonshire Yeomanry destroyed three Tigers in a matter of minutes, one of them reported to have been commanded by SS Tiger tank ace Hauptsturmführer (Captain) Michael Wittman.

PRODUCTION
The Sherman VC Firefly entered production in the autumn of 1943 and was available to British forces during the Normandy campaign. Its 17pdr QF gun substantially improved the odds of survival in combat with German tanks.

Cromwell Mk VIII (1944)

SPECIFICATIONS

DIMENSIONS:	Length: 6.35m (20ft 10in); Width: 2.9m (9ft 6in); Height: 2.49m (8ft 2in)
WEIGHT:	29 tonnes (28.5 tons)
ENGINE:	1 x V-12 Rolls-Royce Meteor powerplant generating 447kW (600hp)
SPEED:	61km/h (37.9mph)
ARMAMENT:	Main: 1 x 75mm (2.95in) QF gun Secondary: 2 x 7.92mm (0.31in) BESA machine guns
ARMOUR:	8–76mm (0.31in–2.9in)
RANGE:	Road: 278km (173 miles); Cross-country: 128.75km (80 miles)
CREW:	5

Perpetuating the British line of cruiser tanks, but finally accounting for the need for a more powerful gun and increased armour protection, the Cromwell Mk VIII made great strides in combat effectiveness against German tanks.

Right: The Cromwell Mk VIII provided a considerable improvement in firepower and armour protection over previous cruiser tank designs. The Cromwell entered combat with British armoured units during the Normandy campaign in 1944.

ARMOUR PROTECTION
With up to 76mm (2.9in) of armour protection, the Cromwell offered its crew a greater chance of survival on the battlefield. Seams and rivets were welded to add extra strength in the final production version of the new tank.

ENGINE
The V-12 Rolls-Royce Meteor petrol engine provided power that preserved the Cromwell's speed advantage despite the added weight of a heavier main gun and enhanced armour protection.

MAIN ARMAMENT
The 75mm (2.95in) QF gun provided the increased firepower necessary for the Cromwell Mk VIII to somewhat even the odds in tank versus tank combat with a new generation of German armoured vehicles.

SECONDARY ARMAMENT
Most versions of the Cromwell mounted two 7.92mm (0.31in) BESA machine guns, one ball-mounted forward in the hull and the other mounted coaxially in the turret.

CROMWELL IN COMBAT

The Cromwell Mk VIII primarily equipped units of the British 7th Armoured Division – the famed Desert Rats. At full strength, the armour complement of a Cromwell regiment included the Mk IV with its 75mm (2.95in) gun, the 95mm (3.74in) howitzer-equipped Mk VIII and the Sherman Firefly, an upgunned British variant of the American M4 Sherman medium tank. Although its main gun was still inferior to those of the German Tiger and Panther tanks, it was a considerable improvement over previous British cruiser tank models.

CROMWELL ADVANCE

The bocage country of Normandy inhibited the Cromwell's advantage of speed, but once the breakout from the hedgerow was achieved the tank kept pace with the rapid movement of infantry across France and into the Third Reich. Here a Cromwell displays its speed, raising clouds of dust during a swift advance.

Tiger II 'King Tiger' (1944)

SPECIFICATIONS

DIMENSIONS:	Length: 7.25m (23ft 10in); Width: 3.72m (12ft 2in); Height: 3.27m (10ft 9in)
WEIGHT:	63.5 tonnes (62.5 tons)
ENGINE:	1 x V-12 Maybach HL 230 P30 petrol engine producing 514kW (690hp)
SPEED:	38km/h (24mph)
ARMAMENT:	Main: 1 x 88mm (3.5in) KwK 43 L/71 high-velocity gun; Secondary: 2 x 7.92mm (0.31in) MG 34 machine guns
ARMOUR:	40–180mm (1.57–7in)
RANGE:	Road: 170km (105 miles); off-road: 120km (70 miles)
CREW:	5

Even as production began on the initial Tiger, the Henschel and Porsche companies were working to develop an even more formidable heavy tank. When Henschel won the contract in October 1943, the result was dubbed the Tiger II or 'King Tiger'.

Right: Although the Tiger II was a formidable foe in combat, fuel shortages and mechanical failures resulted in a number of the massive tanks being abandoned in the field or destroyed by their crews to prevent capture.

PSYCHOLOGICAL IMPACT

The impact of the Tiger II on the battlefields of Europe may best be measured in its psychological effect on Allied soldiers who encountered the armoured giant, or those who believed they had. In reality, the Tiger II was never available in great numbers owing to the German penchant for perceived quality over quantity and the damage inflicted on the country's industrial capacity by continuous Allied bombing. Through the course of World War II, fewer than 500 Tiger IIs were actually completed and deployed during a brief production run from late 1943 through the spring of 1945.

ENGINE
The V-12 Maybach HL 230 P30 petrol engine was also used in Panther medium tanks produced late in the war. In the field, the Maybach powerplant was the source of many mechanical breakdowns.

ARMOUR PROTECTION
The frontal armour of the Tiger II was 150mm (5.9in) thick and sloped 50mm (1.97in), while armour protection for the front of the turret increased to 180mm (7in). Side armour was 80mm (3.15in) thick and sloped at a 25° angle.

MAIN ARMAMENT
The main weapon of the Tiger II heavy tank was the 88mm (3.5in) KwK 43 L/71 high-velocity gun. The weapon's barrel was over 6m (19ft) long.

AMMUNITION STOWAGE
The Tiger II carried a minimum of 80 rounds of armour-piercing and high-explosive 88mm (3.46in) ammunition. While the armour-piercing rounds were for hard targets such as enemy tanks, the high-explosive rounds were devastating to softer targets such as troop concentrations.

ARDENNES OFFENSIVE
The Tiger II reached the battlefield on the Eastern Front in the spring of 1944 and was to play a pivotal role in Hitler's Ardennes Offensive in the West. However, fuel shortages and mechanical problems crippled its combat performance in the field.

Jagdpanzer VI Jagdtiger (1944)

SPECIFICATIONS

DIMENSIONS:	Length: 10.65m (34ft 11in); Width: 3.63m (11ft 11in); Height: 2.95m (9ft 8in)
WEIGHT:	70.6 tonnes (69.5 tons)
ENGINE:	1 x V-12 Maybach HL230 P30 petrol engine generating 522kW (700hp)
SPEED:	38km/h (24mph)
ARMAMENT:	Main: 1 x 128mm (5in) Pak 44 L/55 gun; Secondary: 2 x 7.92mm (0.31in) MG 34 machine guns
ARMOUR:	25–250mm (0.98–9.8in)
RANGE:	Road: 120km (75 miles); Cross-country: 80km (50 miles)
CREW:	6

Although the Jagdtiger, or 'Hunting Tiger,' was the most heavily armed and armoured vehicle deployed during World War II, its ponderous weight, high fuel consumption and inadequate powerplant limited its worth on the battlefield.

Right: The high silhouette of the Jagdtiger made it a conspicuous target on the battlefield. Aside from vulnerability to tank-killer squads the Hunting Tiger was also especially exposed to being spotted and attacked by Allied fighter-bombers.

SECONDARY ARMAMENT
Two 7.92mm (0.31in) MG 34 machine guns protected the Tiger II from infantry attack. One was mounted coaxially in the welded turret, while the other was ball-mounted on the right front hull.

MAIN ARMAMENT
The 128mm (5in) Pak 44 L/55 anti-tank gun was chosen as the primary weapon of the Jagdtiger. It was the heaviest weapon of its kind deployed during World War II.

ENGINE
The V-12 Maybach HL 230 P30 petrol engine was used in Panther medium tanks and the Tiger II heavy tank. The engine was inadequate to power the Jagdtiger efficiently, the heaviest armoured vehicle deployed during World War II.

JAGDTIGER IN COMBAT
Only about 70 examples of the Jagdpanzer VI Jagdtiger were produced by the Nibelungwerk in St Valentin, Germany. Its combat record was mixed. Mechanical failures accounted for numerous losses among the Jagdtigers and the inexperience of some crews resulted in disaster. Tiger tank ace Otto Carius remembered a Jagdtiger commander turning broadside rather than toward the enemy and absorbing several hits that resulted in the deaths of all six crewmen. During a January 1945 encounter, however, a company of Jagdtigers destroyed 11 Sherman tanks, 30 trucks and other vehicles.

SUPERSTRUCTURE
The turret of the Tiger II was removed in favour of a high superstructure in the Jagdtiger, while the hull of the heavy tank was lengthened to accommodate another crewman and the heavy main gun.

CAPTURED JAGDTIGER
American soldiers examine a captured Jagdtiger somewhere in Northwest Europe, late 1944. Note the open doors of the hatch at the rear of the superstructure, the Zimmerit anti-magnetic mine paste applied to the hull and the spare tracks attached to the superstructure.

M24 Chaffee (1944)

SPECIFICATIONS

DIMENSIONS:	Length: 5.49m (18ft); Width: 2.95m (9ft 8in); Height: 2.46m (8ft 1in)
WEIGHT:	18.4 tonnes (18.1 tons)
ENGINE:	Twin Cadillac 44T24 V-8 petrol engines generating combined 220hp (164kW)
SPEED:	56km/h (36mph)
ARMAMENT:	Main: 1 x 75mm (2.95in) M6 gun; Secondary: 2 x 7.62mm (0.3in) Browning machine guns; 1 x 12.7mm (0.5in) Browning machine gun
ARMOUR:	9.5–38mm (0.37–1.5in)
RANGE:	161km (100 miles)
CREW:	5

KOREAN SERVICE

The greatest combat contribution of the M24 Chaffee came during the Korean War of 1950–53. In the early days of the conflict, the Chaffee was available in quantity and it delivered excellent performance in the reconnaissance and infantry support roles. Again, however, it was sometimes compelled to serve in tank versus tank combat and was overmatched by the superb Soviet-built T-34 medium tanks deployed by North Korean forces.

True to its heritage as an armoured vehicle for reconnaissance and infantry support, the M24 Chaffee light tank was a vast improvement over its predecessor, the M3 Stuart, mounting a 75mm (2.95in) main gun and a trio of machine guns. The M24 reached the battlefields of Europe in November 1944. Its numbers were too few, however, to make a definitive impact on Allied operations before the German surrender.

SECONDARY ARMAMENT
Heavily armed for a light tank, the M24 carried a 12.7mm (0.5in) Browning machine gun on the turret hatch and a pair of 7.62mm (0.3in) Browning machine guns coaxially mounted in the turret and in the front hull.

MAIN ARMAMENT
The 75mm (2.95in) M6 gun, adapted from the modified weapon that served aboard the B-25 Mitchell bomber, provided the firepower that had long been lacking in American light tanks.

ARMOUR PROTECTION
The thin armour of the M24, only 38mm (1.5in) at its thickest on the front of the hull, meant that the speedy and upgunned tank was still vulnerable to a variety of German anti-tank weapons.

ENGINE
The twin Cadillac Model 44T24 V-8 petrol engines mounted in the rear of the M24 chassis produced plenty of power for the light tank to manoeuvre in reconnaissance and to maintain contact with advancing infantry units.

M24 IN WORLD WAR II
The M24 Chaffee light tank represented a new generation of American tank development; however, its combat debut in World War II did little to enhance its reputation. Due more to its lack of numbers than inferior performance, only a few dozen Chaffee tanks reached the front prior to the end of the war.

T-34/85 (1944)

SPECIFICATIONS

DIMENSIONS:	Length: 6m (19ft 8in); Width: 2.92 metres (9ft 7in); Height: 2.39 metres (7ft 10in)
WEIGHT:	32 tonnes (31.4 tons)
ENGINE:	1 x 12-cylinder V-2-34 water-cooled diesel engine developing 500hp (375kW)
SPEED:	55km/h (34mph)
ARMAMENT:	Main: 1 x 85mm (3.35in) ZIS-S-53 gun; Secondary: 2 x 7.62mm (0.3in) DT machine guns
ARMOUR:	20–55mm (0.78–2.1in)
RANGE:	300km (188 miles)
CREW:	5

BATTLEFIELD IMPROVEMENT

The T-34/85 brought better combat survivability to Soviet armoured forces. The greater range of the new main weapon and its muzzle velocity of 780mps (2559fps) improved penetration of German armour plating with armour-piercing ammunition. Combat experience revealed the need for additional protection against German anti-tank weapons such as the shoulder-fired Panzerfaust. Additional thin plating or wire mesh was welded into areas around the hull and turret that were susceptible to 'trapping' shells or hollow charges. These were often successful at deflecting otherwise damaging strikes.

The improved firepower of the T-34/85 medium tank came about following analysis of the T-34 performance during the Battle of Kursk in July 1943. Three 85mm (3.35in) weapons were considered before a decision was made to mount the ZIS-S-53.

MAIN ARMAMENT
When the T-34 medium tank's 76.2mm (3in) L-11 gun and later the long-barrelled F-34 were both deemed insufficient in firepower, the new 85mm (3.35in) ZIS-S-53 cannon was installed and the new variant was dubbed the T-34/85.

ENGINE
The T-34/85 powerplant was essentially the same as that of the early T-34, the reliable 12-cylinder V-2-34 water-cooled diesel engine that generated 500hp (375kW).

TURRET
The turret of the T-34/85 was expanded to accommodate three crewmen rather than two, eliminating the need of the tank commander to serve the tank's main weapon.

SUSPENSION
Stronger springs were installed in the T-34/85's Christie suspension system to deal with the heaver turret weight. The suspension was originally designed by American engineer Walter Christie.

FUEL TANKS
The fuel tank capacity of the T-34/85 was reduced from that of the original T-34 due to the redesign of the tank and its added weight. Although the change negatively impacted the T-34/85's range, the firepower gained was worth the price.

TANK COLUMN
A column of T-34/85s stop during the winter offensive of late 1944–early 1945 during the push into Eastern Europe. Approximately 22,500 T-34/85 tanks were produced during the war and production continued into the late 1950s.

IS-3 (1945)

SPECIFICATIONS

DIMENSIONS:	Length: 6.77m (22ft 2in); Width: 3.07m (10ft 1in); Height: 2.44m (8ft)
WEIGHT:	45.8 tonnes (45 tons)
ENGINE:	1 x V-2-IS V-12 diesel powerplant generating 447kW (600hp)
SPEED:	37km/h (22.9mph)
ARMAMENT:	Main: 1 x 122mm (4.8in) D25-T gun; Secondary: 2 x 7.62mm (0.3in) DT or DTM machine guns; 1 x 12.7mm (0.5in) DshK machine gun
ARMOUR:	20–230mm (0.78–9in)
RANGE:	Road: 160km (100 miles); cross-country: 120km (75 miles)
CREW:	4

The last Soviet heavy tank to enter production before the end of World War II, the IS-3 became operational too late to influence the outcome of the war, but nevertheless became a symbol of the Red Army's military might.

Below: This side view shows the 122mm (4.8in) D-25-T gun, developed from the M1931/37 field gun.

ENGINE
The IS-3 was powered by a 12-cylinder, V-2 diesel engine, generating 447 kW (600 hp).

BREECH
Unable to pivot fully on its vertical axis, the breech of the main gun limited the ability to depress the weapon completely.

DRIVER
The driver compartment in the hull was typical of Soviet designs, offering little comfort or storage space.

TURRET
Its rounded cast turret resembled an overturned soup bowl. The turret was small and restricted crew movement.

WAR SERVICE
Although the IS-3 bears something of a family resemblance to preceding Soviet tanks, its design was distinctly different. At the end of World War II, fewer than 30 of the new tank had been completed, but by mid-1946 the number in Red Army service exceeded 2300. Despite the fact that its combat participation in World War II is doubtful, a regiment of the 45.8-tonne (45-ton) machines participated in a victory parade through Red Square on 7 September 1945.

TURRET FEATURES
In the photo at right, the distinctive turret of the IS-3, which was said to resemble an overturned soup bowl or skillet, is easily distinguished. The narrow frontal area and low turret of the IS-3 theoretically reduced the probability of detection and the drawing of enemy fire.

Centurion (1945)

SPECIFICATIONS

DIMENSIONS:	Length: 7.6m (25ft); Width: 3.38m (11ft 1in); Height: 3.01m (9ft 10.5in)
WEIGHT:	52 tonnes (57 tons)
ENGINE:	1 x 12-cylinder Rolls-Royce Mark IVB Meteor engine generating 485kW (650hp)
SPEED:	34km/h (21mph)
ARMAMENT:	Main: 1 x 105mm (4.1in) L7A2 rifled gun; Secondary: Up to 2 x 7.62mm (0.3in) Browning machine guns
ARMOUR:	51–152mm (2–5.9in)
RANGE:	Road: 185km (115 miles); Off-road: 96km (60miles)
CREW:	4

Developed as a cruiser tank during World War II, the British Centurion A41 arrived too late to see action against the German tanks it was intended to defeat. Nevertheless, its service life has lasted more than half a century.

Right: A rear view of an Israeli Centurion during the Six-Day War of 1967.

ENGINE
The Centurion A41 was powered by the 12-cylinder Rolls-Royce Mark IVB Meteor engine, a variant of the Merlin aircraft engine adapted for armour. The Israelis installed the Teledyne Continental AVDS-1790-2R diesel engine in their Sho't variant.

COMMANDER POSITION
To pinpoint a target, the Centurion commander used periscopic rangefinding sights that were mechanically linked to the sights of the gunner. The commander was positioned beneath a rotating cupola on the right side of the turret.

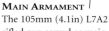

MAIN ARMAMENT
The 105mm (4.1in) L7A2 rifled gun served as main armament on the majority of Centurion tanks, although a limited number were produced mounting the 17pdr and 20pdr QF guns.

ISRAELI USE
The Israeli Defence Force utilized the Centurion effectively during the Six-Day War of 1967 and the 1973 Yom Kippur War. The Israelis modified the Centurion to produce the Sho't variant, which served into the 1990s. The Sho't regularly prevailed during the Yom Kippur War in single combat with Soviet-made Syrian T-54/55 and T-62 tanks. Centurion variants are still active as modified recovery, bridgelaying and troop carrier vehicles.

ARMOUR PROTECTION
Armour protection aboard the Centurion reached 150mm (5.9in) on the turret front. Armour thickness along the welded steel hull was up to 120mm (4.7in) and the side skirts were reminiscent of the earlier German Panther medium tank.

ON EXERCISE
The Centurion compiled an impressive service record during more than half a century with the armoured forces of nations around the world. Its heavy armour protection and accurate 105mm (4.1in) rifled gun made it an enduringly effective weapon.

T-54/55 (1947)

SPECIFICATIONS

DIMENSIONS:	Length: 6.45m (21ft 1in); Width: 3.27m (10ft 8in); Height: 2.4m (7ft 10in)
WEIGHT:	36 tonnes (35.4 tons)
ENGINE:	1 x 12-cylinder V-54 (later V-55) diesel powerplant generating 388kW (520hp)
SPEED:	50km/h (30mph)
ARMAMENT:	Main: 1 x 100mm (3.9in) D10T rifled gun (later D10T2S) Secondary: 1 x 7.62mm (0.3in) PKT machine gun; 1 x 12.7mm (0.5in) DShK machine gun
ARMOUR:	20–205mm (0.79–8in)
RANGE:	500km (300 miles)
CREW:	4

The Soviet T-54/55 main battle tank was produced in greater numbers than any other tank in history. More than 65 years later, it remains in service with the armed forces of numerous small nations and Third World countries.

Below: The T-54/55 tank in profile, with the DShKM machine gun mounted on the turret.

TURRET
The flattened dome turret of the T-54/55 resembled an overturned soup bowl. Its cramped interior impeded crew efficiency and the location of the commander, gunner and loader on the left side meant that a single hit could be lethal to all three.

MAIN ARMAMENT
The T-54/55 was originally armed with the 100mm (3.9in) D10T gun. This was later upgraded to the improved D10T2S with a bore evacuator and improved gun-laying system.

ENGINE
The V-54 12-cylinder diesel engine was prone to mechanical failure due to its poor magnesium alloy construction. The updated V-55 was only partially successful in correcting the problems with the V-54.

HAZARDOUS STORAGE
Fuel and ammunition were stored close together in the hull of the T-54/55, increasing the likelihood of a fire or major explosion in the event of a direct hit.

PROXY WARS AND REVOLUTIONS

The T-54/55 main battle tank has engaged in combat on numerous occasions during its more than 65 years in service. During the Vietnam War, South Vietnamese and American Patton tanks clashed with North Vietnamese T-54s and often got the better of the Soviet-built machines. However, they did not fare as well against the Israeli Centurions during the Six-Day and Yom Kippur Wars.

NBC PROTECTION
With the dawn of the nuclear age, it became necessary to improve survivability of tank and crew in the event of an atomic detonation. A nuclear, biological and chemical (NBC) defence system was installed in the T-54/55 in the 1950s.

IRAQI TANK
In the photo below, an Iraqi T-54/55 lies abandoned after the defeat of Saddam Hussein's army in the 1991 Gulf War.

M41 Walker Bulldog (1951)

SPECIFICATIONS

DIMENSIONS:	Length: 5.8m (19ft 1in); Width: 3.19m (10ft 6in); Height: 2.72m (8ft 11in)
WEIGHT:	23.49 tonnes (23.1 tons)
ENGINE:	1 x Continental AOS-895-3 six-cylinder air-cooled petrol, 500bhp (372kW)
SPEED:	72.4km/h (45mph)
ARMAMENT:	Main: 76mm (3in) M32A1 rifled cannon; Secondary: 1 x 7.62mm (0.3in) M1919A4 coaxial machine gun; 1 x 12.7mm (0.5in) Browning M2 machine gun
ARMOUR:	9.25–31.7mm (0.3–1.25in)
RANGE:	161km (100 miles)
CREW:	4

Implementing lessons learnt in combat during World War II, US engineers developed the M41 Walker Bulldog. This light, air-transportable tank was armed well enough to defend itself and was compatible with parts designed for other armoured vehicles.

TURRET
The cast and welded turret of the M41 was distinguished by its elongated bustle. It accommodated three crewmen.

INTERNAL CONFIGURATION
Divided into three compartments, with the driver to the front, the fighting compartment at centre, and the engine compartment separated by a firewall to the rear, the M41 interior was highly functional, though American crews complained of limited headroom.

MAIN ARMAMENT
The 76mm (3in) M32 main cannon featured an automatic loader, the first to be installed in a US-manufactured tank. The loader was used to select, lift, index, and ram the shell into position, and then to dispense of the empty casings.

ENGINE
The 500hp (374kW), six-cylinder Continental AOS 895-3 engine powered the M41 at up to 72km/h (45mph). A Lycoming engine was also used in some M41s.

DRIVER
The M41 driver sat forwards and to the left in the hull. A drop-out escape hatch was provided through the floor of the hull under the driver's seat.

SUSPENSION
The torsialastic, or rubber-brushed, suspension of the M41 included torsion bars and hydraulic shock absorbers. The drive sprocket was positioned at the rear, with an idler to the front and three return rollers, providing a relatively smooth cross-country ride.

ARVN TANKS
From the mid 1960s, the Army of the Republic of Vietnam (ARVN) were equipped with US M41A3 tanks to build up their armoured force. In one action during Operation *Lam Son 719*, in February–March 1971, a force of M41s destroyed seven T-54s and 16 PT-76s, for only four losses.

BULLDOG IN VIETNAM
Pausing along a street in a South Vietnamese city, the American crewmen of a Walker Bulldog tank watch traffic move past as infantrymen maintain a continuing cordon of security against Viet Cong infiltrators.

AMX-13 (1952)

SPECIFICATIONS

DIMENSIONS:	Length: 4.88m (16ft); Width: 2.5m (8ft 2in); Height: 2.3m (7ft 7in)
WEIGHT:	15 tonnes (14.7 tons)
ENGINE:	1 x SOFAM eight-cylinder V-8 petrol engine
SPEED:	60km/h (37mph)
ARMAMENT:	Main: 1 x 75mm (2.95in) gun Secondary: 2 x 7.5mm (0.29in) or 7.62mm (0.3in) FN1/AAT52 machine guns
ARMOUR:	10–40mm (0.39–1.57in)
RANGE:	Road: 400km (250 miles) Off-road: 250km (150 miles)
CREW:	3

Designed shortly after the end of World War II, the French airmobile AMX-13 light tank was in production into the 1980s and exported to numerous countries. Its many innovations included an oscillating turret and automatic loading system.

SHORTCOMINGS

Despite its innovations and popularity as an export weapon, the performance of the AMX-13 in combat conditions was disappointing. Although it was intended for reconnaissance and infantry support roles, it was at a disadvantage during inevitable encounters with enemy armour. The Israeli Army deployed the AMX-13 during the Suez Crisis of 1956 and the Six-Day War in 1967, but it was withdrawn from service shortly thereafter.

AMMUNITION STORAGE
Since the oscillating turret of the AMX-13 could house only two six-round magazines for the automatic loading system, additional ammunition was stored externally at the rear of the hull.

ENGINE
The basic AMX-13 was fitted with the eight-cylinder SOFAM petrol engine. Later versions were powered by a diesel engine that improved the vehicle's range and reduced the risk of fire.

MAIN ARMAMENT
The initial main armament of the AMX-13 light tank was a 75mm (2.95in) gun patterned after the successful KwK 42 L/70 mounted on the German Panther medium tank during World War II.

TURRET
The early oscillating F-10 turret of the AMX-13 was separated with an upper portion that pivoted to raise and lower the elevation of the 75mm (2.95in) gun. With heavier main weapons, the new F-12 turret was installed.

ARMOUR PROTECTION
The armour protection of the AMX-13 light tank was only 40mm (1.57in) at its maximum thickness. The AMX-13 was vulnerable to any anti-tank weapon in service from deployment to the end of its production.

CAMOUFLAGE
An AMX-13 under camouflage netting. Although this airmobile light tank was innovative in design, it was less than ideal in the field, with limited armour protection and traverse for the main weapon in mountainous terrain.

M48 Patton (1952)

SPECIFICATIONS

DIMENSIONS:	Length: 6.82m (22ft 7in); Width: 3.63m (11ft 11in); Height: 3.1m (10ft 1in)
WEIGHT:	47 tonnes (46.25 tons)
ENGINE:	1 x Continental AVDS-1790-2 V-12 diesel engine generating 559kW (750hp)
Speed:	48km/h (30mph)
ARMAMENT:	Main: 1 x 90mm (3.54in) M41 gun Secondary: 1 x 7.62mm (0.3in) M73 machine gun; 1 x 12.7mm (0.5in) Browning M2 machine gun
ARMOUR:	13–120mm (0.5–4.7in)
RANGE:	Road: 465km (290 miles); Off-road: 300km (180 miles)
CREW:	4

Following the American experience with armour in the Korean War, the development of the M48 Patton medium tank was undertaken. This was the third and most successful in the Patton line of post-war tanks.

Above: The service life of the M48 Patton medium tank has spanned six decades and many remain in service with armed forces around the world. The longevity of the M48 may be attributed in part to its adaptability to upgrades and cost efficiency. This model is employed by the Spanish Army.

ARMOUR PROTECTION
The armour protection of the M48 was improved from the previous tank designs of the Patton series. Turret armour ranged from 75mm (2.95in) on the sides to 110mm (4.3in) across the front, while the hull was armoured up to 120mm (4.7in) on the front glacis.

MAIN ARMAMENT
The main armament of the early M48 Patton medium tank was a 90mm (3.54in) gun. Israeli improvements included the 105mm (4.1in) L7A1 gun, and the United States followed with the heavier weapon. The 105mm is identifiable by its prominent blast deflector.

ENGINE
The Continental ABDS-1790-5B petrol engine was prone to catching fire in the early M48. It was subsequently replaced by a Continental AVDS-1790-2 diesel engine that also improved the tank's operational range.

PATTON PROWESS
The M48 first engaged in combat with Pakistani forces in 1965 and suffered serious losses against the Centurion tanks of the Indian Army. Jordanian M48s were vulnerable due to external petrol tanks during the Six-Day War. The Israeli Defence Force replaced the main 90mm (3.54in) gun with a heavier 105mm (4.1in) weapon and also deployed the M48 during the conflict. US forces sent more than 600 M48s to the Vietnam War.

ESCAPE HATCH
A single escape hatch was placed in the bottom of the M48 Patton medium tank's hull for the crew to exit the tank in case of an emergency.

TRAINING EXERCISE
The 105mm (4.1in) L7A1 main gun and the searchlight sighted with the main gun and gunsights are prominent on this M48 Patton splashing ashore during training exercises. The searchlight generates one million candle power to illuminate distant targets.

PT-76 (1952)

SPECIFICATIONS

DIMENSIONS:	Length: 6.91m (22ft 8in); Width: 3.15m (10ft 4in); Height: 2.33m (7ft 5.6in)
WEIGHT:	14 tonnes (13.7 tons)
ENGINE:	1 x V6B diesel engine on land developing 240hp (179kW); water jet for crossing streams and rivers
SPEED:	Land: 44km/h (27mph); Water: 10.2km/h (6.3mph)
ARMAMENT:	Main: 1 x 76.2mm (3in) D-56TS gun Secondary: 1 x 7.62mm (0.3in) SGMT machine gun; 1 x 12.7mm (0.5in) DShKM machine gun
ARMOUR:	5–20mm (0.19–0.78in)
RANGE:	260km (160 miles)
CREW:	3

The amphibious PT-76 light tank answered the requirement of the Soviet military establishment for a reconnaissance vehicle that could operate on land and water while also providing support for infantry.

Above: The PT 76 maintains a distinct advantage over other amphibious vehicles of its time. The light tank is capable of entering and exiting water without field modification and exposure of the crew to enemy fire.

MAIN ARMAMENT
The original 76.2mm (3in) D-56T gun was later supplanted by the D-56TM and finally the D-56TS, stabilized in two planes and with additional fire-control upgrades.

ARMOUR PROTECTION
The PT-76 was quite thinly armoured to maintain buoyancy in water and achieve reasonable speed on land for reconnaissance operations. Vulnerable to anything heavier than small arms fire, the amphibious tank was protected by a maximum 20mm (0.78in) of armour.

SNORKEL
The prominent snorkel is situated above a ventilator at the rear of the turret and allows oxygen to enter the tank interior while the PT-76 is in water. However, it can also introduce exhaust fumes into the crew and driver compartments.

ENGINE
The V-6B inline water-cooled diesel engine was adequate for the light tank on land, while a water-jet propulsion system moved the PT-76 through water.

FIGHT OR FLEE

The PT-76 was quite stable in water with the exception of heavy surf. This capability was achieved at the expense of armour protection and with hollow road wheels to lighten the tank's overall weight. With armour of just 20mm (0.78in) thickness on the front of the turret, the crew was protected only from small-arms fire up to 12.7mm (0.5in) calibre, small shell fragments and flash burn. A direct hit by anything more substantial was likely to penetrate the hull and disable the vehicle.

HULL CONFIGURATION
The hull configuration of the PT-76 resembles a pontoon or boat and the light tank operates well in amphibious situations, with the exception of heavy surf.

DISTRIBUTION

The PT-76 has seen action around the world, particularly with the North Vietnamese Army during the Vietnam War, with the armed forces of Arab nations during the conflicts with Israel in the 1960s and 1970s, through counterinsurgency operations in Indonesia and into the twenty-first century with Russian troops in Chechnya. For many years, China manufactured an unlicensed copy of the PT-76 and Polish factories built a copy as well.

M60 Patton (1960)

SPECIFICATIONS

DIMENSIONS:	Length: 6.94m (22ft 9in); Width: 3.6m (11ft); Height: 3.2m (10ft 6in)
WEIGHT:	45 tonnes (44.2 tons)
ENGINE:	1 x Continental V-12 AVDS-1790-2 twin-turbo diesel engine generating 560kW (750hp)
SPEED:	48km/h (30mph)
ARMAMENT:	Main: 1 x 105mm (4.1in) M68 gun Secondary: 1 x 7.62mm (0.3in) M73 Browning machine gun; 1 x 12.7mm (0.5in) M85 Browning machine gun
ARMOUR:	150mm (5.9in)
RANGE:	480km (300 miles)
CREW:	4

The M60 main battle tank emerged with significant modifications to the earlier medium M48 Patton. The M60 Patton was the first US armoured vehicle that was truly classified as a main battle tank. Although it relied heavily on the design of the previous M48, it was a marked improvement over the earlier tanks of the Patton series.

Above: Based on the M60A1 Patton main battle tank, the M728 CEV (Combat Engineer Vehicle) mounted a 165mm (6.5in) M135 gun, a licence-built copy of the British L9A1 gun used in British engineer vehicles based on their Centurion tank.

SECONDARY ARMAMENT
A 12.7mm (0.5in) M85 Browning heavy machine gun was mounted on the commander's cupola, while at least one 7.62mm (0.3in) M73 machine gun installed coaxially. Six-round smoke grenade launchers were located on either side of the turret.

MAIN ARMAMENT
The main weapon of the M60 Patton was the 105mm (4.1in) M68 gun, a licence-built version of the fine British L7A1 gun, which was also in use in other contemporary main battle tanks.

ENGINE
The Continental 12-cylinder AVDS-1790-2 turbocharged diesel engine transmitted power through a cross-drive transmission, which was a combined transmission, differential, steering and braking unit for the M60.

ARMOUR PROTECTION
The armour protection of the M60 was up to 150mm (5.9in) thick. It was the only American main battle tank to utilize homogeneous steel armour for protection.

SHOOTING STARSHIP
During 27 years of production from 1960 to 1987, more than 15,000 M60 Patton tanks, as shown in the photo at right, and in all variants were produced. The M60A2 variant, nicknamed the Starship, was modified with a 152mm (6in) weapon system capable of firing the Shillelagh anti-tank missile. The project proved to be a major disappointment with only 550 produced. Most of these were soon placed in storage.

TURRET
The turret of the original M60 main battle tank was similar to the M48. It was replaced in the M60A1 and M60A3 with a needle-nose turret, which reduced the frontal area exposed to enemy fire during combat.

ERA PLATES
The M60 Patton tank is considered by some to be its own main battle tank design and by others as a continuation of the Patton series. This vehicle has some explosive reactive armour (ERA) plates fitted.

T-62 (1961)

SPECIFICATIONS

DIMENSIONS:	Length: 9.34m (30ft 7in); Width: 3.30m (10ft 10in); Height: 2.40m (7ft 10in)
WEIGHT:	40 tonnes (39.3 tons)
ENGINE:	1 x 12-cylinder V-55 water-cooled diesel powerplant generating 433kW (581hp)
SPEED:	Road: 50km/h (31mph); cross-country: 40km/h (24.9mph)
ARMAMENT:	Main: 1 x 115mm (4.5in) U5TS smoothbore gun Secondary: 1 x 7.62mm (0.3in) PKT machine gun; 1 x 12.7mm (0.5in) DshK anti-aircraft machine gun
ARMOUR:	15mm–242mm (0.59–9.53in)
RANGE:	Road: 450km (280 miles) Off-road: 320km (199 miles)
CREW:	4

Only marginally improving on the T-54/55 main battle tank, the T-62 became the primary Red Army tank during the 1960s and was manufactured in large numbers to equip the armoured forces of the Warsaw Pact nations.

Above: The Chinese Type 69 tank shown here was based on a Chinese version of the old Soviet T-54, but with many components copied from the Soviet T-62. The Type 69 became the first independently Chinese-developed main battle tank.

SECONDARY ARMAMENT
The secondary armament of the T-62 included a single 7.62mm (0.3in) PKT coaxial machine gun and a 12.7mm (0.5in) DshK 1938/46 heavy machine gun that the commander had to exit the turret to operate.

MAIN ARMAMENT
The smoothbore 115mm (4in) U5TS gun ushered in a new era as the primary weapon of a main battle tank rather than the previous guns with rifled barrels that had been prevalent for many years.

ENGINE
The 12-cylinder V-55 4-stroke water-cooled diesel engine was an adequate powerplant for the T-62, generating a top speed of 50km/h (31mph) on the road.

LONG T-62 SERVICE
Years after production ceased in the Soviet Union and Czechoslovakia, North Korea produced a variant of the T-62. Following the capture of a T-62 by the People's Liberation Army during border clashes with the Soviets in 1969, the People's Republic of China also produced an unlicensed copy designated the Type 69. Variants of the T-62 included the T-64 tank with an automatic loader, the SU-130 assault gun, a flamethrower tank and an armoured recovery vehicle.

ARMOUR PROTECTION
Even with its frontal hull armour increased to 102mm (4in) and sloped at 60°, the armour protection of the T-62 was considered inadequate by some experts in combat with a new generation of NATO tanks and anti-tank weapons.

SUSPENSION AND TRACTION
A T-62 main battle tank churns up a cloud of dust along a dirt road. The lack of return rollers in the modified Christie suspension is plainly visible. However, the tank did maintain good traction at moderate speed.

Chieftain Mk 5 (1963)

SPECIFICATIONS

DIMENSIONS: Length: 7.52m (24ft 8in); Width: 3.5m (11ft 6in); Height: 2.9m (9ft 6in)

WEIGHT: 54 tonnes (53.1 tons)

ENGINE: 1 x Leyland L-60 No 4 Mark 8 12-cylinder multifuel powerplant generating 560kW (750hp)

SPEED: 50km/h (30mph)

ARMAMENT: Main: 1 x 120mm (4.7in) Royal Ordnance L11A5 rifled cannon Secondary: 1 x 12.7mm (0.5in) L21 machine gun; 1 x 7.62mm (0.3in) L37 GP machine gun

ARMOUR: Classified – estimated up to 203mm (8in)

RANGE: Road: 500km (310 miles); Cross-country: 300km (180 miles)

CREW: 4

Although its origin dated back to the late 1940s, the Chieftain did not enter production until 1963. Intended as a replacement for the Centurion series, the Chieftain exhibited new frontiers in British main battle tank design.

Above: The Chieftain AVRE (Armoured Vehicle, Royal Engineers) carried fascines atop a sloped rail system that deployed bundles of logs to assist in crossing shell holes or other depressions in the terrain.

MAIN ARMAMENT
The main armament of the Chieftain Mk 5 was the 120mm (4.7in) L11A5 L/56 rifled gun. Initially it was laid with tracer fire from a machine gun; however, laser rangefinding equipment was soon installed.

SECONDARY ARMAMENT
Secondary armament included a 12.7mm (0.5in) coaxial machine gun initially used for rangefinding, and a single 7.62mm (0.3in) 8 GP machine gun for infantry and anti-tank defence.

ENGINE
The original diesel engine in the Chieftain was replaced with a Leyland L-60 No 4 Mark 8 12-cylinder multifuel engine. The L-60 had early performance issues as well.

LEADING TANK
With progressively greater armament, speed and armour protection, the Chieftain main battle tank traced its lineage to the infantry and cruiser tanks of the World War II era. With the debut of the Chieftain main battle tank in the early 1960s, Great Britain had assumed a leading role in innovative armoured vehicle design – a far cry from the disappointing combat performance of its most prominent tanks during World War II a quarter century earlier.

ARMOUR PROTECTION
Although some data on armour protection has been classified, the Chieftain was reportedly protected by up to 203mm (8in) on the front glacis. Later, composite armour was applied.

RECOGNITION FEATURES
The Chieftain Mk 5 is easily recognized in the field with its long 120mm (4.7in) rifled gun and the characteristic slope of the front glacis and turret, which does not include a mantlet for the main weapon.

Leopard 1 (1965)

SPECIFICATIONS

DIMENSIONS:	Length: 8.29m (27ft 2in); Width: 3.37m (11ft); Height: 2.39m (7ft 10in)
WEIGHT:	39 tonnes (38.3 tons)
ENGINE:	1 x 10-cylinder MTU MB 838 CaM 500 multi-fuel powerplant generating 619kW (830hp)
SPEED:	65km/h (40mph)
ARMAMENT:	Main: 1 x 105mm (4.1in) Royal Ordnance L7A3 L/52 rifled gun Secondary: 2 x 7.62mm (0.3in) Rheinmetall MG3 or FN MAG machine guns
ARMOUR:	10–70mm (0.39–2.7in)
RANGE:	Road: 600km (373 miles); cross-country: 450km (280 miles)
CREW:	4

The Leopard 1 main battle tank began as a joint venture between Germany and France. When the cooperative effort failed, German designers continued with the development of their own weapon.

Right: The Leopard 1 main battle tank entered service with the army of the Federal Republic of Germany in 1965. It was well armed and utilized state-of-the-art technology but sacrificed armour protection for speed and mobility.

TURRET
The elongated turret with its distinctive bustle was modified a number of times during the course of production. An ammunition resupply hatch was positioned to the left, a searchlight positioned above the main weapon and storage added to the rear.

ENGINE
The 10-cylinder MTU MB 838 CaM 500 multi-fuel engine was powered primarily by diesel fuel and propelled the Leopard 1 at a relatively swift maximum road speed of 65km/h (40mph).

MAIN ARMAMENT
The British Royal Ordnance 105mm (4.1in) L7A3 L/52 rifled gun was built under licence in Germany and equipped the Leopard 1 main battle tank. A limited number of later variants mounted a 120mm (4.7in) gun.

LETHALITY
The powerful 105mm (4.1in) L7A3 rifled gun mounted on the Leopard 1 was popular among numerous countries and set a standard for accuracy. When stabilized, its lethality was enhanced considerably. Manufacturer Krauss-Maffei announced that the incorporation of the stabilization equipment, including a laser rangefinder and integral thermal imaging, increased the probability of a first-round hit from the Leopard's main gun significantly.

ARMOUR PROTECTION
The potential Achilles heel of the Leopard 1 was its lack of armour protection. At 70mm (2.7in) on the front hull and 60mm (2.3in) on the turret glacis, both were sloped, but the thickness remained inadequate.

UPGRADES
In 1971, the West German government authorized a series of upgrades to the Leopard 1, including a major improvement with the stabilization of its main 105mm (4.1in) gun. Improvements continued up to the end of the 1970s.

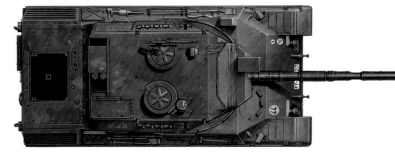

M551 Sheridan (1967)

SPECIFICATIONS

DIMENSIONS:	Length: 6.3m (20ft 8in); Width: 2.82m (9ft 3in); Height: 2.95m (9ft 8in)
WEIGHT:	14.1 tonnes (15.6 tons)
ENGINE:	Detroit 6V-53T 6-cylinder diesel engine
SPEED:	72km/h (44.7mph)
ARMAMENT:	152mm (5.9in) rifled gun/missile system Co-axial: 7.62mm (0.3in) machine gun Turret top: 12.7mm (0.5in) machine gun
ARMOUR:	Aluminium & steel – Max 8mm (0.31in)
RANGE:	560km (348 miles)
CREW:	4

TROUBLESOME GUN/ MISSILE SYSTEM

The solution to the armament problem was an innovative 152mm (5.9in) shell/missile system. While the missiles were used against distance targets and main battle tanks, high-explosive shells were available for general support work or against lighter targets, and could also successfully engage some tanks. However, the gun was found to be inaccurate and its recoil put too much strain on the Sheridan's structure. The shells also posed an explosion risk if the vehicle's very thin armour was penetrated.

The M551 Sheridan was developed in the 1960s to provide US forces with an air-transportable light armoured fighting vehicle. Its gun/missile system was innovative but proved less than satisfactory in practice, and with very light armour the Sheridan was vulnerable to a wide variety of weapons.

Right: An M551 Sheridan, fitted with a shield-mounted 12.7mm (0.5in) machine gun on the turret and an infrared searchlight next to the main armament.

MISSILES
No more than six Shillelagh missiles have ever been fired in anger by the M551 Sheridan.

TURRET
The gunner, loader and commander are housed in the turret, with the driver at the front of the hull.

ARMOUR
Armour is modular, enabling the tank to be stripped down for transport or up-armoured to deal with major threats.

LONG-RANGE ACCURACY
The Shillelagh missile was intended to engage armoured targets out to 3km (2 miles) and was also used on the unpopular M60A2 variant.

AMPHIBIOUS HULL
The M551 Sheridan is amphibious, requiring about two minutes of preparation, and can be carried by a Sea Stallion helicopter.

OPPOSING FORCES
An M551 Sheridan light tank disguised as opposing forces takes time out at a nearby trail during their rotation at the Joint Readiness Training Center. The Sheridan was widely used to represent OPFORS (opposing forces) in exercises, with cosmetic modifications to represent enemy tanks.

Stridsvagn 103B (1967)

SPECIFICATIONS

DIMENSIONS:	Length: 7.04m (23ft 1in); Width: 3.6m (11ft 10in); Height: 2.15m (7ft)
WEIGHT:	38.9 tonnes (38.2 tons)
ENGINE:	1 x Caterpillar 553 gas turbine generating 365kW (490bhp); 1 x Rolls-Royce K60 V-8 multifuel powerplant generating 179kW (240hp)
SPEED:	50km/h (30mph)
ARMAMENT:	Main: 1 x 105mm (4.1in) Bofors L74 L/62 gun Secondary: 3 x 7.62mm (0.3in) FFV machine guns
ARMOUR:	90–100mm (3.54–3.9in)
RANGE:	Road: 390km (240 miles); cross-country: 200km (120 miles)
CREW:	3

Something of an anachronism, the Stridsvagn 103B main battle tank bore a greater resemblance to the tank destroyers of World War II than the main battle tanks of the modern era that it was supposed to defend against.

Above: The long-barrelled L74 gun of the Strv 103 extended well beyond the length of the turretless tank's hull. Bofors, the L74 manufacturer, was one of the premiere weapons producing companies in the world.

ENGINE
The dual powerplant offered maximum range and fuel efficiency and included both a petrol engine and a diesel engine, installed for sprint and cruising situations respectively.

ARMOUR PROTECTION
Since no turret was present to add weight, the maximum armour protection of the Strv 103 hull was substantial, ranging from 90mm (3.54in) to 100mm (3.9in). The front glacis was sloped and horizontal ribs were included to increase the possible deflection of projectiles.

SECONDARY ARMAMENT
The secondary armament consisted of three 7.62mm (0.3in) FFV machine guns, two mounted in the hull and the third in an anti-aircraft position adjacent to the top hatch.

MAIN ARMAMENT
The British Royal Ordnance 105mm (4.1in) L7A3 L/52 rifled gun was built under licence in Germany and equipped the Leopard 1 main battle tank. A limited number of later variants mounted a 120mm (4.7in) gun.

STRIDSVAGN STABILITY

Although the Stridsvagn 103 never fired a shot in anger, it served the defensive purpose for which it was intended admirably. For a turretless tank, it proved versatile in operation. With the 103B an improved powerplant was introduced and in the subsequent 103C the tank was equipped with a bulldozer blade, laser rangefinding equipment and supplemental fuel tanks for increased range. With the 103D, thermal imaging and computerized fire-control equipment were installed. The Strv 103 remained in service with the Swedish military for a quarter of a century, until it was replaced by the German-built Leopard 2 main battle tank in the early 1990s.

HULL CONFIGURATION
The combination driver/gunner and engine compartment was forward in the hull. The position of the engine provided additional protection for the crew. The commander and radio operator were seated in the centre fighting compartment.

GUN AIMING
Since their vehicle did not possess a turret, the crew of the Stridsvagn 103 fired its 105mm (4.1in) gun by turning the entire vehicle and raising or lowering its suspension.

T-72 (1971)

SPECIFICATIONS

DIMENSIONS: Length: 6.95m (22ft 10in); Width: 3.59m (11ft 9in); Height: 2.23m (7ft 4in)

WEIGHT: 41.5 tonnes (40.8 tons)

ENGINE: 1 x V-46 12-cylinder diesel engine generating 780hp (582kW)

SPEED: 60km/h (37mph)

ARMAMENT: Main: 1 x 125mm (4.8in) smoothbore 2A46M high-velocity gun; Secondary: 1 x 7.62mm (0.3in) PKT machine gun; 1 x 12.7mm (0.5in) NSVT anti-aircraft machine gun

ARMOUR: Classified; estimated up to 500mm (19.6in)

RANGE: 460km (290 miles)

CREW: 3

Intended for the export market and the client states of the Soviet Union, the T-72 main battle tank was smaller and faster than other contemporary armoured vehicles but lacked the firepower and protection it needed on the modern battlefield.

Right: The T-72 was deployed with armoured units of the Soviet Red Army stationed within the Soviet Union, while the T-64 equipped forward units that would confront NATO tanks in the early hours of conflict in Europe.

ARMOUR PROTECTION
Composite plating of steel, tungsten, ceramic and plastic protected the front glacis of the T-72 at a thickness of 200m (7.8in). Steel side plates on early models were up to 80mm (3.15in) thick.

SECONDARY ARMAMENT
The coaxial 7.62mm (0.3in) PKT machine gun defended against infantry attack, while a 12.7mm (0.5in) NSVT machine gun atop the commander's cupola was for anti-aircraft defence.

MAIN ARMAMENT
The main armament of the T-72 was the excellent 125mm (4.8in) 2A46M smoothbore gun. The weapon was capable of penetrating the armour of NATO tanks at ranges of over 4000m (4374yd).

ENGINE
The original 12-cylinder V-46 diesel engine was also capable of running on kerosene and benzene. It was later replaced by a larger 839hp (646kW) diesel engine.

T-72S IN ACTION
Since the 1970s the T-72 has seen action in numerous hot spots around the globe. During the 1982 conflict between Israel and Syria in Lebanon, Syrian T-72s proved markedly inferior to Israeli Merkava tanks and scores of the Soviet-supplied tanks were destroyed in combat. The Iraqi T-72s of Saddam Hussein also fell victim to modern US and British Abrams and Challenger tanks in 1991 and 2003. This was partially due to the fact that the T-72s lacked the necessary upgrades to maintain modern battlefield viability

SUSPENSION
The torsion bar suspension of the T-72 supported six cast, rubber-edged wheels with a large drive sprocket and four return rollers. The upper edges of the wheels were protected by spring mounted armour plates.

T-72S ON PARADE
In the photo at right, columns of T-72 main battle tanks parade through Red Square in the Soviet capital of Moscow. The T-72 had been deployed for six years before it made its public debut in 1977.

Merkava (1977)

SPECIFICATIONS

DIMENSIONS:	Length: 7.45m (24ft 5in); Width: 3.7m (12ft 1in); Height: 2.75m (9ft)
WEIGHT:	55.9 tonnes (55 tons)
ENGINE:	1 x Teledyne Continental AVDS-1790-6A 12-cylinder supercharged diesel generating 671kW (900hp)
SPEED:	46km/h (28.5mph)
ARMAMENT:	Main: 1 x 105mm (4.1in) L43.5 M68 gun; Secondary: 3 x 7.62mm (0.3in) FN-MAG machine guns; 1 x 12.7mm (0.5in) M2HB Browning machine gun; 1 x 60mm (2.36in) Soltam popup mortar
ARMOUR:	Classified
RANGE:	Road: 400km (245 miles); off road: 200km (125 miles)
CREW:	4

Designed and built in Israel, the Merkava has received four major upgrades since entering production in 1977. Its radical redesign emphasized crew survivability followed by firepower and mobility.

The Merkava series of main battle tanks was designed and manufactured in Israel, eliminating to a great extent the dependence of the Israeli military on imported tanks and armoured vehicles.

ENGINE
The Merkava IV is powered by the General Dynamics GD833 diesel engine, a substantial upgrade to the original diesel engine and capable of moving the tank at a top road speed of 64km/h (40mph).

MAIN ARMAMENT
The primary weapon of the Merkava main battle tank was initially the 105mm (4.1in) L43.5 M68 gun. This was replaced in later upgrades with the 120mm (4.7in) MG251 and MG253 smoothbore guns capable of firing a variety of ordnance.

TURRET
The low, wedge-shaped turret of the Merkava main battle tank was positioned toward the rear of the hull in a fashion similar to heavy self-propelled artillery weapons. Its design reduced the tank's silhouette considerably.

SECONDARY ARMAMENT
The Merkava IV is armed with up to three 7.62mm (0.3in) FN MAG machine guns for defence against infantry, and a 12.7mm (0.5in) M2HB Browning machine gun intended for defence against attack helicopters (not shown on this model).

RADICAL RETHINK
From the drawing board to the assembly line and the battlefield, the Merkava was a departure from conventional tank design. The engine and diesel fuel tanks were positioned forward in the hull, adding to the armour protection of classified composition but assumed initially to be of homogeneous rolled, cast and welded nickel steel, later augmented by an Israeli adaptation of the British Chobham composite armour. The Merkava turret was moved toward the rear of the hull and fashioned in a low wedge shape to minimize the tank's silhouette. The Merkava was also constructed to serve as a troop carrier or medical evacuation vehicle if necessary.

INTERNAL LAYOUT
The hull design of the Merkava places the engine and diesel fuel tanks forward with the driver to the left of the engine. The commander, gunner and loader are positioned in the turret to the rear of the vehicle. A rear door allows replenishment of ammunition and entry.

INNOVATIONS
An IDF Merkava in action. The Merkava main battle tank does not utilize a turret basket. The floor moves as the turret rotates in acquiring a target. The commander enters and exits the tank through a hatch, dispensing with a cupola that would raise the tank's silhouette.

Leopard 2 (1979)

SPECIFICATIONS

DIMENSIONS: Length: 9.97m (32ft 8in); Width: 3.75m (12ft 3in); Height: 3m (9ft 9in)

WEIGHT: 62.3 tonnes (61.3 tons)

ENGINE: 1 x MTU MB 873 Ka-501 V-12 twin turbo diesel powerplant generating 1479hp (1103kW)

SPEED: 72km/h (45mph)

ARMAMENT: Main: 1 x 120mm (4.7in) Rheinmetall L55 smoothbore gun; Secondary: 2 x 7.62mm (0.3in) MG3A1 machine guns

ARMOUR: Classified; third-generation composite

RANGE: 550km (340 miles)

CREW: 4

LEOPARD LONGEVITY

Continuing upgrades to the Leopard 2 have enhanced performance in a number of areas. The Leopard 2A1 introduced the gunner's thermal sights, improved fuel filters and reengineered ammunition racks, while improved digital radio equipment was installed with the 2A3. The 2A4 included an automated fire and explosion suppression system, better composite turret armour of tungsten and titanium construction, and digital fire control.

The Federal Republic of Germany authorized the production of the Leopard 2 main battle tank in 1977 following two cooperative engineering efforts with the U.S. that ended with each country going its own way in armoured vehicle design.

Above: Top view of the Leopard 2. While traditionally the top armour of tanks has been the thinnest, the introduction of top-attack munitions has led to heavier protection in these areas.

SECONDARY ARMAMENT
A pair of 7.62mm (0.3in) MG3A1 machine guns are mounted on the Leopard 2, one coaxial in the turret and the other pintle-mounted at the loader's hatch. Banks of smoke grenade launchers are installed on either side of the main gun.

ENGINE
The MTU MB 873 Ka-501 diesel engine is standard in the Leopard 2; however, the larger MTU MT 883 has been installed for trials with the EuroPowerPack upgrade.

ARMOUR PROTECTION
Third-generation composite armour with ceramic, tungsten, plastic and hardened steel components provides exceptional protection for the crew of the Leopard 2. Spall liners are installed in crew areas to reduce the volume of shell fragments in the event of a direct hit.

TURRET
Centred on the chassis, the Leopard 2 turret is shaped somewhat like a lozenge. Its flat profile reduces the radar signature and overall silhouette of the tank, although headroom is restricted.

MAIN ARMAMENT
The original main weapon, the 120mm (4.7in) Rheinmetall Waffe L44 smoothbore gun, was later replaced by the longer-barrelled L55, which substantially increased muzzle velocity.

FORDING
A Leopard 2 enters a water obstacle. The tank has a standard fording capability of 1m (3ft 4in), but if fitted with a snorkel device it can extend the depth to 4m (13ft 1in).

Challenger 1 (1982)

SPECIFICATIONS

DIMENSIONS:	Length: 11.55m (37ft 10in); Width: 3.52m (11ft 7in); Height: 2.89m (9ft 6in)
WEIGHT:	62 tonnes (61 tons)
ENGINE:	1 x Rolls-Royce CV 12 diesel or Perkins Engines Company Condor V-12 diesel generating 895kW (1200bhp)
SPEED:	60km/h (37mph)
ARMAMENT:	Main: 1 x 120mm (4.7in) Royal Ordnance L11A5 gun; Secondary: 1 x 7.62mm (0.3in) LA82 machine gun; 1 x 7.62mm (0.3in) L37A2 machine gun
ARMOUR:	Chobham composite, thickness classified
RANGE:	Road: 450km (280 miles); Off-road: 250km (155 miles)
CREW:	4

As its complement of Chieftain tanks was aging, the British Army adopted the Challenger 1 in the early 1980s. Some 420 of these tanks were built and they served as a bridge to the new, more powerful Challenger 2.

Above: The Challenger 1 blended existing technology with numerous upgrades, the tank equipped armoured units of the British Army for nearly two decades, until replaced by the Challenger 2 between 1998 and 2002.

ENGINE
The powerplant of the Challenger 1 was either the Rolls-Royce CV 12 diesel or the Perkins Engines Company Condor V-12 diesel. Their power was comparable and the tank was capable of a top speed of 60km/h (37mph).

SECONDARY ARMAMENT
Two 7.62mm (0.3in) machine guns – an L37A2 atop the commander's cupola and an LA82 coaxially in the turret – were mounted on the Challenger 1 while two banks of smoke grenade launchers were affixed to the hull.

TURRET
The flattened and elongated turret provided ample space for three crew members while also minimizing the tank's silhouette. The commander was provided with nine periscopes for a 360° view of the tank's surroundings.

MAIN ARMAMENT
The 120mm (4.7in) Royal Ordnance L11A5 that had armed the Chieftain main battle tank was retained with the Challenger 1. Already known for its accuracy, the weapon's precision was improved with a new gunsight and fire-control system.

ARMOUR ACCENT
With a primary focus on survivability, the most revolutionary improvement fielded with the Challenger was its Chobham armour, a classified composite that includes ceramic and metal alloys. First developed in the 1960s at the British research facility in Chobham Common, Surrey, the armour is much stronger than conventional steel and reportedly is capable of withstanding an impact five times greater than earlier protection. Chobham was also installed in the American M1 Abrams main battle tank.

ARMOUR PROTECTION
The introduction of revolutionary Chobham composite armour provided greater protection for the crew of the Challenger 1 main battle tank than any previous homogeneous steel or additional plating. Chobham was also adopted by other countries for their own tanks, particularly the US M1 Abrams.

BRITISH SERVICE
The Challenger 1 was accepted by the British Army in December 1982. Its hydro-pneumatic suspension, supporting six road wheels on either side of the hull, functioned well in the desert during the 1991 Gulf War.

M1A1 Abrams (1985)

SPECIFICATIONS

DIMENSIONS:	Length: 7.92m (26ft); Width: 3.66m (12ft); Height: 2.89m (9ft 6in)
WEIGHT:	57 tonnes (56.1 tons)
ENGINE:	1 x Lycoming AGT 1500 gas-turbine powerplant generating 1120kw (1500hp)
SPEED:	67km/h (42mph)
ARMAMENT:	Main: 1 x 120mm (4.7in) L/44 M256 smoothbore gun Secondary: 2 x 7.62mm M240 machine guns; 1 x 12.7mm (0.5in) M2HB machine gun
ARMOUR:	Composite appliqué over homogeneous rolled and welded nickel steel
RANGE:	Road: 500km (310 miles); Cross-country: 300km (180 miles)
CREW:	4

The M1A1 Abrams main battle tank resulted from a major upgrade to the original M1 that entered service with the US Army in 1980. The M1A1 has seen combat service in the Balkans and the Middle East, amassing an impressive record.

SECONDARY ARMAMENT
A 12.7mm (0.5in) M2HB machine gun is mounted near the commander's hatch atop the turret, while one 7.62mm (0.3in) M240 machine gun is installed coaxially in the turret and another on a skate mount atop the loader's hatch.

MAIN ARMAMENT
The 120mm (4.7in) M256 smoothbore, adapted under licence from the German Rheinmetall L44, arms the M1A1 Abrams, replacing the 105mm (4.1in) M68A1 rifled gun, derived from a British Royal Ordnance design, that was mounted on the original M1 tank.

ENGINE
The Lycoming Textron AGT 1500 gas-turbine engine runs much more quietly than contemporary diesel engines and provides enough power for the M1A1 Abrams to reach a top speed of 67km/h (42mph).

M1A1 ABROAD
Although it was initially conceived for combat in Europe, the M1A1 Abrams main battle tank achieved field superiority in the deserts of the Middle East during the 1991 Gulf War and Operation *Iraqi Freedom* in 2003. During the Gulf War, only 18 Abrams tanks were put out of action. Of these, nine were total losses, while nine sustained damage primarily from mines and returned to service. No Abrams crewmen lost their lives. In 2003, American M1A1 tanks destroyed seven Iraqi T-72s in an armoured clash south of Baghdad without loss to themselves.

ARMOUR PROTECTION
Composite armour similar to British Chobham protects the M1A1 and has been upgraded during three decades of service. Modern composite armour includes components of steel, depleted uranium plating, synthetic fibres and ceramic.

AMMUNITION STORAGE
Separated from the crew compartment within the turret, ammunition is stored to the rear in armoured boxes. The storage area is protected by explosive-reactive armour with its top panels designed to blow outward in the event of a direct hit.

FIRING LINE
A unit of M1A1 tanks lets fly with with their 120mm (4.7in) guns. The M1A1's M256 main gun has an effective range of 4000m (4400yd) firing an Armor-Piercing Fin-Stabilized Discarding-Sabot (APFSDS) round with a depleted uranian penetrator.

SPECIFICATIONS

DIMENSIONS:	Length: 9.3m (30ft 6in); Width: 2.71m (8ft 10.5in); Height: 2.55m (8ft 4.5in)
WEIGHT:	22.6 tonnes (22.24 tons)
ENGINE:	Detroit 8V-92TA diesel engine
SPEED:	70km/h (45mph)
ARMAMENT:	Main gun: L7A3 105mm (4.1in) rifled gun; Co-axial: 7.62mm (0.3in) machine gun; Turret top: 12.7mm (0.5in) machine gun
ARMOUR:	23mm (0.9in)
RANGE:	Road: 450km (280 miles)
CREW:	4

Stingray and Stingray II were developed by Cadillac-Gage for the export market. The intention was to provide the mobility and firepower of a larger and far more expensive tank on a lightly armoured hull. Although the project was not a marketplace success, the concept seems entirely viable.

Above: The only export success achieved by the Stingray was with the Royal Thai Army (seen here), which bought 106 models. This did not prevent other versions from being developed and offered for sale.

MAIN GUN
The low-recoil version of the British Royal Ordnance L7 105mm (4.1in) rifled gun is the tank's main asset: it is powerful, and shares most of its ammunition with NATO stocks.

ARMOUR
The Stingray's strength is its speed and manoeuvrability, which has meant it is lightly armoured, with just 23mm (0.9in) maximum on the hull and turret.

CREW
The Stingray has a crew of four: the driver, who sits in the hull front; and a commander, gunner and gun loader/radio operator, who sit in the turret.

SPEED
The Stingray can travel at speeds of up to 70km/h (45mph).

HITTING POWER
The Stingray's armament was the proven L7 105mm (4.1in) rifled gun that was developed in Britain. At the time of the Stingray's entry to the marketplace, this gun was effective against any tank in the world. Even today it remains a credible threat, especially combined with the ability to rapidly outflank a heavier tank force. Armour was much lighter than that of a main battle tank, offering protection against armour-piercing heavy machine-gun ammunition in the frontal arc and small-arms fire elsewhere.

THAI STINGRAYS
The Royal Thai Army is the principal user of the Stingray tank, with 106 of the vehicles in service. Other vehicles in its fleet include the FV 101 Scorpion, the Chinese VT-4 main battle tank and the Ukrainian T-84 Oplot-M main battle tank.

AMX-56 Leclerc (1991)

SPECIFICATIONS

DIMENSIONS: Length: 6.88m (22ft 7in); Width: 3.71m (12ft 2in); Height: 2.46m (8ft 1in)

WEIGHT: 51 tonnes (50.1 tons)

ENGINE: 1 x 12-cylinder SACM V8X-1500 diesel with Suralmo-Hyperbar gas turbine supercharger and Turbomeca TM307B auxiliary power unit generating 1120kW (1500hp)

SPEED: 70km/h (43.5mph)

ARMAMENT: Main: 1 x 120mm (4.7in) GIAT CN120- 26/52 gun Secondary: 1 x 12.7mm (0.5in) coaxial machine gun; 1 x 7.62mm (0.3in) turret machine gun

ARMOUR: Welded steel with SXXI composite and ERA in AZUR upgrade

RANGE: Road: 550km (330 miles); Off-road: 350km (210 miles)

CREW: 3

Entering service in the early 1990s, the AMX-56 main battle tank gave France a main battle tank on par with the performance of other contemporary tanks such as the German Leopard 2 and the US Abrams M1.

Right: The AMX-56 Leclerc entered service with the French armed forces in 1993 and production ceased in late 2007. However, the assembly lines will be reopened if the need should arise.

MAIN ARMAMENT
The 120mm (4.7in) GIAT CN120-26/52 gun is currently utilizing only French ammunition, but it is compatible with NATO rounds. French engineers designed the AMX-56 turret around the main weapon.

CREW POSITIONS
The AMX-56 driver is forward in the hull to the left. The commander and gunner are seated in the turret to the left and right respectively.

SECONDARY ARMAMENT
A 12.7mm (0.5in) M2HB machine gun is mounted coaxially in the turret, while a 7.62mm (0.3in) machine gun, effective against low-flying aircraft, is affixed on the turret top.

ENGINE
The SACM V8X-1500 diesel engine is supplemented by a high-pressure Suralmo-Hyperbar gas turbine supercharger and the Turbomeca TM307B auxiliary power unit is on board.

ARMOUR PROTECTION
The hull and turret of the AMX-56 are welded steel. Their basic armour thickness is increased with modular armour containing Kevlar and ceramics along with tungsten and titanium.

RATE OF FIRE
With a rate of fire up to 12 rounds per minute, the gun is reportedly capable of 95 per cent accuracy at such a pace. It is equipped with an automatic compressed-air fume extractor and thermal sleeve to reduce warping of the barrel. The weapon currently utilizes only French ammunition but is compatible with standardized NATO rounds as well.

POWERPLANT
Seen here on desert manoeuvres, the AMX-56 is powered by a supercharged 12-cylinder diesel engine with an additional auxiliary power unit.

T-90 (1992)

SPECIFICATIONS

DIMENSIONS:	Length: 9.53m (31ft 3in); Width: 3.78m (12ft 5in); Height: 2.22m (7ft 3in)
WEIGHT:	46 tonnes (45 tons)
ENGINE:	1 x Model 84 V84MS diesel powerplant generating 840hp (626kW)
SPEED:	60km/h (37 mph)
ARMAMENT:	Main: 1 x 125mm (4.8in) 2A46smoothbore gun; Secondary: 1 x 7.62mm (0.3in) coaxial machine gun; 1 x 12.7mm (0.5in) anti- aircraft machine gun
ARMOUR:	Steel composite augmented by Kontakt-5 composite with protection equivalent to 1350mm (53in)
RANGE:	550km (340 miles)
CREW:	3

INTERIOR

By NATO standards, the turret of the T-90 is cramped and ergonomically dysfunctional. The commander is seated to the right inside the turret with the gunner to the left, while the driver is centred and forward in the hull. Each crewman is equipped with thermal imaging and laser rangefinding equipment to direct the vehicle, acquire targets and lay the gun accurately. Typically, the driver is further tasked with serving as a field mechanic capable of performing basic maintenance and repair without removing the T-90 from a combat zone.

Although the T-90 main battle tank had been intended as an interim upgrade to the venerable T-72 and the T-80, it has been in service with the Russian armed forces since 1992 and has achieved some export success, selling to countries such as Algeria, India, Syria and Vietnam.

Right: The T-90's centrepiece is its 125mm (4.8in) 2A46 gun, which can fire both shells and missiles. When firing the 9M119 Refleks (NATO designation AT-11 Sniper) anti-tank guided missile, it can hit targets out to 4000m (4374yd).

ENGINE
The 12-cylinder Model 84 V84MS diesel engine powers the domestic T-90 that is fielded by the Russian armed forces, while the T-90S export version is supplied with a 736kW (988hp) 12-cylinder V-92S2 engine.

COUNTERMEASURES
The Shtora-1, or Curtain, system includes infrared jamming equipment, laser-warning capability and aerosol grenades that shroud the tank to confuse the laser tracking beams of enemy weapons systems.

SECONDARY ARMAMENT
A 12.7mm (0.5in) machine gun mounted atop the turret and adjacent to the commander's hatch, along with a 7.62mm (0.3in) coaxial machine gun, provides secondary fire support for the T-90.

MAIN ARMAMENT
The 125mm (4.8in) 2A46 smoothbore gun of the T-90 main battle tank is a holdover from the disappointing T-80. The 2A46 is versatile, capable of firing the Refleks Sniper guided missile against aircraft or armoured targets.

ARMOUR PROTECTION
Kontakt-5 explosive reactive armour protects the T-90 from shaped-charge warheads such as anti-tank missiles, RPGs and mines.

TURRET-MOUNTED WEAPON
In this photograph of a T-90 on manoeuvres, the prominence of the turret-mounted 12.7mm (0.5in) Kord heavy machine gun is striking. The weapon has an effective range of 2000m (2187yd).

M1A2 Abrams (1996)

SPECIFICATIONS

DIMENSIONS:	Length: 9.83m (32ft 3in); Width: 3.66m (12ft) Height: 2.37m (7ft 9in)
WEIGHT:	62 tonnes (61 tons)
ENGINE:	AGT 1500 Lycoming gas turbine powerplant generating 1500hp (1118kW)
SPEED:	Road: 67.6km/h (42mph); Off-road: 54.7km/h (34mph)
ARMAMENT:	Main: 1 x 120mm (4.7in) M256 smoothbore gun Secondary: 2 x 7.62mm (0.3in) M240 machine guns; 1 x 12.7mm (0.5in) M2HB machine gun
ARMOUR:	Composite appliqué armour with equivalent protection estimated up to 960mm (37.7in) of homogeneous rolled steel
RANGE:	426km (265 miles)
CREW:	4

Building on the successful combat record of the M1A1 main battle tank, continuing upgrades include the prominent M1A2 package. Significant enhancements to the tank's computer systems and thermal imaging capabilities have been completed. Entering service with the armoured battalions and cavalry squadrons of the US Army beginning in 1998, the improved M1A2 Abrams was considered a viable option to the costly development of a new main battle tank.

TARGET ACQUISITION
The installation of FLIR (Forward Looking Infrared) sighting equipment replaced older thermal sighting with the upgrade of many existing M1A1 tanks to the M1A2 package, while a few M1A2 tanks were built new with the enhanced system.

ENGINE
The AGT 1500 gas-turbine engine has been out of production since 1992 and development of a replacement engine, the LV100-5 gas turbine, is underway. The gas-turbine engine is substantially quieter than a standard diesel.

SECONDARY ARMAMENT
A 12.7mm (0.5in) M2HB machine gun is mounted near the commander's hatch atop the turret, while one 7.62mm (0.3in) M240 machine gun is installed coaxially in the turret and another on a skate mount atop the loader's hatch.

MAIN ARMAMENT
Although some trials with the 120mm (4.7in) L/55 gun have been conducted, the main armament of the M1A2 Abrams is likely to remain the M256 L/44 smoothbore gun.

ARMOUR PROTECTION
A third-generation composite material based on the original Chobham armour includes plates of depleted uranium and offers protection equivalent to as much as 960mm (37.7in) of rolled homogeneous steel.

EQUIPMENT

The M1A2 is equipped with a commander's independent thermal-imaging viewer, thermal-imaging gunner sights, better navigational and global-positioning equipment, thermal-imaging and integrated display systems for the driver, a comprehensive weapons station with a thermal imager and a digital colour terrain map display. The US military maintained its priorities of crew survivability and early target acquisition linked to accurate fire. Therefore, prominent among the M1A2 upgrades was the installation of the Raytheon two-axis GPS-LOS primary sight, replacing a single-axis sight in the M1A1, to increase the probability of an accurate first round hit significantly.

PEACETIME MANOEUVRES
An M1A2 Abrams on manoeuvres, adopting a hull-down firing position behind raised terrain. The M1A2 SEPv2 (version 2) added a Common Remotely Operated Weapon Station (CROWS) to the turret.

Type 99 (1998)

SPECIFICATIONS

DIMENSIONS:	Length: 11m (36ft); Width: 3.4m (11ft 2in); Height: 2m (6ft 6in)
WEIGHT:	48.9 tonnes (54 tons)
ENGINE:	Turbocharged diesel engine, 1,500 hp (1,119 kW)
SPEED:	80km/h (50mph)
ARMAMENT:	Main gun: 125mm (4.9in) ZPT-98 smoothbore gun; Secondary: Co-axial: 7.62mm (0.3in) machine gun; Commander's cupola: 12.7mm (0.5in) machine gun
ARMOUR:	Classified
RANGE:	Up to 800km (497 miles)
CREW:	3

Chinese tank design during the Cold War era was heavily influenced by Soviet designs – indeed, several Chinese tanks were direct copies of Russian ones. More recently, Chinese tanks have developed a character of their own, with features seen on some Western tanks alongside obvious Russian concepts.

Above: This second-generation Type 85 MBT more clearly shows Russian influences, and has been described as a Chinese T-72. Although similar in shape to the Type 85, the Type 99 is a third-generation tank, with numerous technological improvements.

FUME EXTRACTOR
The bulge on the gun barrel is a fume extractor, preventing toxic propellant fumes from entering the crew compartment.

AUTOLOADER
The Type 99's 125mm (4.9in) smoothbore main gun is fed by a carousel-type autoloader.

ENGINE
The diesel engine used on the Type 99 was derived from the Leopard 2's powerplant.

LASER SYSTEMS
The Type 99 makes extensive use of laser technology. Protection is enhanced by an active laser system, designed to disrupt infrared or laser targeting, and there is a secure laser communications system. So long as tanks are within line of sight of one another they can communicate with virtually no chance of interception – a distinct asset in today's battlespace, where electronic warfare is prevalent. The same system also provides an identification-friend-or-foe capability.

MILITARY PARADE
Type 99 tanks take part in a military parade in China. The Type 99 can launch guided missiles from its main gun. Four missiles are reportedly carried by each tank.

Challenger 2 (1998)

SPECIFICATIONS

DIMENSIONS:	Length: 8.3m (27ft 3in); Width: 3.5m (11ft 6in); Height: 2.5m (8ft 2in)
WEIGHT:	62.5 tonnes (61.5 tons)
ENGINE:	1 x 12-cylinder Perkins Caterpillar CV-12 diesel powerplant generating 1200hp (890kW)
SPEED:	Road: 59km/h (37mph); Off-road: 40km/h (25mph)
ARMAMENT:	Main: 1 x 120mm (4.7in) L30A1 rifled gun; Secondary: 1 x 7.62mm (0.3in) Hughes L94A EX-34 chain gun; 1 x 7.62mm (0.3in) L37A2 GPMG machine gun
ARMOUR:	Chobham Dorchester Level 2, classified properties
RANGE:	450km (280 miles)
CREW:	4

Although retaining the name of its predecessor, the interim Challenger 1, the Challenger 2 main battle tank was almost completely new when it emerged in the late 1990s, as only five per cent of its components are common with the earlier tank.

ARMOUR PROTECTION
Chobham Dorchester Level 2 composite armour, composed of ceramic and steel elements, provides outstanding protection for the Challenger 2 crew. Its thickness and actual protective strength is classified.

SECONDARY ARMAMENT
A 7.62mm (0.3in) Hughes L94A EX-34 chain gun mounted coaxially in the turret and a 7.62mm (0.3in) L37A2 GPMG machine gun affixed near the loader's hatch provide secondary firepower for the Challenger 2 against enemy infantry and low-flying aircraft.

ENGINE
The 12-cylinder Perkins Caterpillar CV-12 diesel engine and David Brown TN54 epicyclical transmission with six forward and two reverse gears offer power and manoeuvrability with the Challenger 2 and generate a top speed of 59km/h (37mph).

MAIN ARMAMENT
The main armament of the Challenger 2 is the 120mm (4.7in) Royal Ordnance L30A1 rifled gun. However, trials have been conducted with the 120mm Rheinmetall L/55 smoothbore gun and it may replace the L30A1.

OPERATIONAL INPUT
The experience gained through deploying Challenger 2s to Iraq has led to several modifications. Although the tanks demonstrated impressive survivability – in one instance a Challenger 2 was hit by 70 RPGs and survived – the lower belly armour was shown to be vulnerable to mines and penetrator charges. In response, explosive reactive armour was replaced with a Dorchester block and the steel underbelly was lined with additional armour as part of the 'Streetfighter' upgrade.

TRACK AND SUSPENSION
The hydrogas variable spring suspension and William Clark defence hydraulically adjusted double pin tracks provide the Challenger 2 main battle tank with great manoeuvrability in any type of terrain.

STEALTH TANK
Equipped with stealth technology to avoid detection by opposing forces, the Challenger 2 main battle tank is capable of closing with the enemy rapidly, acquiring targets and achieving a first hit while maintaining concealment.

Arjun Mk 2 (2014)

SPECIFICATIONS

DIMENSIONS:	Length: 10.64 (34ft 11in); Width: 3.86m (12ft 8in); Height: 2.32 (7ft 7in)
WEIGHT:	53 tonnes (58.5 tons) (Mk2: 61.6 tonnes/68 tons)
ENGINE:	MTU MB 838 Ka 501 diesel engine
SPEED:	72km/h (44.7mph)
ARMAMENT:	Main gun: 120mm (4.7in) rifled gun; Co-axial: 7.62mm (0.3in) machine gun; Turret top: 12.7mm (0.5in) machine gun
ARMOUR:	–
RANGE:	–
CREW:	4

Development of the Arjun main battle tank was heavily influenced by the German Leopard 2. The original Arjun was not a great success, but was the basis for the greatly superior Mk 2 version. It is armed with a 120mm (4.7in) gun that, unusually for such a weapon, is rifled. Development of the Mk 2, however, has been troubled, and at the time of writing (2018) its future status looks uncertain.

Above: A column of Arjun tanks on parade. The Arjun's crew layout is conventional, with the driver in the hull and the commander, gunner and loader in the turret.

REMOTE CONTROLLED WEAPON STATION
The turret-top 12.7mm (0.5in) machine gun can be controlled from within the tank, permitting infantry defence from a position of safety.

BLOW-OUT PANELS
Ammunition storage in the turret has blow-out panels, which will vent an explosion to protect the crew.

SMOKE DISCHARGERS
Banks of smoke dischargers on the rear of the hull can provide instant smoke obscuration when required.

RIFLED GUN
The Arjun's 120mm (4.7in) gun is rifled, giving accuracy advantages over equivalent smoothbores at longer ranges.

ADVANCED FEATURES
Computerized target identification and engagement systems are complemented on the Arjun Mk 2 by panoramic sights and an integrated battle-management system for real-time information sharing. A remotely controlled machine-gun mount provides protection from infantry attack. Fall-off of crew efficiency over time is reduced by attention to ergonomics and crew comfort, which results in lowered fatigue and a subsequent improvement in long-term capability.

HEAVY ARMOUR
The Arjun Mk 2 is protected by composite armour that can be augmented with explosive reactive armour (ERA) panels. Additional protection in the form of an Urban Survival Kit is available.

K2 Black Panther (2014)

SPECIFICATIONS

DIMENSIONS:	Length: 10.8m (32ft 10in); Width: 3.6m (11ft 10in); Height: 2.4m (7ft 10.5in)
WEIGHT:	49.8 tonnes (55 tons)
ENGINE:	MT 833 diesel engine, generating 1,500hp (1,100kW)
SPEED:	70km/h (43mph)
ARMAMENT:	Main gun: 120mm (4.7in) smoothbore gun; Secondary: Co-axial: 7.62mm (0.3in) machine gun Turret top: 12.7mm (0.5in) machine gun
ARMOUR:	-
RANGE:	-
CREW:	3

The armed standoff between North and South Korea has in many ways been a microcosm of the Cold War. South Korean military equipment is intended to provide a qualitative superiority over the more numerous North Korean forces. The K2 Black Panther exploits rapid information exchange to create such an advantage.

OFF-ROAD MOVEMENT
The Black Panther's advanced In-arm Suspension Unit (ISU) gives the suspension automatic adjustment to compensate the all types of terrain and inclines.

TOP ATTACK
The K2 has superior mobility over the preceding K1, with a larger gun capable of firing advanced ammunition. This includes a top-attack munition designed to target the weakest parts of a tank's protection. Tank armour is generally sloped to increase effective thickness against direct-fire impacts, and presents a more or less flat plane against attacks from above. The top-attack munition is fired above the target, deploying a parachute to slow it as it approaches. Once directly over the target, it fires an explosively formed penetrator straight down. This munition has the added advantages that it can be lobbed over an intervening obstacle or fired indirectly from cover or concealment.

MAIN GUN
The 120mm (4.7in) smoothbore gun is fed from a 16-round ready store by an autoloader, with additional ammunition stowed within the hull.

SOPHISICATED ARMOUR
The K2's armour consists of a steel base layer overlaid with modular composite blocks. Reactive armour may also be fitted.

'SOFT KILL'
The K2's defences include a decoy system to 'soft kill' incoming missiles by misdirecting them away from the tank.

CREW
Use of an autoloader enables the K2 Black Panther to operate with a crew of three: driver, gunner and commander.

AMMUNITION
The main gun normally fires tungsten-cored penetrator rounds or high-explosive anti-tank ammunition for 'softer' targets.

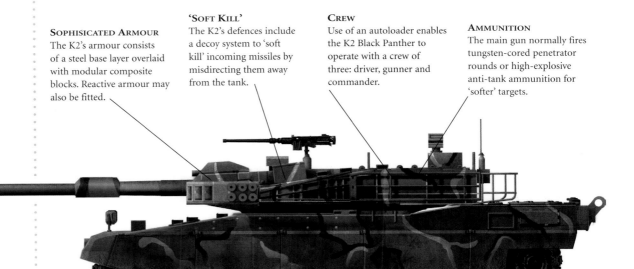

SUSPENSION SYSTEM
The K2's advanced suspension system can be used to increase the elevation of the main gun by lowering the rear of the tank and raising the front.

T-14 Armata (2015)

SPECIFICATIONS

DIMENSIONS:	Length: 8.7m (29ft); Width: 3.5m (11ft 6in); Height: 3.3m (10ft 9in)
WEIGHT:	43.5 tonnes (48 tons)
ENGINE:	A-85-3A turbocharged diesel engine, generating 2000hp (1491kW)
SPEED:	90km/h (55.9mph)
ARMAMENT:	Main gun: 2A82-1M 125mm (4.9in) smoothbore gun; other or additional armament possible; Remote-controlled weapon station: 7.62mm (0.3in) or 12.7mm (0.5in) machine gun
ARMOUR:	–
RANGE:	500km (310 miles)
CREW:	3

Entering Russian service in 2015, the T-14 Armata incorporates a host of advanced features and has been hailed as the first of a new generation of main battle tanks. Whether it lives up to its reputation remains to be seen; other tanks have been lauded as world-beaters at their first appearance.

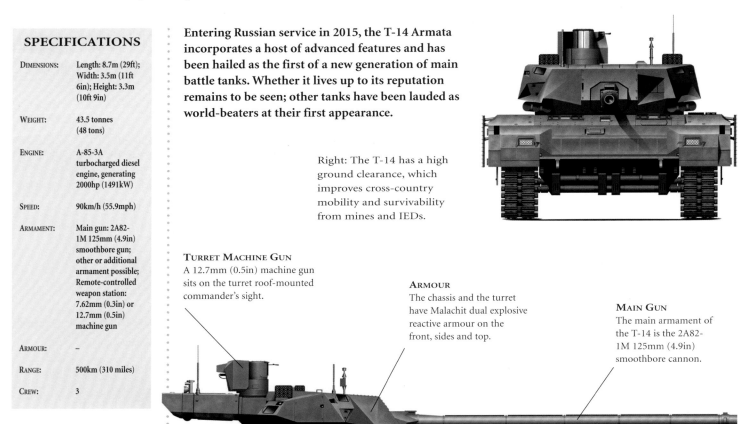

Right: The T-14 has a high ground clearance, which improves cross-country mobility and survivability from mines and IEDs.

TURRET MACHINE GUN
A 12.7mm (0.5in) machine gun sits on the turret roof-mounted commander's sight.

ARMOUR
The chassis and the turret have Malachit dual explosive reactive armour on the front, sides and top.

MAIN GUN
The main armament of the T-14 is the 2A82-1M 125mm (4.9in) smoothbore cannon.

CREW
The T-14 has a crew of three: driver, gunner and commander. The crew is protected by an internal armoured capsule.

MODULAR DESIGN

The T-14 Armata, officially presented to the world in 2015, is constructed on a modular basis. The crew of three is contained in an armoured capsule in the frontal section of the tank, with the engine in a separate compartment at the rear. Between them is the turret mechanism. The turret is unmanned but supports a range of advanced electronics equipment. It contains a 125mm (4.9in) smoothbore gun capable of firing conventional ammunition or guided missiles, and an autoloader that serves the gun. It has been suggested that a 152mm (5.9in) gun could be fitted instead, or perhaps other weapons.

ENHANCED PROTECTION

A T-14 Armata at the 2015 Moscow Victory Day Parade. The T-14 Armata gives its crew enhanced protection by housing them in the hull. A disabling hit to the turret might leave the entire crew unharmed.

Autoblindé Peugeot (1914)

SPECIFICATIONS

DIMENSIONS:	Length (hull): 4.8m (15.75ft); Width: 1.8m (5.9ft); Height: 2.8m (9.19ft)
WEIGHT:	4900kg (10,800lb)
ENGINE:	4-cylinder Renault WC, petrol, 35bhp (26kW)
SPEED:	45km/h (28mph)
ARMAMENT:	1 x 37mm (1.46in) cannon or 1 x 7.62mm (0.3in) MG
SPEED:	Maximum road speed: 40km/h (25mph)
ARMOUR:	4–5.5mm (0.15–0.21in)
RANGE:	140km (85 miles)
CREW:	4 or 5

The Autoblindé Peugeot entered service in WWI as one of the first generation of armoured cars. Armoured cars is literally what they were – French commercial road cars covered with armoured panels. Two such vehicles emerged in late 1914: the AM Renault 20CV and the AC Peugeot 18CV.

POWERPLANT
The four-cylinder petrol engine generated 35bhp (26kW) of power, pushing the vehicle to a maximum speed of 45km/h (28mph).

MAIN GUN
The Puteaux SA 18 37mm (1.46in) main gun actually had a high rate of fire, at a maximum of 15 rounds per minute, although 10rpm was more practical.

ARMOUR
With maximum armour depth of just 5.5mm (0.21in), the Autoblindé Peugeot was scarcely able to keep out rifle-calibre bullets.

ROAD WHEELS
The thin road wheels meant that the vehicle was really only suited to use on roads or firm and relatively smooth ground.

CREW COMPARTMENT
The vehicle held four to five crew members, although the small dimensions of the vehicle meant that the interior was extremely cramped.

VARIANTS
The Renault vehicle was armed with a 7.62mm (0.3in) machine gun, while the Peugeot received a 37mm (1.46in) cannon. The design of the Peugeot and Renault cars was so similar that both armament and armour were interchangeable.

WARTIME SERVICE
About 150 Peugeots were produced during World War I (see right), but the rough conditions of the Western Front quickly revealed the limitations of the vehicle both in terms of off-road performance and in armoured protection. Post-war service included combat with the French Army in Africa, and service with the Polish Army in the 1920s against Russia.

Panhard et Levassor Type 178 (1937)

SPECIFICATIONS

DIMENSIONS:	Length: 4.79m (15ft 8.5in) with gun; Width: 3.5m (11ft 6in); Height: 3.3m (10ft 9in)
WEIGHT:	8.3 tonnes (8.2 tons)
ENGINE:	1 x Renault 4-cylinder petrol, developing 180hp (134kW)
SPEED:	Road speed: 72km/h (45mph); Off-road: 42km/h (26mph)
ARMAMENT:	1 × 25mm (0.98in) cannon; 1 × 7.5mm (0.29in) MG
ARMOUR:	Up to 26mm (1.02in)
RANGE:	300km (190 miles)
CREW:	4

The Panhard 178 was designed in the mid-1930s as a 4 × 4 armoured reconnaissance vehicle for the French Army. Its most common armament was a single 25mm (0.98in) cannon or two 7.5mm (0.29in) machine guns.

GERMAN ADOPTION

The Germans were impressed with the design of the Type 178 and used large numbers under the designation Panzerspähwagen P 204(f). Some of these were turned into anti-aircraft platforms by fitting them with 37mm (1.46in) anti-aircraft guns. A more unusual German variant involved replacing the wheels with railway wheels, and using the vehicle as a form of light armed locomotive. French production of the Type 178 recommenced in August 1944 after the liberation of Paris, though with a larger turret and 47mm (1.85in) gun. These endured in French Army service until 1960.

ARMAMENT
In some versions of the Type 178, the 25mm (0.98in) cannon was replaced by twin turret-mounted 7.5mm (0.29in) machine guns.

TURRET
The APX3 turret could house two men – the commander and the gunner. This turret had frontal armour of 26mm (1.02in).

ENGINE COMPARTMENT
The engine compartment of the Type 178 was set low and tapered, to reduce the overall profile of the vehicle.

FOUR-WHEEL DRIVE
The Type 178 was a four-wheel drive vehicle, giving it a reasonable cross-country performance.

STEERING
The driver could switch the steering between the front and rear wheels, and drive the vehicle backwards using all four main gears.

INVASION OF FRANCE
A German soldier examines a knocked-out and abandoned Panhard Type 178 following the invasion of France, May 1940.

SdKfz 232 (1938)

SPECIFICATIONS

DIMENSIONS:	Length: 8.86m (29ft); Width: 2.2m (7ft 3in); Height: 2.35m (7ft 8in) without masts
WEIGHT:	7.8 tonnes (7.7 tons)
ENGINE:	Büssing-NAG L8V V-8 petrol engine, generating 150hp (112kW)
SPEED:	Maximum road speed of 85km/h (53mph)
ARMAMENT:	Main: 1 x 20mm (0.79in) KwK30 or 38 cannon; Secondary: 1 x 7.92mm (0.31in) MG 34 machine gun
ARMOUR:	8–15mm (0.31–0.59in)
RANGE:	Road range 300km (186 miles)
CREW:	4

SIX WHEELS/EIGHT WHEELS

Six-wheeled cars entered service in 1932, but performed poorly over uneven ground, so eight-wheelers were developed. The most important of these in the early war years was the Panzerspähwagen SdKfz 231, 232 and 233 (8-rad). For some reason, the ordnance department of the German army gave the same number to both six- and eight-wheel armoured cars, so the eight-wheeler was suffixed '8-rad' to distinguish it from the 'other' 232, a 6 × 6 configuration vehicle.

The German Army made much use of armoured cars for reconnaissance during the war and one of their best-known vehicles was the six- and eight-wheeled SdKfz 231 family, which included the SdKfz 232 (8-rad) reconnaissance and communications vehicle.

AERIAL
In order to report their discoveries to armoured and infantry units, the 232 'Achtrads' were fitted with a large frame aerial for a powerful medium-range radio set, and this distinguished it from the otherwise identical SdKfz 231 (8-rad).

MANOEUVRABILITY
For a vehicle expected to make first contact with the enemy, the 'Achtrads' were inadequately armed and armoured. The ability to change direction (the requirement was to do so in under 10 seconds) can be understood in this light.

OFF-ROAD CAPABILITY
The 231 and 232 eight-wheeled cars could cross a trench up to 1.5m (4ft 11in) wide and ford rivers up to 1m (3ft 3in) deep.

WEAPONRY
The 232 (8-rad) was armed with a 20mm (0.78in) KwK 30 cannon and a coaxial MG 34 machine gun.

STEERING AND DIFFERENTIAL
The SdKfz 232 (8-rad) was an excellent off-road vehicle, partly because of its complicated but efficient all-wheel steering and differential system that prevented the inner wheels dragging in turns.

SPECIAL PURPOSE
The crew of a SdKfz 232 (8-rad) mount up in Poland in 1939. The prefix SdKfz meant *Sonderkraftfahrzeug*, or 'special purpose vehicle', and was used for half-tracks, armoured cars and tank destroyers.

SdKfz 251 (1939)

SPECIFICATIONS

DIMENSIONS:	Length: 5.8m (19ft); Width: 2m (6ft 7in); Height: 1.75m (5ft 9in)
WEIGHT:	7.81 tonnes (7.68 tons)
ENGINE:	Maybach HL42 TUKRM six-cylinder petrol engine, 100hp (75kW)
SPEED:	Maximum road speed of 53km/h (33mph)
ARMAMENT:	Differed according to variant
ARMOUR:	6–14.5mm (0.24–0.57in)
RANGE:	Road range of 180km (112 miles)
CREW:	2

The world's first purpose-designed armoured personnel carrier, the SdKfz 251 was used on all fronts and for numerous purposes from mobile howitzer to anti-aircraft gun platform. It was the most numerous German armoured vehicle ever built.

Right: A front view of the SdKfz 251. The standard personnel carrier version could carry 10 fully equipped troops and had a crew of two; note the two vision slits at the front.

MANY VARIANTS

The 251 was used in all theatres of war, in many variants. The 251/1 was fitted with wooden racks for 320mm (12.6in) infantry support rockets, a weapon sometimes known as the 'Stuka on foot'. The 251/16 had dual flamethrower guns. The 251/20 had a large infrared searchlight and was used in conjunction with the IR night sights on some Panther tanks. The 251/22 was a tank-destroyer version with a 75mm (2.95in) PaK 40 anti-tank gun.

ARMOUR
Armour was only 14.5mm (0.57in) at its thickest, which was adequate against heavy machine gun bullets and anti-tank shells.

HULL
Later models had simplified hull construction to speed production, notably all-welded armour as opposed to mainly riveted plates.

ARMAMENT
The base SdKfz 251 had its own armament of a fixed MG 34 machine gun, but there was also a mount for the infantry squad's machine gun.

SLOPING ARMOUR
The sloping of the armoured plates improved the ballistic protection they offered.

ROAD WHEELS
The interleaving road wheels was a feature later used on the Panther and Tiger battle tanks.

FLAMETHROWER VERSION
The Flammpanzerwagen had a 700-litre (153 UK gallons) flame fuel tank, and was used in the infantry assault support role. Here the crew saturate a position with fire.

SdKfz 234/2 (1943)

The SdKfz 234/2 Puma was a fast and well-armed armoured car used for reconnaissance ahead of the main force. There were several variants built in small numbers – the 234/2 had a fully enclosed armoured turret. The small numbers of 234/2s built (101) were distributed to four Panzer divisions and used in Russia and in western Europe.

SPECIFICATIONS

DIMENSIONS:	Length: 6.8m (22ft 4in); Width: 2.33m (7ft 7in); Height: 2.38m (7ft 10in)
WEIGHT:	10.5 tonnes (10.3 tons)
ENGINE:	Tatra 103 V-12 diesel engine, 220hp (164kW)
SPEED:	Road: 53mph (85km/h)
ARMAMENT:	Main: 1 ×50mm KwK 39/1 cannon; Secondary: 1 × 7.92mm (0.31in) MG 34 machine gun
ARMOUR:	9–30mm (0.35–1.18in)
RANGE:	Road: 550km/h (350mph)
CREW:	4

CANNON
The Puma's main armament was a 50mm (1.96in) KwK 39/1 cannon. There was space inside the vehicle for 55 rounds of ammunition.

TURRET
The turret was hand rotated and could be elevated from 10 degrees down to 20 degrees up.

DRIVING POSITION
The Puma had a second backward-facing driving position ahead of the engine. This, together with a gearbox with six forward and six reverse gears, enabled the Puma to be driven equally fast in either direction

DIESEL
Unlike almost all other German armoured vehicles, the Puma had a diesel engine, which was less likely to catch fire if damaged.

PERFORMANCE

The first vehicles served on the Eastern Front, where their good range proved invaluable, though they were complex to maintain, particularly when far from maintenance depots. The heavy main armament also encouraged Puma crews to engage the enemy, thus defeating the vehicle's original purposes. Only 101 turreted 234/2 Pumas were built, but they were followed by similar numbers of 234/3s and 234/4s, which mounted various anti-tank guns in open-topped superstructures.

FACTORY VEHICLE
A factory-fresh Puma is seen attracting a great deal of attention. Production began in September 1943 and ran for one year.

AEC Mk III Armoured Car (1943)

SPECIFICATIONS

DIMENSIONS:	Length: 5.61m (18ft 5in); Width: 2.70m (8ft 11in); Height: 2.69m (8ft 10in)
WEIGHT:	12.7 tonnes (12.5 tons)
ENGINE:	AEC A195 six-cylinder diesel engine, 105hp (78kW)
SPEED:	Road: 58km/h (38mph)
ARMAMENT:	Main: 1 × QF 75mm (2.95in) cannon; Secondary: 1 × 7.92mm (0.31in) Besa machine gun, 1 × 7.62mm (0.303in) Bren light machine gun
ARMOUR:	16–65mm (0.63–2.56in)
RANGE:	Road: 400km (250 miles)
CREW:	4

The AEC armoured cars were heavily armed and effective vehicles, packing the weaponry of a heavy tank. They were adaptable to larger guns as these became available. After the war, some AEC IIIs were supplied to Belgium for its reconnaissance regiments. Total production of the three models was 629 vehicles.

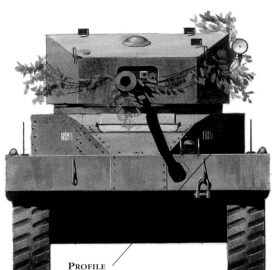

M3 GUN
The AEC Mk III had the 75mm (2.95in) M3 gun used on American medium tanks such as the M3 and many M4 Shermans. The secondary armament was a coaxial 7.92mm (0.31in) Besa machine gun.

CAMOUFLAGE
Camouflage netting was applied to the turret of this AEC Mk III. Local foliage is threaded through the netting to provide some concealment in wooded terrain.

PROFILE
One of the few faults of this car was its high profile and angular appearance, which made it hard to conceal in the observation role.

DRIVE SETTING
The AECs had selectable two- or four-wheel drive and steering with front-wheel drive used only for road travel.

BUS BUILDER

Designed (and built) by a bus manufacturer without any official requirement, the AEC armoured cars proved to be the equal of many tanks of their day and served with distinction in North Africa and Europe. In 1941, the AEC (Associated Engineering Company) of Southall, West London-built an armoured car based on information they had gleaned on fighting in North Africa. This Mk I car was virtually a wheeled tank, with heavy armour, a powerful engine and a 40mm (2pdr) gun, equivalent to that used by most tanks in the desert. Armament was increased on subsequent models in parallel with developments in tank guns. The AEC Mk II was given a three-man electrically traversed turret and a 57mm (6pdr) gun, but the Mk III had a 75mm (2.95in) M3 cannon.

GUN RANGE
An AEC II fires its 57mm (6pdr) gun during fighting for Tripoli in Libya. The gun had an effective firing range of 1510m (1650yd), but a maximum range of 4600m (5000yd).

LVT-4 'Water Buffalo' (1943)

SPECIFICATIONS

DIMENSIONS:	Length: 7.9m (25ft 11in); Width: 3.29m (10ft 9.5in); Height: 2.46m (8ft)
WEIGHT:	11 tonnes (10.8 tons)
ENGINE:	Continental W670-9A, seven-cylinder, radial petrol engine, 250hp (187kW)
SPEED:	Road: 32km/h (20mph)
ARMAMENT:	2 x 12.7mm (0.5in) Browning M2; 3 x 7.62mm (0.3in) Browning M1919 machine guns
ARMOUR:	6–13mm (0.25–0.51in) if added
RANGE:	Road: 480km (300 miles)
CREW:	2–3

The US Marines developed a series of specialized amphibious tractors, or 'AMTRACs', to deliver troops to Pacific island beaches. The LVT-4 Water Buffalo was the most numerous model.

SPEED
The front 'bow' of the LVT-4 had little in the way of seagoing sophistication, but the vehicle could still manage 12km/h (7.5mph) over water, albeit with scant comfort for the crew and other occupants.

ARMOURED HATCH
Initial LVT-4s had two large and two small glass windows at the front of the crew compartment, but these were replaced by a single armoured hatch on the version seen here, the LVT-4 Armoured Cab.

PINTLE-MOUNTED GUNS
As well as a 7.62mm (0.3in) bow machine gun, the LVT-4 was fitted with up to four pintle-mounted machine guns, two of them of 12.7mm (0.5in) calibre.

RAMP
The ramp was operated by a winch and lowered by cables on each side of the cargo compartment.

CREW
The LVT-4 had a crew of two (driver and commander) and could carry up to 24 Marines.

EVOLUTION

The LVT-4 evolved from the earlier tracked landing vehicles LVT-1, -2 and -3, which in turn were descendants of the 'Alligator', a 1930s lightweight tracked amphibious vehicle designed by engineer Donald Roebling for rescue work in the Florida Everglades. In 1937, the US Marine Corps took an interest after an article on the vehicle was published in *Life* magazine Following trials and modifications, 300 LVT (Landing Vehicle, Tracked) -1s were ordered as ship-to-shore cargo carriers. These were constructed by the Food Machinery Company (FMC) in California.

ENGINE
The LVT-4 had the engine moved forward to behind the driver's compartment and a rear ramp fitted. This allowed much easier loading and safer disembarking under fire.

WATER PROPULSION
The LVT-4 was powered in the water by cup-like grousers on the tracks, which propelled the vehicle at up to 12km/h (6.5mph).

LARGE LOADS
With its rear ramp, the LVT-4 could carry wheeled equipment such as Jeeps and light artillery pieces.

IWO JIMA ASSAULT
Packed with US Marines, LVT-2s and LVT-4s lead the assault on the Japanese island of Iwo Jima in 1945. In the Pacific, the Marines valued the LVTs for their ability to cross coral reefs and carry them inland, which landing craft could not do.

T17E1 Staghound I (1944)

SPECIFICATIONS

DIMENSIONS:	Length: 5.49m (18ft); Width: 2.69m (8ft 10in); Height: 2.36m (7ft 9in)
WEIGHT:	13.92 tonnes (13.7 tons)
ENGINE:	GMC 270 six-cylinder petrol engine, 97hp (72kW)
SPEED:	Road: 89km/h (55mph)
ARMAMENT:	Main: 1 x 37mm (1.5in) M6 cannon; Secondary: 2–3 x 7.62mm (0.3in) M1919 Browning machine guns
ARMOUR:	9–44mm (0.35–1.73in)
RANGE:	Road range of 724km (450 miles)
CREW:	5

QUALITIES

The Staghound, with its high speed, good range, thick armour and hydraulically traversed turret, was a popular and effective weapon. It was adaptable for a number of uses, including anti-aircraft (the Staghound AA with twin 12.7mm/0.5in guns) and anti-tank (Staghound Mk III with a Crusader turret and 75mm/2.95in gun).

The Staghound was built in the United States, but used entirely by British and Commonwealth forces during the war. It was powerful, fast and well armed. The 'Staghound' name was actually a British label applied to the T17E1.

FRONT VIEW

In this front view of the Staghound, we can see how the armament presented itself in and on top of the turret and in the front of the hull. The vehicle's combination of speed and firepower made it an excellent reconnaissance and infantry support vehicle.

MACHINE GUNS

The crew of five had up to three 7.62mm (0.303in) Browning machine guns in addition to the main gun. One was pintle-mounted on the turret roof, another was coaxial with the main gun, and the third was in the lower hull.

SEARCHLIGHT

The roof-mounted searchlight was useful for both visibility for the driver and crew but also for target acquisition by the gunner at night.

STOWAGE

The Staghound had stowage hooks for extra fuel containers and crew equipment such as bedrolls and tools.

HATCHES

An advantage of armoured cars over tanks is that an entry/escape hatch can be fitted in the lower fuselage side.

POST-WAR STAGHOUNDS

After the war, Staghounds were supplied to various nations, including Denmark, India and South Africa, and remained in service for some years with the British Army.

Panhard EBR/FL-11 (1951)

SPECIFICATIONS

DIMENSIONS:	Length (gun forwards): 6.15m (20.17ft); Width: 2.42m (7.94ft); Height: 2.32m (7.61ft)
WEIGHT:	13.5 tonnes (13.3 tons)
ENGINE:	1 x Panhard 12-cylinder petrol, developing 200hp (149kW)
SPEED:	Road speed: 105km/h (65mph)
ARMAMENT:	1 x 75mm (2.95in) cannon or 1 x 90mm (3.54in); 2 x 7.5mm (0.29in) or 7.62mm (0.3in) MGs
ARMOUR:	40mm (1.57in)
RANGE:	600km (370 miles)
CREW:	4

French development of an 8×8 armoured car actually began in the 1930s, with a prototype running from 1939. The war interrupted progress, but work resumed in the late 1940, resulting in the highly capable EBR entering production in 1951.

MUNITIONS
The ERB's 90mm (3.5in) gun fired two main types of shell. Its high-explosive (HE) type was intended for use against infantry and their positions and against soft-skinned vehicular targets. By contrast, the heat-explosive anti-tank (HEAT) warhead was the anti-armour munition. Working on shaped-charge principles, the HEAT warhead was capable of penetrating through 320mm (12.6in) of homogenous armour when presented at a 0° angle. Such capabilities meant that even a main battle tank would have to regard the EBR with respect.

MAIN GUN
The main gun on the EBR was initially a 75mm (2.95in) SA49 type, then (in 1954) a higher-powered SA50 version, but most of the armoured cars were later upgraded in the 1960s to a 90mm (3.5in) D921/F1 gun.

TURRET
The FL-11 turret has a full 360° traverse, while the main gun can be elevated between –6° and +13°.

SMOKE DISCHARGERS
Two smoke dischargers are fitted on each side of the hull, providing instant obscuration when required.

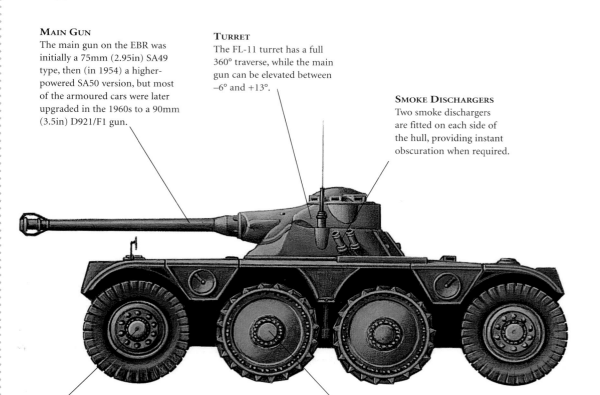

WHEELS
The front and rear wheels are steerable road wheels; the central pairs of wheels are only lowered into contact with the ground when the vehicle goes off-road.

8 × 8 DRIVE
The EBR's 8 × 8 configuration gave it impressive off-road mobility across even the softest ground; with all eight wheels deployed, ground pressure is only 0.7kg (1.5lb) per 1cm^2 (0.16in^2).

VARIANTS
The distinction between the FL-10 and the FL-11 variants of the Panhard EBR lies in the turrets. The FL-10 turret is fitted to the AMX-13 light tank, and features a 75mm (2.95in) cannon fed from two revolver-type magazines, each holding six rounds. The FL-11 turret is specific to the EBR.

M50 Ontos (1955)

SPECIFICATIONS

DIMENSIONS:	Length: 4.88m (16.01ft); Width: 2.68m (8.79ft); Height: 3.35m (10.99ft)
WEIGHT:	11.7 tonnes (11.5 tons)
ENGINE:	1 x Detroit Diesel 6V-53N 6-cylinder diesel, developing 215hp (160kW)
SPEED:	Road: 48km/h (30mph)
ARMAMENT:	6 x 105mm (4.1in)
ARMOUR:	Up to 16mm (0.63in)
RANGE:	185km (115 miles)
CREW:	3

The M50 Ontos was a tank destroyer designed mainly for use as an air-portable vehicle for the US Marine Corps. Its chassis was developed in the early 1950s by GMC, and its weaponry consisted of six M40 105mm (4.1in) recoilless rifles, three mounted either side of a small central turret.

MAIN ARMAMENT
Of the six recoilless rifles fitted to the sides of the vehicles, two of them could be dismounted and used as an infantry weapons.

SPOTTING RIFLES
Attached to the top four guns were 12.7mm (0.5in) spotting rifles. These would fire tracer rounds to assist targeting. Six 105mm (4.1in) rounds were pre-loaded and a further eight were kept inside the vehicle.

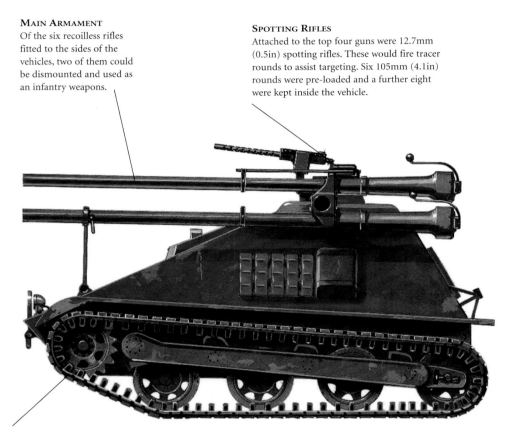

RECOILLESS RIFLES
The M50 Ontos was equipped with six M40 recoilless rifles, which had an effective range of 1350m (1480yd) and a maximum range of 6870m (7513yd). Although the M40 had decent penetration and performance, a major disadvantage of the weapon when applied to the M50 was that the rifles could only be reloaded from the outside, thus exposing the crew to small-arms fire. Also, if multiple weapons were fired together, the enormous back-blast created a highly visible signature of the vehicle's location.

PERFORMANCE
The Ontos was a diminutive vehicle, but it could traverse a vertical obstacle 0.7m (2ft 6in) high and cross a 1.37 (4ft 6in) trench.

US MARINE CORPS VEHICLE
The M50 Ontos turned out to be an excellent fire support weapon for the US Marine Corps in the Vietnam War. It was phased out from USMC use from 1970.

FV601 Saladin (1958)

SPECIFICATIONS

DIMENSIONS:	Length: 4.93m (16.17ft); Wheelbase: 3.048m (10 ft); Width: 2.54m (8.33ft; Height: 2.39m (7.84ft)
WEIGHT:	11.6 tonnes (12.78 tons)
ENGINE:	1 x Rolls Royce B80 Mk.6A, 8 cylinder petrol engine producing 1667 kW (170 hp)
SPEED:	72 km/h (45mph)
ARMAMENT:	Main: 1 x 76mm (3in) L5A1 gun;Secondary: 2 x 7.62mm (0.3in) coaxial machine guns
ARMOUR:	8–16mm (0.32–0.63in)
RANGE:	Road: 400km (249 miles)
CREW:	3

The Alvis Saladin armoured car was placed in service with the armed forces of numerous countries during the 1960s and 1970s, as well as with the United Nations. It proved to be extremely well adapted as a patrol and reconnaissance vehicle.

Right: Another important vehicle from Alvis was the FV603 Saracen, seen here. The Saracen was a versatile APC platform that was extensively repurposed through multiple variants.

WIDESPREAD ADOPTION

The Saladin had been designed in the late 1940s, but it did not enter service with the British Army until 1958. The armed forces of no fewer than 13 countries and those under the flag of the United Nations used the Saladin over the following two decades, with major operators including Indonesia, Jordan, Oman, Tunisia, Uganda and the United Arab Emirates. In British Army service, the Saladins persisted until the early 1980s.

SECONDARY ARMAMENT
For anti-aircraft defence, a 7.62mm (0.3in) Browning machine gun is mounted beside the commander's hatch on the turret. A second 7.62mm (0.3in) machine gun is mounted coaxially in the turret, and two six-round smoke grenade launchers are located on either side of the hull.

TURRET
The manually traversed, steel turret is of all-welded construction and protected by 32mm (1.25in) of armour plating.

COMMANDER POSITION
The commander sees through four periscopes mounted forwards and a fifth swivelling periscope at the rear of the hatch.

MAIN ARMAMENT
The main armament of the Saladin consists of a low-muzzle-velocity 76.2mm (3in) L5 gun. Its maximum effect range is 1000m (3,280ft).

ENGINE
The 170hp (127kW), eight-cylinder Rolls-Royce B80 Mk.6A engine of the Saladin is enclosed in a rear compartment.

GUNNER POSITIONS
His periscope divided into two parts, the Saladin gunner sits to the left of the commander inside the turret and scans the horizon for targets using an upper scope with no magnification and a lower scope with 6 x magnification power.

DRIVER POSITION
The Saladin driver is allowed a maximum field of vision with the hatch, forwards left of the vehicle, folded back completely. In his enclosed compartment, the driver sees through three periscopes.

SALADIN AND SARACEN
An FV601 Saladin and an FV603 Saracen perform joint manoeuvres during British Army training in the 1960s. The familial resemblance between the two vehicles is not coincidental; in fact, they shared many fundamental components.

M113 (1960)

SPECIFICATIONS

DIMENSIONS:	Length: 2.52 m (8ft 3in); Width: 2.69m (8ft 10in); Height: 1.85m (6ft 1in)
WEIGHT:	11.3 tonnes (12.43 tons)
ENGINE:	Detroit Diesel 6V53T, 6-cylinder diesel engine 275hp (205kW)
SPEED:	Speed, road: 61km/h (38mph); amphibious: 5km/h (3mph)
ARMAMENT:	Various but minimum usually 1 x 12.7mm (0.5in) machine gun
ARMOUR:	45mm (1.77in)
RANGE:	480km (298 miles)
CREW:	2 + 11

Conceived as a battle taxi to deliver infantry to combat zones and then withdraw, the M113 armoured personnel carrier evolved into a fighting vehicle. Its chassis has served as the platform for numerous special-purpose vehicles since the 1960s.

Above: The M113 armoured personnel carrier proved to be a remarkable vehicle both in the versatility of its applications and in the reliability of its design and construction. The M113 family of vehicles has been applied to nearly every major functional combat area of the US Army.

WORLD BEATER

The M113 has been judged as one of the most significant military vehicles of the 20th century, on account of both its ubiquity and its utility. To date more than 80,000 of the type have been produced, and despite its 1960s ancestry it is proving hard to replace entirely. More than 60 countries globally have used or continue to use the M113. The range of variants is also truly astonishing. They include mortar carriers, anti-aircraft vehicles, reconnaissance vehicles, radio cars, ambulances, command posts, engineering and recovery vehicles, EOD variants, direction-finding stations, anti-tank vehicles and even versions capable of launching tactical nuclear missiles.

TROOP ACCESS
Combat troops entered and exited the standard vehicle by means of a powered ramp door or through a large rectangular roof hatch.

HULL CONSTRUCTION
The box-like hull of the M113 is watertight, welded aluminium armour, and its forward edges slope at 60 degrees.

MAIN ARMAMENT
The M106 mortar carrier variant with ACAV modifications (shown) mounts a 107mm (4.2in) mortar. This can be fired from inside the troop compartment on a turntable platform or set up outside the vehicle. Its 12.7mm (0.5in) machine gun is protected against small-arms fire by shields.

ENGINE
Early M113s were petrol powered. However, these were modified beginning with the M113A1 in favour of a 275hp (205kW) Detroit Diesel 6V53T powerplant.

TROOP CAPACITY
The interior of the standard M113 armoured personnel carrier is capable of transporting up to 11 combat-ready infantrymen, five seated on benches along either side of the vehicle and another located in an aisle jump seat.

MINIMAL WEIGHT
In the standard APC version, the M113 has just a two-man crew, plus 11 fully armed troops in the rear hull. Despite its size, the M113 had a new aluminium armour that kept overall vehicle weight to a minimum, making it air transportable.

BTR-60PA (1963)

SPECIFICATIONS

DIMENSIONS: Length: 7.56m (24.8ft); Width: 2.825m (7.5ft); Height: 2.06m (6.76 ft)

WEIGHT: 10.2 tonnes (11.24 tons)

ENGINE: 2 x GAZ-40P 6-cylinder petrol engines producing 67 kW (90 hp) each and 134 kW (180 hp) combined

SPEED: Road: 80km/h (49.7mph); Water: 10km/h (6.2mph)

ARMAMENT: 1 × DShK 1938/46 12.7mm (0.5in) heavy machine gun; options for 2 x 7.62mm (0.3in) machine guns

ARMOUR: Welded steel Hull Upper Front: 7mm (0.26in) Hull Lower Front: 9mm (0.35in) Sides: 7mm (0.26in)

RANGE: 500km (311 miles)

CREW: 2 + 16 passengers

Replacing the BTR-152, a converted truck, the development of the BTR-60 and its later variant, the BTR-60PA, began in 1959. Eventually, more than 25,000 of the vehicles were produced in the Soviet Union, equipping the Red Army and the ground forces of Warsaw Pact and other nations.

ARMAMENT
Either a DshK 12.7mm (0.5-in) heavy machine gun or a light 7.62mm (0.3-in) PKT machine gun was mounted above a single hatch positioned behind the commander and driver hatches.

ARMOUR PROTECTION
Frontal hull armour protection was only 9mm (0.35in) thick, while the hull sides varied from 5–7mm (0.2–0.26in).

ACCESS
A lone hatch, opening to the right, was provided above the personnel compartment, while three firing ports were installed on each side of the vehicle. No entry access was available along the sides.

ENGINE
Twin 90hp (67kW), six-cylinder GAZ-40P petrol engines powered the BTR-60 and were prone to catching fire.

BTR-60PA

The BTR-60PA signalled an improvement over the original BTR-60 in that its armoured roof covering for the personnel compartment, thin at only 7mm (0.26 in), offered some protection against shell fragments and small-arms fire from above. However, its complement of up to 14 combat infantrymen were exposed to the enemy while exiting through a top hatch because no exit was possible from the sides.

CAPACITY
Along with its crew of two – a driver and commander – the BTR-60PA carried up to 14 passengers. Later variants added another crewman – a gunner – to man additional armament.

SUSPENSION
The wheeled 8 × 8 vehicle was supported by a torsion bar suspension with two hydraulic shock absorbers on the first and second road wheels of each side, and a single hydraulic shock absorber for the third and fourth road wheels.

KEY FEATURES
Additional features distinguishing the BTR-60PA from its predecessor were the driver's roof-mounted periscope, a heavier machine gun armament, and NBC defences. To assist with ingress and egress, six handrails, grouped in two pairs of three, were attached to the exterior of each side of the vehicle.

BMP-1 (1965)

SPECIFICATIONS

DIMENSIONS:	Length: 6.73m (22ft 1.2in); Width: 2.94m (9ft 8in); Height (to turret top): 2.07m (6ft 9.4in)
WEIGHT:	13.2 tonnes (14.6 tons)
ENGINE:	1 x UTD-20, 6-cylinder 4-stroke V-shaped airless-injection water-cooled multi-fuel 15.8 l (4.17 gallon) diesel producing 300hp (224kW) at 2600 rpm
SPEED:	Road: 65km/h (40mph)
ARMAMENT:	Main: 1x 73mm (2.87in) 2A28 Grom low-pressure smoothbore short-recoil semi-automatic gun (40 rounds); 9S428 ATGM launcher for 9M14 Malyutka (4 + 1 rounds) Secondary: 7.62-mm (0.3-in) PKT coaxial machinegun (2000 rounds)
ARMOUR:	6–33 mm (0.24–1.3in)
RANGE:	Road: 600km (370 miles)
CREW:	3 + 8 passengers

THE IFV

The infantry fighting vehicle (IFV) was a new concept in armoured warfare. Previously, troops had been transported into battle by armoured personnel carriers (APCs), which with their minimal armament and light armour required the protection of heavier combat vehicles. The IFV, by contrast, could not only take troops into action, but it could also provide those troops with heavy fire support and even take on enemy main battle tanks with its gun and missile systems.

The world's first true infantry fighting vehicle, the BMP-1 was heavily armed with cannon and anti-tank guided missiles. It was intended originally to serve as a protected position for infantry to fight from, in the wake of tactical nuclear weapons.

TANK MISSILES
The 9S428 launcher mounted above the 73mm (2.87in) cannon fired the AT-3 Sagger, a wire-guided anti-tank missile, with five rounds on board.

MAIN ARMAMENT
The 73mm (2.87in) 2A28 Grom smoothbore semi-automatic cannon was housed inside a one-man turret. It fired at a rate of eight rounds per minute and had 40 rounds stored in the automatic loader and throughout the hull.

TURRET
Positioned in the centre of the hull, the low, cone-shaped turret housed the 73mm (2.87in) cannon, the automatic loader, and a coaxial 7.62mm (0.3in) machine gun.

TROOP COMPLEMENT
The BMP-1 was capable of transporting up to eight combat-ready infantrymen seated back to back in rows of four in the hull's rear compartment.

ENGINE
The BMP-1 was powered by a 300hp (224kW), six-cylinder UTD-20 engine with a maximum range of 500km (310 miles) cross country or 600km (370 miles) on the road.

ARMOUR PROTECTION
Ranging from 6–33mm (0.24–1.3in) thick, the aluminium alloy armour protection afforded the interior of the vehicle little protection against weapons of heavy calibre.

FOREIGN SERVICE
The BMP-1 has had excellent export success and has been seen in service with countries such as Czechoslovakia, Poland, Germany, Iraq, Greece and India, as well as all the states of the former USSR.

Scimitar (1970)

SPECIFICATIONS

DIMENSIONS:	Length: 4.9m (15ft 9in); Width: 2.2m (7ft 3in); Height: 2.1m (6ft 9in)
WEIGHT:	7.8 tonnes (7.6 tons)
ENGINE:	1 x Cummins BTA 5.9-litre (1.29-gallon) diesel powerplant generating 190hp (142kW)
SPEED:	80km/h (50mph)
ARMAMENT:	Main: 1 x 30mm (1.18in) L21 RARDEN cannon Secondary: 1 x 7.62mm (0.3in) L37A1 machine gun or L94A1 chain gun
ARMOUR:	12.7mm (0.5in)
RANGE:	Road: 645km (400 miles); Cross-country: 450km (280 miles)
CREW:	3

One of a family of reconnaissance vehicles manufactured by the Alvis Company, the FV 107 Scimitar followed the FV 101 Scorpion and excelled in rapid deployment and infantry support.

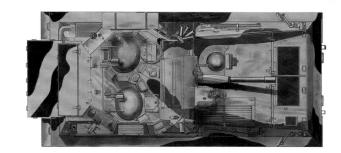

SCIMITAR ON THE SCENE

The FV 107 Scimitar has continued in service for more than 40 years. A combat veteran, the vehicle was deployed in the Falklands War of 1982 as B Squadron, Blues and Royals, providing the only British armoured vehicles used during the short conflict. During the fight to capture the Al Faw peninsula during the 2003 invasion of Iraq, C Squadron of the Queen's Dragoon Guards fielded the Scimitar. The FV 107 was also deployed in the first and second Gulf Wars, Bosnia, Kosovo and Afghanistan. In 2009, the FV 107 was in line for upgrade with the Future Rapid Effect System (FRES), and from 2010 an updated Mk II was developed, largely around improved anti-mine protection.

MAIN ARMAMENT
The 30mm (1.18in) L21 RARDEN cannon may be fired in single shot or automatic mode at a rate of up to 90 rounds per minute. Its muzzle velocity is sufficient to penetrate the side armour of some main battle tanks.

SECONDARY ARMAMENT
The secondary armament of the FV 107 Scimitar has been enhanced through the years. The standard package of the 7.62mm (0.3in) L37A1 machine gun or L94A1 chain gun has at times been augmented with other automatic weapons mounted on the exterior of the hull.

ARMOUR PROTECTION
The rolled and welded aluminium hull is toughened to withstand small-arms fire, blast effect and shockwaves. External armour plating has been added on some vehicles.

ENGINE
The original Jaguar J60 6-cylinder petrol powerplant was later replaced by the Cummins BTA 5.9-litre (1.29-gallon) diesel engine. A more efficient cooling system was added to prolong engine life.

SUSPENSION
The torsion bar suspension stabilized five rubber-edged road wheels on each side of the FV 107 hull, enhancing both road and cross-country performance.

TRANSPORTATION
As shown in the photo here, the Scimitar is easily transportable aboard a flatbed trailer.

Marder (1971)

SPECIFICATIONS

DIMENSIONS:	Length: 6.79m (22.28ft); Width: 3.24m (10.63ft); Height: 2.98m (9.78ft)
WEIGHT:	29.2 tonnes (32.2 tons)
ENGINE:	1 x MTU MB 833 Ea-500 diesel engine producing 441 kW (600 hp)
SPEED:	78km/h (47mph)
ARMAMENT:	Main: 1 x 20mm (0.79in) Rheinmetall MK 20 Rh 202 automatic cannon MILAN ATGM launcher Secondary: 1 x 7.62mm (0.3in) MG3 machine gun
ARMOUR:	Welded steel, protection up to 20 mm (0.79 in) APDS
RANGE:	520km (323 miles)
CREW:	3 + 7

The first infantry fighting vehicle developed and deployed by a NATO country, the Marder entered service in 1971. It has since been joined by the British Warrior and US Bradley amongst others, while retaining its reputation as a highly functional combat support platform.

Right: The Marder's 20mm (0.79in) cannon is mounted on top of the turre but external to the turret housing in order to eliminate the build-up of fumes when the weapon is in action.

TACTICAL VEHICLE

The Marder infantry fighting vehicle combines fire-support capabilities along with transportation of an infantry squad into combat with armour protection. The driver is seated forwards and to the left with the engine compartment on his right, while the commander and gunner occupy the turret directly behind and above the engine. The troop compartment to the rear accommodates six infantrymen seated back to back in groups of three, facing outwards.

MAIN ARMAMENT

The 20mm (0.79in) Rheinmetall Rh.202 cannon is fed by three separate belts, allowing the gunner to change ammunition as combat conditions demand. A MILAN anti-tank guided missile system may also be attached to the turret.

TURRET

The two-man turret houses the commander and gunner and is situated to the right on top of the hull. Capable of 360-degree traverse, it incorporates periscopes for the commander and gunner, while the gunner also has an optical gunsight, which can be replaced with infrared equipment.

SECONDARY ARMAMENT

A coaxial 7.62mm (0.3in) MG3 machine gun was originally complemented by an additional remotely controlled 7.62mm (0.3-n) gun. This was mounted near the rear of the vehicle but was later removed

ENGINE

The MTU MB 883 Ea-500 diesel engine delivers 600hp (441kW) and a top road speed of 78km/h (47mph).

INFANTRY ACCESS

Infantry can engage the enemy dismounted or from inside the Marder, firing through two circular firing ports on either side of the hull. Ingress and egress are accomplished through two roof hatches and a ramp door to the rear.

HULL

Based on a tracked chassis first conceived in the early 1960s, the Marder hull is divided into driving and engine compartments forwards and a troop compartment capable of transporting six fully armed combat infantrymen to the rear.

TRAINING EXERCISE

Photographed during a training exercise, the driver of the German Marder peers through his hatch, while the two-crew turret and its weapons are clearly visible. Sloping armour and reinforced hulls increase survivability.

AAV-7 (1972)

SPECIFICATIONS

DIMENSIONS:	Length: 7.94m (26ft); Width: 3.27m (10.73ft); Height: 3.26m (10.7ft)
WEIGHT:	22.8 tonnes (25.1 tons)
ENGINE:	1 x Detroit Diesel 8V-53T (P-7), Cummins VT 400 903 (P-7A1) 300kW (400hp); or VTAC 525 903 391kW (525hp) (AAV-7RAM-RS)
SPEED:	Road: 64km/h (45mph); Off-road: 13.5km/h (8.2mph)
ARMAMENT:	Main: 1 x Mk 19 40mm (1.57in) automatic grenade launcher (864 rounds) or M242 Bushmaster 25mm (0.98in) (900 rounds) Secondary: 1 x M2HB 12.7mm (0.5in) machine gun (1200 rounds)
ARMOUR:	Up to 45mm (1.77in)
RANGE:	480km (300 miles)
CREW:	3 + 25

For many years the primary amphibious transport vehicle of the US Marine Corps, the AAV-7 was one in a long line of amphibious tracked vehicles designed to insert combat troops and provide fire and logistical support during an inland or cross-country advance.

Above: The primary responsibility of the AAV during an amphibious operation is to spearhead a beach assault. It disembarks from a ship and comes ashore, carrying infantry and supplies to provide a forced entry into the amphibious assault area for the surface assault element.

MAIN ARMAMENT
The AAV7 is equipped with a M242 Bushmaster 25mm (0.98in) chain-fed auto-cannon with 900 rounds.

ARMOUR PROTECTION
With up to 45mm (1.77 in) of protective armour, the AAV7 is lighter than its US Army counterpart, the M2/M3 Bradley Fighting Vehicle, but its capacity is much greater.

INFANTRY ACCESS
The relatively spacious troop compartment of the AAV7 is accessed through a large ramp door at the rear of the vehicle and a pair of roof hatches. Troops are seated on benches facing inwards along the length of the hull and in the centre.

CARGO CAPACITY
The AAV7 is capable of carrying its crew of three along with up to 25 combat-ready Marines. In the logistics support role, it is capable of carrying up to 4.5 tonnes (5 tons) of equipment and supplies.

ENGINE
The General Motors Detroit Diesel 8V53T engine was subsequently replaced by the 400hp (300kW) Cummins VT 400 903 turbocharged diesel engine, which also has multi-fuel capability.

DRIVE TRAIN
The FMC Corporation HS-400-3A1 transmission drives the tracked vehicle with six rubber-coated road wheels on either side and a torsion bar suspension.

FALKLANDS WAR
Although a US vehicle, the AAV-7 has served with several other national operators, including Argentina, within its naval infantry. In 1982 some 20 LVTP-7s (as the AAV was known as the time) were used in the Argentine invasion of the Falkland Islands, and one vehicle was disabled by Royal Marine fire.

NEW REPLACEMENT
The AAV-7 has been the frontline cross-country and urban troop transport vehicle of the US Marine Corps. In 2018 the USMC announced the progressive replacement of the AAV-7 by the BAE/Iveco SuperAV.

Ratel (1976)

The Ratel IFV forms the basis of a family of armoured vehicles designed and manufactured in South Africa for the country's military. Its variants include platforms for anti-tank, mortar, and direct fire support. A number of Ratel have been exported to other countries.

SPECIFICATIONS

DIMENSIONS:	Length: 7.21m (23.66ft); Width: 2.5m (8.2ft); Height: 2.91m (9.56ft)
WEIGHT:	18.5 tonnes (20.39 tons)
ENGINE:	1 x D 3256 BTXF 6-cylinder diesel 210kW (282hp)
SPEED:	Road: 105km/h (65mph) Off-road: 30km/h (18.6mph)
ARMAMENT:	Main: 1 x 20mm (0.79in) semi-automatic cannon Secondary: 1 x 7.62mm (0.3in) MG (coaxial), 7.62mm (0.3in) MG (anti-aircraft), 1 x 7.62mm (0.3in) MG (anti-aircraft), 2 x 2 smoke grenade dischargers
ARMOUR:	Up to 20mm (0.79in)
RANGE:	1000 km (621 miles)
CREW:	3 + 7

ARMOUR PROTECTION
At a maximum of 20mm (0.79in), the Ratel's light armour protects against small arms and shell fragments. An additional armour package protects the underside against mines and IEDs (improvised explosive devices).

SECONDARY ARMAMENT
A coaxial 7.62mm (0.3in) machine gun is mounted in the turret, while a second machine gun of the same size is attached to a rear cupola above the troop compartment. Some Ratel vehicles include a third 7.62-mm (0.3-in) machine gun attached to the turret.

MAIN ARMAMENT
The Ratel 20 (shown) mounts a turreted 20mm (0.79in) semi-automatic cannon or a 12.7mm (0.5in) heavy machine gun for direct fire support, while its variants field such weapons as a 90mm (3.54in) cannon, a 60-mm (2.36in) mortar, or anti-tank guided missiles.

FIRST WHEELED IFV
The South African Ratel was the first wheeled IFV placed into service. Its mobility provided greater reliability and required less maintenance than tracked vehicles in the rugged, arid terrain of the country's border regions, and it had run-flat tyres and reinforced armour for protection against mines. The Ratel was also the first infantry fighting vehicle to install a commander's cupola.

SUSPENSION
The six wheels are each powered, and the vehicle is capable of running on four wheels if necessary.

CAPACITY
The Ratel crew of three, including a commander, driver, and gunner, is augmented with up to seven fully armed combat infantrymen in the troop compartment.

ENGINE
The 282hp (210kW) turbocharged, six-cylinder D3256 BTXF diesel engine generates a top speed of 105km/h (65mph) on the road and 30km/h (18mph) cross country.

CREW LOCATIONS
The driver is located forwards and in the centre of the vehicle with the commander and gunner inside the turret, the troop compartment behind with space for up to seven fully equipped soldiers, and the engine at the rear.

BTR-70 (1976)

SPECIFICATIONS

DIMENSIONS:	Length: 7.53m (24.7ft); Width: 2.8m (9.19ft); Height: 2.23m (7.32ft)
WEIGHT:	11.5 tonnes (11.3 tons)
ENGINE:	1 x ZMZ-4905 8-cylinder petrol, developing 240hp (179kW) at 2100rpm
SPEED:	Road: 80km/h (50mph); Water 5.6km (9mph)
ARMAMENT:	1 x 14.5mm (0.57in) KPVT MG; 1 x coaxial PKT 7.62mm (0.3in) MG
ARMOUR:	Steel (details classified)
RANGE:	600km (370 miles)
CREW:	2 + 9

AMPHIBIOUS VEHICLE

The BTR-70 is a fully amphibious vehicle, with a maximum on-water speed of 5.9km/h (9mph). When in amphibious mode, it is powered by a single water jet at the rear of the vehicle. The driver has to prepare the vehicle to enter water by erecting a trim vane and switching on bilge pumps from within the vehicle. Once back on land, the driver also has a central tyre-pressure regulation system, so that he can adjust type pressure to suit the type of terrain.

The BTR-70 is essentially an improved BTR-60. Its hull is slightly longer than that of the BTR-60, and it features triangular access doors to the troop compartment on both sides, set between the second and third axles. Two roof hatches provide additional access.

TROOP COMPARTMENT
The troop compartment holds nine infantrymen sitting back to back along a central bench.

ARMAMENT
Armament is confined to the small forward turret, and consists of one 14.5mm (0.57in) KPVT machine gun with a coaxial 7.62mm (0.3in) machine gun.

PORTS AND BLOCKS
Three firing ports and a vision block are on each side of the compartment. The two-man crew sit towards the front of the vehicle, and each has three forward and one side-facing periscope.

PEACEKEEPERS
Marines of B Company, 3rd Law Enforcement Battalion, stand atop a Mongolian Armed Forces BTR-70 armored vehicle June 20, 2018, after Khaan Quest 2018 entry control point operations training at Five Hills Area, Mongolia.

M2 Bradley (1981)

SPECIFICATIONS

DIMENSIONS:	Length: 6.55m (21ft 6in); Width: 3.6m (11ft 9in); Height: 2.98m (9ft 9in)
WEIGHT:	27.6 tonnes (27.1 tons)
ENGINE:	1 x Cummins VTA-903T eight- cylinder diesel powerplant generating 447kW (600hp)
SPEED:	66km/h (41mph)
ARMAMENT:	Main: 1 x 25mm (0.98in) McDonnell Douglas M242 chain gun; TOW anti-tank missile launcher Secondary: 1 x 7.62mm (0.3in) M240C machine gun
ARMOUR:	Classified thickness; spaced laminate, steel appliqué and aluminium alloy 7017 explosive-reactive armour
RANGE:	483km (300 miles)
CREW:	3

With its roots in the Vietnam era, the M2/3 Bradley fighting vehicle did not enter service with the US Army until 1981. Even then, controversy swirled around its perceived combat capabilities.

Right: The M2/M3 Bradley fighting vehicle has undergone numerous improvements since entering service. One of these included the Operation Desert Storm (ODS) upgrade following the 1991 Gulf War. Improved fire control, navigation, thermal imaging and command and control have enhanced the vehicle's performance.

MAIN ARMAMENT
The 25mm (0.98in) M242 chain gun, manufactured by McDonnell Douglas, is also known as the Bushmaster. The weapon fires an armour-piercing round with a core of depleted uranium and a high-explosive round.

ANTI-TANK MISSILE
The TOW anti-tank guided missile system is also mounted.

INFANTRY ACCESS
Initially, the M2 Bradley infantry fighting vehicle carried up to seven combat troops. That number was later reduced to six. The M3 cavalry fighting vehicle carries two scout infantrymen.

ARMOUR PROTECTION
The Bradley's aluminium alloy 7017 explosive reactive armour, additional steel plating and spaced laminate armour protect the vehicle against armour-piercing rounds of up to 23mm (0.98in).

URBAN SURVIVABILITY

In 2008, largely inspired by combat experience in Iraq, the British BAe Systems provided the US Bradley force with 952 Bradley Urban Survivability Kits (BUSK). These delivered a package of features to protect the vehicle when operating in hostile urban environments, and include a high-powered directional spotlight, protective mesh for the turret external optics, a lightweight, non-conductive 'dome tent' structure to shield the turret and crew from low-hanging electrical power lines, a commander's 5.56mm (0.223) machine gun, and fire-suppression systems.

DESERT WARRIOR
An M2 Bradley kicks up clouds of dust during a desert manouevre. The M2 proved itself during the 1991 Operation *Desert Storm* in Kuwait and Iraq, destroying large numbers of enemy vehicles, although it proved vulnerable to RPGs and IEDs.

LAV-25 (1983)

SPECIFICATIONS

DIMENSIONS:	Length: 6.39m (21ft 9in); Width: 2.5m (8ft 3in); Height: 2.69m (8ft 10in)
WEIGHT:	12.8 tonnes (12.6 tons)
ENGINE:	1 x Detroit Diesel 6-cylinder diesel, developing 275hp (205kW)
SPEED:	Road: 100km/h (60mph); Water: 12km/h (7.5mph)
ARMAMENT:	Main: 1 x 25mm (0.98in) M242 chain gun; Secondary: 1 x 7.62mm (0.3in) coaxial MG;
ARMOUR:	4.71–9.71mm (0.18–0.38in)
RANGE:	668km (414 miles)
CREW:	3 + 6

The Light Armoured Vehicle 25 (LAV-25) is in most ways a copy of the Swiss MOWAG Piranha, one of the world's most successful armoured personnel carriers. Built by General Motors of Canada, it is an 8 × 8 armoured vehicle with capacity for three crew and six passengers, the latter sitting back to back in the hull rear.

CHAIN GUN
The LAV-25's main weapon is the M242 25mm (0.98in) chain gun, which fires at a cyclical rate of 200 or 500rpm.

ARMOUR
The LAV-25's armour is very light, to a maximum of 9.17mm (0.38in). This protects the crew from small-arms fire and shell splinters, but its main survivability comes from its speed and firepower.

PROPELLERS
The LAV-25 is amphibious (although is not suited to open ocean transit), propellers at the rear driving it to on-water speeds of 12km/h (7.5mph).

DRIVE OPTIONS
The LAV-25's driver can switch between four-wheel and eight-wheel drive options, the latter giving better cross-country performance but at the cost of reduced fuel efficiency.

VARIANTS

Like the Piranha, the LAV-25 has evolved into a large number of variants, including maintenance and recovery vehicles, ATGW carriers, Mobile Electronic Warfare Support System and even an Assault Gun Vehicle armed with a 105mm (4.13in) cannon. The standard turret is usually fitted with a 25mm (0.98in) M242 chain gun and a 7.62mm (0.3in) coaxial machine gun.

AFGHANISTAN PATROL
With interpreters onboard, US Marines conduct a mounted patrol using a LAV-25 near Kandahar, Afghanistan, during Operation *Enduring Freedom*.

Pandur (1986)

SPECIFICATIONS

DIMENSIONS:	Length: 5.7m (18.7ft); Width: 2.5m (8.2ft); Height: 1.82m (5.97ft)
WEIGHT:	13.5 tonnes (13.3 tons)
ENGINE:	Steyr WD 612.95 6-cylinder turbo diesel, developing 240hp (179kW)
SPEED:	Road: 100km/h (60mph)
ARMAMENT:	1 x 12.7mm (0.5in) MG; 2 x 3 smoke grenades launchers; various other configurations
ARMOUR:	Up to 8mm (0.31in)
RANGE:	700km (430 miles)
CREW:	2 + 8

CHASSIS VARIANTS

A common chassis is produced in either 'A' or 'B' variants: 'A' with a raised centre roof and 'B' with a flat roof. Both house a two-man crew. The APC variant has additional space for eight personnel. Pandurs come in a range of variants according to turret or armament configuration. The Pandur Armoured Reconnaissance Fire Support Vehicle, for example, has a Mark 8 90mm (3.5in) gun mounted in a Cockerill LCTS turret, while the Light Armoured Vehicle features the MultiGun Turreted System with 25, 30 or 35mm (0.98, 1.18 or 1.38in) cannon.

The Pandur 6x6 armoured vehicle was developed by Steyr-Daimler-Puch in the mid-1980s. It entered service with the Austrian Army in 1994 and many other armies since.

Right: Belgian soldiers survey the terrain around their Pandur armoured personnel carrier while conducting a simulated defensive operation during exercises, September 2016.

FRONTAL PROTECTION
The Pandur's frontal armour can repel hits from 12.7mm 90.5in) bullets, while the side and rear armour is resistant up to 7.62mm (0.3in) rounds.

GUN TURRET
The standard turret armament is a 12.7mm (0.5in) M2HB machine gun, but other options can be fitted, including heavier cannon.

INTERIOR PROTECTION
The interior of the vehicle features a spall liner, which is a system designed to reduce the effects of metal splintering off the inside of the armour under external impacts.

TROOP COMPARTMENT
The standard troop compartment can hold eight combat-ready soldiers. The doors are located at the rear of the vehicle.

AMPHIBIOUS
The Pandur is an amphibious vehicle, and requires no preparation to enter the water. Amphibious propulsion is provided by water jets on the back of the hull.

REPAIRS
US servicemen assist two Kuwait National Guard soldiers with raising the engine block of a Pandur vehicle at the first ever Transportation and Maintenance Information Exchange and Demonstration at Udairi Range Training site, Kuwait.

BTR-80 (1986)

SPECIFICATIONS

DIMENSIONS:	Length: 7.65m (25.09ft); Width: 2.9m (9.51ft); Height: 2.46m (8.07ft)
WEIGHT:	13.6 tonnes (13.4 tons)
ENGINE:	1 x V8 diesel, developing 260hp (193kW)
SPEED:	Road: 90km/h (56mph)
ARMAMENT:	1 × 14.5m (0.57in) KPVT MG; 1 x coaxial 7.62mm (0.3in) PKT MG
ARMOUR:	(Steel) 9mm (0.35in)
RANGE:	600km (370 miles)
CREW:	3 + 7

FEATURES

The BTR-80 is host to a range of sophisticated features, designed to improve the vehicle's combat functionality. These include include central tyre-pressure regulation (so the driver can adjust tyre pressure to suit the terrain), NBC fittings, and front four wheels steering. It is also fully amphibious, powered by a single waterjet. Four key variants of the vehicle are the BREM-K armoured recovery and repair vehicle; BMM armoured ambulance vehicle; RkhM-4 radiation and chemical reconnaissance vehicle; and 2S23 Nona SVK 120mm self-propelled gun, but there are numerous other sub-variants and spin-offs.

The BTR-80 was part of the steady development of the BTR family which entered production in 1984. Its key contribution to the series was to switch from the two petrol engines of the BTR-60 and BTR-70 to a single powerful V8 diesel.

Above: A column of Ukrainian BTR-80 armoured personnel carriers waits on a road near Yavoriv, Ukraine, 2015.

MG ARMAMENT
The main weaponry is a turret-mounted 14.5m (0.57in) KPVT machine gun and a coaxial 7.62mm (0.3in) PKT machine gun.

GUN TURRET
The gun turret can perform a full 360° rotation, and elevation is from +60º to -4°. The turret can also mount a bank of six 81mm (3.1in) smoke grenade dischargers.

FIRING PORTS
There are three firing ports on each side and one at the front. The front port and the two side ports closest to the front are designed to be forward firing for use with the PK machine gun.

TROOP COMPARTMENT
Seven fully laden soldiers can travel in the BTR-80 as well as the three-man crew, and the troop compartment has a total of seven firing ports.

CONVOY TRAINING
Soldiers with the Armed Forces of Ukraine evacuate a destroyed BTR-80 armored troop transport as they conduct convoy operations training during Operation Rapid Trident in Yavoriv, Ukraine.

Warrior (1987)

SPECIFICATIONS

DIMENSIONS:	Length: 6.3m (20.7ft); Width: 3.03m (9.94ft); Height: 2.8m (9.19ft)
WEIGHT:	25.4 tonnes (28 tons)
ENGINE:	1 x Perkins V-8 Condor diesel producing 550hp (410kW)
SPEED:	Road: 75km/h (46mph)
ARMAMENT:	Main: 1x 30-mm (1.18-in) L21A1 RARDEN cannon Secondary: 1 x coaxial 7.62mm (0.3in) L94A1 chain gun, 1 x 7.62mm (0.3in) machine gun
ARMOUR:	Aluminium and appliqué
RANGE:	660km (410 miles)
CREW:	3 + 7

The FV510 Warrior Mechanized Infantry Combat Vehicle (MICV) was developed to facilitate the changing role of the armoured personnel carrier into a fighting support vehicle. Although its development began in 1972, the Warrior did not enter service with the British Army until 1987.

Above: The Warrior was designed to replace the FV432 APC in the 13 mechanized infantry battalions of the 1st, 3rd, and 4th Armoured Divisions of the British Army based in the Federal Republic of Germany. The transition period would last from 1988–94.

TROOP PROTECTION

One interesting element of the Warrior is that there are no firing ports along the troop compartment. Firing ports are provided to enable the soldiers inside to deliver their own suppressive or return fire from within the vehicle before disembarkation. Yet the inclusion of such ports creates weak points in the side armour. With the Warrior, the British Army opted to omit firing points, focusing on providing the maximum side armour protection for the troops while allowing the vehicle's own integral armament provide any fire suppression or support.

MAIN ARMAMENT
The 30mm (1.18in) L21A1 RARDEN cannon fires several different types of ammunition and is capable of penetrating the armour of other infantry fighting vehicles and numerous main battle tanks of an older generation.

ENGINE
The 550hp (410kW) Perkins Engines Company Condor CV-8 TCA diesel engine powers the Warrior at a top road speed of 75km/h (46mph).

SECONDARY ARMAMENT
An L94A1 coaxial 7.62mm (0.3in) chain gun, two banks of four smoke grenade launchers, and accommodations for LAW or TOW anti-tank missiles round out the potent offensive capability of the Warrior. A second 7.62-mm (0.3-in) machine gun is also mounted on some vehicles.

ARMOUR PROTECTION
The hull of the Warrior is all-welded aluminium capable of withstanding the blast of a 155mm (6.1in) shell from a distance of 10m (33ft) or small-arms fire of a calibre up to 14.5mm (0.57 in). The turret is all-steel construction.

SUSPENSION
Six rubber-coated road wheels with the single-pin TR30 track designed by William Cook Defence are supported by a torsion bar suspension. This provides stability during cross-country manoeuvres.

TROOP COMPARTMENT
Situated to the rear of the vehicle, the troop compartment carries seven fully armed infantry, who exit through a powered rear door rather than a descending ramp.

MOBILITY
An FV510 Warrior on the move. The vehicle's powerplant and suspension have been designed to give it all the off-road traction and mobility required to act in support of Challenger II MBTs. The FV510's maximum cross-country speed is 50km/h 31mph).

B1 Centauro (1988)

SPECIFICATIONS

DIMENSIONS:	Length (with gun): 8.55m (28.05ft); Width: 2.95m (9.68ft); Height: 2.73m (8.96ft)
WEIGHT:	25 tonnes (24.6 tons)
ENGINE:	1 x Iveco MTCA 6-cylinder turbo diesel, developing 520hp (388kW)
SPEED:	Road: 108km/h (67mph)
ARMAMENT:	Main: 1 x 105mm (4.13in) gun; Secondary: 1 x 7.62mm (0.3in) coaxial MG; 1 x 7.62mm (0.3in) turret-mounted MG; 2 x 4 smoke grenade launchers
ARMOUR:	Steel (details classified)
RANGE:	800km (500 miles)
CREW:	4

The Italian B1 Centauro is officially described as a tank hunter. Its armour, however, is light compared to an MBT, and a Centauro crew would rarely tackle an enemy tank in open battle. On top of an IVECO chassis is an OTOBREDA turret armed with a 105mm (4.13in) gun.

GUN
The 105mm (4.13in) OTO-Melara gun is gyro-stabilized, and is of a low-recoil type similar to that of the Leopard II MBT.

ARMOUR
Although the armour of the Centauro could not withstand an MBT shell hit, it is proof up to 20mm (0.79in) and 12.7mm (0.5in) attacks.

TANK KILLER

The B1 Centauro's main weapon is capable of penetrating over 700mm (27.56in) of armour at a range of around 2000m (6550ft) using armour-piercing fin-stabilized discarding-sabot (APFSDS) rounds. Gun handling and targeting are assisted by laser range-finding and a fully computerized fire control system like that used on the Ariete MBT. Although the gun is perfectly capable of tackling enemy heavy armour, in tactical reality it has more been applied in the role of infantry support.

POWERPLANT
The Iveco V6 turbo-charged, after-cooled diesel engine is installed in the front of the vehicle, behind the heavily armoured front hull.

DRIVE CONFIGURATION
All eight wheels of the Centauro provide the drive power, but only the front four actually steer.

MOBILITY
As an 8 × 8 vehicle, the Centauro has good off-road mobility assisted by hydropneumatic suspension and central tyre-pressure regulation.

IN SERVICE
A B1 Centauro on a peacetime exercise. As well as conducting operations in the Balklans in the late 1990s, the Centauro also saw combat service in Iraq in the 2000s, fighting in the Battle of An Nasiriyah in 2003.

BMP-3 (1990)

SPECIFICATIONS

DIMENSIONS:	Length: 7.2 m (23ft 7in); Width: 3.23 m (10ft 7in); Height: 2.3m (7ft 7in)
WEIGHT:	18.7 tonnes (18.4 tons)
ENGINE:	1 x UTD-29M 10-cylinder diesel, developing 500hp (373kW)
SPEED:	Road: 70km/h (43mph)
ARMAMENT:	Main: 1 x 100mm (3.93in) gun; Secondary: 1 x 30mm (1.18in) cannon; 2 x 7.62mm (0.3in) PKT MG
ARMOUR:	Steel (details classified)
RANGE:	600km (370 miles)
CREW:	3 + 7

The BMP-3 entered service in 1990, and is the latest in the BMP range. Classified as an Infantry Combat Vehicle, its extensive armament almost places it in the category of small tank.

Above: Kuwaiti BMP-3s line up for inspection, with their 30mm (1.18in) main cannon covered with dust protectors.

ADVANCED DEFENCE

The BMP-3 incorporates highly sophisticated defensive technologies, both active and passive. For example, the vehicle can be fitted with the Arena-E Defensive aids suite, a Doppler radar system that detects incoming munitions (missiles and shells) and fires a defensive rocket that detonates near the threat, either affecting its flight path or destroying it. This system can also be accompanied by the Shtora electro-optical active protection system, which disrupts the laser designators and laser rangefinders of incoming anti-tank guided missiles.

TROOP COMPARTMENT
Despite the increase in stored ammunition and the consequent extra space this takes up, the BMP-3 takes only one less soldier than the BMP-1 (seven instead of eight), though it is almost a metre (3ft 4in) longer.

SECONDARY WEAPONS
Alongside this weapon is a 30mm (1.18in) cannon, and the turret also bears a 7.62mm (0.3in) PKT coaxial machine gun.

MAIN GUN
Its turret boasts a 2A70 100mm (3.93in) gun which can fire either conventional shells or AT-10 laser-guided ATGWs.

AMPHIBIOUS TRANSPORT
The US Navy offloads a column of BMP-3s at a Kuwaiti port facility from its Elbahia L62 landing craft.

Type 89 (1991)

SPECIFICATIONS

DIMENSIONS:	Length: 6.8m (22.3ft); Width: 3.2m (10.49ft); Height: 2.5m (8.2ft)
WEIGHT:	26.5 tonnes (26 tons)
ENGINE:	1 x 6-cylinder diesel developing 600hp (447kW)
SPEED:	Road: 70km/h (43mph)
ARMAMENT:	Main: 1 x 35mm (1.38in) Oerlikon Contraves cannon; Secondary: 1 x coaxial 7.62mm (0.3in) machine gun; 2 x ATGWs (Jyu-MAT anti-tank missiles)
ARMOUR:	Classified
RANGE:	400km (250 miles)
CREW:	3 + 7

The Mitsubishi Type 89 Mechanised Infantry Combat Vehicle is a true fighting machine. With the dimensions of a small tank, it boasts one 35mm (1.38in) Oerlikon Contraves cannon, a coaxial 7.62mm (0.3in) machine gun, and two preloaded ATGWs (usually Jyu-MAT medium-range missiles).

Above: The Type 89 entered service with the Japan Ground Self-Defense Force in 1989, primarily for armoured reconnaissance and infantry deployment/fire support.

CANNON SYSTEM
The Type 89's Oerlikon Contraves cannon has a dual-feed feed system, which enables the gunner to switch between two different types of ammunition. The types of munition available include high explosive, armour-piercing discarding sabot (APDS) and proximity detonating fragmentation, the latter for attacking enemy personnel who are in covered positions.

MISSILES
The Type 79 Jyu-MAT anti-armour missiles has a range of 4000m (4374yd) and uses a semi-automatic command to line of sight (SACLOS) guidance system.

CREW
A crew of three man the forward section (which includes the engine) and turret of the vehicle, and seven other combat personnel can be transported in the rear.

GRENADE LAUNCHERS
Under each missile unit there is a bank of four smoke grenade launchers, for laying down rapid smoke obscuration.

FIRING PORTS
Six firing ports are provided around the sides and rear of the Type 89 to allow small arms to be deployed against infantry attack.

JGSF ARMOUR
The Type 89 has respectable firepower in the form of its 30mm (1.18in) automatic cannon, but its survivability would be poor if faced with MBTs on an open battlefield. It therefore operates alongside Japan's own MBT, the Type 90.

IAV Stryker (2002)

SPECIFICATIONS

DIMENSIONS:	Length: 6.95m (22.92ft); Width: 2.72m (8.97ft; Height: 2.64m (8.72ft)
WEIGHT:	16.47 tonnes (16.2 tons)
ENGINE:	260kW (350hp) Caterpillar C7
SPEED:	100km/h (62mph)
ARMAMENT:	1 x 12.7mm (0.5in) M2 MG as standard
RANGE:	500km (310 miles)
CREW:	2 + 9

The US Army's Stryker series of infantry fighting vehicles played a key role in Afghanistan, and its mobility and protection have been instrumental during operations in Iraq. The Stryker is actually a family of vehicles rather than a single type, and more than 10 variants have been produced to date.

Above: Army Stryker vehicles of the Stryker Brigade Combat Team kick up plumes of dust as they conduct a patrol near Mosul, Iraq, 2005. These Strykers are from the US 25th Infantry Division.

INFANTRY CARRIER VEHICLE

Developed from earlier Canadian and Swiss armoured vehicle designs, the Stryker entered service with the US Army in 2002 to complement the older M2/M3 Bradleys. Conceived as a method of introducing combat troops to the battlefield rapidly, the basic M1126 Stryker Infantry Carrier Vehicle (ICV) carries up to nine soldiers and is armed with a 12.7mm (0.5in) machine gun or 40mm (1.57in) grenade launcher mounted in the Protector M151 remote weapons station, which may be operated from the relative safety of the vehicle's interior.

WEAPON STATION
The Protector M151 Remote Weapon Station can take a bespoke variety of machine guns, cannon, grenade lauchers and and missiles.

OPTICS
Both the commander and the gunner have periscopes for vision from inside the vehicle, plus the commander has thermal imaging equipment.

ARMOUR
The frontal arc of the Stryker has armour against 14.5mm (0.57in) rounds, while the rest of the vehicle is protected against 7.62mm.

TYRE PRESSURE
The Stryker has a Central Tire Inflation System, which allows the driver to adjust tyre pressures for different terrains.

GROUND CLEARANCE
The Stryker's excellent ground clearance of 533mm (21in) improves crew and vehicle survibility from mine blasts.

AIR TRANSPORTABLE
A US Army Stryker Infantry Carrier Vehicle (ICV) is off-loaded from a C-17 Globemaster III at Andrews Air Force Base, 2002. The Stryker fulfills an immediate requirement to provide combatant commanders with a primary combat and combat support platform.

SPECIFICATIONS

DIMENSIONS:	Length: 7.64m (25ft); Width: 3.2m (10.49ft); Height: 2.97m (9.74ft)
WEIGHT:	17,000kg (37,500lb)
ENGINE:	1 x V8 diesel, developing 210hp (157kW)
SPEED:	Road: 100km/h (62mph)
ARMAMENT:	1 x 30mm (1.18in) 2A42 automatic cannon; 1 x coaxial 7.62mm (0.3in) PKT MG; 1 x automatic grenade launcher; 4 x AT-5 Spandrel ATGWs
ARMOUR:	Not disclosed
RANGE:	600km (370 miles)
CREW:	3 + 10

The BTR-90 was designed during the 1990s and went into production in 2004. In essence it is a larger and better-armoured evolution of the BTR-80, but with a BMP-2 turret and the firepower of a 30mm (1.18in) cannon. It can carry 10 fully armed soldiers within its armoured and amphibious hull.

Above: A BTR-90 stands as part of exhibition of old Soviet era hardware.

WEAPONS SPECTRUM

What makes the BTR-90 distinctive is its armament. All its weaponry is mounted in a single turret located towards the front of the vehicle, and it consists of one 30mm (1.18in) 2A42 automatic cannon, a coaxial 7.62mm (0.3in) PKT machine gun, an automatic grenade launcher, and four AT-5 Spandrel anti-tank missiles. The spectrum of weaponry allows it to engage the enemy infantry, armour and aircraft equally.

CANNON
The cannon armament is the Shipunov 2A42 30mm (1.18in), a dual-feed weapon found on several armoured vehicles and attack helicopters.

TURRET
The commander and gunner both work from the turret. The only other fixed crew member is the driver, who is located in the front hull, just forward of the turret.

TROOP COMPARTMENT
Ten combat-ready troops can be transported in the rear of the vehicle. There are doors on the top and the side of the hull.

WHEELS
The wheels of the BTR-90 have been designed to remain functional even if damaged by mines and small-arms fire; the vehicle can still move with four wheels severely damaged.

HULL
The BTR-90 is fully amphibious without preparation, and there are two water-jet propellers at the rear of the vehicle.

TARGET PRACTICE

This BTR-90 stands as a target on the US Warren Grove Bombing Range in Ocean County, NJ, 2017. Such targets are typically acquired from either former battlegrounds in the Middle East or from US allies equipped with Soviet-era vehicles.

BVS 10 Viking (2005)

SPECIFICATIONS

DIMENSIONS:	Length: 7.5m (24ft 7in); Width: 2.1m (6ft 10.7in); Height: 2.2m (7ft 2.5in)
WEIGHT:	10.6 tonnes (10.4 tons)
ENGINE:	250bhp (183kW) Cummins 5.9l in-line 6-cylinder turbo diesel
SPEED:	Road: 50km/h (31mph); Off-road: 15km/h (9.3mph)
ARMAMENT:	Capacity for 1 x 12.7mm (0.5in) Browning HMG or 1 x 7.62mm (0.3in) MG
ARMOUR:	-
RANGE:	300KM (186 MILES)
CREW:	(front car) Driver + 4 passengers; (rear car) 8 passengers

A collaborative design effort between Britain and Sweden, the BVS 10 entered service with the Royal Marines in 2005. Fully amphibious, the vehicle carries up to four soldiers in its front vehicle and up to eight in the trailer. It is protected by specialized armour and mounts a light machine gun.

VIKING COLUMN
The BvS 10 Viking vehicles drive into training compound during Bold Alligator, Camp Lejeune, N.C., 2017.

STEERING
Steering is provided by hydraulic rams that move both the front and rear cabs in response to the driver's inputs.

DUAL UNIT
The BvS 10, like its similar predecessors, uses a dual-unit set-up, the units connected by an articulated joint for excellent manoeuvrability.

ARMOUR
The vehicle can accept bolt-on armour plates to protect protection against 7.62mm (0.3in) AP rounds and 152mm (6in) shell fragments from a range of more than 10m (32ft 9in).

MULTI-THEATRE CAPABILITIES
The BvS 10 Viking was developed to operate in all conceivable theatres – polar, temperate, desert and tropical. Its powerplant and other systems were purposely designed to function in temperature ranges of –46°C (–51°F) to +46°C (115°F).

AMPHIBIOUS
The vehicle is fully amphibious, although it requires c. 2 minutes of preparation before it can enter the water.

TRACKS
All four tracks are powered continuously, this resulting in superior traction over even the softest of surfaces, such as mud and snow.

FV430 Bulldog Mk 3 (2006)

SPECIFICATIONS

DIMENSIONS:	Length: 5.25m (17ft 2.6in); Width: 2.8m (9ft 2.3in); Height: 2.28m (7ft 5.8in)
WEIGHT:	15.3 tonnes (15 tons)
ENGINE:	179kW (240hp) Rolls-Royce K60 multi-fuel
SPEED:	52km/h (32mph)
ARMAMENT:	1 x 7.62mm (0.3in) MG, plus 2 x 3-barrel smoke dischargers
ARMOUR:	Reactive armour package
RANGE:	580km (360 miles)
CREW:	2 + 10

FV430 FAMILY

The FV430 Mk 3 is one of a family of FV430 vehicles that have been in service with the British Army since the 1960s. This family has included the FV432 APC, the FV433 'Abbott' self-propelled 105mm (4.1in) gun, the FV434 REME (Royal Electrical and Mechanical Engineers) maintenance vehicle and the FV438 Swingfire guided-missile carrier. The Mk 3 was designed to meet an urgent operational requirement for extra armoured vehicles in Iraq and Afghanistan.

The FV 430 Bulldog Mk 3 entered service with British forces in Iraq and Afghanistan late in 2006 in response to the hazards posed by rocket-propelled grenades and improvised explosive devices. Equipped with an extensive reactive armour package, it also carries a remote-controlled 7.62mm (0.3in) machine gun.

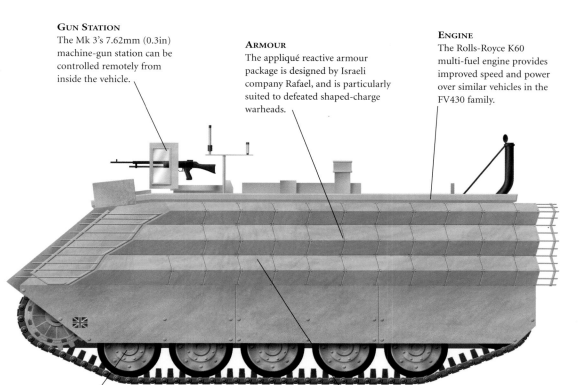

GUN STATION
The Mk 3's 7.62mm (0.3in) machine-gun station can be controlled remotely from inside the vehicle.

ARMOUR
The appliqué reactive armour package is designed by Israeli company Rafael, and is particularly suited to defeated shaped-charge warheads.

ENGINE
The Rolls-Royce K60 multi-fuel engine provides improved speed and power over similar vehicles in the FV430 family.

STEERING
There have been improvements to the Bulldog's steering column, to enhance its manoeuvrability.

ENVIRONMENT
The Bulldog features an air-conditioning system that improves crew comfort when operating in tropical zones.

IRAQ DEPLOYMENT
The first delivery of the upgraded FV430 Mk3 Bulldog vehicles arrived in Iraq just before Christmas 2006 with the RGJ Battalion based at Basra Palace the first to use them on operations. Additional armour provides enhanced safety for driver, commander and troops while other features include air conditioning and an improved engine and transmission for peak performance and reliability.

Artillery & Mortars

The artillery family of weapons covers a particularly broad spectrum of types and capabilities. At the smaller end of the scale, we can include standard infantry mortars, although the label 'light support weapons' might be more accurate. From these, with ranges of just a few thousand metres and delivering diminutive bombs, we scale up through numerous different weapon systems, including field guns, howitzers, rocket launchers and self-propelled guns, to monstrous railway-mounted cannon firing shells weighed by the tonne over ranges measured in dozens of kilometres. Although such monstrous guns are now a thing of the past, through constant innovation in fire control, munitions and portability, artillery has managed to stay relevant to the modern battlefield.

HOWITZER BARRAGE
US Marines with Lima Battery, 3rd Battalion, 12th Marine Regiment fire an M198 medium howitzer near Baghdad, Iraq, 2006.

111

Canon de 75 Mle (1897)

SPECIFICATIONS

GUN LENGTH:	2.72m (9ft)
WEIGHT:	Travelling: 1970kg (4343lb); in action: 1140kg (2514lb)
CALIBRE:	75mm (2.95in)
ELEVATION:	–11° to +18°
TRAVERSE:	6°
SHELL TYPE:	HE, HEAT, shrapnel
MUZZLE VELOCITY:	575m/sec (1886ft/sec)
EFFECTIVE RANGE:	8500m (9295yd)
CREW:	6

The introduction of the French 75mm (2.95in) Model 1897 field gun was a watershed development in the history of modern artillery. This weapon combined a self-contained recoil system, modern sighting, fixed-shell ammunition, a protective shield for the artillerymen servicing the gun and a fast-action breech mechanism. In short, the quick-firing French 75 embodied decades of advances in artillery technology. Superbly designed for use against massed troops in the open, the 75mm (2.95in) gun was indeed a pure field weapon. When war broke out in August 1914, more than 4000 of the guns were already in service with the French Army. More than 21,000 French 75s were produced during a remarkably lengthy period of manufacture, stretching from 1897 to approximately 1940.

Above: A French 75mm (2.95in) field cannon is hauled to its firing position on a horse-drawn limber. The cannon was still in service during World War II.

VERDUN SERVICE

The French 75mm (2.95in) Model 1897 achieved lasting fame during the crucial battles of the Marne in the summer of 1914 and at Verdun during a protracted eight-month struggle from February to September 1916. At Verdun alone, the weapons were reported to have fired an astounding 16 million rounds, accounting for nearly 70 per cent of all the shots fired by French artillery during the battle. More than three million shells were fired in a three-day period during the French offensive in the Verdun vicinity the following spring.

RATE OF FIRE
The cannon's rate of fire was an impressive 15rpm at a maximum range of 6840m (7480yd).

WEIGHT
Initially, a team of six horses was required to haul the gun, which weighed just over 1140kg (2514lb).

SHELL TYPES
The cannon commonly fired two types of ammunition early in the war: a fragmentation or shrapnel shell weighing 5.3kg (11.7lb) and a high-explosive shell of nearly 7.25kg (16lb).

AA VERSION
An anti-aircraft version of the gun, mounted on a truck, was adopted by the army in 1913.

US GUN CREW
The American crew of a French 75mm field cannon loads and fires its weapon with efficiency. A pile of spent shell casings is testimony to the day's work.

Ordnance QF 13pdr (1904)

Developed in 1904 as a result of British experience in South Africa during the Boer War, the Ordnance QF 13pdr (76.2mm/3in) became the Royal Horse Artillery gun for supporting cavalry. Some were sent to India, but most were based in the United Kingdom and were ready to move to France in 1914. Once World War I moved into the trench lines, it had too short a range to be useful and was withdrawn from service. Most were converted into very serviceable anti-aircraft guns and were widely used by the field armies.

SPECIFICATIONS

GUN LENGTH:	1.86m (6ft 2in)
WEIGHT:	1014kg (2235lb)
CALIBRE:	76mm (3in)
ELEVATION:	−5° to +16°
TRAVERSE:	8°
SHELL TYPE:	Shrapnel, HE
MUZZLE VELOCITY:	510m/sec (2673ft/sec)
EFFECTIVE RANGE:	5395m (5900yd)
CREW:	6

RANGE
The 13pdr, a 76mm (3in) weapon, fired a projectile that weighed 5.7kg (12.6lb) to a range of 5395m (5900yd).

TOWING
Batteries normally carried 176 rounds per gun. The gun and its limber was towed by a six-horse team.

RECUPERATOR
The QF 13pdr had a hydraulic buffer and an air recuperator, the latter to return the gun forward after recoil.

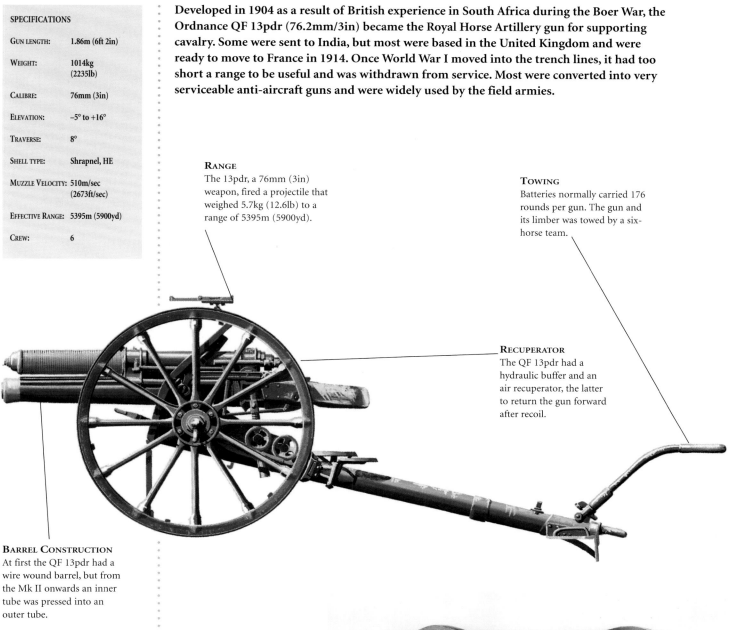

BARREL CONSTRUCTION
At first the QF 13pdr had a wire wound barrel, but from the Mk II onwards an inner tube was pressed into an outer tube.

AA ROLE
As the aircraft emerged as a weapon in its own right during World War I, the 13pdr found new usefulness as a medium anti-aircraft gun. In this role, the weapon served to bridge the inter-war years and was active with the British Army essentially until its evacuation from the continent at Dunkirk in 1940. It was then replaced with a 94mm (3.7in) anti-aircraft weapon.

MOBILE FIELD GUN
The QF 13pdr was no lightweight piece: in action it required six horses to pull into position, the horses arranged in two ranks of three.

Ordnance BL 60pdr (1905)

SPECIFICATIONS

GUN LENGTH:	4.29m (14ft)
WEIGHT:	4470kg (9655lb)
CALIBRE:	127mm (5in)
ELEVATION:	–5° to +21.5°
TRAVERSE:	8°
SHELL TYPE:	HE, shrapnel
MUZZLE VELOCITY:	634m/sec (2080ft/sec)
EFFECTIVE RANGE:	11,247m (12,300yd)
CREW:	7

The heavy artillery of the British Army was serviced by units of the Royal Garrison Artillery. During the fighting on the Western Front, it became readily apparent to the combatants that heavy artillery would be necessary to reduce enemy fortifications successfully. The British actually had gained some experience in this regard during the Boer War; their 60pdr gun was developed with that experience in mind and deployed in 1904. The 60pdr proved to be one of the most popular heavy weapons in the British arsenal, and it remained in service until the end of World War II.

Above: A battery of 60pdr artillery from the Royal Garrison Artillery stands somewhere near Albert, France, March 1918.

RANGE
Wartime modifications improved the transportation of the weapon and increased its range to 11,247m (12,300yd).

WEIGHT
Firing a 127mm (5in) shell a maximum distance of 9418m (10,300yd), the earliest version of the 60pdr weighed nearly 4.5 tonnes (4.4 tons).

AMMUNITION
The QF 60pdr, in common with many guns of this era, used ammunition that consisted of the shell plus separate bagged propelling charges, each of these bags containing either 3.6kg (8lb) of Lyddite or 2.7kg (6lb) of Amatol. The choice of propelling charge was part of the range calculation equation. The shrapnel shells for this gun each contained 397 lead/antimony balls, ejected from the nose of the shell when the munition was detonated by either a timed or a percussion fuze.

TRANSPORT
Initially, the gun was hauled into position by a team of 12 horses. However, a later version, weighing one tonne more, was towed by a steam tractor.

GALLIPOLI
A British 60pdr Mk I battery delivers bombardment from a cliff top at Cape Helles, Gallipoli, possibly in June 1915. The gun has the inscription 'Annie' painted on the barrel. At this moment it is shown at maximum recoil; hence we can see the running-out rods and (between them) the piston rod connected to the hydraulic buffer.

7.7cm FK 96 n.A. (1905)

SPECIFICATIONS

GUN LENGTH:	2.1m (6ft 10in)
WEIGHT:	925kg (2039lb)
CALIBRE:	77mm (3.03in)
ELEVATION:	−13° to +15°
TRAVERSE:	8°
SHELL TYPE:	HE, shrapnel
MUZZLE VELOCITY:	465m/sec (1525ft/sec)
EFFECTIVE RANGE:	7800m (8530yd)
CREW:	5

During the course of World War I, Allied infantrymen came to refer to the report of any German artillery shell as a 'whizz bang', but the term was originally applied to the sound of the 7.7cm (3.03in) field gun, which was the most common artillery weapon in the German arsenal in 1914. More than 5000 of these were with German Army units in the beginning, and the 7.7cm gun was used throughout the conflict. The original design had been introduced in 1896, but the following year saw the debut of the French 75, which rendered the German cannon obsolete. A major redesign effort followed, and the firms of Krupp and Rheinmetall produced the 7.7cm Feldkanone 96 n.A., the initials identifying it as the 'new model'.

Above: The crew of a 7.7cm (3.03in) FK 96 n.A. pose with their gun during the early stages of World War I.

BARREL
The short barrel meant that the muzzle velocity was relatively low, and consequently the range was quite short, although perfectly within the practical limits of infantry support.

BREECH
The breech of the M96 n.A. was a fairly simple and reliable single-motion sliding wedge. It used fixed cartridge ammunition.

GUNLAYER'S SEAT
The gunlayer operated both the elevation and traverse controls, set on the left side of the gun next to the breech.

FRONTLINE SERVICE
Considering German military doctrine of the day, which meant swift manoeuvre and the combined-arms deployment of both infantry and artillery, the 7.7cm (3.03in) gun performed its role well. On the Western Front, static trench warfare robbed the weapon of its advantage of mobility and Allied guns had higher rates of fire and delivered heavier shells, so the 7.7cm often compensated for its shortcomings with sheer weight of numbers. On the more mobile Eastern Front, however, it proved valuable in keeping up with rapidly advancing infantry during offensive operations.

HORSE ARTILLERY
A horse artillery team manhandle a 7.7cm (3.03in) FK 96 n.A. artillery piece through a muddy, bleak landscape in northern France.

Ordnance QF 4.5in Howitzer (1908)

SPECIFICATIONS

GUN LENGTH:	1.8m (5ft 10in)
WEIGHT:	1370kg (3020lb)
CALIBRE:	114mm (4.5in)
ELEVATION:	–5° to +45°
TRAVERSE:	6°
SHELL TYPE:	HE
MUZZLE VELOCITY:	313m/sec (1026ft/sec)
EFFECTIVE RANGE:	6400m (7000yd)
CREW:	6

Introduced in 1909, the Ordnance QF 4.5in howitzer incorporated valuable lessons learned during the Boer War. An improved version went into production in 1917. The QF designation stands for 'quick firing', and more than 3000 of the weapons were produced during World War I. The remarkable service life of the 4.5in howitzer with the British Army extended until the end of World War II.

BARREL
The rifling of the Mk 1 gun had 32 right-hand grooves, the rate of twist increasing as the rifling approached the muzzle.

BREECHBLOCK
The horizontal sliding breechblock design was the first of its type in use with British artillery.

SHELL WEIGHT
The gun's shell, weighing 15.8kg (35lb), was the equivalent of a 114mm (4.5in) round, capable of reaching targets 6400m (7000yd) distant at an elevation of up to 45°.

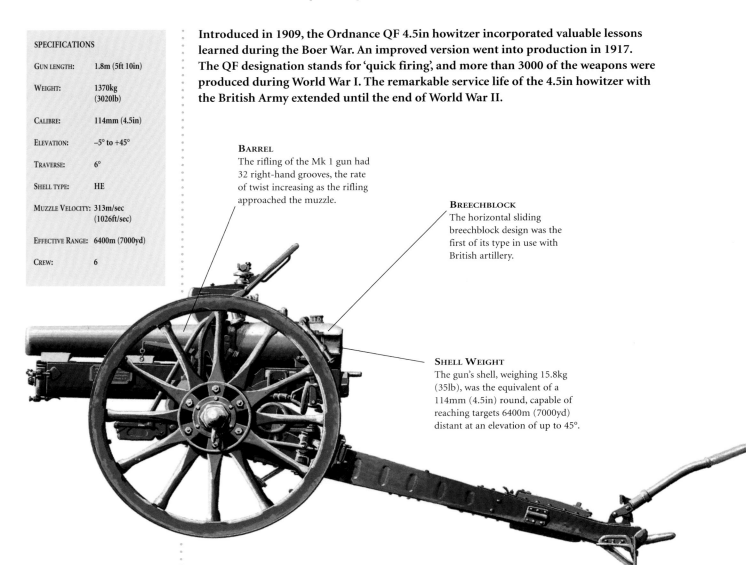

'SUICIDE CLUBS'
Although the 4.5in howitzer was generally a popular field weapon, during World War I it was known for some incidents of catastrophic breech failure in worn guns, incidents that gave the crews the unhelpful nickname of 'Suicide Clubs'. The mechanical problem that caused these malfunctions was solved in the Mk 2 version of the gun.

WESTERN FRONT
A New Zealander crew of a QF 4.5in howitzer gain some respite during the fighting near Le Quesnoy, France, 1918. The 4.5in howitzer entered service with the Royal Field Artillery in 1909 and gradually replaced an outdated 5in howitzer, which saw a great deal of action during the first two years of the war.

Skoda 30.5cm Howitzer (1911)

SPECIFICATIONS

GUN LENGTH:	4.26m (14ft)
WEIGHT:	20,000kg (44,092lb)
CALIBRE:	305mm (12in)
ELEVATION:	+40° to +70°
TRAVERSE:	120°
SHELL TYPE:	HE
MUZZLE VELOCITY:	340m/sec (1115ft/sec)
EFFECTIVE RANGE:	11,300m (12,358yd)
CREW:	15

The Austrians possessed capable, modern artillery, much of which was produced at the Skoda Works. Numerous quality artillery pieces were produced by Skoda and sold to the armed forces of other nations as well. Among the most famous Skoda artillery of the Great War was the 30.5cm (12in) Model 1911 siege mortar, which was deployed by the Germans at Liége.

Right: The Skoda 30.5cm (12in) gun in firing position. Hearing protection was recommended for the crew when the weapon was in use.

RECOIL BRAKE
The two cylinders positioned above the barrel housed the recoil brake; the recuperator cylinders were below the barrel.

IMPACT
When the smaller shell detonated, its killing zone extended more than 393m (430yd), and its impact crater was nearly 8.2m (9yd) deep.

TRANSPORT
The weapon was transported in three sections by a Skoda-Daimler tractor and could be set up to fire in less than an hour.

RATE OF FIRE
Serviced by a crew of 15, the gun could fire 10 rounds in an hour.

UPGRADE
The heavy weapon was capable of firing a 384kg (847lb) shell up to 9601m (10,500yd) or a lighter 287kg (633lb) shell 11,300m (12,358yd). Maximum range was 12,000m (13,125yd). In 1916, an upgraded version extended its range to more than 12,162m (13,300yd), and by the end of the war 40 of these mammoth weapons were in service. Skoda also produced 7.5cm, 10cm and 15cm artillery pieces, which saw service in numerous armies during the war.

DUG-IN WEAPON
An Austro-Hungarian Army 30.5cm (12in) Mörser stands in a dug-in firing position near Brzezany, Ukraine, during the fighting on the Eastern Front during World War I.

Canon de 105mm mle 1913 Schneider (1913)

TYPE · *Field & Heavy Artillery* · **FAMILY** · *Artillery & Mortars*

SPECIFICATIONS

GUN LENGTH:	2.98m (9ft 8in)
WEIGHT:	2300kg (5070lb)
CALIBRE:	105mm (4.13in)
ELEVATION:	0° to +37°
TRAVERSE:	6°
SHELL TYPE:	HE
MUZZLE VELOCITY:	550m/sec (1805ft/sec)
EFFECTIVE RANGE:	12,700m (13,890yd)
CREW:	7

The French 105mm (4.13in) Schneider cannon was manufactured as a result of an initial collaboration between French and Russian designers. The cannon introduced several novel features, including a screw breech that could swing as it opened instead of having to be withdrawn before opening, and a quick-release latch that allowed the gun to be pulled back in the cradle for travelling or removed entirely to a transport wagon.

Above: Finland, July 1941: Finnish artillery operate a 105mm (4.13in) K-29, an ex-Polish Wz 29 Schneider, which was in turn a longer-barrelled version of the mle 1913 with a split trail.

MECHANISM
The mle 1913 featured a new type of hydro-pneumatic recoil system in which the buffer and recuperator were entirely independent of each other.

BREECH
The gun's breech was of the interrupted-screw type, a threaded breechblock screw locking into a correspondingly threaded breech.

TRAIL
The standard mle 1913 had a fixed trail, although some export models are seen with split trails.

EXPORT SUCCESS

The mle 1913 – which had more than proved itself during World War I – was put onto the export market after the end of hostilities in 1918. It was widely adopted – customers included Belgium, Czechoslovakia, Estonia, Finland, Italy (the biggest export buyer), Poland and Yugoslavia, all of whom were rebuilding their armies. It formed the principal gun strength of the French army in 1940. Hundreds of captured guns were put into service by the Germans after the Fall of France.

SOVIET USE
Here a Russian artillery crew fire a mle 1913 Scheider somewhere on the Eastern Front during World War II.

'Big Bertha' (1914)

SPECIFICATIONS

GUN LENGTH:	5.88m (19ft 3in)
WEIGHT:	43,285kg (95,427lb)
CALIBRE:	420mm (16.53in)
ELEVATION:	+40° to +75°
TRAVERSE:	4°
SHELL TYPE:	HE
MUZZLE VELOCITY:	425m/sec (1394ft/sec)
EFFECTIVE RANGE:	12,000m (13,123yd)
CREW:	240

Nicknamed 'Big Bertha', after the wife of the firm's chief, Gustav Krupp, these howitzers were officially designated 42-cm kurze Marinekanone 14 L/12 in Räderlafette ('42-cm short naval canon 14 L/12 on wheeled carriage'). Six of these howitzers were available at the beginning of the war; they were transported either by railway or on a wheeled carriage. The development of the 42cm (16.53in) howitzer had begun in 1900 during Krupp's experimentation with a 35cm (13.7in) weapon. Eight years later, the German Army requested a larger version. The response in 1912 was a 159-tonne (156-ton) howitzer built in five sections for transportation by rail to its assembly point. Later, a more practical 39-tonne (38-ton) howitzer was introduced, which could be moved in the field. It was this weapon that gained the 'Big Bertha' moniker.

SHELL
The gun fired a shell weighing 820kg (1808lb) a distance of up to 12,000m (13,123yd).

RATE OF FIRE
The gun had an approximate rate of fire of 10 rounds per hour.

BOMBARDMENT

In April 1915, an assemblage of 92 heavy German howitzers bombarded the Belgian town of Ypres, and the 42cm (16.53in) Big Bertha fired its shells in pairs from the shelter of the nearby Houthulst Forest. The official British history of World War I noted that the shells 'travelled through the air with a noise like a runaway tramcar on badly laid rails.'

TRANSPORT
The mobile Big Bertha was transported in sections by Daimler-Benz tractors. It took a 200-man crew six hours of strenuous labour to ready it for a firing mission.

REPUTATION
The German 42cm (16.53in) 'Dicke Bertha' – 'Big Bertha'. Aside from being a weapon of great physical destructive power, the Big Bertha was also a tool of German propaganda, and it gained a fearsome reputation among Allied troops.

Paris Gun (1918)

SPECIFICATIONS

GUN LENGTH:	37m (121ft 5in)
WEIGHT:	750,000kg (1,653,466lb)
CALIBRE:	210mm (8.26in)
ELEVATION:	0° to +55°
TRAVERSE:	360°
SHELL TYPE:	HE
MUZZLE VELOCITY:	2000m/sec (6560ft/sec)
EFFECTIVE RANGE:	122km (76 miles)
CREW:	80

Manufactured by Krupp, the Paris Gun was the largest artillery weapon constructed up to that time. From March to August 1918, the Paris Gun reportedly fired 367 shells, about half of which landed within the boundaries of the City of Light. Although the total damage proved relatively insignificant, and its effect on the military situation on the Western Front was negligible, the psychological impact of the weapon was substantial. A total of 256 Parisians were killed and 620 wounded by the gun.

Above: The massive railway gun is shown mounted on its railway carriage. As a weapon the Paris Gun was pointless, but as a technical achievement it was remarkable.

SHELL
Serviced by a crew of 80 sailors of the German Navy, the cannon was capable of firing a 95kg (210lb) shell up to 122km (76 miles), with the projectile actually entering the stratosphere during its flight.

Above: The German Paris Gun. As the tide of war turned in favour of the Allies in 1918, the Paris Gun was apparently destroyed by the Germans rather than being allowed to fall to the enemy.

CAPITAL HIT
On 29 March 1918, a German artillery shell slammed through the roof of the church at St Gervais near Paris, killing 100 people. Tragic though the event was, the source of the bombardment was astounding. The round had been fired by the *Kaiser Wilhelm Geschutz*, also known as the Paris Gun, which had shelled the French capital for the first time a week earlier from the forest area of Coucy, a distance of more than 112km (70 miles).

WEIGHT
The gun weighed 232 tonnes (256 tons); its rifled 210mm (8.3in) barrel was 28m (92ft) long with a 6m (20ft) smoothbore extension.

CARRIAGE
In order to allow the gun to recoil at high elevations without striking the railway track, the carriage was jacked up from the bogies before firing.

10.5cm leFH 18 Light Field Howitzer (1927)

TYPE · *Field & Heavy Artillery* · **FAMILY** · *Artillery & Mortars*

SPECIFICATIONS

GUN LENGTH:	2.98m (9ft 9in)
WEIGHT:	In action: 1985kg (4377lb)
CALIBRE:	105mm (4.13in)
ELEVATION:	0° to +37°
TRAVERSE:	6°
SHELL TYPE:	HE
MUZZLE VELOCITY:	470m/sec (1542ft/sec)
EFFECTIVE RANGE:	10,675m (11,675yd)
CREW:	8

In the late 1920s, the firm of Rheinmetall began developing the 10.5cm (4.13in) leichte Feldhaubitze 18 (leFH 18) light field howitzer. This design work led to the first prototypes being constructed in 1933, and the weapon entered general service in 1935. In general production throughout the second half of the 1930s, the Germans fielded some 5200 leFH 18 howitzers during the September 1939 invasion of Poland. Production continued throughout the war, and it remained the standard weapon equipping the majority of divisional light artillery batteries.

VERSIONS

The leFH 18M (below) was a modified version of the leFH 18. The 18M is easily identifiable by its single-baffle barrel muzzle-break and by its redesigned recuperator and buffer assembly.

WEIGHT

The howitzer weighed 1985kg (4377lb) and fired a 14.8kg (33lb) shell.

INCREASED RANGE

Combat experience in Poland, the West, North Africa and the East in 1939–41 showed that although the howitzer was accurate and reliable, it was heavy to manoeuvre and its range was being outclassed by newer Allied weapons. In response, during 1942 the Germans developed the modified leFH 18M. This howitzer sported a muzzle brake and redesigned recoil system to accommodate a more powerful propellant charge that increased the weapon's maximum range to 12,325m (13,479yd).

MUZZLE VELOCITY

The weapon discharged the shell at a muzzle velocity of 470m/sec (1542ft/sec), enabling it to reach an impressive maximum range of 10,675m (11,675yd).

CHANNEL DEFENCE

Deployed in a seemingly open field position located surprisingly close to the cliff edge overlooking Arromanches, France, is a 7.5cm (2.95in) leFH 18 gun. Probably taken during spring 1944, this bucolic scene was soon replaced by one featuring the full fury of modern industrialized warfare with the D-Day landings.

15cm sIG 33 Heavy Infantry Gun (1927)

SPECIFICATIONS

GUN LENGTH:	1.7m (5ft 6in)
WEIGHT:	1700kg (3750lb)
CALIBRE:	150mm (5.9in)
ELEVATION:	0° to +73° or –4° to +75°
TRAVERSE:	11.5°
SHELL TYPE:	HE, smoke, shaped charge, HEAT
MUZZLE VELOCITY:	241m/sec (783ft/sec)
EFFECTIVE RANGE:	4700m (5140yd)
CREW:	5

In 1927–34, the German Army developed a second, heavy, infantry gun design: the 15cm (5.9in) sIG 33. Limited production and field testing occurred in 1935–37; larger-scale sIG 33 production commenced in 1938. The weapons manufactured were primarily allocated to the cannon companies found within the German infantry regiment. From 1940 onwards, two sIG 33 guns were allocated to the heavy infantry gun platoon found in Waffen-SS Panzergrenadier and infantry regiments.

Above: On the Eastern Front, soldiers of the Waffen-SS *Wiking* Division fit the fuzes into shells for a 15cm (5.9in) sIG 33 gun.

POWER
The short-barrelled (L/11.4) 15cm (5.9in) cannon delivered a high-explosive round out to a maximum range of 4700m (5140yd).

ROUNDS
As well as HE, the gun could also fire smoke, shaped charge and HEAT fin-stabilized (Stielgrenate 42) rounds.

HANDLING
The gun was mounted on a non-split, single-axled, wheeled carriage. The large manoeuvring handle of the sIG 33 positioned on the top of the non-split carriage rear spade is clearly evident in this artwork, as are the early-production spoked wooden wheels.

DIRECT-FIRE SUPPORT
An infantry gun was supposed to be a mobile and manoeuvrable asset that frontline troops could position well forward to provide intimate direct-fire support, particularly if artillery indirect fire was unavailable. At 1700kg (3750lb), however, the sIG 33 was heavy – and also bulky – for such a forward-deployed role. That said, infantry guns could also function as Ersatz indirect-fire artillery pieces in extremis.

SP GUNS
Conventional in design, the sIG 33 was simple and robust and gave no trouble even in the worst conditions, but customers complained of the weight. A self-propelled version of the gun was also produced (seen here), using a variety of different chassis.

15cm sFH 18 Medium Field Howitzer (1934)

SPECIFICATIONS

GUN LENGTH:	4.4m (14ft 5in)
WEIGHT:	5512kg (12,154lb)
CALIBRE:	150mm (5.9in)
ELEVATION:	0° to +45°
TRAVERSE:	60°
SHELL TYPE:	HE, smoke
MUZZLE VELOCITY:	495m/sec (1624ft/sec)
EFFECTIVE RANGE:	13,250m (14,490yd)
CREW:	7

In 1926–30, the firms of Krupp and Rheinmetall produced rival prototypes to the requirement for the army's future standard medium field howitzer. Elements of both designs were amalgamated in 1933, with the latter firm's gun being married to the former's carriage to produce the 15cm (5.9in) schwere Feldhaubitze 18 (sFH 18). Technically, despite its name, this was a 'medium' artillery weapon. Production of the gun commenced in late 1933 and it entered service in 1934. This piece remained the principal German medium field howitzer throughout World War II.

Above: A German 15cm (5.9in) sFH 18 howitzer on the Western Front in 1940, the gun having just returned to battery after firing.

BARREL
The standard 15cm (5.9in) sFH 18 was produced without a muzzle brake (unlike the later 18M variant); this medium howitzer was identifiable by its large recuperator mounted high above the weapon's barrel.

WEIGHT
The weapon weighed 5512kg (12,154lb) and could fire a 43.5kg (96lb) shell out to a maximum range of 13,250m (14,490yd), which was not particularly impressive for a weapon of this calibre.

MODIFIED VERSION
In 1942, a modified version of this weapon was developed: the sFH 18M. This gun fired its round with a larger propellant charge to gain additional range. The increased charge, however, increased the rate of barrel erosion, so the design incorporated a replaceable chamber liner. In addition, the barrel featured a muzzle brake to reduce the stress placed on the carriage during firing.

CARRIAGE
Many of these howitzers were horse-drawn; when in this mobility mode, the weapon's main carriage and rear limbers were transported separately from one another.

LIMITED PERFORMANCE
The 15cm (5.9in) sFH 18 was a prolific field artillery piece on all German fronts in World War II, with a total of 6756 produced between 1939 and 1945. On the Eastern Front, however, the weapon was outclassed by some of the Soviet field guns.

Katyusha Rocket Launcher (1939)

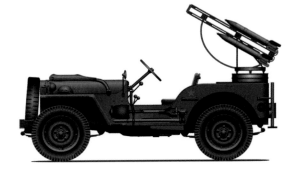

SPECIFICATIONS

ROCKET LENGTH:	1.41m (4ft 7in)
ROCKET WEIGHT:	42.5kg (94lb)
CALIBRE:	132mm (5.2in) M-13 rocket
ELEVATION:	n/a
TRAVERSE:	n/a
SHELL TYPE:	HE
MUZZLE VELOCITY:	n/a
EFFECTIVE RANGE:	8500m (9295yd)
PROPELLANT WEIGHT:	7.2kg (16lb)
CREW:	6

The 82mm (3.2in) M-8 rocket was based on the RS-82 air-launched rocket (RS – *Reaktivnyy Snaryad*, 'rocket-powered shell'). Converting the RS-82 for ground-to-ground use primarily involved enlarging the warhead and motor, but it remained a simple, fin-stabilized, solid-fuel rocket. The type entered service in August 1941; its relatively light weight allowed large numbers to be fired from a single launcher. Medium trucks mounted a bank of rails for no less than 48 rockets, while even jeeps could be fitted with eight-round launchers.

Above: BM-8-8 82mm (3.2in) rocket launcher on a Willys MB jeep. As the Red Army's advance approached the Carpathian Mountains in 1944, the BM-8-8 was hastily developed to ensure that jeeps could give fire support in terrain that was impassable to existing Katyusha vehicles.

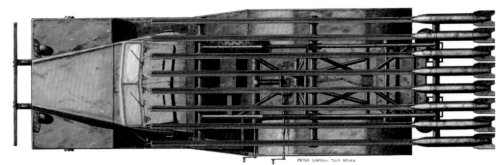

AREA EFFECT

The Katyusha was not an accurate weapon, at least in terms of the individual rockets, but as an area weapon it had enormous destructive capability. A battery of four BM-13 launchers could fire up to 192 rockets in a few seconds, striking over a 400,000sq m (4,300,000sq ft) impact zone. The downside of the system was that once the rockets were fired, it could take about 50 minutes to reload and prepare the battery for the next firing.

MOUNT

The Katyusha did not have a standard vehicular mount. Most commonly it was fitted to trucks, but it was also seen on tractors, trains and even river/naval vessels.

RAIL FIRING

Once the rockets had been loaded onto the rail system, they could be fired as a ripple salvo in just 7–10 seconds.

BM-13-16 ROCKET LAUNCHER

A battery of US-supplied 6 × 4 Studebaker trucks load up their M13 16-rail launchers with 132mm (5.2in) rockets. By the end of the war, more than 10,000 Katyusha launchers of all types had been produced together with 12 million rockets in an estimated 200 factories.

122mm Howitzer M1938 (M-30) (1939)

TYPE · *Field & Heavy Artillery* · **FAMILY** · *Artillery & Mortars*

SPECIFICATIONS

GUN LENGTH: 2.67m (8ft 9in)
L/21.9

WEIGHT: 2450kg
(5401lb)

CALIBRE: 122mm (4.8in)
howitzer Model
1938 (M-30)

ELEVATION: –3° to +63.5°

TRAVERSE: 49°

SHELL TYPE: HE,
HE-fragmentation,
smoke, HEAT,
illumination

MUZZLE VELOCITY: 458m/sec
(1503ft/sec)

EFFECTIVE RANGE: 11,800m (12,904yd)

CREW: 8

By the late 1930s, it was becoming clear to the Soviet military that the Model 1909/37 and the Model 1910/30 howitzers were in need of replacement by an entirely new design: both types were not only outranged by foreign equivalents, but also had poor elevation and traverse. Various 122mm (4.8in) howitzers underwent prolonged service trials in 1938/39, leading to the acceptance of the M-30 in 1940. The design was so successful that production continued until 1960, by which time more than 19,000 had been completed.

Above: A dug-in M-30 fires in support of the Third Belorussian Front's advance on Königsberg in the spring of 1945.

BREECHBLOCK
The breechblock was of the interrupted-screw type. The rate of fire was approximately 5–6rpm.

BARREL
The gun did not have a muzzle brake, increasing the recoil but reducing the visual signature of dust raised up from the ground by a muzzle brake's gas redirection.

BATTLE WINNING
As the Soviet Union's premier piece of divisional artillery, the M-30 had a profound effect on the Red Army's ability to deliver indirect support, especially in the context of the numbers produced. Not only were they extremely powerful in the anti-personnel role, they were also used to destroy field fortifications, minefields and enemy vehicles, purely with their HE shells; by utilizing the BP-60A munition, the gun could also serve in the anti-tank role. Large numbers of captured guns were also used by the Germans, who produced more than a million 122mm (4.8in) shells for this and similar types.

TRAIL
The M-30 had a split trail; in emergencies the gun could be fired with the trail arms together, albeit with a limited traverse.

ANTI-TANK GUN
Although it was primarily an indirect fire weapon, the M-30 did have a significant anti-tank capability after the introduction of the BP-460A HEAT shell in mid-1943, which could penetrate 100–160mm (3.94–6.3in) of armour at 90 degrees.

Ordnance QF 25pdr Mk 2 (1940)

SPECIFICATIONS

GUN LENGTH:	2.4m (7ft 11in)
WEIGHT:	1800kg (3968lb)
CALIBRE:	87.6mm (3.45in)
ELEVATION:	–5° to +40°
TRAVERSE:	On carriage: 8°; on firing table: 360°
SHELL TYPE:	HE, HEAT, smoke
MUZZLE VELOCITY:	532m/sec (1745ft/sec)
EFFECTIVE RANGE:	12,253m (13,400yd)
CREW:	7

One of the most famous artillery pieces of World War II, the 25pdr was designed between the wars to provide the British Army with a versatile weapon that could fulfil the role of both a field gun and a howitzer. The weapon took centre stage during the heavy bombardment that preceded the offensive at El Alamein in 1942. The initial Ordnance QF 25pdrs were essentially heavier guns mounted on the carriages of the old surplus 18pdrs. The carriages had been modernized with pneumatic tyres, and some had been equipped with split trails. A number of these guns, designated Mark I, went to war with the British Expeditionary Force on the continent and were lost during the evacuation at Dunkirk. Simultaneously, however, the Mark II, engineered on a combined basis including gun and carriage, was being deployed with Commonwealth troops and was destined to become one of the best-known artillery pieces of World War II.

Above: A British 25pdr howitzer supports an attack between Tilly and Caen during the fighting for Normandy in June 1944.

MUZZLE BRAKE
The use of the muzzle brake made it possible for the gun to fire the heavier propelling charges.

SIGHTING
As well as an indirect-fire sight, a direct-fire telescope was an integral fitting, used primarily for the anti-tank role.

BREECHBLOCK
Its sliding breechblock enabled the gun to fire 5rpm.

TRAIL
The trail of the 25pdr could be hooked directly to the vehicle; it did not need a separate limber.

DESERT GUN
The battles of the Western Desert between 1940 and 1942 against the Axis were arguably the finest hour of the 25pdr. Being almost 88mm (3.46in) in calibre, the 25pdr was the only gun capable of challenging German heavy armour, as the battles around and to the east of Tobruk would prove the worth of the gun. The fighting there in 1942 saw the 25pdr pitted directly against German tanks; with armour-piercing shot and Super Charge propelling charges, the guns could penetrate 70mm (2.75in) of armour.

FIREPOWER
The 25pdr fired a shell that weighed 11.3kg (25lb) to a range of 12,253m (13,400yd). It had the propellant charge loaded separately to the shell; 'Normal' and 'Super Charge' propellant loads were available.

Wurfgranate 41 (1941)

SPECIFICATIONS

DIMENSIONS:	Length: 6m (19ft 8in); Width: 2.2m (7ft); Height: 3.05m (10ft)
WEIGHT:	7100kg (15,653lb)
CALIBRE:	21cm (8.3in)
ELEVATION:	–5° to +45°
TRAVERSE:	24°
ARMAMENT:	1 x 150mm (5.9in) Nebelwerfer 41 10-barrelled rocket launcher, 1 x 7.92mm (0.31in) machine gun
SHELL TYPE:	HE
MUZZLE VELOCITY:	320m/sec (1000ft/sec)
EFFECTIVE RANGE:	7850m (8584yd)
CREW:	4

The Germans deployed the 15cm (5.9in) Wurfgranate 41 and the 21cm (8.3in) Wurfgranate 42, launched from the multi-barrelled Nebelwerfer mounted on the carriage of the Pak 35/36 gun or fixed atop the SdKfz 4/1 halftrack. Preceding the 15cm and the 21cm rockets were the 28cm (11in) and 32cm (12.6in) Wurfkörper, which were fired from wooden or steel launching frames that doubled as carrying cases. To add mobility to these early rockets, a towed launcher with six frames was constructed; later, mobile launchers were mounted on halftracks and other vehicles.

Above: A small number of 28/32cm (11/12.6in) Nebelwerfer rocket launchers were converted to take the new 30cm (11.8in) Wurfkörper 42 rockets, creating a weapon designated the 30cm Nebelwerfer 42. This one is being camouflaged in a farmer's field somewhere on the Eastern Front.

WURFKÖRPER

In 1942, the 30cm (11.8in) Wurfkörper 42 went into service and was initially fired from the 30cm Nebelwerfer 42 launcher. Among the improvements of the Wurfkörper 42 were a propellant that left a much diminished smoke trail, minimizing the risk of return fire from enemy artillery batteries. Later, a trailer based on the Pak 38 anti-tank gun was introduced, and the weapon could be launched from a halftrack mount as well. The 44.6kg (98.4lb) explosive charge carried by the rocket was large compared to the overall projectile weight of 125.6kg (277lb).

SPIN STABILIZED
The rocket exhaust was pushed out through canted vents in the base of the rocket to achieve a measure of spin stabilization.

LAUNCHER
The launcher unit consisted of six individual tubes, providing an area bombardment effect when launched as a ripple salvo.

HALF-TRACK MOUNT
Heavy but short-range 28cm (11in) or 32cm (12.6in) rockets collectively known as Wurfkörper were fitted to tracked vehicles by the Germans. Often, the mount was the SdKfz 251, a workhorse of the German armed forces. Such vehicles were nicknamed the 'Howling Cow' by German soldiers.

105mm Howitzer M2A1 (1941)

SPECIFICATIONS

GUN LENGTH:	2.31m (7ft 7in)
WEIGHT:	2259kg (4980lb)
CALIBRE:	105mm (3in)
ELEVATION:	–5° to +66°
TRAVERSE:	46°
SHELL TYPE:	HE, smoke, chemical, HEAT, canister
MUZZLE VELOCITY:	472m/sec (1548ft/sec)
EFFECTIVE RANGE:	11,200m (12,248yd)
CREW:	8

The 105mm (3in) howitzer M2A1 was the primary field weapon of US divisional artillery units in World War II. The design for the baseline weapon, the Howitzer M1, was completed in 1928, with the improved M2 variant standardized in 1934 and the M2A1 variant emerging in March 1940. From April 1941 until June 1945, more than 8500 of the M2A1 guns were produced. As well as serving as standard towed field weapons they were also mounted on various vehicles to create self-propelled guns.

Above: During field exercises, US soldiers wrestle a 105mm (3in) M2A1 artillery piece into position. The 105mm M2A1 served as the backbone of US artillery in World War II.

RATE OF FIRE
The howitzer's rate of fire was up to 4rpm, and it incorporated a hydro-pneumatic recoil system and a sliding breechblock.

CARRIAGE
Mounted on the M2A2 carriage, the wheeled weapon was primarily towed into position by the army's 2.3-tonne (2.2-ton) truck.

SELF-PROPELLED GUNS
As World War II progressed, the basic design of the 105mm (3in) howitzer underwent continual revisions, such as the M3, which featured a shortened barrel and was deliverable by aircraft. In terms of self-propelled configurations, the howitzer was mounted on a broad spectrum of vehicles, including the Cletrac MG-2 tracked tractor, the Mack T3 half-track, Medium Tank M3 chassis and Medium Tank M4A3 chassis.

WEIGHT
Heavy for its calibre, the weapon weighed a hefty 2259kg (4980lb).

FIRE MISSION
A 105mm (3in) M2A1 howitzer of the US First Army in operations in Belgium in the March of 1945, shortly after the defeat of Germany's last-ditch Ardennes offensive.

152mm Howitzer M1943 (D-1) (1943)

SPECIFICATIONS

GUN LENGTH:	4.2m (13ft 10in) L/24.6
WEIGHT:	Deployed: 3640kg (8025lb); travelling order: 3600kg (7937lb)
CALIBRE:	152mm (5.98in)
ELEVATION:	–3° to +63.5°
TRAVERSE:	35°
SHELL TYPE:	HE, HE-fragmentation, smoke, chemical, shrapnel
MUZZLE VELOCITY:	508m/sec (1667ft/sec)
EFFECTIVE RANGE:	12,400m (13,560yd)
CREW:	8

Design studies for a mobile 152mm (5.98in) howitzer based on the carriage of the 122mm (4.8in) M-30 and the barrel of the 152mm M-10 began in 1942. The only significant modification was the addition of a muzzle brake to allow the relatively light carriage to absorb the recoil without damage. Trials were carried out in May 1943 and the type was approved for service in August of that year. Production was able to get under way exceptionally quickly using existing stocks of components for the M-30 and M-10.

Right: A battery of 152mm (5.98in) howitzer D-1 Model 1943 artillery of the Third Belorussian Front in action.

RECOIL SYSTEM
The D-1's recoil system, straddling the barrel, consisted of a hydraulic buffer and a hydro-pneumatic recuperator.

SPLIT TRAIL
The split trail was linked directly to the tow vehicle without a limber. On roads, the maximum towing speed was 40km/h (25mph).

MUZZLE BRAKE
The DT-3 muzzle brake was essential to lessen the impact of firing on the lighter M-30 carriage.

PRODUCTION

The D-1 was a very strong design, and more than 2800 were completed between 1943 and 1949. This was, however, actually not a large number of guns compared with many other similar pieces. For example, 17,526 122mm (4.8in) howitzer M1938 (M-30) were produced between 1940 and 1945 alone.

MUSEUM PIECE
A 152mm (5.98in) howitzer D-1 Model 1943 stands outside a museum in St Petersburg, Russia.

105mm Howitzer M3 (1945)

SPECIFICATIONS

GUN LENGTH:	1.88m (6ft 2in)
WEIGHT:	1132kg (2490lb)
CALIBRE:	105mm (4.13in)
ELEVATION:	–9° to +69°
TRAVERSE:	45°
SHELL TYPE:	HE, HEAT, smoke
MUZZLE VELOCITY:	311m/sec (1020ft/sec)
EFFECTIVE RANGE:	7585m (8295yd)
CREW:	7

In 1941, the US Army requested a new 105mm (4.13in) howitzer, capable of being air-lifted, not more than 1134kg (2500lb) in weight and capable of a range of at least 6401m (7000yd), with which to equip their future airborne divisions. The desired result was reached by cutting down the existing M2A1 Howitzer barrel by 686mm (27in) to make the Howitzer T7, and then fabricating a carriage by taking the existing carriage of the 75mm (2.95in) Howitzer M3A1 and the much modified recoil system of the 75mm Pack Howitzer M8. This was standardized as the Howitzer M3 on Carriage M3 in February 1945. More than 2500 were built.

BREECH
The breech mechanism was of the simple sliding-block type, as used on the M1 and M2 howitzers (and variants).

SHIELD OPTION
A shield could be fitted around the barrel to protect the gun crew from small-arms fire, as part of the M3A2 carriage.

BARREL
Because of the M3's short barrel, the gun was used in a number of self-propelled mounts, including half-tracks and armoured cars.

SHELL TYPES
The three main shell types used in wartime US artillery were high-explosive (HE), high-explosive anti-tank (HEAT), smoke and chemical. The latter does not refer to poison gas, but rather to white phosphorous munitions, which not only burst with a dense white smoke – ideal for target marking or obscuration – but that also acted as an incendiary weapon, the phosphorous particles burning with a very intense heat.

TOWING
In keeping with the M3's air-portable status, its main prime mover was the Willys MB or Ford GPW 1/4-ton Jeeps.

AIRBORNE ARTILLERY
American howitzers shell German forces retreating near Carentan, France, 11 July 1944. The M3s were used in North Africa by Infantry Cannon Companies, but this tactical notion was short-lived; for the remainder of the war, the artillery was supplied to armed airborne units only.

OTO-Melara 105mm Mod 56 (1956)

SPECIFICATIONS

GUN LENGTH:	14 calibre: 1.47m (4ft 10in)
WEIGHT:	1273kg (2806lb)
CALIBRE:	105mm (4.13in)
ELEVATION:	–7° to +65°
TRAVERSE:	56°
SHELL TYPE:	HE, smoke, HEAT, illumination
MUZZLE VELOCITY:	416m/sec (1345ft/sec)
EFFECTIVE RANGE:	11,100m (12,140yd)
CREW:	5

The OTO-Melara 105mm Mod 56 was developed in the 1950s to meet demand from many countries for a 105mm (4.13in) howitzer capable of firing the standard US M1 family of ammunition yet light enough to be lifted by the helicopters of the time. This weapon is a pack howitzer; the suspension system allows the weapon to be set high, leaving room for the breech to recoil at high angles of elevation, or low for flat-trajectory firing against tanks and similar targets. As such, it was a highly flexible gun and was widely adopted throughout NATO in the 1950s. Many examples are still in service.

RECOIL CONTROL
To cope with the recoil in a short-barrelled gun, the Mod 56 has a extensive multi-barrel muzzle brake.

PACK LOADS
The Mod 56 can be dismantled into a total of 12 pack loads for easy transportation and storage.

WHEELS
The height of the wheels can be adjusted to suit field and anti-tank use, the anti-tank configuration dropping the overall profile of the gun lower.

US AMMUNITION
In the era of NATO standardization, the OTO-Melara 105mm (4.13in) Mod 56 was designed to have a degree of ammunition commonality with other NATO state members, particularly the United States. It could therefore take the shells used in the American M101 and M102 105mm howitzers.

SPANISH HOWITZER
Spanish Marines man a 105mm (4.13in) Mod 56 howitzer. Other users include Argentina, Greece and the UK.

BM-21 Rocket Launcher (1963)

SPECIFICATIONS

ROCKET LENGTH:	3.226m (10ft 6in)
ROCKET WEIGHT:	77.5kg (170lb)
CALIBRE:	122mm (4.8in)
ELEVATION:	+55°
TRAVERSE:	122°
SHELL TYPE:	HE-fragmentation, incendiary, bomblet
MUZZLE VELOCITY:	690m/sec (2264ft/sec)
EFFECTIVE RANGE:	20.38km (13 miles)
CREW:	3

The Soviet 122mm (4.8in) BM-21 system was developed in the early 1950s. It might be considered to be the successor to the various wartime Katyusha rocket systems, since it uses the same principle of firing a solid-fuel rocket from a bank of launchers mounted on the cargo bed of a 6 × 6 truck. There are also 12- and 36-round variants of the basic launcher mounted on different vehicles.

Above: Reloading the BM-21 takes seven minutes as the rockets have to be slipped into the 40 tubes manually.

40-TUBE LAUNCHER
Instead of the old open rails of the wartime Katyusha, the BM-21 uses closed tubes in a cluster of 40 barrels, on a frame capable of 55° of elevation and 120° of traverse to either side. The rocket can be used with HE-Fragmentation, incendiary or bomblet warheads, and the rocket has four spring-put fins set at a slight angle in order to give the rocket a slow roll to stabilize it in flight.

CAB CONTROLS
The rockets can be fired either from the cab itself or via an external trigger unit connected by a 64m (210ft) cable.

VEHICLE
The standard vehicle in the BM-21 system was the Ural-375D 6 × 6 truck, but the ZIL-131 and Ural-4320 have also been used.

LAUNCHER UNIT
The BM-21 launcher unit had a total of 40 barrels. The rockets can be fired individually, in small groups, or as a complete salvo.

AFGHANISTAN
The rocket launcher's good cross-country mobility have made it ideally suited to operations in countries such as Afghanistan, where its high trajectory fire allows the rockets to penetrate deep valleys.

122mm Howitzer D-30 (1963)

SPECIFICATIONS

GUN LENGTH:	Travelling: 5.4m (17ft 8in)
WEIGHT:	3210kg (7077lb); firing 3150kg (6944lb)
CALIBRE:	121mm (4.8in)
ELEVATION:	−7° to + 70°
TRAVERSE:	360°
SHELL TYPE:	HE-fragmentation, incendiary, bomblet
MUZZLE VELOCITY:	690m/sec (2264ft/sec)
EFFECTIVE RANGE:	15,400m (16,840yd) with HE projectile and 21000m (22,965yd) with rocket-assisted HE projectile
CREW:	7

The Soviet 122mm (4.8in) D-30 howitzer was designed by the F.F. Petrov Design Bureau at Artillery Plant No. 9 at Sverdlovsk to replace the 122mm M1938 (M-30) howitzer, introduced into Soviet service shortly before World War II. The D-30 entered service in the early 1960s and offered several significant advantages, including a range of 15,400 rather than 11,800m (16,840 rather than 12,905yd) and traverse of 360° rather than 49°. The weapon is still in service with 65 countries.

Above: The D-30 122mm (4.8in) howitzer was produced in very large numbers in the USSR, and was also made in China, Croatia, Egypt, Iran, Iraq and Yugoslavia. Substantial numbers are still in service, especially in the Middle East. Iran, for example, has 540 of the type.

MECHANISM

The D-30 has a 4.875m (16ft) barrel with a multi-baffle muzzle brake and a semi-automatic vertical sliding wedge breech mechanism, the recoil system being mounted over the ordnance.

FIRING POSITION

This is the D-30 122mm (4.8in) towed howitzer in firing position with its wheels raised and its trail opened into the three units that provide firing stability when staked at their ends.

FIRING SET-UP

On arrival at the firing position, the crew first unlock the barrel travel lock, which then folds back onto the central trail. The firing jack under the carriage is then lowered to the ground, so raising the wheels, and the outer trails are each spread through 120°. The firing jack is raised until the trail ends are on the ground to provide a stable firing platform after they have been staked to the ground.

SOVIET DISTRIBUTION

In Soviet service, the D-30 was issued on the scale of 36 per tank division (one regiment of two 18-weapon battalions each of three six-gun batteries), and 72 per motor rifle division (each motorized rifle regiment having a battalion of 18 D-30s and the artillery regiment two 18-gun battalions). The Soviets later increased the battery from six to eight guns: each battalion thus had 24 rather than 18 D-30s.

CROATIAN ARTILLERY

A member of the Croatian Defence Council (HVO) Army fires a 122mm (4.8in) Howitzer D-30J field artillery piece during a three-day exercise.

M109 Howitzer (1963)

SPECIFICATIONS

DIMENSIONS:	Length: 9.1m (30ft); Width: 3.1m (10ft 3in); Height: 3.3m (10ft 7in)
WEIGHT:	24.9 tonnes (24.5 tons)
ELEVATION:	−3 to + 75°
TRAVERSE:	360°
ARMAMENT:	Main armament: 1 × M126 155mm (6.1in) howitzer; secondary armament: 1 × 12.7mm (0.5in) M2 machine gun
SHELL TYPE:	HE, ICM, rocket-assisted projectiles, tactical nuclear
MUZZLE VELOCITY:	925m/sec (3034ft/sec)
EFFECTIVE RANGE:	30km (19 miles)
CREW:	6

The primary self-propelled indirect-fire support weapon of the US Army over a period of more than 50 years, the M109 mounts a powerful 155mm (6.1in) howitzer and has demonstrated the ability to decimate distant targets while maintaining the pace of rapid advance.

Above: An M109 makes way at speed. When travelling on road, the M109 can achieve a maximum speed of 65km/h (40mph).

AMMUNITION
The 155mm (6.1in) howitzer is capable of firing high-explosive, Improved Conventional Munitions (ICM) that scatter bomblets, rocket-assisted projectiles, and tactical nuclear weapons. Its rocket-assisted range is 30km (19 miles).

MAIN ARMAMENT
The 155mm (6.1in) howitzer has been a constant feature of the M109; the M284/L39 is mounted with the latest variant, the M109A7.

CHASSIS
The M109 series utilizes the same chassis as the now-retired M108 self-propelled 105mm (4.1in) howitzer, which consisted primarily of components from the M113 armoured personnel carrier. Later improvements moved the driver's position from the turret to a more advantageous location in the hull.

ENGINE
The 328kW (440hp) General Motors Detroit Diesel 8V71T engine is capable of a top road speed of 56km/h (35mph).

CREW
The M109A6 Paladin crew includes a section chief, driver, gunner and assistant gunner. Additional ammunition handlers are sometimes included in the crew.

M109A1
The M109A1 was the first major variant in the series. Its most significant change from the original M109 was its replacement of the M126 gun with a longer-barrelled, 39-calibre M185 gun, increasing maximum range to 18,100m (19,794yd).

Soltam M68 (1968)

SPECIFICATIONS

GUN LENGTH:	5.18m (17ft)
WEIGHT:	Travelling: 9500kg (20,944lb); firing: 8500kg (18,739lb)
CALIBRE:	155mm (6.1in)
ELEVATION:	+52°/–5°
TRAVERSE:	Total 90°
SHELL TYPE:	HE, smoke, illumination
MUZZLE VELOCITY:	253–725m/sec (830–2380ft/sec)
EFFECTIVE RANGE:	Standard HE projectile 21,000m (22,965yd)
CREW:	6

A development of a Finnish design, the Israeli M68 is a split-trail gun-howitzer of reasonable weight and good performance. The carriage has two wheels at the forward end of each trail leg, so they move with the legs as they are opened. There are loose spades that are driven into the ground and then have the trail locked to them by wedges.

Above: The Soltam M68 155mm (6.1in) gun-howitzer in travelling configuration, being towed by a truck. Over the last 30 years, the M-68 has provided the basis for several generations of improved guns.

BARREL
The ordnance of the M68 is 5.18m (17ft) long. It is fitted with a single-baffle muzzle brake, fume extractor and a horizontal breech mechanism.

PROJECTILE
The M68 fires a standard NATO HE projectile weighing 43.7kg (96.3lb) to a maximum range of 21,000m (22,965yd), as well as smoke and illuminating projectiles.

HIGH-VELOCITY SHELLS
The weapon can also fire Soltam-designed projectiles with a higher muzzle velocity (820m/sec or 2690ft/sec compared with 725m/sec or 2380ft/sec) to a maximum range of 23,500m (25,700yd).

FEATURES
The M68 had an efficient muzzle brake and a fume extractor, indicating the use of the same gun in a self-propelled carriage. For movement, the top carriage revolves until the barrel is above the folded trail legs, where it is then locked, and the trail ends are hoisted up and hooked to the towing truck. An unusual feature is the use of a sliding block breech with bag charges, the breechblock having a sealing ring inset in its front face.

WHEELS
Two rubber-tyred road wheels are mounted on each side; a maximum towing speed of 100km/h (62mph) is possible.

FIRING POSITION
The 155mm (6.1in) M68 gun-howitzer in the firing position with trails firmly staked into the ground. The split-trail carriage was unusual for its time: it has four rubber-tyred road wheels, each of which has a hydraulic brake operated from the towing vehicle.

2S3 (1971)

SPECIFICATIONS

DIMENSIONS:	Length: 8.4m (27ft 7in); Width: 3.2m (10ft 6in); Height: 2.8m (9ft 2in)
WEIGHT:	24,945kg (54,880lb)
ELEVATION:	−4° to +60°
TRAVERSE:	360°
ARMAMENT:	Main armament: 1 × 152mm (6in) D-22 gun; secondary armament: 1 × PKT 7.62mm (0.3in) machine gun
SHELL TYPE:	HE, HEAT, smoke, illumination, rocket-assisted projectiles, tactical nuclear
MUZZLE VELOCITY:	925m/sec (3034ft/sec)
EFFECTIVE RANGE:	18.5km (11miles)
CREW:	4

Introduced into the Red Army in 1973, the 2S3 (M1973)152mm (6in) self-propelled gun-howitzer replaced the older D-20 system in artillery regiments of Soviet and Warsaw Pact forces to provide fire support for tank and motorized rifle regiments. The main weapon of the 2S3 could fire a full range of advanced munitions. Its development was authorized in 1967, and it entered service six years later.

Above: A camouflaged 2S3 Akatsiya (M1973), as seen in Russian service in 2008.

CREW POSITIONS
During operation it was normal for two of the crew to stand at the rear of the vehicle and act as ammunition handlers, feeding projectiles via two hatches in the hull rear.

PROTECTION
The vehicle was fitted with nuclear, biological and chemical (NBC) protection and with a tactical nuclear capability, but was not equipped for amphibious operations.

CHASSIS
The chassis was a shortened version of that used for the SA-4 surface-to-air missile system and the GMZ armoured minelayer, both of which were used in the USSR for many years.

COLD WAR STRENGTH
By the 1980s, Western intelligence sources estimated that frontline Soviet armoured and mechanized infantry divisions stationed in East Germany included a battalion of 2S3s, usually totalling 18 vehicles, in their organic artillery regiments. Near the end of the decade, this number had increased to as many as three battalions and up to 54 of the self-propelled guns.

RED SQUARE PARADE
Red Army 2S3 (M1973) self-propelled guns take part in a parade in Moscow's Red Square some time during the 1980s. Developed as a response to the US Army's M109, the 2S3 provided highly mobile fire support for motorized rifle and tank divisions.

FH-70 155mm Howitzer (1974)

SPECIFICATIONS

GUN LENGTH:	6.02m (19ft 9in)
WEIGHT:	Travelling and firing: 9300kg (20,503lb)
CALIBRE:	155mm (6in)
ELEVATION:	+70°/–3°
TRAVERSE:	Total 56°
SHELL TYPE:	HE, smoke, illumination, rocket-assisted projectiles,
MUZZLE VELOCITY:	827m/sec (2713ft/sec)
EFFECTIVE RANGE:	With standard round: 24km (15 miles); with rocket-assisted projectile: 30km (19 miles)
CREW:	8

In 1968, an understanding was signed between the UK and West Germany for the joint development of a 155mm (6in) howitzer that would replace the British 5.5in gun and the American-supplied M114 155mm howitzer. The main requirements the new weapon had to meet included a high rate of fire with a burst-fire capability, increased range and lethality together with a new family of ammunition, high mobility and a minimum of effort for deployment. The UK was team leader for this weapon, which became known as the FH-70.

Above: In addition to its original developers in Britain (illustrated), Germany and Italy, the FH-70 is used by the Saudi Arabian army and the Japanese GSDF.

BARREL
The 6.02m (19ft 9in)-long barrel of the FH-70 has a double-baffle muzzle brake and a semi-automatic wedge-type breech mechanism.

LOADING
The loading system includes a loading tray that presents the projectile to the chamber. A burst rate of three rounds in 13 seconds can be achieved; the normal sustained rate of fire is 6rpm.

AUXILIARY POWER UNIT
The carriage of the FH-70 is of the split-trail type, with an auxiliary power unit mounted on the forward part. This enables the FH-70 to propel itself on roads and across country at a maximum speed of 16km/h (10mph). In addition, the APU provides power for steering, and for raising and lowering the main and trail wheels. When travelling, the ordnance is traversed to the rear and locked in position over the closed trails.

FIRING POSITION
This FH-70 155mm (6in) howitzer is illustrated as it would appear in firing position. The weapon fires a standard high-explosive projectile out to a maximum range of 24km (15 miles).

AMMUNITION
The FH-70 can fire most NATO standard 155mm (6in) ammunition, including guided and extended-range rocket-assisted, but generally is limited to three main types: HE with a weight of 43.5kg (96lb), smoke (base ejection), and illuminating. The last provides one million candelas for one minute.

UNDER TOW
Steyr towing vehicles stand near FH-70 155mm (6in) towed howitzers after transporting them to a defensive position during Operation Desert Shield in 1991.

L118 Light Gun (1976)

SPECIFICATIONS

GUN LENGTH:	Overall length travelling with gun forward: 6.629m (21ft 9in)
WEIGHT:	1860kg (4100lb)
CALIBRE:	105mm (4.13in)
ELEVATION:	−5.5° to +70°
TRAVERSE:	11°
SHELL TYPE:	HE, HESH, smoke, illuminating
MUZZLE VELOCITY:	708m/sec (2320ft/sec)
EFFECTIVE RANGE:	17,200m (18,810yd)
CREW:	6

The Royal Ordnance 105mm (4.13in) Light Gun was designed in the later 1960s as successor to the OTO-Melara Pack Howitzer of the same calibre, and was accepted for service in 1973. Since that time, the weapon has been used successfully in action. More than 1000 such guns have been delivered to the UK and to export customers, including Australia and the US among a total of 19 operators.

Below: The L118A1 Light Gun weighs 1860kg (4100lb) in travelling order. The British Army use a 1-tonne (0.98-ton) Land Rover, a 4 × 4 vehicle able to tow the Light Gun and also carry its crew and some ready-use ammunition. The Land Rover carries two personnel (driver and one passenger) in the cab as well as eight crew in its rear (four on each of two bench seats).

SIGHTING
Direct fire is undertaken with the aid of a telescopic sight incorporating a moving illuminated graticule adjustable for lead when firing at longer ranges against a moving target. There is also a direct-fire night sight. All scales and graticules are illuminated by Trilux-activated light sources, removing the need for onboard electrical batteries.

CARRIAGE
The tyres of the gun's carriage run round the outer edge of the platform, providing for rapid changes of gross azimuth. The platform is connected to the underside of the gun by an assembly of four wire stays.

RATIONALE
The British used the Italian 105mm (4.13in) Mod 56 for some years, but required something air-portable yet more powerful that could fire the ammunition that had been developed for the Abbot SP gun. The 105mm (4.13in) Light Gun L118 was the result, a lightweight gun using a tubular box trail and capable of firing in the howitzer role as well. It is provided with a second barrel, chambered for American 105mm (4.13in) ammunition; if that ammunition is readily available in some distant theatre, the gun is changed to suit.

FIRING PLATFORM
A circular unit of lightweight construction, the Light Gun's firing platform provides a firm base and a high level of gun stability under all operating conditions.

BRITISH SERVICE
The L118 has been combat-proven in the British Army in several contexts, not least in the Falklands War in 1982, when it was the main land-based instrument of artillery support for British troops conducting assaults on Argentine positions.

M198 155mm Howitzer (1978)

SPECIFICATIONS

BARREL LENGTH:	6.09m (20ft)
WEIGHT:	Travelling and firing: 7163kg (15,790lb)
CALIBRE:	155mm (6.1in)
ELEVATION:	−5° to +72°
TRAVERSE:	Total 45°
SHELL TYPE:	HE, rocket assisted, smoke, illumination, area denial, anti-armour mines, laser guided, tactical nuclear
MUZZLE VELOCITY:	684m/sec (2240ft/ sec)
EFFECTIVE RANGE:	With M107 projectile: 18.15km (11 miles); with M549A1 rocket-assisted projectile: 30km (19 miles)
CREW:	7

The M198 became the standard 155mm (6.1in) howitzer of the US Army and Marines from the late 1970s, and replaced the old 155mm M114. The M198 is normally issued to US infantry, airborne and air assault divisions, while mechanized infantry and armoured divisions have the 155mm M109 self-propelled howitzer. In US and Australian use, it is progressively being replaced by the M777 howitzer.

Above: The US Marine Corps (USMC) M198 155mm (6.1in) Howitzer gun crew of 4th Battalion, 14th Marines, Mike Battery, Gun 4 at Camp Fallujah, Iraq, engage enemy targets in support of Operation Iraqi Freedom.

FIRE CONTROL
The fire-control equipment includes an M137 panoramic telescope, two elevation quadrants, and an M138 elbow telescope.

RECOIL MECHANISM
The recoil mechanism is of the hydro-pneumatic type with a variable recoil length.

TRAVELLING
The M198 155mm (6.1in) howitzer is seen in one of its two travelling configurations.

PLATFORM
When the weapon is in the firing position, a firing platform is lowered to the ground under the forward part of the carriage and the wheels are raised clear of the ground.

ADVANCED MUNITIONS
The M198 is able to fire some particularly advanced ammunition types. The M712 Copperhead, for example, is a fin-stabilized laser-guided shell designed to engage hard point targets such as armoured vehicles and bunkers. By contrast, the Area Denial Artillery Munition System (ADAMS) deploys M67 long-duration anti-personnel mines and M72 short-duration anti-personnel landmines, each mine deploying seven tripwires on landing.

GUN DESIGN
The M198 design is quite conventional: a split-trail two-wheel carriage, the wheels of which can be lifted off the ground when firing, and a gun with muzzle brake and screw breech with pad obturation for firing bagged charge. There are two hydro-pneumatic balancing cylinders attached to the cradle to take the weight of the gun. An auxiliary propulsion unit was designed for this gun, but not adopted.

M270 MLRS (1983)

SPECIFICATIONS

DIMENSIONS:	Length: 6.85m (22ft 6in); Width: 2.97m (9ft 9in); Height: 2.59m (8ft 6in)
WEIGHT:	24,950kg (55,000lb)
CALIBRE:	227mm (8.94in)
ELEVATION:	+60° max
TRAVERSE:	194° left or right from stowed position
SHELL TYPE:	Multiple, including anti-armour/ anti-personnel submunitions, guided unitary missiles, mine deployment and chemical warfare
EFFECTIVE RANGE:	M26: 32km (20 miles); M26A1/A2: 45km (28 miles); M30/31: 84km (52 miles)
CREW:	3

The Multiple Launch Rocket System (MLRS) introduced saturation firepower and 'shoot-and-scoot' capability to the US Army. Its mobility and strike capability against ground targets has proven a formidable combination on the battlefield, engaging a variety of targets.

Above: One of the early M270s, as used in Operation Desert Storm. At the time of writing (2018), the M270 is undergoing modernization.

DESCRIPTION

The Vought Multiple Launch Rocket System (MLRS) had its origins in a 1976 feasibility study into what was known as a General Support Rocket System. Following trials, the Vought system was chosen and entered service with the US Army in 1982. These Self-Propelled Launcher Loaders on the chassis of the M2 Infantry Fighting Vehicle carry two pods of six rounds each. The Vought MLRS was licensed to the UK, France, Italy, West Germany and the Netherlands for production. It saw action during the 1991 Gulf War, when Allied MLRS batteries tore large holes in Iraqi defence lines prior to the ground offensive to free Kuwait.

ENGINE
A 373kW (500hp) Cummins Diesel engine powers the MLRS at up to 64km/h (40mph), keeping pace with forward ground units, including the M1 Abrams main battle tank.

CREW
The crew of the MLRS, which includes a driver, gunner and section chief, is capable of firing the system without leaving the protection of the cab, allowing for rapid fire and quick relocation.

MAIN ARMAMENT
The M269 launcher/loader module is capable of firing a variety of rockets against enemy ground targets individually or in a ripple of up to 12 projectiles in less than one minute.

FIRE CONTROL
Advanced fire control capabilities include the use of a global positioning system.

MLRS FIREPOWER
MLRS munitions include the M-77 Dual Purpose Improved Conventional Munition grenade or bomblet, the Ground Launched Small Diameter Bomb, extended range rockets, and guided rockets included with the long-range US Army Tactical Missile System (ATACMS). The system can also fire anti-tank mines, chemical warheads or mine-dispensing munitions.

2S19 Msta (1989)

SPECIFICATIONS

DIMENSIONS:	Length: 7.15m (23ft 5in); Width: 3.38m (11ft); Height: 2.99m (9ft 10in)
WEIGHT:	42,000kg (92,594lb)
CALIBRE:	152mm (6in)
ELEVATION:	–4° to +68°
TRAVERSE:	360°
SHELL TYPE:	Extended-range HE, HEAT, smoke, tactical nuclear and laser-guided
EFFECTIVE RANGE:	Standard ammunition: 24–29km (15–18 miles); rocket-assisted extended range shells: 36km (22 miles)
CREW:	4

The Msta-S self-propelled howitzer is based on the T-72 and T-80 main battle tanks. The gun can use a range of ammunition types, including a laser-guided round intended for use against hard targets such as armoured vehicles and bunkers. For general-purpose use, cluster submunitions or high explosive/fragmentation rounds are used, with extended-range versions available. A jammer-carrying projectile can also be launched to interfere with enemy radio communications.

Above: A 2S19 Msta moves along the Red Square Moscow Victory Parade of 2010.

TOP-MOUNTED MG
A remotely controlled machine gun is mounted on the top of the vehicle for self-defence.

ASSISTED LOADING
An assisted loading system allows a maximum rate of fire of 8rpm using internally stored ammunition; this drops to 6–7rpm using shells loaded from outside.

CHASSIS
The 2S19 is a fusion of two vehicles: it has the suspension and running gear from the T-80 MBT and the powerplant of the T-72 MBT.

ADVANCED VARIANTS

In 2013, the 2S19M2 Msta-SM entered service with Russian forces. This updated variant includes an advanced automatic fire-control system that increases the rate of fire. From 2017, the 2S33 Msta-SM2 went into production. This includes a new 2A79 152mm (6in) cannon, which extends the range of the system out to 40km (25 miles). The replacement of the 2S19 Msta is expected to be the 2S35 Koalitsiya-SV, which has both a greater range and the ability to fire at a cyclical rate of 20rpm.

LONG REACH
The 2S19 Msta-S howitzer on the Parade at Noviy Arbat Street, 2017. The great length of the gun barrel allows it to maximize its muzzle velocity and range.

M777 155mm Howitzer (2005)

SPECIFICATIONS

GUN LENGTH:	5.08m (16ft 8in)
WEIGHT:	3745kg (8256lb)
CALIBRE:	155mm (6.1in)
ELEVATION:	–5° to +70°
TRAVERSE:	Total 45°
SHELL TYPE:	All US and NATO standard 155mm (6.1in) types; M982 Excalibur GPS-guided munition
EFFECTIVE RANGE:	Standard projectile: 24.69km (15 miles); with rocket-assisted projectile: 30km (19 miles)
CREW:	5–7

The M777 Ultralight Field Howitzer enhances the capabilities of heavy field artillery by providing a lighter and more mobile alternative to the M198 towed howitzer that remains in service with the armed forces of numerous countries. The M777 was developed by BAE Systems' Global Combat Systems Division and entered service with the US Army and Marine Corps in 2005. It has also been deployed by Canadian and Australian artillery units.

Above: The M777's lightweight carriage includes two forward stabilizers and two split trails fitted with self-digging spades and dampers. The standard crew is seven.

CONSTRUCTION
The M777 155mm (6.1in) howitzer incorporates titanium and aluminium alloys in its construction. This accounts for a considerable reduction in weight compared with predecessors such as the M198 155mm (6.1in) howitzer.

DIMENSIONS
The M777's overall travelling length is 9.27m (30ft 3in); its height is just 2.26m (7ft 5in).

EMPLACEMENT
The emplacement time for the M777 is just two minutes 10 seconds, compared to more than six minutes for the M198.

RATE OF FIRE
The M777 utilizes a digital fire-control system similar to that which equips the M109A6 Paladin self-propelled howitzer, and is transported by aircraft, helicopter or medium truck. In its most intense mode of fire, the M777 can fire 4rpm for a maximum duration of two minutes, although the sustained rate of fire is 2rpm.

AFGHAN FIRE MISSION
British soldiers fire an M777 155mm (6.1in) Howitzer field artillery gun at identified Taliban fighting positions near the Sangin District Centre area from an undisclosed forward operating base in the Helmand Province of Afghanistan, 2007.

40mm Bofors L/60 (1929)

SPECIFICATIONS

GUN LENGTH:	6.5m (21ft 4in)
WEIGHT:	1981kg (4568lb)
CALIBRE:	40mm (1.57in)
ELEVATION:	−5° to +90°
TRAVERSE:	360°
RATE OF FIRE:	120rpm
MUZZLE VELOCITY:	854m/sec (2802ft/sec)
EFFECTIVE RANGE:	7200m (7874yd)
CREW:	3

If there was such a thing as a universally acclaimed anti-aircraft weapon during World War II, it was, ironically, a gun developed in a neutral country. The Swedish 40mm (1.57in) Bofors traced its origins to a request from the Swedish Navy, and it was being manufactured under licence throughout Europe by the mid-1930s. The weapon provided a high rate of fire, 120 rounds per minute. It was manufactured in a single-barrel mobile mounting for land forces and a dual configuration for naval applications.

CONTINUOUS FEED

The 40mm (1.57in) Bofors could be fired virtually as an automatic weapon because of its continuous feed capability; the spent case was ejected and a new round thrust into the breech until ammunition had been exhausted from the clip.

SIGHTING

The Bofors had reflector sights for aiming by the trainer and layer, while a third crew-member behind them adjusted the lead via a mechanical computer.

MUZZLE VELOCITY

The weapon's high muzzle velocity, 854m/sec (2802ft/sec), contributed to its success as an anti-aircraft gun.

'ONE SHOT, AND IT'S OURS'

When representatives of Bofors visited foreign countries in the 1930s to demonstrate the weapon, their usual comment was, 'One shot, and the contract is ours.' The Germans manufactured the 40mm (1.57in) Bofors in Norway and designated it the 40mm Flak 28 (Bofors), while the United States fabricated it as the 40mm Gun M1. Large numbers of the weapon were also produced by the British Commonwealth.

MARINE GUNNERS

US Marine air defence gunners of the 3rd Defense Battalion man a 40mm (1.57in) Bofors on Bougainville. Each flag painted on the barrel represents a Japanese plane shot down. The weapon was in service in every theatre of World War II, firing a 0.9kg (1.9lb) shell to a maximum ceiling of 7200m (7874yd).

8.8cm Flak 18 (1933)

SPECIFICATIONS

GUN LENGTH:	4.938m (16ft 2in)
WEIGHT:	4985kg (10,992lb)
CALIBRE:	88mm (3.4in)
ELEVATION:	−3° to +85°
TRAVERSE:	360°
RATE OF FIRE:	15–20rpm
MUZZLE VELOCITY:	840m/sec (2690ft/sec)
EFFECTIVE RANGE:	8000m (8748yd) effective ceiling
CREW:	10

The 8.8cm (3.4in) Flak 18 L/56 was the first of several famous 'Flak 88' anti-aircraft gun models that served in the war. During the inter-war years, Krupp collaborated with the Swedish firm Bofors; the Flak 18, which entered service in 1934, was the result. The design of the Flak 18 was highly innovative. The gun was mounted on a novel firing platform of cruciform design, with four outriggers that were extended to provide a stable firing platform. The slightly modified 8.8cm Flak 36 went into production in the late 1930s. Produced in large numbers, the Flak 18, 36 and 37 became the standard German heavy anti-aircraft weapons of World War II.

Right: The 8.8cm (3.4in) Flak gun was such an effective weapon that it naturally gravitated into several static and vehicular variants. Here we see a 8.8cm Flak 18 Selbstfahrlafette auf Zugkraftwagen 12t, the Flak 18 weapon on a half-track mount.

PRODUCTION

In September 1942, some 5184 Flak 18 and Flak 36 weapons were in German service. With production continuing through to almost the end of the war, the number of Flak 18, 36 and 37s in service peaked at 10,704 in August 1944; by February 1945, this total had declined to 8769 weapons.

RATE OF FIRE
With a well-trained crew, the hand-loaded weapon could obtain a maximum rate of fire of 15rpm.

RANGE
The gun fired its high-explosive round with a muzzle velocity of 840m/sec (2690ft/sec) and could obtain a maximum vertical range of 8000m (8748yd).

ANTI-TANK CAPABILITY
Although the weapon was optimized for the anti-aircraft role (for which it fired high-explosive rounds), it also had a useful ground combat capability, firing armour-piercing shells. In the ground role, the gun could penetrate 88mm (3.4in) of vertical armour at a range of 2000m (2187yd).

TOWED 88MM FLAK, SDKFZ 7
The Sdkfz 7 (this one with its canvas roof erected) was the principal prime mover employed for the 8.8cm (3.4in) Flak 18; for movement, the weapon was attached to two single-axle bogie assemblies, a process that took under three minutes.

3.7in QF Gun Mk I (1937)

SPECIFICATIONS

GUN LENGTH:	8.6m (28ft 3in)
WEIGHT:	9317kg (20,541lb)
CALIBRE:	94mm (3.7in)
ELEVATION:	−5 to +80°
TRAVERSE:	360°
RATE OF FIRE:	10–20rpm
MUZZLE VELOCITY:	Mk VI: 1044m/sec (3425ft/sec)
EFFECTIVE RANGE:	Horizontal: 5.6km (3.5 miles); slant: 12km (7.5 miles); ceiling Mk I–II: 9754m (10,667yd)
CREW:	7

Vickers produced the first Ordnance QF 3.7in Mark I, which was capable of firing a 12.9kg (28.4lb) projectile to a ceiling of 9754m (10,667yd). The large weapon weighed 9317kg (20,541lb); the army's requirement that it be mobile could only partially be met due to issues surrounding the carriage, which was improved in the subsequent Mark II and Mark III versions as the war progressed.

Right: A full battery of 12 British QF 3.7in anti-aircraft guns fires skyward at an extremely high trajectory. The occasion was a celebration of victory in Europe, May 1945.

BARREL
The bore of the 3.5in gun featured a sophisticated system of 'RD' (Research Department) Rifling, which worked with the shell design to improve the aerodynamics and velocity of the shell in flight.

FUSE SETTING
The gun was originally hand-loaded, but in 1943 the 'Machine Fuse Setting No 11' was introduced that took a round of ammunition, set the fuse, loaded and fired it, so boosting the rate of fire to 25rpm.

GERMAN USE
Although it was slow to gain the appreciation of gun crews, the 3.7in cannon ultimately proved to be an outstanding performer. By 1941, it was the primary anti-aircraft weapon in use by the British Army. The Germans respected the weapon highly. They used those they captured in coastal defences, renaming them the 94mm Flak Vickers M.39(e), and even manufactured ammunition for them.

MOUNTS
Mobile and static mountings were built, the static having a large counterweight arm above the breech. By the end of the war, most guns had remote power control: all the gunners had to do was load it and clean it.

FIELD GUN
Germany, February 1945: British gunners use an Ordnance QF 3.7in anti-aircraft gun as a field artillery piece, delivering indirect fire on targets along the Siegfried Line.

3.7cm Flak 36 (1937)

SPECIFICATIONS

GUN LENGTH:	3.62m (11ft 10in)
WEIGHT:	1784kg (3925lb)
CALIBRE:	37mm (1.46in)
ELEVATION:	–7° 30' to +90°
TRAVERSE:	360°
RATE OF FIRE:	160rpm
MUZZLE VELOCITY:	820m/sec (2690ft/sec)
EFFECTIVE RANGE:	4800m (5240yd)
CREW:	5

In the late 1930s, the Germans developed the 3.7cm (1.46in) Flak 36 anti-aircraft gun, an upgraded development of the existing 3.7cm Flak 18. The employment of 3.7cm Flak cannon offered the Germans greater range and hitting power than the existing 20mm (0.79in) weapons. The weapon comprised the long-barrelled (L/57) cannon mounted onto either a fixed platform or the new lightweight single-axle wheeled Sonderanhänger 52 carriage. In 1942–44, the firms of Dürkropp, DWM and Skoda produced more than 4500 Flak 36 and Flak 37 weapons.

Above: The 3.7cm (1.46in) Flak guns were just as useful for direct-fire infantry support as they were for anti-aircraft use.

FLASH SUPPRESSOR
Left-side view of a 3.7cm (1.46in)Flak 36 with its gun shield folded down; note the typical conical flash suppressor fitted to the barrel's muzzle.

CHAMBER
The chamber of the Flak 36 was slightly shorter than that of the Flak 18 to accommodate new ammunition types; it had a soft iron driving band rather than copper.

TRAILER
The two-wheeled Sonderanhänger 52 carriage was both light and manoeuvrable, enabling a very quick deployment of the Flak 36 into action.

SIGHTING VARIANTS

The 3.7cm (1.46in) Flak 37 was developed as a variant of the Flak 36. This was identical to the latter, except that it used the Zeiss Flakvisier 37 sighting mechanism rather than the Flakvisier 35 or 36 device used in the Flak 36 weapon; small numbers of the Flak 37 alternatively employed the Flakvisier 40 sighting device.

HALF-TRACK MOUNT

The 3.7cm (1.46in) Flak 18, 36 and 37 guns all found themselves on various vehicular mounts. The gun itself developed a sustained tactical rate-of-fire of 80rpm, and a theoretical maximum cyclic rate-of-fire of 160rpm.

2cm Flak 38 L/65 (1939)

SPECIFICATIONS

GUN LENGTH:	4.08m (13ft 5in)
WEIGHT:	450kg (992lb)
CALIBRE:	20mm (0.79in)
ELEVATION:	−12°to ±90°
TRAVERSE:	360°
RATE OF FIRE:	120–180rpm
MUZZLE VELOCITY:	900m/sec (2953ft/sec)
EFFECTIVE RANGE:	2200m (2406yd)
CREW:	5

In the late 1930s, the Germans developed the 2cm (0.79in) Flak 38, an improved version of the existing ubiquitous 2cm Flak 30, already serving in very large numbers. This new 20mm (0.79in) weapon addressed two of the latter's main deficiencies: its slow sustained tactical rate of fire of 120rpm, and its ammunition feed problems. The weapon typically consisted of the long-barrelled gun, fitted with a well-sloped dual-angle splinter shield, mounted either on a fixed firing platform or a Sonderanhänger single-axle wheeled trailer.

Above: The Flakpanzer 38(t) anti-aircraft AFV mounted the 2cm (0.79in) Flak 38 L/65 cannon onto the rear of the restructured Panzer 38(t) Model M tank chassis; during 1943–44, the Germans produced 142 of these vehicles.

FLAKVIERLING 38

In the late 1930s, Mauser developed for the Kriegsmarine the 2cm (0.79in) Flakvierling 38, a quadruple mounting of the existing Flak 38. The weapon proved so effective that it was subsequently produced for both the Army and the Luftwaffe. The weapon consisted of two vertically paired 20mm (0.79in) cannon situated either side of a pedestal mounting.

WEIGHT OF FIRE

The sustained practical weight of fire of the four combined cannon – 880rpm – was astonishing. Low-flying enemy aircraft that entered the stream of bullets the weapon sent skywards stood a high probability of being downed.

MASS PRODUCTION

Under mass production in 1935–44, the Flak 38 became the Army's standard flak weapon during 1940 and supplanted the 2cm (0.79in) Flak 30, although it never ousted the latter completely. Employed by all branches of the Wehrmacht, it also appeared mounted on various fixed and mobile platforms. The combined total of Flak 30s and 38s in service peaked in March 1944 at 19,692 before declining sharply to 10,531 by February 1945.

HALFTRACK AA GUN

A German Wehrmacht crew gather around a halftrack-mounted Flak 38 in a wood.

Oerlikon 20mm (1939)

SPECIFICATIONS

GUN LENGTH:	2.2m (7ft 3in)
WEIGHT:	68.04kg (150lb)
CALIBRE:	20mm (0.79in)
ELEVATION:	−15° to +90°
TRAVERSE:	360°
RATE OF FIRE:	450rpm
MUZZLE VELOCITY:	820m/sec (2700ft/sec)
EFFECTIVE RANGE:	914m (1000yd)
CREW:	Up to 5

The Swiss 20mm (0.79in) Oerlikon cannon was manufactured in the United Kingdom and many other countries, and was one of the most important weapons of its type in use during World War II. After 1935, the Oerlikon was produced in the United Kingdom for the Royal Navy so that by 1939 there were considerable numbers of this weapon in use.

Right: On the coastline of Normandy in 1944, a British 20mm (0.79in) triple Oerlikon is mounted over a captured German 8.8cm (3.4in) Pak 43 gun emplacement.

MOUNT VARIATIONS

By 1940, Oerlikons were being pressed into service on land mountings of all kinds. Some of these British mountings were simple in the extreme; others, such as the Haszard semi-mobile mount, were much more 'formal'. Later in the war, a triple-gun mounting with the three guns one over the other was placed into production; some of these types of mounts were later used on trucks.

MOUNTING
Although used mainly as a naval weapon, many were employed by land forces. This is the British HB Mk 1 mounting.

FEED
The Oerlikon normally used a 60-round drum magazine for the feed system, but a 20-round box magazine was used on some versions.

BLOWBACK
The Oerlikon was a blowback-operated gun; the action was assisted by the large recoil springs around the barrel that were a recognition feature of the weapon.

NAVAL OERLIKONS
Twin 20mm (0.79in) Oerlikons are cleaned aboard the Indian Navy sloop HMIS *Naradba* late in the war. Still in service at sea after more than 70 years, the Oerlikon is now rarely encountered in towed form.

90mm Gun M2 (1940)

SPECIFICATIONS

GUN LENGTH:	Travelling length: 9.02m (29ft 7in)
WEIGHT:	Complete: 14,651kg (32,300lb)
CALIBRE:	90mm (3.54in)
ELEVATION:	+80°/–10°
TRAVERSE:	360°
RATE OF FIRE:	27rpm
MUZZLE VELOCITY:	823m/sec (2700ft/sec)
EFFECTIVE RANGE:	12,040m (13,167yd)
CREW:	8

The 90mm (3.54in) Gun M2 was a much revised version of the earlier M1; it used a new carriage with a turntable, a power rammer, fuse setter and other changes. This resulted in an excellent gun, but one that was slow and expensive to produce.

Right: The M2 gun (seen here in its travelling configuration) gave a stout defence, most interestingly against the V-1 'Doodlebug' flying bombs launched from the Low Countries. The weapon was also used on the 90mm (3.54in) M36 tank-destroyer.

RATE OF FIRE
The rate of fire was 27rpm under electrical power, or 15rpm via manual operation.

AA FUSING
In late 1944, the 90mm (3.54in) gun was used as one of the first weapons on land to fire the new proximity-fused round, one of the most advanced weapon developments of the war years. Using this fuse, one gunner managed to shoot down an Fw 190 fighter with a single shot during the Ardennes campaign.

COASTAL DEFENCE
The 90mm (3.54in) gun in all its forms was manufactured in large numbers. By August 1945, a total of 7831 of all types had been produced. This total included some guns intended for static mounting only. Some guns were used around the coasts of the continental United States in a dual anti-aircraft/coastal defence role; the M2 (unlike the M1 and M1A1) could depress below the horizontal to engage beach targets below.

EMPLACED GUN
This 90mm (3.54in) M1 anti-aircraft gun is dug in as a beach defence. Other emplacements can be seen in this image, including one at the left rear containing the battery's rangefinder and other related fire-control equipment. In this instance, the gun mount is the M1A1 model; the later M2 mount used a turntable.

M163 Vulcan Air Defense System (1961)

SPECIFICATIONS

DIMENSIONS:	Length: 4.86m (15ft 11in); Width: 2.85m (9ft 4in); Height: 2.59m (8ft 6in)
WEIGHT:	12,310kg (27,139lb)
CALIBRE:	20mm (0.79in)
ELEVATION:	+80° to −5°
TRAVERSE:	360°
RATE OF FIRE:	3000rpm
EFFECTIVE RANGE:	3000m (3280yd)
MUZZLE VELOCITY:	1030m/sec (3380ft/sec)
CREW:	4

The M163 Vulcan Air Defense System (VADS) consists of a 20mm (0.79in) Gatling-type cannon mounted upon an M113 APC chassis. In the early 1960s, Rock Island Arsenal developed two 20mm Vulcan air defence systems. The self-propelled model was based on a modified M113 APC chassis and was designated XM163, while the towed model was the XM167. The M163 was retired from US military service in 1994, after seeing service in the ground-support role during Operation Desert Storm.

RATES OF FIRE
The 20mm (0.79in) cannon has two rates of fire in this application: 1000 and 3000rpm. The former is normally used for engagement of ground targets, while the higher rate of fire is used against aerial targets.

AMMUNITION
Ammunition types that can be fired include APT, TP (target practice), HEI, TPT and HEI-T. All have a muzzle velocity of 1030m/sec (3380ft/sec). Maximum effective range in the anti-aircraft role is 1600m (1750yd) and in the ground role 3000m (3280yd).

TURRET
The turret can be traversed through 360° at a speed of 60° per second.

CHASSIS
The M163 consists of a standard M113 chassis on top of which has been mounted an electrically operated turret fitted with a 20mm (0.79in) six-barrelled M61-series cannon.

VIETNAM DEPLOYMENT
In the early 1960s, Rock Island Arsenal developed a self-propelled air-defence system based on the M113 armoured personnel carrier chassis: this became the M163 Vulcan. GEC began production and the vehicle was soon being deployed to Vietnam, where it was widely used by both US and South Vietnamese troops in a ground-support role. The fast-firing M163 was useful for intense 'reconnaissance by fire' in Vietnam's jungles, although it sometimes lacked distance penetration against reinforced targets.

FIRE CONTROL
In this view of the M163, we can clearly see the AN/VPS-2 range-only radar mounted on the turret. The radar is supplemented by the M61 optical lead-calculating sight.

ZSU-23-4 (1962)

SPECIFICATIONS

DIMENSIONS:	Length: 6.54m (21ft 5in); Width: 3.12m (10ft 3in); Height: 2.58m (8ft 5in)
WEIGHT:	19 tonnes (18.7 tons)
CALIBRE:	23mm (0.9in)
ELEVATION:	−10° to +90°
TRAVERSE:	360°
RATE OF FIRE:	2000rpm
EFFECTIVE RANGE:	1500m (1640yd)
MUZZLE VELOCITY:	970m/sec (3182ftsec)
CREW:	4

The quadruple-barrelled, self-propelled ZSU-23-4 anti-aircraft system proved a formidable weapon in combination with surface-to-air missile batteries. It served as the primary close-support air defence gun for the Soviet Red Army and numerous other nations for three decades.

COMBAT RECORD

The ZSU-23-4 was developed in the 1960s as the replacement for the ZSU-57-2. Although it had a shorter firing range, the radar fire-control and an increased firing rate made the weapon much more effective. The chassis was similar to that of the SA-6 surface-to-air missile (SAM) system and used components of the PT-76 tank. Known to the Soviets as the 'Shilka', the vehicle can create an impassable wall of anti-aircraft fire over an 180° arc. Widely exported, the ZSU-23-4 was particularly effective in Egyptian hands during the Yom Kippur War of 1973, bringing down Israeli aircraft that were forced to fly low by the Egyptian missile defence system. It also saw extensive combat service with the North Vietnamese during the Vietnam War, bringing down numerous American aircraft.

RADAR DETECTION
The RPK-2 Tobol radar, referred to as 'Gun Dish' in the West, was capable of picking up aircraft at a distance of 20km (12 miles) away.

ARMOUR PROTECTION
The maximum armour thickness of 9.2mm (0.36in) in the hull and 8.3mm (0.32in) in the turret was sufficient to withstand only small arms and shell fragments.

MAIN ARMAMENT
Four turret-mounted 23mm (0.9in) AZP-23 water-cooled autocannons with a cyclical rate of fire up to 1000rpm posed a significant threat to helicopters and low-flying aircraft.

TURRET
The welded turret was adapted from the T-54 main battle tank and was fully stabilized to allow accurate fire on the move.

SUSPENSION
The individual torsion bar suspension supported the GM-575 tracked vehicle chassis and included six road wheels with rubber tyres, rear drive sprockets, and one idler wheel on each side.

ENGINE
The 209kW (280hp) six-cylinder V-6R diesel engine was somewhat underpowered for the ZSU-23-4 – which weighed up to 19 tonnes (18.6 tons) – particularly when traversing rugged terrain.

IRAQI WRECK
An Iraqi 'Shilka' lies wrecked in the desert. The ZSU-23-4 is divided into three compartments: the engine situated at the rear; the fighting compartment, housing the commander, gunner and radar operator, in the centre; and the driver forward. Unlike the other crewmen, the driver benefitted from an electric heating system and better air flow.

Flakpanzer Gepard (1970)

TYPE · *Anti-Aircraft Artillery* · FAMILY · *Artillery & Mortars*

SPECIFICATIONS

DIMENSIONS:	Length: 7.68m (25ft 2in); Width: 3.71m (12ft 2in); Height: 3.29m (10ft 10in) radar retracted
WEIGHT:	47,300kg (104,060lb)
CALIBRE:	35mm (1.4in)
ELEVATION:	−5°/+92°
TRAVERSE:	360°
RATE OF FIRE:	550rpm (per barrel)
MUZZLE VELOCITY:	1175m/sec (3850ft/sec)
EFFECTIVE RANGE:	5500m (6015yd)
CREW:	4

The Gepard self-propelled anti-aircraft gun system was designed specifically to protect armoured formations. The system uses the hull of the Leopard 1 main battle tank to carry a welded-steel turret capable of powered traverse through 360° and accommodating the weapon system.

FEATURES

The two 35mm (1.4in) cannon are located externally to avoid the problem of gun gas in the fighting compartment. Ammunition types include high-explosive and armour-piercing. The fire-control system is based on a computer supplied with target data by two radars: the acquisition unit and the tracking unit. Other features are optical sights and a land navigation system. Its radar-controlled guns often work in tandem with teams of infantrymen using the shoulder-fired Stinger anti-aircraft missile, designed to shoot down low-flying fixed-wing aircraft and helicopters.

AIR DEFENCE
Deployed primarily to provide air defence for armoured formations, the Gepard utilizes high-explosive and armour-piercing ammunition fired from a pair of 35mm (1.4in) autocannon.

CYCLIC RATE
Each of the weapons has a cyclic rate of fire of 550rpm, although it is standard procedure to fire bursts of between 20 and 40 rounds.

ENGINE
The engine is a 10-cylinder MTU multi-fuel engine generating 610kW (819hp) and a top speed of 65km/h (40mph).

GERMAN SERVICE
The biggest user of the Gepard, Germany, has had many of these vehicles in storage since 2010; they are being progressively replaced by the 'SysFla', a mobile and stationary air defence system using the LFK NG short-range SAM and the new MANTIS 35mm (1.4in) gun system.

5cm Pak 38 L/60 (1940)

SPECIFICATIONS

GUN LENGTH:	3.2m (10ft 5in)
WEIGHT:	986kg (2169lb)
CALIBRE:	50mm (1.96in)
ELEVATION:	–8° to +27°
TRAVERSE:	65°
SHELL TYPE:	AP, HE
MUZZLE VELOCITY:	AP: 835m/sec (2900ft/sec)
EFFECTIVE RANGE:	AP: 1800m (1969yd), HE: 2600m (2843yd)
CREW:	5

Even before the deficiencies of the 3.7cm (1.46in) Pak 35/36 anti-tank gun had been exposed, Rheinmetall-Borsig had begun developing a more potent replacement weapon, the 5cm Pak 38. This entered service in autumn 1940. The 50mm (1.96in) gun, fitted to a large splinter shield, was relatively light and mounted on an easily manoeuvrable single-axle split-trail carriage. Like many German anti-tank guns, when being moved tactically it was towed by a Sdkfz 251 half-track. In total, Rheinmetall-Borsig manufactured 9504 Pak 38 guns.

Above: The Pak 38 appeared in 1940 after the campaign in France was over. Firing a tungsten-cored armour-piercing shot, it soon showed that it could defeat any Allied tank then in service.

MUZZLE BRAKE
The muzzle brake at the end of the long barrel helped to keep recoil forces to manageable levels.

AMMUNITION
Although the use of tungsten ceased in 1942, the Pak 38 still fired a useful AP/HE shell and remained in use throughout the war, since it was capable of dealing with light tanks and armoured vehicles.

MOUNT
As well as being a towed gun (split trail with tubular legs), the gun was also placed on a wide variety of tracked mountings.

FRONTLINE INTRODUCTION

During the summer 1941 Axis invasion of the Soviet Union, small numbers of 5cm (1.96in) Pak 38 guns equipped a single platoon within the anti-tank companies of elite Army and Waffen-SS motorized divisions. Subsequently, the gun remained in large-scale production in 1942–43, with 8500 examples produced in this period. It became the standard anti-tank weapon of the German Army, gradually replacing the 3.7cm (1.46in) Pak 35/36 in frontline service.

ARTILLERY PIECE
A 5cm (1.96in) PaK 38 (L/60) on display at the Sapun Mountain Memorial complex near Sevastopol. The Pak 38 was the first anti-tank gun to get away from the lightweight 'two men and push it' class of weapon and into the full-scale artillery class, requiring seven men and a tractor.

7.5cm Pak 40 L/46 (1940)

SPECIFICATIONS

GUN LENGTH:	3.7m (12ft 1in)
WEIGHT:	1.5 tonnes (1.37 tons)
CALIBRE:	75mm (2.95in)
ELEVATION:	–5° to +22°
TRAVERSE:	65°
SHELL TYPE:	AP, APCBC, HE
MUZZLE VELOCITY:	APCBC: 792m/sec (2598ft/sec)
EFFECTIVE RANGE:	AP: 2000m (2187yd); HE: 7500m (8202yd)
CREW:	6

Developmental work on a new 75mm (2.95in) anti-tank gun had begun in Germany in 1939 even as work on the 5cm (1.96in) Pak 38 unfolded. To speed up development, the Germans designed the new 7.5cm (2.95in) weapon as a scaled-up copy of the Pak 38. The Pak 40 was a large but low-silhouetted and easy-to-conceal weapon that resembled its smaller progenitor, the Pak 38. The Pak 40 served on all fronts right through until the war's end in May 1945.

Above: A Waffen-SS gun crew man a 7.5cm (2.95in) Pak 40 on the Eastern Front. A large number were taken over at the end of the war and put into service by several European armies trying to re-equip.

EARLY DESIGN
This early-production 7.5cm (2.95in) Pak 40 sports the initial design single-baffle muzzle-brake as well as spoked steel wheels; later examples featured one of two slightly modified muzzle-brake designs.

SHIELD
The long-barrelled (L/46) cannon was fitted to a three-sided angular splinter shield.

BALLISTIC PERFORMANCE
Firing the 7.5cm (2.95in) Panzergrenate Patrone 39 armour-piercing, capped, ballistic-capped (APCBC) round at a muzzle velocity of 792m/sec (2598ft/sec), the gun could penetrate at 500m (547yd) some 135mm (5.3in) of vertical and 106mm (4.2in) of 30-degree sloped armour.

LAYOUT
The gun was mounted on top of a standard-design single-axled, pneumatic-tyred, split-trail carriage.

EASTERN FRONT
The first examples of this new weapon, the 7.5cm (2.95in) Pak 40 L/46, were rushed to the Eastern Front just as the Soviet winter 1941–42 counteroffensive erupted. The troops of the hard-pressed and out-flanked German defensive 'hedgehogs', like those at Velikiye Luki, were relieved when they discovered the new weapon's potent tank-killing powers; it could despatch even the feared T-34 and KV-1 tanks. The only defect was its weight, which led to several being abandoned in retreats in the Russian winter when they became so bogged in mud that the eight-man crew could not move it.

AWAITING TARGETS
A Pak 40 gun crew wait behind their weapon in a well-camouflaged position. The gun was first issued in 1941 and became the standard anti-tank gun for the remainder of the war; as long as the crew kept their nerve and let the tank get close, they could destroy any Allied tank.

3in Gun M5 (1940)

SPECIFICATIONS

GUN LENGTH:	4.02m (13ft 2in)
WEIGHT:	Travelling: 2653kg (5850lb)
CALIBRE:	76.2mm (3in)
ELEVATION:	–5.5° to +30°
TRAVERSE:	46°
SHELL TYPE:	AP, APC
MUZZLE VELOCITY:	AP: 793m/sec (2600ft/sec); APC: 853m/sec (2800ft/sec)
EFFECTIVE RANGE:	1830m (2000yd)
CREW:	6

The 3in Antitank Gun M5 was an improvised weapon using the barrel of an anti-aircraft gun and the breech and carriage of a 105mm (3in) howitzer together with some new components. The gun itself was taken from the 3in Antiaircraft Gun M3, but the chamber had to be altered slightly to take different ammunition. The new gun was modified to take the breech mechanism of the 105mm (3in) howitzer M2A1, then in full-scale production; the same howitzer was used to supply the carriage and the recoil system. The new carriage became the Gun Carriage M1. In this form, the original straight shield of the 105mm howitzer was retained. In time, the shield was modified to have sloping shield plates: this became the Gun Carriage M6.

Above: US soldiers of the 1st Battalion, 327th Glider Infantry Regiment, 101st Airborne Division, fire a 3in M5 anti-tank gun from a barn at Haguenau, France on 31 January 1945.

SHIELD
The protective shield on the original gun was flat, but was sloped with subsequent upgrades to provide improved deflection of bullets and shell fragments.

BARREL
Utilizing the barrel of an anti-aircraft gun gave the M5 the high velocities necessary to puncture armour.

BREECH
The M5's breech was that of the M2 105mm (3in) howitzer, but firing fixed, cased ammunition.

REDISCOVERY

When the M5 was first developed, the ammunition gave problems, and enthusiasm for the gun faded. The problems were solved by early 1944, but by that time the Army was more interested in SP guns and other weapons, so the 3in was more or less forgotten. After the invasion of Europe, it was hurriedly rediscovered and put to good use, since it was the only towed anti-tank gun the Americans had that was bigger than their 57mm (2in) weapon.

WEIGHT ISSUES

In action, the M5 was capable of penetrating up to 84mm (3.3in) of sloping armour at ranges of almost 2000m (2190yd). However, the M5 had a disadvantage in its weight. Rapid movement of the M5 proved to be a major task, and a heavy 6 × 6 truck had to be used to tow the weapon, although lighter tractors could be used on occasions where the terrain permitted.

Ordnance QF 17pdr Gun (1942)

SPECIFICATIONS

GUN LENGTH:	3.56m (11ft 8in)
WEIGHT:	2923kg (6444lb)
CALIBRE:	76.2mm (3in)
ELEVATION:	–6° to +16.5°
TRAVERSE:	60°
SHELL TYPE:	HE, AP, APC, APDS
MUZZLE VELOCITY:	950m/sec (2900ft/sec)
EFFECTIVE RANGE:	3000m (3280yd)
CREW:	7

The Ordnance QF 17pdr was introduced as a prototype in August 1942, and rushed into service in North Africa on the carriage of the 25pdr to address the threat of the new Tiger tanks. Not until 1943, during the Italian Campaign, did the 17pdr gun reach the battlefield in significant numbers. The weapon appeared to be unwieldy, particularly due to the length of its barrel, vertical breechblock and muzzle brake, but it was actually relatively simple to handle. It became the supreme tank killer on the Allied side. As the war neared its end, the gun had become standard among the Royal Artillery.

BREECH
The breech of the 17pdr was a semi-automatic vertical sliding type, which was reliable under intense combat use.

RATE OF FIRE
The rate of fire for such a large gun was impressive, up to 10rpm.

CARRIAGE
The standard mount was a very heavy two-wheeled split-trail type, the bulk of the carriage necessary to absorb the gun's hefty recoil.

PENETRATION
The weapon's armour-piercing discarding sabot (APDS) projectile could penetrate 231mm (9in) of armour plating from a distance of 914m (1000yd).

ARMOURED AND NAVAL APPLICATIONS

Primarily a towed anti-tank gun, the 17pdr was also adapted to tank and self-propelled guns, notably the Valentine, Mk I, Archer, the M10 Achilles and the Sherman Firefly. When the Firefly arrived at the frontlines in 1944, it was one of the most potent armoured vehicles on the battlefield, capable of killing the latest German Panther and Tiger tanks. Large numbers of the 17pdr were also used by the Royal Navy to arm landing craft.

HYBRID GUN
A British 17pdr Mk 2 AT gun mounted on 25pdr carriage, here seen in action at Medenine, North Africa, 1943.

SPECIFICATIONS

GUN LENGTH:	4.18m (13ft 8in) L/42.6
WEIGHT:	1116kg (2460lb)
CALIBRE:	76mm (3in)
ELEVATION:	–5° to +37°
TRAVERSE:	54°
SHELL TYPE:	AP, HE
MUZZLE VELOCITY:	680m/sec (2230ft/sec)
EFFECTIVE RANGE:	13,290m (14,534yd)
CREW:	5

Design of the ZiS-3 began in late 1940. It was essentially a combination of the F-22 USV's barrel and the carriage of the 57mm (2.24in) ZiS-2 anti-tank gun. Despite a lack of official support, the designer, Vasiliy Grabin, took the enormous risk of authorizing production himself and persuaded the Red Army to accept guns for unofficial combat trials. Enthusiastic reports on these guns prompted an official demonstration attended by Stalin. He was deeply impressed by the ZiS-3, describing it as '…a masterpiece of artillery systems design.' With his support, production began in early 1942 with the highest priority; more than 103,000 were completed by the end of the war.

Above: Here, the crew of a ZiS-3 take a break and have something to eat during a quiet period during operations on the Eastern Front.

MUZZLE BRAKE
A muzzle brake was fitted to prevent the recoil damaging the relatively lightweight carriage.

HEIGHT
All anti-tank guns should have a low profile; the ZiS-3 was no exception, with a height of just 1.37m (4ft 6in).

BREECH
The breech was of the semi-automatic vertical sliding-wedge type, taking fixed ammunition.

RATE OF FIRE
The ZiS-3 was a fast-firing gun, with a maximum possible rate of 25rpm.

HANDLING

The ZiS-3 was frequently used in the direct-fire role. A crewman recalled that: 'Two holes were made to the left and right of the gun's wheels – one for the gunner, the other for the loader. ZIS-3 guns didn't require simultaneous presence of the entire crew near the gun… it was usually enough for only one person to be present. The gunner, after firing, could hide himself in his hole while the loader would drive the next shell into the barrel. Now the gunner could take his place, aim, and fire, and the loader would be taking cover at that time. Even after a direct hit into the gun at least one of the two had a chance to survive.'

STREET BATTLE
A Soviet gun crew prepare to fire their ZiS-3 in the shattered streets of Hungary, Budapest, in early 1945.

Ordnance ML 3in Mortar (1932)

SPECIFICATIONS

LENGTH:	1.3m (4ft 3in)
WEIGHT:	52.4kg (115lb)
CALIBRE:	76.2mm (3in)
ELEVATION:	+45° to +80°
TRAVERSE:	11°
SHELL WEIGHT:	4.5kg (10lb)
MUZZLE VELOCITY:	198m/sec (650ft/sec)
EFFECTIVE RANGE:	Mk 1: 1463m (1600yd); Mk 2: 2560m (2800yd)
RATE OF FIRE:	10rpm
CREW:	3

In the late 1920s, the British infantry were asking for some sort of light gun for close support, and there were plans to equip special 'light batteries' of artillery for this role. But financial considerations and manpower questions were very powerful arguments, and at the last moment this design of mortar was accepted instead. A conventional Stokes-type mortar, drop-fired, wartime experience showed that it had insufficient range (2377m/2600yd) compared to its German equivalent, the 81mm (3.18in) Model 34. A new and stronger barrel was designed to fire the same bomb but with a more powerful propelling charge, which put the range up to 2560m (2800yd). This became the Mark 2 mortar; it was to remain in service until replaced by the 81mm (3.18in) mortar in the 1960s.

Above: Australian troops fire a 3in mortar during operations in New Guinea, 1942–44.

EXTRA RANGE

The issue of adding extra range capability to the ML 3in mortar became a constant struggle for British weapon designers during World War II. Most of the efforts focused on manufacturing the barrel of the mortar in heavier weights of steel that could cope with more substantial propellant charges. The work did not pay off; either the barrels bulged or the accuracy was compromised by the more intense recoil.

OPTICAL SIGHT
The optical sight for the mortar was fitted directly onto the barrel tube, a factor that could affect its accuracy.

ELEVATION
The elevation system on the bipod could be adjusted so that mortar shells could be dropped as close as 114m (125yd) from the tube.

BASEPLATE
The octagonal steel baseplate was fitted with spikes to provide additional resistance against slippage under recoil.

MORTAR CREW
British soldiers of the 1st Dorsets target German positions in Hottot, Normandy, with their 3in mortars, July 1944.

sGrW 34 8cm Mortar (1934)

SPECIFICATIONS

LENGTH:	1.14m (3ft 9in)
WEIGHT:	62kg (136lb)
CALIBRE:	81.4mm (3.2in)
ELEVATION:	45° to 90°
TRAVERSE:	Up to 23°
SHELL WEIGHT:	3.5kg (7lb 11oz)
MUZZLE VELOCITY:	174m/sec (571ft/sec)
EFFECTIVE RANGE:	2400m (2625yd) maximum
RATE OF FIRE:	15–25rpm
CREW:	3

STANDARD MORTAR

The sGrW 34 was sturdy enough to survive the rigours of combat and proved a reliable weapon. It soon acquired a good reputation for accuracy, thanks to its RA-35 dial sight, which in contrast to the British mortars had its deflection marked in mils instead of degrees and yards. This medium mortar remained the standard German infantry mortar throughout World War II, being employed in large numbers in every campaign in which the Wehrmacht fought. The weapon was usually operated by a three-man team.

The 8cm schwere Granatwerfer 34 (SGrW 34) medium mortar was the first such weapon to be developed by the Germans, entering service in late 1934. Developmental work had started as far back as 1923. The mortar was actually an 81.4mm (3.2in)-calibre weapon, despite its designation as an 8cm mortar. In the late 1930s, the slightly modified 8cm GrW 34/1 was developed for employment from armoured vehicles, such as half-tracks and tractors.

Right: On the Eastern Front, a German paratrooper mortar team prepare to fire the 8cm sGrW 34.

TRAVERSING GEAR
Side view of an 8cm sGrW 34 medium mortar, with bipod and barrel and base plate; at the top of the bipod is the weapon's traversing gear and elevating mechanism.

BOMB
The weapon fired a decently sized 3.4kg (7.5lb) warhead out to a maximum distance of 2400m (2625yd).

BARREL LENGTH
The mortar was sizable, with a barrel length of 1.14m (3ft 9in) and a weight of 62kg (137lb).

WAFFEN-SS TEAM
A Waffen-SS 8cm sGrW34 mortar crew readies the weapon for action. Note the mortar bombs stacked ready for quick feeding.

SPECIFICATIONS

LENGTH:	Barrel length: 1862mm (73.3in); Bore length: 1536mm (60.47in)
WEIGHT:	Weight in action: 280kg (617lb); Weight travelling: 477.6kg (1052lb)
CALIBRE:	120mm (4.72in)
ELEVATION:	45° to 80°
TRAVERSE:	60°
SHELL WEIGHT:	HE: 16kg (35lb)
MUZZLE VELOCITY:	158m/sec (518ft/sec)
EFFECTIVE RANGE:	6000m (6561yd)
CREW:	6

The Soviet 120mm (4.72in) Model 1938 (120-HM 38) was another scaled-up version of the 82mm (3.2in) Model 1937. It used the same carriage as the 107mm (4.21in) Model 1938, but this was usually attached to a two-wheeled limber with an ammunition box containing 20 bombs. The mortar's firepower and mobility impressed the Germans, who eagerly took any captured examples into service as the 12cm Granatwerfer 378(r). Enthusiastic reports from units issued with these weapons prompted the Germans to manufacture a copy as the 12cm Granatwerfer 42.

Above: A 120-HM 38 on tow behind a Willys MB Jeep. A few ready-use bombs would probably be carried in the towing vehicle, with the main supply in limbers towed by other jeeps.

ADJUSTMENT
Elevation and traverse controls were on the bipod legs, with elevation of 45° to 80° and traverse of 60°.

WEIGHT
With an in-action weight of 280kg (617lb), the 120-HM 38 needed a six-man crew to operate it.

BASEPLATE
The circular baseplate was designed to facilitate rapid changes in traverse without having to raise and move the baseplate itself.

SHIFTING BASEPLATE
Although the 120-HM 38 was a solid combat performer, it did have a tendency for the baseplate to dig into soft ground over extended periods of firing (as many mortars do), necessitating re-aiming. To counteract this, the Soviets introduced a spring-loaded shock absorber mounted on the bipod. This weapon became the 120-HM 43, which is still seen in service around the world today.

STALINGRAD
A 120-HM 38 firing in support of the defenders of Stalingrad, December 1942. Note the hefty dimensions of the shell.

60mm Mortar M2 (1941)

SPECIFICATIONS

LENGTH:	726mm (28.6in)
WEIGHT:	61.7kg (136lb)
CALIBRE:	60mm (2.36in)
ELEVATION:	+40° to +85°
TRAVERSE:	7°
SHELL WEIGHT:	1.33kg (2.94lb)
MUZZLE VELOCITY:	158m/sec (518ft/sec)
EFFECTIVE RANGE:	3008m (3290yd)
RATE OF FIRE:	18rpm
CREW:	3

The US Army began examining mortars in the late 1920s. They eventually bought this design from Edgar Brandt, the French ordnance engineer, and manufactured it under licence in the USA. It was of the usual pattern, a smooth-bore tube on a baseplate, supported by a simple bipod with elevation and traverse mechanism. The firing pin was fixed in the base cap of the tube, and the bomb fired automatically as it was dropped down the barrel.

Above: Two GIs from the US 100th Infantry Battalion fire a 60mm (2.36in) mortar, 1943.

AMMUNITION
The M2 was a basic weapon, fitted with a simple optical sight. It was provided with high-explosive (light and heavy varieties), smoke and illuminating bombs. The latter were found to be useful not only for their usual job of battlefield illumination, but also for anti-tank teams, firing the bomb beyond the enemy tank so as to silhouette it at night. The M57 WP shell could also lay down white phosphorous, which had both obscuration and anti-personnel effects.

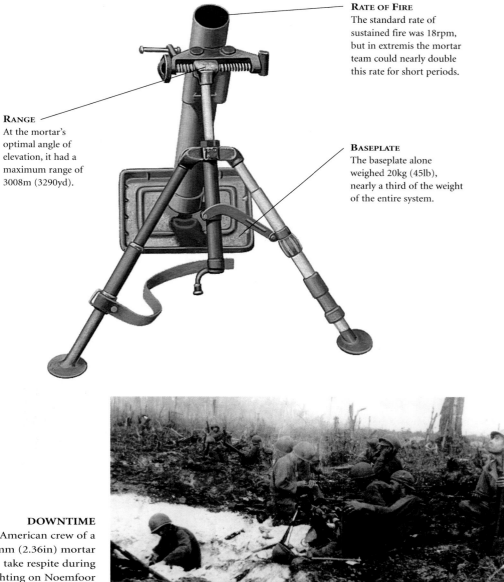

RATE OF FIRE
The standard rate of sustained fire was 18rpm, but in extremis the mortar team could nearly double this rate for short periods.

RANGE
At the mortar's optimal angle of elevation, it had a maximum range of 3008m (3290yd).

BASEPLATE
The baseplate alone weighed 20kg (45lb), nearly a third of the weight of the entire system.

DOWNTIME
An American crew of a 60mm (2.36in) mortar take respite during fighting on Noemfoor Island, in Dutch New Guinea 12 July 1944.

M120 Mortar System (1991)

SPECIFICATIONS

LENGTH:	1.95m (6ft 4in)
WEIGHT:	144.7kg (319lb)
CALIBRE:	120mm (4.7in)
ELEVATION:	45° to 80°
TRAVERSE:	60°
SHELL WEIGHT:	12.6kg (27.8lb)
MUZZLE VELOCITY:	310m/sec (1017ft/sec)
RATE OF FIRE:	16rpm first minute
EFFECTIVE RANGE:	7240m (7920yd)
CREW:	5

The M120 mortar is actually the US rebranding of the Israeli Soltam K6 120mm (4.7in) heavy field mortar. When mounted on the M1064 and M1129 mortar carriers it is known as the M121.

Right: US soldiers from the 25th Infantry Division conduct a live-fire exercise utilizing a RMS6L 120mm (4.7in) mortar system on a M1129 Mortar Carrier, Japan, 2017.

FIRING
Conventional finned bombs are used and are drop-loaded. Firing is activated by a trip mechanism and lanyard; the firing pin can be retracted and locked in the safe position.

LOADING
Marines load a round into a 120mm (4.7in) mortar as they prepare to fire down-range.

SOLTAM K6

The Soltam 120mm (4.7in) K6 is a conventional heavy infantry mortar used by the Israel Defense Forces and a number of other armies. It consists of the usual smoothbore barrel, round baseplate and supporting bipod, all carried on a light two-wheeled trailer in the assembled condition. All that is necessary to bring the mortar into action is to tip the trailer so that the baseplate drops to the ground, then lift the tube and bipod clear and erect them, removing the trailer. The Israel Defense Forces mortars can be mounted in half-tracks or the M113 'Zelda' APC.

TRAINING
Soldiers use a 120mm (4.7in) mortar system on an M1129 mortar carrier during a live-fire event as part of Exercise Orient Shield 2017 at Camp Fuji, Japan.

M224A1 Mortar (2011)

SPECIFICATIONS

BARREL LENGTH: 1m (3ft 4in)

WEIGHT: 21.1kg (47lb)

CALIBRE: 60mm (2.4in)

ELEVATION: 45° to 80°

TRAVERSE: 14°

SHELL WEIGHT: 1.7kg (3.75lb)

RATE OF FIRE: 8–20rpm sustained

EFFECTIVE RANGE: HE: 3490m (3816yd)

CREW: 3

FUZE SYSTEMS

Modern mortar shells have far more versatile fuzing options that the shells of the past. The bombs fired from the M224A1 basically have three fuze options. It has the standard point-detonating fuze, which explodes the bomb on impact, and a timer fuze for controlling the moment of detonation. The M734 multi-option fuze, by contrast, has a rangefinder and collision detection system that detonates the bomb in the position most damaging to the target, whether that be airburst, impact or penetration.

Introduced in 1978, the M224 mortar system was a light and useful support weapon for US air assault, airborne, ranger and light infantry rifle companies. The improved M224A1 entered service in 2011; it reduced the number of components and used lighter materials, reducing weight by 20 per cent compared to the standard M224.

Above: US Marines assigned to the 26th Marine Expeditionary Unit fire an M224A1 60mm (2.4in) mortar system during Exercise Eager Lion in Al Quwayrah, Jordan, 2018.

FIRING
The weapon can be fired either by gravity-dropped shells or by a remote trigger system.

SIGHT UNIT
The M224A1 uses the M64A1 sight unit, which features integral lighting for night and low-light operations.

SHOCK ABSORBER
A spring-type shock absorber takes some of the recoil impact out of firing, making the weapon more accurate in sustained fire.

COMPONENTS
The mortar system consists of the M225A1 tube, M170A1 bipod assembly, M7A1 baseplate, M8 auxiliary baseplate and the M64A1 sight unit.

USMC MORTAR CREW
US Marines operating an M224A1 60mm (2.4in) mortar get into a rhythm feeding shells into the tube. The maximum rate of fire is 18–30rpm for one to four minutes in total.

Aircraft, Helicopters and Drones

Of all the weapon systems featured in this book, military aircraft have arguably made the greatest strides in terms of technological advances. During World War I, the typical fighter aircraft, for example, had a top speed scarcely in excess of 160km/h (100mph), an endurance of a few hours at best, was made of wood, canvas and wire, featured an open cockpit and was armed with one or two synchronized machine guns. Today's fighters, by contrast, can achieve speeds of well over Mach 1 and can range over thousands of kilometres, all while carrying a vast array of air-to-air and ground-attack weapon systems and advanced avionics. Furthermore, we are already entering a future of unmanned aerial vehicles (UAVs); the physical on-board presence of a pilot in the long-term future of combat aircraft is no longer regarded as a certainty.

REFUELLING
An F-15E Strike Eagle refuels from a KC-10 extender boom during an Operation Iraqi Freedom mission.

Fokker E Series (1915)

SPECIFICATIONS

DIMENSIONS:	Length: 7.2m (23ft 7in); Wingspan: 9.5m (31ft 3in); Height: 2.9 m (9ft 5in)
WEIGHT:	610kg (1345lb)
POWERPLANT:	Oberursel 9-cylinder rotary engine, 60kW (80hp)
MAXIMUM SPEED:	140km/h (87mph)
ENDURANCE:	(E.III) 2 hrs 30 mins
SERVICE CEILING:	3000m (9842ft)
CREW:	1
ARMAMENT:	1 × 7.92mm (0.312in) machine gun firing through propeller

The Fokker Eindecker was the first aircraft to be fitted with an interruptor apparatus, which allowed firing of a machine gun through the propeller. It quickly came to dominate the airspace over the Western Front.

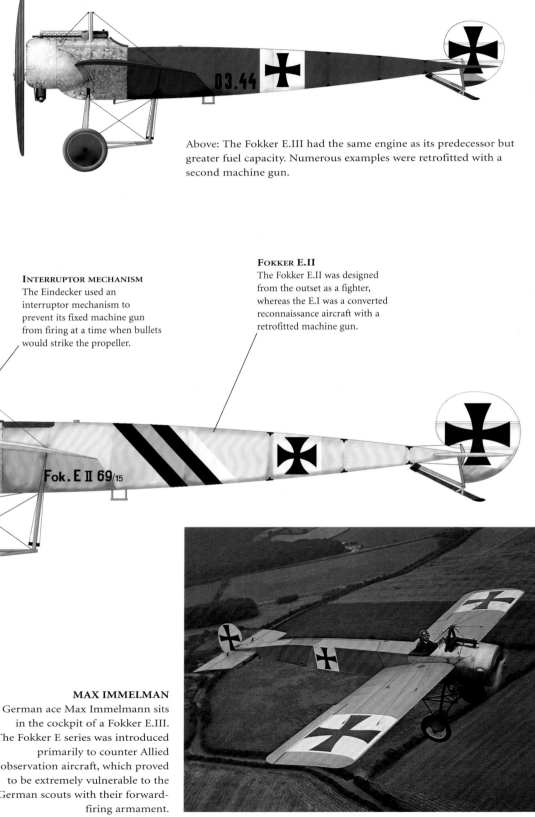

Above: The Fokker E.III had the same engine as its predecessor but greater fuel capacity. Numerous examples were retrofitted with a second machine gun.

ENGINE
The larger engine of the E.IV was not an improvement. Much of the design's previously good manoeuvrability was lost, and the engine was troubled by mechanical issues.

INTERRUPTOR MECHANISM
The Eindecker used an interruptor mechanism to prevent its fixed machine gun from firing at a time when bullets would strike the propeller.

FOKKER E.II
The Fokker E.II was designed from the outset as a fighter, whereas the E.I was a converted reconnaissance aircraft with a retrofitted machine gun.

EINDECKER ACES
In the hands of 'aces' such as Max Immelmann and Oswald Boelke, the Eindecker was extremely effective despite its small numbers. Fewer than 100 were operational on the Western Front at the end of 1915, but they had an effect out of all proportion to the number of aircraft. A handful were sent to the Eastern Front, where they proved just as devastating to the Russian Air Force.

MAX IMMELMAN
German ace Max Immelmann sits in the cockpit of a Fokker E.III. The Fokker E series was introduced primarily to counter Allied observation aircraft, which proved to be extremely vulnerable to the German scouts with their forward-firing armament.

Sopwith Camel (1916)

SPECIFICATIONS

DIMENSIONS:	Length: 5.64m (18ft 6in); Wingspan: 8.53m (28ft); Height: 2.59m (8ft 6in)
WEIGHT:	667kg (1471lb) maximum take-off
POWERPLANT:	Bentley B.R.1 9-cylinder rotary piston engine, 112kW (150hp)
MAXIMUM SPEED:	187km/h (117mph)
ENDURANCE:	2 hrs 30 mins
SERVICE CEILING:	6095m (20,000ft)
CREW:	1
ARMAMENT:	2 × 7.7mm (0.303in) fixed forward-firing Vickers machine guns

Perhaps the most famous British fighter of World War I, the F.1 Camel typified the increasing aerial dominance enjoyed by the Allies from early 1918, but was a handful to fly, demanding the very finest qualities from those who piloted it.

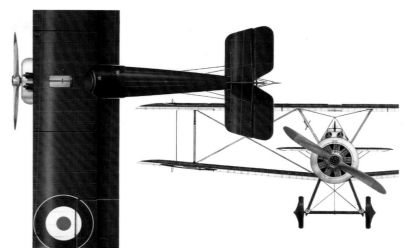

Above: The Camel F6314 was on strength with No. 120 Squadron, part of the newly established Royal Air Force in 1918. The unit saw much action during the German offensive on the Western Front in spring 1918.

CAMELS AT SEA

With the aim of providing aircraft for launch from light cruisers, Sopwith developed a naval version of the Camel. The prototype for the navalized Camel, the FS.1, was equipped with jettisonable wheeled undercarriage for launch, and floats for landing. The wings were shortened and the rear fuselage could be folded for stowage within a warship. From summer 1917, the Camel began to be flown off the decks of warships, now under the revised designation 2F.1. In July 1918, seven bomb-armed Camels flying from the deck of HMS *Furious* attacked the Zeppelin sheds at Tondern, destroying L.54 and L.60. However, only two of the Camels returned safely to the ship.

ARMAMENT
The two synchronized forward-firing Vickers machine guns could be supplemented by up to four 11kg (25lb) bombs carried externally.

CONSTRUCTION
The Camel was built on the basis of a conventional wire-braced wooden box girder structure, with aluminium covering immediately aft of the engine. Further aft, the covering was plywood as far as the rear of the cockpit, while the rear fuselage was covered with fabric.

COLOURS
Late-war RAF Camels wore this dark green scheme. The large letter on the fuselage side indicated the flight to which the aircraft was assigned; in this case, 'B' Flight.

NAVAL CAMEL
The navalized 2F.1 variant differed from the basic Camel in its armament of a single Vickers gun in the port position, supplemented by a Lewis gun above the wing centre section.

Nieuport 17 (1916)

SPECIFICATIONS

DIMENSIONS:	Length: 5.74m (18ft 10in); Wingspan: 8.22m (26ft 11in); Height: 2.4m (7ft 10in)
WEIGHT:	565kg (1246lb)
POWERPLANT:	Le Rhone 9J 9-cylinder rotary engine, 150kW (200hp)
MAXIMUM SPEED:	177km/h (110mph)
ENDURANCE:	1 hr 45 mins
SERVICE CEILING:	5300m (17,390ft)
CREW:	1
ARMAMENT:	1 × 7.7mm (0.303in) Lewis or Vickers machine gun

With a lineage going back to a racing design, the Nieuport 'fighting scouts' were fast and highly manoeuvrable, if rather fragile. They were instrumental in restoring the balance of air power over the Western Front.

Above: Escadrille No3 ('The Storks') originally had other identities and different aircraft, but adopted its definitive form in September 1915 when it was re-equipped with Nieuport 17s.

FIGHTING SCOUTS

Nieuport 11 fighting scouts were important in countering what became known as the 'Fokker Scourge' of 1915–16; a period of dominance by German aircraft. The agile Nieuport was far more effective than earlier designs, and was well liked for its speed and rate of climb. New aircraft appeared at an incredible rate, and any technical advantage was likely to be quickly offset by an improvement in enemy capabilities. Thus a larger and more powerful Nieuport was a necessity almost as soon as the 11 had entered service. The Nieuport 17 was a worthy successor, and was especially important in the air battles over the Verdun and the Somme in 1916. It was highly effective for a time, but eventually had to be replaced with more advanced aircraft. In the meantime, however, 17s were flown by many notable fighter aces including Albert Ball, William Bishop and Georges Guynemer.

GUN
An engine cowling mounting not only made aiming the gun simpler, but also allowed the pilot to more readily clear jams.

WING SURFACES
One design flaw of the Nieuport fighting scouts was a tendency to shed fabric from the upper wing surface, sometimes with catastrophic consequences.

TYPE 17C
A Nieuport 17 in Imperial Russian service. The Nieuport served on both sides during the Russian Civil War (1917–22).

NARROW WING
The narrow lower wing of the Nieuport 17 contributed to its agility and rate of climb, but was fragile. It was replaced by a larger wing on the Nieuport 28.

S.E.5a (1916)

SPECIFICATIONS

DIMENSIONS:	Length: 6.38m (20ft 11in); Wingspan: 8.12m (26ft 7in); Height: 2.89m (9ft 6in)
WEIGHT:	696kg (1535lb)
POWERPLANT:	Hispano-Suiza 8 inline piston engine, 150kW (200hp)
MAXIMUM SPEED:	212km/h (132mph) at 1980m (6500ft)
ENDURANCE:	3 hrs
SERVICE CEILING:	5182m (17,000ft)
CREW:	1
ARMAMENT:	1 × fixed 7.7mm (0.303in) forward-firing machine gun, 1 × trainable 7.7mm (0.303in) machine gun

GRADUAL IMPROVEMENTS

The S.E.5a was subject to continuous refinement. The most celebrated of British scout pilots flew the SE5 and SE5a, of whom the greatest exponent was Major James McCudden, whose total score of 57 aerial victories included 50 while serving with No. 56 Squadron. Other Allied aces to have flown the SE5 and/ or SE5a included Mannock, Bishop, Beauchamp-Proctor and Ball. The last of these, Albert Ball, preferred the French Nieuport, but eventually settled on the S.E.5a, in which he was to lose his life. A squadron that was to see outstanding success with the S.E.5a during World War I, No. 74 received its first aircraft in March 1918. The squadron quickly moved to France where, in its first dogfight, five enemy aircraft were downed for no losses.

Entering service at the same time as the tricky Sopwith Camel, the S.E.5a is today less well known, but was one of the exceptional fighting scouts of its day. It was the mount of famous Allied aces including William Bishop, James McCudden and Edward Mannock.

Right: This S.E.5a was flown by Second Lieutenant P.D. Learoyd of No. 40 Squadron, RFC, based at Bray Dunes aerodrome, in the spring of 1918. No. 40 Squadron was formed in 1916 at Gosport; its ranks included two dozen World War I aces, including Edward Mannock.

GUN ARMAMENT
The S.E.5a usually had one 7.7mm (0.303in) Vickers machine gun fixed in the top of the fuselage to the left of centre, firing through the propeller disc, with a 400-round belt, plus one 7.7mm (0.303in) Lewis machine gun on a Foster mount, with four 97-round drum magazines.

LANDING GEAR
Towards the end of 1917, a stronger landing gear became standard with substantially tapered forward legs. Other modifications included strengthened trailing edges.

EDWARD MANNOCK
This S.E.5a was flown by the highest-scoring British pilot, Captain Edward Mannock VC DSO MC, while serving with No. 74 Squadron. Despite having sight in only one eye, Mannock scored more than 70 kills before his death.

REPLICA S.E.5A
Wearing the colours of No. 24 Squadron, RFC, this is one of a number of replica S.E.5a aircraft that operate as warbirds, some having been produced for film work. At least one original airframe is also still airworthy, and can be seen flying with the Shuttleworth Collection at Old Warden in the United Kingdom.

Fokker Dr.I (1917)

SPECIFICATIONS

DIMENSIONS:	Length: 5.77m (18ft 11in); Wingspan: 7.19m (23ft 7in); Height: 2.95m (9ft 8in)
WEIGHT:	586kg (1291lb) maximum take-off
POWERPLANT:	Oberusel Ur.11 8-cylinder rotary piston engine, 82kW (110hp)
MAXIMUM SPEED:	185km/h (115mph)
RANGE:	300km (185 miles)
SERVICE CEILING:	6100m (20,015ft)
CREW:	1
ARMAMENT:	2 × 7.92 mm (0.31in) IMG 08/15 machine guns

Thanks to the exploits of the legendary 'Red Baron', the Fokker Dr.I has become the archetypal fighter of World War I in terms of the public imagination. Aside from its fame, the Fokker Triplane suffered from a number of operational shortcomings.

Right: A side view of Dr.I 152/17 reveals the characteristic slab-sided fuselage, strut-braced tailplane and fixed landing gear. A key attribute of the Dreidecker was its simple, low-cost construction.

EARLY PRODUCTION
Fokker Dr.I serial number 152/17 was one of a batch of 30 built early in the production run. Assigned to Jasta 11, the aircraft was one of a number flown by Manfred von Richthofen.

TAIL
The 'comma' rudder without a separate fin was a classic trademark of Anthony Fokker's early fighter designs. A tailskid was fitted immediately below the rudder.

LIFTING SURFACE
The impressive agility of the Fokker Dr.I was further enhanced by an additional lifting surface (aerofoil) that enclosed the axle of the fixed main undercarriage.

GUN ARMAMENT
The twin IMG 08/15 'Spandau' guns were arranged side by side in the upper part of the forward fuselage. Air-cooled and belt-fed, the weapons were each provided with 500 rounds of ammunition, housed behind the fuel tank.

CONFIGURATION
In its three-wing layout, the Dr.I was one of a number of contemporary fighting scouts to adopt the proven configuration of the British Sopwith Triplane.

FLYING CIRCUS

Alongside its undoubted prowess in aerial combat, the notoriety of the Dr.I among Allied pilots was certainly sealed by the activities of Manfred von Richthofen's Jagdgeschwader 1 (JG 1), the 'Flying Circus' (or 'Richthofen's Circus'), in which pilots were encouraged to apply eye-catching personalized colour schemes to their mounts. While the propaganda value of JG 1 did serve to exaggerate the capabilities of the Fokker Triplane, the reputation of the Dr.I among German pilots was such that certain leading exponents continued to fly the type even after the arrival of more modern equipment. Although 320 examples were eventually built by the time production ended in May 1918, at no time were there more than 171 Dr.Is in service, making it all the more impressive that it became such a feared foe, and in such a relatively short space of time.

THE 'RED BARON'

Born into an aristocratic family in Silesia in 1892, Manfred Freiherr von Richthofen was the leading air ace of World War I, with 80 aerial victories. Commencing flying training in May 1915, he began his career as an observer on the Eastern Front, before training as a fighter pilot. Transferring to the Western Front, and Jasta 2, he scored his first kill near Cambrai on 17 September 1916, his victim an F.E.2b. After 16 victories in Albatros D.IIs, von Richthofen was given command of Jasta 11, where he scored 40 kills in a period of just six months. He was appointed commander of the first Jagdgeschwader in June 1917; he was leading JG 1 when killed in action on 21 April 1918.

SPAD XIII (1917)

SPECIFICATIONS

DIMENSIONS:	Length: 6.15m (20ft 2in); Wingspan: 7.8m (25ft 8in); Height: 2.12m (6ft 11in)
WEIGHT:	740kg (1631lb) maximum take-off
POWERPLANT:	Hispano-Suiza 8Aa V-8 inline piston engine, 112kW (150hp)
MAXIMUM SPEED:	192km/h (119mph)
ENDURANCE:	2 hrs 15 mins
SERVICE CEILING:	5300m (17,390ft)
CREW:	1
ARMAMENT:	1 or 2 × 7.7mm (0.303in) fixed forward-firing Vickers machine guns

Famed as the colourful mount of the American Expeditionary Air Force's 94th Aero Squadron, the French SPAD XIII was one of the finest Allied fighting scouts of the war. It was also flown by renowned aces Georges Guynemer and René Fonck.

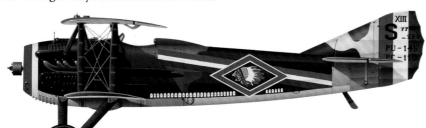

Above: The insignia of the Lafayette Escadrille is worn on the fuselage of SPAD XIII C.1 serial number S7714. Many members of Lafayette joined the 103rd Aero Squadron after the United States entered the war.

CONSTRUCTION
Typical for its day, the SPAD XIII was fabric-covered from behind the cockpit, with aluminium panels for the nose and cowling. The fuselage was constructed of four longerons with spruce struts and stringers.

WING
The construction of the wing was based on hollow spruce box bars with plywood ribs. The leading edges and wingtips were of thin, shaped wooden strip, while the trailing edges were of stretched fabric.

POWERPLANT
Advanced for its day, the water-cooled Hispano-Suiza 8B inline engine was a refined version of the 8A engine that powered the SPAD VII. This V-8 unit was designed by the Swiss engineer Marc Birkigt in 1915 and featured overhead camshafts and single-piece aluminium cylinders.

Above: This French SPAD XIII wears the crowing cockerel insignia of Escadrille SPA 48 along the rear fuselage. French squadron numbers were prefixed by the basic type of aircraft flown by the unit, 'SPA' in this case designating the SPAD fighter.

EDDIE RICKENBACKER
Born in Columbus, Ohio, Edward Rickenbacker was a famous racing driver before the US entered World War I. Enlisting in the US Army as General Pershing's chauffeur, Rickenbacker transferred to the Air Service soon after arriving in France and learned to fly. Rickenbacker then requested a transfer to the front, where he joined the 94th Aero Squadron, a unit that he went on to command. Rickenbacker emerged as the leading US ace of World War I, with 26 confirmed victories. In one remarkable action in September 1918, Rickenbacker tackled a group of seven enemy aircraft, successfully launching an attack that downed two of them.

RICKENBACKER'S SPAD
Eddie Rickenbacker poses with his SPAD XIII on a field somewhere in France. Rickenbacker survived the war and received the Medal of Honor in 1930.

Polikarpov I-16 (1933)

SPECIFICATIONS

DIMENSIONS:	Length: 6.04m (19ft 10in); Wingspan: 8.88m (29ft 1in); Height: 3.25m (10ft 8in)
WEIGHT:	1475kg (3252lb)
POWERPLANT:	M-62 radial piston engine, 820kW (1100hp)
MAXIMUM SPEED:	490km/h (304mph) at 3000m (9845ft)
RANGE:	700km (435 miles)
SERVICE CEILING:	9700m (31,825ft)
CREW:	1
ARMAMENT:	2 × 7.62mm (0.3in) ShKAS machine guns; 2 × 20mm (0.79 in) ShVAK cannons; 6 × unguided RS-82 rockets or up to 500kg (1102lb) of bombs

Given the pace of fighter development in the 1930s, it is all the more remarkable that the Soviet-designed I-16 was essentially the best fighter in the world for a period of six years. It only met its match once pitted against the Luftwaffe's Messerschmitt Bf 109E.

Right: The 29th IAP (*lstrebitel'nyi Aviatsionnyi Polk* or Fighter Air Regiment) was heavily engaged in 1941, using its l-16s to attack German ground forces. It was the first air force unit to receive the Guards title, becoming the 1st Guards IAP during the defence of Moscow on 6 December 1941.

WING STRUCTURE

The I-16 had a metal two-spar wing structure, with trussed KhMA chrome-molybdenum steel alloy centre-section spars and tubular outer spars. Wing ribs were made of dural and skinning was aluminium inboard and fabric outboard. The long ailerons were operated by rods and bell cranks. They could be drooped to act as flaps on landing.

GUN ARMAMENT

Gun armament comprised four 7.62mm (0.3in) ShKAS machine guns, two synchronized in the forward fuselage and two in the wings; the wing machine guns were replaced on some aircraft by two 20mm (0.78in) ShVAK cannon.

COCKPIT

The cramped cockpit was equipped with only rudimentary instruments. No radio or oxygen equipment was fitted, and there was no indicator for the undercarriage. The pilot was provided with a control column with a yoke-type grip, and a cable-cutter for severing the undercarriage retraction cables if they became stuck open.

FUEL LOAD

Fuel was housed in a single tank located in the central fuselage between the cockpit and engine installation. Total capacity was 255 litres (56 gallons). No fuel gauge was fitted in the cockpit; the pilot had to listen to the engine note to determine when fuel was low while keeping a close eye on his watch.

TAIL SURFACES

The tail surfaces were necessarily large to counter the lack of stability caused by the short rear fuselage. Despite the designers' best efforts, the I-16 had only limited stability longitudinally, and needed concentration from the pilot at all times. However, this instability brought great dividends in manoeuvrability at high speeds, where the rod-actuated elevators were noticeably effective.

POLIKARPOV I-153

The I-16's predecessor was the Polikarpov I-153 biplane fighter. This example of the 'Chaika' (seagull) was the first of three restored examples to take to the air in a programme sponsored by the Alpine Fighter Collection at Wanaka in New Zealand in the mid-1990s. It is seen during flight testing in Russia in September 1997.

Messerschmitt Bf 109 (1935)

SPECIFICATIONS

DIMENSIONS:	Length: 9.02m (29ft 7in); Wingspan: 9.92m (32ft 6in); Height: 3.4m (11ft 2in)
WEIGHT:	6600kg (14,551lb) maximum take-off
POWERPLANT:	Daimler-Benz DB 605AM inverted V-12 piston engine, 1342kW (1800hp)
MAXIMUM SPEED:	621km/h (386mph)
ENDURANCE:	720km (447 miles)
SERVICE CEILING:	11750m (38,550ft)
CREW:	1
ARMAMENT:	2 × 13mm (0.51in) MG 131 machine guns and 3 × 20mm (0.79in) MG 151 cannon

The classic Luftwaffe fighter of World War II, the Bf 109 served throughout the conflict in a series of increasingly capable variants. It was the mount for Germany's most celebrated aces, including Erich Hartmann, Gerhard Barkhorn and Hans-Joachim Marseille.

Below: Two views of a Bf 109E-4, the mount of Hans von Hahn, Gruppenkommandeur of I. Gruppe, Jagdgeschwader 3 (JG 3), based at Grandvilliers, France, in August 1940. The 'Tatzelwurm' emblem on the cowling was used throughout I. Gruppe of JG 3.

RECOGNITION MARKINGS
In order to ensure that the Bf 109 would be distinguished from enemy fighters in the heat of battle, yellow or white markings began to be applied in August 1940.

POWERPLANT
In the Bf 109E-4/N sub-variant, power was provided by the DB 601N engine, featuring piston heads with a higher compression ratio and higher-octane fuel.

Below: This Battle of Britain Bf 109E-4 was flown by Helmut Wick, Gruppenkommandeur of I./Jagdgeschwader 2 'Richthofen', based at Beaumont-le-Roger, France in October 1940. Wick was the highest-scoring Luftwaffe ace at the time of his death.

FIGHTER ARM
By making continual improvements to the basic design, the Bf 109 remained viable right until the end of World War II. Despite the appearance of the more capable Fw 109, the Bf 109 remained the backbone of the Luftwaffe fighter arm. The Bf 109 remains associated, therefore, with the legendary aces of the Jadgverband. The top-scoring ace of all time, Erich Hartmann, achieved his 352 victories in the space of three and a half years, all at the controls of a Bf 109.

WING ARMAMENT
Wing armament for the Bf 109E-4 consisted of two MG FF 20mm (0.79in) cannon. This more powerful weapon replaced the two 7.92mm (0.31in) MG 17 machine guns that comprised the original wing firepower.

FIGHTER-BOMBER
The E-4 was the first version to have a fighter-bomber (Jabo) capability, in the form of a simple ETC 500 bomb rack that was carried between the mainwheels. The bomb rack could accommodate four 50kg (110lb) bombs or a single 250kg (551lb) bomb.

SEA PATROL
Operating from an airfield in Greece, Bf 109G-6s of 7./JG 27 patrol over the Adriatic Sea. The two aircraft to the rear are equipped with tropical filters and underwing cannon gondolas.

Hawker Hurricane (1935)

SPECIFICATIONS

DIMENSIONS:	Length: 9.75m (32ft); Wingspan: 12.19m (40ft); Height: 4m (13ft 1in)
WEIGHT:	3583kg (7800lb) maximum take-off
POWERPLANT:	Rolls-Royce Merlin XX V-12 liquid-cooled piston engine, 954kW (1280hp)
MAXIMUM SPEED:	546km/h (339mph)
RANGE:	740km (460 miles)
SERVICE CEILING:	10,850m (35,600ft)
CREW:	1
ARMAMENT:	4 × 20mm (0.79in) cannon plus (intruder) two 227kg (500lb) bombs

The Royal Air Force's first monoplane fighter began a dynasty of Hawker warplanes. The most successful British fighter during the Battle of Britain subsequently excelled in the ground-attack role in North Africa and the Far East.

Below: KZ352 was a Hurricane Mk IIC that served with No. 1 Squadron of the Royal Indian Air Force at Imphal, Manipur, in 1944. This unit conducted 1034 sorties in the defence of Imphal as the Commonwealth forces inflicted a defeat on the Japanese, marking a turning point in the Burma campaign.

COCKPIT
The pilot sat under a heavily framed sliding canopy, protected by armour plate to the rear and a bullet-proof windscreen.

FIN
The fin was constructed around a central stempost, which supported the full-span rudder. The rudder had a small horn at the top and was fitted with a navigation light.

ANTI-TANK HURRICANE
A specialist anti-tank version was the Hurricane Mk IID, armed with 40mm (1.57in) cannon under the wings. The Mk IID appeared in service in 1942 and was primarily engaged in North Africa. A 'universal wing' was the primary feature of the Hurricane Mk IV; this could mount up to eight rocket projectiles or other external stores. Indeed, the Hurricane Mk IV was the first Allied aircraft to deploy air-to-ground rockets, a capability that did much to extend the operational utility of the basic airframe. The Mk IV proved to be the final Hurricane production version.

POWERPLANT
The Hurricane Mk II introduced the Merlin XX engine with two-stage supercharging, driving a three-bladed Rotol propeller.

RUNNING REPAIRS
Throughout its career, the Hurricane retained a fabric-covered rear fuselage. Although antiquated, this proved easier to repair and contributed to survivability.

AIRFRAME IMPROVEMENT
During its production run, the Hurricane benefitted from changes including metal-skinned wings, an enlarged rudder and (on later Mk Is) a ventral underfin.

SCRAMBLE!
Pilots scramble to their Hurricane fighters at RAF Hendon. On 15 September 1940, Hurricanes from No. 504 Squadron at Hendon destroyed eight enemy aircraft and damaged five more.

Mitsubishi A5M 'Claude' (1935)

SPECIFICATIONS

DIMENSIONS:	Length: 7.55m (24ft 9in); Wingspan: 11m (36ft 1in); Height: 3.2m (10ft 6in)
WEIGHT:	1216kg (2681lb)
POWERPLANT:	Nakajima Kotobuki 41 KAI 9-cylinder air-cooled radial engine, 585kW (785hp) at 3000m (9840ft)
MAXIMUM SPEED:	440km/h (273mph)
RANGE:	1200km (746 miles)
SERVICE CEILING:	9800m (32,150ft)
CREW:	1
ARMAMENT:	2 × 7.7mm (0.303in) Type 89 machine guns

When it entered service at the beginning of 1937, the A5M 'Claude' represented a giant leap forwards in carrier-based fighters. Replacing antiquated biplane aircraft, it was the fastest naval fighter in the world and would remain so for almost two years. The A5M was the dominant fighter in the Sino–Japanese conflict, and built up an enviable reputation for strength and agility. By 1942, however, A5Ms were relegated to training duties.

Right: Based on the aircraft carrier *Soryu* during the blockade of the East China Sea in November 1939, this A5M4 was flown by Lieutenant Tamotsu, leader of the *Soryu* fighter element.

WEAPONS
Two 7.7mm (0.303in) Type 89 machine guns were the standard armament for all operational versions of the 'Claude' except the A5M1a, which had two 20mm (0.79in) Oerlikon cannon.

COCKPIT
The 'Claude' had an open cockpit. The pilot often had a gunsight extending from the centre of the windshield.

ENGINE
The Nakajima Kotobuki 41 KAI nine-cylinder radial engine drove a three-bladed propeller. To improve forward visibility from the cockpit, a NACA (National Advisory Committee for Aeronautics) cowling with cooling flaps was fitted.

CARRIER AIRCRAFT
The strict 9-Shi specification of 1934 requested a fighter that was small enough to fit on an aircraft carrier, but that was fast and manoeuvrable. Mitsubishi proposed the Ka-14. Production commenced with the A5M1, which proved in operations that the Japanese had a world-beating fighter. Development led to the more powerful A5M2 and A5M4, which were very impressive in the Sino–Japanese War. Carrier-based A5M4s saw action at the start of World War II in Malaya and the Dutch East Indies. Many A5Ms were used for last-ditch kamikaze raids in 1945.

MARKINGS
Japanese fighters were generally colourfully decorated in their squadron markings. Many aircraft were funded by public subscription and carried the inscription '*Hokokugo*' (patriotism).

OPEN COCKPIT
Pilots of the 'Claude' had to face the elements; this was the last Japanese naval fighter to be fitted with an open cockpit. It did, however, have an exceptional field of view.

Supermarine Spitfire (1936)

SPECIFICATIONS

DIMENSIONS:	Length: 9.11m (29ft 11in); Wingspan: 11.23m (36ft 10in); Height: 3.48m (11ft 5in)
WEIGHT:	3078kg (6785lb) maximum take-off
POWERPLANT:	Rolls-Royce Merlin 45/46/50 V-12 liquid-cooled piston engine, 1074kW (1440hp)
MAXIMUM SPEED:	602km/h (374mph)
RANGE:	756km (470 miles)
SERVICE CEILING:	10,500m (34,450ft)
CREW:	1
ARMAMENT:	Typical: 2 × 20mm (0.79in) cannon and 4 × 7.7mm (0.303in) machine guns

The pre-eminent British fighter of World War II was a thoroughbred with a racing lineage. A masterpiece of design from R.J. Mitchell, the Spitfire is remembered as one of the classic fighters of all time. It saw service in every theatre of combat, from the outbreak of war until the final Allied victory.

Below: This Spitfire Mk IA was flown by South African ace Adolph 'Sailor' Malan in August 1940, when he commanded No. 74 Squadron. By year's end, Malan had 18 victories.

CAMOUFLAGE AND MARKINGS
The RAF Middle East scheme typically comprised dark earth/middle stone upper surfaces with sky or azure below. This aircraft also carries the insignia of No. 7 Wing, SAAF, on the tailfin.

PROPELLER
Engine efficiency was improved through the use of a constant-speed propeller. The propeller pitch automatically adjusted based on the flight regime, ensuring optimum engine operating levels.

Below: This Spitfire Mk V was operated by No. 2 Squadron, No. 7 Wing, South African Air Force (SAAF), part of the Desert Air Force, in July 1943. It first saw action flying from bases in Sicily, and later captured airfields on the Italian mainland.

MK V SPITFIRE
The Mk V, which appeared in March 1941, was the most significant production Spitfire, accounting for 6479 of the total 20,351 aircraft built. As RAF Fighter Command's standard fighter, the Mk V introduced the Merlin Mk 45. This was produced in a number of sub-variants, including the Mk VB with cannon and machine-gun armament, and the Mk VC fighter-bomber with provision for external stores. Most Mk VCs were completed with 'clipped' wings to improve performance at altitudes below 5000ft (1525m). From mid-1941 until mid-1942, the Spitfire Mk VB was the backbone of Fighter Command, until it was superseded by the Mk IX.

VOKES FILTER
For operations in the sandy conditions of the Western Desert, the tropicalized Spitfire was fitted with a Vokes filter under the chin. Later, a low-drag Aboukir filter was introduced.

CANNON
The universal 'C'-type wing included four 20mm (0.79in) Hispano cannon, each of which was provided with 120 rounds of ammunition.

STRENGTHENED STRUCTURE
The beefed-up Mk VC was able to carry bombs in the form of two 113kg (250lb) weapons underwing, or a single 227kg (500lb) bomb under the fuselage.

OVERSEAS SERVICE
The Spitfire first saw overseas service in the form of the Mk V. In March 1942, an initial consignment of these fighters was shipped to Malta in order to defend the island fortress against Axis forces.

Lockheed P-38 Lightning (1939)

SPECIFICATIONS

DIMENSIONS:	Length: 11.53m (37ft 10in); Wingspan: 15.85m (52ft); Height: 3.91m (12ft 10in)
WEIGHT:	5806kg (12,800lb) (empty)
POWERPLANT:	2 × Allison V-1710-111/113 inline piston engines
MAXIMUM SPEED:	667km/h (414mph) at 7620m (25,000ft)
RANGE:	2100km (1300 miles)
SERVICE CEILING:	13,000m (44,000ft)
CREW:	1
ARMAMENT:	1 × 20mm (0.79in) cannon, 4 × 12.7mm (0.5in) machine guns in the nose, plus a bombload of 2 × 726kg (1600lb) bombs or 10 × 70mm (2.75in) rockets

The mighty P-38 was something of an anomaly among the US Army Air Force in World War II: a genuinely successful heavy fighter that was equally capable in the long-range escort role or as a hard-hitting ground-attack aircraft in both European and Pacific theatres. After a successful combat debut, it was soon dubbed the 'fork-tailed devil'.

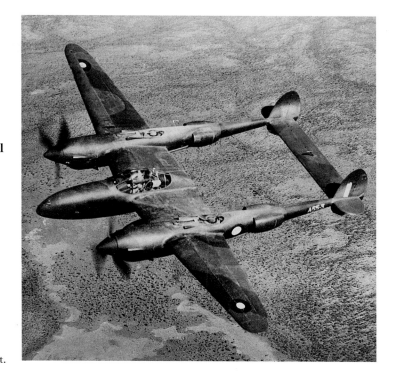

Right: A Royal Australian Air Force photo-reconnaissance Lightning, assigned to No. 1 Photographic Reconnaissance Unit. The RAAF initially received only two F-4s; a third example was subsequently delivered as an attrition replacement.

LIGHT BOMBER

While this P-38J is equipped with the standard 'fighter' nose, a number of J-models were adapted for use in the light bomber role, for which they were fitted with an alternative glazed nose to the centre nacelle for use by a bomb aimer. A bombing radar was another option for this role.

P-38J

The P-38J first saw combat service in August 1943 and was used for long-range penetration fights into the heart of Europe.

FIGHTER ESCORT

The P-38J resulted in a new lease of life for the Lightning, particularly during the 1943 daylight raids by USAAF B-17 and B-24 bombers over Europe. However, in 1944, as deliveries of the P-51 stepped up, the P-38J and the more powerful P-38M came to be used increasingly in the ground-attack role.

BARE METAL

By mid-1944, most USAAF fighters operating in Europe had shed their olive drab/neutral grey finish in favour of bare metal. This provided fractionally more speed in combat.

'LOCO GROUP'

This P-38J-15 was assigned to the 55th Fighter Squadron, 20th Fighter Group, based at Kingscliffe. The unit was known as the 'Loco Group' on account of its train-busting prowess. The 55th used a triangle on the tailfins as its squadron marking. RAF-style letter codes on the tailbooms also indicated the squadron.

Mitsubishi A6M Zero (1939)

SPECIFICATIONS

DIMENSIONS:	Length: 9.12m (29ft 11in); Wingspan: 11m (36ft 1in); Height: 3.51m (11ft 6in)
WEIGHT:	2733kg (6025lb) maximum take-off
POWERPLANT:	Nakajima NK2F Sakae 21 radial piston engine, 820kW (1100hp)
MAXIMUM SPEED:	565km/h (351mph)
RANGE:	1143km (710 miles)
SERVICE CEILING:	11,740m (38,517ft)
CREW:	1
ARMAMENT:	2 × 20mm (0.79in) cannon and 2 × 13.2mm (0.52in) machine guns

Popularly known as the 'Zero', the Mitsubishi A6M was the world's most capable carrier-based fighter at the time of its appearance, out-performing all land-based contemporaries. Latterly outclassed, it remained in service until the end of the war.

Above: The A6M5c sub-variant (93 built) featured improved armament in the form of an additional pair of 13.2mm (0.52in) machine guns fitted outboard of the standard wing cannon.

LIGHTWEIGHT CONSTRUCTION
In order to achieve the eight-hour endurance specific for operations over the Pacific theatre, the Zero employed a very light construction. The result was an airframe that was vulnerable to hits by even rifle-calibre weapons. On occasions, structural failure could result from a high-speed dive.

COCKPIT
The pilot of the A6M2 was not provided with armour plating, a bulletproof windshield or even a jettisonable hood. The multi-panel canopy made use of simple flat plates of glass.

HIGH-PERFORMING
The A6M2 was the IJN's premier fighter during the raid on Pearl Harbor in December 1941, in which eight Zero fighters were lost from the total of 105 involved in the surprise attack on the US Navy fleet. The A6M remained the service's pre-eminent fighter in theatre as fighting extended to Malaya, the Philippines and Burma. Along the way, it demonstrated its superiority against lesser Allied types, including the Brewster Buffalo, Curtiss P-36 and P-40 and Hawker Hurricane fighters. Japan's leading ace of the Pacific war, Saburo Sakai, is believed to have achieved 64 aerial kills in a Zero.

Above: This A6M2 was on strength with the 2nd Sentai, 1st Koku Kentai, and was operating from the carrier *Hiryu* during the Battle of Midway in June 1942. In the course of the battle, the IJN put up large formations of Zero fighters for protection, but these could not prevent the loss of four Japanese carriers to US Pacific Fleet combat aircraft.

ARMAMENT
In addition to the two 20mm (0.79in) cannon that were carried in the wings, a pair of Type 97 machine guns were mounted in the decking of the upper fuselage, forward of the cockpit.

HANDLING
The Zero was equipped with fabric-covered control surfaces. The aircraft was notably agile, but was slower in the roll, and its acceleration in a dive was inferior to Allied counterparts.

NAVAL A6M ZERO
A Mitsubishi A6M Zero of the 12th Naval Air Group Imperial Japanese Navy. Once entering combat in World War II, the highly agile A6M2 proved itself an immediate success, quickly gaining aerial supremacy during the Japanese campaigns in the East Indies and Southeast Asia.

Focke-Wulf Fw 190 (1939)

SPECIFICATIONS

DIMENSIONS: Length: 8.84m (29ft); Wingspan: 10.5m (34ft 5in); Height: 3.96m (13ft)

WEIGHT: (A-8) 3200kg (7060lb)

POWERPLANT: BMW 801D-2 radial piston engine, 1566kW (2100hp)

MAXIMUM SPEED: 654km/h (405mph)

ENDURANCE: 805km (500 miles)

SERVICE CEILING: 11,400m (37,402ft)

CREW: 1

ARMAMENT: 4 × 20mm (0.79in) cannon and 2 × 7.92mm (0.31in) machine guns

At the time of its combat appearance, the Fw 190 was the most capable fighter in service, offering a winning combination of performance and manoeuvrability. Further development ensured it retained its prowess until the end of the war.

Above: 6./JG 26 was based at Coquelles, in the Pas de Calais, in November 1941. It received some of the first production Fw 190A-1s. This example was flown by Walter Schneider.

POWERPLANT
Based on the Fw 190A-5 airframe, the Fw 190F-2 was powered by the BMW 801D-2 14-cylinder two-row radial engine, accommodated in a lengthened mounting.

GUN ARMAMENT
The fuselage upper decking contained a pair of 7.92mm (0.31in) MG 17 machine guns, each with 1000 rounds.

TAILFIN
The robust fin was comprised of two spars; one vertical along the rear, and one angled along the leading edge. The rudder ran the full length of the fin.

THEATRE MARKINGS
Eastern Front theatre markings consisted of a yellow fuselage band, undersides of the wingtips and lower cowling.

BOMB
The early Fw 190F carried a single bomb on an ETC 501 fuselage rack, or four smaller disposable stores on an ER 4 adapter.

NIGHT-FIGHTING
Night-fighting was a specialist role for which the Fw 190A-5/U2 was developed. This was used for *Wilde Sau* (Wild Boar) tactics in which day fighters were used at night, especially in order to counter the 'Window' jamming employed by RAF bombers. The prime exponent of *Wilde Sau* was JG 300, which operated both Fw 190s and Bf 109Gs. The tactics were first employed in August 1943, and eventually proved relatively successful. The Fw 190A-8 became the most numerous *Wilde Sau* fighter.

FW 190A: FIRST INTO COMBAT
Seen here under test in summer 1941 in the form of pre-production Fw 190A-0 series machines (both 'small wing' and the definitive 'large wing' versions), the A-series was the first to enter combat. The operational test unit for the new fighter, dubbed *Würger* (Shrike), was the II. Gruppe of JG 26. Production aircraft began to roll out of the factory in June 1941.

North American P-51 Mustang (1940)

SPECIFICATIONS

DIMENSIONS:	Length: 9.85m (32ft 4in); Wingspan: 11.28m (37ft); Height: 3.71m (12ft 2in)
WEIGHT:	5262kg (11,600lb) maximum take-off
POWERPLANT:	Packard Rolls-Royce Merlin V-1650-7 V-12 liquid-cooled piston engine, 1112kW (1490hp)
MAXIMUM SPEED:	704km/h (437mph)
RANGE:	3347km (2080 miles)
SERVICE CEILING:	12,770m (41,900ft)
CREW:	1
ARMAMENT:	6 × 12.7mm (0.5in) machine guns plus provision for up to 2 × 454kg (1000lb) bombs or 6 × 127mm (5in) rockets

With a strong claim to be the finest piston-engined fighter of World War II, the superlative P-51 emerged from potential obscurity when re-engined with the British-designed Merlin powerplant. It became a war-winning long-range escort after its service entry in late 1943, and later saw combat action in the Korean War.

Above: *Nooky Booky IV* was a P-51K flown by Leonard Carson of the 362nd Fighter Squadron at Leiston, Suffolk, in 1945. Carson was the leading ace of the 357th Fighter Group, with 18.5 victories.

'LITTLE FRIENDS'

The first P-51Bs arrived in England in November 1943 and instantly proved superior in terms of range and high-altitude performance than the P-47 hitherto used as a bomber escort. Furthermore, they were more reliable than the P-38 Lightning. Availability of the Mustang allowed USAAF bombers to receive protection during raids on targets deep inside Germany, and thereby, in concert with RAF Bomber Command, keep up the pressure on the Reich around the clock. Such was the success of the P-51 that it was planned to re-equip all fighter groups of the Eighth Air Force with the fighter. Although this was not realized, by the end of 1944 P-51s equipped no fewer than 15 fighter groups of the 'Mighty Eighth'.

CANOPY
The pilot sat under an aft-sliding, blown 'bubble' canopy; this provided improved visibility compared to the standard canopy on the high-backed P-51B/C.

TAILFIN
Soon after P-51D production commenced, a dorsal fin was added to the tail in order to improve directional stability.

FLAPS
Simple flaps ran along around two-thirds the length of the wing's trailing edge. These were used to reduce speed on landing.

INTAKE
The liquid-cooled engine was provided with a belly-mounted radiator that was fed by this large ventral airscoop. The radiator's location made it vulnerable to ground fire.

ROCKETS
The P-51 could carry zero-length launchers for unguided 127mm (5in) rocket projectiles. The rockets were clipped directly to streamlined mini-pylons.

DAYLIGHT ESCORT
Carrying a long-range drop tank, this P-51D served with the Eighth Air Force's 357th Fighter Squadron, 361st Fighter Group. It was typical of the escort fighters that protected the USAAF 'heavies' on their daylight bombing raids over occupied Europe.

Yakovlev Yak-1/3/7/9 (1940)

SPECIFICATIONS

DIMENSIONS:	Length: 8.55m (28ft); Wingspan: 9.74m (31ft 11in); Height: 3m (9ft 10in)
WEIGHT:	3117kg (6858lb) loaded
POWERPLANT:	Klimov M-105PF V-12 liquid-cooled piston engine, 880kW (1180hp)
MAXIMUM SPEED:	591km/h (367mph)
RANGE:	1360km (845 miles)
SERVICE CEILING:	9100m (30,000ft)
CREW:	1
ARMAMENT:	1 × 20mm (0.79in) cannon and 1 × 12.7mm (0.5in) machine gun

The most important Soviet fighter line of World War II, the Yakovlev series of single-seaters were built in greater numbers than their contemporaries, and scored more victories than all other Soviet fighter types combined.

Above: This Yak-9D was flown by the famous 'Normandie-Niemen' Regiment in 1944. This French-manned unit was established in 1943 and fought with distinction over Byelorussia and Lithuania.

ENGINE
The Yak-3 retained the earlier Klimov M-105PF engine (later redesignated as the VK-105PF), but this featured a further increase in power.

CANOPY
Combined with the lowered rear fuselage deck, the canopy provided excellent all-round vision. The windscreen on the Yak-3 was a one-piece, low-drag model.

STRUCTURE
Optimized for lightness, the Yak-3 employed wooden wings and tail, with plywood and fabric covering. The fuselage was a steel tube with a dural covering fore and plywood/fabric aft.

INTAKE
A large oil cooler intake was installed in the port wing root, replacing the undernose intake installed on previous Yak fighters and providing a useful recognition feature for the Yak-3.

Above: A Yak-3 of the 303rd Fighter Aviation Division, First Soviet Air Army, on the 3rd Ukrainian Front in 1944. Pilot of this aircraft was 303rd commander Georgii Nefedovich, who eventually accumulated 23 kills.

YAK-9

Numerically, the Yak-9 became the most important Soviet fighter of the war, and first saw significant action at Stalingrad. The new fighter replaced most of the earlier wooden components and featured an armament of one 20mm (0.79in) cannon and one 12.7mm (0.5in) machine gun. Production facilities gradually switched over from the Yak-7 to the Yak-9; in the meantime, some features of the former were included in production Yak-7Bs.

WARTIME YAK-9 VARIANTS

Yak-9Bs of the 130th Fighter Aviation Division wear the inscription 'Little Theatre: Front' (i.e., donated by Moscow's Little Theatre to the front). The Yak-9B was a fighter-bomber version, but was produced in only limited numbers. More successful was the Yak-9D long-range version with a range of 1360km (845 miles). The improved Yak-9DD increased that range to 2285km (1420 miles) thanks to additional wing fuel tanks. The Yak-9T and Yak-9K were respectively armed with 37mm (1.45in) and 45mm (1.78in) cannon for anti-tank missions. Last of the wartime line were the strengthened Yak-9M and the Yak-9U with a powerful VK-107A engine.

Vought F4U Corsair (1940)

The F4U had a troubled introduction to service in World War II, but by the end of the conflict it was challenging for a place among the best single-seat fighters of the war. It remained a viable ground-attack aircraft and night-fighter during the subsequent fighting in Korea.

SPECIFICATIONS

DIMENSIONS:	Length: 10.17m (33ft 4in); Wingspan: 12.5m (41ft); Height: 4.5m (14ft 9in)
WEIGHT:	4074kg (8982lb)
POWERPLANT:	Pratt & Whitney R-2800-8 radial engine, 1770kW (2380hp)
MAXIMUM SPEED:	671km/h (417mph) at 6066m (19,900ft)
RANGE:	1617km (1005 miles)
SERVICE CEILING:	12,600m (41,340ft)
CREW:	1
ARMAMENT:	6 × 12.7mm (0.5in) machine guns

PACIFIC WAR ACE
Flown by Lieutenant Ira C. 'Ike' Kepford, leading US Navy ace in the Pacific, during early 1944, this F4U-1A – perhaps the most famous of all the wartime Corsairs – carries Kepford's 16 kill markings in the form of Imperial Japanese rising suns.

CORSAIR CONSTRUCTION
Apart from the highly cranked wing, which could be folded for storage below the carrier deck, the fighter utilized a broadly conventional airframe of all-metal construction. The FG-1 version differed in having fixed rather than folding wings.

GUY BORDELON
Right: This Korean War F4U-5N, named 'Annie Mo', was flown by Lieutenant Bordelon of VC-3, who lived up to his nickname 'Lucky Pierre' when assigned ashore at K-6 under Detachment Dog in mid-1953. Tasked with hunting nocturnal 'Bedcheck Charlie' raiders, Bordelon became the only non-Sabre ace of the war, downing four Yaks and a Lavochkin.

RNZAF CORSAIRS
The Royal New Zealand Air Force received its first Corsairs in March 1944 under Lend-Lease. After the initial deliveries, New Zealand began to assemble its own aircraft. By the time the country stopped building Corsairs in 1945, the RNZAF had acquired 424.

Republic P-47 Thunderbolt (1941)

SPECIFICATIONS

DIMENSIONS:	Length: 11.01m (36ft 2in); Wingspan: 12.43m (40ft 9in); Height: 4.32m (14ft 2in)
WEIGHT:	8800kg (19,400lb) maximum take-off
POWERPLANT:	Pratt & Whitney R-2800-59 radial piston engine, 1716kW (2300hp)
MAXIMUM SPEED:	689km/h (428mph)
RANGE:	2028km (1260 miles)
SERVICE CEILING:	12,800m (42,000ft)
CREW:	1
ARMAMENT:	8 × 12.7mm (0.5in) machine guns; 2 × 454kg (1000lb) bombs underwing; up to 10 × 127mm (5in) unguided rockets

The pugnacious P-47 was one of the stand-out Allied fighters of World War II, equally adept as a long-range bomber escort over occupied Europe or as a potent ground-attack aircraft in theatres that ranged from Burma to the Mediterranean.

Above: A P-47D of the 527th Fighter Squadron, 86th Fighter Group, based in Italy in 1944. As well as pursuing retreating German forces in Italy, the unit flew escort missions for bombers.

Below: A P-47D Thunderbolt of the 56th Fighter Group, US 8th Fighter Command, based at Boxted, England, in 1944. Pilot David C. Schilling flew 132 combat missions with the 56th and scored 22.5 kills.

ENGINE
The P-47 was powered by the reliable Pratt & Whitney R-2800 series Double Wasp. This was an 18-cylinder radial air-cooled unit.

BUBBLE CANOPY
The Block 25 P-47D introduced a bubble cockpit canopy as standard. As a result, the pilot's all-round vision was much improved compared to that found on the earlier 'razorback' models.

WING GUNS
The characteristic staggered wing guns of the P-47D comprised four 12.7mm (0.5in) weapons in each wing, which were useful for strafing softer ground targets.

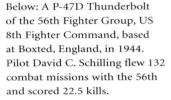

ROCKETS
The P-51 could carry zero-length launchers for unguided 127mm (5in) rocket projectiles. The rockets were clipped directly to streamlined mini-pylons.

FUEL
The main fuel tank in the centre section held 776 litres (205 gallons). This could be augmented by a drop tank under the centreline carrying a further 284 litres (75 gallons).

GROUND-ATTACK SPECIALIST

In all, P-47 production amounted to 15,675 aircraft, making it the most numerous American-made fighter in history. Of this total, a significant number were adapted for ground-attack duties, the P-47D featuring provision for underwing racks that could carry a pair of 454kg (1000lb) bombs. P-47Ds from later production batches had increased external stores capacity, including up to 10 127mm (5in) rockets.

56TH FIGHTER GROUP

This formation of 'razorback' P-47Bs was put up by the 56th Fighter Group in October 1942. The aircraft nearest the camera was flown by one of the leading Thunderbolt aces, Hubert Zemke. The 56th was the leading exponent of the P-47, credited with the destruction of 665.5 aircraft in air-to-air combat. This was more air-to-air kills than any other fighter group in the Eighth Air Force, making it the top-scoring P-47 group during World War II.

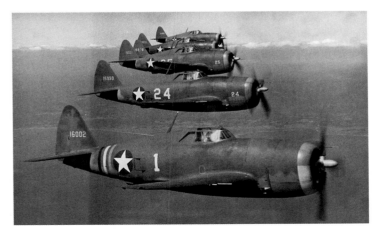

Grumman F6F Hellcat (1942)

SPECIFICATIONS

DIMENSIONS:	Length: 10.24m (33ft 7in); Wingspan: 13.05m (42ft 10in); Height: 3.99m (13ft 1in)
WEIGHT:	6991kg (15,413lb) loaded
POWERPLANT:	Pratt & Whitney R-2800-10W radial piston engine, 1491kW (2000hp)
MAXIMUM SPEED:	612km/h (380mph)
RANGE:	1521km (945 miles)
SERVICE CEILING:	11,369m (37,300ft)
CREW:	1
ARMAMENT:	6 × 12.7mm (0.5in) machine guns, or 2 × 20mm (0.79in) cannon and 4 × 12.7mm (0.5in) machine guns

The best carrier fighter of World War II, the Hellcat built on the earlier success of Grumman's F4F Wildcat. It was responsible for destroying 5156 enemy aircraft in aerial combat – 75 per cent of all US Navy aerial victories in the conflict.

Above: An F6F-5 of VF-27, serving aboard USS *Princeton*, during the Battle of Leyte Gulf, October 1944. VF-27 produced 10 aces, among which the top scorer was Carl A. Brown, Jr (10.5 kills).

Below: This F6F-5P was flown by VF-84, part of Carrier Air Group 84, assigned to the carrier USS *Bunker Hill* in February 1945. The F6F-5P sub-variant was equipped with a rear-fuselage camera installation to provide a tactical reconnaissance capability.

NOSE BAND
The yellow nose band was applied on the cowling during a series of raids on Tokyo. This marking was worn for a period of only two weeks before the cowling reverted to blue.

WING
The wing was comprised of two robust central spars, and the outer panels folded backwards through 90 degress to lie flat against the fuselage for stowage below decks.

DROP TANK
All Hellcat versions were capable of carrying a single 500-litre (150-gallon) auxiliary fuel tank on the fuselage centreline.

BATTLE OF THE PHILIPPINE SEA

Perhaps the most dramatic demonstration of the Hellcat's prowess came during the Battle of the Philippine Sea in June 1944, a huge operation involving 15 US Navy carriers that between them embarked 480 F6Fs, in addition to 222 dive-bombers and 199 torpedo-bombers. In a week-long campaign, the US Task Force 58 destroyed more than 400 Japanese aircraft and sank three carriers. Pilots associated with the Hellcat include the US Navy's 'ace of aces', 34-kill David McCampbell, who shot down nine aircraft in a single engagement in October 1944.

WING ARMAMENT
The usual fixed armament comprised six 12.7mm (0.5in) Browning machine guns mounted in staggered formation. Each weapon was provided with 50 rounds of ammunition. This aircraft also carries six 127mm (5in) rocket projectiles to attack ground targets.

POST-WAR HELLCATS
A radar-equipped F6F-5N night-fighter and three F6F-5s are seen in post-war US Navy service. These brightly marked aircraft were typical of Hellcats that served with 13 reserve units around the United States after VJ-Day.

Messerschmitt Me 262 (1942)

SPECIFICATIONS

DIMENSIONS:	Length: 10.61m (34ft 9in); Wingspan: 12.50m (41ft); Height: 3.83m (12ft 7in)
WEIGHT:	6775kg (14,936lb) maximum take-off
POWERPLANT:	2 × Junkers Jumo 004B-1 turbojets, 8.8kN (1890lb)
MAXIMUM SPEED:	870km/h (541mph)
RANGE:	845km (525 miles)
SERVICE CEILING:	11,000m (36,090ft)
CREW:	1
ARMAMENT:	4 × 30mm (1.18in) cannon

Assured its place in history as the first jet fighter to enter service, the Luftwaffe's Me 262 was the most advanced fighter to reach operational status during World War II, and ushered military aviation into the jet age.

TAIL
Control surfaces included fabric-covered elevators, replaced with stronger metal skins on later production aircraft. The powerful rudder was required to maintain directional stability.

Above: Two views of 'Yellow 8', a Me 262A-1a of 3./JG 7 that was discovered by advancing Allied forces at Stendal in April 1945. The unit emblem of JG 7 was a leaping greyhound.

PILOT
'Yellow 7' was flown by Heinz Arnold, who had scored 42 victories flying piston-engined fighters before transitioning to the jet. He scored seven jet kills in just three weeks before being posted missing in April 1945.

NIGHT-FIGHTER ROLE
The Me 262 saw some limited success in the night-fighter role. A dedicated night-fighter model appeared before the end of the war, in the form of the radar-equipped Me 262B-1a/U1. As a daytime bomber-destroyer, the Me 262 could also be armed with 24 underwing R4M unguided rockets. Ultimately, however, the Me 262 was a case of 'too little, too late' (a total of around 1430 were completed). Despite its undoubted performance advantage, it was unable to alter the course of the war.

ENGINES
Power was provided by a pair of Junkers Jumo 004B-1 axial-flow turbojets. These suffered from poor reliability and limited service life, primarily due to the effects of Allied bombing on production facilities and the lack of certain materials required for the turbine blades.

UNDERNOSE PYLONS
For the fighter-bomber role, undernose stations could accommodate a pair of 250kg (551lb) bombs or a single 500kg (1102lb) weapon, together with related fusing equipment.

ME 262B-1A/U1
The Me 262B-1a/U1 night-fighter was created on the basis of the Me 262B-1a dual-control trainer. The first trials of the night-fighter were undertaken at Rechlin in October 1944, using Lichtenstein SN-2 radar. The production version featured a radar operator in the rear seat and a FuG 218 Neptun V radar that featured a nose-mounted antenna array.

Northrop P-61 Black Widow (1942)

SPECIFICATIONS

DIMENSIONS:	Length: 15.11m (49ft 7in); Wingspan: 20.1m (66ft); Height: 4.46m (14ft 8in)
WEIGHT:	13,472kg (29,700lb) maximum take-off
POWERPLANT:	2 × Pratt & Whitney R-2800-65 radial piston engines, 1491kW (2000hp)
MAXIMUM SPEED:	589km/h (366mph)
RANGE:	4506km (2800 miles)
SERVICE CEILING:	10,090m (33,100ft)
CREW:	3
ARMAMENT:	4 × 20mm (0.79in) cannon, plus 4 × 12.7mm (0.5in) machine guns in later aircraft, with provision to carry up to 4 × 726kg (1600lb) bombs

Without doubt one of the finest night-fighters of the war, the powerful P-61 was one of the few Allied aircraft that was specifically designed for the task. The Black Widow served with particular distinction in the Pacific, often as a night intruder on offensive missions against land and sea targets.

Above: Two views of P-61B serial 42-39403 was fitted with the dorsal gun barbette. Other features of the B-model included a longer nose, Curtiss Electric propellers and four external pylons.

Below: *Midnite Madness II*, a P-61B of the 548th Night Fighter Squadron, US Seventh Air Force, based at Ie Shima in June 1945.

TAIL
The tail unit was attached to the twin booms immediately forward of the fin. The twin fins were equipped with full-span rudders, small tabs and navigation lights.

STABILIZER
The stabilizer joined the twin fins, and utilized a two-spar structure, like the main wing. A full-span elevator was provided.

CREW
The pilot sat in the front cockpit, and also controlled the 20mm (0.79in) cannon. The radar operator was in the upper forward position with responsibility for the gun turret. The rear gunner was in a separate compartment aft of the turret.

STRENGTH
The P-61 was notably robust, thanks to the central 'package' of engine nacelles, inner wings and fuselage. Large carry-through structures maintained the wing spar through the fuselage.

'WIDOW' INTRUDERS

Although always classed as a night-fighter, the P-61B version saw increasing use as a night intruder. It was capable of carrying weapons loads including four 726kg (1600lb) bombs, or four 1136-litre (300-gallon) drop tanks under the wings. Serving in the Far East, some aircraft were further adapted in field in order to carry 127mm (5in) rocket projectiles that were employed against Japanese shipping. In the last 250 P-61Bs, the dorsal turret was reinstated.

ENGINES
The P-61B was powered by a pair of Pratt & Whitney R-2800-65 Double Wasp 18-cylinder two-row radial engines. The 'Dash 65' featured water injection for increased thrust.

DORSAL TURRET
This early P-61A reveals the original General Electric dorsal turret that was subsequently removed after it was found to be prone to buffeting. This was the same turret as used in the B-29. It was armed with four 12.7mm (0.5in) machine guns, each of which was provided with 800 rounds of ammunition.

Lockheed F-80 Shooting Star (1944)

SPECIFICATIONS

DIMENSIONS:	Length: 10.52m (34ft 6in); Wingspan: 12.15m (39ft 10in); Height: 3.45m (11ft 4in)
WEIGHT:	7646kg (16,856lb) maximum take-off
POWERPLANT:	Allison J33-A-35 turbojet, 24.01kN (5400lb)
MAXIMUM SPEED:	956km/h (594mph)
RANGE:	1706km (1060 miles)
SERVICE CEILING:	13,030m (42,750ft)
CREW:	1
ARMAMENT:	6 × 12.7mm (0.5in) machine guns, with up to 907kg (200lb) of external ordnance or 10 × 127mm (5in) rockets

The P-80 (later F-80) holds the distinction of being the first USAF jet aircraft to enter combat. Although it was subsequently outclassed by swept-wing fighters, it provided good service, especially in the fighter-bomber role in the Korean War, and served as the basis for the successful T-33 trainer.

Below: The forward fuselage of the F-80C contained a concentrated battery of six Colt-Browning M2/M3 12.7mm (0.5in) machine guns, supplied with 300 rounds of ammunition per weapon.

Below: A late-production F-80C of the 36th Fighter-Bomber Squadron, 8th Fighter-Bomber Wing, based at Itazuke, Japan, in June 1950. The 36th FBS later converted back to the piston-engined F-51 Mustang, considered more suitable for operations in Korea. It ended the war equipped with F-86 Sabres.

ENGINE
Late-production F-80Cs were powered by an Allison J33-A-35 developing 24.01kN (5400lb) of thrust with water ejection.

KOREAN WAR SERVICE
It was the F-80C that saw service in the Korean War, this being the most modern fighter type available to the Far East Air Force when the conflict broke out. In November 1950, an F-80C flown by Russell J. Brown of the 51st Fighter Interceptor Wing reportedly downed a MiG-15 in what the US claimed was the first conclusive aerial jet combat between two jet fighters. Soviet records indicate that the MiG survived the encounter with Brown's aircraft. Against swept-wing opposition like the MiG-15, however, the Shooting Star was obsolescent and was demoted to the fighter-bomber role.

TIP TANKS
Most F-80s carried tip tanks under the wingtips. These each carried 625 litres (165 gallons) in the standard version of the tank, or 1003 litres (265 gallons) in the later Fletcher type.

BOMBS
In Korea, underwing pylons normally carried 454kg (1000lb) bombs, while alternatives included napalm or up to 10 127mm (5in) unguided rockets.

RATO GEAR
To improve take-off performance when operating at heavier weights, the F-80 could empoy rocket-assisted take-off (RATO) gear, with a single bottle on the underside of the rear fuselage.

Above: In July 1950, Francis B. Clark of the 35th Fighter-Bomber Squadron destroyed a North Korean Yak-9 and damaged another in *Salty Dog*, an F-80C.

Mikoyan-Gurevich MiG-15 (1947)

SPECIFICATIONS

DIMENSIONS:	Length: 10.86m (35ft 7in); Wingspan: 10.8m (33ft); Height: 3.7m (12ft 2in)
WEIGHT:	6045kg (13,327lb)
POWERPLANT:	Kilmov VK-1 Turbojet, 26.5kN (5950lb)
MAXIMUM SPEED:	1075km/h (668mph)
RANGE:	2520km (1565 miles)
SERVICE CEILING:	15,500m (50,840ft)
CREW:	1
ARMAMENT:	1 × 37mm (1.45in) cannon, 2 × 23mm (0.9in) cannon

Experience in World War II indicated that a powerful cannon armament was required to shoot down bombers; machine guns simply did not do enough damage to cripple a large aircraft. An interceptor also had to be fast enough to reach the bombers' altitude before they could penetrate far into friendly airspace.

Below: This Chinese MiG 15 fought during the Korean War for the People's Liberation Army (PLA) in 1950.

MIG-15UTI 'MIDGET'
'Midget' is the NATO reporting name for the MiG-15 UTI two-seat trainer. This example is in Iraqi service c. 1991.

ENGINE
The MiG-15bis used an engine developed from a copy of the Rolls-Royce Nene engine, which powered several contemporary fighters.

WING FENCES
Note the prominent wing fences, which reduce the tendency of swept-wing aircraft to stall due to spanwise (rather than front-to-back) airflow over the wings.

WORLDWIDE SUCCESS
The MiG-15 was primarily built in the Soviet Union, but also in Czechoslovakia and Poland. It served with air forces of various Warsaw Pact nations until the late 1960s, with some remaining in service as trainers after this. The MiG-15 was also adopted by the Chinese air force and by Egypt, where it saw action during the Suez Crisis. A MiG-15 shot down a British-designed Gloster Meteor that was in Israeli service, demonstrating once again the superiority of faster swept-wing fighters over first-generation straight-wing jets.

VINTAGE MIG
A surviving two-seat MiG-15 on display at a modern air show. Some air forces are known to have retained their MiG-15s almost up to the end of the 1990s.

North American F-86 Sabre (1949)

SPECIFICATIONS

DIMENSIONS: Length: 11.84m (38ft 10in); Wingspan: 11.93m (39ft 1in); Height: 4.57m (15ft)

WEIGHT: 9912kg (21,852lb) maximum take-off

POWERPLANT: General Electric J33-GE-3D turbojet, 39.7kN (8920lb)

MAXIMUM SPEED: 1114km/h (692mph)

RANGE: 835km (519 miles)

SERVICE CEILING: 15,485m (50,800ft)

CREW: 1

ARMAMENT: 4 × 20mm (0.79in) cannon and 2 × 227kg (500lb), 340kg (750lb) or 454kg (1000lb) bombs, or 16 × 127mm (5in) rockets

Perhaps the finest jet fighter of its generation, the F-86 won its spurs over Korea and went on to enjoy unprecedented success in a variety of combat roles and with dozens of different air arms around the world, serving for close to 50 years. With nearly 10,000 built, it is the most prolific Western jet fighter of all time.

Below: In the neat undercarriage of the Sabre, the nosewheel unit retracted backwards to lie in the forward fuselage, while the mainwheels retracted inwards to lie in the fuselage.

Below: This F-86D was flown by the 'Geiger Tigers' of the 520th Fighter Interceptor Squadron, Air Defense Command, based at Geiger Field, Washington, in 1955. The three stripes on the fuselage indicate that this is the commander's aircraft.

COCKPIT
The pilot sat below an aft-sliding canopy on a North American ejector seat, in a pressurized cockpit with air conditioning. The display was dominated by a screen for the fire-control system.

INTAKE
Adding radar in the D-model demanded a redesign of the entire nose, which now incorporated an engine intake in the chin position, with air being ducted below the cockpit.

ROCKETS
The 24 Mighty Mouse rockets were the sole armament of the F-86D. These folding-fin weapons were intended to attack bomber formations, each rocket carrying a 3.4kg (7.5lb) warhead.

DROP TANKS
These were fitted to extend range, and were usually of 454-litre (120-gallon) capacity. Internal fuel was carried in the inboard wing sections and in fuselage tanks below the intake trunk and forward part of the engine.

POWERPLANT
The engine in the F-86D was either a J47-GE-17B turbojet, with a very basic afterburner fitted, or the improved J47-GE-33, which offered a significant increase in thrust.

ALL-WEATHER FIGHTER

While the day-fighters are the best-known Sabre variants today, the most numerous member of the family was the F-86D all-weather fighter that was intended for service with Air Defense Command. Originally designated the F-96 on account of its considerable changes, the F-86D incorporated an interception radar and fire-control system and carried an armament of 24 70mm (2.75in) Mighty Mouse rockets in a retractable ventral tray.

KOREAN WAR SABRE

A Korean War F-86E of the 25th Fighter Interceptor Squadron, 51st Fighter Interceptor Wing. The pilot of this aircraft, named Elenore 'E', was William Whisner, an ace with 5.5 MiG kills.

Mikoyan-Gurevich MiG-17 (1950)

SPECIFICATIONS

DIMENSIONS: Length: 11.26m (36ft 11in); Wingspan: 9.63m (31ft 7in); Height: 3.8m (12ft 5in)

WEIGHT: 5350kg (11,770lb) maximum take-off

POWERPLANT: (MiG-17F) Klimov VK-1F afterburning turbojet, 22.5kN (5046lb)

MAXIMUM SPEED: 1145km/h (711mph)

RANGE: 2060km (1280 miles) with drop tanks

SERVICE CEILING: 16,600m (54,450ft)

CREW: 1

ARMAMENT: 1 × 37mm (1.45in) cannon and 2 × 23mm (0.9in) cannon, plus up to 500kg (1102lb) of external stores on underwing pylons

Scourge of the US air arms operating over Vietnam, the MiG-17 was a refinement of the Korean War-era MiG-15, rectifying the earlier fighter's shortcomings. The result was an agile fighter and fighter-bomber that also gave good service in successive battles fought by Arab air forces against Israel into the 1970s.

Below: This MiG-17F wears the colourful markings of an aerobatic team provided by No. 11 Squadron, Indonesian Air Force, which operated the type in the early 1960s.

TAILFIN
The broad-chord fin featured considerable sweep back and a two-section rudder fitted with a lower trim tab. The fin also accommodated a radar warning receiver and gyro compass.

UNDERWING TANKS
Endurance was extended through the use of 400-litre (105-gallon) drop tanks that could be carried underwing. In definitive form, four pylons were provided underwing, although drop tanks could only be carried inboard.

POWERPLANT
This MiG-17 was powered by a VK-1A, the improved version of the original VK-1 that had powered the earlier MiG-15bis. It was based on the RD-45, itself a copy of the Rolls-Royce Nene.

ENGINE INTAKE
The prominent intake divided the incoming airflow as it entered before it was ducted below the cockpit to feed the engine, roughly in line with the wing trailing edge.

NOSEWHEEL
The single nosewheel retracted forward for stowage. The simple undercarriage was designed to enable operations from semi-prepared airfields and rough strips.

'PHENOMENAL'
When the US Air Force encountered the MiG-17 over Vietnam, beginning in 1965, Robin Olds, commander of the 8th Tactical Fighter Wing, described the Soviet-designed fighter as 'a very dangerous little animal. Its manoeuvrability is phenomenal!'

MIG-17 WARBIRDS
The MiG-17's high-subsonic performance, robust construction and the relative availability of both complete aircraft and spare parts have made it a popular performer on the warbird scene. In the US alone there are around 27 privately owned MiG-17s. Many of these originated from Polish production, where locally built variants of the 'Fresco' remained in service until the early 1990s. This particular ex-Polish Air Force example, fitted with underwing smoke generators for airshow performances, was flown by the late Bill Reesman, a former US Air Force and Air Guard pilot who flew 320 combat missions over Vietnam in the F-100 Super Sabre. The jet is now operated by Red Bull.

Dassault Mirage III (1956)

TYPE · *Fighters* · FAMILY · *Aircraft, Helicopters & Drones*

SPECIFICATIONS

DIMENSIONS:	Length: 14.75m (48ft 5in); Wingspan: 8.22m (27ft); Height: 4.5m (14ft 9in)
WEIGHT:	12,700kg (27,998lb)
POWERPLANT:	SNECMA Atar 9C afterburning turbojet, 41.97kN (944 lb)
MAXIMUM SPEED:	2112km/h (1320mph)
RANGE:	3335km (2072 miles)
SERVICE CEILING:	17,000m (55,770ft)
CREW:	1
ARMAMENT:	2 × 30mm (1.1in) cannon plus 4000kg (8818lb) of external stores, typically 2 × Sidewinder or Magic heat-seeking missile plus 1 × Matra R.530 radar-guided missile

Undertaken as a private venture, the delta-wing Mirage III became an enormous export success as well as arming the air force of France. It fought in several conflicts of the mid- to late twentieth century.

ISRAELI MIRAGE
A Mirage IIICJ in Israeli colours, at the time of the 1967 Six-Day War. Although not an outstanding strike aircraft, the Mirage proved to be an excellent air-to-air platform.

DELTA WING
The high sweep of the Mirage III's delta wing resulted in reduced drag at high speeds, while enabling the aircraft to dispense with a conventional tail surface.

TURBOJET ENGINE
The Atar turbojet engine of the Mirage III was used in a variety of Mirage variants and also in the Etendard and Super Etendard naval strike aircraft.

IN SERVICE

The Mirage III was bought by a number of export clients and built under licence in several nations. A major user was Israel, whose pilots contributed to the Mirage's export success by demonstrating its effectiveness in the Six-Day of 1967. More than 80 per cent of Arab aircraft downed in the conflict were at the hands of Mirages, although ground-attack performance was less impressive.

MIRAGE IIICJ
The Mirage IIICJ was primarily an interceptor, designed to climb fast and travel at high speeds in a straight line. The ability to get into missile range of incoming bombers was of extreme importance in the early Cold War years.

WEAPONS
In addition to its two 30mm (1.1in) cannon, the Mirage III could carry around 4000kg (8818lb) of external stores, including missiles, bombs, rocket pods or long-range fuel tanks.

MIRAGES IN THE RAAF
Two Mirage III aircraft of the Royal Australian Air Force take off on a mission during the joint Australian, New Zealand and US (ANZUS) Exercise TRIAD '84.

McDonnell Douglas F-4 Phantom II (1958)

SPECIFICATIONS

DIMENSIONS:	Length: 17.75m (58ft 3in); Wingspan: 11.71m (38ft 5in); Height: 4.95m (16ft 3in)
WEIGHT:	24,766kg (54,600lb) maximum take-off
POWERPLANT:	2 × General Electric J79-GE-8B turbojets, 75.4kN (17,000lb)
MAXIMUM SPEED:	2390km/h (1485mph)
RANGE:	3701km (2300 miles) ferry range
SERVICE CEILING:	18,900m (62,000ft)
CREW:	2
ARMAMENT:	4 × AIM-7 Sparrow air-to-air missiles and up to 4 × AIM-9B/D Sidewinder air-to-air missiles, plus up to 7257kg (16,000lb) of attack weapons

The definitive Western fighter of the Cold War era, the F-4 had it all: performance, advanced avionics and the ability to haul huge quantities of sophisticated weaponry. Originally intended as a carrier fighter for the US Navy, the powerful Phantom remains in frontline service as a fighter-bomber and interceptor.

Below: For anti-shipping work, the F-4EJ Kai can be equipped with the ASM-2 missile, seen here underwing. This turbojet-powered weapon uses infrared guidance for terminal accuracy.

COCKPIT
The backseater was provided with three primary displays that received information from the AN/APR-38, including a threat prioritization system.

STORES OPTIONS
As well as the three types of anti-radar missile, the F-4G could carry a wide range of air-to-ground and air-to-air ordnance, including AGM-65 Maverick missiles, guided bombs and cluster weapons.

FIN CAP
A distinguishing feature of the F-4G was the fin cap that housed a group of receivers for the AN/APR-38. A total of 52 separate receivers were distributed across the airframe, with another prominent group in the enlarged chin pod.

AGM-88 HARM
The HARM homes automatically on hostile radars, providing its receivers are tuned to the correct wavelength. Its high speeds are intended to ensure the radar is destroyed before it can be switched off.

TURBOJETS
The Phantom's superb performance characteristics were the result of its powerful twin-turbojets, fed by fully variable air intakes and exhausting via nozzles with a carefully arranged secondary flow.

PRODUCTION VARIANTS

The initial production model for the US Navy was the F4H-1F (redesignated as the F-4A in September 1962), which succeeded in gaining a number of world speed and time-to-height records. Next in line was the F-4B, of which 649 were built. The B-model had a bulged nose containing an AN/APQ-72 radar, and a raised rear seat. First deployed on carriers in August 1962, it became the standard all-weather fighter for the US Navy and Marine Corps.

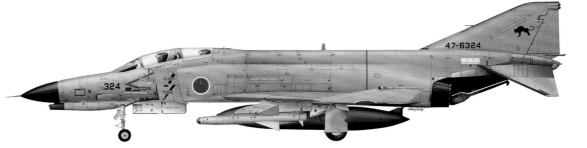

JASDF PHANTOM
An upgraded F-4EJ Kai of the Japan Air Self-Defense Force's 8 Hikotai based at Misawa. The unit had a dual-role ground-attack and anti-shipping assignment.

Mikoyan-Gurevich MiG-21 (1959)

SPECIFICATIONS

DIMENSIONS:	Length: 15m (49ft 2in) with Pitot; Wingspan: 7.15m (23ft 6in); Height: 4.13m (13ft 6in)
WEIGHT:	8725kg (19,325lb) loaded
POWERPLANT:	Tumansky R25-300 afterburning turbojet, 69.62kN (15,650lb)
MAXIMUM SPEED:	2237km/h (1468mph)
RANGE:	1210km (751 miles) on internal fuel
SERVICE CEILING:	17,800m (58,400ft)
CREW:	1
ARMAMENT:	1 × 23mm (0.9in) cannon and 4 × air-to-air missiles or 2 × 500kg (1102lb) bombs

Veteran of more conflicts than any other post-war fighter, the MiG-21 has served with around 60 nations and remains in large-scale frontline service to this day. A plethora of variants and upgrades have been fielded as part of a production run that extended to over 11,000, making it the most prolific supersonic fighter.

TAILFIN
The tailfin is topped by a streamlined fairing for the radar warning receiver. Below this is the rudder, driven by hydraulic power. At the base of the fin is a container for a braking parachute.

CANOPY
Due to the poor rear visibility afforded from the cockpit, the pilot is fitted with a rear-view mirror attached to the canopy. The canopy of the MiG-21M is sideways-opening.

AIR DATA PROBE
A long boom mounted on the nose carries pitot/static heads for the airspeed system as well as pitch/yaw sensor vanes.

CHEAP AND FAST
Small, fast and agile, the MiG-21 was in many ways the antithesis of the increasingly heavy and capable Western fighters that began to be fielded from the early 1960s. The MiG-21, codenamed 'Fishbed' in the West, was originally schemed as a Mach 2-capable bomber interceptor that would be cheap enough to be fielded in significant numbers. In the event, the MiG-21 saw widespread combat service, frequently against its Western counterparts, in war zones ranging from the Middle East to Vietnam and Africa.

UNDERWING STORES
This aircraft carries a typical underwing load of UB-16-57 launchers for 57mm (2.24in) rockets inboard, with French-made MATRA R.550 Magic missiles outboard.

CENTRELINE PYLON
This is plumbed for the carriage of a streamlined 'supersonic' drop tank, carrying 490 litres (129 gallons) of additional fuel.

ROMANIAN MIG-21M
A Romanian Air Force MiG-21M upgraded to Lancer-A standard. While the Lancer A has been withdrawn, in 2014 Lancer-B/Cs continued to serve with two squadrons at two different bases.

Grumman F-14 Tomcat (1970)

The F-14 entered service as a dedicated carrier-based interceptor, built around a powerful fire-control system and long-range missiles. Following the end of the Cold War, the Tomcat was reborn as a multi-role fighter-bomber. In this form, it saw out its career with combat duty over Afghanistan and Iraq.

SPECIFICATIONS

DIMENSIONS:	Length: 19.1m (62ft 8in); Wingspan: 19.45m (64ft 1in) wings spread; Height: 4.88m (16ft)
WEIGHT:	33,724kg (74,348lb) maximum take-off
POWERPLANT:	2 × Pratt & Whitney TF30-P-412 afterburning turbofans, 92.97kN (20,900lb)
MAXIMUM SPEED:	2485km/h (1544mph) 'clean' at high altitude
RANGE:	1233km (766 miles) radius of action with 6 × AIM-7s and 4 × AIM-9s
SERVICE CEILING:	More than 15,240m (50,000ft)
CREW:	2
ARMAMENT:	1 × 20mm (0.79in) rotary cannon plus up to 6577kg (14,500lb) of external ordnance including 4 or 6 × AIM-54 or AIM-7 AAMs plus 2 × AIM-9 AAMs

VARIABLE-GEOMETRY WINGS
The Tomcat's variable-geometry outer wings are equipped with full-span leading edge slats and almost full-span trailing edge flaps. Front-section spoilers provide roll control.

AIM-9 SIDEWINDER
Used for close-in air combat, the AIM-9 is provided with infrared guidance, conferring a 'fire and forget' capability.

REAR FUSELAGE
This includes upper and lower speed brakes in the tapered rear fuselage decking between the engine nozzles. An arrester hook is provided below this decking, lying flush when not required.

VULCAN CANNON
The General Electric M61A1 Vulcan cannon in the nose is provided with 675 rounds of ammunition and can be selected to fire at 4000 or 6000 rounds per minute.

FIRST KILLS
The initial F-14A version entered service in 1972 and saw its first combat in US Navy hands in August 1981, when examples shot down a pair of Libyan Su-22 fighters over the Mediterranean. In another action in January 1989, US Navy Tomcats downed a pair of Libyan MiG-23s over the Gulf of Sidra. Meanwhile, the only export operator, Iran, put its Tomcat fleet to good use during the Iran–Iraq War, in the course of which the type was credited with as many as 64 Iraqi aircraft confirmed destroyed.

AIM-7 SPARROW
The AIM-7 was the primary medium-range air-to-air weapon for the US Navy F-14. The weapon utilizes semi-active radar homing guidance, tracking the fighter's own radar signals reflected from the target.

AIM-54 PHOENIX
The AIM-54 has a range of 150km (93 miles). It is guided initially by the F-14's radar, before acquiring and tracking the target during the mid-course of the engagement. The missile's own on-board active radar is used for guidance in the terminal phase.

Above: The early days of US Navy Tomcat operations saw units wear flamboyant markings. Typical was this F-14A of VF-1 'Wolfpack', on board USS *Enterprise* (CVN 65) in the mid-1970s.

Lockheed Martin F-16 Fighting Falcon (1974)

TYPE · *Fighters* · **FAMILY** · *Aircraft, Helicopters & Drones*

SPECIFICATIONS

DIMENSIONS: Length: 15.03m (49ft 4in); Wingspan: 9.45m (91ft); Height: 5.09m (16ft 8in)

WEIGHT: 12,292kg (27,099lb) maximum take-off

POWERPLANT: General Electric F110-GE-129 afterburning turbofan, 131.48kN (29,588lb)

MAXIMUM SPEED: More than 2125km/h (1321mph) at 12,190m (40,000ft)

RANGE: 1485km (923 miles) radius of action, with 2 × 907kg (2000lb) bombs and 2 × AIM-9 Sidewinder AAMs

SERVICE CEILING: More than 15,240m (50,000ft)

CREW: 1

ARMAMENT: 1 × 20mm (0.79in) rotary cannon and up to 7072kg (15,591lb) of disposable stores carried on 1 under-fuselage, 6 underwing and 2 wingtip hardpoints

In the last 40 years, the F-16 has established itself as the most popular Western fighter in its class, and today serves with 28 nations around the world. The latest production standards and upgrades ensure it will retain its capability well into the twenty-first century, as production continues beyond the 4500-aircraft mark.

Below: US-supplied F-16s arrive for service in the Israeli Air Force in July 1980. These were newly built F-16A/B Block 10 Netz (Sparrowhawk) jets and they equipped Nos. 117 'First Jet' and 110 'Knights of the North' Squadrons.

RADOME
In the F-16A, this houses a Westinghouse AN/APG-66 coherent pulse-Doppler radar, operating in the I/J bands. The antenna is of the planar array (flat plate) type.

TAILFIN
The multi-spar, multi-rib aluminium fin has graphite-epoxy skin and carries a rudder of aluminium honeycomb structure, powered by a servo-actuator. The fin top carries a VHF aerial, anti-collision beacon and directional antennae.

PYTHON 3
Israel has introduced a considerable number of local avionics systems and weapons on its F-16s, including this heat-seeking Rafael Python 3 AAM.

CHANGE OVER TIME
According to the manufacturer, the F-16 has been completed in 138 different configurations from prototype to the latest production model, the F-16V (V for 'Viper', by which name the aircraft is commonly known). Successive changes have taken into account improved cockpit technologies, avionics, sensors and weapons, while at the same time effort has been made to ensure the fighter is more reliable and easier to maintain and support.

INTAKE
Unusual for a high-performance jet fighter, the engine intake is simple, with no moving parts. The location ensures the engine is not starved of air even at high angles of attack.

THE 'BARAK'
In Israeli service the F-16C and F-16D (seen here, top and bottom) are known as the Barak (Lightning). This F-16D wears No. 105 'Scorpion' Squadron markings and carries a GBU-15 glide bomb under its right wing.

Panavia Tornado (1974)

SPECIFICATIONS

DIMENSIONS:	Length: 16.72m (54ft 10in); Wingspan: 8.6m (28ft 2in) maximum sweep; Height: 5.95m (19ft 6in)
WEIGHT:	27,951kg (61,620lb) maximum take-off
POWERPLANT:	2 × Turbo-Union RB.199 Mk 103 afterburning turbofans, 71.50kN (16,075lb)
MAXIMUM SPEED:	2338km/h (1453mph) at 10,975m (36,000ft)
RANGE:	1390km (863 miles) combat radius, with a heavy warload on a typical hi-lo-hi mission
SERVICE CEILING:	More than 15,240m (50,000ft)
CREW:	2
ARMAMENT:	2 × 27mm (1.1in) cannon and up to 9000kg (19,841lb) of disposable stores

Developed as an all-weather strike aircraft and interdictor, by the mid-1980s the multinational Tornado had established itself as arguably the most important combat aircraft in Western Europe. The warplane also served as the basis for a long-range interceptor and a dedicated defence suppression aircraft.

Right: A Tornado ADV of the Royal Saudi Air Force. RSAF Tornado ADVs flew 451 sorties during Operation *Desert Storm*, protecting Saudi airspace against any potential Iraqi intrusion.

REFUELLING PROBE
A detachable retractable inflight refuelling probe can be mounted on the right forward fuselage side, close to the cockpit.

WINGS
The variable-geometry wings are of all-metal construction, with fixed inboard portions and movable outer panels. Instead of ailerons, spoilers are found in each upper surface.

TAILFIN
The all-metal tailfin structure includes a rudder and low-set all-moving horizontal tail surfaces, or 'tailerons'. These can be operated collectively as elevators or differentially.

RADOME
The radar-transparent nosecone accommodated antennae for the Texas Instruments multi-mode forward-looking ground mapping and terrain-following radar. An air data probe is mounted on the tip of the radome.

RECCE EQUIPMENT
In place of conventional cameras, the Tornado GR.Mk 1A was equipped with a sideways-looking infrared system and an infrared linescanner, providing horizon-to-horizon coverage.

COUNTERMEASURES POD
The Swedish-designed BOZ pod is a self-contained microprocessor-controlled chaff and flare dispenser that augments the Sky Shadow electronic countermeasures pod carried under the opposite wing.

AIR DEFENCE VARIANT

With an outstanding RAF requirement for a long-range all-weather interceptor, Panavia developed the Air Defence Version (ADV), which was first flown in October 1979 as the Tornado F.Mk 2. The aircraft accommodated Foxhunter radar and tandem pairs of Sky Flash missiles semi-recessed under a lengthened fuselage. Internal fuel was increased to extend unrefuelled endurance to around four hours 30 minutes.

ECR VERSION

The West German Luftwaffe pioneered the development of the Electronic Combat and Reconnaissance (ECR) version of the Tornado, as a specialist defence suppression aircraft. The heart of the ECR is the internal Emitter Location System (ELS) that enables it to locate and identify hostile radar installations.

Sukhoi Su-27 'Flanker' (1977)

SPECIFICATIONS

DIMENSIONS:	Length: 21.9m (71ft 10in); Wingspan: 14.7m (48ft 3in); Height: 5.93m (19ft 5in)
WEIGHT:	33,000kg (72,751lb) maximum take-off
POWERPLANT:	2 × Saturn/Lyulka AL-31F afterburning turbofans, 122.58kN (27,557lb)
MAXIMUM SPEED:	2280km/h (1417mph) 'clean' at 11,000m (36,090ft)
RANGE:	3680km (2287 miles) at high altitude
SERVICE CEILING:	17,700m (58,071ft)
CREW:	1
ARMAMENT:	1 × 30mm (1.18in) cannon and up to 6000kg (13,228lb) of disposable stores including up to 6 × medium-range and 4 × short-range AAMs

Planned as a Soviet counterweight to the F-15 Eagle, the Su-27 entered service as an air superiority fighter but has demonstrated considerable growth potential, being further developed as a carrier fighter and proving to be an export success.

Right: A specially marked Su-27 'Flanker-B' of the Russian Air Force Training Centre at Lipetsk in the mid-1990s. This unit is tasked with training weapons instructors and developing tactics.

Below: A Su-27 'Flanker-B' of the 582nd Fighter Aviation Regiment, part of the Soviet 4th Air Army based at Chojna, Poland, in 1990. In the same year, this unit withdrew its 32 Su-27s from Poland and relocated to Smolensk, Russia, where it disbanded in 1992.

RADAR
The original Su-27 and Su-27UB uses the N001 radar with a twist-Cassegrain antenna. It can detect a fighter-size target, head-on, at 110–120km (68–75 miles).

SELF-PROTECTION
The self-protection suite includes a radar warning receiver (RWR), a two-pod electronic countermeasures (ECM) system and chaff/flare dispensers.

FIGHTER DEFENCE
The basic 'Flanker' continues to provide the backbone of the Russian Air Force fighter fleet, with 180 examples in service in 2013. These aircraft are undergoing a mid-life upgrade, transforming them into the Su-27SM that is based around a new avionics suite. More recently, Russia has procured three more new-build 'Flanker' versions: the two-seat Su-30M2 and Su-30SM, as well as the thrust-vectoring single-seat Su-35S. The Su-30M2 and Su-30SM are both domestic versions of the significantly improved two-seat derivatives of the 'Flanker'.

IRST
Located ahead of the cockpit, the infrared search and track (IRST) sensor and laser rangefinder is slaved to the radar. It has a high-altitude detection range of 50km (31 miles) against a receding target (in tail-on attack).

R-27 MISSILES
Basic beyond-visual-range weapons for the Su-27 are the semi-active radar-homing R-27R and infrared-homing R-27T (AA-10 'Alamo'), and the extended-range R-27ER and R-27ET derivatives.

ADDITIONAL LIFT
The Su-27 features a prominent leading edge root extension (LERX) that provides additional lift, helping destabilize the heavy radar nose. The starboard wing root contains a 30mm (1.18in) cannon.

Mikoyan MiG-29 'Fulcrum' (1977)

SPECIFICATIONS

DIMENSIONS:	Length: 17.32m (56ft 10in) including probe; Wingspan: 11.36m (37ft 3in); Height: 4.73m (15ft 6in)
WEIGHT:	18,500kg (40,785lb) maximum take-off
POWERPLANT:	2 × Klimov RD-33 afterburning turbofans, 81.39kN (18,298lb)
MAXIMUM SPEED:	2445km/h (1520mph) at high altitude
RANGE:	1500km (932 miles) with standard fuel
SERVICE CEILING:	19,800m (65,000ft)
CREW:	1
ARMAMENT:	1 × 30mm (1.18in) cannon and up to 3000kg (6614lb) of disposable stores carried on 6 underwing hardpoints

Developed by the USSR in response to increasingly sophisticated Western warplanes, the MiG-29 soon established a formidable reputation as an agile dogfighter. Despite its shortcomings, it has continued to undergo development with efforts to extend its range and the addition of a multi-role capability.

TAIL
The twin canted tailfins are combined with all-moving horizontal tail surfaces. Unlike Western counterparts, the early MiG-29s relied on mainly conventional, hydraulically operated flying controls.

AERODYNAMICS
As part of the high-lift, low-drag design ethos, the MiG-29 employs a widely flared wing leading edge root extension, while the intakes for the widely spaced engines are also optimized for high angle-of-attack capability.

STRUCTURE
The MiG-29 was one of the first Soviet aircraft to make extensive use of lightweight aluminium-lithium alloys, reducing overall weight and complexity.

POLISH 'FULCRUMS'
Poland is a NATO member, and the Polish Air Force remains an enthusiastic MiG-29 operator. Poland first ordered nine MiG-29As and three MiG-29UBs, the first of which were delivered in 1989. In 1995, Poland decided to purchase 10 surplus MiG-29s (nine MiG-29As and one MiG-29UB) from the Czech Republic. With the withdrawal from service of Luftwaffe MiG-29s, 22 former East German aircraft (18 MiG-29Gs and four MiG-29GTs) were offered to Poland for a symbolic Euro. The offer was accepted; the first aircraft arrived in Poland in September 2003.

POWERPLANT
In its basic form, the MiG-29 is powered by a pair of RD-33 turbofans, offering increased thrust in afterburning when compared to Western engines, albeit with slightly reduced dry output.

CONTROL SURFACES
The leading edge of the wing is fitted with full-span manoeuvring flaps that are computer-controlled. The trailing edge is outfitted with plain flaps inboard and ailerons outboard.

UPGRADES
In order to continue to operate within NATO, and to extend their service lives, Polish MiGs are being upgraded with a new digital databus with open architecture.

Dassault Mirage 2000 (1978)

SPECIFICATIONS

DIMENSIONS:	Length: 14.36m (47ft 1in); Wingspan: 9.13m (29ft 11in); Height: 5.2m (17ft)
WEIGHT:	15,000kg (33,069lb) maximum take-off
POWERPLANT:	SNECMA M53-P20 afterburning turbofan, 98.06kN (22,046lb)
MAXIMUM SPEED:	2335km/h (1451mph) at high altitude
RANGE:	3333km (2071 miles) with drop tanks
SERVICE CEILING:	16,460m (54,000ft)
CREW:	2
ARMAMENT:	2 × 30mm (1.18in) cannon and up to 6300kg (13,889lb) of disposable stores carried on 5 under-fuselage and 4 underwing hardpoints

Continuing the tradition of delta-winged Dassault fighters, the Mirage 2000 brought the family up to date and established itself not only as the backbone of the French Air Force but also as a genuine success on the export market. The basic fighter has been adapted for roles including nuclear strike and conventional attack.

Below: A Mirage 2000H (known locally as Vajra – Thunderbolt) of No. 1 'The Tigers' Squadron, Central Air Command, Indian Air Force, based at Maharajpura Air Force Station, Gwailor, in the 1990s. A former MiG-21 unit, No. 1 Squadron was the second IAF Mirage 2000 operator after No. 7 Squadron.

Above: A Mirage 2000C of the 5e Escadre de Chasse, as it appeared during Operation *Daguet*, France's contribution to the 1991 Gulf War. The aircraft was one of 14 based in Al Ahsa, Saudi Arabia.

RADAR
The Mirage 2000H was delivered with the Thomson-CSF RDM multi-role radar, which provides continuous-wave target illumination for use with Doppler homing missiles.

SUPER 530 AAM
For air interception, the basic weapon of the Mirage 2000H is the MATRA Super 530D missile, which uses a monopulse continuous-wave Doppler semi-active radar seeker.

WING
Large and lightly loaded, the wing is fitted with automatic leading edge slats for manoeuvrability and two-piece elevons on the trailing edge.

NUCLEAR STRIKE
In 1979, Dassault received a contract to produce two prototypes of a nuclear strike version, which became the Mirage 2000N. Based on the two-seat Mirage 2000B airframe, this features an airframe strengthened for low-level operations, and attack avionics based around the Antilope 5 radar. The primary weapon is the ASMP stand-off nuclear missile. A total of 75 Mirage 2000Ns were built for the French Air Force; the type achieved initial operational capability in 1988.

TARGETING PODS
While the first air-to-ground version of the Mirage 2000, the Mirage 2000N, was not initially equipped with a targeting pod, this omission was addressed in the conventional-optimized Mirage 2000D. The first targeting pods for this model were the PDL-CT (Pod de Désignation Laser-Caméra Thermique), which provided thermal imaging designation, and the ATLIS day-only system.

McDonnell Douglas F/A-18 Hornet (1978)

TYPE · *Fighters* · **FAMILY** · *Aircraft, Helicopters & Drones*

SPECIFICATIONS

DIMENSIONS:	Length: 17.07m (56ft); Wingspan: 11.43m (37ft 6in) without wingtip missiles; Height: 4.66m (15ft 3in)
WEIGHT:	21,888kg (48,253lb) maximum take-off, attack mission
POWERPLANT:	2 × General Electric F404-GE-402 afterburning turbofans, 78.73kN (17,700lb)
MAXIMUM SPEED:	More than 1915km/h (1190mph) at high altitude
RANGE:	More than 3336km (2073 miles) ferry with drop tanks
SERVICE CEILING:	15,240m (50,000ft)
CREW:	1
ARMAMENT:	1 × 20mm (0.79in) rotary cannon and up to 6200kg (13,700lb) of disposable stores

Replacing the F-4 Phantom II in the fleet air defence role, and the A-7 Corsair II attack aircraft, the Hornet brought the US Navy's carrier air wing into a new era with a genuine multi-role carrier fighter. The 'legacy' F/A-18 also continues to serve with the US Marine Corps and a number of export operators.

Below: An F/A-18D of the US Marine Corps' VMFA(AW)-225 armed with 127mm (5in) Zuni unguided rockets underwing, used for target-marking purposes in the forward air controller (airborne) role.

Below: An F/A-18A of Marine Fighter Attack Squadron (VMFA) 314 'Black Knights', aboard the USS *Coral Sea* in the Mediterranean in 1986. The unit was engaged in attacks on Libyan radar sites during Operations *El Dorado Canyon* and *Prairie Fire*.

WINGTIP PYLON
The wingtip hardpoint is normally reversed to carry a version of the Sidewinder AAMs. Seen here is the AIM-9M, which has now been joined by the advanced AIM-9X.

POWERPLANT
The 'legacy' Hornet is powered by the General Electric F404 afterburning low-bypass turbofan, which was derived from the YJ101 engines used in the YF-17.

EXPORT HORNETS
Land-based Hornets have been acquired by seven nations. The first export customer for the type was Canada, which took delivery of 98 single-seat CF-188As and 40 two-seat CF-188Bs between 1982 and 1988. Australia was next, taking 57 F/A-18As and 18 F/A-18Bs. Spain acquired 60 EF-18As and 12 EF-18Bs. Thereafter, export aircraft were all completed to F/A-18C/D standard, comprising 32 F/A-18Cs and eight F/A-18Ds for Kuwait; 26 F/A-18Cs and eight F/A-18Ds for Switzerland; 57 F-18Cs and seven F-18Ds for Finland and eight F/A-18Ds for Malaysia.

RADAR
In the original F/A-18A, two-seat F/A-18B and early C-model aircraft the radar was the Hughes AN/APG-65 multi-mode sytstem, which later gave way to the APG-73.

FUEL
This is carried in four main fuel tanks in the aircraft's spine. The internal total of 5300 litres (1400 gallons) can be supplemented by up to three drop tanks each of 1249-litre (330-gallon) capacity.

KNIGHTHAWKS
An F/A-18C aircraft assigned to Strike Fighter Squadron (VFA) 136 'Knighthawks' unloads a flare over the Persian Gulf before heading into Afghanistan for a close air support mission.

Boeing F-15E Strike Eagle (1986)

SPECIFICATIONS

DIMENSIONS:	Length: 19.43m (63ft 9in); Wingspan: 13.05m (42ft 10in); Height: 5.63m (18ft 5in)
WEIGHT:	36,741kg (81,000lb) maximum take-off
POWERPLANT:	2 × Pratt & Whitney F100-PW-220 afterburning turbofans, 106kN (23,830lb)
MAXIMUM SPEED:	More than 2655km/h (1650mph) at high altitude
RANGE:	1271km (790 miles) radius of action, typical mission with maximum warload
SERVICE CEILING:	18,290m (60,000ft)
CREW:	2
ARMAMENT:	1 × 20mm (0.79in) rotary cannon plus up to 11,000kg (24,250lb) of external ordnance

While the McDonnell Douglas (later absorbed by Boeing) F-15 Eagle established itself as the West's premier air superiority fighter, with a peerless victory to loss ratio of 104:0, further development led to the F-15E Strike Eagle, an all-weather ground-attack aircraft that retains all the air-combat capabilities of the original Eagle.

Below: An F-15E as flown by the commander of the 48th Fighter Wing at RAF Lakenheath. The aircraft is armed for a close support mission, with 14 SUU-30H/B cluster bombs, plus AIM-9s.

RADAR
The F-15E was originally fielded with the AN/APG-70 radar, offering a high-resolution synethic aperture mapping mode. The latest USAF upgrade adds the AN/APG-82(V)1 active electronically scanned array (AESA) radar.

AIM-120 AMRAAM
Carried on the shoulder launch rails, the AMRAAM confers a powerful air-to-air capability, this being a 'fire and forget' missile with active guidance.

WINGS
The wings are based around an extremely strong torque box of light alloy and titanium, to which are attached wingtip sections, flaps and ailerons of aluminium honeycomb.

STRIKE EAGLE SERVICE
The Strike Eagle entered service with the 40th Tactical Training Wing at Luke AFB in 1988. Initial operational deliveries then followed to the 4th TFW at Seymour Johnson AFB, North Carolina. The F-15E made its combat debut during Operation *Desert Storm* in 1991, when its primary mission was to seek and destroy Iraqi 'Scud' mobile ballistic missiles. Since then, the F-15E has been at the forefront of every major US military air campaign.

PAVEWAY LGB
An important weapon for the F-15E, the Paveway laser-guided bomb series includes weapons of 227kg (500lb), 907kg (2000lb) and 2132kg (4700lb). This is a 227kg GBU-12 weapon.

POWERPLANT
The Pratt & Whitney F100 turbofan is a two-stage axial turbofan that offers a very useful thrust-to-weight ratio. The smokeless combustor is provided with air from a 10-stage compressor.

EAGLES OF *ENDURING FREEDOM*
An F-15E from the USAF's 4th Fighter Wing flies over Afghanistan in April 2006. The USAF rotated detachments of F-15Es to Southwest Asia, from where they conducted close air support missions for troops on the ground engaged in rooting out insurgent sanctuaries and support networks. Over Afghanistan, F-15Es typically carried a mix of 227kg (500lb) GBU-12 laser-guided bombs and 907kg (2000lb) GBU-31 GPS-guided bombs, plus up to 500 rounds of ammunition for their M61A1 20mm (0.79in) cannon.

Dassault Rafale (1986)

SPECIFICATIONS

DIMENSIONS:	Length: 15.27m (50ft 1in); Wingspan: 10.8m (35ft 5in); Height: 5.34m (17ft 6in)
WEIGHT:	24,500kg (54,012lb) maximum take-off
POWERPLANT:	2 × SNECMA M88-2 afterburning turbofans, 75kN (16,861lb)
MAXIMUM SPEED:	1913km/h (1189mph) at 11,000m (36,090ft)
RANGE:	1055km (655 miles), low-level with warload and drop tanks
SERVICE CEILING:	16,765m (60,000ft)
CREW:	1
ARMAMENT:	1 × 30mm (1.18in) cannon and up to 9500kg (20,944lb) of disposable stores carried on 14 under-fuselage, underwing and wingtip stations

Described by the manufacturer as an 'omni-role' fighter, the Rafale has excelled in action with both the French Air Force and Navy. Its undoubted capabilities across the combat spectrum have attracted interest on the export market.

Below and right: An early Rafale M of the French Navy. The Rafale is the only non-US fighter cleared to operate from the decks of US carriers, using their catapults and arresting gear.

CANARD CONFIGURATION
The close-coupled canard/delta wing configuration ensures the Rafale remains agile even at high angles of attack.

ENGINES
The M88-2 uses advanced technologies, including integrally bladed compressor disks ('blisks'), and a low-pollution combustor with smoke-free emissions.

REFUELLING PROBE
The refuelling probe is fixed in order to avoid any deployment or retraction problem and is a permanent fixture.

FLIGHT CONTROL
The quadruple-redundant fly-by-wire flight control system provides for longitudinal stability and superior handling performance across three digital channels and one separately designed analogue channel.

STEALTH TREATMENT
Airframe radar cross-section is minimized by using appropriate materials and mould line, including serrated edges to the trailing edge of the wings and canards.

RAFALE IN COMBAT
The Rafale went into combat over Afghanistan in 2006. In 2011, French Air Force and French Navy aircraft engaged in coalition operations over Libya, conducting air superiority, precision strike, deep strike and intelligence, surveillance, target acquisition and reconnaissance (ISTAR) and strike coordination and reconnaissance (SCAR). More recently, French Air Force Rafales have taken a leading role in Mali, helping destroy enemy infrastructure and support friendly troops in contact. The Rafale has also been active against Islamic insurgents in Iraq, flying from its forward base at Al Dhafra in the United Arab Emirates.

AASM HAMMER
The AASM (*Armement Air-Sol Modulaire*, Air-to-Surface Modular Weapon) is a low-cost, all-weather 'fire-and-forget' weapon. Intended to attack targets at long ranges, the AASM is also known as 'Hammer'.

Lockheed Martin F-22 Raptor (1990)

SPECIFICATIONS

DIMENSIONS:	Length: 18.9m (62ft 1in); Wingspan: 13.6m (44ft 6in); Height: 5.1m (16ft 8in)
WEIGHT:	38,000kg (83,500lb) maximum take-off
POWERPLANT:	2 × Pratt & Whitney F119-PW-100 afterburning turbofans, 155.69kN (35,000lb)
MAXIMUM SPEED:	Around 2410km/h (1500mph) at altitude (estimated)
RANGE:	More than 2977km (1850 miles), ferry with 2 external wing fuel tanks
SERVICE CEILING:	15,240m (50,000ft)
CREW:	1
ARMAMENT:	1 × 20mm (0.79in) rotary cannon, plus 2 × AIM-9 AAMs and 6 × AIM-120 AAMs, or (ground attack) 2 × GBU-32 JDAMs and 2 × AIM-120s

Widely regarded as the most capable air superiority fighter in service anywhere in the world, the F-22A is capable of both air-to-air and air-to-ground missions. It has been designed to combine stealth, performance, agility and integrated avionics in a single airframe.

Above: An F-22A wearing the FF ('First Fighter') tail code of the USAF's 1st Fighter Wing, at Langley AIr Force Base, Virginia.

DATALINK
A Raptor pilot can receive information from other F-22s, allowing a radar-silent attack. A Raptor that is outside its missile envelope can thus track a target and covertly send target data to a closer Raptor to make the silent kill.

ENGINES
The two Pratt & Whitney F119 engines allow the Raptor to accelerate to and cruise at speeds of about Mach 1.8 without using afterburners.

ATTACK AIRCRAFT

Although it was originally planned as an air dominance fighter, the F-22 has latterly emerged as a powerful attack aircraft. In the air-to-ground configuration, the aircraft can carry two 907kg (2000lb) GBU-32 Joint Direct Attack Munitions (JDAM) internally and up to eight GBU-39 Small Diameter Bombs (SDBs). Whether carrying JDAMs or SDBs, the Raptor can also carry two AIM-120s and two AIM-9s for self-defence. The F-22A made its combat debut in this role, striking targets in Syria in September 2014.

RADAR
Exploiting its stealthy characteristics, the F-22 has a 'first look, first shot' advantage. The AN/APG-77 active electronically scanned array (AESA) radar can track targets before going electronically silent.

INTERNAL MISSILES
The primary air-to-air weapons are the AIM-9M Sidewinder and the AIM-120C AMRAAM. Weapons are carried in the internal weapons bays, which open up at the very last second as the Raptor 'uncloaks'.

AERODYNAMICS
Advanced aerodynamics, combined with thrust vectoring and cutting-edge flight control systems, provide so-called 'super manoeuvrability'.

US OPERATOR
An F-22A of 27th Fighter Squadron (FS), 1st Fighter Wing (FW), the USAF's first Raptor unit.

Eurofighter Typhoon (1994)

SPECIFICATIONS

DIMENSIONS:	Length: 15.96m (52ft 4in); Wingspan: 10.95m (35ft 11in); Height: 5.28m (17ft 4in)
WEIGHT:	23,500kg (51,809lb) maximum take-off
POWERPLANT:	2 × Eurojet EJ200 afterburning turbofans, 90kN (20,000lb)
MAXIMUM SPEED:	2125km/h (1321mph) at 11,000m (36,090ft)
ENDURANCE:	1390km (864 miles) radius, air superiority mission with 3 drop tanks
SERVICE CEILING:	14,500m (47,570ft)
CREW:	1/2
ARMAMENT:	1 × 27mm (1in) cannon and up to 8000kg (17,637lb) of disposable stores carried on 13 under-fuselage and underwing stations

A European collaborative project, like the Panavia Tornado that preceded it, the Eurofighter Typhoon aimed to provide four of the continent's air forces with a highly capable air defence fighter that would be superior in all respects to the latest generation of Soviet warplanes then coming on line.

Below: The twin 'chin' engine intakes have a hinged lower lip ('varicowl') to ensure good performance at all speeds and angles of attack. An ogival splitter plate removes boundary layer airflow and feeds the engines with clean, fast-moving air.

COCKPIT
Pilot workload is reduced through the use of features such as direct voice input (DVI) and hands on throttle and stick (HOTAS) control functions. This allows single-pilot operations even in the most demanding missions.

ENGINES
The two-spool EJ200 uses a single-stage turbine driving a three-stage fan and five-stage compressor with annular combustion with vaporizing burners. It can cruise at supersonic speeds without afterburning.

PRODUCTION
The first production deliveries of the Typhoon took place in 2003. Eurofighters are being built in three Tranches, or batches. Tranche 1 comprised 148 aircraft: 33 for Germany, 28 for Italy, 19 for Spain and 53 for the UK, plus 15 for Austria, which received some aircraft diverted from Germany. Tranche 2 provided a further 275 aircraft, comprising 79 for Germany, 47 for Italy, 34 for Spain and 67 for the UK, plus 48 for Saudi Arabia. Tranche 3 will see another 200 aircraft produced: 40 for the UK, 31 for Germany, 21 for Italy, 28 for Kuwait, 12 for Oman, 24 for Qatar, 24 for Saudi Arabia and 20 for Spain. Economic changes, however, make all intended deliveries subject to change.

RADAR
The Captor-M mechanically scanned radar's wide field of regard offers significant benefits in both air-to-air and air-to-surface engagements, offering considerable power and aperture for enhanced angular coverage.

AIRFRAME
Only 15 per cent of the Typhoon's surface is metallic, thereby enhancing stealth and protection against radar-based systems. In all, 75 per cent of the aircraft is fabricated from carbon-fibre composites.

AERODYNAMICS
The Typhoon employs a deliberately unstable aerodynamic configuration that delivers superior manoeuvrability at subsonic speeds as well as efficient supersonic capability.

BRITISH PROTOTYPE
DA.2, serial ZH588, was the first British prototype, and is seen armed with AIM-9L Sidewinder missiles. The aircraft was first flown at Warton in April 1994 and is now at the RAF Museum.

Lockheed Martin F-35 Lightning II (2006)

TYPE · *Fighters* · FAMILY · *Aircraft, Helicopters & Drones*

SPECIFICATIONS

DIMENSIONS:	Length: 15.7m (51ft 5in); Wingspan: 10.7m (35ft); Height: 4.38m (14ft 5in)
WEIGHT:	Around 31,750kg (70,000lb) maximum take-off
POWERPLANT:	Pratt & Whitney F135-PW-100 afterburning turbofan, 178kN (40,000lb)
MAXIMUM SPEED:	Around 1931km/h (1200mph) with full internal weapons load
ENDURANCE:	2200km (1367 miles), internal fuel
SERVICE CEILING:	Undisclosed
CREW:	1
ARMAMENT:	1 × 25mm (0.98in) rotary cannon, 2 × AIM-120C AAMs, 2 × 907kg (2000lb) GBU-31 JDAMs

The F-35 is a remarkable and ambitious combat programme that combines stealth, sensor fusion and network-enabled operations in a single airframe. It is built in three variants to replace four frontline types with the US Air Force, Navy and Marine Corps, plus a variety of fighters for at least 10 other countries.

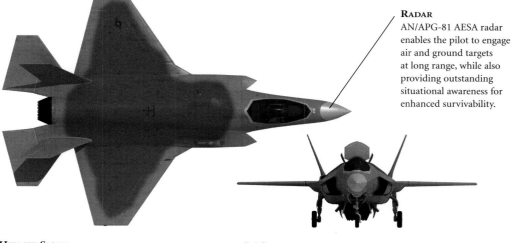

RADAR
AN/APG-81 AESA radar enables the pilot to engage air and ground targets at long range, while also providing outstanding situational awareness for enhanced survivability.

HELMET SIGHT
Real-time imagery is streamed to the helmet, allowing pilots to 'look through' the aircraft. Pilots thus can see the entire environment surrounding them. The helmet also provides pilots with night vision using an integrated camera.

DAS
The Distributed Aperture System (DAS) is the only 360-degree, spherical situational awareness system, sending high-resolution real-time imagery to the pilot's helmet from six infrared cameras mounted around the airframe.

EOTS
The low-drag, stealthy Electro-Optical Targeting System (EOTS) is behind a durable sapphire window. It is linked to the aircraft's integrated central computer through a high-speed fibre-optic interface.

WEAPONS
The internal weapons bay can be complemented by external loads, for example adding four additional JDAMs and two AIM-9X AAMs underwing, complementing two internal JDAMs and two AIM-120s.

STOVL ENGINE
Two primary components provide vertical lift for hover: the LiftFan and 3-Bearing Swivel Module (3BSM). The LiftFan is mounted behind the cockpit. As the aircraft transitions to hover, doors open on top of the aircraft and two counter-rotating fans blow unheated air straight down, producing around half the downward thrust needed. The majority of the remaining vertical thrust is provided by the 3BSM at the rear of the aircraft.

VARIANTS
The F35A is the only version to carry an internal cannon – the 25mm (0.98in) GAU-22/A – and will be the most prolific model. The F-35B is capable of STOVL operation and has a smaller internal weapon bay and reduced internal fuel capacity compared to the F-35A. It is also equipped for the probe and drogue method of aerial refuelling. The F-35C features larger wings and a strengthened undercarriage in order to cope with catapult launches and arrested landings.

JOINT EFFORT
The F-35 makes its initial flight on 15 December 2006 over Fort Worth. The F-35 is in development by the United States and eight other countries: Australia, Canada, Denmark, Italy, the Netherlands, Norway, Turkey and the United Kingdom. Suppliers in all partner countries are producing F-35 components for all aircraft, not just those for their country.

Breguet XIX (1922)

SPECIFICATIONS

DIMENSIONS:	Length: 9.5m (31ft 3in); Wingspan: 14.8m (48ft 8in); Height: 3.69m (12ft 1in)
WEIGHT:	2347kg (5175lb)
POWERPLANT:	Renault 12KD V12 engine, 335kW (450hp)
MAXIMUM SPEED:	234km/h (146mph)
RANGE:	800km (497 miles)
SERVICE CEILING:	7200m (23,600ft)
CREW:	2
ARMAMENT:	1 × Vickers 7.7mm (0.303in) machine gun fixed forward, 2 × Lewis 7.7mm (0.303in) machine guns on observer's mount, 1 × Lewis 7.7mm (0.303in) machine gun on ventral mount

The widely exported Breguet XIX set a record for the first non-stop Paris to New York flight in September 1930. As a warplane, it enjoyed a long and successful career in France, Spain, Greece, Yugoslavia and Poland.

BREGUET BRE.19 A.2
The record-breaking Point d'Interrogation ('Question Mark') was a unique aircraft with an enclosed cockpit, based on a civilian sport variant designated Breguet XIX GR.

WING CONFIGURATION
The Breguet XIX was a sesquiplane design; that is, it had one large wing and a smaller one. Among other advantages, this permitted better downward visibility than identical upper and lower wings.

RECORD BREAKER
At the time of its introduction, the XIX was faster than many fighters, as well as possessing a much greater operating radius. This made it attractive to record-setting pioneers. The first non-stop flight from France to the USA took more than 37 hours – a remarkable feat of endurance for the crew.

IN SERVICE
Essentially an advanced World War I-era design, the Breguet XIX was obsolete by the outbreak of World War II. However, the design gave good service in the 1920s and 1930s during various colonial incidents, rebellions and 'brushfire wars'. Strike aircraft were useful for 'colonial policing' and were at times used to make punitive raids against distant targets. Previously, such a raid would have required a hazardous operation by a 'flying column' of fast-moving ground forces, which still gave no guarantee of reaching the target before rebels or insurgents moved on. Aircraft provided a rapid response to which most colonial opponents had no reply.

POLISH MODEL
A Polish Breguet XIX. These aircraft did not play much part in the defence of Poland in 1939, and were entirely obsolete by then.

ARMAMENT
The twin-Lewis-gun defensive mount was common on many World War I and early inter-war designs, but was ineffective against fast, armoured World War II fighters.

ATLANTIC CROSSING
Flying a Breguet XIX, Maurice Bellonte and Dieudonné Costes performed the first westbound crossing of the North Atlantic, from Paris to New York, in 1930.

Junkers Ju 87 Stuka (1935)

SPECIFICATIONS

DIMENSIONS:	Length: 11.5m (37ft 9in); Wingspan: 13.8m (45ft 3in); Height: 3.9m (12ft 9in)
WEIGHT:	3205kg (7086lb)
POWERPLANT:	Junkers Jumo 211J-1 inverted-Vee piston engine, 1044kW (1400hp)
MAXIMUM SPEED:	410km/h (255mph)
RANGE:	1535km (954 miles)
SERVICE CEILING:	6100m (20,015ft)
CREW:	2
ARMAMENT:	3 × 7.92mm (0.31in) machine guns plus up to 1800kg (3968lb) of external ordnance

The Stuka is remembered as a symbol of the success of Nazi Germany's Blitzkrieg operations in 1939 and 1940. Although rapidly outclassed in its original dive-bomber role, the Ju 87 saw service with the Luftwaffe until the end of the war.

TANK-BUSTING STUKA

The Ju 87G represented a specialist anti-tank aircraft, armed with a pair of 37mm (1.45in) under the wings. This, the final operational version of the Stuka, served with seven *Staffeln*. The Ju 87G had the dive brakes deleted. Although the additional gun armament added considerable weight, the weapons' heavy calibre made them suitable for penetrating the toughest of armoured targets. As an alternative to the guns, the Ju 87G could carry bomb armament.

JUMO ENGINE
In Ju 87B form, the Stuka was powered by a 12-cylinder liquid-cooled Junkers Jumo 211Da engine. This was more powerful than the Jumo 210 in the A-series.

TAILPLANE
To provide additional strength, the Ju 87B's two-spar tailplane was braced by two external struts, replaced on the improved Ju 87D by single aerodynamic struts. The elevators were used in conjunction with aerodynamic brakes to help pull out of a dive.

Below: This Ju 87B-2 was on strength with Sturzkampfgeschwader 77, which flew the type, in different versions, during major operations in World War II, including campaigns in Poland, the Battle of Britain, Greece and the Balkans and, finally, the Eastern Front until 1943.

UNDERCARRIAGE
The robust 'spatted' main undercarriage was a key feature of the Ju 87, although the fairings were often removed to cope with winter conditions on the Eastern Front.

GULL WING
The very strong inverted gull wing was based on a two-spar structure with closely spaced ribs. The centre section was integral with the fuselage. Ailerons and flaps were provided.

Left: The Ju 87G-1 with its twin underwing pods for Bordkanone BK 3.7 (Flak 18) guns. This particular *Kanonenvogel* ('gun bird') served with the 5. Staffel of II./ Schlachtgeschwader 3 based at Jakobstadt, Latvia, in late 1944.

WINTER WARPLANES
Ju 87-Ds wear temporary winter camouflage for operations on the Eastern Front in 1942. The aircraft are armed with AB 500 cluster bomb containers and centreline SC 250 bombs.

Junkers Ju 88 (1936)

SPECIFICATIONS

DIMENSIONS:	Length: 15.58m (51ft 1in); Wingspan: 20m (65ft 7in); Height: 4.85m (15ft 11in)
WEIGHT:	13,100kg (28,880lb) maximum take-off
POWERPLANT:	2 × Junkers Jumo 213E liquid-cooled piston engines, 1342kW (1800hp)
MAXIMUM SPEED:	625km/h (388mph)
RANGE:	2250km (1398 miles)
SERVICE CEILING:	10,000m (32,810ft)
CREW:	3
ARMAMENT:	(Ju 88 A-4) 5 × 7.92mm (0.31in) MG 18J machine guns on multiple mounts; up to 2000kg (4400lb) of ordnance

One of the most versatile warplanes to see service in World War II, the Ju 88 excelled in roles as diverse as medium bomber, anti-shipping strike, close support and night-fighter. It was a mainstay of the Luftwaffe throughout the conflict.

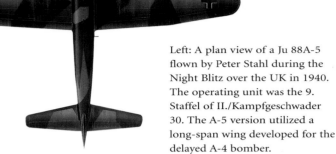

Left: A plan view of a Ju 88A-5 flown by Peter Stahl during the Night Blitz over the UK in 1940. The operating unit was the 9. Staffel of II./Kampfgeschwader 30. The A-5 version utilized a long-span wing developed for the delayed A-4 bomber.

DEFENSIVE ARMAMENT
The pilot had access to a forward-firing MG 15 machine gun that was arranged to fire through the starboard windscreen. One or two similar weapons were usually fitted at the rear of the cockpit.

CREW
The Ju 88A bomber was usually operated by a crew of four: a pilot, co-pilot/bomb aimer, radio operator/ventral gunner and a flight engineer/rear gunner.

BOMB RACKS
Two additional bomb racks, each of 250kg (551lb) capacity, could be fitted below the outer wing panels on the Ju 88A-5.

NIGHT-FIGHTERS
The Ju 88 enjoyed much success as a night-fighter, a role in which it first saw action in summer 1940. The first such aircraft were Ju 88C-2 heavy fighters that were flown as intruders by II./NJG 1, attacking British bomber bases from their base in the Netherlands. First of the dedicated night-fighters was the Ju 88C-6B equipped with FuG 220 Lichtenstein BC radar. Further improvements were manifest in the Ju 88R series, beginning with the R-1 powered by BMW 801 engines, otherwise similar to the Ju 88C-6, and the Ju 88R-2 with uprated BMW 801D engines and with FuG 217 Neptun tail-warning radar.

VENTRAL GONDOLA
As well as being armed with a fourth defensive MG 15, this was used by the bomb aimer.

BOMBLOAD
The Ju 88A-5 was capable of carrying 28 50kg (110lb) bombs internally, while additional weapons, each of up to 500kg (1102lb), could be carried on four racks under the inner wings.

Above: Another KG 30 Ju 88A-5. Based at Westerland-Sylt, the I. Gruppe of this wing was the first to use the Ju 88 in combat. Its initial mission was an anti-shipping attack on British warships in the Firth of Forth on 26 September 1939.

CAPTURED JU 88
A Ju 88A-4, this 3./KG 30 machine landed by mistake at RAF Lulsgate Bottom, after a night raid on Birkenhead in July 1941. It was subsequently throroughly tested by the RAF at Farnborough.

Messerschmitt Bf 110 (1936)

SPECIFICATIONS

DIMENSIONS:	Length: 12.3m (40ft 6in); Wingspan: 16.3m (53ft 4in); Height: 3.3m (10ft 9in)
WEIGHT:	4500kg (9921lb)
POWERPLANT:	2 × Daimler-Benz DB 601B-1 liquid-cooled inverted V-12, 809kW (1085hp) each
MAXIMUM SPEED:	560km/h (348mph)
RANGE:	2410km (1500 miles)
SERVICE CEILING:	10,500m (35,000ft)
CREW:	2/3
ARMAMENT:	2 × 20mm (0.79in) MG FF/M cannon, 4 × 7.92mm (0.31in) MG 17 machine guns, 1 × 7.92 mm (0.31in) MG 15 machine gun; up to 2000kg (4400lb) bombload

Messerschmitt's Bf 110 was one of the Luftwaffe's great hopes at the start of World War II, but the twin-engined *Zerstörer* (destroyer) proved hopelessly vulnerable to single-engined fighter opposition during the Battle of Britain. Nevertheless, it was fast and heavily armed. As the war progressed, it proved to be a solid fighting machine as a long-range fighter and fighter-bomber, as a bomber-destroyer and as a night-fighter.

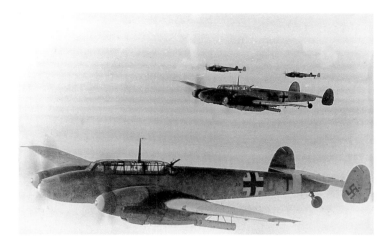

Above: The Bf 110 was without peer when it entered service in 1938 as a long-range heavy 'destroyer' fighter for the Luftwaffe.

ENGINE
All Bf 110s were fitted with the Daimler-Benz DB 601 engine. The prototype had used the DB 600, which was plagued by reliability problems.

NOSE ARMAMENT
There were numerous variants of the Bf 110, with a variety of nose armament. Most early aircraft like this carried four machine guns in the nose and a pair of belly-mounted 20mm (0.79in) cannon.

Above: The Bf 110C-4/B was a fighter-bomber variant. This example served in the Mediterranean with 9/ZG 26 'Horst Wessel', based at Palermo, late in 1940.

COMBAT HANDLING
The Bf 110 was in action in time for the 1939 Polish campaign. That year, the Messerschmitt confirmed its worth as a 'bomber-destroyer' by shooting down nine of 22 RAF Wellington medium bombers on a single mission. This twin-tailed, tailwheel-equipped fighter was rakish and nimble for its size and weight. Pilots found it adequate in combat, although interior space and outside vision left a little to be desired.

DESERT DESTROYER
A Bf 110 kicks up sand as it departs its desert base in North Africa. Its powerful armament was effective in the tank-busting role.

Ilyushin Il-2 Shturmovik (1939)

TYPE · *Ground-Attack Aircraft* · **FAMILY** · *Aircraft, Helicopters & Drones*

SPECIFICATIONS

DIMENSIONS: Length: 11.6m (38ft 1in); Wingspan: 14.6m (47ft 11in); Height: 4.2m (13ft 9in)

WEIGHT: 6380kg (14,065lb) maximum take-off

POWERPLANT: Mikulin AM-38F V-12 liquid-cooled piston engine, 1285kW (1720hp)

MAXIMUM SPEED: 414km/h (257mph)

RANGE: 720km (450 miles)

SERVICE CEILING: 5500m (18,045ft)

CREW: 2

ARMAMENT: 2 × 23mm (0.9in) forward-firing cannon, 2 × 7.62mm (0.3in) forward-firing machine guns, 1 × 7.62mm machine gun in rear cockpit, plus up to 600kg (1320lb) of disposable stores underwing

Built in greater numbers than any other military aircraft in history, the Il-2 was a war-winner for the Soviets, with more than 36,000 built between 1941 and 1955. The ground-attacker was capable of defeating the best-protected German tanks.

Above: This Il-10 was operated by a Soviet Air Force unit based in Poland in 1945. Three regiments took Il-10s into battle before the end of the war in the west, with another active in the Far East.

Below: This Il-2M3 was on strength with the 566th Attack Aviation Regiment, 277th Attack Aviation Division, Soviet Frontal Aviation, and served on the Leningrad front in summer 1944. Flown by squadron commander V.I. Mykhlik, the inscriptions on the fuselage read 'For Leningrad' and 'Revenge for Khristenko', a pilot lost in combat in early 1944.

DEFENSIVE GUN
With the introduction of a second crewman, a 12.7mm (0.5in) UBT machine gun was added on a flexible mount in the rear cockpit.

COCKPIT ARMOUR
The pilot was seated in an armoured tub with a thickness of 5–12mm (0.2–0.5in); this extended to protect the engine. The armour was capable of defeating all small-arms fire.

THE BATTLE OF KURSK

During the Battle of Kursk in the summer of 1943, Vasily Ryazanov, commander of the 1st Attack Aviation Corps, made notably effective use of the Il-2 as part of a combined-arms force that used the Shturmoviks alongside infantry, armour and artillery. Prior to the battle, the Soviets assembled 35 per cent of their entire combat aircraft strength at Kursk; these enjoyed superior maintenance and larger forward fuel reserves than their Luftwaffe counterparts. The Il-2s operated over Kursk in large numbers, harassing German armour and racking up huge victory claims, although their own losses were significant.

ROCKETS
This aircraft is seen unleashing RS-132 unguided rockets from the underwing racks. These weapons were introduced in mid-1941 and were used together with the earlier RS-82. Six RS-132s could be carried, later increased to eight.

ENGINE
The Il-2M3 was powered by a Mikulin AM-38F liquid-cooled V-12, developing 1285kW (1720hp). Introduced in July 1942, it was capable of running on motor fuel.

EASTERN FRONT
The Il-2 first saw combat over the Berezina River in the days after the German invasion began. Losses were initially high. Before long, however, tactics were refined: the Il-2 was typically flown in an echeloned assault by four to 12 aircraft, which attacked their target in a shallow, turning dive.

De Havilland Mosquito (1940)

SPECIFICATIONS

DIMENSIONS:	Length: 12.73m (41ft 9in); Wingspan: 16.51m (54ft 2in); Height: 4.65m (15ft 3in)
WEIGHT:	9798kg (21,600lb) maximum take-off
POWERPLANT:	2 × Rolls-Royce Merlin 76 V-12 liquid-cooled piston engines, 1275kW (1700hp)
MAXIMUM SPEED:	655km/h (407mph)
RANGE:	1143km (710 miles)
SERVICE CEILING:	11,885m (39,000ft)
CREW:	2
ARMAMENT:	4 × 20mm (0.79in) cannon

Immortalized as the 'Wooden Wonder' on account of its construction, the Mosquito was the RAF's most flexible warplane of World War II, excelling as a high-speed reconnaissance aircraft, light bomber, night-fighter, fighter-bomber and anti-shipping aircraft. Its service career lasted well into the 1950s.

Below: Frontal view of a Mosquito B.Mk IV Series II light bomber, which introduced various refinements including extended nacelles, enlarged tailplane and flame dampeners on the exhausts.

CREW
The crew of two were seated side by side in the cockpit, with the pilot on the left. Bulged canopy sides improved rearward vision and an astrodome was provided for navigation by sextant.

WOODEN CONSTRUCTION
The fuselage employed an oval tapering cross-section constructed of balsa, sandwiched between plywood sheets.

FUSELAGE
Internal bracing was provided by wooden bulkheads.

OPERATION JERICHO
On the morning of 18 February 1944, a squadron of RAF Mosquito bombers, flying as low as 15m (50ft) over occupied France, demolished the walls of the civil prison at Amiens in Operation Jericho. The aircraft involved were Mosquito FB.Mk VIs from Nos. 21, 487 and 464 Squadrons, No. 2 Group. The Mosquitoes were covered by Hawker Typhoon fighters, which in the process tangled with Fw 190s near Amiens. Despite poor visibility, the attack succeeded in breaching the prison walls using delayed-fuse 250lb (113kg) bombs, and as such freed 258 prisoners, including a number from the French Resistance. Two Mosquitoes were lost in the course of the raid.

ENGINES
The PR.Mk 34 was powered by either the Merlin 113 on the starboard side and Merlin 114 opposite, or (in the Mk 34A) by a pair of two-stage supercharged Merlin 114A engines.

Above: This Mosquito PR.Mk 34 was flown by No. 81 Squadron, based at RAF Tengah, Singapore, in 1955, as part of the Far East Air Force. A total of 50 of this ultimate mark of photo-reconnaissance Mosquito were completed by Percival.

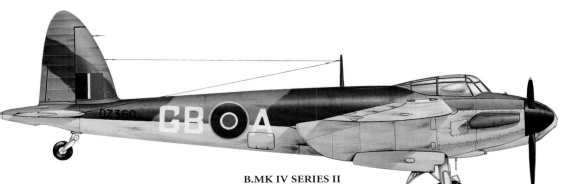

B.MK IV SERIES II
The Mosquito B.Mk IV Series II of No. 105 Squadron, RAF Bomber Command, based at Marham in 1943. The first of these aircraft had been delivered to the unit in late 1942.

Douglas SBD Dauntless (1940)

SPECIFICATIONS

DIMENSIONS:	Length: 10.06m (33ft); Wingspan: 12.65m (41ft 6in); Height: 3.94m (12ft 11in)
WEIGHT:	4924kg (10,855lb) maximum take-off
POWERPLANT:	(SBD-5) Wright R-1820-60 radial piston engine, 895kW (1200hp)
MAXIMUM SPEED:	394km/h (245mph)
RANGE:	1795km (1115 miles)
SERVICE CEILING:	7407m (24,300ft)
CREW:	2
ARMAMENT:	2 × 12.7mm (0.5in) machine guns, 2 × 7.62mm (0.3in) machine guns plus 1020kg (2250lb) of bombs

By the end of the war in the Pacific, the venerable Dauntless dive-bomber was showing its age; nonetheless, its contribution to victory in a succession of key naval battles cannot be overstated and its tally of Japanese shipping is unmatched.

Below: This pre-war SBD-1 wears the markings of the commander of VSB-1, a US Marine Corps squadron based at Quantico, Virginia, in early 1941.

Above: This SBD-4 was operated by VMSB-243, part of the 1st Marine Air Wing, based on Munda on New Georgia, part of the Solomons Islands chain, in August 1943.

TAIL
Both fin and tailplane employed stressed-skin construction. Elevators and rudders were fabric-covered, and tabs were provided on the control surfaces of the tail.

BOMB SIGHT
The pilot was provided with a three-power telescopic sight that protruded through the windscreen and could be used for both gun- and bomb-aiming.

WRIGHT CYCLONE
The SBD-1 was powered by the R-1820-32 Cyclone that developed 746kW (1000hp) on take-off. An intake atop the engine cowling provided carburettor cooling air.

WAR-WINNING
The Dauntless was responsible for sinking a greater tonnage of Japanese shipping than any other aircraft and was central to US naval successes at the Battles of Midway, Coral Sea and the Solomons. This was all the more remarkable considering the fact that the Dauntless was considered obsolescent at the outbreak of the war. Despite its limited performance, it has been recorded that one Navy SBD crew managed to shoot down seven Japanese A6M Zero fighters in a space of just two days.

BOMBS
Underwing pylons could carry 45kg (100lb) bombs, while the main store was carried under the centre section, with a maximum weight of 725kg (1600lb).

USMC SBDS
US Marine Corps SBDs, carrying centreline and underwing bombs, are seen heading for Japanese targets on Rabaul in 1944. The USMC was the second most prolific Dauntless operator, and certainly the most successful outside the US Navy. In all, 20 Marine squadrons flew the Dauntless.

Hawker Typhoon (1941)

SPECIFICATIONS

DIMENSIONS: Length: 9.73m (31ft 11in); Wingspan: 12.67m (41ft 7in); Height: 4.66m (15ft 4in)

WEIGHT: 4010kg (8840lb)

POWERPLANT: Napier Sabre IIC liquid-cooled H-24 piston engine, 1685kW (2260hp)

MAXIMUM SPEED: 663km/h (412mph)

RANGE: 821km (510 miles)

SERVICE CEILING: 10,729mm (35,200ft)

CREW: 1

ARMAMENT: 4 × 20mm (0.79in) Hispano Mk II cannon; 8 × RP-3 air-to-ground rockets; 2 × 227kg (500lb) or 2 × 454kg (1000lb) bombs

An interceptor that failed, the Hawker Typhoon was nearly cancelled before it blossomed into the finest close-support aircraft of World War II. With its pugnacious snub nose, four long-barrelled cannon and whining Sabre engine, the big fighter-bomber wreaked havoc on its foes. Ranging far and wide over the battlefields of northwest Europe, swarms of Typhoons made an indelible mark on the history of warfare.

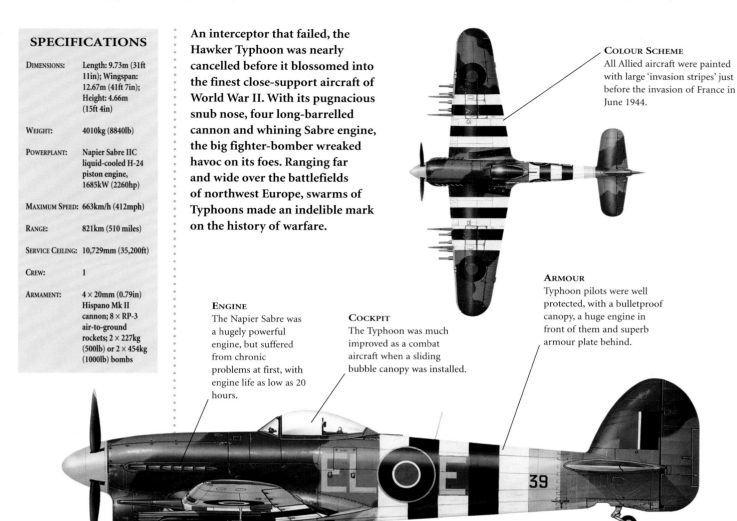

COLOUR SCHEME
All Allied aircraft were painted with large 'invasion stripes' just before the invasion of France in June 1944.

ARMOUR
Typhoon pilots were well protected, with a bulletproof canopy, a huge engine in front of them and superb armour plate behind.

ENGINE
The Napier Sabre was a hugely powerful engine, but suffered from chronic problems at first, with engine life as low as 20 hours.

COCKPIT
The Typhoon was much improved as a combat aircraft when a sliding bubble canopy was installed.

UNDERCARRIAGE
The Typhoon had a wide-track undercarriage, which made it a safe aircraft to use on rough tactical airstrips.

WEAPONS
Originally carrying 12 Browning 7.7mm (0.303-cal.) machine guns, the Typhoon was soon equipped as standard with a harder-hitting fit of four 20mm (0.79in) Hispano cannon and eight 27kg (60lb) rockets.

CLOSE SUPPORT

As a low-level close-support machine, the Typhoon was supreme. It was a superb gun platform, and could carry and deliver with precision a heavy load of bombs or air-to-surface rockets. The climax of the Typhoon's career came in the third week of August 1944, when all of the surviving German forces in northern France were caught in a trap near Falaise. Typhoons, mainly from the RAF's No. 83 Group, unleashed rockets, cannon shells and bombs until hardly one German vehicle was capable of movement.

RP-3 ROCKETS

The RP-3 unguided rocket came to have a 27kg (60lb) semi-armour-piercing (SAP) warhead that was capable of destroying much of the German armour around at the end of the war.

SPECIFICATIONS

DIMENSIONS:	Length: 22.4m (73ft 6in); Wingspan: 19.2m (63ft) wings spread; Height: 5.22m (17ft 1in)
WEIGHT:	45,359kg (100,000lb) maximum take-off
POWERPLANT:	2 × Pratt & Whitney TF30-100 afterburning turbofans, 111.65kN (25,100lb)
MAXIMUM SPEED:	2655km/h (1650mph) clean at 12,190m (40,000ft)
RANGE:	4707km (2925 miles) clean, with maximum internal fuel
SERVICE CEILING:	18,290m (60,000ft)
CREW:	2
ARMAMENT:	Up to 14,228kg (31,500lb) of disposable stores carried in a lower-fuselage weapons bay and on 6 underwing pylons

A controversial aircraft, the F-111 was subject to a troubled development and suffered high-profile combat losses early on. However, once refined, it became almost certainly the most capable precision attack aircraft of its generation, seeing combat over Vietnam and later in raids on both Libya and Iraq.

Right: F-111Fs of the 48th TFW were employed almost exlusively to drop laser-guided bombs during Desert Storm, in this case 907kg (2000lb) GBU-24 Paveway IIIs with penetrator warheads.

FLAPS
The entire trailing edge of the variable-geometry wing was fitted with a powerful double-slotted flap, used to increase lift and, at high angles, drag.

INFLIGHT REFUELLING
Above the fuselage was a receptacle for an inflight refuelling 'flying boom'. Provision was not made for the probe and drogue method of aerial refuelling.

RADOME
This housed the primary attack radar, a multimode General Electric AN/APQ-114, as well as the terrain-following radar, the Texas Instruments AN/APQ-146.

F-111S IN ENGLAND
The first 20th Tactical Fighter Wing (TFW) F-111Es were based at RAF Upper Heyford in September 1970. Six years later, the numbers of 'Aardvarks' in the UK increased significantly when the 48th TFW introduced the latest F-111F model to service at RAF Lakenheath. The F-111 force in the UK made headlines in April 1986 after the Operation El Dorado Canyon raid on Libya by the 48th TFW. After Operation Desert Storm, the F-111s departed the UK, with the last F-111Es leaving Upper Heyford in October 1993.

EXHAUSTS
The engine nozzles were fully variable and were equipped with an unusual translating 'tailfeather' ring, which moved to the rear on take-off, as seen here, in order to reduce drag.

UNDERCARRIAGE
The robust main gear featured large, low-pressure tyres. Combined with long-stroke legs, these permitted no-flare landings to be made at high weights.

INTERNAL BAY
The internal weapons bay was ultimately used mainly for carriage of additional fuel or equipment, including the Pave Tack electro-optical targeting pod in the case of the F-111F.

TARGET DROP
An F-111 of the 20th Tactical Fighter Wing drops unguided bombs on a target range in the UK. Based at RAF Upper Heyford, the 20th TFW was the first of two USAF F-111 wings to arrive in the United Kingdom.

Fairchild A-10 Thunderbolt II (1972)

TYPE · *Ground-Attack Aircraft* · **FAMILY** · *Aircraft, Helicopters & Drones*

SPECIFICATIONS

DIMENSIONS:	Length: 16.26m (53ft 4in); Wingspan: 17.53m (57ft 6in); Height: 4.47m (14ft 8in)
WEIGHT:	22,680kg (50,000lb) maximum take-off
POWERPLANT:	2 × General Electric TF34-GE-100 high-bypass turbofans, 40.32kN (9065lb)
MAXIMUM SPEED:	706km/h (439mph) 'clean'
RANGE:	3949km (2454 miles) with drop tanks
SERVICE CEILING:	13,716m (45,000ft)
CREW:	1
ARMAMENT:	1 × 30mm (1.18in) rotary cannon plus up to 7260kg (16,000lb) of external ordnance on 8 wing and 3 fuselage pylons

Known to those who fly it as the 'Warthog', the A-10 is a tailor-made close-support and anti-tank aircraft, employing the unique GAU-8/A Avenger 30mm (1.18in) cannon. Although it has faced opposition from within the US military, the combat-proven Thunderbolt II has always survived to fight another day.

Above: An A-10A of the 706th Tactical Fighter Squadron, 926th Tactical Fighter Group, as it appeared during Operation Desert Storm wearing the 1980s-era European One camouflage scheme.

TAIL
The A-10 is intended to be able to fly with either half of the twin-finned tail shot away. All parts of the left and right tails are interchangeable.

AMMUNITION
The Avenger cannon can fire three different rounds: high-explosive incendiary, armour-piercing incendiary and training practice.

'WARTHOG' AT WAR
At the end of the Cold War, the USAF considered withdrawing the A-10. In a bid to find a new role, a number of aircraft were redesigned as OA-10As for the forward air control role. The 'Warthog' suddenly received a new lease of life with the 1990 Iraqi invasion of Kuwait: under the 354th Tactical Fighter Wing (Provisional), 152 OA/A-10s from bases in the United States and UK conducted missions with a notable success rate during Operation Desert Storm. As well as two air-to-air victories against Iraqi helicopters, it averaged a kill rate of more than 25 tanks a day. By the end of the war, confirmed A-10 tank kills approached 1000 tanks destroyed.

Above: This A-10A carries a typical Desert Storm mixed weapons load of Mk 20 Rockeye cluster bombs, AGM-65D Mavericks, twin Sidewinders and AN/ALQ-119 electronic countermeasures pod.

STORES STATIONS
Each wing supports four stores stations, with another three under the fuselage, numbered from 1 to 11 from the port wingtip.

AGM-65 MAVERICK
Two primary seeker heads are available for the Maverick air-to-surface missile as carried by the A-10, comprising TV scene magnification and imaging infrared (IIR).

AFGHAN MISSIONS
An A-10 taxis down the flight line at Bagram Air Base, Afghanistan, after flying a close air support mission. The first major action for the A-10 was flown from this base when the aircraft supported Operation Anaconda in March 2002.

SPECIFICATIONS

DIMENSIONS:	Length: 14.12m (46ft 4in); Wingspan: 9.25m (30ft 4in); Height: 3.55m (11ft 8in)
WEIGHT:	14,061kg (31,000lb) maximum short take-off (STO)
POWERPLANT:	Rolls-Royce F402-RR-408 vectored-thrust turbofan, 105.87kN (23,800lb)
MAXIMUM SPEED:	1065km/h (662mph) at sea level
RANGE:	1001km (684 miles) on hi-lo-hi attack mission after STO, with 7 × 227kg (500lb) bombs
SERVICE CEILING:	More than 15,240m (50,000ft)
CREW:	1
ARMAMENT:	1 × 25mm (0.98in) rotary cannon and up to 6003kg (13,235lb) of disposable stores, after STO

With the AV-8B, the US Marine Corps took Britain's first-generation Harrier vertical/short take-off and landing (V/STOL) design and brought this revolutionary aircraft fully up to date. Later aircraft feature radar for a further improvement in capability, and the Harrier II continues to serve aboard US Navy assault vessels.

Above: This AV-8B is illustrated carrying a mixed load of two AGM-65E Mavericks, a pair of Mk 20 Rockeye cluster bombs and AIM-9L/M Sidewinders for self defence.

RADAR
The compact AN/APG-65 radar includes air-to-air and air-to-ground modes and all-digital performance. Terrain-avoidance information is provided for low-level flying.

COCKPIT
Compared to earlier Harriers, this offered a much-improved field of vision thanks to a single-piece wraparound bubble canopy.

REFUELLING PROBE
Normally a standard feature, the bolt-on refuelling probe is retractable and is housed in a streamlined fairing when not in use.

ENHANCEMENTS
USMC AV-8Bs have seen extensive use in Iraq and Afghanistan; the aircraft is now subject to life-extension programmes, addressing the service life of the wing, the vertical tail and some of the subsystems. Life-extension work has focused on the F402-RR-408B powered aircraft, and the TAV-8Bs have also now received the uprated Dash 408B engine. In a bid to increase the AV-8B's utility in its primary close air support mission, the Litening targeting pod has been integrated; this can be used to pass target coordinates to the aircraft's Joint Direct Attack Munitions (JDAM).

AGM-65E MAVERICK
The Marines' AGM-65E version of this missile uses semi-active laser-guidance and a new 136kg (300lb) blast-fragmentation warhead.

ENGINE
This is an uprated version of the British-designed Rolls-Royce Pegasus with improved maintenance characteristics and reliability.

BLACK SHEEP AV-8B
An AV-8B Night Attack jet of VMA-214 'Black Sheep' as it appeared in 1989. Working up during the 1991 Gulf War, the unit made a first foreign deployment with the AV-8B to Iwakuni, Japan, in October of that year.

Lockheed F-117 Nighthawk (1981)

TYPE · *Ground-Attack Aircraft* · **FAMILY** · *Aircraft, Helicopters & Drones*

SPECIFICATIONS

DIMENSIONS:	Length: 20.08m (65ft 11in); Wingspan: 13.2m (43ft 4in); Height: 3.78m (12ft 5in)
WEIGHT:	23,814kg (52,500lb) maximum take-off
POWERPLANT:	2 × General Electric F404-GE-F1D2 turbofans, 48.04kN (10,800lb)
MAXIMUM SPEED:	c. 1040km/h (646mph) at high altitude
RANGE:	c. 862km (535 miles) radius with 1814kg (4000lb) warload
SERVICE CEILING:	11,765m (38,600ft)
CREW:	1
ARMAMENT:	Up to 2268kg (5000lb) of disposable stores

Lockheed's 'stealth' attack aircraft was developed under conditions of utmost secrecy before being propelled to legendary status on account of its combat role during Operation Desert Storm. The aircraft fulfilled a niche role with the US Air Force until it was finally retired from service in 2008.

Above: This F-117A was flown by the commander of the 37th Tactical Fighter Wing. The wing consisted of three units: the 415th TFS, 416 TFS and the 417th Tactical Fighter Training Squadron.

COCKPIT
In original form, this was equipped with Texas Instruments monochrome displays and an array of off-the-shelf instruments taken from other aircraft, including the F/A-18.

STEALTH COATING
Almost every surface of the F-117 was covered with radar absorbent material (RAM). This provided a critical defence against radar detection, but proved laborious and costly to maintain. After each mission, maintenance specialists had to closely examine the aircraft's special coating to identify whether any repairs were needed. If required, the special coatings were reapplied, allowed to cure and then reinspected. Initially applied as individual sheets, the RAM coating was later available in the form of a spray. Where apertures were present in the airframe, and the RAM was interrupted, the area was covered with a fine-mesh grille, smaller than the wavelengths of most detection radars.

WING
This forms a simple aerofoil, with flat surfaces underwing that blend into under-fuselage surfaces to create a single unified lifting surface.

INTERNAL WEAPONS
This F-117A is seen releasing a typical load of two 907kg (2000lb) GBU-27A/B laser-guided bombs fitted with hardened BLU-109/B penetrator warheads.

IRADS
The Infra-Red Acqusition and Designation System (IRADS) was the primary search and attack sensor; it included a forward-looking infrared sensor in front of the cockpit.

RETIREMENT
A total of 59 F-117As were built between 1981 and 1990, six of which were lost in non-combat accidents. Once expected to serve until at least 2018, the USAF retired the F-117 fleet in April 2008 after 27 years of service, in order to free up funds for modernization.

Gotha bombers (1917)

SPECIFICATIONS

DIMENSIONS:	Length: 12.2m (40ft) Wingspan: 23.7m (77ft 9in); Height: 4.5m (14ft)
WEIGHT:	3648kg (8042lb)
POWERPLANT:	2 × Mercedes D.IVa, 193kW (260hp) each
MAXIMUM SPEED:	135km/h (83mph)
RANGE:	840km (522 miles)
SERVICE CEILING:	6500m (21,325ft)
CREW:	3
ARMAMENT:	2 or 3 × 7.92mm (0.312in) Parabellum LMG 14 machine guns; up to 500kg (1100lb) of bombs

The Gotha carried out raids on London and other targets in England, contributing to the belief that 'the bomber will always get through', which shaped inter-war doctrine and the development of more advanced bombers.

GOTHA G.IV
A Gotha G.IV in the colours of Kaghol (Bombing Unit) 3, which made the first daylight raid on London in June 1917.

WEAPONS
The limited field of fire available to the Gotha's defensive machine guns is obvious. A firing tunnel through the rear fuselage provided a novel solution to the problem.

THE GOTHA IN COMBAT
Although it was a slow, unmanoeuvrable and a large target, the Gotha could defend itself with two machine guns – one mounted in the nose and one at the rear of the crew compartment. Fighter pilots quickly learned that the best approach was to attack from behind and underneath, where the bomber had no defensive armament. As a counter, a novel 'firing tunnel' was incorporated on some examples, enabling the rear gunner to see and fire downwards. Gothas also protected one another by flying in close formation, engaging an attacking fighter with fire from several machine guns. This was the forerunner of the 'combat box' tactic used during World War II, and proved effective against the fighters of the day.

GOTHA G.V
This Gotha G.V is wearing camouflage suited to its area of operations on the Western Front in 1918. Gothas undertook raids in the combat zone as well as making long-range attacks on England.

FUSELAGE
The Gotha's fuselage was of plywood and fabric over a frame of wood and steel. Although it was a large target, many hits would go straight through the aircraft without damaging anything important.

PUSHER ENGINES
Removing a section of the trailing wing edge created clearance for the 'pusher' configuration engines. Some ordnance was carried under the wing, but most was in an internal bay.

Boeing B-17 (1938)

SPECIFICATIONS

DIMENSIONS:	Length: 22.78m (74ft 9in); Wingspan: 31.62m (103ft 9in); Height: 5.82m (19ft 1in)
WEIGHT:	32,660kg (72,000lb) maximum take-off
POWERPLANT:	4 × Wright Cyclone R-1820-97 radial piston engines, 895kW (1200hp)
MAXIMUM SPEED:	462km/h (287mph)
RANGE:	3220km (2000 miles) with bombload
SERVICE CEILING:	11,280m (37,000ft)
CREW:	10
ARMAMENT:	13 × 12.7mm (0.5in) machine guns plus a maximum bombload of 7800kg (17,160lb)

The B-17 was a mainstay of the US Eighth Air Force, ranging across occupied Europe as a daylight bomber and experiencing some of the hardest-fought air battles in history. The Flying Fortress also served widely in other theatres and in a variety of different roles.

Above: The B-17C introduced a ventral 'bathtub' that was also used on the B-17D, but had flush waist gun positions instead of blisters. The conspicuous markings date from the pre-1941 period.

Below: Assigned to the 322nd Bomb Squadron of the 91st BG, Chowhound was a Boeing-built B-17G that flew its first operational sortie in January 1944. It was destroyed by flak over Caen in August 1944, with the loss of all but one crewmember.

TOP TURRET
The power-operated Sperry top turret was operated by the flight engineer, who was also responsible for fuel management and basic in-flight repairs.

TAIL GUNS
The B-17 tail gunner sat on a bicycle-type saddle, below a Plexiglas armoured sighting screen. Although twin 12.7mm (0.5in) weapons were the standard fit, some B-17s were modified with a single 20mm (0.79in) cannon in the tail.

DAYLIGHT RAIDS
Typical Eighth Air Force tactics over Europe involved enormous 'box' formations of bombers sent day after day into the heart of the Third Reich, using their strength in numbers and formidable defensive armament to provide protection against Luftwaffe fighters. In the last deep-penetration raid without 'all the way' fighter escort, 291 B-17s and B-24s were sent against the Schweinfurt ball bearing factory in October 1943. The result was 60 bombers posted missing, 17 crashed or written off on return and 121 that suffered some kind of damage. In the face of such mounting losses, the USAAF introduced long-range escort fighters to protect the bombers all the way to the target and back to their bases in eastern England.

COCKPIT
Well laid out and spacious, the cockpit of the B-17 benefitted from Boeing's experience in airliner design. The pilot (and aircraft commander) sat on the right, with the co-pilot on the left.

BOMBLOAD
Although the B-17G could in theory carry a bombload of up to 7800kg (17,160lb), in practice a typical long-range load amounted to 2000kg (4400lb). Bombs included the smallest 0.9kg (2lb) incendiaries up to the heaviest 907kg (2000lb) demolition bombs. Only one of the latter could be carried, due to the dimensions of the bomb bay.

ON THE WAY
Douglas-built B-17Gs of the 881st Bombardment Group (352nd and 533rd Bombardment Squadron) based at RAF Ridgewell head towards their target in occupied Europe.

North American B-25 Mitchell (1939)

TYPE • *Bombers* • FAMILY • *Aircraft, Helicopters & Drones*

SPECIFICATIONS

DIMENSIONS:	Length: 16.12m (52ft 11in); Wingspan: 20.6m (67ft 7in); Height: 4.82m (15ft 10in)
WEIGHT:	15,880kg (35,000lb) maximum take-off
POWERPLANT:	2 × Wright R-2600-13 radial piston engines, 1268kW (1700hp)
MAXIMUM SPEED:	457km/h (284mph)
RANGE:	2414km (1500 miles)
SERVICE CEILING:	6462m (21,200ft)
CREW:	5
ARMAMENT:	6 × 12.7mm (0.5in) machine guns plus a maximum bombload of 1361kg (3000lb)

The USAAF's definitive light/medium bomber of World War II, the B-25 may have served in more campaigns than any other type in that conflict. The aircraft also gave good service in US Navy and Allied hands, and flew the 'Doolittle raid' against Japan in April 1942.

BETTY'S DREAM
A front view of the B-25J from the 499th 'Bats Outta Hell' Bomb Squadron. The aircraft, which carried the individual name Betty's Dream, was fitted with a total of 18 guns, including 12 in the nose.

DORSAL TURRET
Rear protection was provided by a Bendix dorsal turret, armed with two 12.7mm (0.5in) Browning machine guns.

TAIL
The twin tail was based around a two-spar structure, to which leading-edge sections and large control sections were added. A tail turret was added in the B-25J, with the dorsal turret moved forward as a result.

DOOLITTLE'S RAID
On 18 April 1942, a force of 16 17th Bombardment Group B-25Bs led by Lt Col James H. Doolittle took off from the confines of the flight deck of the carrier USS *Hornet*. Thus began a flight of 1184km (714 miles) to strike the Japanese capital, together with other targets at Nagoya, Kobe and Yokohama. After pressing home their attacks, the surviving B-25s made for China, where most force-landed. In recognition for the raid, which had enormous propaganda value, Doolittle received the Medal of Honor. Before the end of the year he was a major general, and took command of the Twelfth Air Force in North Africa.

COCKPIT
The B-25 was flown by a crew of two, comprising the aircraft commander in the left-hand seat and co-pilot/navigator in the right-hand seat. The B-25C/D was equipped with an autopilot.

BOMBLOAD
The deep bomb bay was located between the forward and aft wing carry-through structure. Total internal bomb capacity was 2359kg (5200lb).

Wearing the 'Air Apache' badge on the tail, this B-25J was part of the 345th Bombardment Group (Medium), which moved to Leyte in the Philippines in November 1944. The 'bat wings' nose art was associated with the group's 499th Squadron.

SPECIFICATIONS

DIMENSIONS:	Length: 20.6m (67ft 8in); Wingspan: 33.5m (110ft); Height: 5.5m (18ft)
WEIGHT:	25,000kg (55,000lb) loaded
POWERPLANT:	4 × Pratt & Whitney R-1830-35 or -41 turbosupercharged radial engines, 900kW (1200hp)
MAXIMUM SPEED:	488km/h (290mph)
RANGE:	3300km (2050 miles)
SERVICE CEILING:	8500m (28,000ft)
CREW:	11
ARMAMENT:	Guns: 10 × 12.7mm (0.5in) M2 Browning machine guns in 4 turrets and 2 waist positions; short-range load of 3600kg (8000lb) bombs

Although overshadowed in popular history by the Boeing B-17 Flying Fortress, and latterly by the B-29 Superfortress, the Consolidated B-24 was built in larger numbers (almost 19,000 units) than any other US military aircraft of World War II. It is the most prolific four-engined aircraft in history.

Left: The B-24 had a ferry range (as opposed to a combat range) of 5900km (3666 miles). It was this range capability that led to the VLR (Very Long Range) Liberators, used to patrol across the North Atlantic in the war against German U-boats.

B-24D LIBERATOR TEGGIE ANN
Teggie Ann was the command aircraft of the 'Liberandos', the 376th Bombardment Group. This unit suffered heavy losses following the attacks on the Romanian oil fields at Ploesti in 1944.

LONG WING SPAN
The very long wing span of the USAF B-24s gave the aircraft excellent long range and good performance at high altitude.

REAR GUNNER
The rear gunner fired a pair of 12.7mm (0.5in) machine guns from a powered turret.

PLOESTI RAID
The first major production version, the B-24D with R-1830-43 engines, appeared late in 1941. A policy decision to concentrate B-24s primarily in the Pacific theatre (where the type's long range was used to good effect) resulted in most of the 2738 B-24Ds being deployed against Japan. However, the Eighth and Ninth Air Forces in Europe and North Africa also received the aircraft, one of their outstanding raids being the attack on the Ploesti oil refineries in Romania on 1 August 1943.

B-24D LIBERATOR
The B-24D was the first Liberator to be built in great numbers – a total of 2696.

Handley Page Halifax (1940)

SPECIFICATIONS
(MK III)

DIMENSIONS:	Length: 21.82m (71ft 7in); Wingspan: 31.75m (104ft); Height: 6.32m (20ft 9in)
WEIGHT:	17,178kg (37,870lb) empty
POWERPLANT:	4 x Bristol Hercules XVI radial engine, 1205kW (1615hp) each
MAXIMUM SPEED:	454km/h (282mph)
RANGE:	3000km (1860 miles)
SERVICE CEILING:	7315m (24,000ft)
CREW:	7
ARMAMENT:	5897kg (13,000lb) of bombs; 8 x 7.7mm (.303in) Browning machine guns (four in dorsal turret, four in tail turret); 1 x 7.7mm (.303in) Vickers machine gun in nose

The major partner of the Avro Lancaster in the UK's heavy night bomber forces of World War II, the Halifax was built to the extent of 6178 aircraft. Though generally associated with the air-cooled powerplant of four Bristol Hercules radial engines, the first marks had four liquid-cooled Rolls-Royce Merlin V-12 engines.

Below: This Halifax B.Mk III was part of No. 462 Squadron, Royal Australian Air Force, flying as part of RAF Bomber Command out of Foulsham, Norfolk, in 1945.

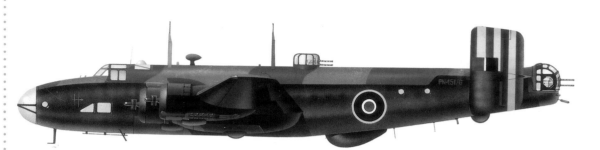

Below: This Halifax Mk I Series I was part of No. 76 Squadron, RAF Bomber Command, and flew from Middleton St George in 1941.

REAR TURRET
The rear turret was armed with four 7.7mm (0.303in) Browning machine guns; together the four guns had a combined cyclical rate of fire of c. 4000rpm.

ROYAL CANADIAN AIR FORCE
Many units and men from Commonwealth and other European countries were evident in the make-up of Bomber Command. Activated on the first day of 1943, No. 6 Group was unique inasmuch as it was not an RAF formation, but rather an element of the RCAF attached to Bomber Command. At maximum, No. 6 Group had 14 bomber squadrons, and in overall terms some 15 different squadrons served with the group. Apart from No. 6 Group, many Canadian personnel served with British and other Commonwealth squadrons, and by May 1945 almost 25 per cent of Bomber Command's personnel was provided by the RCAF.

NOSE TURRET
The original Mk I Halifax had a two-gun nose turret, but from the Mk II Series IA and Mk III the design was simplified to a streamlined perspex nose with a single machine gun.

BOMB LOAD
The Halifax carried a bombload of 5897kg (13,000lb), about 500kg (1100lb) less than the Lancaster but still a powerful complement of ordnance.

HEAVY BOMBER
A few Halifaxes were restored and maintained after the war and still flown in Britain and Canada.

Avro Lancaster (1941)

SPECIFICATIONS

DIMENSIONS:	Length: 21.18m (69ft 6in); Wingspan: 31.09m (102ft); Height: 6.1m (20ft)
WEIGHT:	16,738kg (36,900lb)
POWERPLANT:	4 x Rolls-Royce Merlin XXIV V-12 piston engines, 1223kW (1640hp)
MAXIMUM SPEED:	462km/h (287mph)
RANGE:	4070km (2530 miles) with bombload
SERVICE CEILING:	7470m (24,500ft)
CREW:	7
ARMAMENT:	8 x 7.7mm (0.303in) machine guns, plus bombload comprising one bomb of up to 9979kg (22,000lb) or smaller bombs up to a total weight of 6350kg (14,000lb)

The most celebrated British heavy bomber of World War II, the Lancaster found fame for daring missions such as the 'Dambusters raid' and the attack on the Tirpitz, but achieved greatest impact through its harrowing night-time strategic bombing campaign against Germany.

Below: This Avro Lancaster B.Mk X flew as part of No. 431 'Iroquois' Squadron, Royal Canadian Air Force, as part of RAF Bomber Command in early 1945.

TWIN FINS
Compared to the Manchester with its triple fins, the production Lancaster employed a twin-fin tail unit, with tailfins of considerably increased height.

CREW
A typical Bomber Command complement for the Lancaster consisted of seven men: a pilot, flight engineer, navigator, wireless operator, tail gunner, mid-upper gunner and nose gunner/bomb-aimer.

FUEL CAPACITY
The Lancaster carried a typical fuel load of 9792 litres (2154 gallons), with three tanks in each wing. Additional fuel could be carried in the bomb bay for ferry flights.

NOSE ART
This aircraft, WS-Y, wears colourful nose art based on a character used to promote Youngers brewery. The legend 'Getting Younger Every Day' is worn alongside markings for 41 successful missions.

DAMBUSTERS
In early 1943, Wing Commander Guy Gibson, No. 5 Group RAF, was selected to recruit the best Bomber Command pilots to form a new, elite squadron for a special mission. The result was No. 617 Squadron, which was tasked with perfecting low-altitude flying before being assigned to target three dams in the heart of Germany's industrial Ruhr region, using specialized 'bouncing bombs'. The dams raid of May 1943 was a propaganda success, and one of the most daring bombing missions in history, but its strategic results were limited.

BATTLE OF BRITAIN MEMORIAL FLIGHT
Lancaster PA474 is part of the RAF's Battle of Britain's Memorial Flight and one of only two airworthy survivors of the type. PA474 was completed at Broughton in May 1945, just missing the war in Europe, and was later used for photo-reconnaissance work in Africa during 1948–52.

Boeing B-29 Superfortress (1944)

SPECIFICATIONS

DIMENSIONS:	Length: 30.18m (99ft); Wingspan: 43.36m (142ft 3in); Height: 9.01m (29ft 7in)
WEIGHT:	64,003kg (141,100lb) maximum take-off
POWERPLANT:	4 × Wright R-3350-57 radial piston engines, 1641kW (2200hp)
MAXIMUM SPEED:	576km/h (358mph)
RANGE:	6598km (4100 miles)
SERVICE CEILING:	9695m (31,800ft)
CREW:	10–11
ARMAMENT:	12 × 12.7mm (0.5in) machine guns in remote-controlled turrets, 1 × 20mm (0.79in) cannon and 2 × 12.7mm (0.5in) machine guns in tail, plus bombload of up to 9072kg (20,000lb)

Even without the atomic missions that the type flew against Japan in August 1945, the B-29 – the most advanced heavy bomber of the war – can be considered a war-winner on account of the devastating raids it conducted against the Japanese mainland in the preceding months.

Left: Renton-built B-29A-5-BN serial 42-93869 seen soon after leaving the production line. The huge Wright Duplex Cyclone engines drove 5.05m (16ft 7in)-diameter four-bladed propellers.

SIGHTING BLISTERS
Gunners in the observation blisters on each side of the fuselage also served to check the status of the engines, flaps and undercarriage.

REAR FUSELAGE
A pressurized compartment was found between the rear of the bomb bay and the start of the dorsal fin. This contained the gunners' positions as well as crew rest bunks.

GUNS
The pressurized fuselage demanded the use of remote-controlled gun barbettes, provided in the form of four twin-gun turrets located above and below the fuselage, and one in the tail.

CREW
The typical crew of the B-29 consisted of: pilot, co-pilot, bombardier, flight engineer, navigator, radio operator, radar observer, right gunner, left gunner, central fire control and tail gunner (although the tail gun position might be unmanned).

RADAR
The AN/APQ-13 bombing radar was located between the twin bomb bays. The radome housed a 76cm (30in) rotating dish antenna.

DEVASTATING RAIDS
During their initial nine months of service, the B-29s were employed mainly for high-level daylight raids. However, tactics switched in March 1945, when they began low-level night attacks from the Marianas Islands. These were the most destructive raids of the war in terms of casualties, with the first night-time incendiary raid on Tokyo killing around 80,000 people.

AFTER THE WAR
War-surplus B-29s stand at Kingman Army Air Field, Arizona, after VJ-Day. While many of the B-29s completed before the end of the war met this fate, some of them being disposed of direct from the production line, the Superfortress continued to provide useful service to the post-war US Air Force.

English Electric Canberra (1949)

SPECIFICATIONS

DIMENSIONS:	Length: 19.9m (65ft 6in); Wingspan: 19.5m (64ft); Height: 4.77m (15ft 8in)
WEIGHT:	9820kg (21,650lb)
POWERPLANT:	2 × Rolls-Royce Avon R.A.7 Mk.109 turbojets, 36kN (7400lb) each
MAXIMUM SPEED:	933km/h (580mph)
RANGE:	1300km (807 miles) combat radius
SERVICE CEILING:	15,000m (49,212ft)
CREW:	3
ARMAMENT:	4 × 20mm (0.79in) Hispano Mk V cannon; 3628kg (8000lb) payload, including tactical nuclear weapons

The Canberra was developed to defeat interception by flying too high and too fast to be caught by fighters. After a long career as a strike platform, the Canberra continued to fly as a reconnaissance platform.

NAVIGATION SYSTEM
The upgraded Mk17A featured an improved navigation system and electronic jamming equipment. Its role was to train radar, missile and electronic warfare operators to deal with hostile countermeasures.

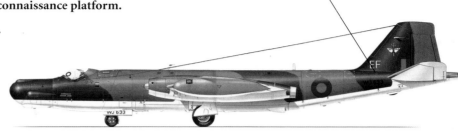

BAC CANBERRA T.MK17
The Canberra T.Mk17 was a specialist electronic warfare training variant, housing its EW suite in a redesigned nose section.

THE CANBERRA IN SERVICE
The first Canberras went into British service in 1951, with an improved version appearing in 1954. The first operational use was during the Malayan Emergency and the Suez Crisis, where the Canberra was sufficiently impressive that the US Air Force adopted it. The arrival of the Valiant, which was the first of the 'V-Bombers' and capable of delivering a larger payload over a longer range, allowed the Canberra to move from a high-altitude bombing role to low-level strike operations. These included tactical strikes, but also delivery of nuclear weapons from low level – the Canberra's high speed enabled it to escape the blast from its weapon. As a result, although the Canberra was phased out of the conventional bombing role in the mid-1960s, some squadrons were retained in the nuclear strike role.

CANBERRA PR.MK 9
The PR.9 photo-reconnaissance variant of the Canberra was still in RAF service until 2006, serving in numerous conflicts during the second half of the twentieth century.

WOODEN TAIL
The wooden tail of the Canberra belonged to an earlier era, but the aircraft was still flying as late as Operation Iraqi Freedom in 2003.

WORLD BEATER
The Canberra proved easy to fly and had few vices, requiring a minimal conversion time from other aircraft. It set several records in the 1950s, including being the first jet aircraft to cross the Atlantic in a non-stop flight.

Boeing B-52 Stratofortress (1952)

SPECIFICATIONS

DIMENSIONS:	Length: 49.05m (160ft 11in); Wingspan: 56.39m (185ft); Height: 12.4m (40ft 8in)
WEIGHT:	229,068kg (505,000lb) maximum take-off
POWERPLANT:	8 × Pratt & Whitney TF33-P-3/103 turbofans, 75.62kN (17,000lb)
MAXIMUM SPEED:	1011km/h (628mph)
RANGE:	14,080km (8800 miles) unrefuelled combat range
SERVICE CEILING:	15,151m (50,000ft)
CREW:	5
ARMAMENT:	c. 31,500kg (70,000lb) of ordnance including bombs, mines and missiles

Still in service after 60 years, the mighty B-52 remains a defiant symbol of American military power, and has served as both a nuclear deterrent and as a frontline type in conflicts extending from Vietnam to the Global War on Terror. As a rolling upgrade programme continues, B-52s are set to serve at least until 2040.

Below: The definitive B-52H, seen in service with the 23rd Bomb Squadron, part of the 5th Bomb Wing at Minot AFB, North Dakota. The unit has flown the B-52 since February 1959.

'WET WING'
The B-52G featured a 'wet wing' that increased maximum fuel capacity to 181,813 litres (48,030 gallons), including 2650 litres (700 gallons) in each of two external wing tanks.

TAIL GUN
The B-52G was the last version to retain the original defensive armament of four Browning machine guns.

SENSORS
For low-level penetration missions, the B-52G was retrofitted with undernose blisters containing low light level TV and forward-looking infrared sensors.

BOMBS
A conventional bombing capability was first included on modified B-52Ds, allowing carriage of up to 105 bombs each of up to 340kg (750lb). The unmodified B-52G, however, could carry only 27 such weapons.

ENGINES
The four pairs of Pratt & Whitney J57-P-43WB turbojets were mounted in four packs of two under the wings. Water injection was provided for take-off.

VETERAN AIRCRAFT
A total of 744 B-52s were built with the last, a B-52H, delivered in October 1962. The first of 102 B-52Hs was delivered to Strategic Air Command in May 1961. The H-model was developed after the cancellation of a planned successor, the North American B-70 Valkyrie. Today, survivors can carry up to 20 AGM-86 Air-Launched Cruise Missiles (ALCMs), and the original tail gun fitting has been deleted altogether.

AFGHANISTAN
A B-52H prepares to take on fuel from a tanker during a close air support mission over Afghanistan. The B-52's contribution to Operation Enduring Freedom began in 2001, and the bomber has excelled in the close air support role, thanks to its ability to loiter high above the battlefield for extended periods and deliver precision-guided munitions in support of the troops below.

Avro Vulcan (1952)

SPECIFICATIONS

DIMENSIONS:	Length: 32.16m (105ft 6in) including probe; Wingspan: 33.83m (111ft); Height: 8.28m (27ft 2in)
WEIGHT:	113,400kg (250,000lb) maximum take-off
POWERPLANT:	4 × Bristol Siddeley Olympus 301 turbojets, 89kN (20,000lb)
MAXIMUM SPEED:	1043km/h (648mph)
RANGE:	7400km (4600 miles) with bombload
SERVICE CEILING:	18,290m (60,000ft)
CREW:	5
ARMAMENT:	Up to 9526kg (21,000lb) of ordnance carried internally

The most successful of Britain's three V-bombers, the Vulcan enjoyed an impressively long service career, starting out as a high-level strategic nuclear bomber and later going into combat as a conventional bomber during the Falklands campaign.

Below: Vulcan B.Mk 2 XM607 was one of the aircraft involved in the first of the 'Black Buck' Falklands raids against Port Stanley airfield, flown on 1 May 1982, and armed with 21 454kg (1000lb) bombs.

REFUELLING PROBE
In the course of Black Buck 6, during a scheduled refuel with a Victor tanker, the refuelling probe was damaged. With not enough fuel to return to Wideawake, the aircraft had to divert to Rio de Janeiro, Brazil.

UPRATED ENGINES
For Black Buck, the Olympus 301 engines were restored to their full 103 per cent power setting, after having been detuned to 98 per cent as a measure to prolong service life.

MODIFICATIONS
Five aircraft were adapted for Black Buck bombing raids, receiving additional ECM equipment and provision for Shrike missiles. Also fitted was the Carousel inertial navigation system for flying over water.

Left: Vulcan B.Mk 2 XM597, stationed at Wideawake Airfield, Ascension Island, during the Falklands campaign of 1982. This aircraft was used on both Black Buck anti-radar attacks and made an emergency landing in Brazil after a raid on the night of 2/3 June.

SHRIKE
During Black Buck 6, XM597 launched two AGM-45 Shrike missiles, which destroyed an Argentine Skyguard anti-aircraft artillery radar stationed in the Falklands.

FALKLAND ISLANDS SWANSONG

The Vulcan force was midway through being wound down when, in April 1982, Argentine forces invaded the Falklands in the South Atlantic. In the course of round trips exceeding 12,870km (8000 miles), and under the codename 'Black Buck', the Vulcans bombed the occupied Port Stanley airfield and related radar installations in the Falklands, putting the runway out of action, albeit only temporarily. The last Vulcans to bow out of service were the K.Mk 2 tankers, finally retired in March 1984.

MARITIME OPERATIONS

Towards the end of the type's career, nine aircraft were modified for the Strategic Maritime Radar Reconnaissance (MRR role) as Vulcan B.Mk 2MRR aircraft. The aircraft were operated by RAF Scampton-based No. 27 Squadron from November 1973 to May 1982, assuming the role from Victor B.Mk 2(SR) aircraft of No. 543 Squadron that were in turn converted as inflight refuelling tankers. Compared to the standard Vulcan bomber, the B.Mk 2MRR received LORAN-C navigation equipment and the terrain-following radar thimble was removed from the nose.

SPECIFICATIONS

DIMENSIONS:	Length: 49.13m (161ft 2in); Wingspan: 50.04m (164ft 2in); Height: 12.12m (39ft 9in)
WEIGHT:	91,800kg (202,380lb)
POWERPLANT:	4 × Kuznetsov/Samara NK-12MP turboprops, 11,185kW (15,000hp) each
MAXIMUM SPEED:	830km/h (516mph)
RANGE:	15,000km (9320 miles)
SERVICE CEILING:	13,716m (45,000ft)
CREW:	7
ARMAMENT:	6–12 cruise missiles; 2 × twin-barrelled 23mm (0.9in) GSh-23 cannon

The remarkable turboprop-powered Tupolev 'Bear' appeared anachronistic when it was first revealed to Western observers in the 1950s, but the quality of the basic design has ensured that it remains in frontline service today as the most numerous long-range strategic bomber within the Russian Air Force inventory.

STANDOFF MISSILE CARRIER
The Kh-20 (AS-3 'Kangaroo') missile was intended to strike both critical land installations and naval targets. During an attack on a warship, the Tu-95K's YaD radar would first determine the position of the target. For missile launch, the Kh-20 would be lowered from its semi-recessed installation into the slipstream below the bomber and its turbojet engine spooled up.

LANDING GEAR
The 'Bear' family features typical Tupolev landing gear, with the four-wheel bogies on each main unit retracting into large fairings on the wing trailing edges, in line with the inner engines. The steerable nose gear comprises twin nosewheels.

DEFENSIVE ARMAMENT
Unlike later models, the original Tu-95 free-fall bomber was provided with three gun installations, positioned dorsally, ventrally and at the tail. Each of these installations was equipped with a pair of 23mm (0.9in) AM-23 cannon, normally provided with 700 (dorsal), 800 (ventral) and 1000 (tail) rounds, respectively.

DEVELOPMENT
The Tu-95 'Bear-A' made its first flight in prototype form on 12 November 1952, but was lost in a crash in May 1953. After a definitive prototype flew in February 1955, production began the following October. While the initial 'Bear-A' had been limited to carrying free-fall ordnance, the first of the missile-carrying 'Bears' was the Tu-95K, armed with a single example of Mikoyan's powerful Kh-20 (AS-3 'Kangaroo'). The Tu-95K 'Bear-B' entered service in 1959. With the carriage of a large cruise missile compromising radius of action, Tupolev set about creating a long-range version of its missile carrier. The result was the Tu-95KD, with in-flight refuelling probe, which entered production as the Tu-95KM 'Bear-C' in 1965.

NK-12 TURBOPROPS
The Tu-95/142 series is powered by four Kuznetsov/Samara NK-12MP turboprops, each developing a maximum of 11,185kW (15,000hp). Each eight-blade propeller unit consists of two four-blade co-axial contra-rotating reversible-pitch propellers.

'BEAR-D'
Known to NATO as the 'Bear-D', the Tu-95RTs was a maritime reconnaissance version that was among the most likely to be encountered by Western air defences during the Cold War. The combination of turboprop engines, capacious internal fuel tanks and in-flight refuelling capability ensured a very long range for overwater patrol.

PATROL FLIGHTS
Beginning in 2007, Russian heavy bombers resumed their long-distance 'patrol' flights, and Tu-95MS and Tu-160 aircraft began increasingly to be intercepted by Western fighters. The 'Bear-H' is equipped for air-to-air refuelling. The location of the fixed refuelling probe directly in front of the cockpit makes this process straightforward.

Tupolev Tu-22M (1969)

SPECIFICATIONS

DIMENSIONS:	Length: 42.46m (139ft 4in); Wingspan: 34.28m (112ft 6in) wings spread; Height: 11.05m (36ft 3in)
WEIGHT:	124,000kg (273,373lb) maximum take-off
POWERPLANT:	2 × Kuznetsov NK-25 afterburning turbofans, 245.18kN (51,115lb)
MAXIMUM SPEED:	2000km/h (1243mph) at high altitude
RANGE:	2200km (1367 miles) radius of action with 1 × Kh-22 at high altitude, part-supersonic
SERVICE CEILING:	14,000m (45,930ft)
CREW:	4
ARMAMENT:	Maximum 24,000kg (52,910lb) of stores, including up to 3 x Kh-22 missiles, 1 x twin-barrel 23mm (0.9in) cannon in tail turret

The appearance of the Tu-22M bomber came as a shock to NATO, and Western navies in particular soon had to find countermeasures to this powerful strike aircraft, the wartime tasks of which would have included missions against carrier battle groups and convoys supporting any conflict on the European continent.

Below: A Tu-22M-3 armed with a Kh-22 missile underwing. This delta-wing missile is made of welded titanium and steel alloys, and powered by a twin-chamber liquid-fuel rocket motor.

Below: A Tu-22M3 of the 924th Naval Missile Carrier Regiment, part of the Russian Navy's Northern Fleet based at Olenya in 1998. Aircraft from this unit were later taken over by the Air Force's 840th Heavy Bomber Aviation Regiment based at Soltsy.

SELF-DEFENCE
The Tu-22M is protected by the Ural system, which includes an infrared missile launch and approach sensor, a radar warning receiver, electronic jammer and chaff/flare dispensers.

TAIL GUN
A twin-barrel 23mm (0.9in) GSh-23M cannon with 750 rounds is carried in a tail turret, remotely controlled using a radar sight and a TV sight.

COCKPIT
The two pilots are seated side by side, with the navigator and weapon system operator to their rear. All crew are provided with KT-1M ejection seats, as well as life-saving dinghies.

FUEL
The two Kuznetsov NK-25 afterburning turbofans are provided with 67,700 litres (17,881 gallons), equivalent to 53,550kg (118,057lb), of internal fuel.

WEAPONS OPTIONS

The primary weapon for the Tu-22M is the Kh-22 (AS-4 'Kitchen') missile, up to three of which can be carried recessed under the fuselage. Kh-22s are provided in versions for high- or low-altitude launch, nuclear or conventional warheads, and with an active radar seeker for anti-ship work or autonomous guidance for use against fixed targets. As well as free-fall bombs, the Tu-22M can also carry mines. In 1989, the Tu-22M3 added new armament in the form of the Kh-15 (AS-16 'Kickback') short-range attack missile, but this was later withdrawn.

KH-22
After launch from high altitude at supersonic speed, the missile accelerates to Mach 3 and a height of 22–23km (72,178–75,459ft). When approaching its target, the missile dives at an angle of around 30°, accelerating to a terminal speed of Mach 4.15.

WING
The variable-geometry wing features large fixed-glove centre sections and hydraulically driven wing panels. Trailing-edge flaps are carried on the fixed glove sections and on the outer wing panels.

FREE-FALL BOMBS
Free-fall bombs can be carried on pylons inside the bomb bay as well as on four external multiple racks: two under the engine air intake trunks, as seen here, and two under the wings.

Northrop B-2 Spirit (1989)

SPECIFICATIONS

DIMENSIONS:	Length: 21.03m (69ft); Wingspan: 52.43m (172ft); Height: 5.18m (17ft)
WEIGHT:	152,635kg (336,500lb) typical take-off
POWERPLANT:	4 × General Electric F118-GE-100 turbofans, 84.52kN (19,000lb)
MAXIMUM SPEED:	About 764km/h (475mph) at high altitude
RANGE:	8334km (5178 miles), hi-lo-hi mission with typical weapons load
SERVICE CEILING:	15,240m (50,000ft)
CREW:	2
ARMAMENT:	Up to 18,144kg (40,000lb) of disposable stores carried in 2 weapons bays in underside of centre section

The bat-winged B-2 stealth bomber is the most expensive warplane ever built, with a price tag of around US$900 million per aircraft. Tricky to maintain, the small fleet of Spirits comprise some of the most potent weapons in the US arsenal.

Below: A B-2 Spirit of the 393rd Bomb Squadron 'Tigers', assigned to the 509th Bomb Wing at Whiteman AFB. The 393rd is complemented by the 13th BS and the 394th Combat Training Squadron, which also operates Northrop T-38 Talon trainers.

Below: Seen here equipped with a spin recovery parachute for early flight tests, B-2 serial 82-1066 (AV-1) was the first Spirit, delivered to the USAF as the Spirit of America in Julyz 1989.

WING PLANFORM
The leading edge is swept at 33 degrees, while the trailing edge features an unusual sawtooth configuration designed to trap radar energy. The engine intakes feature S-shaped curves.

RAM COATING
As well as its radar-defeating shape, the B-2 uses radar-absorbing coatings; these require special maintenance and mean the aircraft requires a considerable support infrastructure.

ENGINES
The four General Electric F118-GE-100 turbofans exhaust through V-shaped outlets set back and above the trailing edges to shield these from ground-based sensors.

DESTRUCTIVE FORCE
In addition to B61 and B83 free-fall nuclear bombs, the Spirit can carry basic and penetrator versions of the 907kg (2000lb) GBU-31 JDAM, and up to 80 of the 227kg (500lb) GBU-38 JDAMs. The Spirit can also accommodate 16 907kg (2000lb) Mk 84 general-purpose bombs, the 2041kg (4500lb) GBU-28 laser-guided bomb, the AGM-154 Joint Stand-Off Weapon, 16 Joint Air-to-Surface Stand-off Missiles (JASSMs) and, most recently, the enormous 13,154kg (29,000lb) GBU-57 Massive Ordnance Penetrator (MOP). If required, the B-2 can also carry Mk 62 Quickstrike sea mines.

CREW
The B-2 has a crew of two pilots, a pilot in the left seat and mission commander in the right, compared to the B-1B's crew of four and the B-52's crew of five.

'FLYING WING'
The design of the B-2 offers the same payload as a conventional aircraft, while weighing less and using less fuel. The weight and drag of the tail unit are also removed, and the wing structure is highly efficient. It also enhances stealth characteristics.

DETERRENT AIRCRAFT
A Spirit breaks away from a tanker after a refuelling mission over the Pacific Ocean. Among the roles performed by the B-2 is as part of the USAF's continuous bomber presence, maintained as a deterrent force in the Asia-Pacific region.

Douglas C-47 Skytrain (1935)

TYPE · *Logistic & Specialist* · **FAMILY** · *Aircraft, Helicopters & Drones*

SPECIFICATIONS

DIMENSIONS:	Length: 19.43m (63ft 9in); Wingspan: 29.11m (95ft 6in); Height: 5.18m (17ft)
WEIGHT:	11,793kg (26,000lb) maximum take-off
POWERPLANT:	4 × Pratt & Whitney R-1830-92 14-cylinder radial piston engines, 895kW (1200hp)
MAXIMUM SPEED:	370km/h (230mph)
RANGE:	2575km (1600 miles)
SERVICE CEILING:	7315m (24,000ft)
CREW:	3
ARMAMENT:	None

The fact that the C-47 remains in frontline military service in the second decade of the twenty-first century goes some way to show the excellence of the basic 1930s design. In World War II, the C-47 played a leading role in decisive air assault and logistical operations in both European and Pacific theatres.

Below: C-47A serial FAC-681 of the Colombian Air Force is seen as it appeared in the 1980s. A former RAF machine, it was later converted as an AC-47 gunship. In 2014, six AC-47T Fantasma gunships remained in Colombian Air Force service.

CABIN
The typical interior layout for trooping operations comprises a row of utility bucket seats fitted along each cabin wall. These can be removed for freighting work.

COCKPIT
While the C-47 captain occupies the usual left-hand seat, the co-pilot sits on the right, and is also responsible for the radios and throttles.

TRANSPORTER

From 1942, the C-47 served as the USAAF's standard transport and glider tug and as such took part in every US airborne operation during the war. General Dwight D. Eisenhower put the C-47 on a pedestal with the bazooka, jeep and atomic bomb as weapons that contributed most to the Allied victory. Among its most incredible wartime exploits were the downing of a Mitsubishi A6M Zero by a pilot who aimed a Browning Automatic Rifle (BAR) into the slipstream before opening fire.

PROPELLERS
Typical propellers for the basic C-47 are these three-bladed Hamilton Standard constant-speed units. The constant-speed unit in the hub controls the pitch of each blade.

FUEL
The main fuel tanks (containing 795 litres/210 gallons) are located in the centre section forward of the wing spar. These are supplemented by two auxiliary tanks (760 litres/201 gallons) aft of the spar.

STATIC LINES
For delivering paratroops, a static line can be provided to open the chutes, rather than relying on a ripcord. A canvas static line is left streaming from the door after each jump.

CASUALTY EVACUATION
Korean War casualties are loaded on a USAF C-47 at a forward airstrip for evacuation to air bases further south. These patients are being evacuated from the front near Hagaru-ri in late 1950.

Consolidated PBY Catalina (1935)

SPECIFICATIONS

DIMENSIONS:	Length: 19.47m (63ft 10in); Wingspan: 31.7m (104ft) Height: 6.15m (25ft 1in)
WEIGHT:	16,066kg (35,420lb)
POWERPLANT:	2 × Pratt & Whitney R1830-92 twin Wasp radial piston engines, 895kW (1200hp)
MAXIMUM SPEED:	288km/h (175mph)
RANGE:	4030km (2520 miles)
SERVICE CEILING:	4000m (15,800ft)
CREW:	8
ARMAMENT:	3 x 7.62mm (0.3in) machine guns, 2 x 12.7mm (0.5in) machine guns; up to 1814kg (4000lb) of bombs or depth chargers

The exceptional flying boat of World War II, the 'Cat' was perhaps all the more remarkable since it had first been ordered for the US Navy back in 1933. It served with great success throughout World War II, and it became the most extensively built flying boat in aviation history.

Below: This OA-10 was with the US Air Force Air Rescue Service in 1947. Built during World War II by Canadian Vickers, it was one of a batch that served from early 1944.

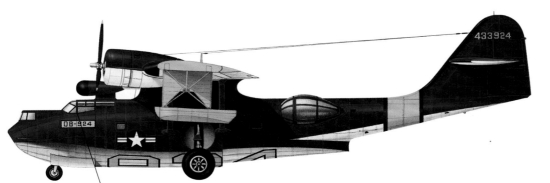

FLIGHT DECK
The pilot and co-pilot sat side by side on the flight deck and were provided with a roof escape hatch for emergencies.

BEAM GUNS
The Catalina carried two 12.7mm (0.5in) machine guns in cupolas on each side of the fuselage.

BOW CABIN
The nose section provided accommodation for one crewmember who acted as an observer. The panel below the station was blind, but would have been used as a bomb-aiming window.

PBY-5A
More than 800 versions of the amphibious version of the PBY-5 were built, mainly for the US Navy. The retractable tricycle landing gear meant it could be used for conventional runways.

AMPHIBIOUS DEVELOPMENTS

Following tests with a retractable tricycle wheel landing gear in the last PBY-4, the final 33 US Navy PBY-5s were completed in the amphibian form, as were 761 PBY-5A aircraft. Following early successful use of the PBY-5 by the RAF's Coastal Command in 1941 as the Catalina Mk I, large orders continued to be placed for the US Navy, additional production being undertaken by Canadian Vickers and Boeing of Canada. A total of more than 500 examples eventually served with the RAF alone, while in Canadian service the PBY-5 was named the Canso.

EARLY DEVELOPMENT
Consolidated first flew the XPBY-5A in November 1939. This was converted with a tricycle-type undercarriage from a PBY-4 and was the first amphibious variant.

Lockheed C-130 Hercules (1954)

SPECIFICATIONS

DIMENSIONS: Length: 29.79m (97ft 9in); Wingspan: 40.41m (132ft 7in); Height: 11.66m (38ft 3in)

WEIGHT: 79,380kg (175,000lb) maximum take-off

POWERPLANT: 4 × Allison T56A-15 turboprops, 3362kW (4508hp)

MAXIMUM SPEED: 556km/h (345mph)

RANGE: 4002km (2487 miles) with maximum payload of 19,686kg (43,400lb)

SERVICE CEILING: 10,060m (33,000ft)

CREW: 5

ARMAMENT: None

The most successful Western military transport of the post-war era, the Hercules has enjoyed an unprecedented production run: it has been built in more than 70 variants, amounting to more than 2400 aircraft. As well as being the backbone of the US tactical airlift fleet, Hercules has been operated by over 60 nations.

Right: The C-130K version was built specifically for British use on the basis of the C-130H, and entered RAF service as the Hercules C.Mk 1, seen here on strength with the Hercules Wing at RAF Lyneham in 1990. This is a C.Mk 1P sub-variant with an inflight refuelling probe above the cockpit.

FLIGHT DECK
In Vietnam, the 'Herc' was usually operated by a flight-deck crew of four: pilot, co-pilot, navigator and systems manager. A loadmaster was also carried.

EXTERNAL TANKS
The C-130E was first to add the two 5148-litre (1360-gallon) underwing fuel tanks that were mounted between the inboard and outboard engines. These imposed a significant drag penalty.

UNDERCARRIAGE
The E-model featured beefed-up landing gear. All versions have included a retractable tricycle-type gear suitable for rough-field operations, and with steerable nosewheels.

LAPES
This aircraft featured a low-altitude parachute-extraction system (LAPES). Bulky cargo was delivered without landing by flying a few metres above the drop zone and releasing into the airstream a parachute attached to the palletized cargo. This pulled the cargo from the hold and off the rear ramp. The pallet then skidded to a stop below.

CARGO HOLD
In addition to different loads of troops, the hold could accommodate various items of cargo, including the 155mm (6.1in) howitzer or various types of small truck or helicopter.

VIETNAM OPS
As an airlifter, the C-130 proved its worth in Vietnam, operating in some of the most remote locations. In its basic form, the C-130 can carry 78 troops, or 92 if a high-density configuration is employed, 64 paratroopers or 74 litter patients. Later in the conflict in Southeast Asia, MC-130 Combat Talons were used to deliver special operations forces and for aerial refuelling. Once fitted with ground-target radar, 20mm (0.79in) Gatling guns, 40mm (1.57in) Bofors gun and, later, a side-firing 105mm (4.1in) howitzer, the Hercules became the AC-130 gunship, which was credited with destroying around 10,000 enemy trucks during the conflict.

RECENT SERVICE
A USAF Hercules from the 320th Air Expeditionary Wing takes off from a landing zone in Afghanistan during Operation Enduring Freedom in October 2002.

Lockheed SR-71 'Blackbird' (1962)

SPECIFICATIONS

DIMENSIONS:	Length: 32.74m (107ft 5in); Wingspan: 16.94m (55ft 7in); Height: 5.64m (18ft 6in)
WEIGHT:	78,017kg (172,000lb) maximum take-off
POWERPLANT:	2 × Pratt & Whitney J58 afterburning turbojets, 144.57kN (32,500lb)
MAXIMUM SPEED:	Mach 3.35 at 24,385m (80,000ft)
RANGE:	5230km (2250 miles) at Mach 3, unrefuelled
SERVICE CEILING:	24,385m (85,000ft)
CREW:	2
ARMAMENT:	None

First revealed in 1964, the aircraft popularly known as the 'Blackbird' remains the world's fastest air-breathing manned vehicle. During the Cold War years in which it served as a strategic reconnaissance platform for the USAF, the Mach 3+ capable SR-71 was effectively immune to interception.

Right: The 64-17978, an SR-71A of the 9th Strategic Reconnaissance Wing, was the first of three 'Blackbirds' to be sent to the Far East during the initial deployment phase, departing Beale for Okinawa in March 1968.

SENSOR BAYS
Four compartments each accommodated an interchangeable pallet carrying sensors including cameras, side-looking radar, infrared linescan and electronic intelligence receivers.

POWERPLANT
The Pratt & Whitney J58 engine was a scaled-down version of the JT9 developed for the XB-70 bomber. Uniquely, it was designed for sustained Mach 3 operations.

RADICAL DESIGN

The secret of the SR-71's awe-inspiring performance lay in a number of innovative design features. First, its use of largely titanium construction allowed it to withstand kinetic heating and retain structural integrity at speeds beyond Mach 3. In order to cope with the aerodynamic drag found at that speed, Johnson's design employed a slim fuselage and very thin delta wings. Integral lifting surfaces, known as chines, were built into the forward fuselage, preventing the nose from pitching down at high speed. Once the aircraft hit Mach 3, the engines were designed to provide just 18 per cent of total thrust, the remainder being derived from suction in the engine intakes and via special exhaust nozzles at the rear of the multiple-flow nacelles.

CHINES
Aerodynamic sharp edges leading aft from either side of the nose along the fuselage provided extra lift and reduced drag and improved directional stability.

UNDERCARRIAGE
The SR-71 employed a tricycle undercarriage with three wheels on each mainwheel strut. The tyres were impregnated with aluminium to reflect heat when retracted.

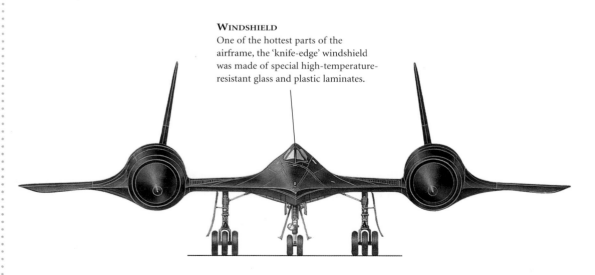

WINDSHIELD
One of the hottest parts of the airframe, the 'knife-edge' windshield was made of special high-temperature-resistant glass and plastic laminates.

FRONT VIEW
The frontal aspect of the SR-71A was dominated by its huge engine nacelles, blended into the wing leading edge, and the broad chines blending the fuselage into the leading edges.

Lockheed C-5 Galaxy (1968)

SPECIFICATIONS

DIMENSIONS:	Length: 75.54m (247ft 10in); Wingspan: 67.88m (222ft 8in); Height: 19.85m (65ft 1in)
WEIGHT:	348,810kg (769,000lb) maximum take-off
POWERPLANT:	4 × General Electric TF39-GE-1C turbofans, 191.27kN (43,000lb)
MAXIMUM SPEED:	890km/h (553mph) at 7620m (25,000ft)
RANGE:	6035km (3750 miles) with maximum payload of 100,228kg (220,967lb)
SERVICE CEILING:	10,360m (34,000ft)
CREW:	5
ARMAMENT:	None

For many years the world's biggest military cargo aircraft, the C-5 Galaxy remains the largest and only strategic airlifter in the US Air Force inventory and can carry more cargo farther distances than any other aircraft. Modified to C-5M Super Galaxy standard, the airlifter will remain in service beyond 2040.

Right and below: A C-5B Galaxy of the USAF's 436th Military Airlift Wing in the European One 'lizard' camouflage scheme worn during the 1980s. The B-model was basically similar to the C-5A, but added the various improvements made during that type's service life.

POWERPLANT
The four General Electric TF39-GE-1C engines are twin-shaft high-bypass turbofans, with a two-stage fan and a 16-stage axial flow compressor. The rear section of the cowling serves as a thrust reverser.

WING
The Galaxy's huge wing is equipped with track-mounted slotted flaps on the trailing edge. These consist of three inboard and three outboard sections. The wing leading edge is fitted with four sealed inboard slat sections, and three slotted outboard sections.

CARGO DOOR
Nose and aft doors open the full width and height of the cargo compartment to permit faster and easier loading.

AIR MOBILITY COMMAND
The C-5 is the largest and most capable asset in Air Mobility Command (AMC) service. Led by a general, the AMC serves as the USAF component of US Transportation Command (TRANSCOM), and is responsible for a single numbered air force, the 18th Air Force/ Air Forces Transportation headquartered at Scott AFB, Illinois. This includes 11 airlift, air mobility and air refuelling wings; two airlift groups, and the 618th Air and Space Operations Center or Tanker Airlift Control Center (TACC), which directs tanker and transport aircraft operations worldwide.

UNDERCARRIAGE
Five sets of landing gear totalling 28 wheels distribute weight. A 'kneeling' system permits lowering the parked aircraft to facilitate drive-on/ drive-off vehicle loading and adjusts the cargo floor to standard truck-bed height.

PAYLOAD
With a payload of six Mine Resistant Ambush Protected vehicles (MRAPs) or up to five helicopters, the C-5 can haul twice as much cargo as any other US airlifter.

TROOP TRANSPORT
As an alternative to the typical cargo load (up to a maximum of 100,228kg/220,967lb), the C-5 can also be adapted for the transport of up to 350 fully equipped troops.

445TH AIRLIFT WING
A Galaxy dwarfs personnel of the USAF's 445th Airlift Wing as the unit receives the first of 11 C-5s in October 2005. An Air Force Reserve Command wing, the 445th previously operated the Lockheed C-141 StarLifter.

E-3 Sentry (1976)

SPECIFICATIONS

DIMENSIONS:	Length: 46.62m (152ft 11in); Wingspan: 44.43m (145ft 9in); Height: 12.6m (41ft 6in)
WEIGHT:	147,418kg (325,000lb)
POWERPLANT:	4 × Pratt & Whitney TF-33 turbofan, 93kN (21,500lb) each
MAXIMUM SPEED:	855km/h (530mph)
RANGE:	7400km (4598 miles)
SERVICE CEILING:	12,500m (41,010ft)
CREW:	4 + 17 AWACS specialists
ARMAMENT:	None

E-3A AWACS SENTRY
Introduced into USAF service in 1977, this Sentry was selected to equip a multinational NATO unit based in Germany.

Essentially a giant flying radar, the E-3 Sentry greatly enhances the capabilities of air combat assets by detecting and tracking targets, and by guiding pilots to where they need to be.

Right: An E-3A, dating from the early 1980s. Most E-3As were later converted to E-3B standard, increasing the AWACS crew from 13 to 17–19.

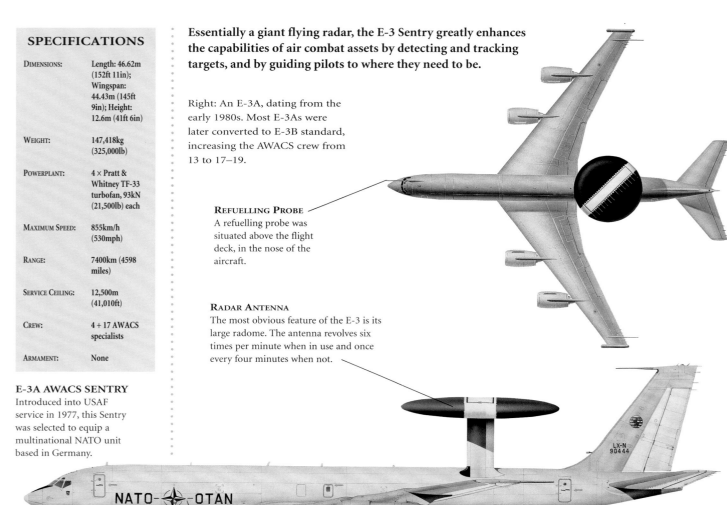

REFUELLING PROBE
A refuelling probe was situated above the flight deck, in the nose of the aircraft.

RADAR ANTENNA
The most obvious feature of the E-3 is its large radome. The antenna revolves six times per minute when in use and once every four minutes when not.

THE E-3 IN SERVICE
The E-3 Sentry is operated by the US Air Force and the RAF under the designation AWACS and AEW respectively. Other users include France and Saudi Arabia. The E-3 entered service in 1977, during the Cold War, and initially was expected to provide early warning and interception of air strikes in a major conflict if one occurred. It has seen service in several smaller conflicts since. The E-3 was highly useful in enforcing the no-fly zone over the Balkans in the 1990s. Operations over Iraq in 1990–91 and 2003 were closer to the E-3's intended role, providing information on enemy movements.

CREW SPACE
The AWACS has a flight crew of four: pilot, co-pilot, navigator and flight engineer. The use of a civilian airframe eliminated the costs required to develop a dedicated platform, and provided plenty of space for crew and electronic systems.

ELECTRONIC EQUIPMENT
Electronic equipment is arranged in bays within the fuselage, grouping equipment used for communications, signal and data processing, command and control, and navigation.

THAILAND EXERCISES
An E-3 Sentry assigned to the 961st AWACS Squadron at Kadena Air Force Base, Japan, takes off during exercises held at Cope Tiger 2002 at Wing 1 Air Base Korat, Thailand.

UH-1 Iroquois (1956)

SPECIFICATIONS

DIMENSIONS:	Main rotor diameter: 14.63m (48ft); Length: 12.31m (40ft 5in); Height 3.77m (12ft 5in)
WEIGHT:	Empty: 2177kg (4789lb); maximum take-off: 3856kg (8483lb)
POWERPLANT:	Lycoming T53-L-11 turboshaft, 820kW (1100hp)
MAXIMUM SPEED:	217km/h (135mph)
ENDURANCE:	383km (237 miles) at sea level
SERVICE CEILING:	5790m (19,000ft)
CREW:	1–4
ARMAMENT:	Up to 3800kg (8300lb) of guns, rockets, missiles and grenades

American soldiers in Vietnam won a prolonged, hand-to-hand battle with North Vietnamese infantry in the Ia Drang Valley in 1965, thanks to a new concept: air cavalry. The Bell UH-1 Iroquois helicopter, or 'Huey', enabled soldiers to move from one firefight to another by air, leapfrogging the enemy and seizing the advantage. The 'Huey' revolutionized warfare, adding a new dimension to air mobility.

Above: A USMC UH-1 Huey helicopter flies in the skies over a forward area refuelling point as it prepares to land and take on fuel in Yuma, Arizona, 2007.

MACHINE GUN
Fitted with twin 7.62mm (0.3in) Browning machine-guns, the UH-1 was a devastating gunship.

ROTOR BLADES
Pilots always checked the glass-fibre rotor blades before a flight to ensure that the surface was not delaminating. They also inspected the so-called 'Jesus nut', which held the main rotor blades securely.

MAIN ROTOR
The large, twin-bladed main rotor had a thick metal leading-edge spar, which allowed pilots to chop through vegetation in confined landing zones.

COMBAT MISSIONS
In combat, UH-1s flew three distinct missions as 'slicks' (troop transports), 'gunships' (armed battlefield helicopters) and 'dust-offs' (medical evacuation aircraft). The Huey was armed with a door-mounted, flexible 7.62mm (0.3in) M60 machine gun; gunship versions carried rocket pods, grenade-launchers or four side-mounted guns. On the battlefield, a soldier might be put into action at the LZ (landing zone) by one 'Huey', given covering fire by another and taken to the field hospital by a third UH-1.

COMPARTMENT
The main compartment could carry up to 10 troops in combat gear or six stretchers. The crew chief supervised loading of cargo, and a gunner operated the M-60 machine gun.

CABIN DOOR
The main cabin door slid backwards to allow the troops to dismount or the gunner to fire. Gunships carried their armament on side-mounted sponsons.

DOOR GUNNER
A Marine readies an M134 7.62mm (0.3in) machine gun mounted in the door of a UH-1 Iroquois helicopter.

MiL Mi-24 'Hind' (1969)

SPECIFICATIONS

DIMENSIONS:	Main rotor diameter: 17.3m (57ft); Length: 19.79m (65ft); Height 6.5m (21ft)
WEIGHT:	Empty: 8400kg (18,400lb); loaded: 12,500kg (27,500lb)
POWERPLANT:	2 × Klimov (Isotov) TV3-117 Series III turboshafts, 1640kW (1500hp)
MAXIMUM SPEED:	310km/h (192mph); maximum cruising speed: 260km/h (161mph)
RANGE:	750km (465 miles) with internal fuel
SERVICE CEILING:	4500m (14,760ft)
CREW:	2–3
ARMAMENT:	1 × 4-barrel JakB 12.7mm (0.5in) Gatling gun in chin turret; 4 × S-8 80mm (3.14in) rocket pods or up to 3460kg (7612lb) of rockets or missiles

The Mil Mi-24 'Hind' is the hammer of the Russian army. A veteran of battles in Afghanistan and Angola and most recently in Chechnya, the Mi-24 is a flying armoured personnel carrier, able to deliver a squad of soldiers and cover them with suppressive fire. Armed with a cannon and powerful laser-guided anti-armour missiles, and now fitted with the latest avionics and new engines, the 'Hind' is a highly potent attack helicopter.

MAIN ROTOR
All Mil helicopters have a clockwise rotating rotor. The rotor head was built to withstand heavy machine-gun fire.

TAIL ROTOR
The original 'Hind-A' had its tail rotor on the starboard side of the tail boom, but it was switched to port soon after production had started.

Below: This Mi-24 'Hind-E' served with the Polish air force's 56th squadron at Inowroclaw, armed with the 'Shturm' AT-6 laser-guided anti-tank missile.

IR JAMMER
Many 'Hinds' have an infrared jammer fitted to counter shoulder-launched heat-seeking missiles such as Stinger and SA-14.

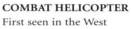

COMBAT HELICOPTER
First seen in the West in 1974, the 'Hind' was designed to carry eight men into frontline positions and support them with air-to-ground fire. The Mi-24 is large and fast, but it is not as agile as Western helicopters. However, aircraft like the AH-64 Apache are designed to engage tanks from hidden hovering positions, which calls for low-speed manoeuvrability. The 'Hind', by contrast, is an offensive weapon, heavily armed and armoured and designed to fly at high speed.

SUPPRESSOR
Large exhaust suppressors are fitted to some 'Hinds' to reduce infrared signature.

STUB WINGS
The stub wings allow the 'Hind' to travel very fast by adding to the lift from the rotor, but by sticking out into the rotor downwash they inhibit low-speed and hovering handling.

WARNING
The tail rotor remains one of the weak points of the 'Hind'. The yellow warning strip has the Russian word for 'danger' painted on it, as ground crews often fail to spot it when it is rotating.

AMERICAN HIND
This Russian-made Mi-24 serves at the US Army Test and Evaluation Center, Threat Support Activity, Las Vegas, Nevada. It provides simulated hostile threats to Search and Rescue operations, to give greater realism.

Lynx (1971)

SPECIFICATIONS

DIMENSIONS:	Main rotor diameter: 12.8m (41ft 12in); Length: 15.24m (49ft 12in); Height: 3.73m (12ft 3in)
WEIGHT:	3030kg (6666lb) empty
POWERPLANT:	2 × Rolls-Royce Gem Gem 42-1 turboshaft engines, each 835kW (1119hp)
MAXIMUM SPEED:	270km/h (168mph)
RANGE:	685km (426 miles)
SERVICE CEILING:	5790m (19,000ft)
CREW:	2 or 3
ARMAMENT:	Multiple machine gun, rocket, missile, gun pod and mine options

Westland and Aérospatiale produced the Lynx, together with the Puma and Gazelle, under the Anglo-French helicopter agreement of 1967. The first of 13 prototypes flew in March 1971; subsequent production included both army and navy versions.

Below: A French Naval Aviation Lynx. The Lynx was acquired for French maritime duties – principally anti-submarine and anti-ship warfare – in 1979.

POWERPLANT
Originally fitted with Gem 41-1 engines, from 1987 the Lynx's powerplant was upgraded to Gem 42-1 standard in the AH.7. These aircraft also have composite rotor blades.

ROOF-MOUNTED SIGHT
British Aerospace, under licence from Hughes, built the Lynx roof-mounted sight. It allows guidance for the TOW missiles.

CABIN
Up to nine soldiers could be carried in the main cabin of the AH.1, or six with full combat equipment.

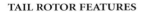

UNDERCARRIAGE
A skid undercarriage allows the helicopter to operate from a variety of surfaces without the risk of sinking into soft ground.

Above: Seen in service with No. 1 Wing, British Army of the Rhine, XZ669 has been converted to AH.7 standard. It is now based at Wattisham, Suffolk, with No. 669 Squadron of No. 4 Regiment, Army Air Corps.

ARMY LYNX
Designated AH.1, the first British Army Lynxes were delivered in 1977. They could carry nine troops, more than 1350kg (3000lb) of external cargo or eight TOW (Tube-launched, Optically-tracked, Wire-guided) missiles, aimed using a sight on the cabin roof. More powerful Gem 41 engines were introduced in the AH.7, in addition to improved avionics and a more powerful tail rotor. This enabled the helicopter to remain in the hover when carrying the heavy loads involved in anti-armour operations.

TOW MISSILES
Hughes manufactured the TOW missiles that are the Lynx's principal anti-tank armament. Optional weapons include air-to-air missiles and gun or rocket pods.

TAIL ROTOR FEATURES
The AH.1 featured a counter-clockwise-rotating tail rotor. On the upgraded AH.7 it was replaced by a more powerful clockwise-rotating unit made from composite materials, which gives better control in the hover. The helicopter here is an AH.9, based on AH.7 but with a wheeled undercarriage and an upgraded gearbox.

AH-64 Apache (1975)

SPECIFICATIONS

DIMENSIONS:	Main rotor diameter: 14.63m (48ft); Length: 14.97m (49ft 2in); Height: 4.66m (15ft 4in)
WEIGHT:	Empty: 5165kg (11,363lb); maximum take-off: 9525kg (20,995lb)
POWERPLANT:	2 × General Electric T700-GE-701 turboshaft engines, 1265kW (1700hp)
MAXIMUM SPEED:	293km/h (182mph)
RANGE:	428km (265 miles)
SERVICE CEILING:	6400m (21,000ft)
CREW:	2
ARMAMENT:	1 × 30mm (1.18in) M230 chain gun cannon, up to 16 AGM-114 Hellfire laser-guided missiles or up to 76 folding-fin rockets; various other combinations of rocket projectiles, guns and missiles

Hughes developed the AH-64 Apache in response to the Warsaw Pact's massive armoured strength. Produced by McDonnell Douglas, the AH-64 can engage tanks, often at a safe distance, even at night and in bad weather. The Apache uses advanced sensors to detect enemy vehicles. It then stalks them, using natural cover as a shield, before rising above the treeline to launch laser-guided Hellfire missiles.

Above: An AH-64 Apache helicopter from 10th Combat Aviation Brigade, 10th Mountain Division, refuels in Jalalabad, Afghanistan, 2007.

TAIL ROTOR
Unusually, the AH-64's tail rotor consists of two twin-bladed units mounted at 55 to each other. This arrangement keeps noise to a minimum.

ROTOR BLADES
Constructed of fibre-glass, stainless steel and composites, the main rotor blades are proof against hits by 23mm (0.9in) cannon shells. They have swept tips for increased performance.

TANK HUNTING

One of the leading battlefield helicopters in the world, the tandem-seat AH-64, which has the gunner forward and pilot aft, uses high-tech sensors, a Chain Gun cannon and far-reaching Hellfire missiles to destroy tanks and other key targets. At night or in bad weather – or even in dust storms, as during Operation Desert Storm – the Apache crew can monitor enemy tank movements, using the PNVS (Pilot's Night-Vision System) and TADS (Target Acquisition and Designation System) to pinpoint and fire at targets. In the Gulf, these sensors and weapons also enabled Apaches to attack Iraqi air defence radar sites.

Above: An AH-64D Apache Longbow from the 3rd Armored Cavalry Regiment (ACR) hovers on the flight line at Forward Operating Base Sykes before a flight mission in Iraq's Ninewa Province.

ROCKETS
A maximum load of 76 folding-fin rockets may be carried, although the configuration shown is almost standard.

AH-64 AT BAGRAM
An AH-64 Apache helicopter from 158th Aviation Regiment waits at Bagram Airfield, Afghanistan, for the helicopter it is escorting, 2007.

UH-60A Black Hawk (1979)

SPECIFICATIONS

DIMENSIONS:	Main rotor diameter: 16.36m (54ft); Length: 19.76m (65ft); Height: 5.13m (17ft)
WEIGHT:	(Army UH-60) Empty: 4819kg (10,600lb); loaded: 9185kg (20,200lb) (Navy SH-60) Empty: 6191kg (13,620lb); loaded: 9926kg (21,837lb)
POWERPLANT:	2 × General Electric T700-GE-701C turboshaft, 1410kW (1890hp) each
MAXIMUM SPEED:	294km/h (183mph)
ENDURANCE:	600km (370 miles)
SERVICE CEILING:	5790m (19,000ft)
CREW:	2 flight crew; 2 crew chiefs/gunners
ARMAMENT:	Usually 2 × 7.62mm (0.3in) door guns, but with a variety of rocket, missile, gun pod and mine options

Sikorsky's UH-60 Black Hawk is one of the most important combat helicopters in service. Special forces soldiers can abseil down from the UH-60 very quickly. This is useful in tight situations where the pilot cannot land safely.

Below: The UH-60A, the first of many versions of the Black Hawk family, saw action during the invasion of Grenada in 1981. The Black Hawk has since been in action in Lebanon, Somalia and both Gulf wars.

Above: US Army Soldiers walk towards the passenger terminal after arriving at Sather Air Base, Iraq, from a UH-60 Blackhawk helicopter, 2008.

MAIN ROTOR
The UH-60's rotor-head and blades were designed to withstand hits from large machine-gun rounds. The gearbox that drives it can run for half an hour after losing its entire oil supply.

EXHAUST
The Black Hawk has an exhaust suppression system that dissipates hot engine gases. This makes the helicopter less of a target for heat-seeking infrared missiles.

NOSE PANELS
The transparent panels in the nose are essential for safe landing in confined spaces.

SURVIVABILITY
The UH-60 was designed with all the years of experience of battle in Vietnam in mind. The low profile of the airframe makes it a difficult target, and safer if it crashes. In an assault landing, the UH-60 comes in fast. Its undercarriage is designed to absorb vertical impacts of up to 45km/h (28mph), dramatically reducing the risk of injury among the helicopter's crew and occupants. If required, the helicopter can be heavily uparmed, including AGM-114 Hellfire laser-guided missiles, AIM-92 Stinger air-to-air missiles and 30mm (1.18in) M230 gun pods.

CABIN
Although the Black Hawk can carry armament, it is essentially a troop carrier. Its cabin and hatches are designed to allow a squad of infantry to get into action fast.

FUSELAGE
The fuselage plan is noticeably broad and long, giving a generous internal capacity while allowing a very flat profile.

URBAN PATROL
A US Army UH-60 Black Hawk helicopter from 227th Aviation Regiment flies over Baghdad, 2007.

MQ-1 Predator (1994)

SPECIFICATIONS

DIMENSIONS:	Length: 8.22m (27ft); Wingspan: 14.8m (48ft 6in); Height: 2.1m (6ft 10in)
WEIGHT:	1020kg (2250lb)
POWERPLANT:	Rotax 914F turbocharged four-cylinder engine, 86kW (115hp)
MAXIMUM SPEED:	217km/h (135mph)
RANGE:	1100km (675 miles)
SERVICE CEILING:	7620m (25,000ft)
ARMAMENT:	2 hardpoints and provisions to carry combinations of: 2 × AGM-114 Hellfire (MQ-1B), 4 × AIM-92 Stinger (MQ-1B), 6 × AGM-176 Griffin air-to-surface missiles

GROUND CONTROL

The Predator is controlled from a ground station, either via a C-band line-of-sight data link or a satellite data link. The latter gives the operators the ability to control Predators from very distant locations indeed; many Predator operations over Afghanistan and Iraq, for example, have been conducted from ground stations based in the United States. The mounted visual/thermographic camera systems enable the pilot to fly the Predator in both daytime and low-light/night conditions.

The Predator is one of the most famous military drones. It has a strange-looking downward-pointing tail and is driven by a propeller at the rear. When it was developed in the early 1990s the Predator was not armed, but today's drones can carry two Hellfire missiles, guided to their target by a laser beam.

Right: Predator drones are used by the armed forces of several countries and also by the CIA, principally for aerial reconnaissance and forward observation roles.

MALE DRONE
Predator is a MALE drone (medium-altitude, long-endurance). This means it can fly fairly high and stay on station (in the target area) for a long time.

DISASSEMBLY
The Predator can be dismantled into six main component parts, for easier transportation to a distant theatre.

DRONE CARRIER
The Predator can carry a smaller drone to the target area, then carry out its own mission after launching it.

ARMED PREDATORS
The Hellfire missile of this US Predator can be seen on its port wing. The first Hellfire tests with the Predator were conducted in February 2001. Recently, the US hunter-killer UAV role has been largely taken by the General Atomics MQ-9A Reaper, developed from the Predator.

RQ-4 Global Hawk (1998)

SPECIFICATIONS

DIMENSIONS:	Length: 14.5m (47ft 8in); Wingspan: 39.9m (131ft); Height: 4.7m (15ft 3in)
WEIGHT:	Empty: 6781kg (14,950lb); Gross weight: 14,628kg (32,250lb)
POWERPLANT:	Rolls-Royce F137-RR-100 turbofan engine, 34kN (7600lb)
MAXIMUM SPEED:	629km/h (391mph)
RANGE:	22,779km (14,154 miles)
SERVICE CEILING:	18,000m (59,000ft)
ARMAMENT:	n/a

Global Hawk was developed to fly at extremely high altitudes and undertake long missions. It is not a combat platform designed to launch missiles at the enemy, but instead undertakes long-range reconnaissance missions over land or sea.

RUDDERVATOR
These V-shaped structures steer and control the drone.

INTEGRATED SENSOR SUITE
The Integrated Sensor Suite (ISS) consists of a synthetic aperture radar (SAR), electro-optical (EO) and thermographic camera (IR) sensors.

POWERPLANT
The powerplant is top-mounted to reduce the ground-detactable heat and noise signatures from the aircraft.

LONG-RANGE SURVEILLANCE
Global Hawk provides detailed surveillance information using its cameras, thermal-imaging equipment and radar. It can stay aloft for more than 35 hours and operates at an altitude of almost 20km (12 miles), high enough that most enemies cannot detect it. The UAV also offers considerable reach: it is designed to fly to a target area more than 1500km (930 miles) away, to remain there for a whole day or more, and then return home safely. To demonstrate its great range, a Global Hawk was flown nonstop from the United States to Australia, setting several records in the process.

PAYLOAD
The RQ-4 can carry a total external payload (principally electronic sensors, cameras and other systems) of 910kg (2000lb).

ANTENNA
The 1.2m-wide (4ft) Ku-wideband satcom antenna provides the main datalink with the ground control station.

INDEPENDENT SYSTEM
Global Hawk can taxi to the runway, take off, fly to its destination, and come home again without direct human control. It can even land itself. If necessary, the drone can be retasked by its controllers and sent to another area or be told to carry out a new mission.

MQ-9 Reaper (2001)

SPECIFICATIONS

DIMENSIONS:	Length: 11m (36ft 1in); Wingspan: 20m (65ft 7in); Height: 3.81m (12ft 6in)
WEIGHT:	Max takeoff weight: 4760kg (10,494lb)
POWERPLANT:	Honeywell TPE331-10 turboprop, 671kW (900hp)
MAXIMUM SPEED:	482km/h (300mph)
ENDURANCE:	c. 30 hours
SERVICE CEILING:	15,000m (50,000ft)
ARMAMENT:	7 hardpoints: up to 680kg (1500lb) on the two inboard weapons stations; up to 340kg (750lb) on the two middle stations; up to 68kg (150lb) on the outboard stations; centre station not used

The Reaper was developed from the MQ-1 Predator; it looks very similar, but the tail section is a distinguishing feature: the Reaper has two fins slanted upward and one pointing straight down. It also has a vastly more powerful engine than the Predator. As well as being capable of attack missions, the Reaper is a versatile sensor platform, equipped with various cameras, thermal imaging equipment, a laser rangefinder, and synthetic aperture radar. It is used in US Homeland Security operations, monitoring coastlines and long borders that would be difficult to patrol at ground level.

MARITIME SECURITY
The United States and a number of allied nations have explored the use of Reaper drones at sea, as part of anti-piracy and maritime security operations. The Reaper has also been approved for use in disaster situations, where it could search for survivors and assess damage to remote areas with its cameras and thermal imagers. The Reaper can remain on station for three times as long as a Predator and can carry out missions over a far greater distance.

TURBOPROP POWER
The Honeywell turboprop engine gives a low speed but impressive levels of endurance and battlefield airspace loitering.

MSTS
The Multi-Spectral Targeting System is a directable unit containing multiple cameras and sensors for reconnaissance and targeting.

MISSILE LOAD
The Reaper can carry up to 14 missiles. It has six external pylons that can carry laser-guided bombs and missiles, GPS-guided bombs, or Stinger and Sidewinder air-to-air missiles.

REAPER OPS
A front view of an MQ-9 preparing to take off. The Reaper began operations in both Iraq and Afghanistan in the summer of 2007.

MQ-8B Fire Scout (2000)

SPECIFICATIONS

DIMENSIONS:	Length: 7.3m (24ft); Rotor diameter: 8.4m (27ft 6in); Height: 2.9m (9ft 8in)
WEIGHT:	1430kg (3150lb)
POWERPLANT:	Rolls-Royce 250, 313kW (420hp)
MAXIMUM SPEED:	213km/h (132mph); Cruise speed: 200km/h (124mph)
ENDURANCE:	8 hours (typical), 5 hours fully loaded
SERVICE CEILING:	6100m (20,000ft)
ARMAMENT:	Options for rocket pods, ASMs and precision-guided bombs

DEVELOPING RECORD

Fire Scout can fly at over 200km/h (124mph) and can stay in the air for more than five hours with a full load. With a lighter load it can fly for up to eight hours. US Navy shipboard deployments of the Fire Scout began in 2008. The type subsequently saw operational service over Afghanistan, Libya (where one was shot down) and off the coast of Africa, the latter in the context of anti-piracy options. By 2013, the Fire Scout had clocked up more than 8000 hours of flight time, including 5000 hours in Afghanistan.

Fire Scout was developed for the US Navy, to provide UAV functions such as surveillance and reconnaissance, targeting information (for both land and naval forces) and fire support. In the latter role, the Fire Scout drone can be armed with Hellfire missiles, Viper Strike laser-guided bombs or a laser-guided rocket system, but it is mainly intended for non-combat duties.

Above: Although it is a diminutive aircraft, the MQ-8B is able to pack a large volume of electronic and combat systems into its airframe, because of the absence of a human pilot.

ROTOR
The original RQ-8A Fire Scout had a three-blade rotor, but performance was improved dramatically in the MQ-8B's four-blade rotor.

RADAR TRACKING
The Fire Scout drone's radar can track multiple contacts at once. It can also be fitted with a landmine/IED aerial detection system.

STUB WINGS
The Fire Scout's stub wings provide a small amount of lift, but also offer a platform for mounting weapon systems and electronics pods.

NAVAL USE
The Fire Scout UAV is used by the United States Navy. Being able to take off and land vertically makes it suitable for use aboard small ships.

Warships

Naval warfare during the twentieth century saw the rise of two major types of warfighting vessel: the aircraft carrier and the submarine. Once it was the capital battleship that stood as the most visible demonstration of naval might. Yet the long-range power-projection of aircraft carriers, and the lethal underwater presence of the submarine, meant that the age of the battleship effectively ended in 1945. Since then, aircraft carriers have taken centre stage on the world's seas, although the bulk of naval work is still performed by a broad range of lesser but often equally advanced warships. New generations of small but highly lethal 'stealth' frigates and destroyers are entering service, and their low visibility and potent over-the-horizon weapon systems are changing the tactical framework of naval warfare for the future.

CARRIER POWER
An elevated bow view of the nuclear-powered aircraft carrier USS *Ronald Reagan* (CVN-76) underway. The *Ronald Reagan* is a Nimitz-class carrier, the ninth of her class.

CSS *Hunley* (1863)

SPECIFICATIONS

DIMENSIONS:	Length: 12m (40ft); Beam: 1m (3ft 4in); Draught: 1.2m (3ft 11in)
DISPLACEMENT:	Surfaced – 6.8 tonnes (6.7 tons)
PROPULSION:	Hand-crank shaft, single screw
SPEED:	Surfaced – 4 knots (7.4km/h; 4.6mph); Submerged – approx. 2 knots (3.7km/h; 2.3mph)
RANGE:	c. 4.8km (3 miles)
ARMAMENT:	1 spar torpedo containing 41kg (90lb) of gunpowder
COMPLEMENT:	8

The intensity of the struggle in the US Civil War forced submarine builders to work fast and take risks. The Confederate submarine *Hunley* underwent three sinkings, drowning its eponymous designer, before it became the first submarine to sink a surface craft. Although on a smaller scale, *Hunley*'s elongated hull form anticipated that of later submarines more closely than most of the early designs.

ARMAMENT
Torpedo spar, with spike and release cord.

SHROUDED PROPELLER
Hunley's propeller was shrouded to avoid entanglements with cables or marine growths, and perhaps also because the original intention was for the vessel to tow its explosive charge.

BALLAST TANKS
The vessel was equipped with two ballast tanks that could be filled with water to submerge the sub and pumped out to raise it again.

ASCENT/DESCENT CONTROL
Just behind the bows, a fin was fixed on each side to a transverse shaft, operated by a lever that changed their angle. Of 1.5m (5ft) length and 203mm (8in) width, they were an early kind of diving plane, enabling the vessel to rise or sink while submerged without changing the water level in the ballast tanks.

ATTACK ON HOUSATONIC

On 17 February 1864, the *Hunley* launched its one and only attack on the steam-powered blockade ship *Housatonic*, a sloop-of-war of 1260 tonnes (1240 tons). Now named in commemoration of *Horace Hunley* – although sometimes referred to as the CSS *Hunley*, it was never officially commissioned as such – the boat was submerged but near enough the surface to create a disturbance. It was spotted by a lookout, but taken to be a plank or a porpoise. Too late, this mistake was rectified. The anchor chain was slipped and the 'porpoise' came under musket fire, which had no effect. The torpedo was rammed against the ship, detached and fired. Traces of copper wire found with *Hunley*'s hull suggest that detonation may have been electrical rather than mechanical.

DETONATION
The effect of the *Hunley*'s torpedo on the *Housatonic* was immediate: five minutes after the explosion, *Housatonic* was sinking in flames. Although *Hunley* was reported to have sent a light signal confirming success, that was its last action – it sank close to its victim, drowning all of its crew.

Intelligent Whale (1866)

SPECIFICATIONS

DIMENSIONS:	Length: 8.75m (28ft 8in); Beam: 2.1m (7ft); Height: 2.7m (9ft)
DISPLACEMENT:	1800kg (4000lbs)
PROPULSION:	Hand-cranked screw
SPEED:	4 knots (7.4km/h; 4.6mph)
ENDURANCE:	10 hours
ARMAMENT:	Hatch for diver – 11.2kg (25lb) mine
COMPLEMENT:	6–13 officers and men

The only surviving US Civil War submersible built in the North, *Intelligent Whale* was intended as a business speculation, but was also an innovative craft using the most advanced technology of its time. The vessel could be submerged by filling compartments with water, and then expelling the water by pumps and compressed air. Litigation and difficulty in finding crews delayed progress and prevented the *Intelligent Whale* from being employed in the Civil War. She was tested in April 1866 by Brigadier General Thomas William Sweeny, who submerged the submarine, exited her in a diving suit, planted an explosive charge on a target and re-entered the submarine. In spite of this successful demonstration, the *Intelligent Whale* gained the reputation of being the 'Disastrous Jonah', sinking three times and drowning her crews. The US Navy ultimately abandoned the project.

BOW
The bow is formed from a hollow cast-iron cone, with a hole at the point to hold a shank with a 165mm (6.5in) diameter ring bolted to its outer end.

SHAPE
Her bulbous shape allowed her to accommodate a crew of 13, but only six were required to operate her. She contained enough air to stay submerged for up to 10 hours and could make a speed of about four knots.

PROPELLER
A three-bladed screw propeller was fitted.

AIR INTAKE AND EXHAUST
Flexible tubes could be attached. The intake system has sometimes been described as a 'snorkel' but information on how it worked (e.g. kept water out) is lacking.

ANCHORAGE
To anchor the craft when submerged, the crew made use of two pieces of 381mm (15in) shot, each weighing 157.5kg (350lb) attached to wire cables wound on windlasses in two watertight boxes.

FLAT-BOTTOMED CRAFT
A photograph taken at the Brooklyn Navy Yard in the 1930s. The towing or mooring ring can be seen, as can the craft's relatively flat bottom.

Gustave Zédé (1893)

SPECIFICATIONS

DIMENSIONS:	Length: 48.5m (159ft); Beam: 3.2m (10ft 6in); Draught: 3.2m (10ft 6in)
DISPLACEMENT:	Surfaced – 264 tonnes (260 tons); Submerged – 274 tonnes (270 tons)
PROPULSION:	2 Sautter-Harlé 268kW (360hp) electric motors, battery powered; single screw
SPEED:	Surfaced – 12 knots (22km/h; 14mph); Submerged – 6.5 knots (12km/h; 7mph)
RANGE:	Surfaced – 220nm (407km; 253 miles) at 5.5 knots (10km/h; 6 mph); Submerged – 105nm (194km; 121 miles) at 4.5 knots (8km/h; 5mph)
ARMAMENT:	1 450mm (17.7in) torpedo tube, 4 Whitehead torpedoes
COMPLEMENT:	19

The French were the most innovative submarine designers of the later nineteenth century; the marine engineer Gustave Zédé (1825–91) was a leading figure. His electrically propelled *Gymnote* was the French Navy's first submarine in 1888, making more than 2000 dives. The larger *Gustave Zédé* was named after him; Zédé had died in 1891.

Above: *Gustave Zédé* skims the surface of the water, some time after reconstruction in the late 1890s.

POWER SUPPLY
The submarine had electric drive only, taking its power from batteries.

ARMAMENT
A 450mm (17.7in) Whitehead torpedo in external cradle. There was a single bow-mounted torpedo tube.

HULL
Gustave Zédé's hull barely showed above the water when surfaced, with only the walk-platform visible. For 10 years after launching, it was the largest submarine in the world. To contemporaries, it was 'a giant'.

COMBAT TRIALS

In the early hours of 3 July 1901, *Gustave Zédé* entered Ajaccio harbour in Corsica undetected, on a combat trial against 'friendly' shipping. The submarine fired an unarmed torpedo at the battleship *Charles Martel*, flagship of the Second Division, striking the hull. An observer wrote: 'The presence of the submarine was not suspected until a curious shock was sustained and a white furrow was perceived on the surface of the sea....'

CELEBRATED ARRIVAL

The submarine's arrival in Marseille in 1898 drew a large crowd, eager to see this new form of maritime combat vessel. One of the ship's first major journeys, under her own power, was from Toulon to Marseille – a distance of 66km (41 miles).

USS *Holland* (1897)

SPECIFICATIONS

DIMENSIONS:	Length: 16.4m (53ft 10in); Beam: 2.6m (8ft 6in); Draught: 2.6m (8ft 6in)
DISPLACEMENT:	Surfaced – 65 tonnes (64 tons); Submerged – 75 tonnes (74 tons)
PROPULSION:	Otto engine developing 34kW (45hp) with 1 E.D. electric motor developing 56kW (75hp), single screw
SPEED:	Surfaced – 8 knots (14.8km/h; 9mph); Submerged – 5 knots (9.2km/h; 5.7mph)
RANGE:	1150nm (2129km; 1323 miles)
ARMAMENT:	1 457mm (18in) bow torpedo tube, 2 torpedoes; 2 Zalinski pneumatic cannon (one later removed)
COMPLEMENT:	6

Named for its Irish-American designer John P. Holland, this was the first submarine to be commissioned into the United States Navy. Among many other novel features, it was the first submarine to incorporate separate power sources for running on the surface and when submerged.

Above: The fifth *Holland* submarine for Britain's Royal Navy, commissioned in 1902 and designated Holland 5. A periscope and torpedo tube were incorporated.

POWER SUPPLY
As in subsequent submarines, the batteries in *Holland* were placed centrally close to the keel, their weight helping to maintain the boat's trim.

CLINOMETER
Among the numerous aids pioneered on the *Holland* was the clinometer, devised by Frank T. Cable. This enabled the vessel's pilot to check the submarine's angle from the horizontal.

PROPELLER
One of J.P. Holland's original ideas was that the propeller of the submarine should be placed beyond the steering gear. It was only with difficulty, after early testing of the *Holland*, that he was persuaded to have the large three-bladed screw moved inboard of the rudder.

'AERIAL TORPEDO'
The Zalinski cannon, or 'dynamite gun', fired a level shot just above the surface. It was known as the 'aerial torpedo'. On 27 March 1898, in Staten Island Sound, the *Holland* tested its forward gun for the Navy. The gun was aimed at Tottenville on Staten Island and was charged with only 270kg (600lb) of compressed air instead of the 450kg (1000lb) Holland had wanted. When fired, the 1m-long (3ft 3in), 22.5kg (50lb) wooden dummy projectile ran forward just under 300m (980ft).

NAVAL TRIALS
The first *Holland* design for Britain's Royal Navy, and the Royal Navy's first submarine, on trials in 1900. It is preserved at the Royal Navy Submarine Museum, Gosport, Hampshire.

B-Class (1904)

SPECIFICATIONS

DIMENSIONS:	Length: 41m (135ft); Beam: 4m (13ft 5in); Draught: 3.15m (10ft 4in)
DISPLACEMENT:	Surfaced – 292 tonnes (287 tons); Submerged – 321 tonnes (316 tons)
PROPULSION:	16-cylinder gasoline engine, 450kW (600hp); electric motor, 130kW (180hp), single screw
SPEED:	Surfaced – 12 knots (22km/h; 14mph); Submerged – 6.5 knots (12km/h; 7.4mph)
RANGE:	1110nm (2055km; 1277 miles) at 12 knots (22.2km/h; 14mph), surfaced
ARMAMENT:	2 457mm (18in) torpedo tubes, 2 reload torpedoes
COMPLEMENT:	15

By 1901, the British Admiralty had dropped its complacent attitude to submarines and begun to take them seriously, both as a threat and as a potential new weapon. The B-class marked a real step forward.

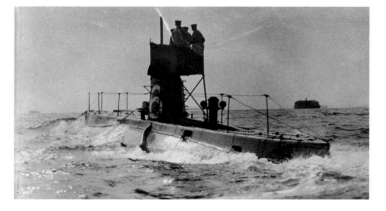

Right: HMS *B-6* off Portsmouth Harbour. A compass binnacle is mounted on the quarter deck aft of the tower.

NAMING CONVENTIONS
British submarines were assigned identification letters and numbers only until 1914, when names began to be used on new vessels.

SHROUDING
Canvas shrouding could be lashed around the railings to protect the minimal accommodation for Watch Officer and lookout when running on the surface.

COMBAT SUCCESS
During World War I, in the ill-fated Dardanelles campaign, the exploits of the submarines were among the few successful aspects. The B-class, by 1915 provided with a Maxim gun for surface defence, had several encounters with Austrian seaplanes in the course of 81 Adriatic patrols; *B-11* captured a seaplane's crew on 17 January 1916. *B-10* was the first submarine to be sunk by air attack, during a bombing raid on Venice on 9 August 1916. Although refloated, it was further damaged by a fire and scrapped.

POWER SUPPLY
Gasoline was a dangerous fuel because of the fumes it gave off and its high flammability. From around 1904, the French Navy began experimenting with diesel engines, but the Royal Navy did not use diesel until the advent of its D-class submarines, after the Electric Boat contract ended in 1910.

RADIO COMMUNICATIONS
Unsuccessful attempts were made to use wireless transmission from the B-class in 1903. After more experiments in 1910 with B-3 and B-4, most of the class had short-range radio from 1914, effective up to about 48km (30 miles).

ARMAMENT
By the start of World War I, the boats could carry the 457mm (18in) Mark VIII torpedo. This had a warhead of 150kg (330lb) of TNT and two settings for range and speed: 2300m (2515yd) at 35 knots (64.8km/h; 40.2mph); or 3700m (4046yd) at 29 knots (53.7km/h; 33.3mph).

OBSERVATION PLATFORM
In HMS *B-5*, the observation platform was extended aft on some members of the class, supported on metal struts, hidden here by canvas shrouding.

U-9 (1910)

SPECIFICATIONS

DIMENSIONS:	Length: 57.3m (188ft); Beam: 6m (19ft 7in); Draught: 3.5m (11ft 6in)
DISPLACEMENT:	Surfaced – 431.8 tonnes (425 tons); Submerged – 610 tonnes (601 tons)
PROPULSION:	4 Körting kerosene engines; electric motors; single screw
SPEED:	Surfaced – 14.2 knots (26.2km/h; 16.3mph); Submerged – 8 knots (14.8km/h; 9.2mph)
RANGE:	3356nm (6215km; 3862 miles) at 8.6 knots (15.9km/h; 9.8mph)
ARMAMENT:	4 450mm (17.7in) torpedo tubes, 2 reloads; 1 37mm (1.5in) deck gun
COMPLEMENT:	29

Although already an obsolescent design by the outbreak of war in 1914, *U-9* caused a sensation in the early weeks of World War I by sinking three British cruisers in the North Sea in the course of a single hour.

Right: A cross-section through *U-9*, which had a beam of 6m (19ft 7in). Operational spaces were extremely cramped for the crew of 29 men.

BATTLE BRIDGE
The top of the conning tower was the 'battle bridge', occupied by a watch crew of officer, petty officer and seaman lookout. They had to be secured by safety lines in rough weather.

ARMAMENT
From 1915, *U-9* would be fitted with a 37mm (1.46in) SK L/40 deck gun.

ATTACK SUB
In August 1914, *U-9* was commanded by an exceptionally able officer, Kapitänleutnant Otto Weddigen, the first submarine commander to reload his torpedo tubes while submerged. Early on 22 September 1914, *U-9* sighted the British cruisers *Cressy*, *Aboukir* and *Hogue* in the North Sea, steaming NNE without zigzagging. Patrols were supposed to maintain 12–13 knots (22.2–24km/h; 13.8–14.9mph) and zigzag, but the old cruisers were unable to maintain that speed and the zigzagging order was widely ignored. *U-9* manoeuvred to attack; this began at 6.25am, the submarine reloading frequently. All three cruisers were sunk in less than an hour, with the loss of nearly 1500 British lives.

DESCENT SPEED
These early double-hulled U-boats had a very slow dive-time: *U-9* required seven minutes. This was not seen as a problem until wartime conditions prevailed, especially when facing the disguised merchantmen known as Q-ships, and later air attacks.

AIR INTAKE/RELEASE
The diving station consisted of 24 levers on each side of the submarine, allowing air to be released from or forced into the ballast tanks.

POWER SUPPLY
Batteries were placed below the living space and were constantly monitored for release of poisonous hydrogen. Ventilation tubing ran along both sides of the boat.

RETURN TO BASE
Crewmembers stand at the salute as *U-9* returns to its base, somewhere off the Baltic coast.

HMS *E-11* (1914)

The E-class submarines were the main element in the Royal Navy's attack submarine force during World War I, operating in the North and Baltic seas, the Mediterranean and the Dardanelles. In some respects inferior to U-boats, they still gave distinguished service.

SPECIFICATIONS

DIMENSIONS:	Length: 55.17m (181ft); Beam: 6.91m (22ft 8in); Draught: 3.81m (12ft 6in)
DISPLACEMENT:	Surfaced – 677 tonnes (667 tons); Submerged – 820 tonnes (807 tons)
PROPULSION:	2 Vickers diesel engines developing 1192kW (1600hp); 2 313kW (420hp) electric motors; 2 screws
SPEED:	Surfaced – 14 knots (25.9km/h; 16.1mph); Submerged – 9 knots (16.6km/h; 10.3mph)
RANGE:	3579nm (6628km; 4118 miles) at 10 knots (18.5km/h; 11.5 mph)
ARMAMENT:	5 457mm (18in) torpedo tubes; 1 6-pdr QF deck gun
COMPLEMENT:	30

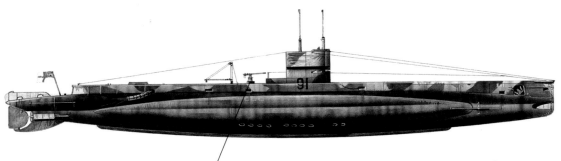

12-pounder QF guns were installed on the walking deck, either immediately aft of the tower or on the extreme end of the deck.

COMMUNICATIONS
A dismountable radio mast could be stowed immediately aft of the tower.

SURFACE CAMOUFLAGE
In the Dardanelles campaign, *E-11* was painted in camouflage colours rather than in standard Royal Navy grey.

EXHAUST VENT
Diesel engine exhaust, alongside walk-deck.

SUBMARINE CONSTRUCTION

A total of 56 E-class submarines were built in the UK between 1911 and 1917, although submarines of this class remained in service until 1922. Although the German U-boats have attracted much historical attention, the Royal Navy's Submarine Service operated the world's largest fleet of submarines at the beginning of the war.

BEAM TUBES
The beam tubes fired to port (forward tube) and starboard (after tube) respectively. They were opened laterally to load the torpedoes. Impracticable in action, they were hard to aim and required the boat to come to a stop for firing.

POWER SUPPLY
E-11 was fitted with two battery sets for the electric motors, each consisting of 112 cells, with a combined weight of around 230 tonnes (226 tons).

NAVAL KILLS

During a 20-day patrol in *E-11*, Lieutenant-Commander Martin Nasmith sank one gunboat, two ammunition ships, two transports and two further supply ships. Nasmith became the third submarine commander to be awarded a VC in the Dardanelles campaign. On 8 August 1915, *E-11* sank the Turkish pre-dreadnought *Barbaros Hayreddin* with torpedoes.

Deutschland (1916)

SPECIFICATIONS

DIMENSIONS:	Length: 65m (213ft 3in); Beam: 8.8m (28ft 10in); Draught: 5.3m (17ft 5in)
DISPLACEMENT:	Surfaced – 1536 tonnes (1512 tons); Submerged – 1905 tonnes (1875 tons)
PROPULSION:	2 6-cylinder Viertakt diesel engines 588kW (800hp); electric motors; twin screws
SPEED:	Surfaced – 12.4 knots (22.9km/h; 14.2 mph); Submerged – 5.2 knots (9.6km/h; 6mph)
RANGE:	13,130nm (24,316km; 15,109 miles) at 9 knots (16.6km/h; 10.3mph)
ARMAMENT:	6 500mm (20in) torpedo tubes, 18 torpedoes; 2 150mm (5.9in) deck guns
COMPLEMENT:	29 (merchant); 56 (military)

First as a cargo-carrier that made two voyages across the Atlantic, then as armed submarine cruiser *U-155*, *Deutschland* demonstrated the rapid development of German U-boat design and technology during World War I.

Right: The engine-room passageway in *U-155*. Note the massive spanners stowed at the side.

EXHAUST VENT
Diesel engine exhaust pipe.

ATTACK PERISCOPE
As *U-155*, an attack periscope tube was stepped in the deck forward of the tower.

MERCANTILE FORM
The profile shows the boat in its original unarmed mercantile form. Three were built like this and four were converted to combat boats while under construction. The addition of two 150mm (5.9in) deck guns radically changed the appearance.

PROPELLERS
New larger propellers were fitted as part of the U-boat conversion in the hope of improving speed. The diesel and electric motors could drive the shaft simultaneously, although only for limited periods, to obtain maximum speed.

DERRICKS
The derricks over the cargo hatches were dismountable.

U-155 ARMAMENT

Six torpedo tubes were fitted beneath the deck and outside the pressure hull. Although two internal bow tubes were later installed, little use was made of them. *U-155*'s guns were large enough to tackle an armed merchant vessel or an anti-submarine Q-ship, although their recoil put heavy stress on the mountings made in a deck not intended for such a purpose.

DEUTSCHLAND IN THE UNITED STATES

Deutschland enters the port of Baltimore, July 1916, with a raw materials cargo for trade. The US flag is at the foremast, the Imperial German flag at the aftermast, with the German Merchant Navy ensign at the stern.

UC-25 (1916)

SPECIFICATIONS

DIMENSIONS:	Length: 49.45m (162ft 3in); Beam: 5.28m (17ft 4in); Draught: 4m (13ft 1in)
Displacement:	Surfaced – 400 tonnes (390 tons); Submerged – 480 tonnes (470 tons)
Propulsion:	2 6-cylinder diesel engines, 370kW (500hp); 2 Siemens-Schukert motors, 340kW (460hp); twin screws
Speed:	Surfaced – 11.5 knots (21.2km/h; 13.2 mph); Submerged – 7.2 knots (13.3km/h; 8.2mph)
Range:	9260nm (17,149km; 10,656 miles) at 7 knots (12.9km/h; 8mph)
Armament:	3 500mm (20in) torpedo tubes, 7 torpedoes; 18 UC200 mines; 1 88mm (3.5in) deck gun
Complement:	26

The Imperial German Navy's Type UC-II class consisted of 64 small but powerfully armed submarines; these turned out to be perhaps the most versatile and effective U-boats of World War I.

Below: UC-II class *UC-74*, commissioned on 26 November 1916, was at sea when Germany surrendered in November 1918. It made for Kiel, but ran out of fuel and was interned at Barcelona on 21 November 1918. Later handed over to France, it was broken up in 1921.

FOREDECK
The front portion of the foredeck is raised above the level of the gun platform as a fairing over the mine tubes. These discharged through the boat's bottom.

TORPEDO TUBES
The bulges on the forward part of the hull hold the forward torpedo tubes.

REAR TORPEDO
A single stern torpedo tube was fitted.

ARMAMENT
The 88mm (3.5in) KL/30 deck gun was a standard fitting on the UC-II boats.

ANCHOR
The bow compartment holds the anchor and cable, lowered through the bottom.

FIRST COMMAND

In March–August 1918, Karl Dönitz, future supreme commander of the U-boat fleet, became captain of *UC-25*, his first command. On a mission between 17 July and 7 August 1917, *UC-25* slipped through the Otranto Barrage, narrowly avoiding air attacks with depth charges south of Corfu. Entering the Sicilian harbour of Augusta, it sank a ship that Dönitz possibly believed to be the British depot ship HMS *Cyclops*, but that was later identified as an Italian cargo vessel.

NAVAL BASE
A Type UC-II boat at an unidentified base, probably Pola, Croatia, as the submarine is rigged for breaching defence netting. Pola was the chief naval base of the Austro-Hungarian Navy.

Surcouf (1929)

SPECIFICATIONS

DIMENSIONS:	Length: 110m (360ft 10in); Beam: 9.1m (29ft 9in); Draught: 9.07m (29ft 8in)
DISPLACEMENT:	Surfaced – 3302 tonnes (3250 tons); Submerged – 4373 tonnes (4304 tons)
PROPULSION:	2 diesel motors 5667kW (7600hp); 2 electric motors 2535kW (3400hp)
SPEED:	Surfaced – 18.5 knots (34.2km/h; 21.2mph); submerged – 8.5 knots (15.7km/h; 9.7mph)
RANGE:	10,000nm (18,520km; 11,507 miles) at 10 knots (18.5km/h; 11.5mph)
ARMAMENT:	8 551mm (21.7in) and 4 400mm (15.75in) torpedo tubes; 2 203mm (8in) guns, 2 37mm (1.5in) guns, 4 8mm (0.3in) Hotchkiss machine guns
COMPLEMENT:	118

Intended as an oceanic commerce raider and built to beat international restrictions, this huge French submarine even carried a floatplane and was the largest in the world from 1929 until 1943. The cause of its loss, with no signal or message, remains unclear.

FLOATPLANE
A Besson MB-41-0 floatplane with a 400-km (248-mile) range was originally carried in a hangar behind the tower. After a crash landing in July 1933, it was replaced by an MB-41-1 model. Both were wood-framed. In 1938, a Breguet gyroplane was tested as a possible replacement.

ARMAMENT
The 203mm (8in) guns and gun-laying equipment were not new, as many guns in good condition were available from decommissioned surface ships. The twin turret weighed 185 tonnes (182 tons) and could be ready to fire within three minutes of surfacing, sending a 120kg (264lb) shell a distance of 27,500m (90,223ft).

COLOUR SCHEME
Originally painted in French naval grey, *Surcouf* was repainted in 'dark Prussian blue' from 1934 until 1940. From then on, it was painted in two-tone grey.

HOLDING CELL
Although the design provided for a 5m (16ft) motorboat, it was unusable and *Surcouf* never carried one on active service. The submarine was also said to have prison space for 40 men, but this was also usable as a cargo space.

SECRET LAUNCH
Laid down at Cherbourg naval dockyard on 3 October 1927, *Surcouf* was launched in secret on 18 October 1929. As usual with French submarines, it had a double hull. The superstructure had a massive appearance, with the conning tower located behind a double gun turret and forward of the aircraft hangar. On the surface it was powered by two Sulzer diesel engines of 5667kW (7600hp). The electric motors, delivering 2535kW (3400hp), were supplied by the Compagnie Générale.

IN BRITISH WATERS
Surcouf, carrying the designation number 17P, close to the Royal Navy's submarine base at Faslane, on the Firth of Clyde, in 1940.

USS *Nautilus* (V-6) (1930)

SPECIFICATIONS

DIMENSIONS:	Length: 113m (370ft 9in); Beam: 10m (32ft 10in); Draught: 4.8m (15ft 9in)
DISPLACEMENT:	Surfaced – 2773 tonnes (2730 tons); Submerged – 3962 tonnes (3900 tons)
PROPULSION:	From 1942 – 4 GM 16-278A two-cycle diesels each of 1200kW (1600hp); 2 GM 8-2168A diesel generators of 300kW (400hp) each; 2 Westinghouse 950kW (1270hp) electric motors; twin screws
SPEED:	Surfaced – 18 knots (33.3km/h; 20.7mph); Submerged – 11 knots (20.3km/h; 12.6mph)
RANGE:	9380nm (17,371km; 10,794 miles) at 11 knots (20.3km/h; 12.6mph)
ARMAMENT:	6 533mm (21in) torpedo tubes; 2 152mm (6in) guns
COMPLEMENT:	88

To some experts, *Nautilus* (originally named and designated *V-6*) was the first true submarine: not a surface ship that could submerge for limited periods, but a vessel capable of staying underwater for lengthy periods without needing to draw any sustenance from the surface.

Right: The relative size of *V-6* is clear as it rests alongside an S-class boat in a fitting-out basin, probably Mare Island.

ARMAMENT
The deck guns were designed for the secondary battery of Lexington-class battlecruisers and South Dakota-class battleships, but were only installed in Omaha-class cruisers. They fired a 47kg (105lb) shell to a range of 21,310m (69,914ft) at their maximum elevation of 25°.

FREEBOARD
Nautilus had a high freeboard, with the gun deck raised above the outer hull, giving the guns a wider bearing and greater range.

HEAVY GUNS
Nautilus carried the heaviest artillery of any US submarine. Two 152mm (6in) deck guns were carried, forward and aft of the tower, requiring built-out Mark 17 wet mountings, and capable of firing a 47kg (105lb) shell to a maximum range of 21,310m (23,305yd) at the maximum elevation of 25°. To its original six 533mm (21in) torpedo tubes, four externally mounted tubes were added in a 1941–42 refit. It could carry up to 38 torpedoes, with 12 mounted externally.

FUEL RESERVES
With extra fuel in some ballast tanks, *Nautilus* had an extended operating range of 25,000nm (46,300km; 28,769 miles) at 5.7 knots (10.5km/h; 6.5mph).

EMBRASURES
Modification of *Nautilus* was complete by 31 March 1942. It included the addition of four external torpedo tubes, two facing aft, two forward. Embrasures were made in the upper side of the outer hull, just in front of the forward gun, for the new forward tubes.

CONSTRUCTION
A view of the early stage of *Nautilus*'s construction at Mare Island, California, in 1929, with the scaffolding uprights in place for the hull fabrication.

U-47 (Type VIIB) (1938)

SPECIFICATIONS

DIMENSIONS: Length: 66.5m (218ft); Beam: 6.2m (20ft 3in); Draught: 4.7m (15ft 6in)

DISPLACEMENT: Surfaced – 765 tonnes (753 tons); Submerged – 871 tonnes (857 tons)

PROPULSION: 2 GW diesel engines, 2088kW (2800hp); 2 AEG GU 460/8-276 double-acting electric motors, 552kW (740hp); twin screws

SPEED: Surfaced – 17.2 knots (31.8km/h; 19.7mph); Submerged – 8 knots (14.8km/h; 9mph)

RANGE: Surfaced – 8700nm (16,112km; 10,011 miles) at 10 knots (18.5km/h; 11.5mph)

ARMAMENT: 5 533mm (21in) torpedo tubes, 14 torpedoes; 1 88mm (3.5in) gun, 1 20mm (0.79in) flak gun

COMPLEMENT: 44

U-47 made world headlines and won glory in Germany by its daring entry into the British Scapa Flow naval anchorage in the Orkney Islands on 14 October 1939, when it sank the battleship HMS *Royal Oak* before making a successful getaway.

ARMAMENT
The early VIIBs had their 20mm (0.79in) flak gun mounted on the aft deck. This was not ideal, as the tower created a dead firing zone, and it took time to get the gun into action and for the crew to return inside the U-boat in an emergency. For these reasons, it was decided to move the gun to the aft end of the conning tower. Re-siting took place over the winter of 1939–40. To accommodate the gun, the rear of the platforms had to be completely rebuilt.

SURFACE CAMOUFLAGE
Colours of wartime U-boats varied at different times, but were almost always in shades of grey, usually in two tones; Dunkelgrau 51 ('dark grey', although actually more like medium grey) above the surfaced waterline, and Schiffsbodenfarbe III Grau ('hull colour grey') below.

Below: This frontal view shows the bulges of the Type VIIB's increased fuel capacity.

PROPAGANDA VICTORY
For the attack at Scapa Flow, new G7e electric wakeless torpedoes were deployed. The battleship *Royal Oak* was hit by four torpedoes and sank with the loss of more than 800 crew. Although by chance most of the British fleet had left Scapa Flow two days previously, and *Royal Oak* was an elderly battleship, the venture was one of the most daring, skilful and hazardous ever carried out by a submarine: it was a tremendous propaganda victory for the Nazi regime.

POWER SUPPLY
Diesel engines in Type VIIB submarines were normally either MAN Type M6 V40/46 with forced induction by Buchi supercharger, developing 1043kW (1400hp) and weighing 39.1 tonnes (38.5 tons), or the slightly heavier Germania Werft GW Model e.v. 40/46, also with forced induction, with the same power rating and weighing 44 tonnes (43.4 tons).

PROTECTION
Protectors were fitted to forward and aft diving planes.

TWIN RUDDERS
Type VIIB had twin rudders rather than the single rudder of the VIIA boats; its stern tube was brought inside the pressure hull.

POST-ATTACK CELEBRATIONS
Following the attack at Scapa Flow in October 1939, the crew of U-47 celebrate for photographers, complete with a visiting band.

U-459 (Type XIV) (1941)

SPECIFICATIONS

DIMENSIONS:	Length: 67.1m (220ft); Beam: 9.4m (30ft 10in); Draught: 6.5m (21ft 4in)
DISPLACEMENT:	Surfaced – 1688 tonnes (1661 tons); Submerged – 1932 tonnes (1901 tons)
PROPULSION:	2 GW supercharged 4-stroke, 6-cylinder diesel engines developing 2350kW (3160hp); 2 Siemens-Schukert 2GU 345/38-8 double-acting electric motors, 550kW (740hp), twin screws
SPEED:	Surfaced – 14.5 knots (26.8km/h; 16.6mph); Submerged – 6.3 knots (11.6km/h; 7.2mph)
RANGE:	12,350nm (22,872km; 14,212 miles)
ARMAMENT:	2 37mm (1.5in) guns, 1 20mm (0.79in) gun
COMPLEMENT:	53

U-459, first of the 10 boats of Type XIV, was the Kriegsmarine's first purpose-built refuelling and supply submarine, a large boat intended to intensify the Atlantic war by enabling attack vessels to spend longer periods at sea.

Right: A transfer operation, in anything other than a flat calm, was a tricky business. A Type VIIB is being refuelled while another waits.

INTERNAL LAYOUT
Compartments from stern to stem were: workshop; motor rooms; engine room; galley; control room with pumps, magazine and provisions below; captain's and officers' cabins (port side) – W/T and hydrophone room (starboard side); wardroom (port side, with after battery room below) – petty officers' mess (starboard side); chief petty officers' mess (port side with forward battery below) – ratings' mess (starboard side); bow compartment. The main provisions store was situated below the mess room.

LOADING HATCH
Lightweight cranes could be rigged for high-line transfer of boxed goods and of replacement or injured crewmen, although a rubber dinghy was more often used.

AA ARMAMENT
The Type XIV's only armament was anti-aircraft weapons for self-defence. Two 37mm (1.5in) cannons were fitted, one forward and one aft of the bridge, and a single 20mm (0.79in) on a platform aft. These were upgraded in 1943 after the fifth patrol, with the gun platform behind the conning tower widened and armoured; a second platform was fitted just aft of the original. The original 20mm (0.79in) cannon on the old gun platform was replaced by a pair of twin 20mm cannon; the new aft gun platform mounted either a 37mm (1.5in) cannon or, more usually, a quadruple 20mm (0.79in) cannon known as a Vierling.

FUEL TANKS
The transfer hose was 152m (500ft) long, made up of sections connected by clasp joints, with an internal diameter of 89mm (3.5in). In *U-459* there was an additional 8m (26ft 3in) length of rubber-impregnated linen hose, to which an 8m (26ft 3in) length of armoured hose was connected to prevent chafing where the hose left the supply boat.

EMBLEM
To U-boat crews, *U-459* was also known as *das Elefant*, being large and grey.

SINKING
U-459 slowly sinks after a battle with two RAF Wellington aircraft on 24 July 1943. Nineteen of the crew were killed; 41 were taken prisoner.

Type XXI (1943)

SPECIFICATIONS

DIMENSIONS:	Length: 76.7m (251ft 7in); Beam: 6.6m (21ft 7in); Draught: 6.3m (20ft 8in)
DISPLACEMENT:	Surfaced – 1621 tonnes (1595 tons); Submerged – 1819 tonnes (1790 tons)
PROPULSION:	2 MAN M6V40/46KBB supercharged 6-cylinder diesel engines, 2908kW (3900hp); 2 SSW GU365/30 double-acting electric motors, 3654kW (4900hp); 2 SSW GV232/28 silent electric motors; twin screws
SPEED:	Surfaced – 15.7 knots (29km/h; 18mph); Submerged – 17.2 knots (31.8km/h; 19.7mph)
RANGE:	15,500nm (28,706km; 17,837 miles) at 10 knots (18.5km/h; 11.5mph)
ARMAMENT:	6 533mm (21in) torpedo tubes, 23 torpedoes, or 17 torpedoes plus 12 TMC mines; 4 20mm (0.79in) flak guns
COMPLEMENT:	57

Known as the *Elektroboot*, this was the submarine with which Grand Admiral Dönitz expected to reinvigorate Germany's war at sea and gain control of the Atlantic routes. It was a superb design, but came too late to influence events.

Below: A profile view of a Type XXI. In total, 118 submarines of this type were commissioned between 1943 and 1945.

AIR INTAKE
Despite its advantages, the snorkel needed to be used with care. The intake pipe drew in air for the crew as well as the engines, letting the entire hull volume act as an air buffer. If the valve was suddenly closed, the diesels could run on for a short time, but would use all internal air, with fatal consequences for the crew. Air supply had to be constantly monitored in order to stop the diesels whenever the valve closed. Eventually, this process was automated.

RADAR
Radar equipment was a FuMB Ant 3 Bali radar detector and antenna and a FuMO 65 Hohentwiel U1 radar with Type F432 D2 transmitter.

STREAMLINING
All external mountings were retractable when submerged. The 20mm (0.79in) flak guns were in streamlined housings on the tower (actually designed for 30mm/1.18in cannon).

ELECTRICAL POWER
Greater electrical power, with three times the battery capacity of the Type VIIC, gave the class a much wider underwater range, enabling it to traverse the Bay of Biscay at a depth that minimized the risk of detection. It took between three and five hours to recharge the batteries with the snorkel once every two or three days if travelling at a moderate 4–8 knots (7.4– 14.8km/h; 4.6–9.2mph); the Type XXI was thus much less in danger from the air attacks that were increasingly responsible for sinking U-boats.

PASSIVE/ACTIVE SONAR
In the Type XXI, an improved Gruppenhorchgerät (GHG) passive sonar system was fitted beneath the keel; a new active system, Unterwasser-Ortungsgerät Nibelung, enabled detection and attack of enemy shipping without optical contact – another revolutionary feature.

TORPEDO SALVO
Once a Type XXI had located a convoy, data collected by sonar was to be converted and automatically set in the new LUT (Lageunabhängiger Torpedo) torpedoes, which were then fired in spreads of six. This guided torpedo could be fired regardless of the target's bearing and steer an interception course programmed by the torpedo computer. The probability of hits on targets longer than 60m (200ft) was calculated at 95 per cent.

HOME PORT
Tugboats attend to a Type XXI as it comes into port. From the condition of the port installations, this looks like a late 1943 or early 1944 image.

I-400 (1943)

SPECIFICATIONS

DIMENSIONS:	Length: 122m (400ft); Beam: 12m (39ft 4in); Draught: 7m (23ft)
DISPLACEMENT:	Surfaced – 5306 tonnes (5223 tons); Submerged – 6670 tonnes (6560 tons)
PROPULSION:	4 diesel engines developing 6720kW (7700hp); 2 electric motors, 3360kW (4200hp); twin screws
SPEED:	Surfaced – 18.7 knots (34.6km/h; 21.5mph); Submerged – 12 knots (22.2km/h; 14mph)
RANGE:	37,500nm (69,450km; 43,154 miles) at 14 knots (25.9km/h; 16.1mph)
ARMAMENT:	8 533mm (21in) torpedo tubes, 20 Type 95 torpedoes; 1 140mm (5.4in) gun; 4 25mm (1in) AA cannon
COMPLEMENT:	144 (157 including aircraft crews)

The multi-hulled Japanese Sen-Toku I-400 class were the largest submarines built by any country before the appearance of nuclear-powered SSBNs, with by far the greatest power and longest range. Envisaged for strategic roles, they were never actually deployed on an operational mission.

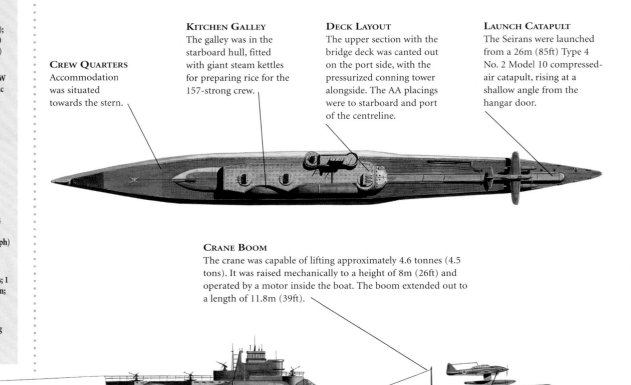

KITCHEN GALLEY
The galley was in the starboard hull, fitted with giant steam kettles for preparing rice for the 157-strong crew.

DECK LAYOUT
The upper section with the bridge deck was canted out on the port side, with the pressurized conning tower alongside. The AA placings were to starboard and port of the centreline.

LAUNCH CATAPULT
The Seirans were launched from a 26m (85ft) Type 4 No. 2 Model 10 compressed-air catapult, rising at a shallow angle from the hangar door.

CREW QUARTERS
Accommodation was situated towards the stern.

CRANE BOOM
The crane was capable of lifting approximately 4.6 tonnes (4.5 tons). It was raised mechanically to a height of 8m (26ft) and operated by a motor inside the boat. The boom extended out to a length of 11.8m (39ft).

SUBMARINE-LAUNCHED ATTACK FLOATPLANE
The key assembly points of the aircraft were marked with fluorescent paint so that they could be assembled in darkness.

HARDER-HITTING MUNITIONS

The Japanese fleet had the most effective torpedoes available during World War II. The Type 95 (smaller submarine version of the Type 93), developed from 1928, used pure oxygen to burn kerosene instead of the compressed air and alcohol used in other nation's torpedoes. This gave them a range of up to 12km (7.5 miles), roughly double that of their Allied counterparts, and also reduced their wake, making them harder to notice and avoid. The Type 95 also had by far the largest warhead of any submarine torpedo – initially 405kg (893lb), and increased to 550kg (1210lb) late in the war.

SURRENDER
Following the Japanese surrender on 15 August 1945, *I-400* and *I-401* sit alongside the submarine tender USS *Proteus*.

USS *Tench* (1944)

SPECIFICATIONS

DIMENSIONS:	Length: 95m (311ft 8in); Beam: 8m (27ft 4in); Draught: 5.18m (17ft)
DISPLACEMENT:	Surfaced – 1600 tonnes (1570 tons); Submerged – 2455 tonnes (2416 tons)
PROPULSION:	Diesel-electric, 4 Fairbanks-Morse 38D8-1/8 10-cylinder opposed piston engines, 4023kW (5400hp); 2 low-speed direct-drive GE motors, 2041kW () 2740hp; twin screws
SPEED:	Surfaced – 20.25 knots (37.5km/h; 23.3mph); Submerged – 8.75 knots (16.2km/h; 10mph)
RANGE:	11,000nm (20,372km; 12,658 miles) at 10 knots (18.5km/h; 11.5mph)
ARMAMENT:	10 530mm (21in) torpedo tubes, 28 torpedoes; 1 127mm (5in) deck gun
COMPLEMENT:	81

The submarines of the Tench class were developed versions of the previous Gato and Balao classes, fitted with improved interior machinery and ballast tank arrangements. A total of 29 were completed for the United States during or immediately following World War II, but most never made a war patrol.

GUPPY 1A REFIT PROGRAMME (1951)
The profile shows *Tench* in wartime form. Under Guppy IA, the pointed fleet bow was retained and the motors, already slow-speed type, were not modernized, although the auxiliary diesel generator was replaced by air-conditioning equipment. With the Guppy project, the tower ceased to hold a control station and came to be known as the sail (US) or fin (Britain).

HULL
Below the waterline, the hull of the *Tench* was almost spherical in shape.

LF LOOP ANTENNA
This was mounted between the periscopes, although later Tench-class boats had it mounted on a bracket aft of the SJ mast.

DIVE PLANES
Forward diving planes were stowed ready tilted in dive position so that when extended they would immediately force the bow down. Diving to periscope depth could be achieved in 30–40 seconds.

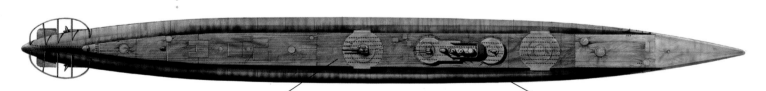

WARTIME SERVICE
Deployed to Pearl Harbor, *Tench* made three wartime patrols, sinking four Japanese ships and several small craft. Its first patrol was as a member of a 'co-ordinated attack group', modelled on the German wolfpack, with USS *Sea Devil*, *Balao* and *Grouper*. The four submarines rotated patrol/attack, weather-reporting, photographic-reconnaissance and lifeguard duties.

FAIRWATER
The fairwater has been minimized: the extent of the lip on the after gun platform is so great as to require a support stanchion.

BALLAST TANKS
Re-planning of the ballast tanks allowed space for an additional four torpedoes compared with the Balao and Gato boats.

CONVERSION
The *Tench* after undergoing Guppy 1A conversion. 'Guppy' stood for Greater Underwater Propulsion Power Program.

USS *Nautilus* (1954)

SPECIFICATIONS

DIMENSIONS:	Length: 97m (323ft 6in); Beam: 8.4m (27ft 6in); Draught: 6.6m (21ft 9in)
DISPLACEMENT:	Surfaced – 3589 tonnes (3533 tons); Submerged – 4168 tonnes (4102 tons)
PROPULSION:	1 S2W pressurized water-cooled reactor, geared steam turbines; 10MW (13,400hp), 2 screws
SPEED:	Surfaced – 22 knots (40.7km/h; 25.3mph); Submerged – 25 knots (46.2km/h; 28.7mph)
RANGE:	Unlimited
ARMAMENT:	6 533mm (21in) torpedo tubes
COMPLEMENT:	105

Breaking new ground as history's first nuclear-powered submarine, USS *Nautilus* (SSN 571) was actually the sixth ship in US Navy history to take that name. The new powerplant offered a genuine revolution in submarine performance.

Right: The US Navy's eighth nuclear submarine, USS *Skate* (SSN-578), emulated the sub-Arctic transit made by *Nautilus*, but actually surfaced very close to the North Pole, on 11 August 1958.

STEEL PLATE
The hull is formed of HY-42 steel plate, of 290 MPa (2704 ton/sq ft) yield strength. The improved HY-75 steel used on later boats was not available until the mid-1950s.

CREW QUARTERS
Although the power and propulsion units took up almost half the boat, *Nautilus* still provided more crew facilities and comfort than any previous submarine, with accommodation on two decks.

NUCLEAR REACTOR
The reactor compartment, with the reactor, primary coolant circuit and steam generators, was not accessible when the reactor was operating.

CONTROL ROOM
This includes navigation equipment, steering, diving valve controls and operators of the diving planes.

TORPEDO LAUNCH TECHNOLOGY
The six forward tubes used air-powered piston ejection pumps, which forced a slug of water through a slide valve behind the torpedo to push it out, rather than the pulse of air used in previous designs.

BREAKING RECORDS
On 17 January 1955, *Nautilus* went to sea for the first time. In the next two years, it covered distances unthinkable for a conventional submarine, breaking all previous records for underwater speed and distance. After more than two years of operation and evaluation, *Nautilus* was refuelled in April 1957. On the first core, it had steamed a total of 62,562 nautical miles (115,864km; 71,995 miles), more than half of which was submerged.

NORTH POLE
At 11.15pm on 3 August 1958, *Nautilus* reached the geographic North Pole, the first vessel in history to do so. Here we see *Nautilus* at New York City, 25 August 1958, on its return from under the Arctic icecap.

Sturgeon Class (1966)

SPECIFICATIONS

DIMENSIONS:	Length: 89m (292ft 3in); Beam: 9.7m (31ft 8in); Draught: 8.8m (28ft 10in)
DISPLACEMENT:	Surfaced – 3698 tonnes (3640 tons); Submerged – 4714 tonnes (4640 tons)
PROPULSION:	1 S5W pressurized water reactor, 2 S5W steam turbines; single screw
SPEED:	Surfaced – 15 knots (27.7km/h; 17.2mph); Submerged – 25 knots (46.2km/h; 28.7mph)
RANGE:	Unlimited
ARMAMENT:	4 533mm (21in) torpedo tubes; Harpoon and Tomahawk missiles, torpedoes or mines
COMPLEMENT:	109

This class of nuclear-powered SSNs formed the core of the US Navy's attack and espionage submarine fleet in the later stages of the Cold War, carrying a range of tactical missiles, special mission gear and detection equipment.

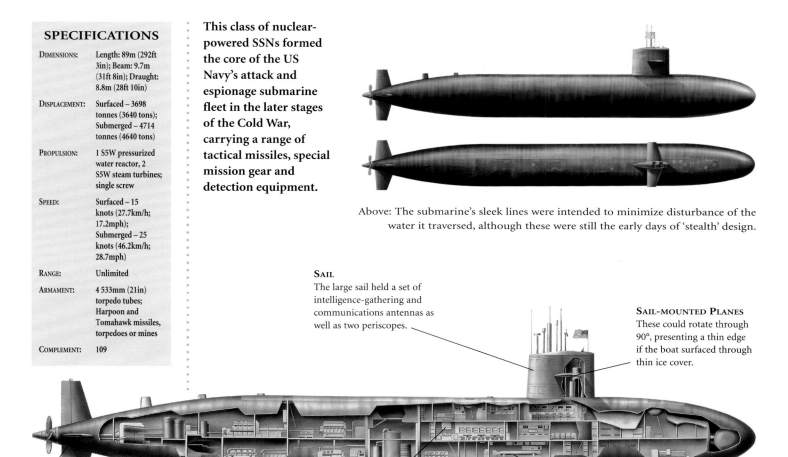

Above: The submarine's sleek lines were intended to minimize disturbance of the water it traversed, although these were still the early days of 'stealth' design.

SAIL
The large sail held a set of intelligence-gathering and communications antennas as well as two periscopes.

SAIL-MOUNTED PLANES
These could rotate through 90°, presenting a thin edge if the boat surfaced through thin ice cover.

ARMAMENT
Outwards-canted torpedo tubes. Up to 21 reload weapons were carried, including both Mk 48 and Mk 48 ADCAP torpedoes, four sub-Harpoon missiles, up to eight Tomahawk missiles and a maximum of four SUBROC ASW missiles.

INTERNAL LAYOUT
The five-compartment arrangement of the Permit-class hull was retained in the design of Sturgeon: bow compartment with diesel generator; operations compartment with torpedo room beneath; reactor compartment; auxiliary machinery room no. 2 and engine room.

SONAR ARRAY
The Sturgeon class first towed the TB-16 Fat Line sonar array; this comprised a 630kg (1400lb) acoustic detector array, 8.6cm (3.5in) in diameter and 73m (240ft) long, attached to a 731m (2400ft) coaxial cable 9.4mm (0.37in) diameter and weighing 202.5kg (450lb). Later the TB-23 Thin Line array, with greater sensor capacity, was used.

ATTACK BOAT
The Sturgeon class was equipped to carry the Harpoon missile, the Tomahawk cruise missile and a mixed load of torpedoes, including Mk 14 Mod 6, Mk 37 and Mk 37TS, Mk 48 and Mk 48 ADCAP. Bow positioning of the BQQ-2 active and BQQ-7 passive sonar sphere required the Mk 63 torpedo tubes that were positioned immediately aft of the array to be canted some 15° outwards.

NORTH POLE
Sturgeon-class USS *Billfish* (SSN 676) surfaces at the North Pole, 30 March 1987. Note the vertically turned diving planes on the sail.

HMS *Resolution* (1966)

SPECIFICATIONS

DIMENSIONS:	Length: 129.5m (425ft); Beam: 10.1m (33ft); Draught: 9.1m (30ft)
DISPLACEMENT:	Surfaced – 7620 tonnes (7500 tons); Submerged – 8535 tonnes (8400 tons)
PROPULSION:	1 Vickers-RR PWR1 pressurized water reactor, steam turbines, 20,507kW (27,500hp)
SPEED:	Surfaced – 20 knots (37km/h; 23mph); Submerged – 25 knots (46.2km/h; 28.7mph)
RANGE:	Unlimited
ARMAMENT:	16 Polaris A3TK SBM; 6 533mm (21in) torpedo tubes
COMPLEMENT:	154

The Resolution class of four vessels were the Royal Navy's first ballistic missile submarines. HMS *Resolution* fired the RN's first nuclear-capable Polaris missile on 15 February 1968, taking over the nuclear deterrent role from the Royal Air Force.

Right: A Royal Air Force Sea King helicopter winches a crewmember up from the deck of HMS *Resolution*.

MAIN TURBINE
'Rafting' of the machinery to minimize contact with the hull was a British idea. The US Navy was sceptical for some years before being won over to what is now a standard practice.

SONAR TRANSDUCER
Situated in the nose of the submarine.

RUDDER
The two-level rudder gave a distinctive tail-end look when the boat was surfaced.

ACCOMMODATION
The crew quarters included the mess, bunk space and galley.

REACTOR COMPARTMENT
PWR1 was the first reactor plant designed and manufactured by Rolls-Royce for the British nuclear submarine programme. The first core, based on an American design, was fitted to the Valiant and Resolution classes.

ARMAMENT
Polaris was a US-developed two-stage solid-fuel rocket 9.4m (31ft) long, with a diameter of 1.4m (4ft 6in). Three versions were produced between 1960 and 1971, when phasing out began. Version A-1 carried a one-megaton nuclear warhead 2200km (1400 miles). A-2 had the same warhead, but a range of 2700km (1670 miles). A-3 could carry three 200-kiloton warheads a distance of 4500km (2800 miles); this was adapted by the UK for the A-3TK Chevaline system, fitted with decoy warheads and electronic jammers for penetrating ballistic missile defences.

MISSILE CONTROL
The missile control station on HMS *Resolution*. With its complement of Polaris nuclear missiles, *Resolution* was capable of the near-simultaneous destruction of multiple Soviet towns and cities.

USS *Los Angeles* (1974)

SPECIFICATIONS

DIMENSIONS:	Length: 110.3m (362ft); Beam: 10m (32ft 10in); Draught: 9.9m (32ft 6in)
DISPLACEMENT:	Surfaced – 6180 tonnes (6082 tons); Submerged – 7038 tonnes (6927 tons)
PROPULSION:	1 GE S6G pressurized water reactor, 2 turbines, 26MW (35,000hp) single shaft; auxiliary Magnetek motor
SPEED:	Surfaced – 20 knots (37km/h; 23mph); Submerged – 33 knots (61.1km/h; 37.9mph)
RANGE:	Unlimited
ARMAMENT:	4 533mm (21in) torpedo tubes; Tomahawk Land Attack missiles, Harpoon SSM
COMPLEMENT:	133

USS *Los Angeles* (SSN-688) was the lead ship of the Los Angeles class. Defined as fast attack submarines and escorts for carrier battle groups, they are in fact versatile craft that have undertaken a variety of combat, escort and intelligence-gathering missions over the years.

Below: In the 1990s, construction cost of a Los Angeles-class submarine was $900,000,000. Extension of its service life by 12 years is estimated to cost $200,000,000.

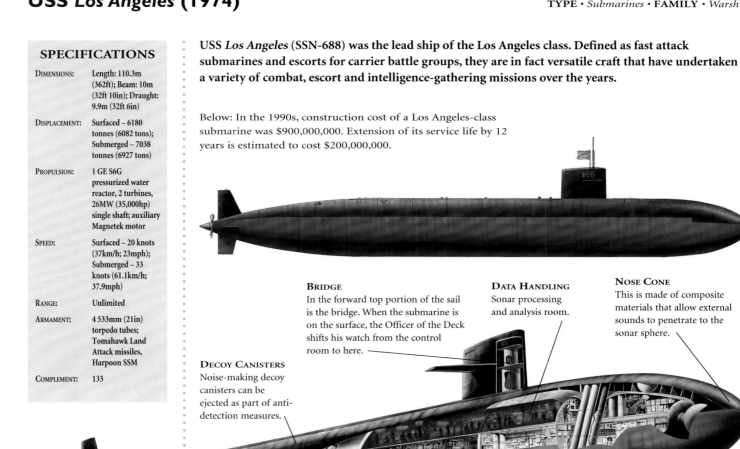

BRIDGE
In the forward top portion of the sail is the bridge. When the submarine is on the surface, the Officer of the Deck shifts his watch from the control room to here.

DATA HANDLING
Sonar processing and analysis room.

NOSE CONE
This is made of composite materials that allow external sounds to penetrate to the sonar sphere.

DECOY CANISTERS
Noise-making decoy canisters can be ejected as part of anti-detection measures.

HULL CONSTRUCTION
The hull is formed from HY-80 high-tensile steel 76mm (3in) thick, with a test depth of 290m (950ft).

ARMAMENT
Torpedo and missile storage room holding 24 weapons, also housing controls for the vertical cruise missile launch tubes.

MESS DECK
Mess and berthing deck, plus galley. Hot meals are prepared four times a day, in line with the six-hour watches.

TOMAHAWK MISSILES
The class is armed with both the land-attack and anti-ship version of the Tomahawk missile from Raytheon. The land-attack Tomahawk has a range of 2500km (1550 miles). A TAINS (Tercom Aided Inertial Navigation System) guides the missile towards the target, flying at subsonic speed at an altitude of 20m (65ft) to 100m (330ft). Block III improvements include an improved propulsion system and Navstar Global Positioning System (GPS) capability.

CONTROL CENTRE
Crewmembers of Los Angeles class USS *Oklahoma City* (SSN-723) at the control centre during the course of an exercise.

Project 705 Lira (Alfa Class) (1977)

SPECIFICATIONS

DIMENSIONS:	Length: 81m (265ft 9in); Beam: 9.5m (31ft); Draught: 8m (26ft 3in)
DISPLACEMENT:	Surfaced – 2845 tonnes (2800 tons); Submerged – 3739 tonnes (3680 tons)
PROPULSION:	BM-40A liquid-metal reactor, 2 steam turbines, single screw
SPEED:	Surfaced – 20 knots (37km/h; 23mph); Submerged – 42 knots+ (77.7km/h+; 48.3mph+)
RANGE:	Unlimited
ARMAMENT:	6 533mm (21in) torpedo tubes; 18 torpedoes or 21 RPK-2 Vyuga missiles or 36 mines
COMPLEMENT:	31

In 1971, the Soviet Union completed the world's first titanium-hulled submarine, which was also the fastest. A revolutionary design in almost every way, including a new kind of compact nuclear reactor, it was the precursor of a bold new class of attack submarines.

Above: Images of the *Liras* are quite rare. The fine streamlining of the sail is evident in this aerial view.

PROPELLER PODS
The single screw was adopted for Project 705 almost simultaneously with the Project 671 (Victor II) second-generation SSN design. To provide these submarines with emergency propulsion and, in suitable circumstances, low-speed and ultra-quiet manoeuvres, both classes were fitted with small two-blade propeller 'pods' on their horizontal stern surfaces.

ESCAPE CHAMBER
The sail contained an escape chamber above the control room that could hold the entire crew – another unique feature of the class.

CONTROL INTEGRATION
This was the first submarine to have integrated combat information and control systems, providing integration of navigation, tactical handling and weapons deployment.

CUTTING EDGE
By 1985, the Soviet Navy had at least six operational Lira-class boats. They were so different to any previous Russian (or other) submarine that it took almost 10 years for the US Navy to appreciate their remarkable and highly advanced qualities. As alert high-speed interceptors, they were not used on screening missions or patrol duties. Kept in port in a state of readiness, when a target was detected they would set out and move at speed to the target's last known location. The fastest submarines yet built, they could reach a top 'burst speed' of 45 knots (83km/h; 51.7mph). Pursuit and detection – and potential destruction – was their task, aided not only by speed but by the highest levels of automation yet seen in a submarine.

TITANIUM HULL
This material gave 30 per cent lower mass, 25 per cent lesser displacement and 10 per cent increase in speed compared to steel plate.

AUTOMATED PROCEDURES
Only two central compartments, for control and living space, were manned. In the other four compartments, procedures were automated. The original proposals envisaged a crew of only 18.

ARMAMENT
In addition to SET 65A and SAET 60 torpedoes, the submarine could carry the RPK-2 Vyuga (Blizzard) ASW missile, given the NATO designation SS-N-15 Starfish. This was a ballistic missile capable of carrying a 200-kiloton nuclear warhead.

SAIL SECTION
A section of the sail top could be opened to provide a cockpit with wind/water screen for surface observations.

USS Ohio (1979)

SPECIFICATIONS

DIMENSIONS:	Length: 170.7m (560ft); Beam: 12.8m (42ft); Draught: 11.1m (36ft 5in)
DISPLACEMENT:	Surfaced – 16,764 tonnes (16,499 tons); Submerged – 18,750 tonnes (18,450 tons)
PROPULSION:	1 S8G pressurized water reactor, 2 steam turbines developing 44,742kW (60,000hp), single screw
SPEED:	Surfaced – 24 knots (44.4km/h; 27.6mph); Submerged – 28 knots (52km/h; 32.2mph)
RANGE:	Unlimited
ARMAMENT:	4 533mm (21in) torpedo tubes. SSBN: 24 Trident C4 SLBMs; SSGN: 152 Tomahawk cruise missiles
COMPLEMENT:	155

The Ohio class remains the basis of America's strategic nuclear deterrent until the 2030s. The largest submarines built for the US Navy, all 18 have undergone substantial modification and updating programmes in the early twenty-first century.

Below: The paint scheme for the Ohio class has varied between a combination of red (below the surfaced waterline) and black (above the waterline) – see cutaway – and all-black, as above.

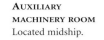

SONAR ROOM
Under A-RCI, the system can be upgraded by improving processing without changing the sensors. It integrates the boat's sonar arrays, running more advanced algorithms and providing more comprehensive data on the surrounding environment.

AUXILIARY MACHINERY ROOM
Located midship.

COMMUNICATIONS
The radio room.

STERN PLANES
These may be fitted with vertical stabilizing fins.

CREW QUARTERS
Includes accommodation for Special Forces.

CLASS LEADER
USS *Ohio*, the class leader, was laid down as SSBN-726 at the General Dynamics Electric Boat Yard, Groton, Connecticut, on 10 April 1976 and launched on 7 April 1979. The largest submarine yet built for the US Navy, it was commissioned on 11 November 1981 as SSBN-726 and equipped with 24 Trident C-4 ballistic missiles with multiple independently targeted warheads, set in parallel rows of 12. The class is powered by the S8G pressurized water reactor, providing steam to two geared turbines.

ARMAMENT
The Mk 48 ADCAP (Added Capability) torpedo has a 292kg (650lb) warhead, a range of 32km (20 miles) and a speed of 50 knots (92.5km/h; 57.5mph).

CONVERTED VESSEL
USS *Ohio* as converted to SSGN, carrying two Dry Deck Shelter (DDS) modules. 'SSGN' refers to the primary armament being cruise missiles: the 'G' in the abbreviation stands for 'Guided', the 'SS' standing for 'Submarine' and 'N' for 'Nuclear-powered'.

Le Triomphant (1994)

SPECIFICATIONS

DIMENSIONS:	Length: 138m (453ft); Beam: 17m (55ft 9in); Draught: 12.5m (41ft)
DISPLACEMENT:	Surfaced – 12,842 tonnes (12,640 tons); Submerged – 14,565 tonnes (14,335 tons)
PROPULSION:	1 Type K15 pressurized water reactor supplying 150MW (201,150hp), turbo electric drive; pump-jet propulsor; 2 SEMT-Pielstick 8 PA 4 v 200 SM diesel auxiliaries
SPEED:	Surfaced – 20 knots (37km/h; 23mph); Submerged – 25 knots (46.2km/h; 28.7mph)
RANGE:	Unlimited
ARMAMENT:	16 M45/TN75 SLBM; 4 533mm (21in) torpedo tubes
COMPLEMENT:	111

In 1997, *Le Triomphant* entered service as the first of the French Navy's latest class of SSBN. Three more were commissioned between 2000 and 2010. Since then, at least one has been permanently on patrol, armed with 16 M45 ballistic missiles.

Right: *Le Triomphant* entering the port of Cherbourg, the location of the Cherbourg Naval Base.

NOISE BAFFLE ZONE
Located between the sonar sphere in the nose and the torpedo room.

EMERGENCY EXIT
Hatch of aft exit/ escape tower.

POWER SUPPLY
Le Triomphant was the first submarine to be fitted with a ducted propulsor. The pump-jet system delivers 30,500kW (41,500hp).

FIXED VERTICAL FINS
As with some other submarines (e.g. USS *Ohio*), fixed vertical fins can be mounted at the ends of the stern diving planes. Their function may be as stabilizers, or they may be linked to the sonar system.

ARMAMENT
The F21 heavyweight torpedo from DCNS is a dual-purpose anti-ship and anti-submarine weapon. Weighing 1.3 tonnes (1.4 tons), it can be launched in swim-out or push-out modes. It incorporates a new-generation acoustic head from Thales Underwater Systems, in addition to an impact/ acoustic fuse warhead. Operational depth is from 10m (33ft) to 500m (1640ft). It has electric propulsion based on a silver oxide-aluminium (AgO-Al) primary battery, with a speed of up to 50 knots (92.5km/h; 57.5mph), a range of more than 50km (31 miles) and endurance of one hour.

COLLISION
Le Triomphant at sea, with crew on deck in survival suits. In a rather embarrassing incident for both the British and the French, on 3–4 February 2009, *Le Triomphant* and the British submarine HMS *Trident* collided with each other at low speed in the Atlantic, both sustaining repairable damage.

Kursk (1994)

SPECIFICATIONS

DIMENSIONS:	Length: 154m (505ft 2in); Beam: 18.2m (60ft); Draught: 9m (29ft 6in)
DISPLACEMENT:	(Minimum): Surfaced – 13,600 tonnes (13,400 tons); Submerged – 18,300 tonnes (18,000 tons)
PROPULSION:	2 OK-650b reactors, 380MW (509,580hp), steam turbines 7.4MW (100,000hp), 2 screws
SPEED:	Surfaced – 16 knots (29.6km/h; 18.4mph); Submerged – 32 knots (59km/h; 37mph)
RANGE:	Unlimited
ARMAMENT:	2 650mm (25.4in) and 4 533mm (21in) launch tubes; 24 P-700 3M45 missiles; 24 torpedoes
COMPLEMENT:	118

Kursk (K-141) was one of the Oscar II class, the largest attack submarines yet built. It was the first Russian nuclear submarine to be completed after the break-up of the Soviet Union in 1990.

Below: The Oscar I submarine profile. Note the closed covers of the missile silos.

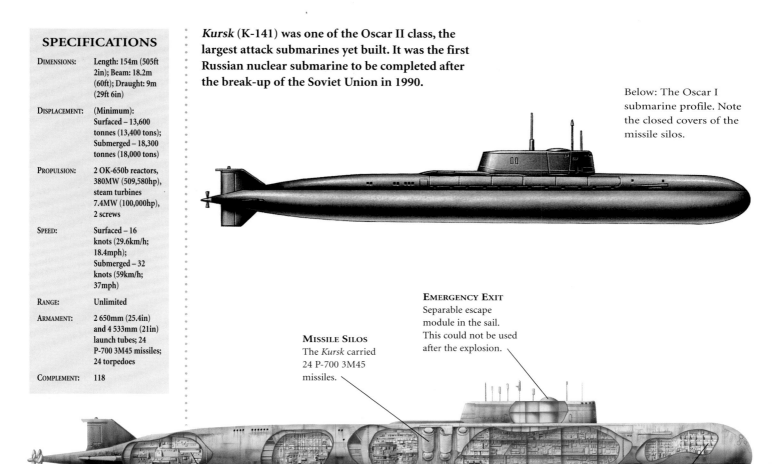

EMERGENCY EXIT
Separable escape module in the sail. This could not be used after the explosion.

MISSILE SILOS
The *Kursk* carried 24 P-700 3M45 missiles.

STERN COMPARTMENT
The survivors of the explosion gathered here, close to the aft escape hatch.

TORPEDO ROOM
This is where the fatal explosion happened on the *Kursk*.

FATAL EXPLOSION

The Oscar II boats were considered to be highly capable and reliable, so the abrupt sinking of *Kursk* during exercises in the Barents Sea on 12 October 2000 was at first attributed to an undersea collision. A violent explosion, equivalent to 4.5 on the Richter scale, was recorded on Norwegian seismographs. Immediate rescue attempts, soon aided by Norway and Britain, were frustrated by surface storms and poor underwater visibility. In total, 23 crewmembers survived the initial event and took refuge in the stern compartment, but attempts to pump oxygen into the hull were unsuccessful and robot vehicles failed to access the emergency hatch in time to rescue them. All 118 persons on board ultimately perished.

OPERATIONS

Kursk moored at Vidyaevo (Ara Bay) submarine base in May 2000, three months before the disaster. *Kursk* had been operational since December 1994, when it was commissioned, although during that time it made only one mission: a six-month deployment to the Mediterranean during the summer of 1999.

USS *Seawolf* (1995)

SPECIFICATIONS

DIMENSIONS:	Length: 107m (351ft); Beam: 12m (40ft); Draught: 10.9m (35ft 9in)
DISPLACEMENT:	Surfaced – 8738 tonnes (8600 tons); Submerged – 9285 tonnes (9138 tons)
PROPULSION:	1 GE S6W pressurized water reactor, 2 turbines rated at 38.8MW (52,000hp); one Improved Performance Machinery Program Phase II secondary propulsion motor; propulsor
SPEED:	Surfaced – 18 knots (33.3km/h; 20.7mph); Submerged – 35 knots (64.8km/h; 40.2mph)
RANGE:	Unlimited
ARMAMENT:	8 660mm (25.9in) launch tubes for Mk 48 torpedoes, Tomahawk or Sub-Harpoon missiles; 50 torpedoes
COMPLEMENT:	140

The culmination of the USA's Cold War attack submarine designs, the Seawolf class was intended to replace the Los Angeles class and to restore US dominance over Russia's new generation of fast stealth submarines. However, in changing circumstances, only three were built.

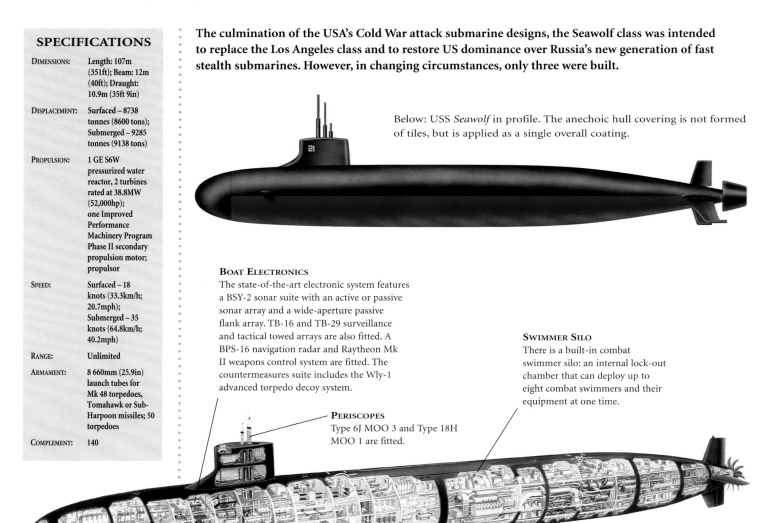

Below: USS *Seawolf* in profile. The anechoic hull covering is not formed of tiles, but is applied as a single overall coating.

BOAT ELECTRONICS
The state-of-the-art electronic system features a BSY-2 sonar suite with an active or passive sonar array and a wide-aperture passive flank array. TB-16 and TB-29 surveillance and tactical towed arrays are also fitted. A BPS-16 navigation radar and Raytheon Mk II weapons control system are fitted. The countermeasures suite includes the Wly-1 advanced torpedo decoy system.

SWIMMER SILO
There is a built-in combat swimmer silo: an internal lock-out chamber that can deploy up to eight combat swimmers and their equipment at one time.

PERISCOPES
Type 6J MOO 3 and Type 18H MOO 1 are fitted.

HULL CONSTRUCTION
HY-100 steel has a tensile yield strength of 690 MPa (6433 tons/ sq ft). Construction of *Seawolf* was dogged by problems of weld cracking; an estimated two years' work on hull construction had to be abandoned until a technical solution was reached.

COMBAT CAPABILITY
The eight 660mm (25.9in) tubes enable silent 'swimout' launches of Mk 48 torpedoes. They also launch a variety of other missiles, including Sub-Harpoon anti-ship missiles and Tomahawk land attack cruise missiles with a range of 1700km (1050 miles), as well as remotely controlled vehicles. A mix of 50 torpedoes, Sub Harpoons and Tomahawks can be carried. Combat data system, fire control, countermeasures and sonar equipment, all fully up-to-date when *Seawolf* was commissioned in 1997, have been upgraded.

ARMAMENT
Seawolf carries 50 torpedoes/ missiles or 100 mines. The two-deck torpedo room can engage multiple targets simultaneously through the Raytheon Mk II fire control system.

SEA TRIALS
USS *Seawolf* is seen here on pre-commissioning sea trials in Narragansett Bay, 3 July 1996. She was commissioned on 19 July 1997.

Type 039 (Song) (1999)

SPECIFICATIONS

DIMENSIONS:	Length: 74.9m (245ft 8in); Beam: 8.4m (27ft 6in); Draught: 5.3m (17ft 4in)
DISPLACEMENT:	Surfaced – 1700 tonnes (1673 tons); Submerged – 2286 tonnes (2250 tons)
PROPULSION:	4 MTU 16V 396S E84 diesels, 18,148kW (24,360hp), single screw
SPEED:	Surfaced – 15 knots (27.7km/h; 17.2mph); Submerged – 22 knots (40.7km/h; 25.3mph)
RANGE:	Undisclosed
ARMAMENT:	6 533mm (21in) torpedo tubes, 18 torpedoes/missiles or 24–36 mines
COMPLEMENT:	60

Given the reporting name of 'Song' by NATO, the Type 039 – an ocean-going multi-role SSK – is the first submarine to have been completely designed, built and fitted out in China.

Right: Submariners pose on the deck of a Song submarine, at an unidentified location.

SAIL
The original Type 039 boat had a stepped sail. On Type 039G, the sail is teardrop-shaped, narrowing sharply to the rear. Its top deck is open.

SONAR
To enhance passive search capabilities, a low-frequency sonar of French Thomson-CSF TSM-2255 design is mounted on the flanks. Its maximum range is in excess of 30km (18.6 miles) and it can track four targets simultaneously.

SKEW PROPELLER
The propeller is designed to minimize pressure fluctuations on the blade to reduce cavitation (the formation of bubbles and consequent noise).

ARMAMENT

The 039 class are currently equipped with YJ-82 cruise missiles for underwater launching. The YJ-82 is a highly effective surface skimmer with a 120-km (75-mile) range, and a warhead of 165kg (363lb). There are six 533mm (21in) bow torpedo tubes for torpedoes and anti-ship missiles, including Yu-3 acoustic-homing anti-submarine torpedoes and Yu-4 passive acoustic-homing anti-ship torpedoes. Yu-4 has a speed of 30 knots (55.5km/h; 34.5mph) and a range of 6km (3.7 miles). The submarine can alternatively carry 24 to 36 tube-launched naval mines.

ON MANOEUVRES
Song-class submarines advancing in line abreast, in a photo intended to display Chinese naval power.

USS *Virginia* (2003)

SPECIFICATIONS

DIMENSIONS:	Length: 115m (377ft 3in); Beam: 10m (33ft); Draught: 9.7m (32ft)
DISPLACEMENT:	Surfaced – undisclosed; Submerged – 7900 tonnes (7800 tons)
PROPULSION:	1 S9G pressurized water reactor, 29.4MW (40,000hp); 2 steam turbines; United Defense pump jet propulsor
SPEED:	Surfaced – undisclosed; Submerged – 25 knots (46.2km/h; 28.7mph)
RANGE:	Unlimited
ARMAMENT:	12 vertical BGM-109 Tomahawk cruise missile tubes; 4 53mm (21in) torpedo tubes; 38 weapons
COMPLEMENT:	135

USS *Virginia* (SSN-774) entered the world stages as the lead boat in its class upon its commissioning in 2004. A key feature of the craft is its use of photonic masts, which meant that the control room could be located lower in the hull than possible with optical periscopes.

Right: USS *Virginia* at sea. The deck markings indicate the location of rescue hatches.

COST-EFFECTIVE REDESIGN

As part of the Virginia-class Block III contract, the US Navy redesigned approximately 20 per cent of the submarine to reduce future acquisition costs and improve operational effectiveness. Most of the changes were made in the bow: the air-backed sonar sphere has been replaced with a water-backed Large Aperture Bow (LAB) array, reducing acquisition and life-cycle costs and providing enhanced passive detection capabilities. The redesigned bow also replaces the 12 Vertical Launch System (VLS) tubes with two large-diameter 213.3cm (84in) Virginia Payload Tubes (VPTs), each capable of launching six Tomahawk cruise missiles. The VPTs simplify construction, reduce acquisition costs and offer greater payload flexibility. These alterations were successfully tested during sea trials in North Dakota in August 2014.

MULTI-FUNCTION MAST
The multi-function mast incorporates submarine high data rate (sub HDR) multiband satellite communications systems allowing simultaneous communication at super high frequency (SHF) and extremely high frequency (EHF).

PHOTONIC MASTS
The submarines have two Kollmorgen AN/BVS-1 photonic masts rather than optical periscopes. Sensors mounted on the non-hull-penetrating photonic mast include LLTV (low-light TV), thermal imager and laser rangefinder.

DUCTED PROPULSOR
With non-rotating nozzle.

AIRLOCK CHAMBER
A built-in nine-man airlock chamber allows access and egress.

ELECTROMAGNETIC REDUCTION
An advanced electromagnetic signature reduction system has been incorporated from USS *California* (SSN-781) and retrofitted in earlier boats.

BOW AND CHIN SONAR ARRAYS
For detecting other vessels.

OVERHAUL

USS *Virginia* arriving at Portsmouth Naval Shipyard on 7 September 2010 for a major overhaul. It returned to active service on 5 May 2012.

Astute Class (2007)

SPECIFICATIONS

DIMENSIONS:	Length: 97m (318ft); Beam: 11.3m (37ft); Draught: 10m (33ft)
DISPLACEMENT:	Surfaced – 7000 tonnes (6889 tons); Submerged – 7400 tonnes (7283 tons)
PROPULSION:	1 RR PWR2 Core H reactor, 2 turbines, single shaft, propulsor
SPEED:	Surfaced – undisclosed; Submerged – 29 knots (53.7km/h; 33.3mph)
RANGE:	Unlimited
ARMAMENT:	6 533mm (21in) launch tubes for Spearfish torpedoes/ Tomahawk Block IV TLAM; 38 weapons
COMPLEMENT:	135

Britain's latest fast-attack SSN class is named after HMS *Astute*. It is intended to be formed of seven boats over a construction period extending towards 2020 and with a service life continuing towards the mid 21st century.

Right: About to take to the water – *Astute* at the BAE Systems construction yard, Barrow-in-Furness, June 2007.

INTERNAL LAYOUT
Manoeuvring (machinery control) room with switchboard room below and diesel generator room on keel deck.

COMMUNICATION AND OPTRONIC OBSERVATION MASTS
No optical periscope was included in *Astute*'s design.

ESCAPE TOWERS
The Astute class have two up-to-date escape towers: the Logistic Escape Tower (LET) aft and a Forrard Escape Tower (FET). Escapees are encased in protective suits with a breathing system. When the pressure inside the tower matches the external pressure, the upper lid will open and the escapee will rise safely to the surface.

WINCH GEAR
Additional stowage for towed sonar.

MAIN MACHINERY MOUNTING RAFT
Located to the rear of the submarine.

ACCESS POINT
Weapons loading hatch and Gemini craft (six-person inflatable) stowage.

WEAPONS STORAGE COMPARTMENT
Anti-shock mounting provides adaptable protection according to the number of weapons stored on each stowage tier. The launch system uses an air turbine pump to achieve a positive launch firing mechanism. The ATP displaces a volume of water to launch a weapon. A programmable firing valve controls the ATP firing air profile, allowing the system to match the launch requirements precisely to a range of variables, including weapon type, boat speed and depth.

FIRST DEPLOYMENT
Astute close to its home base at Faslane, Scotland. The submarine's first operational deployment saw it spend a full eight months at sea.

Type 094 (Jin Class) (2007)

SPECIFICATIONS

DIMENSIONS:	Length: 135m (442ft 11in); Beam: 12.5m (41ft); Draught: 8m (26ft 3in)
DISPLACEMENT:	Surfaced – 8128 tonnes (8000 tons); Submerged – 11,176 tonnes (11,000 tons)
PROPULSION:	Nuclear reactor, single screw
SPEED:	Surfaced – undisclosed; Submerged – 20 knots+ (37km/h+; 23mph+) (estimated)
RANGE:	Unlimited
ARMAMENT:	12 JL-2 SLBMs; 6 533mm (21in) torpedo tubes
COMPLEMENT:	Undisclosed

China's second-generation nuclear-powered SSBN has significantly extended the country's range of potential strategic engagement. No details about the Jin's internal arrangements have been officially released, but analysis of external images enables experts to make conjectures about the internal layout and key features, with a high degree of probability.

Above: A Type 094 at sea. It shows the typical basic features of a ballistic missile submarine, with a raised fairing over the missile launchers. The sail is partly merged into the fairing to improve hydrodynamics.

LAUNCH TUBES
Silos for 12 launch tubes for the JL-2 SLBM, each capped with up to six nuclear warheads.

ARMAMENT
Chinese torpedoes are assumed to be based on Russian models and to include in their range a development of the Shkval 'rocket torpedo' that travels at high speeds enveloped in its own bubble of gas to avoid water resistance.

HULL CONSTRUCTION
The Jin hull is modelled on that of the Xia class, but the design is smoother, more integrated and more sophisticated.

CONTROL ROOM
Navigation, fire control, countermeasures and sonar systems may be less technically advanced than on American and Russian submarines, although the successor Type 096 will certainly show significant upgrading of these aspects.

SLBM STOWAGE
The Jin class reportedly will carry 12 JL-2 (NATO designation CSS-N-5 Sabbot) SLBMs. Other armament includes six 533mm (21in) torpedo tubes. American intelligence suggests that the PLAN (People's Liberation Army Navy) is also developing a typical range of countermeasures including decoys, chaff, electronic jamming and thermal shielding.

MISSILE TUBES
Two Type 094 Jin-class submarines moored at the Hainan Island naval complex. The nearer has its missile tubes open. These submarines carry 12 JL-2 SLBMs with a range of 7200km (4500 miles).

Soryu (2009)

SPECIFICATIONS

DIMENSIONS:	Length: 84m (275ft 7in); Beam: 9.1m (30ft); Draught: 8.5m (27ft 11in)
DISPLACEMENT:	Surfaced – 2900 tonnes (2854 tons); Submerged – 4200 tonnes (4134 tons)
PROPULSION:	2 Kawasaki 12V 25/25 SB-type diesels; 4 Kawasaki-Kockums V4-275R Stirling engines, single screw
SPEED:	Surfaced – 13 knots (24km/h; 14.9mph); Submerged – 20 knots (37km/h; 23mph)
RANGE:	6100nm (11,297km; 7019 miles) at 6.5 knots (12km/h; 7.4mph)
ARMAMENT:	6 533mm (21in) launch tubes for torpedoes; Sub-Harpoon missiles, mines
COMPLEMENT:	65

The first boat of the Soryu class, named after the Japanese Imperial Navy aircraft carrier *Soryu*, was commissioned in 2009. Translated from Japanese, it means 'Blue Dragon'. A class of 10 is planned, all of them named after dragons in Japanese mythology.

Right: A Soryu-class boat making full surface speed. Under the surface it would be almost undetectable.

MASTS
In stem to stern order, the masts are search radar, ESM, air induction and exhaust.

NOISE REDUCTION
A rubber-based covering is believed to be the secret of *Soryu*'s extreme quietness. On-board electronic equipment also has this covering to mute any noise. Even the light bulbs have had their sound signatures extracted.

EXHAUST DISCHARGE
Stirling-AIP burns pure oxygen and diesel fuel in a pressurized combustion chamber whose pressure is higher than the external water pressure, allowing exhaust products to be discharged overboard without using a compressor to dissolve in the sea. This procedure reduces infrared signature and noise emission levels.

LONG-RANGE ATTACK
The class is armed with six HU-606 533mm (21in) torpedo tubes for the Type 89 torpedoes and UGM-84 Sub-Harpoon anti-ship missiles. Type 89 is a wire-guided torpedo with active and passive homing modes. It has a maximum speed of 130km/h (80mph), can engage targets within a range of 50km (31 miles) and carries a high-explosive warhead of 267kg (588lb). The Harpoon has a range of more than 124km (77 miles) and speed of 864km/h (536mph). Weapon stowage capacity is believed to be the equivalent of 20 heavyweight torpedoes/ Harpoon missiles or 10 torpedoes/Harpoon missiles plus 20 (smaller) mines.

TORPEDO ROOM
Type 89 is a wire-guided torpedo with active and passive homing modes. It has a maximum speed of 130km/h (80mph) and can engage targets within a range of 50km (31 miles). The torpedo can carry a warhead of 267kg (588lb).

GROUNDING KEELS
These enable *Soryu* to sit silently on the seabed.

HULL CONSTRUCTION
Like the Oyashio class, the Soryu class has a 'hybrid' hull structure that is partially double and partially single. The hull is divided into six compartments.

PEARL HARBOR VISIT
With garlanded sail, Soryu-class *Hakuryu* (commissioned 14 March 2011) arrives at Joint Base Pearl Harbor-Hickam on a goodwill visit on 6 February 2013.

INS *Arihant* (2015)

SPECIFICATIONS

DIMENSIONS:	Length: 110m (361ft); Beam: 11m (36ft); Draught: 9m (29ft 6in)
DISPLACEMENT:	Surfaced – 6000 tons (5900 tons); Submerged – undisclosed
PROPULSION:	1 pressurized water reactor, 83MW (111,000hp), single screw
SPEED:	Surfaced – 15 knots (27.7km/h; 17.2mph); Submerged – 24 knots (44.4km/h; 27.6mph)
RANGE:	Unlimited
ARMAMENT:	6 533mm (21in) launch tubes; 30 torpedoes; 12 K-15 SLBM
COMPLEMENT:	96

With the home-built SSBN *Arihant*, India has become the sixth country to construct and operate nuclear submarines. An ongoing programme for further vessels, both missile carriers and attack boats, has been announced by the Indian government. Some 110m (361ft) long and 11m (36ft) in beam, the submarine has a main control room and an auxiliary control room, while the complete power and propulsion plant and associated systems occupy the rear half of the hull.

AB-2 STEEL
AB-2 is a high-yield strength, low-carbon, low-alloy steel with nickel, molybdenum and chromium. It has excellent weldability and good ductility even in welded sections. Its yield strength of 690 MPa (6433 tons/sq ft) is equivalent to the USA's HY-100 rating.

MISSILES
Arihant has successfully test-fired an unarmed Sagarika B-05 missile produced by India's Defence Research Development Organisation (DRDO). It has a 700-km (440-mile) range and is capable of carrying a nuclear warhead.

PROPELLER
Arihant is driven via a seven-bladed fixed-pitch propeller with cruciform vortex dissipators. An emergency back-up drive is provided by two diesel engines of 370kW (496hp) giving a speed of 4 knots (7.4km/h; 4.6mph).

ANECHOIC COVERING
An Indian-developed anechoic covering said to be made of 100mm (4in)-thick rubber-based tiles, each containing thousands of tiny voids, is applied to the outer hull. It is intended to absorb the pulses emitted by active sonar and reduce and distort the return signal, while also attenuating the sounds emitted by the vessel itself.

SONAR
In the hull sides, twin flank-array sonars and Israeli-designed Rafael broadband expendable anti-torpedo countermeasures are fitted.

K-15 MISSILES
With underwater ballistic missile launch capability, the boat carries 12 K-15 Sagarika submarine-launched ballistic missiles (SLBMs). With a 1000kg (2200lb) warhead, the missile has a 700–750-km (434–465-mile) range. This is a significant limitation, since the submarine has to move close to enemy shores to launch its missiles, although with a 180kg (396lb) warhead, the range extends to 1900km (1200 miles).

PLANNED PRODUCTION
Arihant in the course of sea trials. It is interesting to compare its shape with the contemporary Chinese Jin class. At the time of writing, it is unclear how many of the Arihant-class submarines are to be produced, with three to six being likely.

HMS *Furious* (1917)

Originally intended as a cruiser, *Furious* became the first warship in regular use as an aircraft carrier, undergoing successive conversions from partial to full flight deck. With HMS *Argus,* it was one of only two ships to serve as a carrier in both world wars.

Below: HMS *Courageous*, although built on an identical hull, had a different design as a carrier to *Furious*. The best form of the carrier was still being explored.

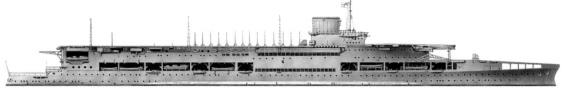

SPECIFICATIONS

DIMENSIONS:	Length: 224.1m (735ft 2in); Beam: 26.8m (88ft); Draught: 8.3m (27ft 3in)
DISPLACEMENT:	22,900 tonnes (22,500 tons); 26,900 tonnes (26,500 tons) deep load
PROPULSION:	18 Yarrow boilers, 4 Brown-Curtis geared turbines, 4 shafts, 67,113kW (90,000shp)
SPEED:	30 knots (56km/h; 34.5mph)
RANGE:	7480nm (13,850km; 8610 miles) at 10 knots (18.5km/h; 11.5mph)
ARMAMENT:	10 BL 140mm (5.5in) Mk 1 guns, 6 QF 102mm (4in) AA guns
AIRCRAFT:	36
COMPLEMENT:	795

GUNS
The guns were mounted laterally at main deck level on partial sponsons.

FLY-OFF DECK
Initially, the lower fly-off deck was laid over the forecastle, tapering with the bow.

PROFILE
The profile shows the carrier's appearance in World War II, with guns and direction-finding equipment forward of the flight deck.

EXHAUST
Exhaust gases were ducted out at the stern in the space between the flight deck and the hangar roof – a bad location for planes landing, flying into the wind.

AIRCRAFT
The Sopwith Camels first carried on *Furious* were not designed for carriers. In the 1920s, a few types adapted for naval use appeared, including the Avro Bison and Blackburn R-1 Blackburn spotter planes, the Blackburn Dart torpedo bomber, the Westland Walrus reconnaissance plane and the Gloster Mars X Nightjar and Fairey Flycatcher, both fighters. In 1940, *Furious* was carrying Fairey Swordfish and Gloster Sea Gladiators.

SECURE LANDING
HMS *Courageous*, showing the bow flight deck. Note the cranes to port and starboard. In 1931, this became the first British carrier to mount transverse arrester wires to make landings more secure.

HMS *Eagle* (1924)

SPECIFICATIONS

DIMENSIONS:	Length: 203.5m (667ft 6in); Beam: 35.1m (115ft); Draught (max.): 8.1m (26ft 8in)
DISPLACEMENT:	(Standard): 22,200 tonnes (21,850 tons)
PROPULSION:	32 Yarrow boilers, 4 geared turbines, 37,000kW (50,000shp)
SPEED:	24 knots (44km/h; 28mph)
RANGE:	4800nm (8900km; 5500 miles) at 16 knots (29.6km/h; 18.4mph)
ARMAMENT:	9 152mm (6in) guns, 5 102mm (4in) AA guns
AIRCRAFT:	24
COMPLEMENT:	791

Like all the first-generation carriers, *Eagle* was not originally intended for the role, and retained much of its battleship appearance even after conversion to an aircraft carrier.

Right: The Fairey Flycatcher was developed in 1922 as a single-seat fighter and served on all British aircraft carriers of the era. Its forward section was metal; the rear section, wings and tail were fabric-covered wood. Some 192 Flycatchers were built up to 1930.

FLIGHT DECK
Eagle was the first carrier to have an island structure on the flight deck, establishing the convention that it would be positioned on the starboard side of the ship.

ISLAND
Eagle was the ship that confirmed the starboard placement of the island, although its island, with a huge tripod mast, was larger than most.

AIRCRAFT AND FITTINGS
Nine 152mm (6in) guns were mounted on the main deck. Armour consisted of a 114mm belt (4.5in), deck armour of 25–38mm (1–1.5in) and 102mm (4in) transverse bulkheads. Two aircraft lifts were fitted, one just forward of the island, the other at the stern. *Eagle*'s battleship-type hull restricted it to carry a maximum of 24 aircraft, usually only 20–21. On its final mission, it was carrying 20 Sea Hurricanes; at earlier stages in World War II it flew Fairey Swordfish, Fairey Flycatchers, Gloster Sea Gladiators and Fairey Fulmars.

ENGINE ROOM
The engine room instruments were ordered prior to purchase by the British. Uniquely for a British warship, they were calibrated in metric units and labelled in Spanish.

TORPEDO BLISTERS
Eagle was fitted with torpedo blisters intended to be capable of absorbing a charge of 52kg/cm2 (750psi).

CAMOUFLAGE
The profile shows *Eagle* in 1942 camouflage paint.

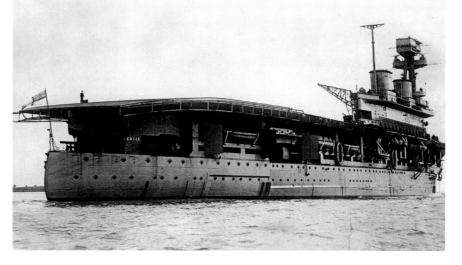

FLIGHT DECK
Eagle in the 1930s. While the forward end of the flight deck conformed to the hull shape, at the stern it was canted out to provide a broader landing area.

Akagi (1927)

SPECIFICATIONS

DIMENSIONS:	Length: 260.6m (855ft); Beam: 31.4m (103ft); Draught: 8.8m (29ft)
DISPLACEMENT:	37,084 tonnes (36,500 tons); 41,961 tonnes (41,300 tons) full load
PROPULSION:	19 Kampon boilers, 4 turbines, 4 shafts, 41,013kW (55,000shp)
SPEED:	31 knots (57.3km/h; 35.6mph)
RANGE:	10,000nm (18,520km; 11,510 miles) at 14 knots (25.9km/h; 16.1mph)
AIRCRAFT:	91
ARMAMENT:	6 354mm (8in) guns, 12 120mm (4.7in) guns, 14 twin 25mm (1in) AA guns
COMPLEMENT:	1630

Flagship of Japan's Pearl Harbor attack fleet, and flagship at the start of the Battle of Midway, *Akagi* participated in major action in the early stages of the Pacific War.

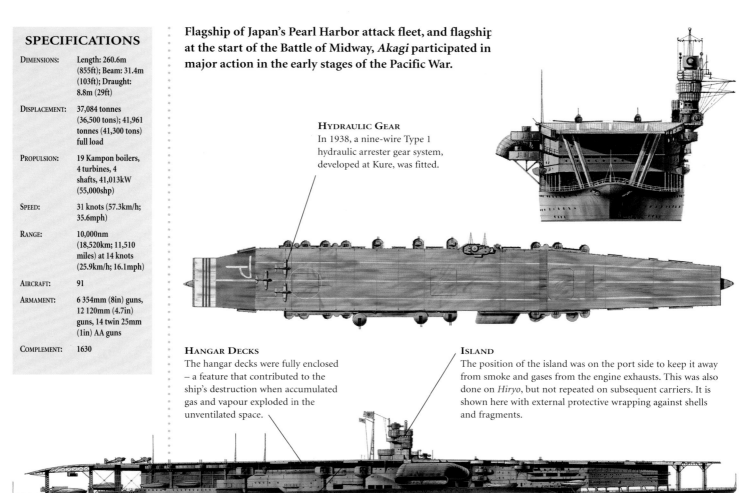

HYDRAULIC GEAR
In 1938, a nine-wire Type 1 hydraulic arrester gear system, developed at Kure, was fitted.

HANGAR DECKS
The hangar decks were fully enclosed – a feature that contributed to the ship's destruction when accumulated gas and vapour exploded in the unventilated space.

ISLAND
The position of the island was on the port side to keep it away from smoke and gases from the engine exhausts. This was also done on *Hiryo*, but not repeated on subsequent carriers. It is shown here with external protective wrapping against shells and fragments.

PEARL HARBOR ATTACK

On 7 December 1941, *Akagi* launched two waves of aircraft, the first including 15 dive-bombers, 12 torpedo planes and ten fighter planes; the second formed of eight dive-bombers and nine fighters. The Japanese carriers lost 29 aircraft in the attack, while, apart from the loss of five battleships and damage to numerous other warships, the US lost 239 aircraft in simultaneous raids on the airfields. *Akagi*'s torpedo bombers were responsible for the destruction of USS *Oklahoma* and *West Virginia*. It was a shattering display of naval air power.

FLIGHT DECK
From 1938, the flight deck was 249.2m (817ft 6in) long. The flight decks of Japanese carriers were wood-laid, with the planks running longitudinally rather than transversely as in US carriers.

FUNNEL
The funnel had a large vent on the starboard side. Water could be sprayed into the smoke as it left the funnel, making it heavier so that it would not roll up and over the flight deck and interfere with flight operations.

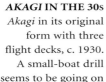

***AKAGI* IN THE 30s**
Akagi in its original form with three flight decks, c. 1930. A small-boat drill seems to be going on in the foreground.

USS *Lexington* (CV-2) (1927)

SPECIFICATIONS

DIMENSIONS:	Length: 270.66m (888ft); Beam: 32.12m (105ft 5in); Draught: 10.15m (33ft 4in)
DISPLACEMENT:	38,284 tonnes (37,681 tons); 43.744 tonnes (43,055 tons) full load
PROPULSION:	16 water-tube boilers, turbo-electric drive, 134,226kW (180,000shp), 4 shafts
SPEED:	33.25 knots (61.5km/h; 38mph)
RANGE:	10,500nm (19,456km; 12,075 miles) at 15 knots (27.7km/h; 17.2mph)
ARMAMENT:	8 203mm (8in), 12 127mm (5in) guns
AIRCRAFT:	63
COMPLEMENT:	2791

Laid down first as a battlecruiser, *Lexington* was redesigned as a carrier and taught the US Navy much about sea flying in the 1930s. In 1942, it played a key part in the Battle of the Coral Sea before succumbing to fire after heavy attacks.

Above: The Grumman SF-1 was a two-seater scout version of the FF-1 fighter plane that had been introduced in 1933. In 1936, *Lexington*'s air group included 18 Grumman SF-1s.

FUNNEL
Lexington's massive funnel structure, separate from the island, gave it a unique and easily recognizable profile. A gallery was built below the funnel cap in the 1937–38 refit and a CXAM radar grid was mounted on its top forward edge in October 1941.

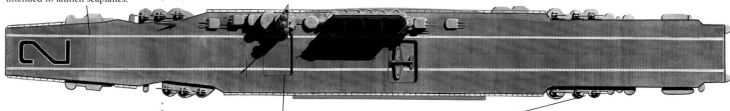

CATAPULT
Until 1936, the ship carried a flywheel-powered F Mk II catapult on the starboard bow, intended to launch seaplanes.

DESTRUCTION
On 8 May 1942, during the Battle of the Coral Sea, *Lexington* was hit by two aerial torpedoes on the port side near the bow as well as three bombs, and it caught fire. At first the fires appeared to have been extinguished, but leaking vapour from ruptured fuel tanks built up and exploded at 12.47, causing a series of further explosions. The ship developed a heavy list to port, and its captain gave the order to abandon at 17.00. There were 216 fatalities and 2770 survivors. Its orphan aircraft were redeployed to *Yorktown*.

HANGAR DECK
The hangar deck was enclosed; the explosion of gasoline vapour in the confined space resulted in uncontrollable fire on 8 May 1942, a major factor in the ship's loss.

ARMAMENTS
Original armament was eight 203mm (8in) guns in quadruple turrets, 12 127mm (5in) and 48 28mm (1.1in) guns. It is probable that if they were fired to port (across the deck) the blast would have damaged the flight deck. The guns could be depressed to −5° and elevated to +41°.

US NAVAL BASE
USS *Lexington* with other American warships at Hawaii, 1930. There had been a naval station at Pearl Harbor since 1908, but it was much enlarged in the 1930s.

Hiryu (1937)

SPECIFICATIONS

DIMENSIONS:	Length: 227.4m (746ft 1in); Beam: 22.3m (73ft 2in); Draught: 7.9m (26ft)
DISPLACEMENT:	17,577 tonnes (17,300 tons); 22,403 tonnes (20,250 tons) full load
PROPULSION:	8 Kampon Ro boilers, 4 geared turbines, 4 shafts; 114,000kW (153,000shp)
SPEED:	34.3 knots (63.5km/h; 39.5mph)
RANGE:	10,330nm (19,130km; 11,890 miles) at 18 knots (33.3km/h; 20.7mph)
AIRCRAFT:	73
ARMAMENT:	12 127mm (5in), 31 25mm (1in) AA guns
COMPLEMENT:	1100

The Imperial Japanese Navy was building up its carrier force in the late 1930s, with *Soryu* and *Hiryu* as fast carriers added to the fleet in 1937 and 1939. Both were to become victims of the Battle of Midway.

Below: *Soryu* was slightly smaller in overall dimensions than *Hiryu*, but the main difference between the two sister ships was the location of the island. *Soryu*'s was positioned to starboard.

SISTER SHIP
Both ships had similar tower-type islands, although differently located, and *Hiryu*'s had an additional deck level. Both had masts rising from flight-deck level, although again of different design.

RISING SUN
A large *Hinomaru* or rising sun was painted on *Hiryu*'s flight deck, ironically providing a 'bullseye' target for US dive-bombers.

FIRE CURTAINS
Fire curtains and insulation on carriers of all navies in the 1930s and 1940s made extensive use of asbestos, whose toxic properties were not realized at the time.

MIDWAY ENDING
The Battle of Midway (4–7 June 1942) was a turning point in the naval war in the Pacific. During this epic confrontation, the Japanese lost four aircraft carriers – *Akagi*, *Kaga*, *Soryu* and *Hiryu* – plus one heavy cruiser. *Hiryu* was hit by multiple bomb and torpedo strikes by waves of aircraft from the US carriers, and fire raged uncontrollably aboard. The ship eventually sank, with the loss of 389 crewmembers.

HANGARS
Both *Soryu* and *Hiryu* retained the two-level enclosed hangar design of earlier carriers such as *Kaga*. The height of the lower hangar, at 4.3m (14ft), restricted the type of plane that could be carried.

BEAM
Hiryu's beam was 1.2m (4ft) greater than *Soryu*'s, giving the ship a 20 per cent increase in interior space as well as greater stability.

MAKING SPEED
Hiryu making speed during its sea trials in April 1939. Both it and *Soryu* were fast ships, capable of 34 knots (63km/h; 39mph) or more.

USS *Yorktown* (CV-5) (1937)

TYPE · *Aircraft Carriers* · FAMILY · *Warships*

SPECIFICATIONS

DIMENSIONS:	Length: 251.4m (824ft 9in); Beam: 33.4m (109ft 6in); Draught: 7.9m (25ft 11in)
DISPLACEMENT:	20,100 tonnes (19,800 tons); 25,900 tonnes (25,500 tons) full load
PROPULSION:	9 B&W boilers, 4 Parsons turbines, 89,000kW (120,000shp)
SPEED:	32.5 knots (60.2km/h; 37.4mph)
RANGE:	12,500nm (23,200km; 14,400 miles) at 15 knots (27.7km/h; 17.2mph)
ARMAMENT:	8 127mm (5in) 38-cal guns, 4 quad 280mm (1.1in) 75-cal guns, 24 .50-cal machine guns
AIRCRAFT:	90
COMPLEMENT:	2217

The first of the US Navy's large purpose-built carriers, *Yorktown* saw fierce action in the Pacific War. Fatally crippled in the Battle of Midway, it was abandoned and subsequently torpedoed.

Above: The Curtiss SBC Helldiver dive-bomber was the last biplane type acquired by the US Navy, in 1938. The *Yorktown* included Helldivers from 1943–45.

CATAPULT
Until 1943, a lateral-firing catapult was installed on the hangar deck for use in emergencies.

TORPEDO
Torpedoes were held in an armoured box on the hangar deck just aft of the island.

FLIGHT DECK
The flight deck was formed of Douglas fir planks, 7.6cm (3in) thick and 15.2cm (6in) wide, laid over steel sheet 2.5mm (0.1in) thick. Metal aircraft tie-down strips were laid every 1.2m (4ft).

CRASH BARRIERS
Crash barriers were mounted forward of the forward elevator.

HANGAR DOORS
Shutter-type doors on each side allowed for closure of the separate hangar sections.

MIDWAY VICTORY
Off Midway on 4 June 1942, *Yorktown* sent out reconnaissance planes, confirming the Japanese positions. An initial American attack by torpedo bombers was turned back with massive losses, but the SBD Dauntless dive-bombers from both *Enterprise* and *Yorktown* reached the Japanese carriers at the same time. Their onslaught was devastatingly successful, reducing *Akagi*, *Kaga* and *Soryu* to flaming hulks.

ARRESTER WIRES
Arrester wires were mounted forward and aft on the flight deck.

BATTLE DAMAGE
Smoke billows up after *Yorktown* is struck by a Japanese dive-bomber in the Battle of Midway, June 1942.

USS *Enterprise* (CV-6) (1938)

SPECIFICATIONS

DIMENSIONS:	Length: 251.4m (824ft 9in); Beam: 34.9m (114ft 5in); Draught: 7.9m (25ft 11in)
DISPLACEMENT:	21,336 tonnes (21,000 tons); 32,573 tonnes (32,060 tons) full load
PROPULSION:	9 B&W boilers, 4 Parsons geared turbines, 89,484kW (120,000shp), 4 shafts
SPEED:	32.5 knots (60.2km/h; 37.4mph)
RANGE:	12,000nm (23,200km; 14,400 miles) at 15 knots (27.7km/h; 17.2mph)
AIRCRAFT:	90
ARMAMENT:	8 127mm (5in) 38-cal guns, 8 twin and 6 quad 40mm (1.57in) Bofors guns, 50 20mm (0.79in) Oerlikon guns
COMPLEMENT:	1224

The seventh US ship to carry the name, the 'Big E' took a prominent part in all the great Pacific campaigns of World War II, surviving bombs and kamikaze attacks to gain both battle scars and stars as the most decorated US ship of the war.

Right: The Douglas TBD Devastator torpedo-bomber entered service in 1937. At the Battle of Midway in 1942, 41 Devastators were launched from USS *Hornet*, *Enterprise* and *Yorktown* to attack the Japanese fleet.

DECK TRACTORS
Deck tractors and trolleys speeded up the loading of torpedoes and bombs. This was done on the flight deck, whereas the Japanese practice was to send up ready-loaded planes from the hangars.

ISLAND
Aft of the pilot house and navigation bridge, the island also held a flag officer's suite and operations room as well as the captain's sea cabin.

FRESH WATER TANKS
These were kept in the depths of the ship.

WAR RECORD

Enterprise's war record encompassed the destruction of 911 enemy aircraft, the sinking of 71 ships and severe damage to a further 192. It gained the greatest number of battle honours of any US warship, including 20 battle stars. On three separate occasions, the Japanese declared they had sunk *Enterprise*, but she survived the war and was eventually scrapped in the late 1950s.

RADAR FITTING
Enterprise after RCA-CXAM radar had been fitted. The absence of aircraft suggests it has accomplished a delivery trip, perhaps in late 1941.

HMS *Ark Royal* (1938)

SPECIFICATIONS

DIMENSIONS:	Length: 208m (682ft); Beam: 28.9m (94ft 10in); Draught: 8.73m (27ft 10in)
DISPLACEMENT:	22,352 tonnes (22,000 tons); 28,163 tonnes (27,720 tons) full load
PROPULSION:	6 Admiralty boilers, 3 Parsons geared turbines; 76,807kW (103,000shp)
SPEED:	31 knots (57km/h; 36mph)
RANGE:	7600nm (14,100km; 8700 miles) at 20 knots (37km/h; 23mph)
ARMAMENT:	16 110mm (4.5in) DP guns, 32 2-pdr 40mm (1.57in) pom-pom guns, 32 12.7mm (0.5in) AA guns
AIRCRAFT:	60
COMPLEMENT:	1580

The third *Ark Royal*, the first carrier to bear the name, saw intensive action in the early part of World War II in the Atlantic, the Norwegian Sea and finally the Mediterranean.

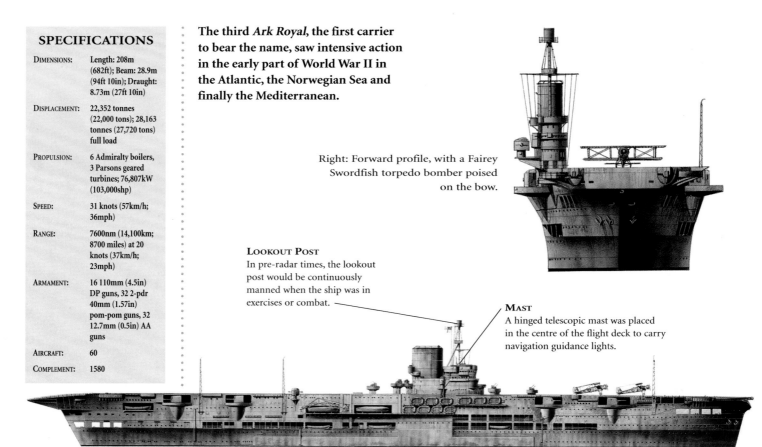

Right: Forward profile, with a Fairey Swordfish torpedo bomber poised on the bow.

LOOKOUT POST
In pre-radar times, the lookout post would be continuously manned when the ship was in exercises or combat.

MAST
A hinged telescopic mast was placed in the centre of the flight deck to carry navigation guidance lights.

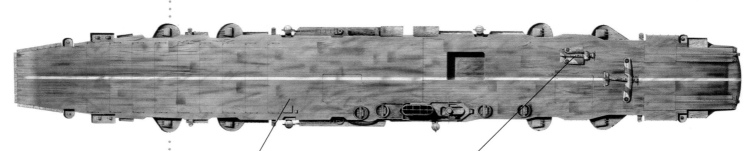

FLIGHT DECK
Ark Royal's flight deck was 20m (66ft) above the waterline. Its length exceeded that of the keel by 36m (118ft).

FOLDING WINGS
Almost from the start, naval aircraft were made with folding wings to fit lifts and maximize use of hangar space. The first naval aircraft with folding wings was the British Shorts Folder seaplane in 1913.

BISMARCK RUN

Early in 1941, *Ark Royal* delivered desperately needed fighters to Malta, then was deployed to the Atlantic to search for the battleships *Scharnhorst* and *Gneisenau*. In May, the hunt changed to *Bismarck*. Swordfish planes launched and landed in stormy conditions, with the flight deck pitching 15m (50ft) and more. *Ark Royal* kept the German battleship under surveillance on 26 and 27 May and fired the torpedoes that disabled its steering gear.

PRE-WAR VESSEL
Ark Royal seen from the port side, in original condition, June 1938. The ship had been laid down in September 1935, launched in April 1937, and commissioned in December 1938.

USS *Lexington* (CV-16) (1938)

SPECIFICATIONS

DIMENSIONS:	Length: 250m (820ft); Beam: 28m (93ft); Draught: 10.41m (34ft 2in)
DISPLACEMENT:	27,534 tonnes (27,100 tons); 36,962 tonnes (36,380 tons) full load
PROPULSION:	8 boilers, 4 Westinghouse geared turbines, 110,00kW (150,000shp), 4 shafts
SPEED:	33 knots (61km/h; 38mph)
RANGE:	15,440nm (28,564km; 17,756 miles) at 15 knots (27.7km/h; 17.2mph)
ARMAMENT:	12 127mm (5in) 38-cal guns, 4 twin, 4 single; 8 quad 40mm (1.57in) 56-cal and 46 20mm (0.79in) 78-cal AA guns
AIRCRAFT:	110
COMPLEMENT:	2600

This Essex-class carrier was laid down in July 1941 with the name *Cabot*, but was later renamed *Lexington* in honour of the US vessel sunk at the Battle of Coral Sea. Launched on 23 September 1942, the new *Lexington* saw extensive service throughout the remainder of the war.

Right: *Lexington*'s appearance after major modifications carried out between 1953 and 1955.

RADARS
SG and Mk 4 radars were fitted.

ISLAND
Lexington as it looked in 1945 with a remodelled island. SK radar was fixed to the starboard side of the funnel.

HANGAR BAYS
The three hangar bays had 3600sq m (40,000 sq ft) of space.

MACHINE ROOMS
The machinery rooms were arranged en echelon (alternately located) for maximum survivability.

PAINT SCHEME
Lexington usually sported a blue camouflage paint scheme (Measure 33); this, together with four successive Japanese claims that it had been sunk, gained it the nickname of 'The Blue Ghost'.

AVIATION FUEL
The ship's fuel bunkers held 5,955,000 litres (1,500,000 gals) plus 1,747,000 litres (440,000 gals) of aviation fuel.

ORDNANCE
The forward magazines held 635 tonnes (625.5 tons) of aviation ordnance.

BATTLE OF THE PHILIPPINE SEA

Planes from *Lexington* were in action in the Battle of the Philippine Sea, 19–20 June 1944, contributing to what became known as 'the Great Marianas Turkey Shoot' in which Japanese aircraft, other than suicide planes, were virtually cleared from the skies. *Lexington* continued on campaign through that summer, joining in another major battle in Leyte Gulf, where it helped sink the battleship *Musashi* and the light carriers *Chitose* and *Zuiho*. On its own, it sank the fleet carrier *Zuikaku* on 24–25 October.

POST-WAR SERVICE

Lexington under way on 12 November 1943. The ship had a long service life after World War II. She was recommissioned in 1955 after a major modernization programme, and served as both an active and a training carrier before being struck off in 1991.

Jun'yo (1942)

SPECIFICATIONS

DIMENSIONS:	Length: 219.3m (719ft 7in); Beam: 26.7m (87ft 7in); Draught: 8.15m (26ft 9in)
DISPLACEMENT:	24,526 tonnes (24,140 tons); 28,753 tonnes (28,300 tons) full load
PROPULSION:	6 Mitsubishi boilers, Mitsubishi geared turbines, 41,906kW (56,250shp)
SPEED:	26 knots (48km/h; 30mph)
RANGE:	10,000nm (18,500km; 11,500 miles)
AIRCRAFT:	53
ARMAMENT:	(Original): 6 twin 127mm (5in) Type 89 DP guns, 8 triple 25mm (1in) Type 96 AA guns
COMPLEMENT:	1224

Jun'yo was laid down as a passenger liner and underwent conversion to a carrier in order to boost Japan's already considerable naval air power. It was one of two Japanese carriers to survive action in World War II.

Right: *Jun'yo* anchored at Sasebo naval base, southern Japan, in 1945.

MAST POSITIONING
Unusually, the mainmast was positioned aft of the funnel, although a small mast was mounted at a later stage just forward of it.

GAS DISPERSION
Jun'yo's funnel was angled out to starboard at 25° to help disperse hot gases away from the flight deck.

RADAR
Type 13 air search radar was fitted in September 1944.

ISLAND
This was almost entirely sponson-supported.

ROCKET PLACEMENT
In September 1944, six racks of 30-tube launchers for 127mm (5in) phosphorus rockets were fitted, three on each side, on stern sponsons. These rockets were armed with multiple incendiary shrapnel charges on a time fuse.

ZUIHO
Zuiho (below), commissioned in 1940, was another pre-planned conversion. It was launched as a submarine tender. Classed as a 'light carrier', it had less than half the displacement of *Jun'yo*. It was sunk in the Battle of Cape Engaño, on 25 October 1944.

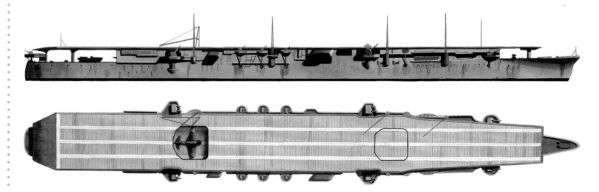

USS *Intrepid* (1943)

SPECIFICATIONS

DIMENSIONS:	Length: 250m (820ft); Beam: 28m (93ft); Draught: 10.41m (34ft 2in)
DISPLACEMENT:	27,534 tonnes (27,100 tons); 36,962 tonnes (36,380 tons) full load
PROPULSION:	8 boilers, 4 Westinghouse geared turbines, 4 shafts, 110,00kW (150,000shp)
SPEED:	33 knots (61km/h; 38mph)
RANGE:	15,440nm (28,564km; 17,756 miles) at 15 knots (27.7km/h; 17.2mph)
AIRCRAFT:	110
ARMAMENT:	12 127mm (5in) 38-cal guns, 4 twin, 4 single; 8 quad 40mm (1.57in) 56-cal and 46 20mm (0.79in) 78-cal AA guns
COMPLEMENT:	2600

Despite being the most frequently hit US carrier in World War II, *Intrepid* served in the US Navy for more than 30 years on missions from Pacific battles to spacecraft recovery. It remains today as one of the four surviving Essex-class carriers, albeit as a museum vessel.

Right: forward and aft profiles of USS *Intrepid*.

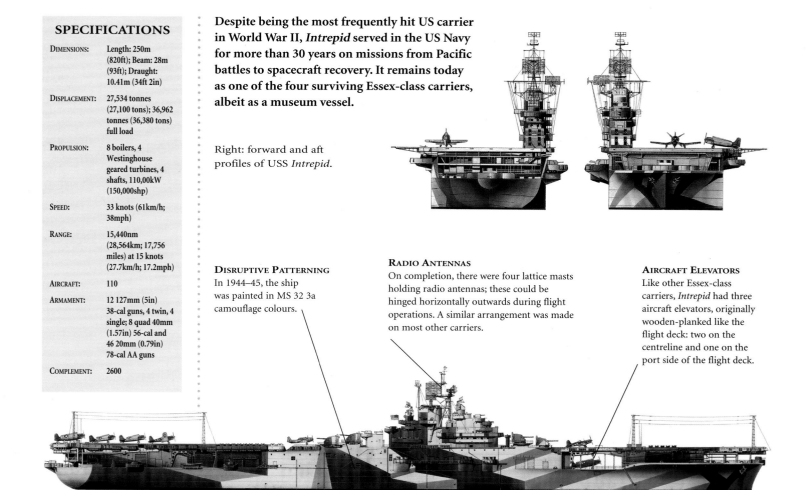

DISRUPTIVE PATTERNING
In 1944–45, the ship was painted in MS 32 3a camouflage colours.

RADIO ANTENNAS
On completion, there were four lattice masts holding radio antennas; these could be hinged horizontally outwards during flight operations. A similar arrangement was made on most other carriers.

AIRCRAFT ELEVATORS
Like other Essex-class carriers, *Intrepid* had three aircraft elevators, originally wooden-planked like the flight deck: two on the centreline and one on the port side of the flight deck.

AIRCRAFT
The *Intrepid* carried 110 aircraft of various types, including Hellcats and Helldivers. In the vessel's post-war modernization, she received a much more heavily reinforced flight deck, to take the weight and impact of modern jet aircraft.

FLIGHT DECK
The flight deck area was 262.8m × 32.9m (862ft 2in × 107ft 11in).

CATAPULT
Intrepid was commissioned with one H-4A catapult. By 1945, it had two H-4B in position at the bow.

JET AIRCRAFT
Intrepid off Guantanamo Bay naval base, Cuba, in February 1955, between its two modernizations. McDonnell F2H Banshee jet fighters are on the flight deck.

Shinano (1944)

Shinano was to have been a Yamato-class battleship, but changing needs brought conversion to the largest carrier yet built. It was sunk, however, even before it went into operational service.

SPECIFICATIONS

DIMENSIONS:	Length: 265.8m (872ft 1in); Beam: 36.3m (119ft 1in); Draught: 10.3m (33ft 10in)
DISPLACEMENT:	65,800 tonnes (64,800 tons); 73,000 tonnes (72,000 tons) full load
PROPULSION:	12 Kampon boilers, 4 geared turbines, 110,000kW (150,000shp), 4 shafts
SPEED:	27 knots (50km/h; 31mph)
RANGE:	10,000nm (18,500km; 11,500 miles)
ARMAMENT:	8 twin 127mm (5in) Type 89 guns, 35 triple 25mm (1in) Type 96 guns, 12 28-barrel 127mm (5in) rocket launchers
AIRCRAFT:	139
COMPLEMENT:	2400

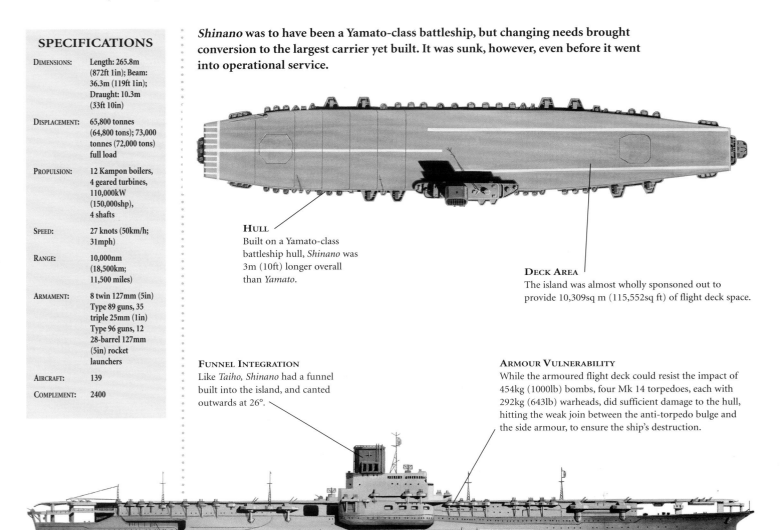

HULL
Built on a Yamato-class battleship hull, *Shinano* was 3m (10ft) longer overall than *Yamato*.

DECK AREA
The island was almost wholly sponsoned out to provide 10,309sq m (115,552sq ft) of flight deck space.

FUNNEL INTEGRATION
Like *Taiho*, *Shinano* had a funnel built into the island, and canted outwards at 26°.

ARMOUR VULNERABILITY
While the armoured flight deck could resist the impact of 454kg (1000lb) bombs, four Mk 14 torpedoes, each with 292kg (643lb) warheads, did sufficient damage to the hull, hitting the weak join between the anti-torpedo bulge and the side armour, to ensure the ship's destruction.

KAMIKAZE CARGO

Shinano was transporting 30 Ohka MXY-7 rocket-powered attack aircraft when it was sunk by submarine attack on 29 November 1944. These were kamikaze craft, essentially human-guided flying bombs, with a 1200kg (2650lb) high-explosive bomb forming the nose of the craft. Normally transported beneath Mitsubishi G4M2e 'Betty' bombers, they would be released and would then glide towards the target vessel. The pilot would then fire the solid-fuel rocket motors, attaining a diving speed of up to 1000km/h (600mph) on the final approach, and crash-dive his plane on to the target.

HULL TYPE
Shinano was built on the same hull type as its 'twin', the super-battleship *Yamato*, seen here on sea trials on 20 October 1941. *Yamato* was sunk on 7 April 1945.

USS *Midway* (1945)

SPECIFICATIONS

DIMENSIONS:	Length: 295m (968ft); Beam: 34.4m (113ft); Draught: 10.7m (35ft)
DISPLACEMENT:	45,720 tonnes (45,000 tons); 60,960 tonnes (60,000 tons) full load
PROPULSION:	12 boilers, 4 turbines, 158,000kW (212,000shp), 4 shafts
SPEED:	33 knots (61km/h; 38mph)
RANGE:	12,000nm (22,200km; 13,800 miles)
AIRCRAFT:	145
ARMAMENT:	18 127mm (5in) 54-cal Mk 16 guns, 84 Bofors 40mm (1.57in) guns, 68 Oerlikon 20mm (0.79in) AA cannon
COMPLEMENT:	3443

A wartime design but not commissioned until after the conflict had ended, *Midway* was the first of a new generation of USN carriers, and underwent major changes through a working life of almost half a century.

Below: Until 1955, the USS *Midway* was the largest ship in the world – so large that it was unable to pass through the Panama Canal.

SIZE
Midway was the largest warship in the world until 1955. An overall width of 31.45m (136ft) prevented it from using the Panama Canal. Atlantic–Pacific transits had to be made via Cape Horn.

FLIGHT DECK
A Midway-class armoured flight deck was not part of the hull structure, as in British Navy carriers, but part of the ship's superstructure, mounted above the hull. Subsequent US classes followed the British format.

LENGTH
The flight deck's length was 304m (997ft 5in).

FUEL CAPACITY
Ship and aviation fuel storage capacity was 13.26 million litres (3.5 million gals).

HULL
The hull was subdivided into 2000 compartments, with 18 deck levels.

WORK IN PROGRESS
Midway has been described as the most-altered of any aircraft carrier to cope with the increasing requirements of heavy jet planes. Deck reinforcement, new steam catapults, new arresting gear, jet blast deflectors and strengthened elevators were all needed. The two major refits transformed the ship's appearance, first with the angled flight deck and then with deck enlargement. Most of its guns were gone by 1963, and by 1990 it was armed with two eight-cell Sea Sparrow missile launchers and two Phalanx CIWS. Final loaded displacement was around 71,120 tonnes (70,000 tons).

OPERATION *FROSTBITE*
Midway among scattered ice floes in Operation *Frostbite*, an Arctic cruise in March 1946. On deck are SB2C Helldivers and F4U-4 Corsairs.

HMS *Eagle* (1951)

SPECIFICATIONS

DIMENSIONS:	Length: 247.4m (811ft 10in); Beam: 34.4m (112ft 9in); Draught: 10.13m (33ft 3in)
DISPLACEMENT:	37,400 tonnes (36,800 tons); 47,000 tonnes (46,000 tons) full load
PROPULSION:	8 boilers, 4 geared turbines, 4 shafts, 113,000kW (152,000shp)
SPEED:	31 knots (57km/h; 36mph)
RANGE:	7000nm (13,000km; 8050 miles) at 18 knots (33.3km/h; 20.7mph)
ARMAMENT:	16 114mm (4.5in) guns, 61 40mm (1.57in) AA guns
AIRCRAFT:	60
COMPLEMENT:	2500

The Royal Navy's largest carrier at the time, *Eagle* played a major role in British and NATO naval operations until the decision to drop fleet carriers was taken in the late 1960s.

Below: HMS *Eagle* before acquiring an angled flight deck.

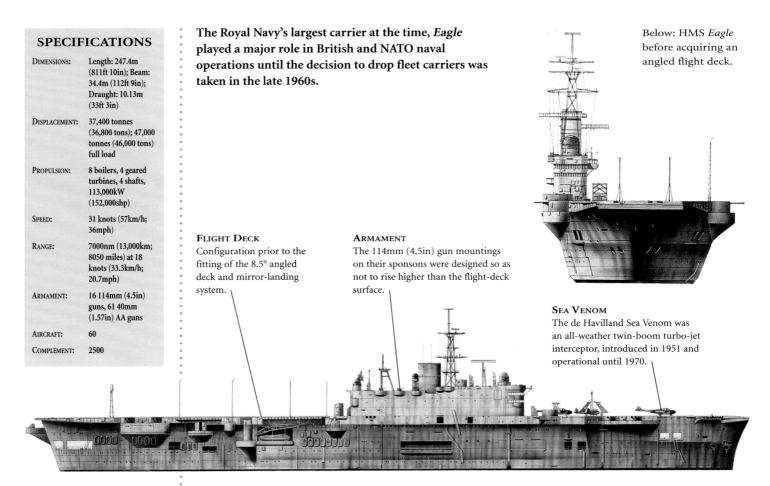

FLIGHT DECK
Configuration prior to the fitting of the 8.5° angled deck and mirror-landing system.

ARMAMENT
The 114mm (4.5in) gun mountings on their sponsons were designed so as not to rise higher than the flight-deck surface.

SEA VENOM
The de Havilland Sea Venom was an all-weather twin-boom turbo-jet interceptor, introduced in 1951 and operational until 1970.

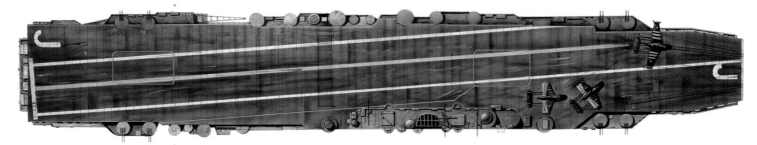

DESIGN DETAILS

In the established Royal Navy design, the hangar was an all-round armoured box structure, beneath a flight deck 25–100mm (1–4in) thick, and with 25mm (1in) sides and deck. Along the waterline, 100mm (4in) armour was fitted. Aircraft capacity (pre-1964) was 60, with two hydraulic catapults mounted at the bow.

OFFICIAL DUTIES
HMS *Eagle* with crew manning the railings to mark a ceremonial visit to Wellington, New Zealand, in August 1971.

USS *Forrestal* (1955)

SPECIFICATIONS

DIMENSIONS:	Length: 326.14m (1070ft); Beam: 39.6m (130ft); Draught: 11.3m (37ft)
DISPLACEMENT:	60,610 tonnes (59,650 tons); 82,402 tonnes (81,101 tons) full load
PROPULSION:	8 B&W boilers, 4 Westinghouse geared turbines, 190,000kW (280,000shp), 4 shafts
SPEED:	33 knots (61km/h; 38mph)
RANGE:	7995nm (14,806km; 9200 miles)
AIRCRAFT:	85
ARMAMENT:	(Original): 8 127mm (5in) 54-cal Mk 42 guns
COMPLEMENT:	5540

Forrestal **introduced the concept of the super-carrier and was the lead ship of its class. These were the last US carriers to be conventionally powered.**

Below: USS *Forrestal* as seen in 1979, by which time it had been reclassified as a 'Multi-purpose Aircraft Carrier'.

RUDDERS
Originally *Forrestal* had three rudders. The centre rudder was found to be unnecessary and was welded as an extension of the keel.

MAST
The mainmast could be folded in order to clear bridges.

RADAR ANTENNAS
In the original design there was no island, although the hull design was the same. Radar antennas were mounted on retractable poles.

CATAPULT LAUNCH
Four jets could be launched in one minute with all catapults in action, although often one or more were under service or repair.

INTERNAL LAYOUT
The five-compartment arrangement of the Permit-class hull was retained in the design of *Sturgeon*: bow compartment with diesel generator; operations compartment with torpedo room beneath; reactor compartment; auxiliary machinery room no. 2 and engine room.

COMBAT MISSIONS

In June 1967, the ship was deployed to Vietnam, but had been engaged in combat missions for only four and a half days when, on 29 July, it suffered the worst accident on a US surface ship since World War II. A Zuni rocket, accidentally fired from a F-4 Phantom, struck an armed and loaded A-4 Skyhawk. The resultant series of explosions and fires broke holes in the flight deck; fire and further explosions rapidly spread through the lower decks. At the time, the ship was on Yankee Station off the Vietnamese coast and launching combat flights. The flight deck fire was put out quickly with the help of sprays from nearby ships, but damage crews fought inside the hull for 24 hours to extinguish the flames. The incident cost the lives of 134 men.

DEPLOYMENT
Forrestal cruising off the Philippines, August 1967, as American involvement in Vietnam increased.

HMS *Hermes*/INS *Viraat* (1959)

In service with the Royal Navy from 1959 to 1984, *Hermes* achieved fame at home as flagship of the British naval force in the Falklands War of 1982. It then had a second career with the Indian Navy until 2016, being decommissioned in 2017.

SPECIFICATIONS

DIMENSIONS:	Length: 225.2m (738ft 10in); Beam: 27.4m (90ft); Draught: 8.5m (27ft 11in)
DISPLACEMENT:	23,000 tonnes (22,638 tons); 28,000 tonnes (27,559 tons) full load
PROPULSION:	4 Admiralty 3-drum boilers, 2 Parsons SR geared turbines, 57,000kW (76,000shp), 2 shafts
SPEED:	28 knots (52km/h; 32mph)
RANGE:	7000nm (13,000km; 8050 miles) at 18 knots (33.3km/h; 20.7mph)
ARMAMENT:	10 40mm (1.57in) Bofors AA guns
AIRCRAFT:	30
COMPLEMENT:	2100

Right: Sea Harrier FRS Mk 1. The Hawker Siddeley (later British Aerospace) single-seater V/STOL multi-role combat plane was in service with the RN Fleet Air Arm between 1981 and 2006.

Below: This profile shows *Hermes* post-1980 with bow ramp and modernized radar systems.

RADAR
Type 965 air search radar replaced the large Type 984 in the 1970s.

HELICOPTERS
Hermes carried Westland Sea King ASW helicopters.

SEA HARRIER
These served with the Fleet Air Arm from 1980 to 2006. Sea Harriers shot down 20 Argentinian aircraft in the Falklands conflict.

ON-BOARD ENTERTAINMENT
Hermes was probably the only carrier to stage a circus performance in the hangar (October 1961). A horse race was run inside it in March 1976.

CONTAMINATION MEASURES
Hermes was the first British carrier to be designed so that internal accommodation, including the boiler and turbine rooms, could be sealed off and controlled remotely in the event of encountering radioactive contamination.

ANTI-SUBMARINE
A further alteration was made in 1976 to make *Hermes* an anti-submarine support ship at a time when NATO and Soviet submarines were shadowing one another in the Atlantic. This was followed by yet another change of role after a refit between 20 March 1980 and 12 May 1981, which gave the ship a 12° ski jump on the port foredeck to enable short take-off Sea Harrier jets to be carried.

WORK-UP TRIALS
Hermes after a two-year refit, doing work-up trials in the Moray Firth, Scotland, in March 1966. During the late 1960s, the carrier worked closely with the Royal Australian Navy (RAN), and was even offered to the RAN.

Clemenceau (1960)

SPECIFICATIONS

DIMENSIONS:	Length: 265m (869ft); Beam: 51.2m (168ft); Draught: 8.6m (28ft)
DISPLACEMENT:	22,710 tonnes (22,352 tons); 32,000 tonnes (31,496 tons) full load
PROPULSION:	6 Indret boilers, 4 turbines, 94,000kW (126,000shp), 2 shafts
SPEED:	32 knots (59km/h; 37mph)
RANGE:	7500nm (13,875km; 8625 miles) at 18 knots (33.3km/h; 20.7mph)
AIRCRAFT:	38
ARMAMENT:	8 100mm (4in) 55-cal Mod 53 guns
COMPLEMENT:	1338

France's first modern aircraft carrier was an important element in President Charles de Gaulle's policy of military independence and boosting national grandeur. Very much a symbol of French power, *Clemenceau* had many operational deployments in European and Pacific waters, mostly in support of French actions and policies, although also as part of international peacekeeping operations.

Above: An F-8E(FN) Crusader fighter jet lands on the flight deck of the *Clemenceau*. The *Clemenceau* carried eight Crusaders. The Crusader was the last American fighter with guns as the primary weapon.

DECK
The landing area on *Clemenceau* was 165m (543ft) by 29.5m (97ft), at 8.5° to the ship's axis.

ANTENNA
Tactical air navigation system antenna.

PROXIMITY RADAR
Proximity radar DRBV-23.

WEAPONS CONTROL RADAR
Weapons control radar DRBC-31.

AIRCRAFT
Clemenceau and *Foch* mainly flew French-built naval aircraft, apart from the Crusaders and guests. In the 1960s, the air wing was six F-8E (FN) fighters, 18 Etendard IVM fighter-bombers and eight Alizé ASW planes. By 1990, the complement was ten F-8E (FN), 16 Super Etendard, three Etendard IVP, seven Alizé planes and two Alouette III helicopters.

NATIONAL PRIDE
Clemenceau at sea. Its sister ship, *Foch*, went on to service in the Brazilian navy as the *São Paulo*.

USS *Enterprise* (CVN-65) (1961)

SPECIFICATIONS

DIMENSIONS:	Length: 342.3m (1123ft); Beam: 40.5m (132ft 9in); Draught: 12m (39ft)
DISPLACEMENT:	84,626 tonnes (76,515 tons)
PROPULSION:	8 Westinghouse A2W reactors, 4 steam turbines, 208,600kW (280,000shp), 4 shafts
SPEED:	33.6 knots (62.2km/h; 38.7mph)
RANGE:	Unlimited
AIRCRAFT:	2 Sea Sparrow launchers, 2 RIM-116 RAM launchers, 2 20mm (0.79in) Phalanx CIWS
AIRCRAFT:	90
COMPLEMENT:	5828

The world's first nuclear-powered carrier, this became the US Navy's third-longest serving surface ship, commissioned from 1961 to 2012, and making a total of 24 active deployments.

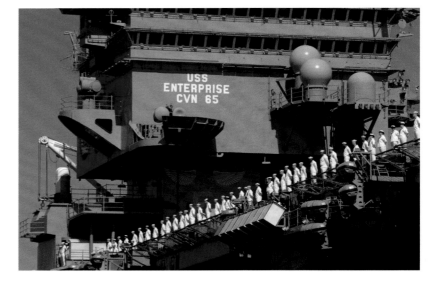

Right: Crewmen man the railings as *Enterprise* leaves Naval Station Norfolk on a scheduled deployment on 2 May 2006.

FLOODLIGHTS
Floodlights were mounted on the mast in the 1960s to aid in night raids during the Vietnam War.

BRIDLE-CATCHER RAMPS
Enterprise was the last USN operational carrier to have bridle-catcher ramps at the catapult ends, which extended over the bow.

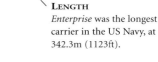

PROPELLER
Four five-blade propellers each weighed 35 tonnes (34 tons).

LENGTH
Enterprise was the longest carrier in the US Navy, at 342.3m (1123ft).

PERSIAN GULF

After the 11 September 2001 attacks on New York and Washington, *Enterprise*, then in the Persian Gulf area, joined in missile and bombing raids on Al-Qaeda and Taliban targets in Afghanistan before returning to Norfolk. The next combat mission was in support of the invasion of Iraq, September 2003–February 2004, providing continuous air cover for the ground troops and carrying out bombing and missile strikes.

KEEPING STATION
Guided missile frigate USS *Taylor*, fast combat support ship USNS *Supply*, and USS *Enterprise* keep station as the supply ship replenishes the carrier's avgas tanks, 2006.

HMS *Fearless* (1965)

SPECIFICATIONS

DIMENSIONS:	Length: 160m (520ft); Beam: 24m (80ft); Draught: 6.4m (21ft)
DISPLACEMENT:	12,802 tonnes (12,600 tons); 15,138 tonnes (14,900 tons) full load
PROPULSION:	2 B&W Y24A boilers, 2 EE turbines, 2 shafts, 8203kW (11,000shp)
SPEED:	21 knots (39km/h; 24mph)
RANGE:	10,000nm (18,500km; 11,500 miles)
AIRCRAFT:	5
ARMAMENT:	2 BMARC GAM B01 20mm (0.79in) single mounts, 2 20mm (0.79in) Vulcan Phalanx CIWS
COMPLEMENT:	580

Designed as a highly specialized assault ship capable of operating landing craft and helicopters in any part of the world, *Fearless* played a central part in amphibious operations during the Falklands War (1982), and later served as a training ship.

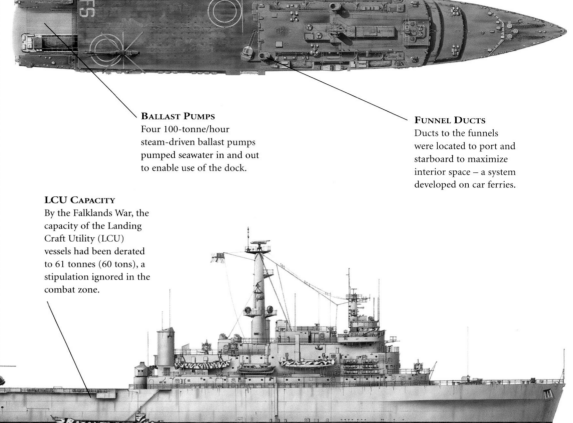

BALLAST PUMPS
Four 100-tonne/hour steam-driven ballast pumps pumped seawater in and out to enable use of the dock.

FUNNEL DUCTS
Ducts to the funnels were located to port and starboard to maximize interior space – a system developed on car ferries.

LCU CAPACITY
By the Falklands War, the capacity of the Landing Craft Utility (LCU) vessels had been derated to 61 tonnes (60 tons), a stipulation ignored in the combat zone.

CRANE
The mobile gantry crane from Houlder and SCX Special Projects could lift 4.5 tonnes (4.5 tons).

HELICOPTERS
Fearless had no permanently assigned aircraft, but could operate up to four Sea King HC4 assault or multi-role helicopters from two take-off positions on the flight deck. With smaller helicopters such as Gazelles, and allowing for folding rotor blades, six aircraft could be transported. The flight deck, above the dock, was 51 × 23m (165 × 75ft) and could take helicopters up to the size of the RAF Chinook or the US Marine Corps CH53E. The utility Sea King or Wessex could carry an underslung load of up to 2267kg (5000lb). No hangar was provided.

JOINT EXERCISE
Fearless off the coast of North Carolina on 9 May 1996, during a NATO Combined Joint Training Field Exercise. It was in the 1960s that the concept of the multi-role assault ship grew up alongside that of the aircraft carrier, with an eye on tactical deployment.

Moskva (1967)

SPECIFICATIONS

DIMENSIONS:	Length: 196.6m (645ft); Beam: 35m (115ft); Draught: 7.6m (25ft)
DISPLACEMENT:	14,800 tonnes (14,567 tons)
PROPULSION:	2 shaft steam turbines, 4 pressure fire boilers, 75,000kW (100,000shp)
SPEED:	31 knots (57km/h; 35.4mph)
RANGE:	14,000nm (25,928km; 16,110 miles) at 12 knots (22km/h; 14mph)
AIRCRAFT:	18 helicopters
ARMAMENT:	1 twin SUW-N-1 launcher, 2 twin SA-N-3 missile launchers
COMPLEMENT:	850, including air wing

Moskva was the first helicopter carrier built for the Russian Navy, completed in 1967 to counteract the threat from the US nuclear-powered missile submarines that began to enter service in 1960. A central block dominated the vessel and housed the major weapons systems.

Right: The Krasina-class vessels were other Soviet anti-submarine ships of the 1960s and 1970s; note the batteries of SS-N-12 SSN missiles on the deck.

FLIGHT DECK
The flight deck measures 86m (282ft) by 34m (111ft 6in) and has four mesh-covered landing areas; a fifth landing area is located in the centre of the ship.

RADAR MAST ASSEMBLY
Moskva had an extensive radar and surveillance suite aboard, including the Top Sail (air warning) system and the 'Head Net A' 2D air surveillance and surface search radar.

AIR DEFENCE
Primary air defence came from eight twin SA-N-3 'Goblet' SAM launchers with 48 missiles.

HELICOPTERS
The vessel carried a total of 18 Kamov Ka-25 'Hormone-A' anti-submarine helicopters.

STRATEGIC PURPOSE
The cruiser *Moskva* and its sister ship *Leningrad* were designed primarily to hunt and destroy NATO strategic missile submarines in the North Sea, North Atlantic, Baltic and Indian Ocean. They would also act as command vessels for larger anti-submarine hunter-killer groups. In reality, however, their systems were soon outdated; both ships were decommissioned in the 1990s.

AIRCRAFT HANGAR
This stern perspective of the *Moskva* provides a view directly into the ship's hangar space, which was wide enough to store two helicopters side by side along its 15m (49ft) length.

USS *Nimitz* (1975)

TYPE • *Aircraft Carriers* • FAMILY • *Warships*

SPECIFICATIONS

DIMENSIONS:	Length: 317m (1040ft); Beam: 40.8m (134ft); Draught: 11.3m (37ft)
DISPLACEMENT:	110,250 tonnes (100,020 tons)
PROPULSION:	2 Westinghouse A4W reactors, 4 steam turbines, 4 shafts
SPEED:	31.5 knots (58.3km/h; 36.2mph)
RANGE:	Unlimited
ARMAMENT:	2 Sea Sparrow, 2 RIM-116 missile launchers; 2 Phalanx CIWS; 2 .50-cal machine gun mountings
AIRCRAFT:	90
COMPLEMENT:	5680

This was the lead ship of a class of ten nuclear-powered super-carriers, considered to be the 'centrepiece' of US naval strength, both in deterrence and attack.

Below: Described as 'floating airfields' or 'movable pieces of sovereign territory', the Nimitz-class's great extent is displayed in the plan view of the class leader.

Below: The bow-on view displays the remarkable breadth of the Nimitz-class flight deck compared to the beam of the hull.

DECK SIZE
Overall deck length is 332.8m (1092ft), and width is 76.7m (251ft 10in). It is covered with an anti-slip coating.

DEFLECTOR
Jet blast deflector.

HULL PROTECTION
With such a vast hull, anti-corrosion measures are vital. The US Navy Research Laboratory has done much work on the design and protection of CVN hulls, using Impressed Current Cathode Protection rather than zinc sacrificial anodes, to keep the problem to a minimum.

ANTI-AIRCRAFT MISSILES
Sea Sparrow launcher.

CLOSE-IN WEAPON SYSTEM
Phalanx CIWS.

COMBAT SORTIES

In March 2003, *Nimitz* supported the US–British invasion of Iraq in Operation *Iraqi Freedom* as flagship of a Carrier Battle Group that comprised Carrier Air Wing 2, with USS *Constellation* (CV-64), the cruisers *Valley Forge* and *Bunker Hill*, destroyers *Higgins* and *Milius*, frigate *Thach*, fast combat support ship *Rainier* and nuclear submarine *Columbia*. *Nimitz* launched more than 6500 sorties against targets in Iraq during this six-month mission, in which it launched the F/A-18F Super Hornet and E-2C Hawkeye 2000 aircraft on their first combat flights.

HELICOPTER LIFT-OFF
A CH-46 Sea Knight of Helicopter Combat Support Squadron Six lifts off from *Nimitz*'s flight deck as the carrier returns from a deployment on Operation *Southern Watch* in the Persian Gulf in 1993.

Kiev (1975)

SPECIFICATIONS

DIMENSIONS:	Length: 273.1m (896ft); Beam: 31m (102ft); Draught: 8.95m (29ft 5in)
DISPLACEMENT:	31,018 tonnes (30,530 tons); 42,032 tonnes (41,370 tons) full load
PROPULSION:	4 geared steam turbines, 4 shafts, 100,000kW (140,000shp)
SPEED:	32 knots (59km/h; 37mph)
RANGE:	13,500nm (25,000km; 15,500 miles) at 18 knots (33.3km/h; 20.7mph)
AIRCRAFT:	32
ARMAMENT:	2 12-barrel RBU-6000 ASW launchers, 1 twin SUW-N-1 launcher for FRAS 1 missiles; 2 twin SA-N-3 and 2 twin SA-N-4 SAM launchers, with 122 missiles; 4 twin SS-N-12 SSM launchers with 16 reloads; 2 twin 76mm (3in) cannon, 8 ADMG 630 30mm (1.18in) six-barrel Gatling CIWS; 10 533mm (21in) torpedo tubes
COMPLEMENT:	2042

Described as a 'heavy aviation cruiser', *Kiev* was the Soviet Navy's answer to the requirement of multi-role warships in the 1970s, and was Russia's first carrier for fixed-wing aircraft.

Above: Starboard side view of *Kiev*.

ANTENNA
The spherical cover holds a High Pole IFF antenna.

HEAT-RESISTANT TILES
Special tiles were fitted on the flight deck to absorb the heat of the Yak-38 Forger's vertical lift jet engines.

ANTI-SUBMARINE MEASURES
Two RBU-6000 ASW rocket launchers and an SUW-N-1 ASW missile launcher are positioned on the foredeck, forward of the 76mm (3in) dual-purpose gun.

SONAR
LF hull-mounted sonars were fitted.

DEPLOYMENTS

Kiev and its sister ships were widely deployed; these were the first ships capable of giving air fighter cover to Soviet naval craft, with two assigned to the Northern and two to the Pacific fleet. Kiev's designation as a 'cruiser with aircraft' enabled it to pass through the Bosphorus (forbidden to carriers of any nation) despite protests, and conduct trials in the Mediterranean before making for its home port at Severomorsk.

AERIAL VIEW
A magnified aerial image gives a close-up view of *Kiev*'s substantial armament. The vessel was sold to China as a museum ship in 1996.

USS *Tarawa* (1976)

SPECIFICATIONS

DIMENSIONS:	Length: 250m (820ft); Beam: 32m (106ft); Draught: 7.9m (26ft)
DISPLACEMENT:	40,030 tonnes (39,400 tons); 40,673 tonnes (40,032 tons) full load
PROPULSION:	2 boilers, 2 geared steam turbines, 2 shafts, 57,419kW (77,000shp)
SPEED:	24 knots (44.4km/h; 27.6mph)
RANGE:	10,000nm (19,000km; 12,000 miles) at 20 knots (37km/h; 23mph)
ARMAMENT:	2 8-cell Mk 25 Sea Sparrow BPDMS launchers, Mk 49 RAM missile system, 2 Vulcan Phalanx CIWS mountings, 6 25mm (1in) automatic cannon
AIRCRAFT:	43
COMPLEMENT:	960

This ship and the others in its class were built in order to transport, land and support US Marine troops on any coastline in the world, as the core of an Amphibious Readiness Group.

Right: *Tarawa* carried up to eight AV-8B Harrier II V/STOL planes, in addition to helicopters, on missions to the Persian Gulf and other world trouble spots. The sea-stained hull sides suggest a long deployment is close to ending.

BOILERS
The two boilers were the largest yet made for the US Navy, but the ship earned a Gold Award for energy conservation in 2007.

LOW-SPEED MANOEUVRES
A 671kW (900hp) bow thruster enabled lateral movement at low speeds.

CRANE
The crane was used to hoist LCMs on to the deck.

MEDICAL FACILITIES
A 300-bed hospital was installed, with four operating rooms and three dental surgery rooms.

BALLAST PUMPS
Ballast pumps can fill and empty the tanks with 12,192 tonnes (12,000 tons) of sea water when lowering and raising the dock.

FUNCTIONALITY
Bunk accommodation had to be provided for 1703 Marines, their vehicles and stores. Most of the interior of the hull was a vast multi-level warehouse, with the elevators set on the centreline, and a system of conveyor belts and monorails to transport items in palletized loads for easy stacking and storing. Inclined ramps allowed vehicles to access the well deck for loading onto landing craft, or the flight deck for helicopter lifting.

HARRIER TAKE-OFF
During a Persian Gulf deployment, an AV-8B Harrier II of Marine Medium Helicopter Squadron 166 (Reinforced) takes off from *Tarawa*.

HMS *Invincible* (1980)

The development of the VSTOL jet fighter transformed this ship from a helicopter carrier to a much more potent and capable warship, underlined by its role in the Falklands War.

SPECIFICATIONS

DIMENSIONS:	Length: 210m (689ft); Beam: 36m (118ft); Draught: 8.5m (29ft)
DISPLACEMENT:	16,256 tonnes (16,000 tons); 22,352 tonnes (22,000 tons) full load
PROPULSION:	4 R-R Olympus gas turbines, 4 shafts, 84,500kW (112,000shp)
SPEED:	28 knots (52km/h; 32mph)
RANGE:	7000nm (13,000km; 8050 miles) at 18 knots (33km/h; 20mph)
AIRCRAFT:	22
ARMAMENT:	2 GAM-B01 20mm (0.79in) guns; 3 Goalkeeper CIWS
COMPLEMENT:	1051

RUNWAY
Planes had 170m (518ft) of runway length for take-off.

FIRE CONTROL
Type 909 Mod 1.

RADAR
Type 996 surface search radar.

DECK LAYOUT
There were seven deck levels within the hull.

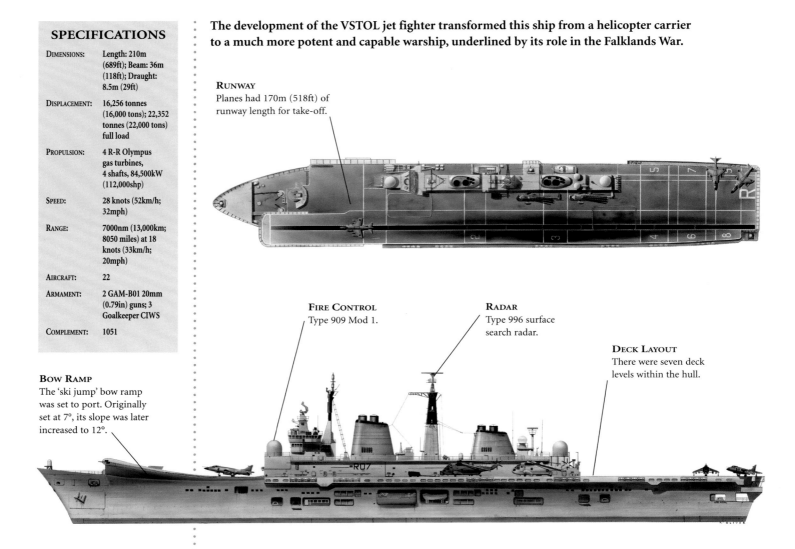

BOW RAMP
The 'ski jump' bow ramp was set to port. Originally set at 7°, its slope was later increased to 12°.

AIRCRAFT MISSION
The air group carried varied according to mission. Up to 24 aircraft could be carried after modification, including nine Harrier GR7 or GR9 planes. Sea King ASaC Mk7 early warning reconnaissance, Merlin HM.1 ASW and Sea King and Chinook general-purpose helicopters were also carried. *Invincible* was understood to have storage facilities for nuclear weapons.

'SKI-JUMP' TAKE-OFF
A Sea Harrier launches from the deck ramp of HMS *Invincible*.

Admiral Kuznetsov (1995)

SPECIFICATIONS

DIMENSIONS:	Length: 305m (1001ft); Beam: 72m (236ft); Draught: 11m (36ft)
DISPLACEMENT:	53,848 tonnes (53,000 tons); 59,537 tonnes (58,600 tons) full load
PROPULSION:	8 boilers, 4 turbines, 4 shafts, 149,000kW (200,000shp)
SPEED:	29 knots (54km/h; 33mph)
RANGE:	8000nm (14,800km; 9200 miles)
ARMAMENT:	12-launcher Granit anti-ship SS-N-19 missiles; 24 vertically mounted Klinok launchers; Kashtan multi-functional CIWS; 6 AK630 AD 30mm (1.18in) AA guns
AIRCRAFT:	50
COMPLEMENT:	2100

The flagship of Russia's fleet, the ship's original purpose was to provide support for submarines against air attack, but it is now also used on power-projection missions.

Right: The Sukhoi Su-33 is a naval version of the land-based Su-27: a single-seat multi-role aircraft. It has been in service since 1994. Its home base is with the 279th Shipborne Fighter Aviation Regiment (KIAP) at Severomorsk.

ARRESTING GEAR
Kuznetsov is known to have experienced problems with its arresting gear while engaged in air strikes against Syrian targets in late 2016.

RADAR
Radars include D/E band air and surface target acquisition radar, F-band surface search, G/H band flight control, I-band navigation, and four K-band fire-control radars for the Kashtan air defence system.

FLIGHT DECK
The flight deck area is 14,700sq m (158,229sq ft); two aircraft lifts are fitted on the starboard side.

TARGET ENGAGEMENT
The Klinok defence system can fire a missile every three seconds and engage four targets simultaneously, with a range of almost 15km (10 miles).

BOW RAMP
Kuznetsov's lack of a catapult launcher restricts the payload of aircraft, which have to take off from the bow ramp.

SHORT TAKE-OFF AND VERTICAL LANDING

The first aircraft carried were Sukhoi Su-27K, MiG 29K and Yakovlev Yak-41M. Later these were replaced by Yak-43 and Su-33. The Sukhoi Su-33 naval aircraft (Flanker-D in NATO code) has short, broad wings and a reinforced undercarriage specifically for STOVL launches and landing. It carries a 30mm (1.18in) cannon and six R-27 and 4 R-73 air-to-air missiles, plus other bombs and rockets according to mission. Helicopters may include Ka-31 airborne early warning craft, Ka-27-Ld Helix, Ka-27 PLO and Ka-27-S. The Ka-27 ASW helicopters are equipped with surface search radar, dipping sonar, sonobuoys and magnetic anomaly detectors.

MEDITERRANEAN CRUISE

A port beam view of *Admiral Kuznetsov* in the Mediterranean south of Italy, making its way back to the Northern Fleet base at Severomorsk.

HMS *Ocean* (1998)

SPECIFICATIONS

DIMENSIONS:	Length: 203.4m (667ft); Beam: 35m (115ft); Draught: 6.5m (21ft)
DISPLACEMENT:	21,500 tonnes (21,200 tons)
PROPULSION:	2 Crossley Pielstick 16 PC2.6 V 200 diesels, 2 shafts, 17,557kW (23,904bhp)
SPEED:	18 knots (33.3km/h; 20.7mph)
RANGE:	7000nm (13,000km; 8000 miles)
AIRCRAFT:	18
ARMAMENT:	3 Vulcan Phalanx Mk 15 CIWS and 8 Oerlikon/BMARC GAM-BO3 20mm (0.79in) guns in 4 twin mountings
COMPLEMENT:	365

The Royal Navy's only Landing Platform Helicopter is equipped for giving air support to littoral operations and for ASW warfare.

Below: High blank sides and a reduction of extraneous detail mark modern warship design in an era in which 'stealth' is at a premium and protection against radiation has to be allowed for.

By 1998, HMS *Ocean* was a third-generation Royal Navy approach to the design and operation of a multi-role amphibious warfare command ship.

LANDING CRAFT VEHICLE PERSONNEL
The LCVPs are mounted on box-section davit arms 6m (18ft 4in) long, each weighing 4 tonnes (3.9 tons), with twin pivot points, operating on a winch and reeved rope system that must be kept permanently ready for use.

HULL DESIGN
This shows the 'car ferry' construction style, which has an estimated service life of 20 years.

LCVP DIMENSIONS
Ocean's four LCUP Mk 5 are 15.7m (51ft 6in) long and weigh 24 tonnes (23.6 tons) fully loaded. They can travel 210nm (389km; 241 miles) at a maximum speed of 25 knots (46.2km/h; 28.7mph).

HELICOPTER CARRIER
The flight deck, 170 × 33m (557 × 108ft) has six landing and six parking spots. *Ocean* has carried Sea King HC4/Merlin troop lift and Lynx or WAH-64 Apache attack helicopters. It has also flown Agusta Westland AW 159 Wildcats, Boeing Chinooks and Blackhawks. The ship has now been sold to the Brazilian Navy.

PILOT TRAINING
Pilot training in the course of an Arabian Gulf deployment in December 2012. A UH-60 Black Hawk from the 111th Aviation Regiment gets landing guidance from a Leading Aircraftman.

Charles de Gaulle (2001)

SPECIFICATIONS

DIMENSIONS:	Length: 261.5m (858ft); Beam: 64.3m (211ft 3in); Draught: 9.4m (30ft 11in)
DISPLACEMENT:	37,085 tonnes (33,530 tons); 42,500 tonnes (41,830 tons) full load
PROPULSION:	2 K15 reactors, 2 Alstom steam turbines, 2 shafts, 61,000kW (83,000shp)
SPEED:	27 knots (50km/h; 31mph)
RANGE:	Unlimited
ARMAMENT:	2 8-cell Sylver launchers for MBDA Aster 15 SAMs, 2 6-cell Sadral launchers for Mistral missiles and 8 Giat 20F2 20mm (0.79in) cannon
AIRCRAFT:	40
COMPLEMENT:	1950

Flagship of the Marine Nationale, *Charles de Gaulle* is the only non-American nuclear-powered aircraft carrier and the only nuclear-powered surface ship in a European navy.

Below: *Charles de Gaulle* in outline. Compared to American carriers, the island is set relatively far forward.

ISLAND
The island design shows concern to maximize stealth characteristics. Even in such a large ship this might help to conceal its identity.

PRESSURE VENTS
Although no funnel is needed, the island incorporates steam safety-valve vents to release excessive pressure in the turbine and catapult systems.

FINS
The SATRAP (système automatique de tranquillisation et de pilotage) system for launching planes in high wind and sea conditions combines lateral stabilization with two sets of retractable fins with the movement of 12 22-tonne (21.6-ton) rolling weights mounted on rails below the flight deck, whose movement can compensate for weight adjustment of take-offs.

NUCLEAR POWER
A conventionally powered carrier needs to refuel every three or four days, and its activity on deployment is constrained by the availability and speed of a support tanker, whereas *Charles de Gaulle* runs for 7.5 years between refuellings and can carry oil to supply three escorts for ten days as well as 3400 tonnes (3346 tons) of aviation fuel. Sufficient provisions are carried for 45 days at sea.

REFIT
Charles de Gaulle moored at the naval base, Toulon, while undergoing a technical refit in December 2012. In 2015 and 2016, the carrier conducted anti-ISIS operations in the Persian Gulf and Mediterranean.

USS *Ronald R. Reagan* (2003)

SPECIFICATIONS

DIMENSIONS:	Length: 332.8m (1092ft); Beam: 40.8m (134ft); Draught: 11.3m (37ft)
DISPLACEMENT:	113,600 tonnes (101,400 tons)
PROPULSION:	A4W nuclear reactors, 4 steam turbines, 4 shafts, 194,000kW (260,000shp)
SPEED:	30 knots (56km/h; 35mph)
RANGE:	Unlimited
AIRCRAFT:	90
ARMAMENT:	2 RIM-162 Evolved Sea Sparrow 8-cell MK 29 SAM medium range launchers, 2 RIM-116 21-cell RAM short range missile surface-to-air launchers, CIWS
COMPLEMENT:	5680

Flagship of the world's largest navy, this huge carrier displays a number of alterations and additions to the earlier ships of the Nimitz class. The convention of naming super-carriers after US presidents began with *John F. Kennedy* (CV-67) in 1968. It has been criticized by some, especially for selecting recent incumbents. When Congress laid down rules for the naming of warships in 1862, aircraft carriers were scarcely dreamt of.

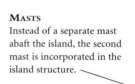

MASTS
Instead of a separate mast abaft the island, the second mast is incorporated in the island structure.

BOW BUBBLES
Just under the flight deck at the bow is the control station for the power, tension and launching of each of the forward catapults.

DECK DIMENSIONS
The full width of the flight deck is 76.8m (252ft).

BOW
A new form of bulbous bow was fitted to this ship, adding 122 tonnes (120 tons) to bow weight compared to its class-fellows' 611 tonnes (601 tons), improving forward buoyancy and smoothing the vessel's passage through water to the benefit of stability.

STRIKE GROUP MAKE-UP
A Carrier Strike Group is currently formed with a Nimitz-class carrier at the centre. A nuclear submarine of the Los Angeles or Virginia classes is also part of the group. Typically it might include two guided missile cruisers of the Ticonderoga class, with two destroyers of the Arleigh Burke or Spruance classes, armed primarily with anti-air missiles, and two frigates of the Oliver Hazard Perry class, armed primarily for anti-submarine warfare, flanking the group.

STRIKE GROUP
USS *Enterprise* (CVN-65) leads its strike group in the Atlantic Ocean on 7 May 2006. Other ships are guided missile frigate USS *Nicholas*, guided missile cruiser USS *Leyte Gulf*, guided missile destroyer USS *McFaul*, and fast combat support ship *Supply*. The group has a 'surge deployment' addition in the guided missile destroyer *James E. Williams*.

Liaoning (2012)

SPECIFICATIONS

DIMENSIONS:	Length: 304.5m (1000ft); Beam: 73.15m (240ft); Draught: 10.97m (36ft)
DISPLACEMENT:	Approx 53,050 tonnes (52,215 tons); 59,100 tonnes (58,169 tons) full load
PROPULSION:	Gas turbine, unconfirmed, 4 shafts
SPEED:	Not known
RANGE:	Not known
ARMAMENT:	3 Type 1130 SAM; 2 H/PJ11 CIWS
AIRCRAFT:	40 fixed wing and rotary aircraft
COMPLEMENT:	2586

Originally an aircraft-carrying cruiser of the Soviet Navy, this ship was transformed into China's first carrier and the prototype for a new class of carriers. The ship follows the *Kuznetsov* form, with a 12° 'ski-jump' bow ramp to assist take-off, and arrester wires for landing, but no catapult, putting it in the STOBAR (Short Take-Off But Arrested Recovery) category.

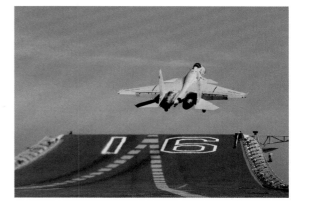

Right: A Chinese Navy J-15 fighter takes off from *Liaoning* during training exercises in the South China Sea, 2 January 2017.

RADAR
Liaoning mounts active phased array radar capable of tracking air and surface targets to 150km (93 miles), along with Sea Eagle radar capable of a 250-km (155-mile) surface search.

NON-SLIP GRIP
A zinc chromate non-slip surface covers the flight deck.

LANDING SYSTEM
Improved Fresnel Lens Optical Landing System.

AIR DEFENCE SYSTEM
The FL 3000N CIWS is similar to the Raytheon RIM-116 Rolling Airframe Missile. Its fire-and-forget design locks on to the target immediately after launch and it travels at a speed of Mach 2.5.

AIR WING

Liaoning's air wing consists of 24 Shenyang J-15 multi-role fighters, which are Chinese-built and modified versions of Russia's Sukhoi-33. On 23 November 2012, J-15 fighters first landed on the ship. A range of helicopters has also been observed on *Liaoning*, including Changhe Z-18 transport, Z-18J AEW, Z-18F ASW and Harbin Z-9D SAR helicopters, also Kamov Ka-31 Helix AEW helicopters.

COMMISSIONING

Liaoning at Dalian shipyard in its home province, on 25 September 2012, the day it was commissioned into the People's Liberation Army Navy, confirming China's big step towards air superiority in the southwest Pacific region.

HMAS *Canberra* (2014)

SPECIFICATIONS

DIMENSIONS:	Length: 230.8m (757ft 4in); Beam: 32m (105ft); Draught: 7m (23ft 2in)
DISPLACEMENT:	27,940 tonnes (27,500 tons); 27,534 tonnes (27,100 tons) full load
PROPULSION:	1 GE LM2500 gas turbine; 2 MAN 16V32/40 diesel generators, 2 Siemens azimuth thrusters, 22,000kW (29,502hp)
SPEED:	19 knots (35km/h; 22mph)
RANGE:	9000nm (17,000km; 10,000 miles)
ARMAMENT:	4 x Rafael Typhoon 25mm remote weapons systems; 6 × 12.7mm (0.5in) machine guns
AIRCRAFT:	18 helicopters
COMPLEMENT:	358

Australia's largest warship is a state-of-the-art amphibious warfare vessel, capable of playing a variety of roles, particularly enhancing the Australian Navy's off-shore capabilities.

Right: *Canberra* moored at Fleet Base East, Sydney Harbour, in June 2015.

MAST HEIGHT
At 46.8m (142ft 7in) above the waterline, *Canberra*'s mast would have just 40cm (15.7in) clearance when passing under Sydney Harbour Bridge.

LANDING CRAFT
The four LCM 1E landing craft have an endurance of 190nm (389km; 242 miles). They can 'comfortably' hold 120 personnel with full combat load, but this can be stretched to 170.

DECK LAYOUT
There are three main decks below the flight deck: the hangar deck with storage also for light vehicles and cargo; the main accommodation deck; and the well dock, 69.3 by 16.8m (211ft 3in by 51ft) that occupies the stern part of the ship, with heavy vehicle accommodation forward of it. The dock normally holds four LCM 1E landing craft, but is fitted for other types, including US and British variants, both conventionally engined craft and air-cushion LCAC vessels. The lower deck can hold armoured vehicles of up to 65 tonnes (64 tons), which allows for the 60-tonne (59-ton) Abrams battle tank.

TWIN DECKS
There are two decks for heavy and light vehicle storage.

PROPELLER
Thruster propellers are 4.5m (15ft) in diameter.

HMAS *ADELAIDE*
A close-up view of HMAS *Adelaide*'s bow section contrasts the sculptured appearance of the ship's bow with the straight-sided boxy hull: in effect a floating dock plus garage. *Adelaide* is the second of the Canberra-class vessels.

Izumo class (2015)

SPECIFICATIONS

DIMENSIONS:	Length: 248m (814ft); Beam: 38m (125ft); Draught: 7.5m (25ft)
DISPLACEMENT:	19,800 tonnes (19,500 tons); 27,432 tonnes (27,000 tons) full load
PROPULSION:	COGAG system, 4 LM2500IEC gas turbines, 2 shafts
SPEED:	30 knots (55.5km/h; 34.5mph)
RANGE:	Undisclosed
ARMAMENT:	2 Phalanx CIWS; 2 SeaRAM missile launchers
AIRCRAFT:	28
COMPLEMENT:	470

Classed as 'helicopter destroyers' to avoid contravention of Japan's constitution, the two ships of the Izumo class are fast and powerful multi-role warships. The Izumo class are the largest vessels yet built for the Japanese Maritime Self-Defence Force (JMSDF).

Above: *Izumo* at sea. Unlike US ships, the Japanese carriers are rarely depicted with aircraft parked on the flight deck.

EDGE ELEVATOR
The deck edge elevator is 14 × 15m (42ft 6in × 45ft 9in); the forward one is 20 × 13m (61ft × 39ft 7in).

CLOSE-IN WEAPON SYSTEM
Mk 15 20mm (0.79in) CIWS.

MISSILES
Sea RAM missile launcher.

BOW
Novel tapered square-end bow design with a single anchor.

SONAR
QQQ-23 bow-mounted sonar.

ASW FUNCTION
The steady build-up of China's submarine strength has kept the JMSDF's submarine detection skills both challenged and well-honed. ASW is the prime function of the Izumo class, although HADR relief operation is also emphasized. Defensive armament comprises two 20mm (0.79in) Phalanx CIWS mountings and two Mk 31 RIM-116 Sea-RAM missile launchers. The forward CIWS is set on the starboard side of the flight deck; all other weapons are mounted on sponsons or on the island.

AIRCRAFT CAPACITY
Stern view of *Izumo*. Japan's helicopter destroyers can accommodate large aircraft like the MV-22 Osprey of the US Marine Corps.

HMS *Queen Elizabeth* (2017)

SPECIFICATIONS

DIMENSIONS:	Length: 284m (932ft); Beam: 72.97m (239ft 5in); Draught: 10.97m (36ft)
DISPLACEMENT:	71,730 tonnes (70,600 tons)
PROPULSION:	2 RR Marine Trent MT30 gas turbines, 2 shafts, 71,520kW (96,000shp)
SPEED:	27 knots (50km/h; 31mph)
RANGE:	10,000nm (18,500km; 11,500 miles)
AIRCRAFT:	40
ARMAMENT:	3 Phalanx CIWS
COMPLEMENT:	1450

The two ships of the Queen Elizabeth class will be the largest carriers and largest warships built for the Royal Navy. Both ships are STOVL type carriers, intended to embark the Lockheed-Martin F-35C multi-role jet, itself still in development as the carriers near completion.

Above: HMS *Prince of Wales* is expected to be commissioned in 2020. The ship is currently planned to carry up to 40 F-35B Lightning II stealth multirole fighters and Merlin helicopters.

REAL-TIME MAPPING
To get around the complex interior, crew can use a special Platform Navigation app in hand-held devices.

AIR CONTROL
Aft air control island.

ISLAND
Forward island with navigation bridge, topped by long-range radar.

RUDDERS
The steering gear is supplied by Rolls-Royce as an integral system, including hydraulic power units, control and alarm systems. The twin rudders have 'twisted design' blades to reduce cavitation.

WASTE DISPOSAL
A pyrolysis compartment deals with shipboard waste by compaction and incineration.

MOORING DECKS
The forward mooring deck with winches and cables is at the bow below the ramp. The stern has port and starboard mooring decks.

LEAN-MANNING
Lean-manning is an essential feature of these carriers. A crew of 679, no greater than that of the much smaller Invincible class, can operate the ship due to extensive automation and the use of bulk handling, palletized loads, specialist mechanical equipment and computerized inventory controls. The 'highly mechanized weapons handling system' is based on commercial warehouse picking and conveying systems, controlled from one central point.

FITTING OUT
Queen Elizabeth fitting out at Rosyth Dockyard, some time in 2016. The carrier was commissioned into the fleet on 7 December 2017.

USS *Gerald R. Ford* (2017)

SPECIFICATIONS

DIMENSIONS:	Length: 332.8m (1092ft); Beam: 40.8m (134ft); Draught: 11.3m (37ft)
DISPLACEMENT:	113,600 tonnes (101,400 tons)
PROPULSION:	2 A4W nuclear reactors, 4 steam turbines, 4 shafts, 194,000kW (260,000shp)
SPEED:	30 knots (56km/h; 35mph)
RANGE:	Unlimited
ARMAMENT:	2 RIM-162 Evolved Sea Sparrow 8-cell MK 29 SAM medium range launchers, 2 RIM-116 21-cell RAM short range missile surface-to-air launchers, CIWS
AIRCRAFT:	90
COMPLEMENT:	5680

The first of a new generation of nuclear-powered super-carriers, this ship is intended to maintain and extend the US Navy's preponderance for decades to come. The carrier was formally commissioned on 22 July 2017.

Left: On 26 January 2013, the giant Newport News crane lowers the carrier's 555-tonne (546-ton) island precisely into place.

MAST
The mast is formed of composite materials, carrying communications, search and tracking links.

DUAL-BAND RADAR
DBR is the first system using an automated central controller and two sets of active-array radars operating at different frequencies.

WEAPON HANDLING
The ship has 11 advanced outboard weapons elevators integrated with the internal weapons handling systems.

MOORING
Stopping and holding a ship of this size is an exercise in itself. The mooring system can pay out 29m (90ft) of chain in five seconds.

ISLAND
Positioning of the island so far aft allows for relocation of the aft starboard aircraft elevator to a position closer to mid-ship. With three elevators compared to the Nimitz-class four, Ford will have a higher launch rate.

WEAPON SYSTEMS

The ship will carry around 75 aircraft, including fighter and strike planes, as well as transport, reconnaissance and other specialist craft, such as unmanned aerial vehicles (UAV). The basis of the air wing will be the F-35C carrier variant of the Lightning II Fighter, with stealth characteristics and hacking/jamming ability in addition to a formidable weaponry including AIM-120 AMRAAM air-to-air and air-to-surface guided missiles, two GBU-31 JDAM guided bombs, eight GBU-38 bombs and a 35mm (1.4in) GAU-22A series cannon. Its total payload is 8160kg (17,993lb) and its operational radius is 1100km (440 miles).

AT ANCHOR
Gerald R. Ford in the James River, the anchorage for the National Defense Reserve Fleet, 11 June 2016.

INS *Vikrant* (2018)

SPECIFICATIONS

DIMENSIONS:	Length: 259m (850ft); Beam: 58m (190ft); Draught: 8.4m (28ft)
DISPLACEMENT:	38,100 tonnes (37,500 tons); 40,640 tonnes (40,000 tons) full load
PROPULSION:	4 GE LM2500+ gas turbines, 2 shafts, 80,000kW (107,281hp)
SPEED:	28 knots (52km/h; 32mph)
RANGE:	7500nm (13,875km; 8625 miles) at 18 knots (33km/h; 21mph)
AIRCRAFT:	36
AIRCRAFT:	4 OTO Melara 76mm (3in) DP guns, Barak 1 and Barak 8 SAM launchers, AK-630 CIWS
COMPLEMENT:	1560

India's first home-built aircraft carrier is helping to expand and develop the country's military technology, but also suffering delays in commissioning.

Right: *Vikrant* is a STOBAR carrier, capable of handling short take-off aircraft, but without a catapult.

RADAR
Active electronically scanned array radars (AESA) work across a band of frequencies, with long-range aircraft detection up to 400km (250 miles).

TURBINES
The LM2500+G4 turbines can develop full power within ten minutes.

DECK AREA
The flight deck area is 10,000sq m (110,000sq ft).

AIRCRAFT CAPACITY
There is capacity for 36 aircraft, although hangar space for only 17. The aircraft complement will be formed from multi-role Mikoyan MiG-29K folding-wing STOL planes and Ka-31 AEW and Ka-28 ASW helicopters, as well as HAL-Dhruv general utility helicopters.

RADAR PROFILE
The island superstructure is shaped in order to minimize its radar profile; note also the rounded edge of the flight deck.

PREPARED FOR LAUNCH
The carrier's hull is decorated for the launch, and Cochin Shipyard workers gather to watch, on 12 August 2013.

USS *Monadnock* (1864)

SPECIFICATIONS

DIMENSIONS:	Length: 76m (250ft); Beam: 16.36m (53ft 8in); Draught: 3.73m (12ft 3in)
DISPLACEMENT:	3454.5 tonnes (3400 tons)
PROPULSION:	Twin shafts, horizontal return connecting rod engines, 4 Martin boilers
SPEED:	10 knots (18.5 km/h; 11.5 mph)
RANGE:	–
ARMAMENT:	4 375mm (15in) SB guns
ARMOUR:	Sides: 125mm (5in); Turrets: 250mm (10in); Deck: 37mm (1.5in)
COMPLEMENT:	150

The first *Monadnock* was the only monitor of the Miantonomoh class to see action during the American Civil War. Later it passed through the Straits of Magellan on a cruise from Philadelphia to San Francisco.

VENTILATION
A ventilation shaft for the engine room was placed abaft of the funnel.

TURRETS
Internal diameter of the turrets was 7m (23ft).

PILOT HOUSES
Pilot houses were mounted on each turret, with a light hurricane deck between.

DECK
The deck was 0.79m (31in) above the waterline.

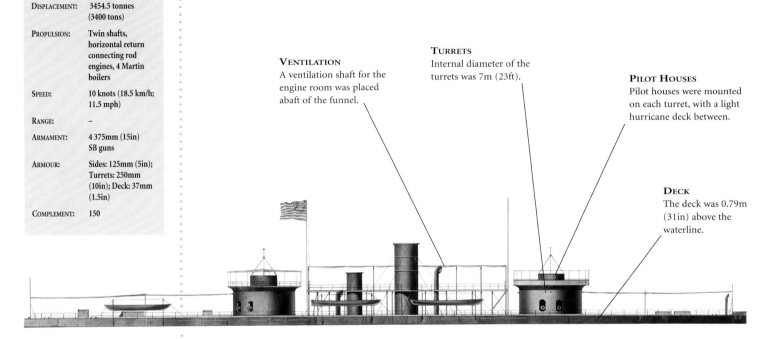

CIVIL WAR SERVICE

Monadnock steamed to Norfolk, Virginia, where Commander Enoch G. Parrott took command on 20 November 1864. On 13 December it left for the assault against Fort Fisher, in North Carolina, joining Rear-Admiral David Porter's North Atlantic Blockading Squadron on 15 December. Four days later, the vessel joined the fleet assembled to attack Confederate defences on the Cape Fear River. On the morning of Christmas Eve, it closed the entrance of the river and bombarded Fort Fisher throughout the day. The following morning, it resumed shelling as 2000 Union troops landed north of the fort. The attack failed but was renewed on 13 January 1865, with *Monadnock* again shelling the fort's defences. Firing continued until the last gun on the sea face was silenced. During the action, *Monadnock* was struck five times.

DOWNTIME
Sailors aboard *Monadnock* take a break from duties for a photograph. Note the improvised sun awning that has been strung over one of the gun turrets.

HMS *Devastation* (1873)

SPECIFICATIONS

DIMENSIONS:	Length: 86.9m (285ft); Beam: 19m (62ft 4in); Draught: 8.4m (27ft 6in)
DISPLACEMENT:	8464 tonnes (9330 tons)
PROPULSION:	Penn direct acting trunk engines, 2 screws, 4959kW (6650hp)
SPEED:	14 knots (26km/h; 16mph)
RANGE:	4700nm (8704km; 5408 miles) at 10 knots (18.5km/h; 11.5mph)
ARMAMENT:	(1873): 4 305mm (12in) MLR guns
ARMOUR:	Belt: 305–216mm (12–8.5in); Breastwork: 305–250mm (12–10in); Turrets: 356–250mm (14–10in); Conning tower: 228mm (9in); Deck: 76–50mm (3–2in)
COMPLEMENT:	358

HMS *Devastation*, the first seagoing turret ship, carrying the heaviest guns yet, was a highly controversial design. However, its big-gun layout, and its reliance on engines only, without sails, proved successful against the critics' prophecies of doom, and gave many pointers to further development.

ARMOUR WEIGHT
Compared to the 5452-tonne (5365-ton) ironclad *Audacious* of 1870, which had an armour weight of 15.3 per cent of displacement, *Devastation*'s armour protection was 27.2 per cent of displacement – a huge improvement.

HULL SIDES
The hull sides were parallel for two-thirds of the ship's length, another original feature in an age when warships' sides normally curved from stem to stern.

FREEBOARD
The freeboard of the low armoured deck was no more than 1.37m (4ft 6in) above the waterline, but higher than American monitors and calculated to give an effective margin of buoyancy.

COAL LOAD
Devastation carried 1633 tonnes (1607 tons) of coal, an exceptional amount for the time.

COAL POWER
Although *Devastation* was a highly modern vessel for its time, it was still born in the era of steam, and was thus acutely dependent on coal as its energy supply. At maximum capacity, the ship could carry 1372 tonnes (1350 tons) of coal, giving her a range of 3550 nautical miles (6570km; 4090 miles) at 12 knots (22km/h; 14mph). For steam generation, the vessel also carried a 30.4-tonne (30-ton) load of water.

APPEARANCE
Comparison with some of the other illustrations will show how *Devastation*'s appearance was very unlike that of the established notion of how a battleship should look in 1873.

Imperator Alexander II (1891)

SPECIFICATIONS

DIMENSIONS:	Length: 105.6m (346ft 6in); Beam: 20.4m (66ft 11in); Draught: 7.85m (51ft 9in)
DISPLACEMENT:	9392 tonnes (9224 tons)
PROPULSION:	Twin shafts, vertical compound engines, 12 cylindrical boilers, 6181kW (8289hp)
SPEED:	15.3 knots (28.3km/h (17.6mph)
RANGE:	4440nm (8223km; 5110 miles) at 8 knots (15km/h; 9mph)
ARMAMENT:	2 305mm (12in), 4 229mm (9in), 8 152mm (6in) guns; 10 47mm (1.9in), 10 37mm (1.5in) Hotchkiss revolving guns; 5 381mm (15in) torpedo tubes
ARMOUR:	Belt: 356–102mm (14–4in); Bulkheads: 152mm (6in); Barbettes: 254mm (10in); Conning tower: 203mm (8in); Deck: 64mm (2.5 in)
COMPLEMENT:	616

Intended to assert Russian domination of the Baltic Sea, the design of *Imperator Alexander II* reflected the ongoing debate about whether big guns should be placed in barbettes or turrets. The ship was laid down at the New Admiralty Yards, St Petersburg, in November 1885 and launched in July 1887. Completion was not until June 1891.

Above: *Imperator Alexander II* bedecked in flags during a port call.

MASTS
Each of the two masts featured a large fighting top, reflecting French influence on the design.

DESIGN
A two-level wheel and charthouse structure is cantilevered out from the superstructure.

TURRET
The 'turret' is really a lightly armoured shelter that turns with the guns.

BRIDGE
The after flying bridge extends the full width of the ship.

MAIN GUNS

The main guns were Model 1877, made at the Obukhov State Works, St Petersburg, to a Krupp design, firing 331.7kg (731.3lb) shells with a maximum range of 5090m (5570yd) at an elevation of 60 degrees. Five torpedo tubes were carried: two in the bows, two midships and one in the stern. The hull was of steel and the armour was up-to-date compound-type with a full-length belt. Its engines were made at the Baltic Works, St Petersburg.

RENAMING

Imperator Alexander II served in the Russian fleet until 1922, although with the Russian Revolution in 1917 its name became unacceptable in Soviet eyes. Thus, in May 1917 the ship was renamed *Dawn of Freedom*. During her service years, the ship operated as part of the Baltic Fleet and the Mediterranean Squadron.

USS *Maine* (1895)

SPECIFICATIONS

DIMENSIONS:	Length: 98.9m (324ft 4in); Beam: 17.4m (57ft); Draught: 6.5m (21ft 5in)
DISPLACEMENT:	6062 tonnes (6682 tons)
PROPULSION:	8 boilers, 2 N.F. Palmer inverted vertical triple expansion engines, 6930kW (9293hp)
SPEED:	16.45 knots (30.4km/h; 18.8mph)
RANGE:	Not known
ARMAMENT:	4 254mm (**10in**) guns, 6 152mm (6in) guns, 7 6-pdr and 8 1-pdr guns; 4 457mm (18in) torpedo tubes
ARMOUR:	Belt: 305mm (12in); Turrets: 203mm (8in); Conning tower: 254mm (10in); Deck: 102mm (4in)
COMPLEMENT:	374

Despatched to Havana, Cuba, at a time of high international tension to 'show the flag' and protect US interests, *Maine* blew up in an explosion whose cause would remain a subject of controversy for more than three-quarters of a century.

TURRETS
The two main turrets were not counterbalanced: if both were trained in one direction, the ship heeled. After *Maine* and *Texas*, the echelon turret placement was dropped.

Deck plan: the echelon placement of the gun turrets was made necessary by the raised forecastle and poop decks – an aspect of design that would disappear in future USN battleships.

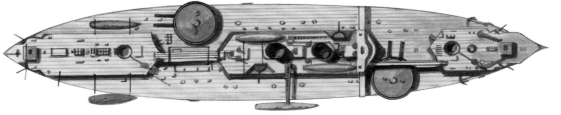

FIGHTING TOPS
Each fighting top held a 1-pounder gun, part of the anti-torpedo boat defences (note also the searchlights). These guns fired 0.5kg (1.1lb) shells to a range of approximately 3200m (3500yd).

EXPLOSION

Cuba in 1897 was still a Spanish colony, but an independence struggle was underway. *Maine* was despatched to Havana in a show of force, arriving on 25 January 1898 and anchoring in the harbour. On 15 February, at 21:40, there was a huge explosion in the forward part of the hull and the ship was wrecked, with 252 crew dead and missing. An attack could not be ruled out. A US court of inquiry decided that *Maine* had been blown up by a mine, although how, or by whom, was not clear.

COAL BUNKERS
Coal bunkers were placed between the forward 254mm (10in) magazine and the outer hull. Spontaneous combustion here may have caused the fatal explosion.

ARMAMENT
152mm (6in) guns were fitted in casemates at the bow and stern, to give supplementary fore and aft fire.

WRECKED VESSEL
The part-submerged wreck of *Maine* lay in Havana harbour from 1898 to 1914. The incident hastened the Spanish–American War, which began on 21 April 1897.

Mikasa (1902)

SPECIFICATIONS

DIMENSIONS:	Length: 131.7m (432ft); Beam: 23.2m (75ft 6in); Draught: 8.28m (27ft 6in)
DISPLACEMENT:	13,789 tonnes (15,200 tons)
PROPULSION:	25 Belleville watertube boilers, 2 vertical triple-expansion engines, 11,185kW (15,000hp), 2 screws
SPEED:	18 knots (33km/h; 21mph)
RANGE:	9000nm (17,000km; 10,000 miles) at 10 knots (18.5km/h; 11.5mph)
ARMAMENT:	4 305mm (12in) guns, 14 152mm (6in) guns, 20 12-pdr, 8 3-pdr, 4 2.5-pdr guns, 4 457mm (18in) torpedo tubes
ARMOUR:	Belt: 229–102mm (9–4in); Bulkheads: 305mm (12in); Deck: 76mm (3in); Main turrets: 254–203mm (10–8in)
COMPLEMENT:	830

Admiral Heihachiro Togo's flagship, and Japan's largest battleship in the Russian–Japanese War of 1905, the British-built *Mikasa* was involved in two fierce battles, in the Yellow Sea and at Tsushima. Later sunk, and raised, it is the only surviving battleship of the pre-Dreadnought era.

EMBLEM
The emblem on the bow is the Japanese imperial symbol of the chrysanthemum.

TOPMAST
The high topmasts supported aerial wires for radio communication.

BRIDGE
Flying bridges fore and aft carried searchlights on each side.

PAINT COLOUR
Mikasa as preserved is painted in 'battleship grey', but this paint finish, with the triple-stripe funnels, was ordered for its original completion.

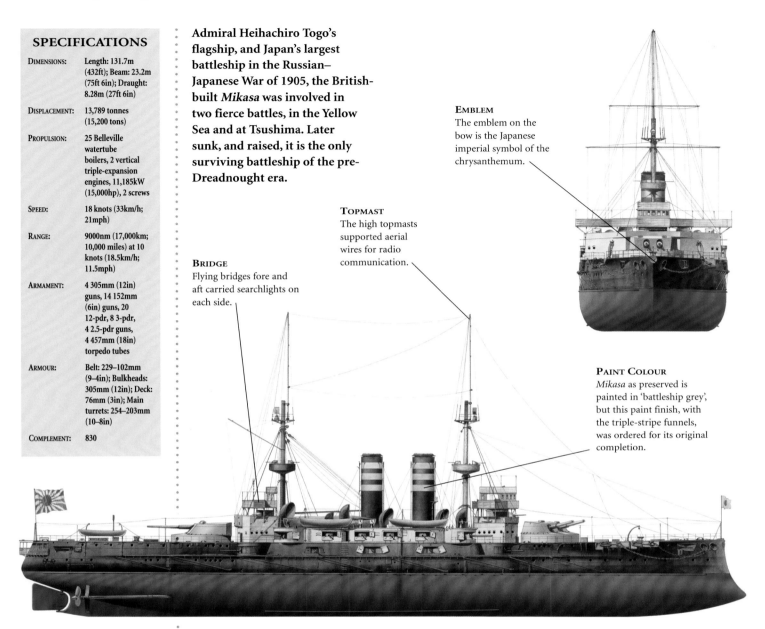

TSUSHIMA

The battle of Tsushima was fought in the waters between Japan and Korea on 27–28 May 1905. Although the Japanese had only four battleships against the Russians' eight, they had a much larger number of other craft – altogether 89 vessels against the Russians' 28. The result was a Nelsonian-scale victory for Togo, with seven Russian battleships and 14 other enemy vessels sunk, for the loss of three torpedo boats. *Mikasa* took some 40 strikes, although no major damage was done.

BRITISH ORIGINS
Mikasa in drydock at the Royal Navy yard, Portsmouth, England, early 1902, before making the voyage to join the Imperial Japanese Navy.

HMS *Dreadnought* (1906)

SPECIFICATIONS

DIMENSIONS:	Length: 160.4m (527ft); Beam: 25m (82ft); Draught: 8.1m (26ft 6in)
DISPLACEMENT:	16,238 tonnes (17,900 tons); 19,817 tonnes (21,845 tons) full load
PROPULSION:	18 Babcock & Wilcox boilers, 4 Parsons turbines, 19,649kW (26,350hp), 4 screws
SPEED:	21 knots (39km/h; 24mph)
RANGE:	6620nm (12,260km; 7618 miles) at 10 knots (18.5km/h; 11.5mph)
ARMAMENT:	10 305mm (12in) guns, 27 12-pdr guns, 5 457mm (18in) torpedo tubes (submerged)
ARMOUR:	Belt: 279–102mm (11–4in); Bulkhead: 203mm (8in); Barbettes: 279–102mm (11–4in); Turrets: 279mm (11in); Conning tower: 279–203mm (11–8in)
COMPLEMENT:	773

A new era of fast, big-gun battleships was inaugurated by the appearance of HMS *Dreadnought*. Similar ships were already being planned or considered by other navies: consequently, instead of assuring British dominance, the effect was to start a naval arms race.

Below: *Dreadnought* was revolutionary in that she was equipped primarily with an 'all-big-gun' main armament of 305mm (12in) guns, rather than having the mix of primary and secondary guns common to most warships prior to her commissioning in 1906.

REAR TRIPOD
The secondary control station on the rear tripod was replaced in 1917 by a lighter searchlight platform.

FOREFUNNEL
The positioning of the forefunnel was one of the few minus points of the design.

BROADSIDE
When the eight-gun 305mm (12in) salvo was first fired, an expert observer noticed no more than 'a muffled roar and a bit of a kick' on the ship.

RUDDERS
Two parallel rudders were fitted, centre-mounted, abaft of the inner screws, contributing to the ship's excellent handling qualities.

HULL
The hull shape was carefully worked out to ensure that the required speed of 21 knots (39km/h; 24mph) could be achieved on the least horsepower.

FASTEST BATTLESHIP
Another revolutionary aspect of the new ship was its motive power. Turbines had never been applied to a battleship before, but when fitted to *Dreadnought* she was faster than any other battleship, mechanically more reliable, more economical on fuel, and provided infinitely better working conditions in the engine room.

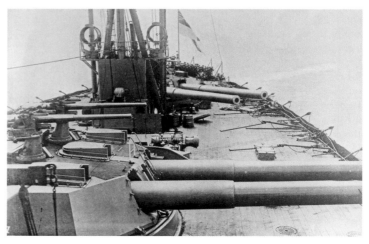

AFT GUNS
A view of *Dreadnought*'s guns at the aft of the ship, with 305mm (12in) turrets in the foreground and at the rear and QF 12-pounders in between. Also note the twin searchlights mounted to aid the guns in night-firing actions.

Vittorio Emanuele (1908)

SPECIFICATIONS

DIMENSIONS:	Length: 144.6m (474ft); Beam: 22.4m (73ft); Draught: 8.58m (28.1ft)
DISPLACEMENT:	13,914 tons (14,137 tonnes)
PROPULSION:	Twin shafts, 2 triple expansion engines, 14,484kW (19,424hp)
SPEED:	21.36 knots (39.56km/h; 24.58mph)
RANGE:	10,000nm (19,000km; 11,500 miles) at 10 knots (18.5km/h; 11.5mph)
ARMAMENT:	2 305mm (12in), 12 200mm (8in), 16 76mm (3in) guns; 2 450mm (17.7in) torpedo tubes
ARMOUR:	Belt: 248mm (9.8in); Turrets: 203mm (8in); Conning tower: 250mm (10in); Deck: 38mm (1.5in)
COMPLEMENT:	764

Second of the four-strong Regina Elena class, this pre-dreadnought took part in operations in the Italo–Turkish War. Although also active in World War I, the ship saw no further combat.

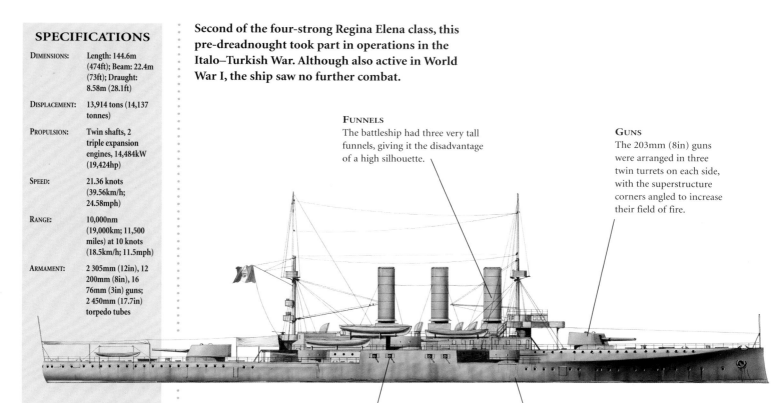

FUNNELS
The battleship had three very tall funnels, giving it the disadvantage of a high silhouette.

GUNS
The 203mm (8in) guns were arranged in three twin turrets on each side, with the superstructure corners angled to increase their field of fire.

CLOSE-RANGE DEFENCE
Close-range defense against torpedo boats was provided by a battery of sixteen 76mm (3in) 40-calibre guns.

WATERLINE
Fear of torpedo strikes below the waterline belt from Austrian submarines kept the ship out of the Adriatic Sea during World War I.

VITTORIO CUNIBERTI

Designed by Vittorio Cuniberti, chief constructor of the Italian Navy, a believer in the 'all-big-gun' battleship concept and a highly influential figure in warship design, *Vittorio Emanuele* was laid down at Cantieri di Castellammare di Stabia on 18 September 1901, launched on 12 October 1904, and completed on 1 August 1908. Cuniberti modified his principles considerably for the class, which carried only two heavy guns and a large array of 'semi-heavy' 200mm (8in) guns, rather than his ideal of 12 305mm (12in) guns. The two main guns were carried in single turrets with sloping sides. After 1912, machine guns were mounted on the tops. Two torpedo tubes were fitted below the waterline.

WARTIME SERVICE
Vittorio Emanuele under way during World War I. Prior to 1914, the ship had seen some combat during the Italo–Turkish War of 1911–12, but during the subsequent world war she was never actually committed to battle, on account of the fear that she would be lost to enemy submarines.

HMS *Indomitable* (1908)

SPECIFICATIONS

DIMENSIONS:	Length: 172.8m (567ft); Beam: 23.97m (78ft 7.7in); Draught: 7.6m (25ft)
DISPLACEMENT:	17,373 tons (17,652 tonnes); 20,078 tons (20,400 tonnes) full load
PROPULSION:	Quadruple shafts, Parsons turbines, 31 Babcock & Wilcox boilers, 30,570kW (41,000shp)
SPEED:	25.5 knots (47.2km/h; 29.3mph)
RANGE:	–
ARMAMENT:	8 305mm (12in)/45-cal, 16 102mm (4in)/45-cal QF guns; 7 Maxim guns; 5 457mm (18in) torpedo tubes
ARMOUR:	Belt: 152–100mm (6–4in); Bulkheads: 180–152mm (7–6in); Barbettes: 180–50mm (7–2in); Turret faces: 180mm (7in); Conning tower: 250–152mm (10–6in); Deck: 65–20mm (2.5–0.75in)
COMPLEMENT:	784

The three ships of the Invincible class were the first battlecruisers, powered by turbines and carrying eight 305mm (12in) guns, but with relatively light armour protection. The battlecruiser was a new concept in naval technology.

Above: The 305mm (12in) guns sit amidship on HMS *Indomitable*.

VULNERABLE TURRET
Indomitable's sister ship *Invincible* was destroyed at Jutland when 'Q' turret (starboard amidships) was struck by a shell from *Derfflinger*: 1026 on board were killed in the magazine explosion.

GUNS
The 102mm (4in) guns, completely open until 1917, were mounted on top of the 305mm (12in) turrets.

FIREPOWER
At Jutland, *Indomitable*'s guns hit *Derfflinger* three times, and *Seydlitz* and *Pommern* once each, in the course of firing 175 305mm (12in) shells.

ENHANCEMENTS
In 1917, a director tower was added, searchlights were mounted around the aft funnel, and aircraft platforms installed on the wing turrets.

DEPLOYMENTS

In August 1914, *Indomitable* was engaged in pursuit of the German battleships *Breslau* and *Goeben*, then joined the Dardanelles blockade. It was in action at the Battles of the Dogger Bank and Jutland, sustaining no damage, and was with the 2nd Battle Cruiser Squadron from June 1916 to January 1919.

TURBINE POWER
Smoke pours from *Indomitable*'s three funnels as she makes way in the company of another Invincible class battlecruiser, HMS *Inflexible*. The ships of this class were powered by two paired sets of Parsons direct-drive turbines, which could deliver a speed of 25.5 knots (47.2km/h; 29.3mph).

USS *South Carolina* (1910)

SPECIFICATIONS

DIMENSIONS:	Length: 137.9m (452ft 8in); Beam: 24.5m (80ft 5in); Draught: 7.49m (24ft 7in)
DISPLACEMENT:	14,515 tonnes (16,000 tons); 16,238 tonnes (17,900 tons) full load
PROPULSION:	12 Babcock & Wilcox boilers, 2 vertical 4-cylinder triple-acting engines developing 12,304kW (16,500hp), 2 screws
SPEED:	18.5 knots (34km/h; 21mph)
RANGE:	5000nm (9260km; 5753 miles) at 10 knots (18.5km/h; 11.5mph)
ARMAMENT:	8 305mm (12in) guns, 22 88mm (3in) QF guns, 2 underwater 533mm (21in) torpedo tubes
ARMOUR:	Belt: 305–228mm (12–9in); Casemates and barbettes: 254–203mm (10–8in); Turrets: 304mm (12in); Deck: 38mm (1.5in); Conning tower: 305mm (12in)
COMPLEMENT:	869

Striking power and staying power were seen as more important than speed by the US Navy. This two-strong class mounted a formidable eight-gun 305mm (12in) broadside, and their superfiring turrets were to become the standard arrangement for capital ships.

SIGHTS
Sights were fitted on the turret sides, rather than on the tops, to avoid blast impact.

SIDE ARMOUR
Side armour reached a maximum thickness of 305mm (12in) alongside the main magazines.

AA GUNS
AA guns replaced the searchlights on the crane pole platforms in 1918.

TURRET DESIGN
Drawn up before HMS *Dreadnought*, this was the first battleship planned with all its big guns in centreline turrets (though the first design incorporated two single turrets to port and starboard).

GUNNERY
The ship's arc of fire was around 270 degrees. The 305mm (12in) guns had 13.72m (45ft) barrels weighing 47.85 tonnes (47.09 tons) and fired 390kg (870lb) shells with an extreme range of 18,000m (20,000yd) at their maximum elevation of 15 degrees. The rate of fire was three rounds a minute at peak performance. The secondary armament of 22 76mm (3in) guns was intended for defence against torpedo boats. This was altered in 1917, with 14 76mm (3in) guns, two 76mm (3in) AA guns and four 1-pounder guns.

LEADING DESIGNS
South Carolina and *Michigan* set the pattern of pre-1914 US battleship silhouettes with their gun arrangement, basket masts and tall, capped funnels.

USS *Utah* (1911)

SPECIFICATIONS

DIMENSIONS:	Length: 159m (521ft 6in); Beam: 26.9m (88ft 3in); Draught: 8.7m (28ft 6in)
DISPLACEMENT:	22,669 tons (23,033 tonnes)
PROPULSION:	Quadruple shafts, Parsons turbines, 12 boilers, 20,880kW (28,000shp)
SPEED:	21 knots (39km/h; 24.2mph)
RANGE:	5776nm (10,700km; 6650 miles) at 10 knots (18.5km/h; 11.5mph)
ARMAMENT:	10 305mm (12in)/45-cal, 16 127mm (5in)/51-cal guns; 2 530mm (21in) torpedo tubes
ARMOUR:	Belt: 279mm (11in); Turret faces: 305mm (12in); Conning tower: 292mm (11.5in); Deck: 38mm (1.5in)
COMPLEMENT:	1001

Utah and *Florida* were the US Navy's most powerful battleships when commissioned in 1911, although by that time the USS *Wyoming*, with 12 305mm (12in) guns, was already launched.

Right: A stern view of the *Utah* at the New York Review.

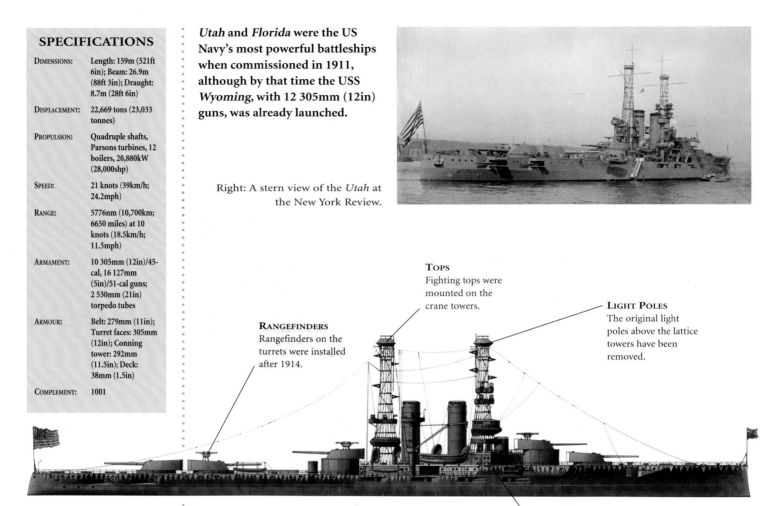

TOPS
Fighting tops were mounted on the crane towers.

LIGHT POLES
The original light poles above the lattice towers have been removed.

RANGEFINDERS
Rangefinders on the turrets were installed after 1914.

DESIGN
The illustration shows *Utah* as it was around 1923. Several alterations were made to the control and signalling positions on the masts during World War I.

SERVICE RECORD

Utah's war service began with the US occupation of Vera Cruz, Mexico, where it and *Florida* landed marines on 21 April 1914. From 6 April 1917, it was based at Chesapeake Bay for engineering and gunnery training until 30 August 1918, when it crossed the Atlantic to Bantry Bay, Ireland, as flagship of Battleship Division 6, patrolling the Western Approaches to the British Isles. During the inter-war years, *Utah* made several ceremonial, diplomatic and operational tours, serving in European, South American and US waters. On 7 December 1941, *Utah* was terminally damaged by the Japanese air attacks against Pearl Harbor, where the ship had been based since the previous September.

PUGET SOUND
USS *Utah* (AG-16) at the Puget Sound Naval Shipyard, Bremerton, Washington, on 18 August 1941, having undergone rearmament and fresh applications of paint camouflage.

Derfflinger (1913)

SPECIFICATIONS

DIMENSIONS:	Length: 210.4m (690ft 3in); Beam: 29m (95ft 2in); Draught: 9.2m (30ft 3in)
DISPLACEMENT:	23,750 tonnes (26,180 tons); 27,857 tonnes (30,707 tons) full load
PROPULSION:	18 boilers, Parsons turbines, 4 screws
SPEED:	26.5 knots (49km/h; 30mph)
RANGE:	5300nm (9816km; 6100 miles) at 14 knots (25.9km/h; 16.1mph)
ARMAMENT:	(1916) 8 305mm (12in) guns, 12 150mm (5.9in) guns, 4 88mm (3.4in) guns, 4 88mm (3.4in) AA guns, 4 500mm (19.6in) torpedo tubes
ARMOUR:	Side belt: 300–150mm (12–6in); Bulkhead: 250–100mm (9.8–3.9in); Conning tower forward: 300mm (11.8in); Aft: 200mm (7.8in); Barbettes: 260mm (10.2in); Turrets: 270mm (11in); Deck: 30mm (1.18in); Funnels: 165mm (6.5in); Conning tower: 305mm (12in)
COMPLEMENT:	1112–1182

Germany's battlecruisers, built in response to Britain's, were better armoured than their British counterparts, although not as fast. With the three ships of the Derfflinger class, the Imperial German Navy also first made use of the 305mm (12in) gun.

Right: This aerial view from 1917 shows the fine lines of *Derfflinger*'s hull design. The location is the Jade River, Kiel Naval Base.

FOREFUNNEL
Derfflinger was the only ship of the three in the class to have the forefunnel slightly higher than the after funnel.

AA GUNS
Derfflinger was the first German capital ship fitted with 88mm (3.4in) AA guns.

BULKHEAD
A weak point of the design was the non-provision of an anti-torpedo bulkhead behind the broadside torpedo compartment – this was a major contribution to the fate of *Lützow*.

FOREMASTS
The three Derfflinger-class ships were the only German battlecruisers fitted (after May 1916) with tripod foremasts, very broadly based with the side poles straddling the bridge structure.

MAIN TURRETS
This was the only German battlecruiser class with superfiring main turrets.

BATTLE OF JUTLAND
The Battle of Jutland, fought on 31 May–1 June 1916, was the only large-scale sea battle of World War I. *Derfflinger* was in action from around 15:38 on 31 May until the last moments of the battle in the early hours of 1 June, firing 385 shells from the main guns, 235 rounds from the secondary armament and a single torpedo. In total, 157 of the crew were killed and 26 were wounded.

BROADSIDE FIRE
Derfflinger fires a massive broadside from its eight 305mm (12in) guns. Each shell weighed up to 405kg (893lb), so theoretically the battleship could put a total of 3240kg (7128lb) of ordnance onto a target at any one moment, out to a maximum range of 41,300m (45,200yd).

HMS *Royal Oak* (1914)

SPECIFICATIONS

DIMENSIONS:	Length: 189m (620ft 6in); Beam (with bulge): 31.2m (102ft 2in); Draught: 8.7m (28ft 6in)
DISPLACEMENT:	25,991 tonnes (28,650 tons); 30,390 tonnes (33,500 tons) with bulges
PROPULSION:	18 Yarrow boilers, Parsons geared turbines developing 30,000kW (40,000hp), 4 screws
SPEED:	23 knots (42.6km/h; 26.5mph)
RANGE:	4200nm (7400km; 4600 miles) at 10 knots (18.5km/h; 11.5 miles)
ARMAMENT:	8 381mm (15in) Mk 1 guns, 12 152mm (6in) guns, 8 102mm (4in) guns, 4 533mm (21in) torpedo tubes
ARMOUR:	Belt: 330mm (13in); Turret faces: 330mm (13in); Barbettes: 254mm (10in); Bulkhead: 152mm (6in); Deck: 51–25mm (2–1in)
COMPLEMENT:	997

One of a class of five battleships intended for fighting in line with the main fleet, *Royal Oak* was engaged at Jutland. It was the first capital ship to be sunk in World War II, torpedoed at anchor in Scapa Flow by a German U-boat.

Above: *Royal Oak* shows its powerful lines in this pre-war photograph.

FUNNEL
Royal Oak was the only ship of the Revenge class not to be fitted with a funnel cowl.

SEARCHLIGHT TOWERS
The searchlight towers were built up round the funnel in 1917–18.

SECONDARY BATTERY
This was the last RN battleship class with a main deck secondary battery on each side.

AIRCRAFT LAUNCHER
This view shows *Royal Oak* as it looked in 1939, with aircraft launcher on 'X' turret and luffing crane.

TORPEDO BULGE
The blister shape of the torpedo bulge is apparent. Total armour weight was 7484 tonnes (7365 tons).

REVENGE CLASS

Beginning with HMS *Ramillies*, the British Revenge class were the first battleships to be fitted with anti-torpedo bulges, or 'blisters', adding 4m (13ft) to the beam. In *Royal Oak*, the bulges were heightened in 1927, almost reaching the battery deck. The five ships in the class were: *Revenge*, *Resolution*, *Royal Oak*, *Royal Sovereign* and *Ramillies*.

FIREPOWER

This view of the *Royal Oak* shows her forward 318mm (15in) guns. During the Battle of Jutland, *Royal Oak* fired on both *Derfflinger* and *Seydlitz*, hitting both in the engagement, although without inflicting critical damage.

USS *Texas* (1914)

USS *Texas* saw service in both world wars in the Atlantic, the Mediterranean and the Pacific. The first US warship to launch an airplane, it still survives as a museum ship at La Porte in its name state.

SPECIFICATIONS

DIMENSIONS:	Length: 174.5m (572ft 7in); Beam: 29m (95ft 3in); Draught; 8.7m (28ft 5in)
DISPLACEMENT:	24,494 tonnes (27,000 tons)
PROPULSION:	14 boilers, 2 vertical triple-expansion engines developing 20,954kW (28,100hp), 2 screws
SPEED:	21 knots (38.8km/h; 24mph)
RANGE:	8000nm (14,816km; 9206 miles)) at 10 knots (18.5km/h; 11.5mph)
ARMAMENT:	10 356mm (14in) guns, 21 127mm (5in) guns, 4 533mm (21in) torpedo tubes
ARMOUR:	Belt: 304–254mm (12–10in); Deck: 76mm (3in); Turrets: 356mm (14in); Barbettes: 305mm (12in); Conning tower: 305mm (12in)
COMPLEMENT:	1530

TORPEDO PROTECTION
Blister anti-torpedo protection increased the beam to 32.33m (102ft 1in) and worsened the ship's already poor handling qualities.

PROFILE
As commissioned in 1914, *Texas* had two basket masts, set closely fore and aft of two equal-size funnels, giving it a quite different profile to the post-1935 form shown here.

GUNS
Triple-mount 305mm (12in) guns were originally intended to be fitted. In 1941, the elevation of the 356mm (14in) guns was raised from 150 to 300, increasing their range.

RADAR AERIAL
In December 1938, *Texas* was fitted with a CXZ radar aerial above the bridge.

BASKET MASTS
The basket masts were replaced by tripods quite early in 1925.

TAKE-OFF PLATFORM

The take-off platform was originally fitted to *Texas*'s 'B' turret during the 1919 refit at the New York Navy Yard. It was used to launch a British Sopwith Camel aircraft. Use of aircraft on capital ships began in 1914–18 and was initiated by the British. The key item was a floatplane that could be launched by catapult, land on water and be craned back on to the parent vessel. Aircraft were used for reconnaissance and were more versatile than tethered balloons, which were also used.

Above: The deck plan shows the post-conversion layout, with single funnel and tripod mainmast set aft of the centre turret.

BATTLE HONOURS

A photograph of USS *Texas*, circa 1914, just back from foreign waters, its main guns and basket mast prominent. Although the battleship saw only limited combat in World War I, in World War II she was involved in coastal bombardment actions off the shores of France, including on D-Day.

Fuso (1915)

SPECIFICATIONS

DIMENSIONS:	Length: 205m (672ft 6in); Beam: 10.08m (33ft 1in); Draught: 8.6m (28ft)
DISPLACEMENT:	35,512 tonnes (39,145 tons) full load
PROPULSION:	6 Kampon boilers, 4 Kampon steam turbines developing 55,927kW (75,000hp), 4 shafts
SPEED:	24.5 knots (45.4km/h; 28.2mph)
RANGE:	11,800nm (21,900km; 13,600 miles) at 16 knots (30km/h; 18mph)
ARMAMENT:	12 356mm (14in) guns, 14 152mm (6in) guns (1938), 8 127mm (5in) guns, 16 132mm (5.2in) AA guns in quadruple mountings
ARMOUR:	Side belt: 305–102mm (12–4in); Main turrets: 297–114mm (11.7–4.5in); Casemate: 152mm (6in); Deck: 132–51mm (5.2–2in)
COMPLEMENT:	1396

The first 'super-dreadnought' of the Imperial Navy to be both designed and built in Japan, *Fuso* was the world's largest battleship when commissioned. In original form, it showed a mix of British and Japanese influences; later modifications changed its appearance entirely, giving it an unmistakable profile.

The two profiles here, from 1915 (below) and 1933 (bottom), illustrate the remarkable change in *Fuso*'s appearance after modernization. Completely new machinery was also installed.

TURRETS
The arrangement of No.3 and No.4 turrets was unusual; the location of the central turret magazines in the same region of the ship as the oil bunkers may have contributed to the ship's fate.

CATAPULT
A Type Kure Shiki 2 Go 4 Gata catapult was mounted on No.3 turret in the 1930–33 modernization.

GUNS
The original 356mm (14in) guns elevated from 00 to 300. Post-1933, elevation was between −50 and 430, with a maximum range of 35,450m (38,770yd). The Tetsukodan armour-piercing shell weighed 673.5kg (1485lb) and the high-explosive shell, 01-Shiki Tsujodan, 625kg (1378lb).

FLOATPLANES
Japanese capital ships carried the following floatplanes (with dates indicating entry into service): Nakajima 90-11 (1927), Nakajima 90-11b (1933), Kawanishi 94-1 (1935), Kawanishi 95 (1938) or Mitsubishi F1 M (1938). All were biplanes, and were used primarily for reconnaissance duties, patrolling the skies looking for US vessels to give advance warning and targeting information.

SEA TRIALS
Fuso undergoing trials in 1915. It was one of very few battleships to have six heavy gun turrets. The battleship was sunk on 25 October 1944 at the Battle of Leyte Gulf.

HMS *Hood* (1918)

TYPE · *Surface Warships* · FAMILY · *Warships*

SPECIFICATIONS

DIMENSIONS:	Length: 262m (860ft 7in); Beam: 31.8m (104ft 2in); Draught: 9.8m (32ft)
DISPLACEMENT:	37,376 tonnes (41,200 tons)
PROPULSION:	24 Yarrow small-tube boilers, Brown-Curtis geared turbines developing 107,381kW (144,000hp)
SPEED:	31 knots (57km/h; 35.4mph)
RANGE:	5332nm (9870km; 6132 miles) at 20 knots (37km/h; 23mph)
ARMAMENT:	8 381mm (15in) guns, 12 140mm (5.5in) guns, 4 102mm (4in) AA guns, 6 533mm (21in) torpedo tubes
ARMOUR:	Belt: 305–152mm (12–6in); Bulkheads: 127–102mm (5–4in); Deck: 76–19mm (3–0.75in); Barbettes: 305–127mm (12–5in); Turrets: 381–279mm (15–11in); Conning tower: 279–229mm (11–9in)
COMPLEMENT:	1433

Of majestic appearance and fine proportions, *Hood* was seen as the 'ultimate' battlecruiser. Completed too late for World War I, by the next war its deficiencies were apparent even before its fatal confrontation with *Bismarck*.

MAST
The mast configuration was often altered: the top section of the mainmast was removed by 1941. *Hood* was the last RN battleship to have masthead control tops.

BOILERS
The new small-tube boilers provided 107,381kW (144,00hp) for the same weight as HMS *Renown*'s boilers, which produced 83,518kW (112,000hp).

HULL
The long hull made the ship subject to heavy bending stresses. The ratio of hull to beam was 8.239/1.

DEFLECTOR
The ship floated more than 1m (3ft 6in) deeper than originally planned, and a deflector was placed to keep bow seas clear of 'A' turret.

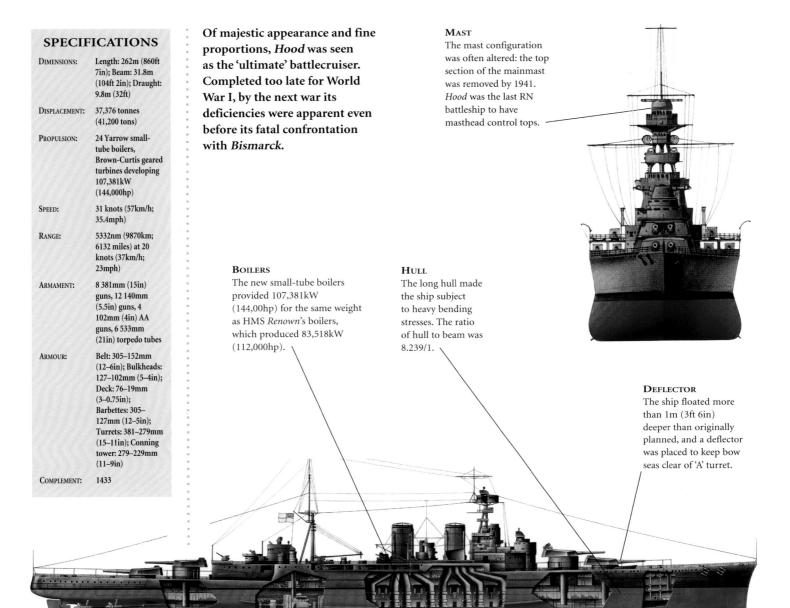

DEVASTATING END

On 22 May 1941, *Hood* was flagship of Vice Admiral Holland's Battle Cruiser Force, sent with HMS *Prince of Wales* to intercept *Bismarck* and *Prinz Eugen*, south of Greenland. Two days later, while exchanging gunfire with the German ships at a range of around 22,860m (25,000yd), *Hood* was struck by a shell from *Bismarck*. The shell pierced the ship's magazine, and *Hood* exploded at 06:00 on 24 May and sank a few minutes later. Only three of the crew survived.

WORLD CRUISE

Hood as photographed in 1924 off the coast of Australia. Accompanied by the battlecruiser *Repulse*, *Hood* set out on a world cruise in November 1923. The objective of the cruise was to remind the Dominions of their dependence on British sea power. They returned home 10 months later having visited South Africa, India, Australia, New Zealand and Canada.

HMS *Rodney* (1927)

SPECIFICATIONS

DIMENSIONS:	Length: 216.8m (710ft); Beam: 32.4m (106ft); Draught: 9.1m (30ft)
DISPLACEMENT:	30,799 tonnes (33,950 tons); 34,473 tonnes (38,000 tons) full load
PROPULSION:	8 3-drum boilers with superheaters, Brown-Curtis geared turbines developing 33,556kW (45,000hp)
SPEED:	23 knots (26.5 mph; 42.6 km/h)
RANGE:	14,300nm (26,500km; 16,470 miles) at 12 knots (22km/h; 14mph)
ARMAMENT:	9 406mm (16in) guns, 12 152mm (6in) guns, 6 119mm (4.7in) AA guns, 8 2-pdr pom-poms, 2 622mm (24.5in) torpedo tubes, underwater
ARMOUR:	Belt: 356mm (14in); Bulkheads: 356–76mm (14–3in); Barbettes: 381mm (15in); Turret faces: 406mm (16in); Deck over magazines: 158mm (6.25in); Deck over machinery: 76mm (3in)
COMPLEMENT:	1314

Of unusual design with all the heavy guns mounted forward, *Rodney* was one of the two Royal Navy battleships built under the terms of the Washington Naval Treaty of February 1922, and was the only British warship to carry 406mm (16in) guns.

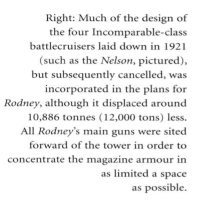

Right: Much of the design of the four Incomparable-class battlecruisers laid down in 1921 (such as the *Nelson*, pictured), but subsequently cancelled, was incorporated in the plans for *Rodney*, although it displaced around 10,886 tonnes (12,000 tons) less. All *Rodney*'s main guns were sited forward of the tower in order to concentrate the magazine armour in as limited a space as possible.

MACHINERY
Rodney's machinery arrangement was unusual, with the eight Admiralty boilers placed abaft the engine room with its two Brown-Curtis geared turbines. This was in order to keep the funnel as far away from the tower as possible.

AA GUNS
The final AA armament fitted was 16 40mm (1.6in), 48 2-pounder pom-pom and 61 20mm (0.79in) guns.

TRIPLE TURRETS
These were the first British battleships to carry heavy guns in triple turrets and the only ones with 406mm (16in) guns.

FLUSH DECK
These were the first RN battleships to be fully flush-decked since HMS *Lord Nelson* (1908).

TOWER LAYOUT
The five-deck tower design, with integrated mast, had been planned for the battlecruisers and carried directors for the various gun groups, Admiral's bridge, torpedo control station, signalling and navigation bridges. A pedestal above the bridge turret carried an AA gun position initially, but in 1935–36 the platform was enlarged to carry new fire-control equipment. *Rodney* and *Nelson* were the last British battleships to be built with separate conning towers.

BIG GUNS
Shells for the 406mm (16in) guns being loaded from a supply vessel during World War II. Each one weighed 1198kg (2641lb). Details of rangefinding and radar equipment can be seen. In theory, the guns could fire abaft the beam; in practice this proved impossible, the blast smashing even reinforced glass windows and damaging the tower structure.

Deutschland/Lützow (1933)

SPECIFICATIONS

DIMENSIONS:	Length: 186m (610ft 3in); Beam: 20.6m (67ft 6in); Draught: 7.2m (23ft 7in)
DISPLACEMENT:	10,659 tonnes (11,750 tons); 14,424 tonnes (15,900 tons) full load
PROPULSION:	4 9-cylinder double-acting 2-stroke MAN diesel engines developing 40,268kW (54,000hp), Vulcan gearboxes, 2 screws
SPEED:	28 knots (52km/h; 32mph)
RANGE:	8700nm (16,110km; 10,010 miles) at 19 knots (35km/h; 22mph)
ARMAMENT:	6 280mm (11in) guns, 8 150mm (5.9in) guns, 3 88mm (3.5in) guns, 8 500mm (19.7in) torpedo tubes
ARMOUR:	Belt: 80–60mm (3.1–2.4in); Bulkheads: 45–40mm (1.8–1.6in); Deck: 45–40mm (1.8–1.6in); Barbettes: 150–50mm (5.9–2in); Turrets: 140–85mm (5.5–3.3in); Conning tower: 150–50mm (5.9–2in)
COMPLEMENT:	619

Signalling the re-creation of a sea-going German Navy, *Deutschland* (renamed *Lützow* in 1939) was the first of a class of 'pocket battleships' that included *Admiral Graf Spee*. It was the first major warship to be powered by diesel engines.

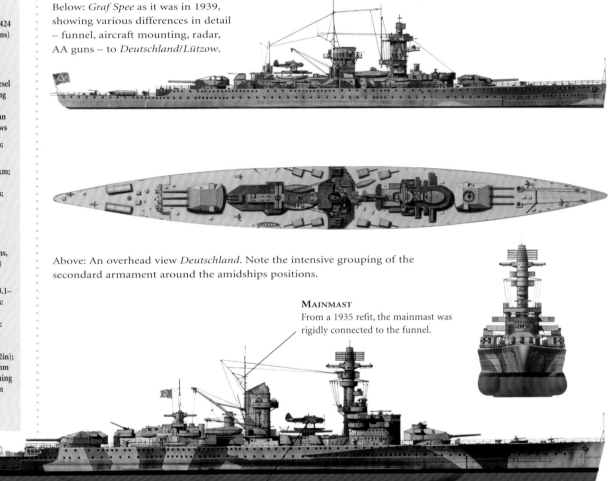

Below: *Graf Spee* as it was in 1939, showing various differences in detail – funnel, aircraft mounting, radar, AA guns – to *Deutschland/Lützow*.

Above: An overhead view *Deutschland*. Note the intensive grouping of the secondard armament around the amidships positions.

MAINMAST
From a 1935 refit, the mainmast was rigidly connected to the funnel.

ARMOUR COVERS
Protective armoured covers were fitted over the torpedo tubes shortly after commissioning.

AIRCRAFT
Deutschland was the only ship in the class to carry its two aircraft between tower and funnel (fitted in 1935).

POCKET BATTLESHIP

The term 'pocket battleship', first used outside Germany, was not intended as a compliment, but it became clear that *Deutschland* and its two sister ships, *Admiral Scheer* (1934) and *Admiral Graf Spee* (1936), had to be taken seriously as commerce raiders. Apart from providing a maximum speed of 28 knots (52km/h; 32mph, the engines gave a wide operational range of 8700nm (16,120km; 10,016 miles) at 19 knots (35km/h; 22mph).

ADMIRAL GRAF SPEE

Admiral Graf Spee in 1939. It and *Admiral Scheer* had angular bridge tower structures, different to *Lützow*'s. *Seetakt* radar, primarily for gunnery, was fitted to *Graf Spee* in 1939: the rangefinder or telemeter is prominent at the top.

De Ruyter (1936)

SPECIFICATIONS

DIMENSIONS:	Length: 170.9m (560ft 8in); Beam: 15.7m (51ft 6in); Draught: 5.1m (16ft 9in)
DISPLACEMENT:	6650 tonnes (6545 tons)
PROPULSION:	Twin shafts, Parsons geared turbines, 6 Yarrow boilers, 49,216kW (66,000shp)
SPEED:	32 knots (59km/h; 37mph)
RANGE:	6800nm (12,600km; 7800 miles) at 12 knots (22km/h; 14mph)
ARMAMENT:	7 150mm (5.9in) guns; 10 40mm (1.5in) AA guns
ARMOUR:	Belt: 50mm (2in); Bulkheads: 33mm (1.3in); Turret faces: 100mm (3.9in); Deck: 33mm (1.2in)
COMPLEMENT:	435

This Dutch light cruiser of the mid-1930s incorporated many advanced features. It was sunk in the Battle of the Java Sea in February 1942 after a combined Allied fleet was resoundingly defeated by a Japanese cruiser force during the invasion of Java.

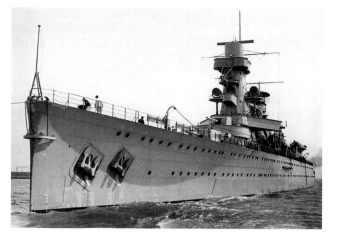

Right: A fine view of the bows of *De Ruyter*. The ship was built on a budget, and unfortunately lacked decent armour and AA protection.

AA GUNS
The ten 40mm (1.5in) Bofors AA guns were directed by an effective Dutch Hazemeyer Signaal control system.

GUNS
The 150mm (5.9in) guns fired 46kg (101.5lb) shells at a high muzzle velocity: 899m (2950ft) per second.

CATAPULT AND FLOATPLANES
De Ruyter carried a Heinkel 18m (59ft) catapult and two Fokker CX1W floatplanes.

ARMOUR
Although the tower looked well armoured, it was only lightly protected, like the rest of the ship.

TURRET
The single-gun super-firing turret could fire star-shells.

BATTLE OF JAVA SEA

As a large Japanese convoy escorted by cruisers and destroyers moved towards Java, a regrouped Allied force set out to intercept it. In the subsequent Battle of the Java Sea on 27 February 1942, torpedoes proved more effective than gunnery. Around 23:30, *De Ruyter*, already hit by shells, was struck by one or more 'Long Lance' torpedoes from the Japanese heavy cruiser *Haguro*. Almost at the same time, the Dutch cruiser *Java* was hit by a 'Long Lance' from the cruiser *Nachi* and sank. Fire broke out on *De Ruyter*; at 02:30 on 28 February it sank with the loss of 345 of its crew.

MAIN GUNS
De Ruyter lets fly with her 150mm (5.9in) main guns. The wrecks of *De Ruyter* and *Java* were located on 1 December 2002 by specialist divers, and named as war graves.

Scharnhorst (1939)

SPECIFICATIONS

DIMENSIONS:	Length: 235m (772ft); Beam: 30m (98ft 5in); Draught: 9.7m (31ft 9in)
DISPLACEMENT:	29,121 tonnes (32,100 tons), 34,564 tonnes (38,100 tons) full load
PROPULSION:	12 Wagner HP boilers, 3 Brown-Boveri geared turbines developing 119,312kW (160,000hp)
SPEED:	31 knots (57km/h; 35.4mph)
RANGE:	8800nm (16,298km; 10,127 miles) at 19 knots (35km/h; 22mph)
ARMAMENT:	9 280mm (11in) guns, 12 150mm (5.9in) guns, 14 105mm (4.1in) guns, 16 37mm (1.5in) and 10 20mm (0.79in) AA guns, 6 533mm (21in) torpedo tubes
ARMOUR:	Belt: 350–200mm (13.8–7.9in); Bulkheads: 200–150mm (7.9–5.9in); Deck: 50–20mm (2–0.79in); Barbettes: 350–200mm (13.8–7.9in); Turrets: 350–200mm (13.8–7.9in); Conning tower: 350–100mm (13.8–3.9in)
COMPLEMENT:	1968

Often referred to as the first German battleship to be constructed since World War I, *Scharnhorst*, the first of the two to be launched, was actually laid down and commissioned after *Gneisenau*. Despite being sister ships, there were numerous minor differences between them.

Above: Deck plan: the 150mm (5.9in) secondary guns are clearly visible from this perspective, as are the many smaller 37mm (1.5in) and 20mm (0.79in) AA guns.

FUEL CAPACITY
Maximum fuel capacity was 5624 tonnes (5535) tons of oil, giving a range of 8800nm (16,298km; 10,127 miles) at 19 knots (35km/h; 22mph).

BOATS
Three picket boats, two motor yawls, five cutters, one motor pinnace and one motor launch were carried.

PROPULSION
Diesel propulsion had been originally intended for both ships, but no diesel engines could produce the necessary power output per shaft, and 12 Wagner extra-high pressure boilers drove the turbines.

OUTLINE
A general resemblance of outline between *Scharnhorst*, *Gneisenau*, *Bismarck* and *Tirpitz* was deliberately planned in order to confuse their identities.

CONVOY ACTION

By the end of 1943, *Scharnhorst* was the Reich's only operational capital ship. With a force of five destroyers under Rear Admiral Bey, it was sent on 25 December to attack Convoy JW55B en route for Murmansk, and came under fire from the guns of the battleship *Duke of York*, with four escorting destroyers. A combination of torpedoes and shell fire finally destroyed *Scharnhorst*. It sank at 19:44 on 26 December, in 290m (950ft) of water, with the loss of 1803 men.

NAVAL SALUTE
Scharnhorst's crew salutes that of *U-47* as it returns to Kiel after sinking HMS *Royal Oak* in September 1939.

Richelieu (1940)

SPECIFICATIONS

DIMENSIONS:	Length: 247.9m (813ft); Beam: 33m (108ft); Draught: 9.7m (32ft)
DISPLACEMENT:	16,170 tonnes (15,910 tons)
PROPULSION:	3 Blohm & Voss steam turbines, 3 three-blade propellers, 98MW (132,000shp)
SPEED:	32 knots (59km/h; 37mph)
RANGE:	8,500nm (15,740km; 9780 miles)
ARMAMENT:	8 20.3cm (8in) guns, 12 10.5cm (4.13in) SK C/33 guns, 12 3.7cm (1.46in) SK C/30 guns, 8 20mm (0.79in) C/30 guns (20 × 1), 6 53.3cm (21in) torpedo tubes
ARMOUR:	Belt: 70–80mm (2.8–3.1in); Armour deck: 20–50mm (0.79–1.97in); Turret faces: 105mm (4.13in)
COMPLEMENT:	42 officers, 1340 enlisted men

The newly commissioned *Richelieu* was attacked by Allied ships after the fall of France. It later was taken over by Free French forces and played a part in the struggle against the Axis powers both in European and Far Eastern waters.

Right: From 1943, *Richelieu*, as France's largest battleship, was a powerful symbol of Free France while the country lay under German occupation.

BOILERS
Richelieu's new type pressure-fired boilers supplied the highest power rating of any battleship until the US Iowa class in 1943.

SEAPLANES
Three Loire 130 seaplanes were carried from July 1941 until late 1942.

PROPELLER SHAFTS
Both starboard shafts were severely damaged in the air attack of 8 July 1940.

QUADRUPLE TURRETS
Fire from the quadruple turrets was improved from 1948, when retarders were fitted to the outer guns, giving them a delay of 60 milliseconds – enough to avoid mutual dispersional effects of simultaneously fired shells.

CONSTRUCTION CHANGES

During construction, numerous changes were made to the original design, which had the funnel placed between the main and aft towers. The funnel and aft tower were merged into a single structure, with the funnel angled sharply towards the stern. Despite the ever-increasing size and displacement of capital ships, designers were always looking for possible ways to save weight, if only to reuse it elsewhere, and this was one solution.

WARTIME PAINTWORK
Richelieu in early 1946, probably at Singapore and about to sail home, still with wartime hull paintwork, intended to disguise the true length of the ship.

Bismarck (1940)

SPECIFICATIONS

DIMENSIONS:	Length: 251m (793ft); Beam: 36m (118ft); Draught: 9.3m (31ft)
DISPLACEMENT:	44,905 tonnes (49,500 tons)
PROPULSION:	12 Wagner HP boilers, 3 Brown-Boveri geared turbines developing 111,982kW (150,170hp)
SPEED:	29 knots (53.7km/h; 33.3mph)
RANGE:	8870nm (16,430km; 10,210 miles) at 19 knots (35km/h; 22mph)
ARMAMENT:	8 380mm (15in) guns, 12 150mm (5.9in) guns, 16 105mm (4.1in) guns, 16 37mm (1.5in) guns, 12 20mm (0.79in) AA guns
ARMOUR:	Belt: 320–80mm (12.6–3.1in); Bulkheads: 220–45mm (8.6–1.7in); Deck: 120-80mm (4.3–1.7in); Barbettes: 340–220mm (13.4–8.6in); Turrets: 360–180mm (14.2–7in)
COMPLEMENT:	2291

Bismarck and *Tirpitz* represented the peak of German battleship design in terms of size, armament, speed and staying power. However, *Bismarck*'s first combat mission, although including a major success, was also its last.

Right: Adolf Hitler inspects the almost-completed *Bismarck* at the Gotenhafen (Gdynia) naval base on 5 May 1940.

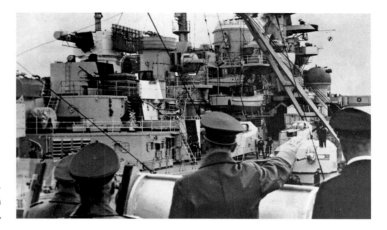

RADAR EQUIPMENT
Bismarck carried FuMO radar equipment on the forward and aft rangefinders and the foretop, although blast concussion disabled it. It also had hydrophone detectors.

SEARCHLIGHTS
Seven 1.5m (59in) diameter searchlights were carried, one on the foremast, four each side of the funnel and two abaft the mainmast.

MAIN TURRETS
German practice was to name the main turrets – A, B, C, D – as Anton, Bruno, Cäsar and Dora.

BOW ANCHORS
Three bow anchors were carried, two on the port side and one stern anchor (also port side). Each anchor weighed 9500kg (20,944lb).

ENGINE
Initial plans for propulsion – later dropped – featured turbo-electric drive, in a compact arrangement with boilers on each side, the generator in the middle, and an electric motor for each shaft.

HUNTING BISMARCK

Bismarck and *Prinz Eugen* left Gdynia on 18 May 1941 to raid merchant shipping routes in the Atlantic. On 24 May, the battlecruiser HMS *Hood* was sunk by *Bismarck*'s fifth salvo. A huge Allied three-day pursuit followed, and *Bismarck* was hit by Swordfish torpedo bombers from HMS *Ark Royal* on 26 May, jamming the port rudder. On 27 May at 08:47, the battleships HMS *Rodney* and *King George V* opened fire. By around 10:00, all *Bismarck*'s guns were disabled and the order was given to scuttle. Hit by more British torpedoes, it sank with 1977 of the 2221 people on board.

ATLANTIC RAID
Bismarck photographed from *Prinz Eugen*, en route to the Atlantic, 19–20 May 1941. The camouflage paint represents a false bow and stern, to minimize the ship's great size.

Vittorio Veneto (1940)

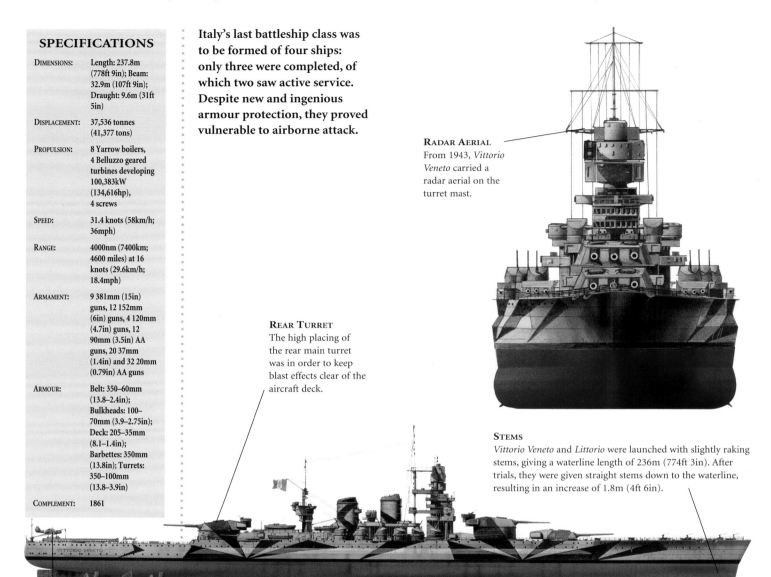

SPECIFICATIONS

DIMENSIONS:	Length: 237.8m (778ft 9in); Beam: 32.9m (107ft 9in); Draught: 9.6m (31ft 5in)
DISPLACEMENT:	37,536 tonnes (41,377 tons)
PROPULSION:	8 Yarrow boilers, 4 Belluzzo geared turbines developing 100,383kW (134,616hp), 4 screws
SPEED:	31.4 knots (58km/h; 36mph)
RANGE:	4000nm (7400km; 4600 miles) at 16 knots (29.6km/h; 18.4mph)
ARMAMENT:	9 381mm (15in) guns, 12 152mm (6in) guns, 4 120mm (4.7in) guns, 12 90mm (3.5in) AA guns, 20 37mm (1.4in) and 32 20mm (0.79in) AA guns
ARMOUR:	Belt: 350–60mm (13.8–2.4in); Bulkheads: 100–70mm (3.9–2.75in); Deck: 205–35mm (8.1–1.4in); Barbettes: 350mm (13.8in); Turrets: 350–100mm (13.8–3.9in)
COMPLEMENT:	1861

Italy's last battleship class was to be formed of four ships: only three were completed, of which two saw active service. Despite new and ingenious armour protection, they proved vulnerable to airborne attack.

RADAR AERIAL
From 1943, *Vittorio Veneto* carried a radar aerial on the turret mast.

REAR TURRET
The high placing of the rear main turret was in order to keep blast effects clear of the aircraft deck.

STEMS
Vittorio Veneto and *Littorio* were launched with slightly raking stems, giving a waterline length of 236m (774ft 3in). After trials, they were given straight stems down to the waterline, resulting in an increase of 1.8m (4ft 6in).

AIRCRAFT
Ro 43 reconnaissance aircraft were carried. *Littorio* in 1942 carried floatless Reggiane 2000 fighters that could be launched from the ship, but had to find a landing ground on shore.

SISTER SHIPS

One sister ship, *Littorio*, renamed *Italia* after Italy's surrender in 1943, was scrapped in 1952–54. The other, *Roma*, was sunk by German 'Fritz X' radio-controlled glide bombs on 9 September 1943 in the Strait of Bonifacio, the bombs dropped by German Dornier Do 217s. *Vittorio Veneto* herself survived the war and was scrapped in 1951–54.

SEASONAL CAMOUFLAGE
Various styles of camouflage paint were applied during *Vittorio Veneto*'s wartime action, depending on the season and mission. Here it is probably at Taranto in 1940.

Yamato (1941)

The Japanese Yamato class were to be 'super-battleships': bigger, more heavily armed and better protected than anything else afloat. Intended to enforce Japan's mastery of the Pacific, they made a minimal contribution to the country's war effort.

SPECIFICATIONS

DIMENSIONS:	Length: 263m (862ft 9in); Beam: 36.9m (121ft 1in); Draught: 10.39m (34ft 1in)
DISPLACEMENT:	61,698 tonnes (68,010 tons); 65,008 tonnes (71,659 tons) full load
PROPULSION:	12 Kampon HP boilers, 4 Kampon turbines developing 111,855kW (150,000hp), 4 screws
SPEED:	27 knots (50km/h; 31mph)
RANGE:	7200nm (13,330km; 8280 miles) at 16 knots (29.6km/h; 18.4mph)
ARMAMENT:	9 460mm (18.1in) guns, 12 155mm (6.1in) guns, 12 127mm (5in) guns, 24 25mm (0.98in), 4 13.2mm (0.52in) AA guns
ARMOUR:	Belt: 410mm (16in); Deck: 230–200mm (9.1–7.9in); Barbettes: 546–50mm (21.5–2in); Turrets: 650–193mm (19.7–11.8in); Torpedo
COMPLEMENT:	2500

HULL
The hull shape was carefully worked out to bear the huge stresses. The stem design was estimated to reduce water resistance by 8.2 per cent; the overall design gave a power saving of 11,797kW (15,820hp).

MAIN DECK
Gas pressure when the main guns fired prevented stowage of boats on the main deck: they were housed under cover below the top deck, alongside the hangar and 'C' turret.

GUNS
By April 1945, the ship carried 24 127mm (5in) twin-barrelled AA guns, 87 triple-barrelled and 63 single-barrelled 25mm (0.98in) AA guns.

Above: The deck plan reveals the distinctive hull shape, reaching maximum beam towards the stern. The 'wings' carried Type 96 25mm AA guns in triple mounts.

TURRET
The turret was formed of two concentric armoured cylinders, the inner one of 1.5m (4ft 10in) containing a hoist for four men.

FATE OF THE *YAMATO*
Despite their evident power, both the *Yamato* and her equally impressive sister ship *Musashi* would not survive the war. *Yamato*'s last sortie was a one-way suicide mission against US invasion forces around Okinawa. Detected before her guns could have an impact, the great ship was destroyed in a relentless attack by US carrier aircraft on 7 April 1945.

ARMOURED DECK
The armoured deck was designed so that it could be pierced only by bombs of 1000kg (2200lb) or more, dropped from a height exceeding 2400m (7800ft).

AIR ATTACK
Yamato at speed, photographed from an American warplane while under bomb attack in the Leyte Gulf sea battle, 25 October 1944.

Tirpitz (1941)

SPECIFICATIONS

DIMENSIONS:	Length: 251m (823ft 6in); Beam: 36m (118ft 1in); Draught: 9.3m (30ft 6in)
DISPLACEMENT:	38,283 tonnes (42,200 tons); 46,992 tonnes (51,800 tons) full load
PROPULSION:	12 Wagner superheated boilers, 3 Brown-Boveri geared turbines developing 102,906kW (138,000hp)
SPEED:	30 knots (56km/h; 34.8mph)
RANGE:	8870nm (16,430km; 10,210 miles) at 19 knots (35km/h; 22mph)
ARMAMENT:	8 380mm (15in) guns, 12 150mm (5.9in) guns, 16 105mm (4.1in) guns, 16 37mm (1.5in) and 12 20mm (0.79in) AA guns
ARMOUR:	Belt: 320–80mm (12.6–3.1in); Bulkheads: 220–45mm (8.6–1.7in); Deck: 120–80mm (4.3–1.7in); Barbettes: 340–220mm (13.4–8.6in); Turrets: 360–180mm (14.2–7in)
COMPLEMENT:	2065

Sister ship to *Bismarck*, *Tirpitz* had similar qualities of power and resistance. Although its active service was very limited, the fact of its presence tied up substantial British resources until its ultimate destruction.

Right: *Tirpitz* is depicted below in 'Paint Scheme K', which it carried between March and July 1944. The camouflage style was frequently changed to confuse aerial observers.

Below: The deck plan is essentially the same as that of *Bismarck*. Comparison with the cutaway profile below shows how much space was taken up by machinery, barbettes and magazines.

MAINMAST
A 'spotting top' observation post high on the mainmast was removed in 1942.

SEARCHLIGHTS
Protective domes cover searchlight positions alongside the funnel.

FUNNEL
At first black, the funnel cowling was painted silver or light-grey from 1942. The catwalk from funnel platform to tower was added in 1942.

STEM
The revised 'Atlantic' stem was fitted to *Tirpitz* before launching.

CRANES
The cranes were fitted one deck higher and slightly further forward than in *Bismarck*.

SUPERSTRUCTURE
The open fore part of the superstructure, hardly higher than 'B' turret, was rimmed out to deflect blast from gunfire.

DESTROYING TIRPITZ

On 12 November 1944, 32 Lancaster bombers of the RAF's 9 and 617 Squadrons, converged on *Tirpitz* from 09:35. The ship's main guns opened up on them from long range, but there was no aerial opposition from the Luftwaffe. The Lancasters scored at least two direct hits and four near misses with 'Tallboy' 5080kg (11,199lb) bombs carrying around 3000kg (6614lb) of high explosive. The most destructive hit was between the aircraft catapult and funnel, which blew a massive hole in the side armour.

WARSHIP WRECK
Several hundred British and Russian aircraft made attacks on the *Tirpitz* over almost three years, and many were shot down before the battleship was finally eliminated (see photo). *Tirpitz* did not have a 'glorious' career, but its influence on the Arctic war was important.

USS *Indiana* (1942)

SPECIFICATIONS

DIMENSIONS:	Length: 210m (680ft); Beam: 32.9m (107ft 8in); Draught: 8.9m (29ft 3in)
DISPLACEMENT:	34,446 tonnes (37,970 tons); 40,387 tonnes
PROPULSION:	8 Foster Wheeler boilers, 4 Westinghouse geared turbines developing 96,941kW (130,000hp)
SPEED:	27 knots (50km/h; 31mph)
RANGE:	15,000nm (27,750km; 17,245 miles) at 15 knots (27.7km/h; 17.2mph)
ARMAMENT:	9 406mm (16in) guns, 20 127mm (5in) guns, 24 40mm (1.6in) and 50 20mm (0.79in) AA guns
ARMOUR:	Belt: 310–22mm (12.2–0.87in); Bulkheads: 279mm (11in); Barbettes: 439–287mm (17.3–11.3in); Turrets: 457–184mm (18–7.25in); Deck: 152–146mm (6–5.75in)
COMPLEMENT:	1793

The second ship of four in the South Dakota class, *Indiana* and its sister ships saw extensive action during World War II, all of it in Pacific Ocean campaigns.

Right: USS *Indiana* at anchor in Hampton Roads, Virginia, on 8 September 1942. Work appears to be in hand on the 406mm (16in) guns.

Below: The South Dakota class was relatively compact in form – 210m (680ft) long compared to the preceding North Carolina's 222.1m (728ft 8in) – but of almost the same beam, and capable of considerably greater speed.

CRANES
The heavy boat cranes by the aft superstructure were carried only on *Indiana* and *Massachusetts*.

AA GUNS
A 40mm (1.6in) four-barrelled AA gun was placed on 'B' turret in 1944.

AIRCRAFT
A Vought OS 2 U-1 Kingfisher is on the catapult. Two were carried.

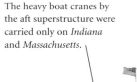

LAYOUT

These were the first American ships to be given inclined internal side armour, reaching from the armoured deck to the inner bottom and 310mm (12.2in) thick, tapering to 25mm (1in). This layout gave the ships a long indented inward-angled stretch of the central hull, just below the flush deck, rather reminiscent of the old casemate structure. Torpedo bulges were not fitted to this class, but a splinter protection deck placed 0.8cm (2ft 7in) below the main armour deck was a new feature.

AIR DEFENCE
South Dakota's anti-aircraft batteries in action against low-flying Japanese torpedo bombers in the Battle of the Santa Cruz Islands, 26 October 1942.

Iowa (1943)

SPECIFICATIONS

DIMENSIONS:	Length: 270.4m (887ft 2in); Beam: 33.5m (108ft 3in); Draught: 11.5m (38ft)
DISPLACEMENT:	47,173 tonnes (52,000 tons); 52,118 tonnes (57,450 tons) full load
PROPULSION:	8 Babcock & Wilcox boilers, 4 GE steam turbines developing 158,088kW (212,000hp), 4 screws
SPEED:	33 knots (61km/h; 38mph)
RANGE:	12,937nm (23,960km; 14,890 miles) at 12 knots (22km/h; 14mph)
ARMAMENT:	9 406mm (16in) guns in 3 turrets, 20 127mm (5in) guns, 60 40mm (1.6in) AA guns
ARMOUR:	Belt: 310mm (12.2in); Barbettes: 440–287mm (17.3–11.3in); Turret faces: 500mm (19.7in); Deck: 152mm (6in)
COMPLEMENT:	1921

Lead ship of the US Navy's last and largest class of battleships, pennant number BB61, *Iowa* was planned and built as a 'supership', to have a combination of armament, speed and armour superior to that of any other nation.

Below: The profile shows Iowa-class USS *Missouri* as it appeared in 1944–45. It was on board *Missouri* that Japan's surrender was formally signed on 2 September 1945, ending World War II.

FUNNEL
Black paint on the funnel caps was a post-World War II alteration.

GUNS
The 406mm (16in) guns were Mark VII, of 50 calibre compared to *Indiana*'s 45 calibre. On 20 January 1989, one of them fired a shell to a distance of 43,300m (47,350yd), believed to be a record.

TORPEDO PROTECTION
Below the waterline, tanks filled with oil or water lined the side outside the belt armour to detonate torpedoes and absorb the shock.

ANTI-AIRCRAFT DEFENCES

By the time *Iowa* entered service, the vulnerability of capital ships to air attack was very well known to the Allied forces. Consequently, a massive battery of AA guns was fitted. A length 48.5m (159ft) greater than *South Dakota* allowed for more mountings, and the extra 8164 tonnes (8035 tons) provided a more substantial platform. In 1943, it carried 80 40mm (1.6in) Bofors guns and 49 20mm (0.79in) AA Oerlikon cannon mounted on both sides of the superstructure

KOREAN WAR
Iowa firing its full broadside to starboard against shore targets in North Korea, in mid-1952. The blast effect on the sea's surface is very noticeable.

Kirov Class (1977)

SPECIFICATIONS

DIMENSIONS:	Length: 250m (827ft); Beam: 28.5m (94ft); Draught: 9.1m (3 ft)
DISPLACEMENT:	25,401 tonnes (28,000 tons) full load
PROPULSION:	2-shaft CONAS, nuclear-powered with steam turbine boost producing 104.4 MW (140,000 shp)
SPEED:	32 knots (59km/h; 37mph)
RANGE:	1000nm (1852km; 1150 miles) at 30 knots (56km/h; 34.8mph); essentially unlimited with nuclear power at 20 knots (37km/h; 23mph)
ARMAMENT:	10 533mm (21in) torpedo tubes; 20 SS-N-19 Shipwreck cruise missiles; 14 SS-N-14 cruise missiles; rocket launchers, and guns
ARMOUR:	76mm (3in) plating around reactor compartment
COMPLEMENT:	800

When the Soviet Union launched the missile cruiser *Kirov* in December 1977, she was the largest warship – apart from aircraft carriers – built by any nation since World War II. She was reminiscent of the battlecruisers of bygone years.

Right: A view of *Kirov's* bridge and mainmast, showing some of its array of sensors and radar units.

SENSORS
Kirov carried a formidable array of sensors, including air/surface search radar, fire-control radar, and hull-mounted sonar. The Voskhod MR800 Top Pair search radar was mounted on the foremast.

ARMAMENT
The primary armament of the *Kirov* was the Granit (SS-N-19 'Shipwreck') long-range anti-ship missile. 20 missiles were installed under the upper deck, mounted at an angle of 60 degrees.

BOW
One of the prominent features of the Kirov-class warships was the sharply raked bow, a feature of all Soviet warships designed in the latter years of the Cold War.

AIRCRAFT
The cruiser was equipped to carry three Kamov Ka-25 'Hormone-A' or Ka-27 'Helix' helicopters. On board were 18 aircrew, two crews being assigned to each helicopter. While the primary role of the Ka-25 helicopters was submarine hunting, the Ka-27 helicopters also acted as missile guidance aircraft, providing target data for the ship's SS-N-19 anti-ship missiles.

MACHINERY
Kirov's propulsion system was based on a combination of nuclear power and steam turbine. Two nuclear reactors were coupled to two oil-fired boilers, which superheated the steam produced in the reactor plant to increase the power output available during high-speed running.

COMPARTMENTS
The main machinery was arranged in three compartments: one compartment housed the two nuclear reactors; the other two housed the geared-turbine units and steam boilers respectively.

RFS ADMIRAL USHAKOV
Kirov was renamed *Admiral Ushakov* in 1992. In total, four ships of the planned five Kirov class were commissioned between 1980 and 1998, the fifth ship being cancelled in 1990.

Type 22 (1979)

SPECIFICATIONS

DIMENSIONS:	Batch 1: Length: 131.2m (430ft); Beam: 14.8m (48ft); Draught: 6.1m (20 feet)
DISPLACEMENT:	4500 tonnes (4429 tons)
PROPULSION:	2 Rolls-Royce Olympus TM3B gas turbines, 40MW (54,000shp); 2 Rolls-Royce Tyne RM1C cruise gas turbines, 7.2MW (9700shp)
SPEED:	30 knots (56km/h; 34.8mph)
RANGE:	4500nm (8890km; 5524 miles) at 18 knots (33km/h; 21mph)
ARMAMENT:	Batch 3: 2 Sea Wolf anti-air missile launchers; 2 Quad Harpoon missile launchers; 2 triple Magazine launched anti-submarine torpedo tubes; 1 114mm (4.5in) Mk.8 gun; 2 20mm (0.78in) GAM-BO1 guns; 1 Goalkeeper CIWS
COMPLEMENT:	222

In total, some 14 Type 22 frigates would be produced for Royal Navy service between 1979 and 1990. They were initially intended to be anti-submarine vessels, but over the course of their development and deployment they came to perform numerous other roles, from providing air-defence screens to counter-piracy operations.

Right: A Lynx helicopter flies over the bows of HMS *Beaver*. Each Type 22 could carry one or two Lynx Mk 8 helicopters, armed with anti-ship and anti-submarine missiles.

HULL
The Type 22 design went through three evolutions, denoted by Batch numbers. In each evolution, the hull length was increased, with Batch 3 at 148.1m (486ft).

EXOCET LAUNCHERS
The four Exocet missile launchers on the foredeck were replaced in the Batch 3 ships by the classic 114mm (4.5in) Mk 8 gun.

SEAWOLF
At the rear of the ship are 2 × 6 GWS25 Seawolf SAM launchers, these providing the ships with a point-defence system against air attacks.

FALKLANDS SERVICE
Two Type 22 frigates served in the Falklands War in 1982: HMS *Brilliant* and HMS *Broadsword*. During their time in theatre, both ships came under heavy Argentine attack. *Brilliant* was slightly damaged by aerial cannon fire, while *Broadsword* was hit by a bomb that passed through the ship, disabling a Lynx helicopter on the way, but thankfully exiting the vessel before exploding. Between them the two vessels shot down five Argentine aircraft (*Broadsword* shared one with HMS *Antelope*).

HMS *BROADSWORD*
HMS *Broadsword* was the lead ship of the Type 22 class. Laid down on 7 February 1975, she was commissioned on 4 May 1979. The ship was sold to the Brazilian Navy on 30 June 1995 and renamed *Greenhalgh*.

Sovremennyy Class (1980)

SPECIFICATIONS

DIMENSIONS:	Length: 156m (512ft); Beam: 17.3m (56.8ft); Draught: 6.5m (21.3ft)
DISPLACEMENT:	7203 tonnes (7940 tons)
PROPULSION:	2 shaft steam turbines, 74.6MW (100,000hp)
SPEED:	32 knots (59km/h; 37mph)
RANGE:	3406nm (6307km; 3920 miles) at 18 knots (33.3km/h; 20.7mph)
AIRCRAFT:	1 Ka-25 Helix helicopter
ARMAMENT:	2 × 4 SS-N-22 Sunburn Moskit SSM; 2 × 1 SA-N-7 Gadfly SAM; 4 130mm (5.1in) guns; 4 30mm (1.18in) AK-630 Gatling guns; 4 553mm (21in) torpedo tubes; 2 x RBU-1000 ASW rockets
ARMOUR:	–
COMPLEMENT:	350

The name *Sovremennyy* translates from the Russian as 'modern.' The designation was ideally suited to this formidable class of destroyer, its weapon systems upgraded to counter the American Spruance-class multi-role destroyers.

HELICOPTER
Sovremennyy-class ships are fitted with a helicopter pad for one Kamov Ka-25 ASW helicopter, which can operate up to 200km (125 miles) from the parent vessel.

COMBAT SYSTEMS
The ship's combat systems can use target-designation data from the ship's active and passive sensors, from other ships in the fleet, from surveillance aircraft, or via a communications link from the ship's helicopter.

ANTI-SUBMARINE WEAPONS
The destroyer has two double 533mm (21in) torpedo tubes and two six-barrel RBU-1000 anti-submarine rocket launchers, with 48 rockets. The rocket is armed with a 55kg (122lb) warhead and has a range of 1000m (1094yd).

ARMAMENT
The Sovremennyy class is armed with 44 air-defence missiles, eight anti-ship missiles, torpedoes, mines, long-range guns and a sophisticated electronic warfare system.

MACHINERY
Sovremennyy (decommissioned in 1998) was powered by two steam turbine engines, each producing 37.3kW (50,000hp), together with four high-pressure boilers driving two fixed-pitch propellers. The ship's maximum speed was just under 33 knots (61km/h; 38mph) and its range was 3406nm (6307km; 3920 miles) at 18 knots (33.3km/h; 20.7mph).

SAM LAUNCHERS
In this aerial surveillance shot of a Sovremennyy-class vessel, we can see the quad SS-N-22 surface-to-air (SAM) missile launchers towards the front of the vessel. Most of this class of destroyer have now been decommissioned, although some remain in Russian service and others have been sold into the Chinese Navy.

Ticonderoga Class (1983)

SPECIFICATIONS

DIMENSIONS:	Length: 173m (567ft); Beam: 16.8m (55ft); Draught: 10.2m (234ft)
DISPLACEMENT:	Approx. 9800 tonnes (9645 tons)
PROPULSION:	4 General Electric LM2500 gas turbines, 60,000kW (80,000shp)
SPEED:	32.5 knots (60 km/h; 37.4 mph)
RANGE:	6000nm (11,000km; 6835 miles) at 20 knots (37km/h; 23mph)
ARMAMENT:	2 61-cell Mk 41 vertical launch systems, containing 122 cruise, SAM, SSM and anti-submarine missiles; 8 Harpoon missiles; 2 Mk 45 Mod 2 127mm (5in)/54-cal lightweight gun; 2 25mm (1in) Mk 38 gun; 2 Phalanx CIWS; 2 Mk 32 torpedo tubes
COMPLEMENT:	400

The Ticonderoga class of guided-missile cruisers forms a critical power element of today's US Navy. In total, 27 of this type have been built. At the time of writing, five early vessels have been decommissioned, while the rest remain on active service.

Above: This aerial view of a Ticonderoga-class vessel shows the sleek lines of the primary design; the hull lines are largely based on those of the earlier Spruance-class destroyers.

AEGIS COMBAT SYSTEM
The ACS is a combat suite that allies advanced command and decision technology to a weapon control system, linked mainly to the Phalanx CIWS and the Mk 41 VLS.

VERTICAL LAUNCHING SYSTEM
Located just behind the 114mm (4.5in gun), the Mk 41 VLS can fire a variety of missile types, including cruise missiles, SAMs and anti-ship weapons, meaning that multiple missiles are kept in readiness simultaneously.

AEGIS CAPABILITY
The Ticonderoga class includes the Aegis Ballistic Missile Defense System, which enables the vessels to track, engage and destroy incoming ballistic missiles and even, potentially, satellites in a low-Earth orbit. To test that capability, on 20 February 2008, *Lake Erie* fired an SM-3 missile at a dead US satellite as it was just about to re-enter Earth's atmosphere. The DoD announced that the missile had indeed achieved a direct hit on the target.

REAR HELICOPTER DECK
The Ticonderoga-class vessels can operate two Sikorsky SH-60B or MH-60R Seahawk LAMPS III helicopters.

USS TICONDEROGA (CG-47)
CG-47 is the fifth United States Navy vessel named for the Capture of Fort Ticonderoga in 1775.

Type 23 Frigate (1987)

SPECIFICATIONS

DIMENSIONS: Length: 133m (434ft 4 in); Beam: 16.1m (52ft 10 in); Draught: 7.3m (24ft)

DISPLACEMENT: 3810 tonnes (4200 tons) full load

PROPULSION: CODLAG (Combined Diesel-electric and Gas) with 4 1510kW (2025shp) Paxman Valenta 12CM diesel generators powering two GEC electric motors delivering 2980kW (4000shp) and 2 Rolls-Royce Spey SM1A delivering 23,190kW (31,100shp) to 2 shafts

SPEED: 28 knots (52km/h; 32mph)

RANGE: 9000nm (16,668km; 10,360 miles) at 15 knots (27.7km/h; 17.2mph)

AIRCRAFT: 1 Lynx HMA8 or Merlin HM1 helicopter

ARMAMENT: 2 quadruple Harpoon launchers; 1 Sea Wolf GWS.26 VLS; 2 twin 324mm (12.75in) torpedo tubes; 1 114mm (4.5in) Mk 8 DP gun; 2 x DS 30B 30mm (1.18in) AA guns, 2 CIWS

COMPLEMENT: 181

The Type 23 light anti-submarine frigate was conceived in the late 1970s to replace both the Leander class, developed in the 1950s, and the 1960s-vintage Type 21. The new type was intended to be the backbone of the British Royal Navy's surface ship anti-submarine force.

Right: The Type 23 vessels still form the backbone of the Royal Navy's frigate force, with 13 vessels in service at the time of writing.

SENSORS
The Duke-class Type 23 frigates have a range of powerful sensors for communications and to detect the enemy in the air, on the surface or underwater. Information from the sensor suite is fed into the vessel's sophisticated BAe SEMA command system.

MISSILES
The Type 23s are armed with two quadruple Harpoon launchers and were the first ships to be fitted with the vertical-launch Sea Wolf anti-aircraft missile, which is boosted vertically until it clears the ship's superstructure.

GUNS
The frigates were originally equipped with a BAe Systems RO Defence 114mm (4.5in) Mk 8 Mod 0 gun with a range of 22km (14 miles) against surface and 6km (3.7 miles) against airborne targets. These were gradually replaced with the electrically driven Mk 8 Mod 1, *Norfolk* being the first to be so equipped in 2001.

MACHINERY
The Type 23 vessels use a Combined Diesel-Electric and Gas (CODLAG) system of propulsion, with electrical motors powered by diesel generators, but gas turbines used for higher speeds.

ACCOMODATION
Much emphasis was placed on crew comfort and safety in the design of the Type 23s. For example, foam mattresses were replaced with sprung mattresses to reduce the risk of fire.

SUPERSTRUCTURE
Designed for an anti-submarine role, the ship's superstructure is angled to minimize radar reflections, shrinking her 133m (434ft) hull so that it has the radar signature of a fishing boat. Such 'stealth' capability has become an important characteristic of most modern destroyers and frigates.

ONBOARD HELICOPTERS
The Type 23s carry a single helicopter, either a Lynx HMA8 or, as seen here, a Westland Merlin HM2, armed with anti-submarine or anti-ship missiles.

Arleigh Burke Destroyer (1991)

SPECIFICATIONS

DIMENSIONS:	Flight I: Length: 154m (505ft); Beam: 20m (66ft); Draught: 9.3m (30ft 6in)
DISPLACEMENT:	Flight I: 8315 tonnes (8184 tons)
PROPULSION:	4 General Electric LM2500 gas turbines, each 19,570kW (26,250bhp)
SPEED:	30 knots (56km/h; 35mph)
RANGE:	4400nm (8100km; 5030 miles) at 20 knots (37km/h; 23mph)
ARMAMENT:	Multiple missile configurations from a Mk 41 Vertical Launch System; 2 Mk 141 Harpoon missile launchers; various cannon and CIWS configruations; 2 or 6 torpedo tubes
COMPLEMENT:	c. 300

Named after a distinguished US Navy admiral, the Arleigh Burke class of guided missile destroyers are the foundation of the US Navy's combat surface fleet, with some 68 vessels completed to date (2018) and more planned for the future. Each ship can deploy more than 100 missiles of various types, ranging from Tomahawk cruise missiles through to RIM-161 ballistic defence missiles and Harpoon SSMs.

Right: An Arleigh Burke class destroyer underway. The class has been built in several evolutions known as 'Flights', the most modern being Flight IIA.

PHALANX
The Phalanx CIWS is a radar-guided multi-barrel 20mm (0.79in) cannon, used for engaging fast incoming threats with a stream of shells, fired at between 3000 and 4500rpm.

NAVAL GUN
5in (127mm) Mk 45 Mod 1 dual-purpose gun.

STEALTH DESIGN
The destroyers use smooth-angled surfaces as much as possible to reduce the radar signature.

USS COLE
On 12 October 2000, the USS *Cole*, an Arleigh Burke class destroyer, was attacked in Aden harbour by suicide bombers, who piloted a small craft against the side of the American warship and detonated a 300kg (660lb) charge. In total, 17 crewmembers were killed by the explosion, which ripped a huge hole in the side of the vessel. The damage was eventually repaired, and the ship returned to service in 2001.

SUPPORT MISSION
The guided missile destroyer USS *Arleigh Burke* (DDG 51) steams through the Mediterranean. *Arleigh Burke* was deployed in the Mediterranean Sea in 2003, conducting missions in support of Operation Enduring Freedom.

Visby (2002)

SPECIFICATIONS

DIMENSIONS:	Length: 72.6m (238ft); Beam: 10.4m (34ft); Draught: 2.5m (8.2ft)
DISPLACEMENT:	590 tonnes (650 tons)
PROPULSION:	CODAG, 2 Honeywell TF 50 A gas turbines, total rating 16MW (21,446shp), 2 MTU Friedrichshafen 16V 2000 N90 diesel engines, total rating 2.6MW (2385hp)
SPEED:	40 knots (74km/h; 46mph)
RANGE:	2500nm (4600km; 2860 miles) at 15 knots (27.7km/h; 17.2mph)
AIRCRAFT:	Helicopter pad
ARMAMENT:	1 57mm (2.24in) Mk3 gun; 8 RBS15 Mk 2 anti-ship missile; plus mines and depth charges
COMPLEMENT:	43

The Visby-class corvette is the latest class of corvette to be deployed with the Royal Swedish Navy after the Göteborg and Stockholm classes. The vessel has many stealth features, and the first two ships became operational early in 2010.

STRUCTURE
The hull is constructed with a sandwich design consisting of a PVC core with a carbon fibre and vinyl laminate. Its angular design reduces its radar signature.

ARMAMENT
Visby was designed to carry eight RBS15 anti-ship missiles, mines and depth charges, and vertical-launch surface-to-air missiles, but it was decided not to install the latter. A rapid-firing 57mm (2.24in) Bofors gun is mounted.

SYSTEMS
Visby carries hull-mounted, variable-depth and towed-array sonar systems. The vessel is fitted with a Condor CS-3701 Tactical Radar Surveillance System and a Ceros 200 fire control radar system.

ROVs
The corvette is equipped with a compartment for housing and launching remotely controlled vehicles (ROVs) for hunting and destroying mines.

AIRCRAFT
Visby can carry one helicopter, such as the AgustaWestland A109M. A helicopter hangar was originally planned, but was deleted because it was considered too cramped. The helicopter is able to land, take off and refuel from a platform on the upper deck.

MACHINERY
Visby is powered by four Vericor TF50A turbines for high speed, plus two diesels for low speed with double flexible mountings, with encapsulated noise-absorbant housings.

HMS *HELSINGBORG*
HMS *Helsingborg* is the second of the Visby class corvettes, launched in June 2003 and delivered for naval service in April 2006. In total, the class consists of five vessels.

Type 45 Destroyer (2009)

SPECIFICATIONS

DIMENSIONS:	Length: 152.4m (500ft); Beam: 21.2m (69.5ft); Draught: 7.4m (16.4ft)
DISPLACEMENT:	8092 tonnes (9000 tons) deep load
PROPULSION:	2 Rolls-Royce WR-21 gas turbines producing 21.5MW (28,819shp), 2 Converteam electric motors producing 20MW (26,808shp)
SPEED:	29 knots (53.7km/h; 33.3mph)
RANGE:	7000nm (12,964km; 8055 miles) at economical speed
AIRCRAFT:	1 Lynx HMA8 or 1 Westland Merlin HM1 helicopter
ARMAMENT:	1 PAAMS Air Defence System SYLVER CLS of Aster 15 and Aster 30 missiles; 2 Phalanx CIWS; 1 BAE 114mm (4.5in) Mk 8 mod 1 gun; 2 30mm (1.18in) guns
COMPLEMENT:	190

The Type 45 destroyer is a state-of-the-art air defence destroyer programme, designed to replace the Type 42 destroyers in service with the British Royal Navy. The Type 45s are also known as the Daring class after the lead ship of the same name.

RADAR
Daring's SAMPSON radar is said to be capable of tracking an object the size of a tennis ball travelling at three times the speed of sound.

AIR DEFENCE
The Type 45 design uses the Principal Anti-Air Missile System (PAAMS), a joint British, French and Italian design. The PAAMS system is able to control and coordinate several missiles in the air at once.

FLIGHT DECK
The Type 45 has a large flight deck that can accommodate helicopters up to and including the size of a Chinook. The ship can also take up to 700 people if necessary to support a civilian evacuation from war zones or natural disasters.

PROPULSION
The Type 45 is the first warship to use an all-electric propulsion system. This removes the need for a gearbox on the ship, which considerably simplifies maintenance and also reduces the amount of lay-up time.

STEALTH FEATURES
The Type 45 incorporates signature reduction features, including the elimination of right angles and reduced equipment on deck. The infrared signature is reduced by cooling devices on the funnels.

ACCOMODATION
The Type 45 is able to embark up to 60 troops (over and above its own complement) and their equipment, and support them with a modern medical facility that can provide surgical capability.

GUN FITTING
Although the Type 45 is at the cutting edge of naval technology, it has retained a forward gun, in this case the 114mm (4.5in) Mk 8 naval gun. Past lessons have shown that, in general, omitting a gun armament is a tactical mistake.

DDX (Zumwalt Class) (2016)

SPECIFICATIONS

DIMENSIONS:	Length: 183m (600ft); Beam: 25.6m (84ft); Draught: 8.4m (28ft)
DISPLACEMENT:	14,798 tonnes (14,564 tons)
PROPULSION:	2 Rolls-Royce Marine Trent-30 gas turbines and emergency diesel generators
SPEED:	30.3 knots (56km/h; 35mph)
RANGE:	–
ARMAMENT:	Aircraft: 1 SH-60 or MH-60R helicopter, 3 MQ-8 Fire Scout VTUAVs. Weapons: 20 MK 57 VLS modules; Evolved Sea Sparrow Missile (ESSM); Tactical Tomahawk Vertical Launch Anti-Submarine Rocket (ASROC); 2 155mm (6.1in) Advanced Gun System; 2 Mk 110 57mm (2.24in) gun (CIWS)
COMPLEMENT:	142

LAND AND SURFACE ATTACK

The Zumwalt class will be armed with two 155mm (6.1in) guns capable of firing 12 rounds per minute at targets up to 100 nautical miles (185km; 115 miles) distant, for land attack and engagement of surface combatants. Missile armament includes Tactical Tomahawk cruise missiles in vertical launch tubes dispersed around the hull. Doing this, rather than concentrating them in one area, reduces the effects of damage on the ship's ability to fight and the possibility of a single hit crippling the vessel's armament.

The Zumwalt class of advanced multi-mission destroyers is currently under development for use by the United States Navy. The project has been revised at times to meet changing requirements and to take advantage of new technologies. Rather than being optimized for 'blue water' operations in the open ocean, the Zumwalt class is primarily aimed at the littoral environment close to the shore.

Right: The stealth features of the Zumwalt class are so sophisticated that despite being larger than an Arleigh Burke destroyer, they have the same radar signature as a fishing boat.

AVIATION DECK

The large aviation deck and hanger can accommodate two SH-60 helicopters.

HULL

The hull uses a 'tumblehome' configuration, sloping inwards rather than outwards above the waterline. Combined with the use of advanced materials, this greatly reduces radar return.

STEALTH FEATURES

Thermal and acoustic emissions are kept to a minimum, and advanced low-probability-of-intercept radars are utilized, improving 'stealth' characteristics even when actively emitting radar pulses.

MISSILE LAUNCH

An artist's impression of the Zumwalt class in action. At the time of writing (2018), one vessel – the *Zumwalt* – has been commissioned and two others are estimated for commissioning in 2019. However, the US Navy plans to build more of the less expensive Arleigh Burke class, which follows a far more traditional design.

Small Arms

In one sense, small-arms technology has made relatively few advances since 1945, at least in terms of the core principles of how they work. Despite their futuristic appearance, modern military firearms still fire propellant-filled cartridges from a variety of blowback, gas and recoil-operated systems, much as they did in World War II. Yet advances have come in the material construction, modularity and sighting of small arms. Today's weapons are lighter, more instinctive to aim, often have precision optical sights as standard, and can accept a variety of tactical attachments on integral rails.

SPECIAL FORCES WEAPON
A US Navy SEAL conducts training with his FN SCAR assault rifle, fitted with a suppressor. The SCAR is one of a new generation of infantry rifles, and is available in both 5.56mm and 7.62mm calibres.

Adams Revolver (c. 1851)

SPECIFICATIONS

DIMENSIONS:	Length: 330mm (13in)
	Barrel Length: 190mm (7.48in)
WEIGHT:	1.27kg (2.79lb)
CALIBRE:	.51in
OPERATION:	Double-action revolver
FEED:	5-round cylinder
MUZZLE VELOCITY:	213m/sec (700ft/sec)
EFFECTIVE RANGE:	30m (32yd)

One of the most important weapons of the mid-nineteenth century was the Adams revolver. This weapon can be considered a British equivalent of the Colt in terms of its significance, as it was the first successful double-action revolver. At first muzzle-loading, later guns in the Adams family were adapted for centrefire cartridges.

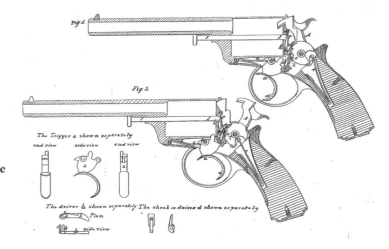

Above: US patent diagram for the 1855 Beaumont-Adams revolver, a weapon developed on the Adams framework by Lieutenant Frederick E.B. Beaumont of the Royal Engineers.

BARREL
The comparatively long barrel gave the gun good forward stability in a steady hand, giving reasonable accuracy over the weapon's effective range.

ROBERT ADAMS (1810–70)
Robert Adams was a landmark figure in the history of British firearms design. A manager at the London-based arms manufacturers George and John Dean, Adams broke new ground in 1851 with the patent for his Adams Self-Cocking Revolver, a design of such importance that he was made a partner in the firm.

CYLINDER
A drawback of the Adams concerned safety. Being a double-action only revolver, when the cylinder was fully loaded with cap, powder and ball the hammer rested on a live cap, raising the prospect of accidental discharges.

DOUBLE ACTION
The Adams revolver was self-cocking only; there was no external hammer spur for cocking the weapon manually for single-shot mode. The only way to fire the gun, therefore, was to pull the trigger through its full cycle.

IMPROVED VERSIONS
The innovation of Lieutenant Frederick Beaumont in 1855 is evident in the hammer spur of this boxed weapon. Beaumont improved the action of the basic Adams, enabling it to fire in both single- and double-action modes. The Beaumont-Adams was adopted as an official British Army service pistol in 1855.

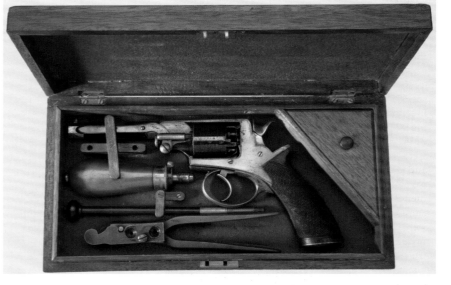

Colt M1851 Navy & 1860 Army (1851/1860)

SPECIFICATIONS

Navy Colt

DIMENSIONS:	Length: 328mm (12.91in)
	Barrel Length: 190mm (7.5in)
WEIGHT:	1.02kg (36oz)
CALIBRE:	0.36in
OPERATION:	Single-action revolver
FEED:	6-round cylinder
MUZZLE VELOCITY:	300m/sec (980ft/sec)
EFFECTIVE RANGE:	40m (44yd)

Army Colt

DIMENSIONS:	Length: 349mm (13.74in)
	Barrel Length: 203mm (8in)
WEIGHT:	1.25kg (44oz)
CALIBRE:	.44in
OPERATION:	Single-action revolver
FEED:	6-round cylinder
MUZZLE VELOCITY:	220m/sec (725ft/sec)
EFFECTIVE RANGE:	40m (44yd)

Two major Colt variants saw use in the American Civil War (1861–65): the M1860 'Army' Colt, chambered in .44 calibre, and the M1851 'Navy' Colt, which was chambered for .36. A new 'Navy' revolver, the M1861, based on the 'Army' design, was fielded, but did not achieve commercial success.

Below: There was almost no visual distinction between the two Colts, although here we see, at the top, a particularly ornate ceremonial version of the M1851 Navy.

LOADING LEVER
The hinged loading lever beneath the barrel was used to tamp down each ball firmly atop the powder in the cylinder, the ball fitting tightly to prevent gas escape on firing.

CAP AND BALL
The early Colts were 'cap-and-ball' pistols: each cylinder was individually loaded with a bullet, powder and percussion cap.

SIX-SHOOTER
Both the 1851 and 1860 were six-shot weapons. The Navy weapon had a slightly shorter cylinder than the Army variant.

SINGLE ACTION
Both revolvers were single-action only. The hammer was drawn back and cocked before firing, resulting in a very light trigger pull.

DEMAND FOR COLTS
The number of guns in circulation following the Civil War did little to reduce demand. As the dust of war settled and the migration westward began, the Colt company supplied arms to the frontiersmen by the ton. Then came the defining moment in the development of modern firearms: the point at which flintlocks were pronounced dead and cap-and-ball weapons were eclipsed by unitary metallic cartridge weapons. Samuel Colt's revolvers were at the forefront of the firearms revolution and truly deserve their place in history.

COLTS FOR THE COMMON MAN
It was not uncommon for soldiers to display revolvers proudly during photographic portrait sittings, as we see here on the left. The price of an 1860 Army Colt was about $20, which was quite expensive for the time; the later 1865 model was reduced to $14.50.

Borchardt C/93 (1893)

SPECIFICATIONS

DIMENSIONS:	Length: 279mm (11in)
	Barrel Length: 165mm (6.5in)
WEIGHT:	1.1kg (2.56lb)
CALIBRE:	7.65 × 25mm
OPERATION:	Short recoil
FEED:	8-round detachable box magazine
MUZZLE VELOCITY:	326m/sec (1070ft/sec)
EFFECTIVE RANGE:	100m (109yd) with stock

One example of a ground-breaking but ultimately less than useful weapon is the Borchardt C/93. This masterpiece of engineering was unwieldy and fragile due to the protruding mechanism for recoil operation. Its significance, however, was that the Borchardt was the first self-loading handgun, fed from a detachable box magazine.

Above: A top view of the Borchardt's toggle-joint recoil system, which worked on similar principles to that used in the Maxim machine gun.

TOGGLE LOCK
The toggle lock 'broke' upwards when the gun recoiled, allowing the empty case to eject upwards and clear of the gun.

SELF-LOADING PISTOLS
Self-loading semi-automatic pistols offered two major advantages over revolvers: 1) a higher magazine capacity (most revolvers were limited to just six rounds) and 2) faster reloading times, as preloaded magazines could be kept at the ready and switched over in seconds. On the negative side, semi-automatic pistols were less reliable than revolvers, being more prone to stoppages.

MAGAZINE
The pistol's detachable box magazine held eight rounds of 7.65mm ammunition. Many early semi-auto pistols had fixed top-charged magazines.

RECOIL OPERATION
The Borchardt used the force of recoil to power the gun through its extraction and ejection phases.

CARBINE PISTOL
Although the Borchardt pistol was functional and sold in significant numbers until it was discontinued in 1898, it was undeniably heavy and awkward to use. It therefore came supplied with a detachable wooden stock to turn the pistol into a carbine. The stock also functioned as a holster.

Mauser C/96 (1896)

SPECIFICATIONS

DIMENSIONS:	Length: 312mm (12.25in)
	Barrel Length: 139mm (5.5in)
WEIGHT:	1.25kg (2.75lb)
CALIBRE:	7.63 × 25mm
OPERATION:	Short recoil
FEED:	10-round integral magazine
MUZZLE VELOCITY:	434m/sec (1425ft/sec)
EFFECTIVE RANGE:	Up to 100m (109yd)

Looking somewhat ungainly to the untrained eye, the Mauser C/96 was actually a powerful, well-balanced and accurate weapon. Only the success of other handguns and calibres prevented it from achieving greater historical prominence.

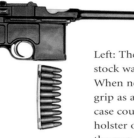

Left: The C/96's shoulder stock was an ingenious design. When not fitted to the pistol grip as a stock, the wooden case could also serve as a holster or carrying case for the gun.

SHORT RECOIL
During recoil, the barrel and bolt would recoil together for a short distance before disconnecting and allowing the bolt to return fully to the rear.

HAMMER
In the original C/96, the large hammer actually obscured the rear sight when it was forward as a reminder to cock the gun.

CARTRIDGE
The 7.63 × 25mm Mauser cartridge had a bullet weight of 5.57g (86 grains).

MAGAZINE
To load the integral magazine, the bolt was opened and held back, and rounds pushed down into the magazine from a stripper clip.

UPDATED VERSIONS

During the 1920s and 30s, the C/96 was the subject of some significant revision. To evade the Versailles Treaty restrictions on pistol barrel length and calibre, the 'Bolo' model was calibrated again for 7.63mm and its barrel length reduced to 99mm (3.38in). During the 1930s, Mauser also noted that some Spanish gunmakers had produced full-auto copies of the C/96. In response, Mauser officially produced the M712 model, which featured 10- or 20-round detachable magazines and a selective-fire capability via a simple bar level selector on the left-hand side of the frame.

LOADING

Here we see the Mauser C/96 with its bolt in the rearmost position (note the cocking action on the hammer) and a stripper clip positioned for loading the magazine.

SPECIFICATIONS

DIMENSIONS:	Length: 223mm (8.75in)
	Barrel Length: 102mm (4in)
WEIGHT:	0.87kg (1.92lb)
CALIBRE:	9 × 19mm Parabellum
OPERATION:	Short recoil
FEED:	8-round box magazine
MUZZLE VELOCITY:	380m/sec (1274ft/sec)
EFFECTIVE RANGE:	50m (55yd)

The infamous Luger P-08 pistol is instantly recognizable in profile and action. It was a desirable acquisition for any Allied infantryman fighting against the Germans during both World Wars.

Above: The Artillery Model Luger, which came with a shoulder stock and 32-round 'snail' magazine, was little more than an experiment. By the end of World War I, submachine guns such as the Bergmann MP18 were better options for portable firepower.

OPERATING THE LUGER

To fire the Luger, the first step is to insert a filled eight-round magazine into the pistol grip. Interestingly, the steep angle of the pistol grip – and, therefore, the magazine feed – means that the magazine is fitted with an ammunition draw-down device to make it easier for the operator to add fresh rounds into the top of the magazine. If the full eight rounds are loaded, the magazine cannot be inserted into the gun if the toggle lock is down; the lock needs to be in the pre-cocked position. To cock the gun with a magazine holding fewer than eight rounds, the operator first releases the safety (the gun cannot be cocked if the safety is on), grips the circular nuts either side of the toggle lock, draws them up and releases them. This action allows the first round to be stripped from the magazine and chambered – the gun is now ready to fire. When the magazine is empty, the toggle lock will lock in the open position.

FIRING PIN
The Luger is fired via a spring-loaded striker, here shown held in its cocked position ready for release when the trigger is pulled.

TOGGLE-LOCK JOINT
Here is the central joint of the toggle lock; this breaks upwards during recoil to allow cartridge extraction and ejection.

HINGE SYSTEM
This spring-loaded hinge mechanism allows the toggle lock to break upwards above the axis of the bore during the recoil phase.

TRIGGER MECHANISM
The Luger's trigger mechanism could be its Achilles' heel; many users complained of poor pull qualities and unreliability.

MAGAZINE
The P-08's single-stack magazine held eight rounds at full capacity.

SIDEARM
A German infantryman clutches a Luger P-08, supplementing his already considerable load of weaponry and ammunition, including a stick grenade and a belt of 7.92mm cartridges.

Colt M1911 (1911)

SPECIFICATIONS

DIMENSIONS:	Length: 216mm (8.5in)
	Barrel Length: 127mm (5in)
WEIGHT:	1.13kg (2.49lb)
CALIBRE:	.45 ACP
OPERATION:	Short recoil
FEED:	7-round box magazine
MUZZLE VELOCITY:	253m/sec (830ft/sec)
EFFECTIVE RANGE:	70m (77yd)

Few guns have the instant recognizability and potent reputation of the Colt M1911. Millions have been made and sold, and for more than 70 years it was the standard handgun for the US armed forces.

Above: The Colt M1911 has been produced in dozens of variants. Here is the Colt Ace, chambered for the low-powered .22 LR cartridge to provide a low-recoil and low-cost training weapon.

SLIDE
Here the slide is in its rearward position at full recoil. Note how the rear of the barrel has tilted downwards, disengaging its top ribs from the slide grooves.

FIRING PIN
The firing pin spring returns the firing pin to position after the recoil and return phases.

COLT POWER

The Colt M1911 was a formidable gun to fire – recoil was heavy, requiring strong hands and a lot of training to recover quickly between shots – but the gun had awesome reliability. The effect on target of the 15.16g (230-grain) .45 ACP round was also beyond question, as it delivered both a deep and a broad penetration track. In short, it was a manstopper. Moreover, the mechanism was of such simple and successful design that to this day a large percentage of the world's handguns are modelled directly on this configuration. Colt weapons in this series still sell in large volumes to civilian, military and law-enforcement markets, with little change to the essential principles. More than 40 different nations have either bought or licence-produced the M1911 since its creation.

SWINGING LINK
Here is the swinging link, responsible for pulling the barrel down to disengage it from the slide during recoil.

MAGAZINE
The M1911's magazine holds a total of seven .45 ACP rounds. The magazine drops out unassisted when the release catch is pressed.

HAMMER
The hammer can be placed in half-cock and full-cock positions, although the half-cock is vulnerable to accidental discharge.

M1911 TRAINING
US Army personnel on a firing range get accustomed to the M1911A1. One of the reasons for the shift to 9mm in the 1980s was the amount of time it took to train an inexperienced soldier on a .45 handgun.

Webley Mk V & Mk VI (1913 & 1915)

SPECIFICATIONS

DIMENSIONS:	Length: 286mm (11.25in)
	Barrel Length: 152mm (6in)
WEIGHT:	1.09kg (2.4lb)
CALIBRE:	.455 British Service
OPERATION:	Double-action revolver
FEED:	6-round cylinder
MUZZLE VELOCITY:	200m/sec (655ft/sec)
EFFECTIVE RANGE:	50m (55yd)

The most famous revolvers in British service at this time were made by Webley & Scott. Two stalwarts of World War I were the Mk V and Mk VI. The 'classic' was the Mk IV, which, like its predecessors, was a heavy but powerful weapon using a break-open ('tip-down') mechanism rather than a hinged cylinder.

Above: When the Webley's action was opened as shown, an automatic extractor removed the spent cartridge cases from the cylinders.

ACTION
The Webley was a double-action revolver, the trigger pull both drawing back and releasing the hammer.

TRENCH WARFARE
Conditions in the trenches were not kind to soldiers or their weapons, but the Webley developed a reputation for reliability in the most horrific conditions. In close-quarters trench fighting, rifles were simply too unwieldy, so handguns, knives and a range of improvised clubs saw frequent and brutal use. A 'revolver-bayonet' was available for the Webley pistol for use in such circumstances, although it was not particularly effective.

BARREL LENGTHS
The standard Mk V barrel was 100mm (4in), but it also came in 130mm (5in) and 150mm (6in) versions.

GRIP
The Mk V gun shown here was largely the same as the Mk VI, but had a rounded grip as opposed to the squared-off grip of the Mk VI.

MANSTOPPER
For combat use, one of the main advantages of the Mk VI was its heavy 17g (265-grain) .455in calibre. Although it was relatively slow in terms of muzzle velocity, the broad lead bullet carried with it a heavy terminal impact for its victims, although it also delivered substantial recoil.

Colt Detective Special (1927)

SPECIFICATIONS

DIMENSIONS:	Length: 171mm (6.7in)
	Barrel Length: 54mm (2.13in)
WEIGHT:	0.6kg (1.31lb)
CALIBRE:	.38 Special
OPERATION:	Double-action revolver
FEED:	6-round cylinder
MUZZLE VELOCITY:	400m/sec (1312ft/sec)
EFFECTIVE RANGE:	25m (27yd)

A small revolver useful for concealed carry, the Colt Detective Special became a weapon of choice for many plain-clothes detectives. This weapon, which entered production in the 1920s, was based on the standard Colt police revolver, fitted with a short or 'snub' barrel only 54mm (2.13in) long.

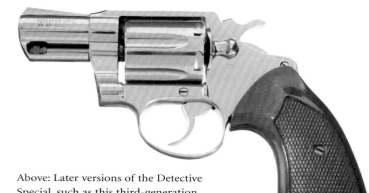

Above: Later versions of the Detective Special, such as this third-generation nickel model, had a shrouded fitting for the extractor rod beneath the barrel.

EASY CARRY
Chambered for .38 Special ammunition, the Detective Special is light enough to be carried in comfort for long periods, and can be drawn quickly from a concealed holster. Its principal drawback was its particularly short barrel, which compromised its accuracy, although in reality it would only be used at close quarters anyway. In the 1950s, the Detective Special was redesignated the Model D.1.

ACTION
The Detective Special is a double-action pistol, with a 'Positive Safety Lock' hammer-block mechanism.

SIGHTS
Ramped front sights were introduced into the Detective Special range from 1947, the gun having previously had a simple 'half-moon' blade.

CALIBRE
The Detective Special came with a six-round cylinder, beating competitors offering only five-shot compact revolvers.

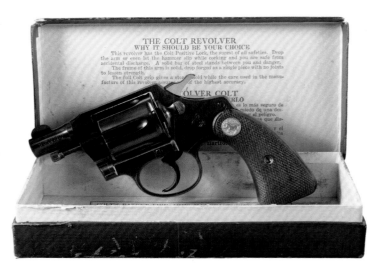

FIRST GENERATION
The boxed revolver here is the first generation of the Detective Special, produced from 1927. It is visually defined from some of the later variants by its unshrouded ejector rod and its half-moon front sight. Its dimensions were kept small by the short barrel, the narrow distance between grip and trigger guard, and its slim frame.

Browning GP35 HP (1935)

SPECIFICATIONS

DIMENSIONS:	Length: 197mm (7.75in)
	Barrel Length: 118mm (4.65in)
WEIGHT:	0.9kg (2.19lb)
CALIBRE:	9 × 19mm Parabellum
OPERATION:	Manual
FEED:	Short recoil
MUZZLE VELOCITY:	335m/sec (1110ft/sec)
EFFECTIVE RANGE:	50m (55yd)

To judge the quality of the Browning GP35 High-Power (HP), we need only note that, since its development in the 1920s and 30s, more than 90 nations have adopted it as a standard side-arm.

Above: The Browning Double Action (BDA) was introduced in the 1980s. As its name states, it has a double-action mechanism, meaning that the hammer can be fully operated by the trigger.

GP35 ADVANTAGES

Produced by Fabrique Nationale of Belgium (although initially a Browning design), the GP35 was an exceptional weapon. It had the reliability of an M1911 but with a radically enhanced ammunition capacity and the smooth-shooting characteristics of a 9mm weapon, with rapid recovery between shots. The Belgians produced 59,000 of the guns before they were occupied in 1941, whereupon the Germans manufactured 329,000, designated Pistole 640(b); most of these went to the Waffen-SS and the Fallschirmjäger. Conversely, the British produced the weapon in small numbers. (FN's chief designer, Dieudonné Saive, and his team had escaped to the UK.) Inglis of Canada had made 151,816 models by 1945 for the Chinese Army.

BARREL
The barrel is locked to the slide via two lugs that engage in cams in the slide.

HAMMER
In the single-action HP, the hammer is cocked by the action of pulling back and releasing the slide.

RETURN SPRING
The return spring beneath the barrel returns the slide to the forward position after the recoil phase.

TRIGGER
When the trigger is pulled, it pushes up a trigger level against a sear level to release the hammer.

MAGAZINE
The Browning magazine has a double-stack configuration, which increases capacity without overly increasing the magazine length.

BRITISH VARIANT

The L9A1 was the British military version of the HP following revisions to the design in the early 1960s. Despite new weapons entering service, this one is still found in British hands today.

Walther P38 (1938)

SPECIFICATIONS

DIMENSIONS:	Length: 213mm (8.38in)
	Barrel Length: 127mm (5in)
WEIGHT:	0.96kg (2.11lb)
CALIBRE:	9mm Parabellum
OPERATION:	Short recoil
FEED:	8-round box magazine
MUZZLE VELOCITY:	350m/sec (1150ft/sec)
EFFECTIVE RANGE:	50m (55yd)

At the beginning of World War II, the Wehrmacht was looking to replace the Luger P-08 as the standard military service pistol. The weapon that stepped into its shoes was the Walther P38, of which nearly 600,000 were made between 1939 and 1945.

Right: The P38 has very clean lines that suggest a well-balanced pistol. In terms of sights, it has a U-shaped notch for the rear sight and a front sight blade fitted in an integral mount.

LOCKED BREECH
Here a cartridge is in the chamber with the slide and breech locked together by a falling wedge.

HAMMER
The hammer could be cocked either by the thumb, trigger or the motion of the slide in recoil.

BARREL
The barrel of the P38 is 127mm (5in) long and features six grooves with a right-hand twist.

TRIGGER
The P38 had a double-action/single-action trigger system, meaning it could be fired from a hammer-uncocked position just by pulling the trigger.

POST-WORLD WAR II SERVICE

The sheer numbers of P38s produced during the war ensured that the handgun would go on to have a lively post-war career through war surplus and new production. On the Soviet side of the Cold War divide, many P38s remained either in civilian hands or went into police use, with the Nazi markings erased. In the West, most of the security forces under American jurisdiction initially had American firearms, and from 1945 to 1957 no military P38s were made. However, things changed with the formation of the Bundeswehr in 1955. Germany once more had a military force that needed kitting out, and it was announced that the P38 would be the standard service pistol. Walther therefore had to gear up again for pistol production. (Walther was now based at Ulm-Donau, the previous factory having been destroyed by the Soviets towards the end of the war.) Thus the P38 gained a new life, although it was now called the P1.

MILITARY HANDGUN
Here a British Army soldier familiarizes himself with the operation and firing characteristics of the P38. The weapon featured some modern innovations when it first emerged, including a loaded chamber indicator and a decocker safety lever.

Beretta 92 & 93R (1976)

SPECIFICATIONS (93R)

DIMENSIONS:	Length: 240mm (9.45in)
	Barrel Length: 156mm (6.14in)
WEIGHT:	1.12kg (2.47lb)
CALIBRE:	9 × 19mm Parabellum
OPERATION:	Short recoil
FEED:	15- or 20-round detachable box
MUZZLE VELOCITY:	375m/sec (1230ft/sec)
EFFECTIVE RANGE:	50m (55yd)
RATE OF FIRE:	1100rpm

The Beretta 92 was introduced in 1976, and its 92SB variant was the eventual winner of the extended trials for a new US military service pistol in the 1980s. The Beretta 92 is a fairly conventional modern semi-automatic. It has an ambidextrous safety and magazine release and can be fired double-action on the first shot or manually cocked. Magazine capacity is 15 rounds of 9mm Parabellum, offering good firepower.

The Beretta 92 has been produced in a number of different variants, often related to the configuration of single-action and double-action mechanisms.

FULL-AUTO OPTION
The Beretta 92 has been a popular standard law enforcement sidearm, also used by many private owners. An 'assault pistol' version, the 93R, was available from the late 1970s. Fitted with a tiny foregrip and an extended magazine, the 93R can deliver three-round bursts. Yet even with the optional stock, a full-automatic pistol is not the most controllable of devices. Although the 93R is in use with Italian governmental protection officers, it has not achieved widespread popularity. A suppressed version of the standard 92F is also available to military users.

BARREL
While the standard Beretta 92 had a barrel length of 217mm (8.54in), the 93R extended it out to 240mm (9.45in).

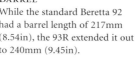

FRONT GRIP
The folding metal front grip of the 93R provides only limited additional stability for the user, although recoil control was also aided by a muzzle brake.

EXTENDED MAGAZINE
Even the 20-round extended magazine would be emptied quickly if the firearm was used continually in three-round burst mode.

UNIVERSAL HANDGUN
Modern handguns are designed for ease of use in the hands of part-trained personnel. These Iranian women are training with 9mm Beretta 92 pistols as members of the Civil Militia, although their formal stances are hardly realistic for actual combat.

IMI Desert Eagle (1979)

SPECIFICATIONS

DIMENSIONS:	Length: 260mm (10.25in)
	Barrel Length: 152mm (6in)
WEIGHT:	1.7kg (3.75lb) for .357; 1.8kg (4.1lb) for .44; 2.05kg (4.5lb) for .50
CALIBRE:	.357, .44 or .50 Magnum
OPERATION:	Gas
FEED:	9 rounds (.357 Magnum); 8 rounds (.44 Magnum); 7 rounds (.50 Magnum), detachable box magazine
MUZZLE VELOCITY:	436 m/sec (1430ft/sec) for .357; 448m/sec (1470ft/sec) for .44
EFFECTIVE RANGE:	100m (109yd)

The original Desert Eagles, chambered for .357 and .44 Magnum, are both extremely powerful weapons. As if this were not enough, a massive .50-calibre version followed.

Above: A British Army paratrooper tests out the Desert Eagle, the intense recoil evident on his face and body.

BARREL
Depending on the variant, the Desert Eagle has been produced in two different barrel lengths, 152mm (6in) and 254mm (10in).

HANDLING THE EAGLE

The standard Desert Eagle is a huge and bulky handgun, quite unsuitable for concealed carry but offering massive stopping power. Its nine-round magazine (for the .357 Magnum) allows reasonable sustained fire, although such an awesome weapon is difficult to control despite being designed to cut felt recoil to manageable levels.

GAS OPERATION
Unlike most other handguns, the Desert Eagle is a gas-operated weapon. Gas ported off just beneath the front of the barrel provides the motive force to drive the slide backwards and perform extraction and ejection.

ROTATING BOLT
Allied to the gas mechanism is a rotating bolt, configured much like those found on military assault rifles. The gun's operating system allows the use of more powerful cartridges than those for regular handguns.

CARTRIDGE CHOICE
Over its production lifetime, the Desert Eagle has been offered in a variety of calibres, all of them potent. The largest – .50 Action Express – generates a muzzle energy of 1965J (1449ft lbf). By comparison, a typical 9mm round has 481J (355ft lbf) of energy.

Glock 17 (1982)

SPECIFICATIONS

DIMENSIONS:	Length: 188mm (7.4in)
	Barrel Length: 114mm (4.49in)
WEIGHT:	0.65kg (1.44lb)
CALIBRE:	9 × 19mm Parabellum
OPERATION:	Short recoil
FEED:	17-round box magazine
MUZZLE VELOCITY:	350m/sec (1148ft/sec)
EFFECTIVE RANGE:	50m (55yd)

The Glock was a truly revolutionary weapon. Its clean lines are made possible by a lack of external controls. Rather than the traditional safety catch, the Glock uses passive safety mechanisms on the trigger, firing pin and firing pin lug; the weapon will not fire unless the trigger is deliberately pulled.

Right: Many modern Glocks feature grooved lower front frames to accept all manner of tactical accessories, such as lights and laser aiming systems.

SLIDE
The slide and the barrel are the main metal parts of the Glock. The Glock's overall profile is kept low; the axis of recoil is kept close to the shooter's hand, aiding quick recovery between shots.

ACTION
The Glock is a striker-fired pistol (it has no internal hammer). Once the gun is loaded, trigger pull alone will then fire the weapon.

HIGH CAPACITY
Invented by Austrian Gaston Glock, the first Glock handgun was the Glock 17. The '17' designator was derived from the weapon's magazine capacity – an awesome 17 rounds of 9mm Parabellum, double-stacked in the detachable box magazine. The firepower offered by such a large magazine, coupled with good marketing and overall simplicity of use, made the Glock 17 a winner. It has been adopted by police and military forces worldwide and is a popular sidearm for civilian weapon users.

FRAME
The frame is formed from a durable polymer, which gave the firearm the nickname of 'the Plastic Pistol'.

TRIGGER SAFETY
A trigger safety lever is built directly into the trigger itself; both trigger and integral lever must be pulled together to enable the gun to fire.

GLOCK POPULARITY
The Glock has been produced in a great many variants, offering a wide range of options when it comes to size, magazine capacity and calibre. Today the Glock is the world's most popular handgun. In the United States alone, some 65 per cent of law enforcement officers carry Glocks.

SIG P320 (2014)

SPECIFICATIONS
(P320 X5 Full-size)

DIMENSIONS:	Length: 216mm (8.5in)
	Barrel Length: 127mm (5in)
WEIGHT:	1kg (2.2lb)
CALIBRE:	Various (see text)
OPERATION:	Short recoil
FEED:	10- or 21-round box magazine
MUZZLE VELOCITY:	360m/sec (1181ft/sec)
EFFECTIVE RANGE:	50m (55yd)

US ARMY HANDGUN

On 19 January 2017, the US Department of Defense announced that the P320 MHS variant had won the Modular Handgun System trials, and thus would become the standard US Army handgun, replacing the Beretta M9 (the military version of the Beretta 92 FS). The weapon is produced in two sizes for military service: the M17 (full size) and M18 (compact).

The SIG P320 is one of a new generation of modular pistols, created by the German SIG Sauer company and produced from 2014. Its modular construction means that frame, slide and barrel can be changed around the internal stainless steel fire-control unit to switch the weapon between different calibres: 9 × 19mm Parabellum, .357 Sig and .40 S&W.

ACTION
The P320 is a short-recoil-operated, locked-breech pistol; the rear of the barrel locks into the gun's ejection port before firing.

Above: A P320 with its slide locked back, the barrel clearly tilted upwards after being disengaged from the slide during the recoil phase.

RAIL
P320s feature a true Mil-std. M1913 rail at the front of the frame, to accept a wide range of tactical accessories.

GRIP
In keeping with its highly modular design, all P320 handguns are offered with options of three glass-filled polymer grip module sizes: small, medium and large.

CIVILIAN MODELS

Texas governor Greg Abbott takes to the firing range with a P320 with an optional suppressor fitted. The TACOPS (Tactical Operations) variant of the P320 comes with an extended barrel threaded at the front to take the suppressor. The version also comes with an extended 21-round magazine.

Dreyse Needle Gun (1841)

SPECIFICATIONS

DIMENSIONS:	Length: 1100mm (43.25in)
	Barrel Length: 700mm (27.5in)
WEIGHT:	4.6kg (10lb)
CALIBRE:	13.6mm
OPERATION:	Single-shot, bolt-action, breech-loading
MUZZLE VELOCITY:	295m/sec (960ft/sec)
EFFECTIVE RANGE:	600m (656yd)
RATE OF FIRE:	–

The Dreyse Needle Fire Rifle was named after the firing mechanism that initiated its unusual cartridge. The Needle Rifle saw action as early as 1849, during unrest in Dresden, and again during the Prussian campaign in Denmark, but it was in the war with Austria in 1866 that it truly demonstrated its potential. Almost at a stroke, existing cap-and-ball muzzle loaders became obsolete.

Above: A cutaway diagram of the Needle Gun operating mechanism. The thinking behind having the primer at the front of the cartridge, rather than the rear, was to improve the efficiency of combustion.

BOLT ACTION
The long needle-like firing pin was actually the rifle's Achilles' heel, as it frequently broke under intensive combat use.

SIGHTS
The sights consisted of a simple V-notch rear sight and a post front sight, requiring great user skill for accuracy over long ranges.

CALIBRE
While von Dreyse created the Needle Gun in 15mm calibre, it was adopted for Prussian Army service in 1836 in a smaller 13.6mm.

FIRING MECHANISM
The cartridges for the Needle Gun were composed of an acorn-shaped bullet glued into a paper case. The gunpowder filled much of the case, up to a papier-mâché wad that contained the cartridge's priming powder, located directly behind the rear of the projectile (not at the base of the cartridge, as with modern weapons). This configuration required a long, needle-like firing pin that, when released, would drive through the full length of the cartridge to strike the priming powder.

TRANSFORMATION
The Needle Gun was essentially the first bolt-action, breech-loading rifle, and it completely changed the face of infantry firepower. During Prussia's campaigns of the 1840s, 50s and 60s, it played a major role in Prussia's victories over its enemies, who could not produce comparable rates of fire or accuracy with their muzzle-loaders.

Chassepot Carbine (1866)

SPECIFICATIONS (CARBINE)

DIMENSIONS:	Length: 1175mm (46.25in)
	Barrel Length: Not available
WEIGHT:	Not available
CALIBRE:	11mm
OPERATION:	Single shot, bolt action
MUZZLE VELOCITY:	410m/sec (1345ft/sec)
EFFECTIVE RANGE:	1000m (1094yd)
RATE OF FIRE:	–

The Chassepot was an excellent weapon, chambered for an 11mm round. From 1873 onward (as the renamed Gras rifle) it used a metallic cartridge. It was a single-shot, bolt-action weapon, and in trained hands could deliver between eight and 15 aimed shots every minute. The carbine version was developed for cavalry and light infantry.

Right: The bolt action of the Chassepot was reliable and quick. Its main problem was that of fouling caused by the paper and powder residues.

SIGHTS
Chassepot sights were graduated out to a maximum of 1600m (1750yd), although effective range was less than half that.

SEALING RING
The Chassepot bolt featured a rubber sealing ring on its face to ensure a gas-tight seal on firing.

CALIBRE
The Chassepot's 11mm calibre was significantly smaller than that of the Dreyse Needle Gun, but it generated higher muzzle velocities and flatter trajectories.

BREECH LOADING

The Chassepot rifle was part of the breech-loading revolution that emerged during the nineteenth century. What made the Chassepot ground-breaking was the way that its bolt-action mechanism was allied to a new paper cartridge – one that had the percussion cap in the base of the cartridge rather than beneath the bullet (like the Dreyse Needle Gun opposite). This meant that the length of the firing pin could be reduced, improving reliability and lock time (the interval from trigger pull to cartridge ignition).

COMBAT USE
Here we see a French infantryman taking aim with his Chassepot carbine. Chassepots were used extensively during the Franco–Prussian War (1870–71), where it demonstrated advantages over the Prussian weapons in terms of rate of fire and accuracy.

Martini-Henry (1871)

SPECIFICATIONS

DIMENSIONS:	Length: 1310mm (51.5in)
	Barrel Length: 850mm (33.25in)
WEIGHT:	4.7kg (10.34lb)
CALIBRE:	45in
OPERATION:	Single-shot, falling-block action
FEED:	Single shot
MUZZLE VELOCITY:	400m/sec (1310ft/sec)
EFFECTIVE RANGE:	600m (656yd)
RATE OF FIRE:	–

The Martini-Henry rifle was the result of combining a seven-groove rifling system invented by Alexander Henry and the falling-block breech mechanism devised by Frederich Martini. The resulting weapon was simple, robust, easy to maintain and accurate. It was adopted for service with the British army in 1871 and served until the end of the 1880s, when it was replaced by the Lee-Metford.

Right: A classic portrait of a late nineteenth-century British infantryman, armed with the Martini-Henry rifle. The Martini-Henry was one of the last single-shot types used as a standard weapon by the British, replaced by the magazine-fed bolt-action Lee-Metford in 1888.

BARREL HEAT
The Martini-Henry's recoil was not excessive, but the barrel did become hot very quickly. Many users wrapped cloth or leather around the barrel to protect their hands.

LEVER ACTION
Depressing the lever drops the breechblock (hence the 'falling-block' designation) and cocks the weapon while extracting the spent round. A round is manually placed in the breech and the weapon brought to firing condition by returning the level to its initial position.

CLEANING ROD
The Martini-Henry could suffer from heavy fouling from the black-powder cartridges; the cleaning rod was stored in a pipe beneath the barrel.

BRITISH BREECHLOADERS
Breech-loading rifles represented a significant increase in infantry firepower, giving troops a massive advantage over opponents equipped with weapons of previous generations. Britain was at the time engaged in a great deal of colonial warfare, pitting small but well-equipped and disciplined forces against large numbers of opponents far from support, so this capability was vital to the defence of the Empire. Sighted out to 1372m (1500yd), the Martini-Henry possessed good stopping power and was capable of rapid fire at need.

IMPERIAL RIFLE
Seen here in the hands of Royal Marines in the late nineteenth century, the Martini-Henry became an iconic weapon of the British imperial period. It was robust and immensely powerful, although the power could mean seriously bruised shoulders over prolonged combat firing.

Mosin-Nagant M1891/30 Rifle (1891/1930)

SPECIFICATIONS

DIMENSIONS:	Length: 1016mm (40in)
	Barrel Length: 508mm (20in)
WEIGHT:	4kg (8.8lb)
CALIBRE:	7.62 × 54R
OPERATION:	Bolt action
FEED:	5-round integral box magazine
MUZZLE VELOCITY:	766m/sec (2514ft/sec)
EFFECTIVE RANGE:	600m (656yd)
RATE OF FIRE:	–

The foremost weapon of the soldiers of Russia, both revolutionaries and counter-revolutionaries, was the Mosin-Nagant rifle, which dated from the 1890s. Like most Russian weapons, it was capable of functioning in the truly horrible conditions that were normal in Russia, and was thus an ideal weapon for the trenches of World War I.

Below: The M1891/30 was a Soviet-era refinement of the original rifle, with shortened dimensions, improved sights and manufacturing modifications for cheaper and faster production.

BOLT MECHANISM
The two-piece bolt was generally judged to be more complicated than was really necessary, though it gave little trouble in use.

SIGHT MOUNT
The M1891/30 could be adapted to take a telescopic sight, which sat just above the chamber. Such sniper rifles required a longer, angled bolt handle to avoid clashing with the sight.

MAGAZINE
The top cartridge of the five-round magazine was kept free of spring pressure, to aid the loading process.

CLEANING ROD
The Mosin-Nagant's cleaning rod was stored integrally in a pipe that ran through the gun's wooden fore-end, beneath the barrel.

MOSIN-NAGANT M1938 CARBINE
A shortened ('carbine') version of the venerable Mosin-Nagant rifle, the M1938 was sufficiently accurate to be used as a sniping weapon. It retained the same five-round internal magazine as the original rifle.

SNIPER USE
Guards Junior Sergeant A.M. Yaremchoock of the Kalininsky Front operating as a sniper in 1942. He is armed with a Mosin Model 1891/30 rifle with a 4 × PE telescopic sight. The M1891/30 weighed 3.47kg (7.6lb) empty, had a muzzle velocity of 811m/sec (2661ft/sec) and, although a modernization of an old design, was robust and reliable. With a tradition of hunting in some extremely harsh terrain, soldiers conscripted from rural parts of the Soviet Union made excellent snipers.

SMLE (1903)

SPECIFICATIONS

DIMENSIONS:	Length: 1132mm (44.57in)
	Barrel Length: 640mm (25.19in)
WEIGHT:	3.94kg (8.69lb)
CALIBRE:	.303in
OPERATION:	Bolt action
FEED:	10-round detachable box magazine
MUZZLE VELOCITY:	617m/sec (2025ft/sec)
EFFECTIVE RANGE:	1000m (1094yd)
RATE OF FIRE:	–

The Short Magazine Lee Enfield (SMLE) was the quintessential combat bolt-action rifle. Introduced in 1903, it initially met with scepticism from much of the military community, although its performance in World War I silenced its detractors.

BOLT SYSTEM
A cutaway image of the SMLE's bolt action, trigger group and magazine. When the rifle was cocked, the cocking piece at the rear of the bolt remained held to the rear, a visible indicator that the rifle was ready to fire.

REAR SIGHT
The rear sights on the original Mk I SMLE were adjustable for both windage and range, the latter in 25yd increments from 200 to 2000yd (183–1830m).

MAGAZINE SPRING
The magazine of the SMLE held 10 rounds, and was loaded via two five-round chargers.

FRONT SIGHT
The front sight blade was protected by two wings to shield it from damage. In practical terms, the iron sights were best used at ranges under 600m (656yd).

FURNITURE
The SMLE was distinctive in that its wooden furniture ran all the way to the front. The bayonet boss protrudes at the front of the rifle, just beneath the muzzle.

SLING
The adjustable sling was made of webbing, and it signalled the shift from leather to webbing in British equipment manufacture.

BOLT ACTION
The Lee-Enfield action cocked the firing pin when the bolt was closed rather than opened, and rear-mounted locking lugs meant the bolt handle could be placed closer to the operator.

INTERMEDIATE RIFLE
The rifle was extremely robust, not least by virtue of the wooden furniture that ran all the way to the muzzle, giving the weapon its distinctive snub-nosed appearance. The intermediate dimensions of the gun were eventually acknowledged as a definite bonus in the context of trench warfare, where its more manageable length made it better for combat in confined terrain. Its bolt action was fluidly smooth to operate; in the hands of a well-trained infantryman, the SMLE could run through 15 rounds per minute.

BAYONET FITTINGS
British soldiers take the surrender of two Germans during action on the Western Front in World War I. Note the length of the Pattern 1907 bayonets fitted to the SMLEs.

M1903 Springfield (1903)

SPECIFICATIONS

DIMENSIONS:	Length: 1097mm (43.19in)
	Barrel Length: 610mm (24in)
WEIGHT:	3.94kg (8.68lb)
CALIBRE:	.30 M1903/.30 M1906
OPERATION:	Bolt action
FEED:	5-round internal box magazine
MUZZLE VELOCITY:	853m/sec (2798ft/sec)
EFFECTIVE RANGE:	1000m (1094yd)
RATE OF FIRE:	–

The Springfield M1903 is a legendary weapon in the history of US firearms. It provided the American soldier with a weapon capable of handling the latest generation of high-pressure cartridges.

Below: The M1903A4 was a moderately successful conversion of the obsolescent bolt-action service rifle. Its main drawback was that the scope prevented the use of a charger to rapidly load the magazine.

BOLT ACTION
The M1903's bolt action was indebted to that of Mauser rifles, with two main locking lugs plus a safety lug.

LADDER SIGHT
The rear ladder sight on the .30-06 M1903 was graduated out to 2400yd (2195m); if the ladder sight was laid flat, the soldier used a simple open-notch battle sight set to 500m (550yd).

TRIGGER GROUP
The trigger group of the M1903 was essentially that of the earlier Krag-Jorgensen rifle.

BARREL
The M1903 had a 610mm (24in) barrel rifled with four grooves on a right-hand twist.

WARTIME SERVICE
The Springfield M1903 would be carried into action through World War I and into the next world war, although from the early 1940s it was progressively replaced by the M1 Garand semi-automatic rifle as the standard US military rifle. The definitive World War II version was the M1903A3, which was introduced in May 1942 and featured some production improvements plus the installation of a rear aperture sight rather than a leaf sight.

WORLD WAR I RIFLE
US 'Doughboys' ready themselves for deployment to the Western Front in 1917, with their Springfield rifles stacked up in front of them, hung with their webbing equipment and water bottles.

Kar 98k (1935)

SPECIFICATIONS

DIMENSIONS:	Length: 1110mm (43.7in)
	Barrel Length: 600mm (23.62in)
WEIGHT:	3.9kg 8.6lb)
CALIBRE:	7.92 × 57mm Mauser
OPERATION:	Bolt action
FEED:	5-round integral magazine
MUZZLE VELOCITY:	745m/sec (2444ft/sec)
EFFECTIVE RANGE:	500m (547yd) with iron sights
RATE OF FIRE:	–

There is little glamorous or exciting about the Kar 98k, it being a conventional 7.92mm bolt-action rifle based on the original Gewehr 1898. Yet it should not be underestimated. From 1935 to 1945, the Kar 98k was the principal firearm of one of the world's most professional armies.

MAGAZINE
Five rounds were pressed down into the magazine against the magazine spring, fed one at a time by the bolt action.

Above: The Gewehr 98 equipped the German Army throughout World War I, with stocks also being used in World War II.

STOCK
At first the stocks were made of solid walnut, but from 1938 they were constructed of plywood laminates.

REAR SIGHT
The rear tangent sight was graduated to 2000m (2187yd) in 100m (109yd) increments.

BOTTOM PLATE
The magazine bottom plate was formed from a continuation of the trigger guard.

FRONT SIGHT
From 1939, the front sight of the Kar 98k was hooded to shield it from sun glare and protect it from damage.

SOUND DESIGN

The Kar 98k had many virtues. It was extremely reliable and safe to operate, the bolt having in effect three locking lugs that ensured the 7.92 × 57mm Mauser cartridge was locked safely in the chamber on firing. The mechanism could also handle all manner of hard punishment on the battlefield, and just a basic field clean and light oiling a few times a week would ensure that it remained serviceable for years, if not decades. The pistol-grip stock, as opposed to the straight 'English' style stock of earlier rifles, fitted very comfortably in the hand.

SNIPER WEAPON
When the Kar 98k was fitted with a telescopic sight, as seen here, it had an effective range of 1000m (1094yd). The man on the left appears to have a Soviet PPD 40 SMG.

M1 Garand (1936)

SPECIFICATIONS

DIMENSIONS:	Length: 1103mm (43.5in)
	Barrel Length: 610mm (24in)
WEIGHT:	4.37kg (9.5lb)
CALIBRE:	.30-06
OPERATION:	Gas-operated semi-automatic
FEED:	8-round internal magazine
MUZZLE VELOCITY:	853m/sec (2800ft/sec)
EFFECTIVE RANGE:	500m (547yd)
RATE OF FIRE:	–

It is no exaggeration to say that the M1 Garand changed the face of infantry firepower. As history's first self-loading rifle adopted as an army standard, it gave the US forces in World War II an unprecedented advantage in small-unit combat.

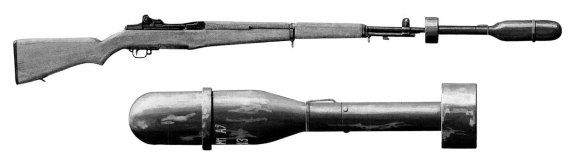

Above: The M1 could be fitted with an M7 grenade launcher. The grenade fitted over the barrel and was propelled by the gases generated from special blank cartridges.

REAR SIGHT
The M1 had an adjustable rear peep sight; the small aperture was lined up quickly with the front blade and the target.

STOCK
The Garand's stock was a solid affair. The curve of the pistol grip behind the trigger could vary according to the manufacturer.

COCKING HANDLE
With the handle drawn back to its rear position and locked, the bolt was opened for loading the gun.

GAS CYLINDER
The gas cylinder for the operating piston was located just beneath the M1's barrel.

SAFETY CATCH
The M1's safety catch was located just in front of the trigger guard, and was engaged when it was pulled back against the guard.

GAS OPERATION
The M1 was a gas-operated weapon. Propellant gases were tapped off from the barrel near the muzzle to drive back a piston that in turn worked the operating system through the cycle of unlocking and driving back the bolt. The spent cartridge case was extracted and ejected. The bolt mechanism moved to the rear until checked and driven forward once more by the main spring to lift and chamber a fresh round.

M1 MYTHS
A US infantryman unloads M1 fire on his enemies. Some myths have grown up around the Garand. One is that the eight-round magazine could not be topped up when it was partially empty – it was either eight rounds or nothing. Modern practical demonstrations, however, have proved that idea to be false.

M1 Carbine (1942)

SPECIFICATIONS

DIMENSIONS:	Length: 905mm (35.65in)
	Barrel Length: 457mm (18in)
WEIGHT:	2.48kg (5.47lb)
CALIBRE:	.30in M1 Carbine
OPERATION:	Gas
FEED:	15- or 30-round box magazine
MUZZLE VELOCITY:	593m/sec (1950ft/sec)
EFFECTIVE RANGE:	300m (328yd)
RATE OF FIRE:	900rpm (M2 Carbine)

The M1 Carbine began life as something of a marginal concept in the US arsenal. Yet this intermediate-power weapon embedded itself in American consciousness and became the most mass-produced US firearm of World War II.

Below: The M1 Carbine had a light, slender layout that made it a very convenient weapon to handle in combat. It only weighed 2.48kg (5.47lb) when empty.

REAR SIGHT
This is the Type 2 rear sight, an aperture-type sight that could be adjusted for both windage and elevation.

BOLT
The bolt is moved by gas pressure via an operating rod, which is in turn powered by the short-stroke piston mechanism.

MAGAZINE
The M1 had a 15- or 30-round detachable box magazine.

GAS CYLINDER
The gas cylinder beneath the barrel contained a short-stroke piston that delivered the motive power to cycle the operating rod and bolt.

BARREL
The M1's barrel had an overall length of 457mm (18in) and a four-groove, right-hand rifling configuration.

PRODUCTION
Incredibly, such was the popularity of the weapon that 5.5 million M1s were produced during the war years. In both the European and Pacific theatres, the M1 was valued for its quick-shooting characteristics and portability.

CLOSE-QUARTERS WEAPON
Armed with an M1 Carbine, a US Marine awaits the signal to go into battle to recapture Guam from the Japanese, July 1944. Although the .30in M1 Carbine round was somewhat underpowered, its practicality for close-quarters fighting made it popular.

FG 42 (1942)

SPECIFICATIONS

DIMENSIONS:	Length: 940mm (37in)
	Barrel Length: 508mm (20in)
WEIGHT:	4.5kg (9.92lb)
CALIBRE:	7.92 × 57mm Mauser
OPERATION:	Gas operated
FEED:	20-round box magazine
MUZZLE VELOCITY:	760m/sec (2495ft/sec)
EFFECTIVE RANGE:	500m (547yd)
RATE OF FIRE:	750rpm

In many fields of technology, the Germans were ahead of their time during World War II. A case in point is the Fallschirmjägergewehr 42 (FG 42) rifle, a truly remarkable weapon the effect of which was limited by wartime politics.

Below: As shown here, the FG 42 was fed by a 20-round box magazine and could be fitted with a stiletto-style bayonet.

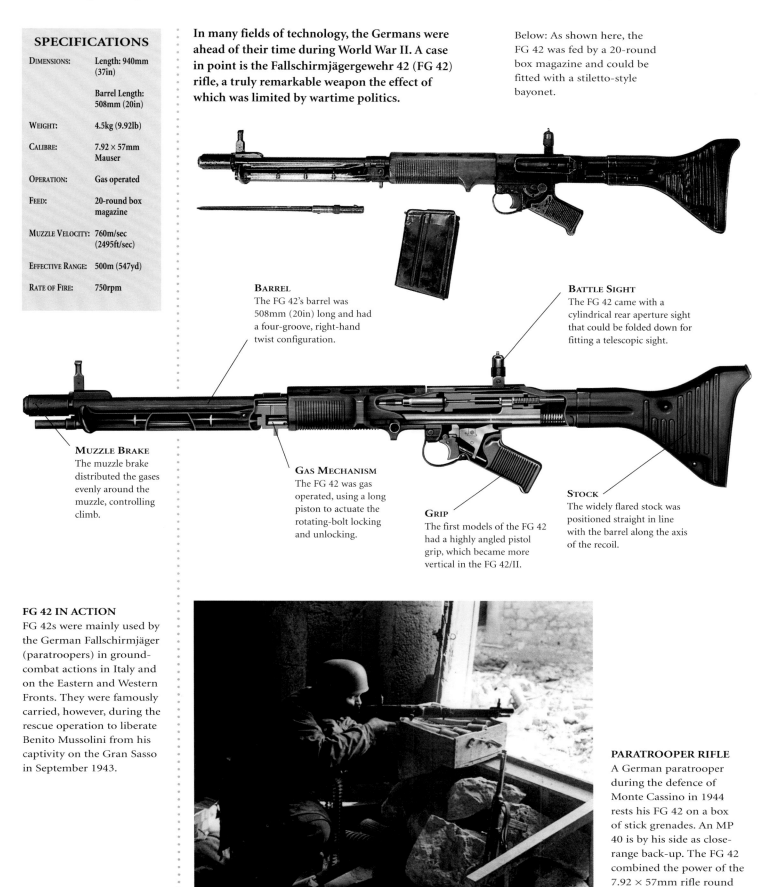

BARREL
The FG 42's barrel was 508mm (20in) long and had a four-groove, right-hand twist configuration.

BATTLE SIGHT
The FG 42 came with a cylindrical rear aperture sight that could be folded down for fitting a telescopic sight.

MUZZLE BRAKE
The muzzle brake distributed the gases evenly around the muzzle, controlling climb.

GAS MECHANISM
The FG 42 was gas operated, using a long piston to actuate the rotating-bolt locking and unlocking.

GRIP
The first models of the FG 42 had a highly angled pistol grip, which became more vertical in the FG 42/II.

STOCK
The widely flared stock was positioned straight in line with the barrel along the axis of the recoil.

FG 42 IN ACTION

FG 42s were mainly used by the German Fallschirmjäger (paratroopers) in ground-combat actions in Italy and on the Eastern and Western Fronts. They were famously carried, however, during the rescue operation to liberate Benito Mussolini from his captivity on the Gran Sasso in September 1943.

PARATROOPER RIFLE
A German paratrooper during the defence of Monte Cassino in 1944 rests his FG 42 on a box of stick grenades. An MP 40 is by his side as close-range back-up. The FG 42 combined the power of the 7.92 × 57mm rifle round with the handling of an assault rifle.

MP44/StG44 (1943)

SPECIFICATIONS

DIMENSIONS:	Length: 940mm (37in)
	Barrel Length: 419mm (16.5in)
WEIGHT:	5.22kg (11.48lb)
CALIBRE:	7.92 × 33mm *kurz*
OPERATION:	Gas
FEED:	30-round detachable box magazine
MUZZLE VELOCITY:	685m/sec (2247ft/sec)
EFFECTIVE RANGE:	400m (437yd)
RATE OF FIRE:	500rpm

Although originally named the MP43 (MP stood for Maschinenpistole), the weapon that became known as the Sturmgewehr 44 (StG44) can be considered the first true assault rifle. Chambered for the shortened 7.92 × 33mm *kurz* (short) ammunition, the StG44 provided greater range than a submachine gun but similarly controllable full-auto firepower.

Above: A German infantryman with his StG44 slung around his neck, this view showing the substantial proportions of the weapon. Altogether, about 426,000 of these rifles were produced.

GAS OPERATED
The StG44 was a gas-operated weapon, the gas tapped off from the barrel into the gas cylinder above, where the action was driven by a piston.

ASSAULT RIFLE
Fed from a 30-round magazine and firing at 500rpm, the StG 44 was effective out to 400m (437yd) or more. Its shortened cartridge had reduced range, power and accuracy over the battle rifles of the period, but this was offset by the volume of fire and reduced recoil. Lighter cartridges also allowed personnel to carry more ammunition, which was necessary given the high rate of expenditure when using automatic fire. The StG44 was sufficiently successful that it was copied or used as the basis of other weapons in many nations, and proved the concept of the lightweight, automatic assault rifle that is still in use today.

CONSTRUCTION
The StG44 was built to high standards and was robust. Heavy construction may have been a factor in the weapon's impressive resistance to horrific weather conditions on the Eastern Front, but the gun was also heavy to use.

SELECTOR
The StG44's selector is a push-button device located just behind the safety catch. Troops were trained to use semi-automatic fire as much as possible, switching to full-automatic in emergencies such as close combat with submachinegun-armed opponents.

TACTICAL ADVANTAGES
The MP44/StG44 quickly demonstrated its tactical value in action. Once the importance of its increase in firepower had been fully realized, the rifle became a priority weapon and urgent requests were made to suppliers. Most of the weapons went to the Eastern Front.

AK-47/AKM (1949)

SPECIFICATIONS

DIMENSIONS:	Length: 880mm (34.65in)
	Barrel Length: 415mm (16.34in)
WEIGHT:	4.3kg (9.48lb)
CALIBRE:	7.62 × 39mm
OPERATION:	Gas operated
FEED:	30-round box magazine
MUZZLE VELOCITY:	600m/sec (1970ft/sec)
EFFECTIVE RANGE:	c. 300m (328yd)
RATE OF FIRE:	600rpm

The AK series of assault rifles have quite literally transformed the world's security situation. With more than 100 million of the family (including all variants) produced, the AK is the most mass-produced weapon in history.

Below: The Chinese Type 56 is a near-identical copy of the AK rifle, manufactured from 1956 and still in service with Chinese forces today. An estimated 15 million have been produced.

BOLT GROUP
The bolt is of a rotating type, the bolt locking into the barrel extension via two very strong locking lugs on the bolt head.

GAS CYLINDER
The AK's gas cylinder is located above the barrel and holds the piston that engages with the bolt carrier.

BORE
The AK has a chromium-lined bore that is highly resistant to wear and corrosion.

STOCK
In addition to the wooden stock seen here, AKs are commonly fitted with a folding metal skeleton stock.

MAGAZINE
The distinctive curved magazine of the AK holds 30 7.62 × 39mm cartridges.

SIMPLICITY

AKs are extremely simple to use, which is one of the reasons they have achieved such impressive global popularity. To fire the weapon, just hinge a magazine into place, drop the selector level to either semi- or full-auto mode, cock, draw and release the cocking handle, and pull the trigger. The other key reasons for the rifle's success are its immense durability, the simplicity of cleaning and repair, its low cost and its massive distribution.

US TEST FIRING
US Marines from 1st Platoon, Echo Company, 3rd Assault Amphibious Battalion, 1st Marine Division, fire AKM assault rifles provided by the Mongolian armed forces.

EM2 (1951)

SPECIFICATIONS

DIMENSIONS:	Length: 889mm (35in)
	Barrel Length: 623mm (24.5in)
WEIGHT:	3.41kg (7.52lb)
CALIBRE:	7 × 44mm (.280 British)
OPERATION:	Gas
FEED:	20-round box magazine
MUZZLE VELOCITY:	771m/sec (2530ft/sec)
EFFECTIVE RANGE:	500m (547yd)
RATE OF FIRE:	450–600rpm

The first bullpup weapon was developed just after World War II. Designated the EM-2, this highly innovative weapon was chambered for a special 7mm round and fed by a 20-round magazine behind the trigger assembly.

Above: A disassembled EM2, showing (at the top) the operating rod, return spring and bolt. The EM2 used a flap-locking system, flaps on the sides of the bolt locking out into rececesses on the inner wall of the receiver.

SIGHT
Another innovation of the EM2 was the fact that it had an optical sight built fitted directly onto the rifle's carrying handle.

BARREL
Despite the gun's overall short length, the barrel – at 623mm (24.5in) – was actually longer than that of an M14 rifle.

RECEIVER
The receiver of the EM2 was designed with careful thought about how to prevent the ingress of dust and dirt.

BULLPUP LAYOUT

The EM2 was of a bullpup design. In this type of layout, the magazine is located behind the trigger group, rather than in front of it as found on the majority of assault rifles, and the end of the receiver sits against the operator's shoulder. The advantage of this layout is that the weapon's overall dimensions can be reduced, while at the same time keeping the full-length barrel that ensures a high muzzle velocity. The main disadvantage was the complexity, and therefore the cost, of the operating mechanism.

HANDLING

The EM2 was a fine weapon. Light and well-balanced, it offered battle rifle accuracy in a short package, making it ideal for urban or mechanized combat. It was killed off, however, by the political considerations surrounding the adoption of the 7.62 × 51mm cartridge as the NATO standard.

FN FAL/L1A1 SLR (1954)

SPECIFICATIONS

DIMENSIONS:	Length: 1053mm (41.46in)
	Barrel Length: 533mm (21in)
WEIGHT:	4.31kg (9.5lb)
CALIBRE:	7.62 × 51mm NATO
OPERATION:	Gas
FEED:	20-round box magazine
MUZZLE VELOCITY:	853m/sec (2800ft/sec)
EFFECTIVE RANGE:	600m (656yd)
RATE OF FIRE:	Varies according to model

The FN FAL ranks alongside the AK as one of history's most successful firearms. In total, more than 70 countries have adopted the rifle over its lifetime, with users appreciating the weapon's reliability and hard-hitting reach.

Below: An Argentine model of the FN FAL, with a folding stock rather than the traditional fixed wooden or plastic butt stock.

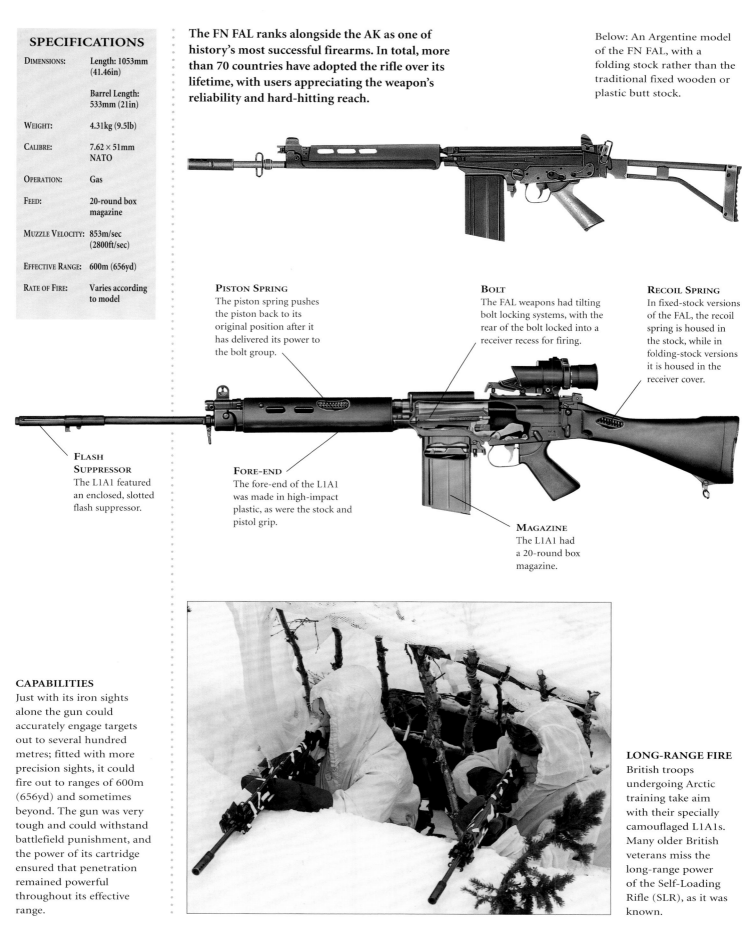

PISTON SPRING
The piston spring pushes the piston back to its original position after it has delivered its power to the bolt group.

BOLT
The FAL weapons had tilting bolt locking systems, with the rear of the bolt locked into a receiver recess for firing.

RECOIL SPRING
In fixed-stock versions of the FAL, the recoil spring is housed in the stock, while in folding-stock versions it is housed in the receiver cover.

FLASH SUPPRESSOR
The L1A1 featured an enclosed, slotted flash suppressor.

FORE-END
The fore-end of the L1A1 was made in high-impact plastic, as were the stock and pistol grip.

MAGAZINE
The L1A1 had a 20-round box magazine.

CAPABILITIES

Just with its iron sights alone the gun could accurately engage targets out to several hundred metres; fitted with more precision sights, it could fire out to ranges of 600m (656yd) and sometimes beyond. The gun was very tough and could withstand battlefield punishment, and the power of its cartridge ensured that penetration remained powerful throughout its effective range.

LONG-RANGE FIRE
British troops undergoing Arctic training take aim with their specially camouflaged L1A1s. Many older British veterans miss the long-range power of the Self-Loading Rifle (SLR), as it was known.

CETME Model 58 (1957)

SPECIFICATIONS

DIMENSIONS:	Length: 1015mm (40in)
	Barrel Length: 450mm (17.72in)
WEIGHT:	4.4kg (9.7lb)
CALIBRE:	7.62 × 51mm NATO
OPERATION:	Delayed blowback
FEED:	20- or 30-round box
MUZZLE VELOCITY:	786m/sec (2580ft/sec)
EFFECTIVE RANGE:	600m (656yd)
RATE OF FIRE:	550–600 rpm

Originally chambered for 7.92mm, the CETME Model 58 went into production in several versions, capable of firing 7.62mm and later (in the Model L/LC) 5.56mm ammunition. Although it remained in service with the Spanish and other armed forces for many years, the CETME never really caught on.

Right: A Spanish serviceman checks the firing mechanism of a CETME Model 58 rifle.

FLUTED CHAMBER
The CETME rifle had a fluted chamber: grooves in the wall of the chamber allowed gas to circulate around the case, allowing for easier extraction.

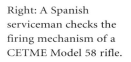

BIPOD
A useful addition was an integral bipod for stabilized firing. This bipod could be neatly folded back against the fore-end.

FORE-END
The perforated steel fore-end allowed for a more efficient barrel cooling than an enclosed fore-end.

BLOWBACK
The Model 58 used a roller-delayed blowback system, in which rollers on the bolt, pushed out into recesses in the receiver, kept the bolt locked until the pressure had dropped to safe levels for unlocking.

FOREIGN ORIGINS
The Model 58 took its inspiration from two main sources. The first was an experimental German wartime design, the StG45, which used a roller-delayed blowback mechanism. The designer of this mechanism, Ludwig Vorgrimler, and another StG45 designer, Theodor Löffler, then went to work for CEAM of France. There they helped design a .30 Carbine rifle called the Modèle 1950, which had a similar appearance to the CETME Model 58. Ludwig Vorgrimler went on to work for CETME in the 1950s.

SPANISH SERVICE RIFLE
Derived from a German design, the CETME Model 58 was adopted by the Spanish military as its standard service rifle. Originally chambered for a light cartridge, later versions adopted the 7.62mm NATO round.

M14 (1959)

SPECIFICATIONS

DIMENSIONS:	Length: 1117mm (44in)
	Barrel Length: 558mm (22in)
WEIGHT:	3.88kg (8.55lb)
CALIBRE:	7.62 × 51mm NATO
OPERATION:	Gas
FEED:	20-round box magazine
MUZZLE VELOCITY:	853m/sec (2800ft/sec)
EFFECTIVE RANGE:	800m (875yd)
RATE OF FIRE:	750rpm

The M14 was a transitional phase in the history of US military small arms. Introduced into service in the late 1950s, it was intended to replace several weapons, specifically the M1 Garand, M1 Carbine, M3 Grease Gun and the BAR.

REAR SIGHT
The M14's rear sight was of the aperture type. Wheels on the side adjusted windage and elevation.

MAGAZINE
The size of the 7.62 × 51mm cartridges meant that the rifle had only a 20-round magazine capacity.

GAS PISTON
The gas piston in the M14 is connected to an operating rod that drives the bolt through its recoil, extraction and ejection stages.

STOCK
Three materials were used for the M14 stock: walnut, then birch followed by fibreglass.

M1 HERITAGE

The M14's ancestry in the M1 Garand rifle is most apparent in the gun's receiver and stock configuration, and most different in its 20-round box magazine and exposed barrel. Both weapons had similar performance characteristics in terms of range and penetration.

ENDURING RIFLE
Showing that the M14 still has some life left in it yet, a US soldier fires the rifle in Afghanistan in 2011. The M14 has a hard-kicking 'retro' feel that many modern soldiers love.

Heckler & Koch G3 (1959)

SPECIFICATIONS

DIMENSIONS:	Length: 1025mm (40.35in)
	Barrel Length: 450mm (17.71in)
WEIGHT:	4.4kg (9.7lb)
CALIBRE:	7.62 × 51mm NATO
OPERATION:	Roller-delayed blowback
FEED:	20-round box magazine
MUZZLE VELOCITY:	800m/sec (2625ft/sec)
EFFECTIVE RANGE:	400m (437yd) with iron sights
RATE OF FIRE:	500–600rpm

Four assault/battle rifles have dominated the last 50 years of warfare: the AK, M16, FN FAL and the Heckler & Koch G3. More than 50 nations have used the latter in earnest, the weapon being a relatively cheap but trustworthy rifle.

Below: In this cutaway, the bolt is in its forward position having chambered and fired a cartridge. Two locking rollers delay the rifle's blowback cycle until pressures are at safe levels.

DRUM SIGHT
The rear drum sight gives the soldier range adjustments from 100m (109yd) to 400m (437yd).

FORE-END
Two versions of the fore-end are available: a slender ventilated model and a wider unventilated type.

FLASH HIDER
The flash hider features six lozenge-shaped cuts to divert propellant gas.

MAGAZINE
The G3 takes steel or aluminium magazines in double-stack configuration.

FULL-AUTO OPTION
Despite the fact that the G3 fires the powerful 7.62 × 51mm NATO round, it is still a selective-fire weapon. On full-auto it will race through the 20-round box magazine at 500–600rpm, although semi-auto rifle is the tactically preferred option for accurate shooting and for ammunition conservation.

SELECTOR
The G3's selector switch is on the left side of the receiver, but it also has a selector indicator on the right side.

ACCURIZED MODEL
A German soldier patrols the streets of Mazar-e-Sharif, Afghanistan, July 2011, with his accurized G3SG/1. The Taliban and al-Qaeda forces have largely relied upon AK rifles and RPK and PKM machine guns; the G3 is able to match and even exceed the AK in particular for range and power.

M16 (1963)

SPECIFICATIONS

DIMENSIONS:	1006mm (39.63in)
	Barrel Length: 508mm (20in)
WEIGHT:	3.58kg (7.89lb)
CALIBRE:	5.56 × 45mm NATO
OPERATION:	Gas
FEED:	30-round box magazine
MUZZLE VELOCITY:	1000m/sec (3280ft/sec)
EFFECTIVE RANGE:	Up to 600m (656yd)
RATE OF FIRE:	600–940rpm

As the standard-issue weapon of most of the US armed forces, the M16 rifle (and the M4 Carbine version) are universally familiar, a fact that can veil the controversy surrounding the rifle's introduction back in the 1960s.

Below: The M16A4 is the latest version of the M16, with a removable carrying handle. Its selective fire options are configured to safe, semi-auto fire and a useful three-round burst fire.

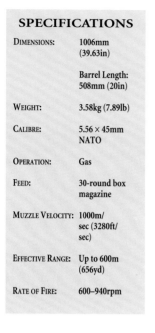

CARRYING HANDLE
The carrying handle incorporates the rear sight, which sits 63.5mm (2.5in) above the bore.

FORE-END
The fore-end, like the pistol grip and stock, is made from high-impact plastic material.

RECOIL SPRING
The recoil spring is housed in the stock, giving a straight recoil path into the operator's shoulder.

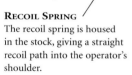

BOLT GROUP
Having a direct-impingement gas system, the M16 needs scrupulous cleaning to prevent carbon build-up around the bolt.

EARLY CONTROVERSY

When the M16 was first introduced into combat service in Vietnam, it was plagued with problems related to fouling and stoppages, and earned an initially terrible reputation for unreliability. Many of the issues were related to the ammunition type issued and improper cleaning instructions. When these problems were rectified, and the M16A1 version emerged with its chrome-lined chamber, the reliability of the weapon improved significantly.

LIGHT WEAPON
A US soldier in Vietnam opens fire with his M16A1. After initial problems with the rifle, many soldiers came to appreciate the M16's lightness and rapid firepower, especially in close-quarters jungle conditions.

SVD Dragunov (1963)

SPECIFICATIONS

DIMENSIONS:	Length: 1225mm (48.20in)
	Barrel Length: 610mm (24in)
WEIGHT:	4.31kg (9.5lb)
CALIBRE:	7.62 × 54R
OPERATION:	Gas
FEED:	10-round detachable box magazine
MUZZLE VELOCITY:	828m/sec (2720ft/sec)
EFFECTIVE RANGE:	800m (875yd)
RATE OF FIRE:	–

Unlike some other armed forces, the Russian Army has always placed a high value on snipers. The SVD (Snaiperskaya Vintovka Dragunova), or Dragunov, rifle is an excellent tool in the right hands.

Above: The AK ancestry is clearly evident in the SVD, externally and internally. Yet the components and build process of the SVD are precision-manufactured to give the weapon its long-range accuracy and consistent groupings.

OPTICS
The Dragunov SVD comes with a good set of iron sights, but is usually paired with a 4 × optical telescopic sight. It can take a range of other accessories, including infrared and high-magnification sights.

AMMUNITION
Built around the standard AK-47 action, the SVD is chambered for 7.62 × 54R ammunition that is not compatible with standard infantry rifles.

BARREL
With its long, heavy barrel, the semi-automatic SVD is accurate out to 800m (875yd). Fairly light for a sniping weapon, the SVD is nevertheless as rugged as all Russian equipment.

MARKSMAN USE
The SVD rifle was not intended specifically for snipers in the usual sense, but was meant to be carried by a trained soldier within an infantry squad – what we would today call a 'designated marksman'. This marksman would be able to engage targets beyond the usual ranges managed by combat troops, out to about 600m (656yd). The rifle does make an excellent pure sniping weapon, however, and has seen considerable service in this role.

SOVIET DOCTRINE
During the Soviet era, doctrine required an SVD-armed marksman to be included in every infantry platoon. This soldier was tasked with engaging high-value targets such as officers and support gunners while his squad mates carried out more general combat roles.

M21 (1969)

SPECIFICATIONS

DIMENSIONS:	Length: 1118mm (44in)
	Barrel Length: 560mm (22in)
WEIGHT:	5.27kg (11.6lb)
CALIBRE:	7.62 × 51mm NATO
OPERATION:	Gas
FEED:	20-round box magazine
MUZZLE VELOCITY:	853m/sec (2800ft/sec)
EFFECTIVE RANGE:	800m (875yd)
RATE OF FIRE:	–

The M21 Sniper Weapon System (SWS) rifle is an evolution of the M14 rifle, with the standard rifle transformed through the addition of a precision barrel and advanced optical sights.

Below: The M21 sniper rifle is instantly recognizable as being based upon the M14 rifle; indeed, it is easy to mistake an M14 fitted with a scope for an M21.

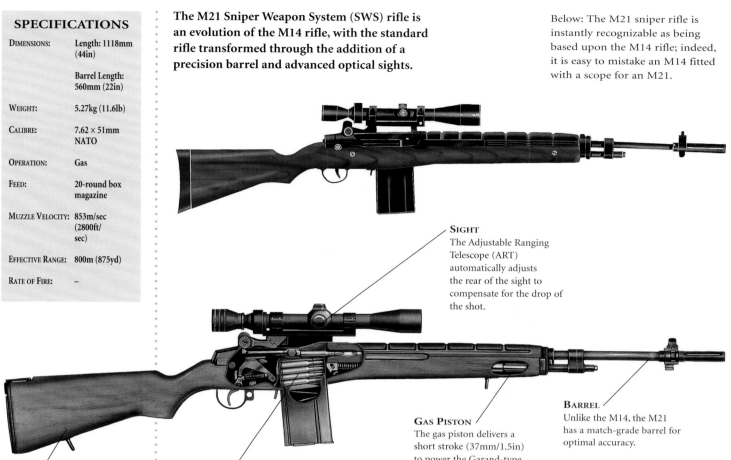

SIGHT
The Adjustable Ranging Telescope (ART) automatically adjusts the rear of the sight to compensate for the drop of the shot.

BARREL
Unlike the M14, the M21 has a match-grade barrel for optimal accuracy.

GAS PISTON
The gas piston delivers a short stroke (37mm/1.5in) to power the Garand-type operating rod.

STOCK
A classic walnut stock would in time be replaced by a fibreglass version.

MAGAZINE
The M21 takes the standard 20-round detachable box magazine.

DEVELOPMENT

The first rifle, which went into service in 1969 as the XM21, was developed with a walnut stock, but this was eventually replaced with a fibreglass version in 1975, the synthetic material having better resistance to distortion in humid conditions. (This rifle's name became the M21 in 1972.) Otherwise, the weapon was the standard rotating-bolt, gas-operated rifle as the M14, although it omitted the full-auto fire mode that was never necessary for a sniper weapon. The feed remained the 20-round box magazine as standard, although small five- or 10-round capacity magazines were available.

SNIPER TRAINING
Two USAF personnel conduct sniper training. The man on the left is armed with a Springfield Armory M21, while the soldier on the right has a bolt-action M24 rifle.

Galil (1973)

The Galil rifle was a solution to Israel's rifle requirements based on lessons learnt during the 1967 Six-Day War. The result was a particularly robust and practical firearm, well suited to Israeli operations.

SPECIFICATIONS

DIMENSIONS:	Length: 979mm (38.54in)
	Barrel Length: 460mm (18.11in)
WEIGHT:	4.35kg (9.59lb)
CALIBRE:	5.56 × 45mm NATO
OPERATION:	Gas
FEED:	35- or 50-round box magazine
MUZZLE VELOCITY:	950m/sec (3117ft/sec)
EFFECTIVE RANGE:	600m (656yd)
RATE OF FIRE:	650rpm

GAS PISTON
The gas piston sits above the barrel; the piston rod is attached to the bolt carrier.

ROTATING BOLT
The Galil's rotating-bolt mechanism follows the same principle as that used on the AK-47.

Above: The Galil ARM bipod is extremely well designed. It includes a bottle-opening feature (to stop soldiers using the lips of magazines) and, when folded, aids quick magazine loading.

SIGHTS
The standard Galil iron sights are configured for taking shots out to 500m (547yd).

DESIGN FEATURES
The furniture consists of a high-impact plastic fore-end and pistol grip, plus a tubular steel stock that can be folded forward against the side of the receiver for storage or easy transportation. In terms of the ammunition feed, the standard option is a curved 35-round box magazine, although standard M16 magazines can be used with a special adapter. The ARM version of the rifle also comes with a bipod fitted just in front of the fore-end to turn the Galil into a light machine gun, or to stabilize it for accurate single shots. For sights, there is a front post adjustable for windage and elevation, enclosed in a protective hood, and a rear sight with two apertures preset for firing at 0–300m (0–328yd) and 300–500m (984–1640ft). Both sights also have self-luminous tritium capsules for night shooting.

FORE-END
The fore-end on the ARM is enlarged compared to the standard rifle to hold the bipod legs when they are folded.

STOCK
The Galil stock hinges to fold against the left side of the receiver.

MAGAZINE
The standard mag holds 35 rounds, although high-capacity 50-round versions are available.

IN ACTION WITH THE IDF
An Israeli soldier on an urban deployment with his Galil. The Galil was developed as a way to strike a good compromise between the Uzi submachine gun and the FN FAL rifle, the two standard weapons of the Israel Defense Forces during the 1960s and early 70s. The Galil also provided a better response to the AKs that were almost universal issue among opposing Arab armies.

AK-74 (1974)

SPECIFICATIONS

DIMENSIONS:	Length: 930mm (36.6in)
	Barrel Length: 400mm (15.8in)
WEIGHT:	3.6kg (7.94lb)
CALIBRE:	5.45 × 39mm M74
OPERATION:	Gas
FEED:	30-round box magazine
MUZZLE VELOCITY:	900m/sec (2952ft/sec)
EFFECTIVE RANGE:	500m (547yd)
RATE OF FIRE:	650rpm

The AK-74 was part of a general shift towards small calibres and ultra-high velocities in assault rifles during the 1960s and 70s. In most respects, the AK-74 was an AK rifle rechambered for the new 5.45 × 39mm round.

Below: The AKS-74U is an ultra-compact version of the AKS-74. The very short barrel reduces the weapon's muzzle velocity to about 735m/sec (2411ft/sec).

SIGHTS
The sights of the AK-74 rifles are optimized for a practical combat range of 400m (437yd).

BOLT CARRIER
The bolt carrier transfers the rearward force of the gas piston into rotational and rearward movement of the bolt.

ROTATING BOLT
The AKS-74 uses the same rotating-bolt gas-operated mechanism as used in the AKM.

AKS-74 VARIANT
The AKS-74 differs from the AK-74 by having a side-folding tubular metal stock, locked when folded by a spring-loaded catch on the receiver.

LIMITED DISTRIBUTION
The picture below shows a youth in Afghanistan enthusiastically nurturing a AK-74 – Afghanistan was the first combat outing for the AK-74. About five million AK-74s have been produced; this is far fewer than the 7.62mm AKs, which have far cheaper and more accessible ammunition.

Steyr AUG (1977)

The Steyr AUG is, at first glance, an outlandishly awkward-looking weapon. Yet appearances are deceptive – the AUG is actually an outstanding assault rifle, being accurate, tough, easy to use and well balanced.

SPECIFICATIONS

DIMENSIONS:	Length: 790mm (31.10in)
	Barrel Length: 508mm (20in)
WEIGHT:	3.6kg (7.93lb)
CALIBRE:	5.56 × 45mm NATO
OPERATION:	Gas
FEED:	30- or 42-round box magazine
MUZZLE VELOCITY:	970m/sec (3128ft/sec)
EFFECTIVE RANGE:	300m (328yd)
RATE OF FIRE:	650rpm

Above: The Steyr AUG A1 has been fitted with a 407mm (16in) carbine barrel and is finished in either olive green or black furniture.

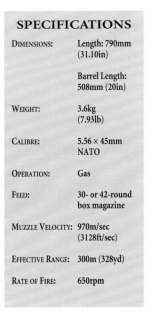

HAMMER
The AUG's hammer is made of plastic, and its force comes from a coil spring.

BARREL
The barrel is fitted with a three-pronged flash suppressor and the muzzle can fit any NATO-standard rifle grenade.

GRIP
The front grip is used to stabilize the hold and facilitate barrel changes.

BOLT
The bolt has seven lugs, which rotate into barrel recesses to provide secure locking before the gun is fired.

MAGAZINE
The extremely tough translucent plastic magazine shows at a glance the number of cartridges left.

CONSTRUCTION

The AUG's construction relies heavily on the use of tough synthetic materials. The stock is made from fibreglass-reinforced polyamide 66, and the sights can be configured for left- or right-handed users. The magazines are made from a clear plastic, which usefully allows the operator to see exactly how many rounds are left before he runs empty. Much of the trigger group is also made of plastic – even the weapon's hammer.

OPTICAL SIGHT
An Austrian soldier armed with a Steyr AUG rifle illustrates the convenience of the high-mounted optical sight, which aligns naturally with the eye when the user is in the prone position.

FAMAS (1978)

SPECIFICATIONS

DIMENSIONS:	Length: 757mm (29.8in)
	Barrel Length: 488mm (19.21in)
WEIGHT:	3.6kg (7.96lb)
CALIBRE:	5.56 × 45mm NATO
OPERATION:	Delayed blowback
FEED:	25- or 30-round box magazine
MUZZLE VELOCITY:	960m/sec (3150ft/sec)
EFFECTIVE RANGE:	300m (328yd)
RATE OF FIRE:	900–1000rpm

The FAMAS joins the Steyr AUG and the British SA80 as the most successful of the post-war bullpup designs. Known as 'Le Clarion' (The Bugle) by French troops, it has served in numerous conflicts since the late 1970s.

MODERN BAYONETS
Some modern assault rifles, including the FAMAS rifles used by these French Foreign Legion soldiers, still retain bayonets. The FAMAS bayonet is based on the older M1949/56 design, albeit with a new plastic scabbard and a web belt hanger. Note how the bayonet mounts above the muzzle, not below. The bayonets of other armies include more features and utility functions.

BOLT
The FAMAS is a delayed-blowback gun, the recoil of the bolt retarded by a lever that engages with a recess in the receiver.

CARRYING HANDLE
Like the M16 and AUG, the FAMAS' carrying handle contains the weapon's standard iron sights.

SELECTOR
The selector switch has three options: safe, semi-auto and full-auto.

BARREL
The FAMAS barrel is 488mm (19.21in) long and has a rifling configuration of three grooves with a right-hand twist.

HAMMER
The FAMAS hammer and trigger group sits well back in the stock, connected to the trigger by a trigger bar.

BIPOD FITTING
The FAMAS is an extremely compact weapon, although its bullpup arrangement allows it to retain an appreciably long barrel of 488mm (19.21in). One interesting feature on a weapon of this size is the folding bipod, which is standard. This bipod allows the rifle to be used over the full spectrum of the 5.56mm round's performance.

FIRING THE FAMAS
A US Marine with 2nd Battalion, 3rd Marine Regiment, fires a FAMAS assault rifle on Plum Base Range, New Caledonia, France, in 2011.

Vektor R4 (1980)

SPECIFICATIONS

DIMENSIONS:	Length: 1005mm (35.97in) stock extended; 740mm (29.13in) stock folded
	Barrel Length: 460mm (18.11in)
WEIGHT:	4.3kg (9.48lb)
CALIBRE:	5.56 × 45mm M193
OPERATION:	Gas
FEED:	35- or 50-round detachable box magazine
MUZZLE VELOCITY:	980m/sec (3215ft/sec)
EFFECTIVE RANGE:	300–500m (328–547yd)
RATE OF FIRE:	650rpm

South Africa was for a long time subject to an international arms embargo, which led to the development of an impressive arms industry. One of its products was the Vektor family of rifles, which was based on the Israeli Galil and included many of that weapon's best features.

Above: A right-side view of the R4. The selector lever is indebted to the design of the AK-47.

CHARGING HANDLE
Although the charging handle is on the right side of the gun, the handle itself is angled upwards to enable cocking with either arm.

OPERATING SYSTEM
Like the Galil, the R4 uses a gas-operated rotating-bolt mechanism, based mainly on that of the Finnish Valmet M62, in turn derived from the AK mechanism.

BIPOD
When the integral bipod (Not shown) is used with 50-round magazines, the R4 can partly take the role of a light machine gun.

MAGAZINES
The R4 magazines are made from a synthetic material to reduce the costs of manufacture, especially as magazines are so frequently lost in combat.

MODIFICATIONS

The Vektor R4 is largely a licence-produced copy of the Israeli Galil ARM, but with some local variations. The metal stock, for example, is made from fibreglass-filled nylon, which is less prone to heat build-up than the Galil's metal version. The stock is also a little longer, to suit general South African physical dimensions. Like the ARM, the R4 has an integral folding bipod.

FOLDING STOCK
A Vektor R4 in the hands of a UN peacekeeper in 2013. This viewpoint gives a clear perspective on the stock hinge. The stock can be folded forward to sit along the right side of the receiver, which makes the rifle more convenient for carrying aboard vehicles.

M16A2 (1982)

SPECIFICATIONS

DIMENSIONS:	Length: 990mm (39in)
	Barrel Length: 508mm (20in)
WEIGHT:	2.86kg (6.3lb)
CALIBRE:	5.56 × 45mm M193
OPERATION:	Gas operated
FEED:	30-round detachable box magazine
MUZZLE VELOCITY:	1000m/sec (3280ft/sec)
EFFECTIVE RANGE:	600m (656yd)
RATE OF FIRE:	600–940rpm

The M16A2 was the principal US service rifle for many years, although its shorter, lighter M4 Carbine variant replaced it in many units. The A2 was designed to fire improved 5.56mm ammunition and is limited to three-round bursts rather than full-automatic fire. A heavier barrel adds to the weapon's overall weight, which is also increased by a generally heavier and more robust construction.

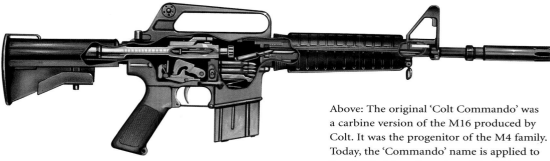

Above: The original 'Colt Commando' was a carbine version of the M16 produced by Colt. It was the progenitor of the M4 family. Today, the 'Commando' name is applied to the shortest-barrel version of the M4.

REAR SIGHT
The M16A2 had an improved rear sight that could be easily adjusted for windage and range.

BARREL
The barrel of the M16A2 had new rifling with a 1 in 7 twist to fire NATO standard SS109 type (M855).

DEFLECTOR
The deflector fitting just behind the ejection port deflects ejecting cases away from the face of left-handed shooters.

FLASH SUPPRESSOR
The flash suppressor for the M16A2 was closed at the bottom to reduce the dust signature created when firing the rifle close to the ground.

THE 5.56MM NATO

Alongside the 7.62 × 51mm round, the 5.56 × 45mm has become the standard of NATO, Western and many international forces. The 5.56mm offers a considerably lower recoil than the 7.62mm, thereby reducing training times and making full-auto fire more controllable. It is also a physically lighter round, meaning that a soldier can carry more ammunition for a given weight. The 5.56mm compensates for its light weight with an extremely high velocity, in the region of 1000m/sec (3280ft/sec).

GRENADE LAUNCHER
This soldier undergoing rifle training has his M16A2 fitted with an under-barrel 40mm M203 grenade launcher. Note the metal M203 mount handguard fitted around the rifle fore-end, with its flip-up sight on the front just behind the rifle's main sight.

PSG-1 (1985)

Futuristic in appearance, but actually descended from a design of the 1940s, the Heckler & Koch PSG-1 (Präzisionsschützengewehr) is based on the G3 assault rifle.

SPECIFICATIONS

DIMENSIONS:	Length: 1208mm (47.56in)
	Barrel Length: 650mm (25.6in), 4 grooves, rh
WEIGHT:	8.1kg (17.86lb)
CALIBRE:	7.62 × 51mm NATO
OPERATION:	Roller-locked delayed blowback
FEED:	5-, 10- or 20-round detachable box magazine
MUZZLE VELOCITY:	815m/sec (2675ft/sec)
EFFECTIVE RANGE:	800m (875yd)
RATE OF FIRE:	–

Above: The original PSG-1, this specimen is without a bipod. Being a heavy gun, some form of front support was essential for accurate shooting.

SCOPE
No iron sights are fitted to the PSG-1. The original version of the rifle was fitted as standard with a Hensoldt ZF 6 × 42 PSG1 scope.

STOCK
The stock is fully adjustable for both length, drop and cheek position, the latter especially important to ensure consistent eye alignment with the sight.

SNIPING RANGES

A semi-automatic weapon fed from 5-, 10- or 20-round magazines, the PSG-1 provides excellent accuracy at ranges of up to 800m (875yd), making it suitable for most battlefield sniping tasks. Law-enforcement snipers often shoot from under 100m (109yd), so achieving a one-shot kill with a PSG1 is not a problem for a police marksman.

TRIPOD
An optional tripod mount gives the gun superb muzzle control across a wide angle of fire.

BOLT-ACTION V. SEMI-AUTO

A PSG-1, seen here with the 5- or 20-round magazines. The use of bolt-action or semi-auto sniper rifles has been a topic of hot debate. Bolt-action weapons are generally more accurate, as they seat each round more carefully, limiting damage on the bullets. Semi-auto sniper rifles are not quite as accurate, especially over very long ranges, but they offer fast follow-up shots.

SA80 (1985)

SPECIFICATIONS

DIMENSIONS:	785mm (30.9in)
	Barrel Length: 518mm (20.39in)
WEIGHT:	4.98kg (10.98lb)
CALIBRE:	5.56 × 45mm NATO
OPERATION:	Gas
FEED:	30-round box magazine
MUZZLE VELOCITY:	940m/sec (3048ft/sec)
EFFECTIVE RANGE:	600m (656yd)
RATE OF FIRE:	650–800rpm

The SA80's career has been mired in controversy and politics. At first it was not a popular weapon with British forces, but following a significant upgrade to the L85A2 variant it has steadily gained their respect.

Right: Designed for armoured fighting vehicle (AFV) crew, the L22A1 Carbine is a radically shortened version of the SA80; note the lack of fore-end and its replacement by a vertical grip.

RETURN SPRING
The return spring runs along the top of the stock, controlling the recoil in direct line with the shooter's shoulder.

SUSAT SIGHT
The SUSAT sight provides 4× magnification and a pointer illuminated by a Trilux lamp.

GAS CYLINDER
The gas cylinder sits above the barrel. The gas from the barrel enters the cylinder and drives back the piston rod, bolt carrier and bolt.

CAM STUD
The cam stud in the bolt fits into a recess in the bolt carrier. The interaction between the two unlocks the bolt from the breech.

AFGHANISTAN MODIFICATIONS

The L85A2 has been heavily field-modified during the course of British Army operations in Afghanistan. The standard fore-end has been replaced with a Picatinny quad-rail assembly that is fitted with a vertical foregrip for rapid handling of the weapon in close-quarters fighting. The rail can also take the Light Laser Marker, tactical flashlights, the L123A3 (H&K AG36) underslung grenade launcher and other fittings. Steel magazines have been replaced with lighter, tougher EMAG polymer magazines. Most significant has been the replacement of the SUSAT sight by more advanced optics, such as the ACOG 4× and the ELCAN Specter 4×, often backed by the Shield-produced Mini Sight Reflex Red-Dot, again to enhance close-quarters fighting capabilities.

TRUSTED WEAPON
British troops in Afghanistan conduct a patrol with their L85A2s. Despite severe reliability problems in the L85A1 rifle predecessor, the L85A2 is currently one of the most reliable assault rifles in the Western world, with a mean round between failure rate of about 25,000 rounds.

Barrett M82A1 (1989)

SPECIFICATIONS

DIMENSIONS:	Length: 1549mm (60.98in)
	Barrel Length: 838mm (33in)
WEIGHT:	14.7kg (32.14lb)
CALIBRE:	.50 BMG
OPERATION:	Short recoil
FEED:	11-round box magazine
MUZZLE VELOCITY:	843m/sec (2800ft/sec)
EFFECTIVE RANGE:	1500m (1640yd)
RATE OF FIRE:	–

The Barrett M82A1 set a formidable new standard in the world of sniper rifles. Here was a rifle capable of wrecking a truck engine block at more than a mile away, delivering its destruction with the devastating .50-calibre BMG cartridge.

Below: The Barrett M82A1, shown here stood on its bipod, which is mounted just beneath the fore-end. Note that the Barrett is also now offered in .416 Barrett calibre, with this version having a non-detachable magazine.

BIPOD
The bipod assembly has retractable legs and extending feet, and can be detached from the receiver if necessary.

IRON SIGHTS
As well as the optical sight, the Barrett has a rear aperture peep sight graduated from 100m to 1500m (109yd to 1640yd) in 100m intervals.

SCOPE RAIL
The scope rail extends nearly the full length of the receiver, and can take a variety of optical and night-vision scope types.

STOCK
The stock of the gun is integral with the receiver, producing an extremely strong structure.

MUZZLE BRAKE
The muzzle brake absorbs about 70 per cent of the gun's recoil forces.

ANTI-MATERIEL RIFLE
Although the Barrett is used against human targets on occasion, the rifle's overarching purpose is as an anti-materiel rifle. The power and size of the round make it suitable for destroying vehicle, aircraft and boat engines, radar equipment, communications equipment and many other targets, all for the cost of a single bullet rather than an expensive missile. It is also used against enemy personnel behind protective cover, such as brick walls.

HEAVY SNIPING
A US Army sniper with Bravo Company, 502nd Infantry Regiment, 101st Airborne Division, stands ready to engage targets during a combat mission on the outskirts of Baghdad in 2005.

M4 Carbine (1994)

SPECIFICATIONS

DIMENSIONS:	Length: 840mm (33.07in) stock extended; 760mm (29.92in) stock retracted
	Barrel Length: 368mm (14.49in)
WEIGHT:	2.54kg (5.6lb)
CALIBRE:	5.56 × 45mm NATO
OPERATION:	Gas
FEED:	20- or 30-round box magazine
MUZZLE VELOCITY:	920m/sec (3020ft)
EFFECTIVE RANGE:	300m (328yd)
RATE OF FIRE:	700–1000rpm

The M4 Carbine has, in many cases, replaced the M16A2 as the standard rifle of the US armed forces. Although its issue is not without controversy, a survey of US troops found that more than 90 per cent were happy with the weapon.

Above: An M4 Carbine fitted with the M68 Close Combat Optic. This sight is a battery-powered red-dot type, which is watertight down to 25m (27yd).

PICATINNY RAIL
The Picatinny rail system around the fore-end provides a flexible surface for fitting tactical devices and a vertical grip.

STOCK
The telescoping stock can be adjusted to fit the precise length of pull of each individual soldier.

ROTATING BOLT
Internally, the M4 uses the same rotating-bolt system as found in the M16A2 rifle.

M203 GRENADE LAUNCHER
The M203 is a single-shot 40mm grenade launcher with an effective range of 150m (164yd).

FLASH SUPPRESSOR
Carbines tend to have excessive muzzle flash, which the M4 partly controls with a flash suppressor.

SHARED DESIGN

The M4 is essentially a shortened M16A2, sharing about 80 per cent of its parts with the rifle and working on the same gas-operated, rotating-bolt mechanism. Its big difference from the rifle is the length. With its multi-position telescoping stock extended, it is 840mm (33.07in), dropping to 760mm (29.92in) with the stock pushed in. The biggest length saving comes from shortening the barrel from the M16A2's 508mm (20in) down to 368mm (14.49in). The fitting of a Rail Adapter System (RAS) to the carbine transforms the gun into the M4 Modular Weapon System (MWS), which can take all manner of extra fittings.

ON PATROL
US soldiers in Iraq in 2010, both armed with M4 Carbines. The soldier on the left has an AN/PEQ-2 Target Pointer/Illuminator/ Aiming Light (TPIAL) fitted to the front of his firearm to assist with target acquisition and accuracy.

Heckler & Koch G36 (1995)

SPECIFICATIONS

DIMENSIONS:	Length: 999mm (39.3in) stock extended; 758mm (29.8in) stock retracted
	Barrel Length: 480mm (18.9in)
WEIGHT:	3.63kg (8lb)
CALIBRE:	5.45 × 45mm NATO
OPERATION:	Gas operated
FEED:	30-round box magazine or 100-round drum magazinev
MUZZLE VELOCITY:	920m/sec (3020ft/ sec)
EFFECTIVE RANGE:	800m (875yd)
RATE OF FIRE:	750rpm

The Heckler & Koch G36 embodies the very latest thinking in assault rifle construction and modular layout. With its optional tactical fittings, the G36 can transform its capabilities in seconds.

Right: A G36-armed soldier keeps careful watch during a medical exercise. As well as military use, the G36 has proved very popular in law enforcement; it is a standard weapon among UK firearms officers, for example.

POLYMER CONSTRUCTION
The polymer materials used in construction are incredibly durable yet also light compared to steel parts.

SIGHT
The optical sight here can be supplemented with a detachable red-dot sight for close-quarters shooting.

BARREL
The barrel is free-floating and has a chrome-lined bore with a six-groove rifling twist.

MAGAZINE
The 30-round magazines are made from translucent plastic. Standard M16 magazines can be accepted via an adapter.

STOCK
The folding stock is hinged at the receiver, and can be folded along the right side of the gun.

MODULARITY

The G36 is an extremely accurate rifle, not least on account of its free-floating barrel arrangement. Its 30-round box magazine is made of translucent polymer, so the operator can always see how many rounds are left before it runs empty. Clips on the magazines allow them to be linked together for rapid changes. The G36 is designed for extremely easy maintenance and modular improvement, so can be disassembled by the user without the need for any tools. The trigger unit comes as a separate component, so it is straightforward to change the selective-fire modes.

SIGHT OPTIONS
A German soldier fires an H&K G36 rifle in Kosovo in 2001. Note how he can instantly switch his eyeline between the optical sight and the reflex sight.

OICW/XM29 (1996)

SPECIFICATIONS

DIMENSIONS:	Length: 890mm (35.04in)
	Barrel Length: KE (kinetic energy) – 250mm (9.84in); HE (high explosive) – 460mm (18.11in)
WEIGHT:	5.5kg (12.13lb)
CALIBRE:	5.56 × 45mm NATO and 20 × 85mm HE
OPERATION:	Gas
FEED:	KE – 20- or 30-round box; HE – 5-round box
MUZZLE VELOCITY:	KE – 750m/sec (2460ft/sec); HE – 180m/sec (590ft/sec)
EFFECTIVE RANGE:	KE – 600m (656yd); HE – 1000m (1094yd)
RATE OF FIRE:	KE – 700–1000rpm

The Objective Infantry Combat Weapon (OICW) programme was intended to give the battle rifle a whole new set of lethal capabilities and modular options. The XM29 was the winning prototype within the programme.

Right: Developed by Alliant Techsystems and Heckler & Koch, the OICW/XM29 combines a 5.56mm-calibre rifle based on the H&K G36 with a 20mm weapon that gives infantry personnel extra firepower.

SIGHTING
A top-mounted computer-assisted sighting system features a laser rangefinder, thermal night-vision capabilities, and up to 6× optical telescopic sight.

GRENADE LAUNCHER
The semi-automatic 20 × 28mm smart grenade launcher is fed from a five-round box magazine.

SMART MUNITIONS
The XM29 includes a laser rangefinder and internal electronics that allow a 20mm round to be fused to a distance found by the laser. This allows soldiers to 'shoot around corners' by detonating a 20mm shell over or beside cover used by enemy personnel. The OICW would allow each infantryman to take on some of the roles of support weapons, doing away with the need for specialists equipped with grenade launchers, or at least ensuring that, if a 'hard' target or one needing indirect fire is encountered, there is a suitable weapon available to every member of the squad.

CARBINE
The kinetic energy element is an unslung 5.56mm carbine working on a standard gas-operated rotating-bolt mechanism.

XM29 COMPONENTS
This breakdown of the XM29 shows all the major components that create the weapon. The general OICW programme has largely ceased, having produced no unitary battlefield weapon, although there have been several spin-off products, particularly relating to the smart grenade launcher.

FIRE-CONTROL COMPUTER

VIDEO CAMERA, 6X SCOPE AND LASER RANGEFINDER

LIGHT-LEVEL DETONATION AND ON/OFF CONTROLS

18-IN. TITANIUM 20MM BARREL

10-IN. STEEL 5.56 MM BARREL

SAFETY, SINGLE SHOT AND 2-ROUND BURST SELECTOR

BAYONET

SINGLE TRIGGER FIRES BOTH BARRELS

5.56MM KINETIC ROUND AND 30-SHOT CLIP

20MM HIGH-EXPLOSIVE ROUND AND 6-SHOT CLIP

SLING

SPECIFICATIONS (AK-103)

DIMENSIONS:	Length: 943mm (37.1in) stock extended ; 705mm (27.8in) stock folded
	Barrel Length: 415mm (16.3in)
WEIGHT:	3.6kg (7.9lb)
CALIBRE:	7.62 × 39mm
OPERATION:	Gas operated
FEED:	30-round box magazine
MUZZLE VELOCITY:	715m/sec (2346ft/ sec)
EFFECTIVE RANGE:	500m (547yd)

Kalashnikov also manufactures AK rifles that use ammunition other than the Russian armed forces' standard 5.45mm. These include the AK-101 and the AK-103, which take 5.56 × 45mm NATO and 7.62 × 39mm ammunition, respectively. Large stockpiles of the latter still exist in former Warsaw Pact nations.

INTERNATIONAL EXPORT
As seen here, the AK-103 has been adopted as the standard weapon of the Venezuelan Army, with limited production beginning in 2012–13 but full-scale production in 2019.

AK AMMUNITION

The AK-47, and subsequent major variants such as the AKM, were based squarely around the 7.62 × 39mm intermediate cartridge. The big change in AK calibre came in 1974, with the introduction of the AK-74 firing the 5.45 × 39mm round. Like the introduction of the 5.56mm NATO cartridge in the West, the 5.45mm round was designed to deliver higher velocities and to reduce physical effects such as recoil and load-carrying burden.

FURNITURE
The AK-103 is designed to take rail mounts around the fore-end for fitting optical sights and tactical accessories, such as this foregrip.

FOLDING STOCK
The hinged stock can be folded against the side of the receiver. Solid and skeleton stocks are available.

CALIBRE
The use of 5.56mm and the old 7.62mm cartridges in weapons such as the AK-101 and AK-103 reflect international commercial realities and opportunities, especially the ability to sell into markets already familiar with those calibres.

RECEIVER
The AK-103 receiver and internal mechanism basically follow the same structure as that of most AK rifles, reducing training times.

QBZ-03 (2003)

SPECIFICATIONS

DIMENSIONS:	Length: 950mm (37in) stock extended; 725mm (28.5in) stock folded
	Barrel Length: not available
WEIGHT:	3.5kg (7.7lb)
CALIBRE:	5.8 × 42mm or 5.56 × 45mm NATO
OPERATION:	Gas
FEED:	30-round box magazine
MUZZLE VELOCITY:	930m/sec (3051ft/sec)
EFFECTIVE RANGE:	400m (437yd)
RATE OF FIRE:	650rpm

The QBZ-03 was added to China's small-arms arsenal in 2003. It demonstrates the steady move away from the Type 56, a copy of the AK, towards a truly modern assault rifle.

Below: The QBZ-03 is, in many respects, a conventional gas-operated, rotating-bolt assault rifle. It is built to high standards, however, with a heavy use of synthetic materials and good attention to ergonomics.

RECEIVER
The receiver is in two halves: an upper half holds the barrel and bolt group; the lower half holds the trigger group, stock, mag aperture and grip.

FOLDING STOCK
Folding the stock along the right side of the receiver reduces the overall length to 725mm (28.5in).

BAYONET
A bayonet can be attached around the flash suppressor, which can also accept rifle grenades.

FORE-END
The fore-end, pistol grip and stock are made of tough but light polymer materials.

SELECTOR SWITCH
The small selector switch gives semi-auto or full-auto options.

MAGAZINE
Magazine capacity is 30 rounds. The magazines are made from a polymer material.

LIGHT CONSTRUCTION

The rifle uses the latest construction techniques and materials, including a polymer stock, pistol grip and fore-end. These materials keep the rifle's weight under control – its empty weight is 3.5kg (7.7lb). The stock is a folding type; when not in use it can be swung and locked against the side of the receiver for storage or transportation. The fore-end has an extended heat shield, and is vented to allow for barrel cooling.

BAYONET FITTING
The QBZ-03 is shown here with bayonet fitted. The view of the right side of the gun clearly shows the ejection port and the cocking handle beneath it.

SPECIFICATIONS

DIMENSIONS:	Length: 940–840mm 36.9–33in) w/ adjustable stock
	Barrel Length: 420mm (16.5in)
WEIGHT:	4.4 kg (9.8lb)
CALIBRE:	5.56×45mm
OPERATION:	Manual
FEED:	30-round STANAG magazine
EFFECTIVE RANGE:	550m (point target); 700m (area target)
RATE OF FIRE:	Sustained: 36rpm

The M27 Infantry Automatic Rifle (IAR) is a major shift in US military acquisition. In 2018, it was announced that the M27 would become a future standard rifle of the US Marine Corps, replacing the M4A1 but also the M249 light machine gun.

Right: The M27 IAR is based upon the Heckler & Koch 416 and features a gas-operated short-stroke piston action with a rotating-bolt mechanism.

BARREL
The M27 has a highly accurate free-floating barrel, meaning that the barrel is not in contact with any of the furniture around it.

MOUNT
Four rails can take a variety of accessories. The standard sight is the the Trijicon ACOG Squad Day Optic (SDO).

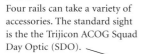

BIPOD
The separate Harris bipod replaces the original grip pod system, which had the bipod legs inside the foregrip.

CALIBRE DEBATE

The M27 is the product of a long and complex debate in the United States Marine Corps about the best way to achieve fire supremacy. Simplifying greatly, part of the debate resolves around those who see fire supremacy as coming mainly from sheer weight of fire, and those who advocate more accurate fire. The M27 represents a victory for the latter, although the controversy will certainly continue. With its integral bipod and cyclic 700rpm rate of fire, each M27 will have the potential to put down suppressive full-auto fire, but also accurate shots of longer ranges, this capacity compensating for the limitations of the 30-round magazine feed.

COMBAT TESTING

Combat testing of the M27 began in 2011, when a small number of troops from 1st Battalion, 3rd Marines took the new rifle to Afghanistan. Initial suspicion towards the rifle, particularly from M249 gunners, seems to have been overcome, the IAR being lighter and easier to maintain than the LMG.

M110 Semi-Automatic Sniper System (2008)

SPECIFICATIONS

DIMENSIONS:	Length: 1028mm (40.5in)
	Barrel Length: 508mm (20in)
WEIGHT:	6.94kg (15.3lb) loaded
CALIBRE:	7.62 × 51mm NATO
OPERATION:	Gas
FEED:	10- or 20-round box magazine
MUZZLE VELOCITY:	784m/sec (2571ft/sec)
EFFECTIVE RANGE:	800m (875yd)
RATE OF FIRE:	–

Out to 800m (875yd) range, the M110 Semi-Automatic Sniper System (SASS) is lethally accurate, and it has been a popular weapon of snipers and designated marksmen since its introduction into service in 2008.

WEIGHT
With a sniper scope, bipod and fully loaded magazine, the M110 SASS can be quite a heavy weapon, weighing around 6.94kg (15.3lb).

Right: A left-side view of the M110 SASS. Note the full-length rail across the top of the fore-end and receiver.

OPTICAL SIGHT
The standard optical sight fitting is a Leupold 3.5–10× variable power daytime optic, although other sights can be mounted.

STOCK
The stock can be incrementally adjusted for length of pull, according to the user's preference.

MAGAZINE
The rifle has the option of 10- or 20-round box magazines.

BIPOD
The detachable bipod is a fully swivelling type made by Harris Bipods.

BARREL
The heavy match-grade barrel is free-floating. It incorporates a flash hider and (just in front of the fore-end) a sound suppressor mount.

SOUND SUPPRESSOR
The M110 can be fitted with a sound suppressor that provides a 30db noise reduction over the standard shot. The suppressor unit is a stainless steel component that is 362mm (14.25in) long and weighs 0.89kg (1.96lb). The sound suppressor mount allows the quick fitting and detachment of the mount when required. The shooter, however, needs to be aware that the rifle's zero will shift when the suppressor is fitted.

SNIPER ROLES
A US Army soldier watches for enemy activity in Kajaki, Afghanistan, in 2011, observing through the scope of his M110 SASS. Snipers perform a broader range of duties than is commonly realized. Aside from their familiar duty of killing enemy personnel, they also conduct reconnaissance and intelligence gathering, often from concealed forward positions. Tactically, they might also perform over-watch duties, or restrict enemy ability to move against a position.

FN SCAR (2009)

SPECIFICATIONS

DIMENSIONS:	Length: 889mm (35in) with stock extended; 826mm (32.5in) with stock fully retracted
	Barrel Length: 330mm (13in)
WEIGHT:	3.5kg (7.7lb)
CALIBRE:	7.62 × 51mm NATO
OPERATION:	Gas
FEED:	10- or 20-round box magazine
MUZZLE VELOCITY:	714m/sec (2342ft/sec)
EFFECTIVE RANGE:	300m (328yd)
RATE OF FIRE:	600rpm

The FN Special Operations Forces Combat Assault Rifle (SCAR) sets the benchmark for modern modular rifles. By changing the barrel, calibre and optional fittings, the SCAR can be configured for different tactical roles.

Below: The SCAR Mk 16 rifle pictured here has the standard barrel length, and shows the iron sights in their upright position.

TACTICAL RAIL
The tactical rail runs along the full length of the top of the receiver, and here has an optical sight fitted; the iron sights hinge down flat when not used.

STOCK
The polymer stock is telescoping for a precision fit to the user's body.

MAGAZINE
This version of the SCAR takes either 10- or 20-round magazines.

BARREL
The SCAR barrels are free-floating for accuracy and feature efficient flash hiders at the muzzle.

ADAPTABLE WEAPON
Strictly speaking, the SCAR is not a single rifle but rather a family of rifles. The foundations of the family are two receivers: 1) the Mk 16, chambered for the 5.56 x 45mm NATO round; and 2) The Mk 17 receiver, designed for the 7.62 x 51mm NATO cartridge. Each receiver can then take a variety of barrel lengths. For the Mk 16, the available lengths are: Close Quarters Combat (CQC) barrel – 254mm (10in); standard barrel – 356mm (14in); and long barrel – 457mm (18in).

SEAL SCAR
A US Navy SEAL in Afghanistan takes aim with his SCAR. With the optical sight fitted, the soldier will be able to take shots out to ranges of about 600m (656yd).

SPECIFICATIONS

DIMENSIONS:	945mm (37.2in) stock extended; 725mm (28.5in) stock folded Barrel Length: 415mm (16.3in)
WEIGHT:	3.3kg (7.28lb)
CALIBRE:	Various (see text)
OPERATION:	Gas
FEED:	30-round box, 60-round casket or 95-round drum magazines
MUZZLE VELOCITY:	900m/sec (2953ft/sec) with 5.45 × 39mm
EFFECTIVE RANGE:	600–800m (656–874yd)
RATE OF FIRE:	700rpm

The AK-12 is interesting as a next stage in the evolution of the history of the AK rifle. Like many modern assault rifles, it places the emphasis on modularity and accessories.

Below: The AN-94 is an even more sophisticated alternative to the AK-12. It uses a blowback shifted pulse mechanism in which two burst-fire shots are felt as one recoil sensation.

TOP RAIL
The top rail runs for the complete length of the receiver to take scopes and other accessories.

STOCK
The stock is fully adjutable for both length of pull and cheek weld.

TACTICAL GRIP
A rail beneath the weapon is often used for a tactical grip for close-quarters work.

MUZZLE BRAKE
The large muzzle brake features threading to accept NATO-standard rifle grenades.

CALIBRE CHANGE
One of the key selling points of the AK-12 is its modular approach to calibre. The weapon is designed to be easily modified for different calibres, largely by changing the barrel unit. In its 'Light' form, the AK-12 can be switched between the following cartridges: 5.42 × 39mm, 5.56 × 45mm, 6.5 × 39mm Grendel and 7.62 × 39mm. The 'Heavy' version of the rifle will take more powerful rifle cartridges, such as the 7.62 × 51mm NATO round. This approach to the calibre makes good business sense, as it opens the rifle up to every conceivable export market.

FULL-AUTO FIRE
During the production of the AK-12, there has been some debate about whether it is right to include a full-auto fire option, as many regard this as wasteful of ammunition. The AK-12, however, does retain that option; in fact, it takes the cyclical rate up to 700rpm, faster than the AK-74.

Bergmann MP 18 (1918)

SPECIFICATIONS

DIMENSIONS:	Length: 812mm (31.97in)
	Barrel Length: 196mm (7.75in)
WEIGHT:	4.19kg (9.25lb)
CALIBRE:	9 × 19mm Parabellum
OPERATION:	Blowback
FEED:	32-round helical drum
MUZZLE VELOCITY:	380m/sec (1274ft/sec)
EFFECTIVE RANGE:	200m (219yd)
RATE OF FIRE:	400rpm

Although not the world's first submachine gun (SMG), the Bergmann MP 18 was the concept's first expression in a viable physical format. Within 20 years, more armies in the world would have their own SMGs.

Below: An MP 18 with its distinctive 32-round 'snail' magazine. An adapter prevented the magazine from being pushed too far into the magazine well.

FEED MECHANISM
The MP 18 had its magazine wide-mounted on the left of the stock, meaning that the gun's centre of gravity changed significantly during firing.

RECOIL SPRING
The recoil spring alone held the bolt in place at the point of firing.

STOCK
The MP 18 had simple but very durable hardwood furniture, with a grooved grip in the fore-end.

BARREL JACKET
The 196mm (7.75in) barrel was protected along its entire length by a ventilated barrel jacket.

FIRING PIN
The MP 18 was prone to accidental discharges if the bolt was left in the closed position on a round and the gun then received a hard knock.

TRIGGER
The operator of the MP 18 would need to learn good trigger control to avoid excessive ammunition consumption.

STORMTROOPERS

The MP 18 was something of a revelation to those who first used them or faced them. In the hands of German stormtrooper soldiers, trained to overwhelm their opponents through fire and manoeuvre, the blasts of 9mm down the length of a trench or in a point-blank urban landscape were horribly effective.

SECURITY USE
The MP 18 served on with some German police and security units throughout the 1920s, 30s and into World War II, although it was modified to take straight box magazines, as seen in this photograph.

Thompson M1928 (1928)

SPECIFICATIONS

DIMENSIONS:	Length: 857mm (33.75in)
	Barrel Length: 266mm (10.5in)
WEIGHT:	4.88kg (10.75lb)
CALIBRE:	.45 ACP
OPERATION:	Delayed blowback
FEED:	18-, 20- or 30-round box magazine of 50- or 100-round drum magazines
MUZZLE VELOCITY:	280m/sec (920ft/sec)
EFFECTIVE RANGE:	c. 200m (219yd)
RATE OF FIRE:	600–700rpm

It was the great firearms designer John T. Thompson who actually coined the term 'submachine gun' (SMG). Although the United States somewhat lagged behind Germany in SMG development, Thompson quickly helped play catch-up.

Below: The M1928A1 variant made some simplifications for military use, such as having a horizontal fore-end instead of a front pistol grip. Note the adjustable Lyman rear ladder sight.

BLISH LOCK
Here is the sliding Blish Lock component, which locked under the high immediate pressures of firing but released the bolt as pressures dropped.

REAR SIGHT
The Lyman rear sight could be adjusted to a range of 600yd (584m), although this was well beyond the gun's effective range.

COMPENSATOR
The compensator directed muzzle gases upwards, producing a counter-force to recoil-induced muzzle climb.

GRIP
The front pistol grip, combined with the effect of the Cutts Compensator, made the Thompson controllable on full-auto fire.

MAGAZINE
The 30-round box magazine (seen here) became the most popular magazine option for Thompson users.

BUTT
The M1928 had a removable stock in which the gun's oiling bottle was stowed.

OPEN-BOLT WEAPON
The Thompson submachine gun is an open-bolt weapon. In mechanical terms, what this means is that the bolt is held to the rear before firing, rather than closed up to the breech (which would be characteristic of a closed-bolt weapon). When the trigger is pulled, the sear releases the entire bolt, which runs forward, strips a new cartridge from the magazine, feeds it and fires it in one action.

BRITISH THOMPSONS
British soldiers proudly display their M1928 Thompsons, all fitted with the 50-round drum magazine. These were heavy and rattling, and were generally swapped for stick magazines.

MP 38/MP 40 (1938)

SPECIFICATIONS

DIMENSIONS:	Length: 832mm (32.75in) stock extended; 629mm (24.75in) stock folded
	Barrel Length: 248mm (9.75in)
WEIGHT:	3.97kg (8.75lb)
CALIBRE:	9 × 19mm Parabellum
OPERATION:	Blowback
FEED:	32-round box magazine
MUZZLE VELOCITY:	380m/sec (1247ft/sec)
EFFECTIVE RANGE:	100m (109yd)
RATE OF FIRE:	500rpm

The most striking feature of the MP 38, and its more cost-effective successor, the MP 40, was its near all-metal design. Even the wooden stock seen on traditional weapons had been replaced with a metal skeleton stock, which also folded beneath the gun to facilitate easy storage.

Below: This exploded view of the MP 40 shows the main constituent parts of the weapon. During the war, different sub-assemblies were often sent to small workshops for production.

SEAR
The sear lever restrains the bolt at the rear when the gun is cocked; pulling the trigger releases the bolt to strip, chamber and fire the round.

BARREL HOOK
The MP 38 and MP 40 featured a hook beneath the barrel, intended to lock onto the rim of a vehicle to stabilize and control the fire.

BLOWBACK
Here the bolt (in red) has fed and fired a 9mm cartridge, the firing pin running through the centre of the bolt.

STOCK
The folding metal stock could be hinged forward, the hinged butt stock then resting flush underneath the receiver.

WAR TESTING

The MP 40 was a popular weapon among German troops, because for close-range combat it was far more advantageous than the standard-issue Kar 98k rifle, with its five-shot magazine and bolt action. The MP 40 was controllable to fire, and delivered decent accuracy at ranges of around 100m (109yd).

STALINGRAD
Two German troops at Stalingrad, armed with MP 40s. The Soviet–German war brought the MP 40 in competition with the Soviet PPSh 41, which demonstrated far greater reliability and firepower. The biggest issue with the MP 40 was misfeeding from the single-stack magazine.

MAS 38 (1939)

SPECIFICATIONS

DIMENSIONS:	Length: 734mm (28.9in)
	Barrel Length: 224mm (8.82in)
WEIGHT:	2.87kg (6.33lb)
CALIBRE:	7.65 × 19.5mm Longue
OPERATION:	Blowback
FEED:	32-round box magazine
MUZZLE VELOCITY:	351m/sec (1152ft/sec)
EFFECTIVE RANGE:	200m (219yd)
RATE OF FIRE:	600rpm

French wartime armament production included the MAS 38 submachine gun, which was unusual for several reasons. The bolt was able to travel unusually far, being returned to position by a very long spring situated in the butt. The barrel and stock were offset slightly, giving the weapon a 'broken' appearance but helping to control recoil; this was not great anyway, owing to the low power of the 7.65mm round used by the weapon.

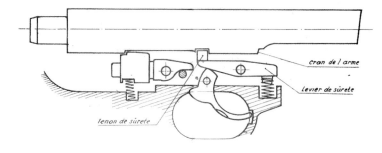

Above: The essential simplicity of the MAS 38 operating system is evident from this technical diagram.

STOCK
The unusually long and rather awkward-looking stock contained a tube for the recoil spring.

STRAIGHT-IN-LINE
In modern firearms manufacture, it has been desirable to have the top of the stock as much in line with the top of the receiver and the barrel as possible, as this configuration directs the recoil straight back into the operator's shoulder, reducing muzzle climb and improving accuracy. The MAS 38, although not perfectly straight-in-line, approached that ideal; when combined with the low-power cartridge this made it highly accurate.

RECEIVER
The body of the MAS 38 was made of machined rather than stamped steel, which made the firearm very robust.

EJECTION PORT
Not seen in this view, the ejection port included a spring-plate cover that opened automatically when the gun was cocked.

MAGAZINE
The magazine held a total of 32 rounds of the 7.65mm ammunition.

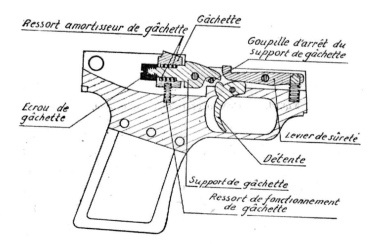

TRIGGER MECHANISM
There was no separate safety switch on the MAS 38. Instead, the safety was built into the trigger itself – pushing the trigger forward locked the bolt into place. The weapon only fired on full-auto mode; it had no single-shot option.

Sten Mk 2 (1941)

SPECIFICATIONS

DIMENSIONS:	Length: 762mm (30in)
	Barrel Length: 196mm (7.75in)
WEIGHT:	2.95kg (6.5lb)
CALIBRE:	9 × 19mm Parabellum
OPERATION:	Blowback
FEED:	32-round box magazine
MUZZLE VELOCITY:	380m/sec (1247ft/sec
EFFECTIVE RANGE:	100m (109yd)
RATE OF FIRE:	550rpm

The Sten gun is not a sophisticated weapon on any level. Crudely manufactured and not always reliable in action, it nevertheless ensured that the British Army had a serviceable submachine gun (SMG) to take into action from 1941 to 1945.

Below: Introduced in 1944, the Sten Mk 5 was a much-refined version of the Mk 2, with wooden fore-grip.

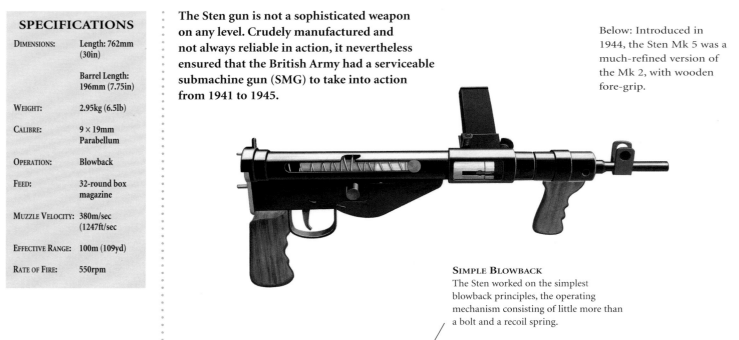

SIMPLE BLOWBACK
The Sten worked on the simplest blowback principles, the operating mechanism consisting of little more than a bolt and a recoil spring.

STOCK
The Sten's tubular metal stock came in two versions: a wire frame or a single-tube version.

SLEEVE
Unscrewing the barrel sleeve allowed the user to remove and clean the barrel.

BOLT
The Sten was an open-bolt weapon, meaning that the bolt was held to the rear when the gun was cocked; pulling the trigger released the bolt to strip, feed and fire a cartridge in one movement.

TRIGGER
The Sten triggers were crude and not always reliable.

RESISTANCE USE

The Sten gun was issued in large numbers to various resistance groups around the world, from France to Southeast Asia. As a resistance weapon, the Sten had many advantages. First, it was cheap, so it did not cost the Allies much to give away free firearms. Second, once the Sten was broken down into its constituent parts, it could be contained in a very small package, making it ideal for covert delivery into the hands of resistance fighters. By firing the 9mm Parabellum round, the Sten also gave fighters an accessible ammunition type – plenty of ammunition could be captured from the Germans.

RESISTANCE FIGHTER
A French Resistance fighter armed with a Sten gun and an American officer with a Browning pistol take cover during the liberation of Paris, August 1944.

PPSh-41 (1941)

SPECIFICATIONS

DIMENSIONS:	Length: 838mm (33in)
	Barrel Length: 266mm (10.5in)
WEIGHT:	3.64kg (8lb)
CALIBRE:	7.62 × 25mm
OPERATION:	Blowback
FEED:	35-round box magazine or 71-round drum magazine
MUZZLE VELOCITY:	500m/sec (1640ft/sec)
EFFECTIVE RANGE:	150m (164yd)
RATE OF FIRE:	900rpm

One word sums up the performance of the PPSh-41: reliability. Regardless of the weather conditions, the type of use or the number of rounds put through the gun, the PPSh-41 would just keep on firing.

Right: The PPSh-41 was a masterpiece of functional engineering. With a 900rpm rate of fire, it could empty the 71-round drum magazine in about five seconds.

RECOIL SPRING
Being a blowback weapon, the PPSh-41's recoil spring provided the pressure to close the bolt against the breech.

BOLT
The sides of the PPSh-41 bolt featured recesses to control the ingress of dirt and other foreign bodies.

BARREL HINGE
For cleaning, the barrel hinged forward on the receiver just in front of the magazine housing.

SELECTOR
The PPSh-41's selector switch was located within the trigger guard, just in front of the trigger.

MAGAZINE
The cartridges in the 71-round drum magazine were placed under spring tension for feeding into the gun.

ROBUST SERVICE

Georgi Shpagin created the PPSh-41, certainly one of the finest SMGs ever made. Its defining characteristic was trustworthy reliability. It was of a straightforward open-bolt blowback type, to keep the design simple. The mechanism was highly tolerant of dirt intrusion, having a certain 'looseness' to cope with foreign bodies, and the barrel was chrome-lined for durability. All the soldier had to do was keep the weapon reasonably clean and properly lubricated (kerosene was often used during the extreme winter months) and it would be utterly dependable.

SHORT-RANGE FIREPOWER
Red Army troops make an assault from a trench position armed with PPSh-41s and Mosin-Nagant rifles. The PPSh-41s would come into their own within ranges of 150m (164yd).

Austen (1942)

SPECIFICATIONS

DIMENSIONS:	Length: 845mm (33.25in) stock extended; 552mm (21.75in) stock folded
	Barrel Length: 196mm (7.75in)
WEIGHT:	3.98kg (8.75lb)
CALIBRE:	9 × 19mm Parabellum
OPERATION:	Blowback
FEED:	28-round box magazine
MUZZLE VELOCITY:	380m/sec (1246ft/sec)
EFFECTIVE RANGE:	150m (164yd)
RATE OF FIRE:	500rpm

Another effort to create something better than the Sten, but that was not much more expensive, was the Australian Austen SMG. Combining features of the MP40 and the Sten, the Austen was a robust and effective weapon chambered for 9mm Parabellum.

LENGTH
With a length of only 552mm (21.75in) with the metal stock folded, the Austen was very handy at close quarters but was edged out by the more reliable Owen.

MAGAZINE
The 28-round magazine fed from the side, above a canted foregrip.

FOREGRIP
The foregrip provided an improved control of recoil when compared to the Sten, especially in sweaty tropical conditions.

MECHANISM
The Austen's receiver, barrel and trigger mechanism were directly copied from the Sten.

GERMAN INFLUENCE
Although recognizably derived from the Sten, the Austen was also indebted to certain features of the German MP 40, particularly the design of the mainspring, bolt and the folding metal stock. Yet the Austen was never really able to escape the unreliability issues that blighted the Sten, and the rival Australian Owen submachine gun proved far more successful and popular.

PARATROOPER WEAPON
Because of its folding stock, the Austen was suitable for deployment by airborne troops. Here we see an Australian paratrooper from the Parachute Battalion Training Centre armed with an Austen Mark 1.

M3A1 'Grease Gun' (1942)

SPECIFICATIONS

DIMENSIONS:	Length: 762mm (30in) stock extended; 577mm (22.75in) stock folded
	Barrel Length: 203mm (8in)
WEIGHT:	3.7kg (8.15lb)
CALIBRE:	.45 ACP
OPERATION:	Blowback
FEED:	30-round box magazine
MUZZLE VELOCITY:	275m/sec (900ft/sec)
EFFECTIVE RANGE:	100m (109yd)
RATE OF FIRE:	450rpm

Britain had the Sten, Germany had the MP 40 and the Soviet Union had the PPSh-41. But in the early 1940s, the United States had yet to develop its own submachine gun (SMG) suitable for wartime mass production.

Left: A suppressed version of the M3A1 was built during World War II for use by the Office of Strategic Services (OSS).

BUDGET FIREARM

To satisfy the requirements of rapid wartime production, the M3 was simplified to its most essential elements. Much of the gun was manufactured from basic metal stamping, welding and riveting processes, making manufacturing quick and low-cost. From its introduction in 1943 until the end of the war in 1945, a total of 622,163 were produced. Not always popular, the M3 and the improved M3A1 nevertheless gave thouands of US troops portable .45-calibre firepower.

EJECTION PORT COVER
The hinged ejection port cover also acted as a basic safety. When it was closed, projections on the cover clicked into notches on the bolt, holding the bolt in place.

BARREL
The M3 barrel was 203mm (8in) long and had a four-groove, right-hand twist configuration.

BLOWBACK
When a cartridge was fired, the recoil forces imparted to the empty case drove back the unlocked bolt.

TRIGGER
The M3A1 had no selective-fire system, so single shots had to be delivered by careful trigger control alone.

STOCK
The extendable stock also acted as a cleaning rod and a disassembly tool to unscrew the barrel cap.

MAGAZINE
The M3 magazine had a poor single-stack design that was the main cause of feed problems.

POST-WAR USE
ARVN irregulars line up during the Vietnam War, armed with M3 'Grease Guns'. The M3 had a large number of post-war users, including China, Greece, Morocco and Thailand. M3s were still found in use in the 1990s.

Sterling L2A1 (1953)

SPECIFICATIONS

DIMENSIONS:	Length: 690mm (27.16in) stock extended; 483mm (19in) stock folded
	Barrel Length: 198mm (7.79in)
WEIGHT:	2.72kg (6lb)
CALIBRE:	9 × 19mm Parabellum
OPERATION:	Blowback
FEED:	34-round box magazine
MUZZLE VELOCITY:	390m/sec (1280ft/sec)
EFFECTIVE RANGE:	200m (219yd)
RATE OF FIRE:	550rpm

The Sterling submachine gun served for more than four decades with the British Army. It was also adopted by dozens of other countries around the world, being one of the most reputable SMGs of the post-war era.

Below: The Sterling's overall dimensions can be reduced instantly by collapsing the stock, although it is not recommended to fire the gun in the stock-folded position.

FRONT SIGHT
The Sterling's front sight is adjustable for windage.

FEED
The Sterling had a side-mounted magazine holding 34 rounds, a legacy of the Sten.

BOLT
Note the large size of the bolt, which also features an integral striker in its face.

STOCK
With the stock folded, the overall length of the gun is reduced by 207mm (8.1in).

BARREL
The Sterling's barrel is 198mm (7.79in) long and has a six-groove, right-hand twist configuration.

MAGAZINE LOCATION
The barrel is protected by a full-length ventilated jacket, and the magazine feed is from a curved and side-mounted 34-round detachable box magazine. The location of the magazine separated the Sterling from most other world SMGs, but the gun actually balances extremely well around the pistol grip. Furthermore, by having the magazine at the side, the Sterling allowed soldiers to get fully into the prone position while still retaining easy control over magazine loading and removal.

BRITISH MAINSTAY
British Army soldiers undergo training during the early 1980s. The officer in the foreground is armed with a Sterling submachine gun, while behind him soldiers carry an L1A1 SLR and L7A2 general-purpose machine gun, a variant of the FN MAG.

Uzi (1954)

SPECIFICATIONS

DIMENSIONS:	Length: 650mm (25.6in) stock extended; 470mm (18.5in) stock folded
	Barrel Length: 260mm (10.23in))
WEIGHT:	3.7kg (8.15lb)
CALIBRE:	9 × 19mm Parabellum
OPERATION:	Blowback
FEED:	25- or 32-round box magazine
MUZZLE VELOCITY:	400m/sec (1312ft/sec)
EFFECTIVE RANGE:	200m (219yd)
RATE OF FIRE:	600rpm

The Uzi's profile has a near-universal recognizability. It was one of a new generation of post-war submachine guns that adopted a telescoping bolt and pistol-grip mounted magazine.

Below: The Mini Uzi measures 600mm (23.62in) with its stock extended and 360mm (14.17in) with its stock folded. Rate of fire is a fast 950rpm.

BOLT
The Uzi is an open-bolt blowback weapon; the telescoping bolt wraps around the rear end of the barrel.

STOCK
The folding stock hinges beneath the rear of the receiver and locks into place.

BODY
Grooves in the receiver work to channel dirt and debris away from the operating parts.

GRIP
The pistol grip incorporates the magazine, magazine release catch and grip safety mechanism.

CONTROLLABILITY

On account of its small size and the location of the magazine, the Uzi was also very well balanced, making it controllable under full-auto fire. This was essential – the weapon has a cyclical rate of 600rpm, which meant that an Israeli squad could lay down some very heavy fire over the gun's effective range of about 200m (219yd). The rear aperture sight could be flipped between 100m (109yd) and 200m with just thumb pressure.

BORDER PATROL
Israeli troops patrol near the Gaza border in 1955. The Uzi proved itself to be excellent for urban and close-quarters warfare, although less convincing for open battlefield combat.

Heckler & Koch MP5 (1966)

SPECIFICATIONS

DIMENSIONS:	Length: 680mm (26.77in)
	Barrel Length: 225mm (8.85in)
WEIGHT:	2.55kg (5.62lb)
CALIBRE:	9 × 19mm Parabellum
OPERATION:	Delayed blowback
FEED:	15- or 30-round box magazines
MUZZLE VELOCITY:	400m/sec (1312ft sec)
EFFECTIVE RANGE:	200m (219yd)
RATE OF FIRE:	800rpm

Highly accurate, even on full-auto fire, the MP5 has helped to keep the submachine gun concept alive to the present day. Designed during the 1960s, it has become the weapon of choice for many elite law enforcement and military units specializing in hostage rescue and counter-terrorist actions.

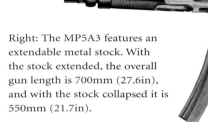

Right: The MP5A3 features an extendable metal stock. With the stock extended, the overall gun length is 700mm (27.6in), and with the stock collapsed it is 550mm (21.7in).

REAR SIGHT
The standard rear sight on an MP5 is a drum aperture type.

LOCKING ROLLERS
The MP5 is a blowback gun, with rollers attached to the side of the bolt providing a delay to the blowback recoil.

COCKING HANDLE
Located on the left side of the fore-end, the MP5's cocking handle is non-reciprocating.

MAGAZINE
The MP5 takes either 15- or 30-round magazines.

MP5 FAMILY

The MP5 is really a family of firearms, consisting of numerous variants designed to suit all requirements from the users. The base models are essentially the MP5A2, which features a rigid synthetic polymer buttstock, and the MP5A3, with a collapsible metal buttstock. There is also the MP5K, which was introduced in the 1970s as a highly concealable weapon for counter-terrorist forces. The MP5K is basically an MP5A2 but minus the stock and with a shortened barrel – 115mm (4.53in) as opposed to the standard 225mm (8.85in). A front pistol grip is added to give some additional stability in the absence of a stock, and the rate of fire climbs to 900rpm.

SPECIAL FORCES FIREARM
A US Navy SEAL, in firing position armed with an MP5-N submachine gun, sets up a security perimeter on the upper deck of the USNS *Leroy Grumman* during a search and seizure exercise.

FN P90 (1980)

SPECIFICATIONS

DIMENSIONS:	Length: 400mm (15.75in)
	Barrel Length: 263mm (7.75in)
WEIGHT:	2.8kg (6.17lb)
CALIBRE:	5.7 × 28mm FN
OPERATION:	Blowback
FEED:	50-round detachable box magazine
MUZZLE VELOCITY:	850m/sec (2800ft/sec)
EFFECTIVE RANGE:	200m (219yd)
RATE OF FIRE:	800–1000rpm

Like the Calico M950, the Fabrique Nationale P90 can be classified in various ways. Some call it a submachine gun, some a carbine. Its makers term it a Personal Defence Weapon, and cite its role as a defensive weapon for personnel whose duties do not normally include small arms combat, such as vehicle crews and artillerymen.

SIGHTS
The P90 is fitted with the Ring Sights MC-10-80 reflex sight, which was specifically designed for the P90.

MAGAZINE
The magazine lies across the top of the receiver, with the cartridges at 90 degrees to the bore. A turntable device rotates the cartridges when feeding them.

BLOWBACK
Internally, the P90 uses a standard blowback system. The weapon fires from a closed bolt to maintain its accuracy.

GRIP
The P90 has a thumbhole grip that, despite its appearance, is actually very comfortable. Operating controls are fully ambidextrous.

NEW CALIBRE

Apart from its futuristic appearance and layout, one of the most interesting elements of the P90 is the choice of calibre – 5.7 × 28mm FN. This is a bottlenecked cartridge developed by FN in the late 1980s and early 1990s, specifically in response to NATO investigations into possible high-power replacements for the 9mm round. The 5.7mm offers performance that approaches that of many assault rifles, and can penetrate certain types of body armour at ranges of 200m (219yd).

MAGAZINE LAYOUT
The P90 has a highly distinctive patented magazine layout. The value of configuring the magazine in this way is to reduce the dimensions of the weapon and to keep its weight well balanced. The magazines are made from a semi-transparent polymer.

BXP (1984)

SPECIFICATIONS

DIMENSIONS:	Length: 607mm (23.9in) stock extended; 387mm (15.2in) stock folded
	Barrel Length: 208mm (8.2in), 6 grooves, rh
WEIGHT:	2.5kg (5.5lb)
CALIBRE:	9 × 19mm Parabellum
OPERATION:	Blowback
FEED:	22- or 32-round box magazine
MUZZLE VELOCITY:	370m/sec (1214ft/sec)
EFFECTIVE RANGE:	200m (219yd)
RATE OF FIRE:	1000–1200rpm

VERSATILITY

As well as being very well made, mostly from stainless steel, the BXP has some interesting features. It can accept a compensator to reduce felt recoil or a suppressor to reduce noise levels, and can even launch rifle grenades. While this capability will not be needed in most security applications, it does add to the overall versatility of the weapon.

The South African BXP, chambered for 9mm Parabellum, represents an interesting compromise between machine pistol and carbine-type SMGs. It is configured like an Uzi, with a wraparound bolt and 208mm (1.18in) barrel in a package just 387mm (15.2in) long. The weapon, however, comes with an ingenious folding metal stock that doubles as a foregrip when not in use.

Above: Although the BXP has an extremely high rate of fire, it is so well balanced that it can be fired one-handed.

SAFETY CATCH
The manual safety catch is ambidextrous, with the operator able to select between 'safe' and 'fire' on both sides of the firearm.

TRIGGER
In the military version of the BXP, the trigger pull controls semi-auto (half-pull) and full-auto (full-pull) modes.

FRONT GRIP
As seen here, when the stock is folded the shoulder pad acts as a foregrip, providing extra stabilization.

PRODUCT OPTIONS

Here we see three BXPs surrounded by various optional fittings, including the suppressor (the weapon on the right), which substantially extends the length of the firearm. Semi-auto-only versions are available on the civilian market.

Calico M950 (1990)

SPECIFICATIONS

DIMENSIONS:	Length: 365mm (14.3in) with 50-round mag
	Barrel Length: 152mm (6in), 6 grooves, rh
WEIGHT:	1kg (2.2lb)
CALIBRE:	9 × 19mm Parabellum
OPERATION:	Delayed blowback
FEED:	50- or 100-round detachable helical magazine
MUZZLE VELOCITY:	390m/sec (1276ft/sec)
EFFECTIVE RANGE:	100m (109yd)
RATE OF FIRE:	750rpm

Although chambered in .22LR or 9mm Parabellum, both pistol calibres, the Calico M950 is really more of a carbine-type weapon. Shaped like a large handgun with a curious cylinder (the magazine) on top, the Calico has enough barrel shrouding to allow a two-handed grip more suited to a submachine gun or rifle than a pistol.

Above: The variant shown here is the Calico M960A, a version fitted with a telescoping stock for improved handling.

MAGAZINE
The magazine sits longitudinally atop the receiver, which keeps most of the the weight of the gun closer to the user's grip hand and body.

FIREPOWER
The M950's long barrel allows accurate fire out to about 100m (109yd), and the 50- or 100-round helical feed magazine offers impressive capacity. Most of the extensive range (the M950 is the baseline for a total of eight models) fire semi-auto only, but full-auto versions are available to security and military users.

EJECTION
The spent cartridge cases are ejected from a port just in front of the trigger guard.

ACTION
The action of the M950 is roller-delayed blowback, essentially the same as that used in the H&K MP5.

WEIGHT MANAGEMENT
When the M950, or its variants, are fitted with a full 100-round magazine, the total gun weight rises to a hefty 2.63kg (5.79lb). In such cases, the optional foregrip is a useful practical addition for controlling the weight.

Gatling Gun (1878)

SPECIFICATIONS

DIMENSIONS:	Length: 965mm (38in)
	Barrel Length: 610mm (24in)
WEIGHT:	34kg (75lb)
CALIBRE:	.45-70
OPERATION:	Manual
FEED:	400-round drum magazine
MUZZLE VELOCITY:	400m/sec (1310ft/sec)
EFFECTIVE RANGE:	600m (656yd)
RATE OF FIRE:	c. 300rpm

The Gatling gun was a genuine revolution in firepower. It was the most successful of the hand-cranked machine guns to enter service in the nineteenth century, and the Gatling principles are still in operation in electrically powered variants.

Left: The Gatling Model 1893 Bulldog. This later version of the Gatling was a compact model in .40in or .44in calibres. It weighed only 20kg (44lb) and featured 457mm (18in) barrels

MAGAZINE
As the operating handle of the gun was turned, the cartridges were progressively aligned and fed into the chambers via a carrier mechanism. This type of magazine held 240 rounds.

CRANK MECHANISM
The locks, carrier and barrel set were mounted on the same longitudinal shaft, which meant that the major operating parts stayed in perfect alignment as the crank handle was turned.

SHIP-MOUNTED GATLING GUNS

For much of the early history of machine guns, these weapons were more regarded as forms of artillery than extensions of the small-arms family. In both the Royal Navy and the US Navy, therefore, Gatlings were given shipboard mounts to enhance naval firepower at targets under ranges of 1000m (1094yd). During the American Civil War (1861–65), for example, eight Gatlings were fitted to Union river gunboats to deliver ship-to-shore fire, or to pepper the decks of Confederate rivals.

MOUNT
A variety of mounts were made for the Gatling, which allowed for controlled traverse and elevation to deliver fire at ranges in excess of 600m (656yd).

BARREL SET
The 10-barrel set of the 1874 Gatling meant that during a complete 360-degree cycle of operation five barrels were in the loading and firing phase, and five were in the extraction and ejection phase.

LOCK CYCLINDER
The lock cyclinder contained a firing pin and cartridge extractor for each barrel.

BRITISH GATLINGS
British troops proudly stand by their Gatling guns in Afghanistan in the 1880s. The high rate of fire provided by the Gatling was much valued in warfare against mass tribal enemies.

Madsen Light Machine Gun (1902)

SPECIFICATIONS

DIMENSIONS:	Length: 1145mm (45in)
	Barrel Length: 585mm (23in), 4 grooves, rh
WEIGHT:	9kg (20lb)
CALIBRE:	Various from 6.5mm to 8mm
OPERATION:	Recoil
FEED:	25-, 30- or 40-round box magazine
MUZZLE VELOCITY:	c. 700m/sec (2300ft/sec) depending on calibre
EFFECTIVE RANGE:	c. 600m (656yd)
RATE OF FIRE:	450rpm

The Danish Madsen light machine gun, first produced in 1897 and in service from 1902, saw combat in the Russo–Japanese War and finally ceased production in 1955. The Madsen was based on the Martini rifle and, weighing less than 10kg (22lb), it was a true light machine gun that could be carried by a member of a rifle squad.

Above: The Madsen, which was fitted with an integral bipod, effectively introduced the concept of the light machine gun.

MAGAZINE
The top-mounted magazine had no feed lips, instead relying on an external clip to hold the cartridges in place; the clip popped out to the side of the receiver when the magazine was loaded.

BARREL
The Madsen could perform quick barrel changes, the whole barrel and action sliding out in one piece.

CHARGING HANDLE
The charging handle was located on the right side of the gun, and was of a non-reciprocating type.

EJECTION
Spent cases were pulled from the chamber by an extractor and thrown out the bottom of the gun, via a curved ejection ramp.

OPERATION
The most intriguing element of the Madsen was its recoil operating mechanism. Instead of using a conventional horizontally oscillating bolt, the Madsen had a rising and falling block action, rather like that in a Martini-Henry rifle. This system, which was complex but worked well, meant that the horizontal movement of the barrel and action was only about 31mm (1.25in), but this was still sufficient to feed cartridges of c. 76mm (3in) length.

CANNON VARIANT
The Madsen was produced in many different variants over its lifetime, the operating system providing suitable for adaptation to various calibres. The weapon seen here is a 20mm cannon Madsen, developed for mounting aboard ships.

Maxim Gun/MG 08 (1908)

SPECIFICATIONS

DIMENSIONS:	Length: 1175mm (46.25in)
	Barrel Length: 721 mm (28.4 in)
WEIGHT:	26.44kg (58.29lb)
CALIBRE:	7.92 × 57mm Mauser
OPERATION:	Short recoil
FEED:	250-round belt
MUZZLE VELOCITY:	892m/sec (2925ft/sec)
EFFECTIVE RANGE:	1000m (1094yd)
RATE OF FIRE:	300–450rpm

The Maxim gun was essentially the world's first true machine gun. Developed by the relentless ingenuity of Hiram Maxim, it utilized the power of recoil to cycle the action, moving away from the hand-cranked principles of weapons such as the Gatling. Such was the sound nature of Maxim's design that machine guns based directly on the Maxim were still in service in the late 1960s and beyond. The German MG 08, alongside the British Vickers and Russian M1910, were the most influential derivatives.

Right: This British .303in Maxim gun is set in a naval mount; the Maxim proved popular in naval use for close-in protection.

GREAT WAR GUN
German forces received a Maxim-type machine gun, the Maxim Maschinengewehr 08, in the years running up to the start of the Great War. Water-cooled, this weapon could sustain 450 rounds per minute almost indefinitely. Initially fielded on a heavy steel mount weighing more than 60kg (132lb), the 08 eventually gained a bipod mount, bringing the overall weight of the gun and mount down to a rather more manageable 26.44kg (58.29lb). Like the original Maxim, the MG 08 was effective out to around 2000m (2187yd), and it was devastating when sweeping along the wire-festooned approaches to a defensive position.

WATER COOLED
A large water-filled jacket wrapped around the barrel, which served to prevent the barrel overheating during sustained fire.

TOGGLE LOCK
The Maxim-type guns used a toggle-lock system of locking, which was robust enough to withstand the repeated impacts of recoil and loading.

BELT FEED
The MG 08 was chambered for a fairly heavy 7.92 × 57mm round, feeding in 250-round belts.

MAXIM M1910
Mounted on a clumsy and extremely heavy carriage, this Red Army-operated Maxim 1910 fires on Finnish troops near Viborg in 1940. The vast weight of this artillery-style Sokolov mount would have reduced the Maxim's mobility, making it a primarily defensive weapon.

Lewis Gun (1911)

SPECIFICATIONS

DIMENSIONS:	Length: 1283mm (50.5in)
	Barrel Length: 666mm (26.25in)
WEIGHT:	11.8kg (26lb)
CALIBRE:	.303in
OPERATION:	Gas
FEED:	47-round pan magazine
MUZZLE VELOCITY:	c. 745m/sec (2450ft/sec)
EFFECTIVE RANGE:	1000m (1094yd)
RATE OF FIRE:	550rpm

The Lewis Gun signalled an important diversification in the world of small arms. It was a true light machine gun, a weapon that could be carried and operated by a two-man team during assault movements.

Above: The Lewis's folding leaf rear sight was graduated to 2000yd (1830m). In reality, the gun was better put to use at ranges of 600–1000m (1968–3280ft).

BARREL SHROUD
The aluminium barrel shroud contained fins to act as heat sinks for the barrel.

RECOIL SPRING
The operating rod was toothed, and the teeth engaged with a cog that wound the helical recoil spring.

GAS PISTON
The gas piston was driven backwards by the force of propellant gas tapped off near the muzzle.

BARREL
The Lewis barrel measured 666mm (26.25in) and had a six-groove, left-hand twist configuration.

AERIAL LEWIS GUNS
The Lewis gun took firepower to the skies during World War I and beyond. Even before the conflict, it was showing how it could transform an aircraft's combat capabilities: in June 1912, the Lewis became the first machine gun fired from an aircraft, a Wright Model B Flyer crewed by Captain Charles Chandler and Lieutenant Roy Kirtland.

LEWIS ASSAULT
A soldier of the New Zealand Rifle Brigade (Earl of Liverpool's Own) readies his Lewis gun prior to moving forward. The bipod mount was ideal for low-profile prone shooting positions.

Vickers Machine Gun (1912)

SPECIFICATIONS

DIMENSIONS:	Length: 1155mm (45.5in)
	Barrel Length: 723mm (28.5in)
WEIGHT:	18.1kg (40lb)
CALIBRE:	.303in
OPERATION:	Short recoil
FEED:	250-round fabric belt
MUZZLE VELOCITY:	745m/sec (2450ft/sec)
EFFECTIVE RANGE:	2000m (2187yd)
RATE OF FIRE:	450rpm

The Vickers was a true workhorse machine gun. Built to a high standard of finish and capable of hours of sustained fire, it left its mark on half a century of warfare across numerous theatres and conflicts.

Below: This cutaway image shows not only the feed mechanism, but also the barrel running through the lower part of the jacket, terminating in the muzzle booster device at the front.

COCKING LEVER
Once a belt of .303in ammunition had been fed into the gun, the cocking lever was drawn back twice to load the first round into the chamber.

CONDENSING CAN
Steam generated from within the barrel jacket was channelled down into a condensing can via a rubber hose.

WATER COOLANT
The water-coolant system ensured that the barrels rarely overheated. The jacket held 4.3 litres (7.3 imperial pints) of water, and as the barrel warmed up through sustained fire the water would literally boil inside the jacket. The resultant steam was siphoned off via a hose into a condensing can, where it would become water again and could by tipped back into the jacket.

TRIPOD
The tripod mount gave an extremely stable platform for sustained fire at long ranges.

AMMUNITION
The Vickers fired from a 250-round canvas belt; each belt weighed 10kg (22lb).

AA VICKERS
The Vickers also found use as an anti-aircraft gun during World War I; here we see an infantry team with the gun at high elevation for obtaining aerial targets.

Hotchkiss Modèle 1914 (1914)

SPECIFICATIONS

DIMENSIONS:	Length: 1270mm (50in)
	Barrel Length: 775mm (30.5in)
WEIGHT:	23.6kg (52lb)
CALIBRE:	8mm Lebel
OPERATION:	Gas
FEED:	24- or 30-round metallic strip or 249-round strip/belt
MUZZLE VELOCITY:	725m/sec (2380ft/sec)
EFFECTIVE RANGE:	2000m (2187yd)
RATE OF FIRE:	600rpm

Most automatic weapons at the time of the Great War used fabric belts to feed cartridges into the mechanism, but other systems were available. Early Hotchkiss weapons used a rigid metal strip holding 24 or 36 rounds, which worked well enough, but when the Hotchkiss Mle 1914 was fielded it used what may well have been the first example of the disintegrating metal belt.

Below: The Hotchkiss machine gun was first introduced in the 1890s, but the success of its design meant that it served through both world wars and into the post-war period, with recorded uses in the French Indochina War (1945–54).

BARREL FINS
The brass barrel fins were meant to accelerate barrel heat loss, a function that largely failed.

PISTOL GRIP
Unlike the Maxim-type paddle triggers, the Hotchkiss used a conventional pistol grip.

FEED
A string of 3-round metal strips was connected together to create a continuous belt feed, the standard number of rounds on the belt being 249.

MOUNT
The Hotchkiss was a tripod-mounted gun, but weight was a problem – the total weight of the gun and tripod was about 50kg (110lb).

GAS OPERATED
The gun itself was a reliable gas-operated weapon normally chambered for the 8mm Lebel cartridge. It was effective to 2000m (2187yd) or more and, although its weight precluded much mobility, was considered good enough to be taken into service by France, Britain, the US and other nations. After the Great War, it gained considerable overseas popularity, being sold in Central and South America as well as in Europe.

ANTI-AIRCRAFT GUN
French troops man a Hotchkiss M1914 sometime during World War I. They appear to be training for the anti-aircraft role.

BAR (1918)

SPECIFICATIONS

DIMENSIONS:	Length: 1219mm (48in)
	Barrel Length: 610mm (24in)
WEIGHT:	8.8kg (19.4lb)
CALIBRE:	.30 M1906
OPERATION:	Gas
FEED:	20-round detachable box magazine
MUZZLE VELOCITY:	808m/sec (2650ft/sec)
EFFECTIVE RANGE:	1000m (1094yd)
RATE OF FIRE:	500–650rpm ((M1918, M1922, M1918A1)

John Browning saw the advantage of a machine gun that could keep up with infantry, and in 1917 he designed the Browning Automatic Rifle (BAR). Chambered for .30-06, the same ammunition used in standard infantry rifles, the BAR was fed by a 20-round detachable box magazine and could fire on full-automatic or single shots as a self-loader.

Above: A US soldier takes aim with his BAR. The sights could be adjusted to ranges of up to 1500yd (1372m).

LOCKING
The BAR bolt featured a locking wedge that was cammed up into a recess located in the distinctive hump atop the receiver.

STOCK
A monopod stock rest could be fitted into a hole in the underside of the stock, although it rarely was.

GAS SYSTEM
The BAR was a gas-operated gun that fired from an open bolt. The gas cylinder runs beneath the barrel.

BIPOD
The bipod had legs that could be adjusted for height – useful for when lying in the prone position.

US POPULARITY
Although a BAR could burn through its entire magazine very quickly at 350 or 550 rounds per minute, the firepower it offered in a package only twice as heavy as an infantryman's rifle made it popular with the troops. The standard BAR came equipped with a bipod, but this was often removed to save weight. It served in both World Wars and was not withdrawn until 1957. Even then, it was retained for special applications, including VIP protection, for many years afterwards.

BAR GUNNER
A typical World War II US infantry rifle squad of 12 men would consist of nine riflemen with M1 Garands or M1 Carbines, one BAR gunner, and two NCOs with either Garands, Carbines or SMGs.

M1919 Browning (1919)

SPECIFICATIONS

DIMENSIONS:	Length: 1041mm (41in)
	Barrel Length: 610mm (24in)
WEIGHT:	14.05kg (31lb)
CALIBRE:	.30in
OPERATION:	Short recoil
FEED:	250-round fabric belt
MUZZLE VELOCITY:	853m/sec (2800ft/sec)
EFFECTIVE RANGE:	c. 2000m (2187yd)
RATE OF FIRE:	500rpm

The Browning M1919 was a masterpiece of design. Despite being a weapon that dates back to the end of World War I, versions of the M1919 are still found in action today with some modern armies.

Below: The Browning M1919A4 is here seen on its tripod. The tripod could sit very low to the ground, making it ideal for establishing the gun in defensive earthworks.

BOLT
The large bolt here has just fed a cartridge into the chamber; note the firing pin sat ready to strike the cartridge primer.

BARREL
Encased in a ventilated jacket, the M1919 barrel was 610mm (24in) long and had a four-groove, right-hand pattern of rifling.

JACKET
The M1919's jacket provided protection for the barrel, allowed for an easier barrel change, and was ventilated to allow barrel cooling.

PISTOL GRIP
Like the M1917, the M1919 series retained the pistol grip and single trigger format.

PROVEN RELIABILITY

The Browning system had almost unnerving reliability. During one demonstration firing exercise in May 1917, a single gun fired 20,000 rounds non-stop, then repeated the same feat for good measure. Provoking suspicion in the army board, Browning later presented another gun that ran through 28,920 rounds in 48 minutes and 12 seconds. The army quickly placed a major order, and 68,000 M1917s were made by the end of the war.

SURPLUS M1919s
French troops in Indochina in 1951 use an M1919 in their war agains the Viet Minh. The French utilized large numbers of war surplus M1919s in their post-war conflicts.

M2 Browning .50-cal (1933)

SPECIFICATIONS

DIMENSIONS:	Length: 1653mm (65.1in)
	Barrel Length: 1143mm (45in)
WEIGHT:	38.22kg (84lb)
CALIBRE:	.50 BMG
OPERATION:	Short recoil
FEED:	110-round metallic belt
MUZZLE VELOCITY:	898m/sec (2950ft/sec)
EFFECTIVE RANGE:	2000m+ (2187yd+)
RATE OF FIRE:	450–550rpm

It is hard to overstate the sheer power of the Browning M2 machine gun. With a design little changed in 80 years, it still delivers crushing firepower over ranges of many thousands of metres.

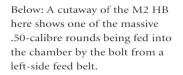

Below: A cutaway of the M2 HB here shows one of the massive .50-calibre rounds being fed into the chamber by the bolt from a left-side feed belt.

TRIGGER
Unlike the M1919, the M2 uses spade grips and a butterfly trigger, giving excellent physical control over manoeuvring and firing the weapon.

QUICK CHANGE BARREL (QCB)
With the QCB kit fitted, the operator of the M2HB ('Heavy Barrel') can change the barrel in 10 seconds or less.

BARREL
The M2HB barrel is 1143mm (45in) long and has a rifling configuration of four right-hand grooves.

CHARGING HANDLE
The charging handle can be mounted on the left- or right-hand side of the gun.

TRIPOD
The M3 tripod weighs 20kg (44lb) and allows fixed or mobile elevation and traverse.

LONGEVITY

The M2's endurance as a heavy machine gun is astonishing. Despite the first variant in the series, the M1921, appearing in the early 1920s, its descendants are still serving with dozens of military forces around the world today, including the US Army and Marine Corps. Partly this success is due to the exceptionally robust design of the gun, but it is also due to the sheer power of the .50 Browning Machine Gun (BMG) round that was specifically developed for the weapon, and that has few equals in terms of range, penetration and destructive force on its target.

DESTRUCTIVE POWER

For those on the receiving end, the M2's power is quite simply devastating. During Operation *Iraqi Freedom* in 2003, US Army sergeant Paul Ray Smith virtually held off a company-sized Iraqi force with an M2 HB mounted atop a damaged infantry vehicle. During the action, he was mortally wounded, but his fire made a significant contribution to more than 50 enemy killed.

MG 34 (1934)

SPECIFICATIONS

DIMENSIONS:	Length: 1219mm (48in)
	Barrel Length: 627mm (24.7in)
WEIGHT:	11.5kg (25.35lb)
CALIBRE:	7.92 × 57mm
OPERATION:	Short recoil
FEED:	50-round belt
MUZZLE VELOCITY:	755m/sec (2480ft/sec)
EFFECTIVE RANGE:	2000m (2187yd)
RATE OF FIRE:	800–900rpm

The MG 34 was an exceptional weapon, one that terrorized Allied forces during World War II and served as the model for a new type of firearm: the general-purpose machine gun (GPMG).

Right: This MG 34 is set on the Lafette 34 tripod mount with an optical sight. The mount had a searching fire device that would index the gun up and down slightly as it recoiled in the mount.

BARREL
The barrel had a quick-change facility, with a change recommended after every 250 rounds of rapid fire.

SADDLE DRUM
Here is the 75-round saddle drum magazine; changing the gun's top cover was required for belt feed.

BOOSTER
A booster cone at the muzzle accelerated the rearward recoil force.

TRIGGER
The two-section trigger gave single shots (top half) or full auto (bottom half) fire selection.

BOLT
The MG 34 used a rotating bolt head to lock the bolt to the barrel extension before firing.

GPMG

The fire from the MG 34 was devastating in and of itself, but what made the MG 34 supreme was its flexibility; it was a true 'general-purpose' machine gun. On a tripod mount it could be used to deliver sustained direct and indirect fire at designated targets. The Lafette mounts could be fitted with optical sights that enabled the gun crew to control fire out to nearly 4km (2.5 miles) range. When mounted on its bipod alone an assault team could carry it forward to provide mobile suppressive fire.

SEARCHING FIRE
This MG 34 is set on the Lafette 34 tripod mount with an optical sight. The mount had a searching fire device that would index the gun up and down slightly as it recoiled in the mount.

Bren Gun (1938)

The Bren gun was the antithesis of the German MG 42. Magazine fed, it was accurate and had a comparatively sedate rate of fire. Yet to those who relied on it in combat, the Bren was a weapon held in high regard.

SPECIFICATIONS

DIMENSIONS:	Length: 1156mm (42.9in)
	Barrel Length: 635mm (25in)
WEIGHT:	10.35kg (22.38lb)
CALIBRE:	.303in
OPERATION:	Gas operated
FEED:	30-round box magazine
MUZZLE VELOCITY:	731m/sec (2400ft/sec)
EFFECTIVE RANGE:	500m (547yd)
RATE OF FIRE:	500rpm

Right: The rimmed .303in rounds were stacked in an angular fashion in the magazine, which necessitated that the magazine follow a curved profile. Here we see the round at the point of firing.

REGULATOR
The gas regulator controlled the volume of gas passing from the barrel into the gas piston.

MAGAZINE
A 30-round magazine could be emptied in about four seconds of continuous fire.

BIPOD
The Bren Mark 1 had a collapsible bipod; this was converted to a fixed version in some later variants.

PISTON
The gas piston featured vents in the wall to allow gas to escape once the piston had travelled far enough backwards.

TRIGGER
A selector lever just above the trigger provided safe, single-shot or full-auto positions.

RECOIL SPRING
The Bren's recoil spring was located in the butt stock. The gun has excellent 'straight-in-line' recoil characteristics.

ABBREVIATED NAME
The new weapon was put into production at the Royal Small Arms Factory at Enfield Lock in 1937 and called the Bren. The name itself was derived from a combination of 'BRno' – the Czech city where its progenitor, the Zb vz. 26, was designed – and 'ENfield', the UK production centre. In 1938, the weapon went into British Army and Commonwealth service as the Bren Mark 1.

TAKING AIM
A British infantryman takes aim with his Bren in the China–Burma–India (CBI) theatre. The Bren was more accurate than many machine guns, but a simple manual traverse would still deliver a broad pattern of impact on the target.

MG 42 (1942)

SPECIFICATIONS

DIMENSIONS:	Length: 1219mm (48in)
	Barrel Length: 533mm (21in)
WEIGHT:	11.5kg (25.35lb)
CALIBRE:	7.92 × 57mm Mauser
OPERATION:	Short recoil
FEED:	50-round belts
MUZZLE VELOCITY:	755m/sec (2480ft/sec)
EFFECTIVE RANGE:	2000m (2187yd)
RATE OF FIRE:	1200rpm

The MG 42 needs almost no introduction. This astonishing weapon became the benchmark for machine-gun design during World War II and beyond, and gained a fearsome battlefield reputation that still stands to this day.

Below: This view of the right-hand side of the MG 42 clearly shows the slot in the barrel jacket, through which barrel change could be performed in around five seconds.

BOLT
Here the bolt is pushing the cartridge into the chamber, the bolt locked by two rollers forced outwards into barrel-extension recesses.

RECOIL SPRING
The MG 42's powerful coil spring had to cope with punishing 1200rpm rates of fire.

MUZZLE BOOSTER
The muzzle booster increased the recoil effect on the barrel, thereby increasing the gun's rate of fire.

BARREL
The MG 42's barrel was 533mm (21in) long and had a four-groove right-hand rifling pattern.

BELT-FED SYSTEM
The 50-round ammunition belts could be joined together to produce a sectionally disintegrating belt.

STOCK
The 'straight-in-line' stock focuses the recoil forces straight back into the operator's shoulder.

DOMINATING FORCE

In total, more than 420,000 MG 42s were produced between 1942 and 1945. The Allies were lucky that the numbers were not higher. In combat on all fronts, the presence of just one MG 42, let alone several working together, could send an entire Allied company to ground. The intense rate of fire produced by the gun meant that just a one-second burst would unleash 20 high-velocity rounds that had a lethal range of well over a mile. Those hit by such a blast would be physically shattered, and those around them would be forced to take and hold solid cover.

EASTERN FRONT
A German soldier on the Eastern Front has his MG 42 at the ready. The rear sight was graduated in 100m (109yd) intervals to 2000m (2187yd).

RPD (1953)

SPECIFICATIONS

DIMENSIONS:	Length: 1041mm (41in)
	Barrel Length: 520mm (20.5in)
WEIGHT:	7kg (15.43lb)
CALIBRE:	7.62 × 39mm M1943
OPERATION:	Gas operated
FEED:	100-round metallic belt
MUZZLE VELOCITY:	735m/sec (2410ft/sec)
EFFECTIVE RANGE:	600m (656yd)
RATE OF FIRE:	700rpm

In many ways, the RPD is not the best example of a light machine gun (LMG), being vulnerable to some significant feed and firepower issues. Yet, despite its 60-plus year existence, it still persists in active service around the world.

CARTRIDGE
The 7.62 × 39mm cartridge can struggle to provide all the power required for the gun's operating cycle.

BOLT
The RPD bolt is locked by locking flaps being pushed out into recesses in the receiver.

BIPOD
The recoil impulse of the 7.62 × 39mm cartridge is fairly low, so control of fire from a bipod is not a problem.

DRUM MAGAZINE
The 100-round metallic link belt is coiled up in a drum feed, although a loose belt feed is also optional.

RECOIL SPRING
The RPD's recoil spring is located inside the gun's stock to improve the weapon's stability.

DRUM MAGAZINE

The gun is belt fed, with the 100-round metallic belt coiled up inside a large drum magazine located neatly beneath the receiver. The magazine fitting was a useful tactical addition, as the gun had the ammo capacity that came from a belt feed but the portability that came from a magazine feed. Note, however, that the RPD was not dependent on the magazine; it could feed from a loose belt if required. The cyclic rate of fire for the RPD was 700rpm.

RPD GRIP
US Marine Corporal Markus P. Czirban sights in with a Degtyarov RPD during familiarization training in 2014. Note the recommended grip, with the left hand on the stock.

M60 (1957)

SPECIFICATIONS

DIMENSIONS:	Length: 1067mm (42in)
	Barrel Length: 560mm (22.04in)
WEIGHT:	8.61kg (18.98lb)
CALIBRE:	7.62 × 51mm NATO
OPERATION:	Gas
FEED:	Disintegrating link belt
MUZZLE VELOCITY:	860m/sec (2821ft/sec)
EFFECTIVE RANGE:	1500m (1640yd)
RATE OF FIRE:	550rpm

The M60 has been historically known as the 'Pig'. Despite this unaffectionate nickname, it remains in service today with US forces, mostly seen fitted as a helicopter door gun.

Left: The M60E3 was a distinct improvement over the earlier versions of the weapon. Note that the bipod and gas cylinder are now a separate unit to the barrel.

HEAT GUARD
A plastic heat guard is wrapped around the rear of the barrel and lower receiver.

FIRING PIN SPRING
Here we see the spring-loaded firing pin running through the centre of the rotating-bolt mechanism.

OPERATING ROD
The operating rod spring delivers the motive power to drive the operating rod and bolt forward during loading and chambering.

TRIGGER
The M60 is purely a full-auto weapon, although the steady rate of fire means it is simple to fire off single shots through trigger control.

GAS CYLINDER
Gas is tapped off from the barrel into the cylinder, and drives back the piston rod to provide power for extraction and ejection.

VARIANTS

Several versions of the M60 have been specifically designed for vehicular mounting (M60E2) or as helicopter armament (M60B, C and D), and have been relatively successful in these capacities. Furthermore, the US military now has another more thoroughly modernized version, the M60E4 (or Mk 43 Mod 0 in Navy parlance), made by US Ordnance.

TRIPOD MOUNT
A US Marine gunner and assistant gunner man their M60E3 machine gun during a joint services exercise. This weapon has a tripod mount to aid sustained fire.

FN MAG (1958)

SPECIFICATIONS

DIMENSIONS:	Length: 1250mm (49.2in)
	Barrel Length: 546mm (21.5in)
WEIGHT:	10.15kg (22.25lb)
CALIBRE:	7.62 × 51mm NATO
OPERATION:	Gas
FEED:	Metal link belt
MUZZLE VELOCITY:	853m/sec (2800ft/sec)
EFFECTIVE RANGE:	1500m (1640yd)
RATE OF FIRE:	750rpm

The FN MAG perfectly embodies the concept of the general-purpose machine gun (GPMG). It has been hugely successful, with some 200,000 of the weapons manufactured, and it is used by more than 80 countries.

Below: The British-produced L7A1 version of the FN MAG, originally developed for infantry use. It was known by the nickname 'Jimpy', after the abbreviation GPMG.

GAS PORT
The gas port aperture is controlled by a regulator. On the British L7 this had 10 positions.

TRUSTED
The MAG is a hard-hitting weapon, accurate and dependable under the most adverse conditions and easy to handle. Its design was inspired by two particular sources: the feed mechanism of the German MG 42 and the breech mechanism of the Browning Automatic Rifle (BAR). Both of these were proven weapons in their own right; hence the MAG has gained a reputation for solid reliability.

BIPOD
The MAG's bipod is height adjustable, making it simple to configure for prone or upright positions.

BELT FEED
The belt is loaded into the gun with the feed tray cover open and the leading round sat against the cartridge stop.

RECOIL SPRING
The recoil spring must be resilient enough to handle repeated oscillations at 750rpm.

VEHICLE MOUNTS
The FN MAG has been used on dozens of different vehicle types during its life. These include light and heavy tanks (including the Scorpion, M1 Abrams and Stridsvagn 103), armoured personnel carriers (APCs), infantry combat vehicles such as the US Bradley and LAV-25, light vehicles such as the Humvee and numerous helicopters (examples include the Black Hawk, Lynx and the Chinook).

RPK (1961)

SPECIFICATIONS

DIMENSIONS:	Length: 1041mm (41in)
	Barrel Length: 589mm (23.2in)
WEIGHT:	4.76kg (10.5lb)
CALIBRE:	7.62 × 39mm M1943
OPERATION:	Gas, air-cooled
FEED:	30- or 40-round box or 75-round drum
MUZZLE VELOCITY:	732m/sec (2400ft/sec)
EFFECTIVE RANGE:	800m (875yd)
RATE OF FIRE:	600rpm

Although the Soviets already possessed a light machine gun in the form of the RPD, it was decided to design a better weapon to replace it. The result was the RPK, which was essentially a Kalashnikov AKM rifle conversion. The original assault rifle can clearly be seen in the RPK, although the machine gun version has a longer, heavier barrel and a bipod.

Right: The 75-round drum magazine gives the gunner better suppressive fire, although it increases the overall weight.

BARREL
Although the RPK's barrel is longer and heavier than the regular rifle, is is still non-changeable, meaning the weapon is not capable of prolonged sustained fire.

BIPOD
The RPK has a basic integral bipod to stabilize the shooting position. It cannot be adjusted for height.

STOCK
The fixed wooden RPK stock is derived from that of the RPD. A folding stock is available on the RPKS model.

HEAT ISSUES

The RPK can deliver 600rpm out to about 800m (875yd), but since it is not possible to change the barrel it quickly overheats at sustained high rates of fire. It will survive for a time, but like all scaled-up assault rifles this weapon is not really capable of true machine gun firepower. However, with 30- or 40-round magazines or a 75-round drum available in a weapon weighing little more than an assault rifle, the extra firepower offered by the RPK has been attractive enough for many nations to adopt it.

ASSAULT WEAPON

For a machine gun, the RPK is not a heavy weapon, weighing 4.76kg (10.5lb) empty. Of course, the loaded magazines add considerable weight: here an Iraqi soldier has taped two 40-shot box magazines together for quick mag changes.

PK (1961)

SPECIFICATIONS

DIMENSIONS:	Length: 1160mm (45.67in)
	Barrel Length: 658mm (25.9in)
WEIGHT:	9kg (19.84lb)
CALIBRE:	7.62 × 54R
OPERATION:	Gas
FEED:	Non-disintegrating belt
MUZZLE VELOCITY:	825m/sec (2706ft/sec)
EFFECTIVE RANGE:	1000m (1094yd)
RATE OF FIRE:	700rpm

The PK machine gun is partly an evolution of the AK-47, using the same rotating-bolt principle. Like the AK, it also exhibits great reliability and firepower. More than a million of these weapons have been produced.

Left: The PK mechanism is extremely simple inside compared to many modern machine guns; hence it is known for its reliability and ease of maintenance.

REAR SIGHT
The PK's rear sight is an adjustable leaf type graduated from 0 to 1500m (0–1640yd) in 100m (109yd) increments.

BARREL
The exterior of the barrel is fluted, a measure to save weight and also to assist with cooling.

FLASH SUPPRESSOR
The flash suppressor has five elongated vents and is screwed onto the barrel via a threaded section.

BELT FEED
The non-disintegrating belts come in 25-round sections, combined to a maximum of 250 rounds.

STOCK
The skeleton stock contains a cleaning and maintenance kit.

BIPOD
The adjustable front bipod is attached to the gas cylinder; its right leg contains a gun cleaning rod.

THE PK FAMILY
The basic PK is the core member of quite a large family of weapons. The PKS, for example, is a tripod-mounted variant, while the PKT is a version adapted for co-axial fitting in armoured vehicles. One of the most popular variants is the PKM, a modernized weapon with a lighter barrel (although unfluted) and some manufacturing improvements.

AFGHAN ISSUE
An Afghan National Police (ANP) officer mounts a PKM general-purpose machine gun to a turret while working with US Marines at a police station in Delaram, Afghanistan, in 2009.

FN Minimi/M249 SAW (1974)

SPECIFICATIONS

DIMENSIONS:	Length: 1040mm (40.56in)
	Barrel Length: 466mm (18.34in)
WEIGHT:	6.83kg (15.05lb)
CALIBRE:	5.56 × 45mm NATO
OPERATION:	Gas
FEED:	100- or 200-round belt; 30-round box magazine
MUZZLE VELOCITY:	915m/sec (3000ft/sec)
EFFECTIVE RANGE:	1000m (1094yd)
RATE OF FIRE:	750–1100rpm

Until recently, 5.56mm was considered a light machine gun and rifle calibre rather than one suitable for a true GPMG. This assumption was challenged by the Fabrique Nationale Minimi, which is in service with the US military as the M249 SAW (Squad Automatic Weapon).

Below: The Minimi Mk 3 Para version has been highly popular with international forces, who appreciate its more compact dimensions.

QUICK-CHANGE BAR
A hot barrel can be quickly removed by releasing the barrel lock and twisting out the barrel using the affixed handle.

THE M249 SAW
The Minimi, designated as the M249 Squad Automatic Weapon (SAW), was adopted by the US military in the early 1980s. It was acquired primarily as a weapon that could replace the 7.62mm M60 with a lighter and more portable alternative, but one that could still boost the firepower of the infantry squad. Similar considerations also informed the British acquisition of the Minimi; the British use the standard and Para variants, designated L108A1 and the L110A2 respectively.

FEED
The Minimi has feed apertures for both box magazines and belts; the box magazines are standard infantry 5.56mm types.

STOCK
Minimis are produced in various different stock configurations, including solid synthetic and folding skeleton versions.

SQUAD WEAPON
A US support gunner fires his M249 light machine gun from a natural position reinforced with a few sandbags. The M249 uses the same ammunition as infantry rifles in the squad, but its 200-round box affords it huge firepower.

CETME Ameli (1982)

SPECIFICATIONS

DIMENSIONS:	Length: 970mm (38.19in)
	Barrel Length: 400mm (15.75in)
WEIGHT:	6.35kg (14lb) standard; 5.2kg (11.46lb) lightweight
CALIBRE:	5.56 × 45mm NATO
OPERATION:	Gas, air-cooled
FEED:	100- or 200-round boxed belt
MUZZLE VELOCITY:	875m/sec (2870ft/sec)
EFFECTIVE RANGE:	1000m (1094yd)
RATE OF FIRE:	850 or 1200rpm

Another very good 5.56mm-calibre GPMG is the CETME Ameli. It looks like a German MG3, but is in fact only related in that CETME engineers have in the past used German ideas such as the roller-locking blowback system developed by Heckler & Koch. This system is indeed used in the Ameli and has proven reliable even at 850 or even 1200 rounds per minute.

FEED
The Ameli is a belt-fed gun, the belts either being loose or contained in belt boxes that hang on the receiver.

BOLT
The Ameli's rate of fire can be adjusted by using bolts of different weights, the lightest bolt giving a rate of 1200rpm.

BARREL
The Ameli barrel is a quick-change type. Different barrel rifling twist rates are available to suit the SS109 or M193 5.56mm cartridges.

ASSAULT WEAPON

The Ameli is typical of several modern machine guns that stray between the categories of light machine gun and general-purpose machine gun. The 5.56mm calibre makes it an LMG in terms of its cartridge performance, but its belt feed, quick-change barrel and ability to take various mounts (including vehicular and aircraft mounts) makes it more along the lines of a GPMG. It has also been referred to as an 'assault' machine gun, because it is light and compact enough to be handled in dynamic infantry manoeuvres.

FLUTED BARREL
The quick-change style air-cooled barrel is equipped with a slotted flash suppressor. The barrel has a chrome-lined bore with six right-hand grooves and a rifling twist rate that is designed specifically for use with 5.56×45mm NATO rounds.

L86 Light Support Weapon (1985)

SPECIFICATIONS

DIMENSIONS:	Length: 900mm (35.43in)
	Barrel Length: 646mm (25.43in)
WEIGHT:	5.4kg (11.9lb)
CALIBRE:	5.56 × 45mm NATO
OPERATION:	Gas operated
FEED:	30-round detachable box magazine
MUZZLE VELOCITY:	970m/sec (3182ft/sec)
EFFECTIVE RANGE:	600m (656yd)
RATE OF FIRE:	700rpm

The move from 7.62mm GPMGs to lighter 5.56mm Squad Automatic Weapons such as the British LSW makes theoretical sense in many ways – a support weapon based on the current service rifle can share components, spares and ammunition, and any rifleman can take up the support weapon and use it effectively.

SIGHT
The LSW uses the same Sight Unit Small Arms, Trilux, (SUSAT) as the standard rifle, although it is now also seen with the popular ACOG.

BARREL
The barrel is 128mm (5in) longer than the standard rifle, producing marginally higher muzzle velocities and therefore improved range and accuracy.

REAR GRIP
The LSW features a rear vertical grip behind the pistol grip. This is held with the left hand to provide a more controlled grip, as long as the front of the barrel is supported on the bipod or another surface.

CONTROVERSY
The LSW has struggled to find its tactical home in the British Army. Since the 1980s, its two primary roles – that of a designated marksman rifle and of a light machine gun – have essentially been replaced by weapons better suited to these roles, such as the 7.62mm L129A1 rifle and the 5.56mm Minimi machine gun.

PRECISION RIFLE
Although the LSW was designed primarily to provide suppressive fire as a light machine gun, it was quickly discovered that its impressive accuracy made it suitable for medium-range single-shot marksmanship.

Glossary

AA – anti-aircraft

AAM – air-to-air missile

ailerons – a pair of hinged flight-control surfaces on an aircraft's wings used for controlling roll

ASM – anti-ship missile or anti-submarine missile

blowback – a system of firearms operation in which the weapon's cycle is powered by the rearward pressure imparted to the empty cartridge case just after firing

bolt – the moving part of a firearm responsible for feeding and chambering a cartridge, but also including the firing pin, extractor and sometimes ejector components

bore – the inside of a gun barrel

breech – the opening at the rear of a gun into which a cartridge, shell or ammunition component is inserted into the chamber

bridge – the room or platform from which a ship is commanded, and where the ship's wheel is often located

broadside – when all main guns of a warship are turned either port or starboard and fired simultaneously

bullpup – in firearms, when the action of the weapon is located behind the trigger group

carbine – a shortened version of a rifle

chamber – in firearms or artillery, the chamber is the space at the rear of the barrel in which ammunition is seated prior to firing

coaxial – a coaxial machine gun is mounted in an armoured vehicle turret alongside the main gun, turning in sympathy with the turret

delta wing – aircraft wings that form the shape of a large triangle

direct fire – shooting at targets that can be seen in direct line of sight, using a relatively flat trajectory

director – a mechanical or electronic computer used in artillery systems to calculate how to hit a moving target

double action – in handguns, a double-action firearm is one in which a single pull of the trigger both cocks and releases the hammer to fire

draught – the distance from the waterline to the keel of a ship

elevators – in aircraft, flight control surfaces usually at the rear of the aircraft, responsible for controlling pitch

ERA – explosive reactive armour

fairwater – a US term of a submarine's sail (q.v.)

ferry range – the maximum range an aircraft can fly

fore-end – the front furniture section of a firearm

freeboard – on a ship, the distance from the waterline to the upper deck

gas operated – a self-loading firearm powered through its operating cycle by propellant gas tapped off after firing

gunlayer – the person responsible for aiming an artillery piece

HEAT – High-Explosive Anti-Tank (shell)

HESH – High-Explosive Squash Head (shell)

IFV – Infantry Fighting Vehicle

indirect fire – shooting at targets that are beyond or hidden from direct line of sight, using an arcing trajectory

interrupter gear – a mechanical system introduced in World War I fighter aircraft to enable machine guns to fire through the arc of the propeller without hitting the propeller blades

island – the command centre for the flight deck of an aircraft carrier

leading edge – the front edge of an aircraft wing

limber – a two-wheeled cart designed to support the trail of an artillery piece

Mach – in aeronautics, a Mach number is used to denote an aircraft's speed relative to the speed of sound, e.g. Mach 1 means the speed of sound, Mach 2 twice the speed of sound, and so on

MBT – Main Battle Tank

muzzle brake – a muzzle fitting on artillery pieces and some large firearms, used to reduce the velocity of recoil

muzzle velocity – the speed of a bullet or shell as it leaves the muzzle of the barrel

NBC – Nuclear, Biological, Chemical

payload – the carrying capacity of

an aircraft, usually measured by weight

PDW – Personal Defence Weapon

percussion fuze – an artillery fuze designed to detonate the main shell charge when the shell strikes a physical object

receiver – the main body of the firearm that contains the weapon's principal operating parts

recoil operated – a self-loading firearm that uses the force of recoil to perform its core mechanical actions

sail – on a submarine, the sail is the tower-like structure on the upper hull; it provides vertical stability and in older submarines

SAM – surface-to-air missile

semi-automatic – a firearm that fires a single shot with each pull of the trigger, reloading automatically between shots

single action – in handguns, a single-action firearm requires the hammer to be cocked manually or through other mechanical process; pulling the trigger does not cock the hammer, only releases it

smoothbore – denotes the bore of a gun that has no rifling

STOVL – (aircraft) Short Take-off Vertical Landing

superstructure – the parts of a ship built above its hull and main deck, other than masts and rigging

suppressor – in firearms, a suppressor is a muzzle attachment that reduces the noise of firing; often incorrectly known as a silencer

tailplane – on an aircraft, lifting surfaces fitted either side of the tail

trail – the part of an artillery carriage used for towing the gun and for emplacing it

UAV – Unmanned Aerial Vehicle (a drone)

VSTOL – Vertical/Short Take-off and Landing

Below: US Marines train with an M1A1 Abrams main battle tank in 2009. The M1 is the main battle tank of the United States Army and Marine Corps, and is also used by the armed forces of Egypt, Kuwait, Saudi Arabia and Australia.

Index

2cm (0.79in) Flakvierling 38 147

2cm Flak 38 L/65 147

2S19 Msta 141

2S19M2 Msta-SM 141

3.7cm (1.46in) Flak 37 146

3.7cm Flak 36 146

3.7in QF gun Mk 1 145

3in gun M5 155

5cm Pak 38 L/60 153

7.5cm Pak 40 L/46 154

7.7cm FK 96 n.A. 115

7TP Polish light tank 16

8.8cm Flak 18 144

10.5cm leFH 18 light field howitzer 121

15cm sFH 18 medium field howitzer 123

15cm sIG 33 heavy infantry gun 122

40mm Bofors L/60 143

42-cm kurze Marinekanone 14 L/12 in Räderlafette (Big Bertha) 119

60mm Mortar M2 161

76.2mm divisional gun M1942 (ZiS-3) 157

90mm gun M2 149

105mm (4.13in) K-29 118

105mm howitzer M2A1 128

105mm howitzer M3 130

122mm howitzer D-30 133

122mm howitzer M1938 (M-30) 125

152mm howitzer M1943 (D-1) 129

A

AAV-7 95

Abbott, Greg 363

Aboukir (cruiser) 253

Adams revolver 350

Adams, Robert 350

Adelaide, HMAS 308

Admiral Graf Spee 329

Admiral Kuznetsov 303

Admiral Ushakov (formerly *Kirov*) 339

AEC Mk I armoured car 84

AEC Mk II armoured car 84

AEC Mk III armoured car 84

Afghanistan
aircraft carriers 296
APC 93, 99, 109
bombers 226
drones 242, 244, 245
field howitzer 142
fighter aircraft 194, 201, 202
infantry fighting vehicles 106
ground-attack aircraft 215, 216
helicopters 238, 240
logistic and specialist aircraft 233
machine guns 416, 432
rifles 380, 385, 391, 398–9, 400
rocket launcher 132
surface warships 344

Agusta Westland AW 159 Wildcats 304

AH-64 Apache 240

AH-64D Apache Longbow 9

air aces 166, 170, 171, 173, 176, 178, 180–5, 189

aircraft carriers 246–7, 279–312

airlifters 233, 235

AK-12 401

AK-47/AKM 375

AK-74 385

AK-101 & AK-103 396

Akagi 281, 283, 284

AKS-74U 385

Alizé ASW planes 295

Alouette III helicopters 295

American Civil War 248, 249, 313, 351, 416

Amiens, France 211

amphibious vehicles
aircraft 232
all terrain armoured vehicles 108
armoured personnel carriers 95, 97, 99–101, 107
tanks 58, 63
tractors 85
AMTRACs 85

AMX-13 56

AMX-56 Leclerc 71

AN-94 rifle 401

An Nasiriyah, Battle of (2003) 103

Angola 238

anti-aircraft artillery 143–9

anti-armour guns 153–7

anti-ISIS operations 305

anti-magnetic mine paste 49

anti-personnel mines 139

anti-submarine ships 294, 298, 306, 340, 314, 343

anti-tank guns 153–7

Ardennes Offensive 48, 128, 149

Argentine army 95
see also Falklands War

Argentine rifle 377

Arihant, INS 278

Arjun Mk 2 76

Ark Royal, HMS 286, 333

Arleigh Burke destroyer 344

armour, Chobham armour 68

armoured doctrine 13

armoured personnel carriers 79–109

Army of the Republic of Vietnam (ARVN) 55, 409

Arnold, Heinz 185

Arromanches, France 121

Astute Class 275

Atlantic, crossing of 206, 225

Atlantic War (WWII)
aircraft carriers 286
bombers 221
submarines 260–1
surface warships 325, 333

Austen SMG 408

Australian air force 177, 191, 222

Australian aircraft carriers
Adelaide, HMAS 308
Canberra, HMAS 308

Australian submachine guns, Austen 408

Austrian armoured personnel carriers
Pandur 100

Austrian artillery
Skoda 30.5cm howitzer 117

Austrian handguns
Glock 17 362

Austrian rifles
Steyr AUG 386

Autoblindé Peugeot 79

AV-8B Harrier II 216

AV-8B Harrier II V/STOL planes 301

Avro Bison 279

Avro Lancaster 223

Avro Vulcan 227

B

B-5, HMS 252

B-6, HMS 252

B-24 Liberator 221

B-Class submarines 252

B1 Centauro 103

Balao, USS 263

Balkans
armoured reconnaissance vehicles 93
ground attack aircraft 207
logistic and specialist aircraft 236
tank hunter 103
tanks 69

Ball, Albert 168, 169

BAR 422

Barbaros Hayreddin (dreadnought) 254

Barkhorn, Gerhard 173

Barkmann, Ernst 39

Barrett M82A1 392

bayonets 368, 373, 387, 397

Beauchamp-Proctor 169

Beaumont-Adams revolver 350

Beaumont, Frederick 350

Beaver, HMS 340

Belgian handguns
Browning GP35 HP 358

Belgian machine guns
FN MAG 430
FN Minimi/M249 SAW 433

Belgian rifles
FN FAL/L1A1 SLR 377

FN SCAR 400
Belgian submachine guns
  FN P90 413
Bellonte, Maurice 206
Beretta 92 & 93R 360
Bergmann MP 18 402
Big Bertha 119
Billfish, USS 265
Bishop, William 168, 169
Bismarck 286, 327, 333
Black Buck raids, Falklands 227
Blackburn planes 279
BM-8-8 82mm (3.2in) rocket
  launcher 124
BM-21 rocket launcher 132
BMP-1 92
BMP-3 104
Boeing B-17 Flying Fortress
  219
Boeing B-29 Superfortress 224
Boeing B-52 Stratofortress 226
Boeing Chinooks 297, 302, 304
Boeing F-15E Strike Eagle 201
Boelke, Oswald 166
bombers 218–30
Borchardt C/93 352
Bordelon, Lt. 182
Bougainville 143
Bradley Urban Survivability
  Kits (BUSK) 98
Breguet XIX 206
Bren gun 426
Brilliant, HMS 340
Britain, Battle of
  fighters 173, 174
  ground attack aircraft 207,
    209
British aircraft carriers
  Ark Royal, HMS 286
  Eagle, HMS 280, 292
  Fearless, HMS 297
  Furious, HMS 279
  Hermes, HMS 294
  Invincible, HMS 302
  Ocean, HMS 304
  Queen Elizabeth, HMS 310
British all-terrain armoured
vehicles
  BVS 10 Viking 108
British anti-aircraft artillery
  3.7in QF gun Mk 1 145
  Oerlikon 20mm 148
British anti-armour guns

Ordnance QF 17pdr gun 156
British armoured cars
  AEC Mk III armoured car
    84
  FV601 Saladin 89
British armoured
  reconnaissance vehicles
  Scimitar 93
British artillery
  FH-70 155mm howitzer 137
  L118 light gun 138
  Ordnance BL 60pdr 114
  Ordnance QF 4.5in howitzer
    116
  Ordnance QF 13pdr 113
  Ordnance QF 25pdr Mk 2
    126
British bombers
  Avro Lancaster 223
  Avro Vulcan 227
  English Electric Canberra
    225
  Handley Page Halifax 222
British fighters
  Hawker Hurricane 174
  Panavia Tornado 196
  S.E.5a 169
  Sopwith Camel 167
  Supermarine Spitfire 176
British forces
  1st Dorsets 158
  7th Armoured Division 47
  21st Army Group 46
  79th Armoured Division 43
  Desert Rats 47
  No. 669 Squadron of No. 4
    Regiment, Army Air Corps
    239
  RFC No.24 Squadron 169
  RFC No.50 Squadron 169
  RFC No.74 Squadron 169
British forces (RAF)
  20th Tactical Fighter Wing
    214
  48th Tactical Fighter Wing
    201, 214
  No.6 Group 222
  No.21 Squadron 211
  No.76 Squadron 222
  No.81 Squadron 211
  No.83 Group 213
  No.105 Squadron 211
  No.464 Squadron 211
  No.487 Squadron 211

No.504 Squadron 174
  No.617 Squadron 223
British ground-attack aircraft
  De Havilland Mosquito 211
  Hawker Typhoon 213
British handguns
  Adams revolver 350
  Webley Mk V & Mk VI 356
British helicopters
  Lynx 239
British infantry combat vehicles
  Warrior 102
British machine guns
  Bren gun 426
  Gatling gun 416
  L86 light support weapon
    435
  Lewis gun 419
  Maxim gun/MG 08 418
  Vickers machine gun 420
British mortars
  Ordnance ML 3in mortar
    158
British rifles
  EM2 376
  Martini-Henry 366
  SA80 391
  SMLE 368
British submachine guns
  Sten Mk 2 406
  Sterling L2A1 410
British submarines
  Astute Class 275
  B-Class 252
  E-11, HMS 254
  Resolution, HMS 266
British surface warships
  Devastation, HMS 314
  Dreadnought, HMS 318
  Hood, HMS 327
  Indomitable, HMS 320
  Rodney, HMS 328
  Royal Oak, HMS 324
  Type 22 340
  Type 23 frigate 343
  Type 45 destroyer 346
British tanks
  Centurion 53
  Challenger 1 68
  Challenger 2 75
  Chieftain Mk 5 61
  Churchill AVRE 42
  Churchill Mk IV 31

Churchill Mk VII Crocodile
    43
  Cromwell Mk VIII 47
  Crusader III 30
  Mark V Male 12
  Mk III Valentine Infantry
    Tank 25
  Mk VI Crusader I Cruiser
    Tank 30
  Sherman Crab Mine-
    Clearing Tank 45
  Sherman VC Firefly 46
  Vickers 6-ton Light Tank 16
  Whippet 13
Broadsword, HMS 340
Brown, Carl A. 184
Brown, Russell J. 187
Browning GP35 HP 358
Browning, John 422
Browning L9A1 358
BT-5 17
BT-7 17
BTR-60PA 91
BTR-70 97
BTR-80 101
BTR-90 107
Budapest, Hungary 157
Bunker Hill, USS 184, 299
Burma campaign (WWII) 25,
    174, 178, 183
BVS 10 Viking 108
BXP 414

C
Cabot, USS see Lexington, USS
(CV-16)
Calico M950 415
camouflage
  aircraft 207, 235
  aircraft carriers 289
  surface warships 333, 334,
    336
  tanks 14, 21, 56
Canadian air force 222, 223
Canadian armoured personnel
carriers
  LAV-25 99
Canberra, HMAS 308
Canon de 75 Mle 112
Canon de 105mm mle 1913
  Schneider 118
Carius, Otto 49
Carson, Leonard 180
Centurion 53

Centurion (Sho't variant) 53
CETME Ameli 434
CETME Model 58 378
CH-46 Sea Knight 299
CH53E helicopter 297
Challenger 1 68
Challenger 2 75
Changhe Z-18 307
Char B1 bis 22
Charles de Gaulle 305
Charles Martel (battleship) 250
Chassepot Carbine 365
Chechnya 58, 238
Chieftain AVRE 61
Chieftain Mk 5 61
Chinese aircraft carriers
   Liaoning 307
Chinese fighters
   Shenyang J-15 fighter 307
Chinese forces 17, 188
Chinese helicopters 307
Chinese rifles
   QBZ-03 397
   Type 56 rifle 375
Chinese submarines
   Type 039 (Song) 273
   Type 094 (Jin Class) 276
Chinese tanks
   Type 69 60
   Type 85 MBT 74
   Type 99 74
Chinook helicopters 297, 302, 304
Chitose (light carrier) 287
Chobham armour 68, 73, 75
Christie, J. Walter 17
Churchill AVRE 42
Churchill AVRE Mortar, Recoiling Spigot, Mark II 42
Churchill Mk IV 31
Churchill Mk VII Crocodile 43
Clark, Francis B. 187
Clemenceau 295
Cole, USS 344
Colombian Air Force 231
Colt Detective Special 357
Colt M1851 Navy & 1860 Army 351
Colt M1911 355
Columbia (submarine) 299
Consolidated PBY Catalina 232
Constellation, USS (CV-64) 299

Coral Sea, Battle of (1942) 212, 282
Coral Sea, USS 200
Costes, Dieudonné 206
Courageous, HMS 279
Cressy (cruiser) 253
Croatian Defence Council (HVO) Army 133
Cromwell Mk VIII 47
Crusader III 30
Crusader tanks 30
Cuba 316
Cuniberti, Vittorio 319
Curtis SBC Helldiver 284
Czechoslovakia 24
Czirban, Markus P. 428

D
D-Day 43, 46, 223
Dambusters Raid 223
Danish machine guns
   Madsen light machine gun 417
Dardanelles campaign 320, 252, 254
Dassault Mirage 2000 199
Dassault Mirage III 191
Dassault Rafale 202
Dawn of Freedom (formerly Imperator Alexander II) 315
DDX (Zumwalt Class) 347
De Havilland Mosquito 211
De Havilland Sea Venom 292
De Ruyter 330
Derfflinger 323, 324
Deutschland/Lützow 329
Deutschland (U-155) 255
Devastation, HMS 314
Dogger Bank, Battle of 320
Dönitz, Karl 256
Doolittle, James H. 220
Douglas C-47 Skytrain 231
Douglas SBD Dauntless 212, 284
Douglas TBD Devastator 285
Dreadnought, HMS 318
Dreyse Needle Gun 364
drones 242–5
Duke of York, HMS 331
Dutch surface warships
   De Ruyter 330

E
E-2C Hawkeye 2000 299
E-3 Sentry 236
E-11, HMS 254
Eagle, HMS 280, 292
Egyptian forces 151, 188
   see also Suez Crisis; Yom Kippur War
Eisenhower, Gen Dwight D. 231
El Alamein (1942) 30, 126
Elektroboot 261
EM2 rifle 376
English Electric Canberra 225
Enterprise, USS (CV-6) 284, 285
Enterprise, USS (CVN-65) 194, 296, 306
Etendard IVM fighterbombers 295
Etendard IVP 295
Eurofighter Typhoon 204
Exercise Eager Lion (2018) 163
Exercise Orient Shield (2017) 162

F
F-8E (FN) fighters 295
F-8E(FN) Crusader fighter 295
F-15C Eagle fighters 9
F-15E Strike Eagle 164–5
F-16C Falcon 9
F/A-18F Super Hornet 299
F4U-4 Corsairs 291
Fairchild A-10 Thunderbolt II 215
Fairey Flycatcher 279, 280
Fairey Fulmars 280
Fairey Swordfish 280, 286
Falaise, France 213
Falklands War (1982)
   aircraft carriers 294, 297, 302
   armoured personnel carriers 95
   armoured reconnaissance vehicles 93
   artillery 138
   bombers 227
   surface warships 340
FAMAS 387
Fearless, HMS 297
FG 42 373
FH-70 155mm howitzer 137

field guns 112, 114, 115
fighter aircraft 166–205
fighter-bombers 173
First Gulf War *see* Gulf War (1991)
Flakpanzer Gepard 152
flamethrower tanks 43, 82
floatplanes 257, 262, 325, 326, 330
flying boats 232
FN FAL/L1A1 SLR 377
FN MAG 430
FN Minimi/M249 SAW 433
FN P90 413
FN SCAR 348–9, 400
Foch 295
Focke-Wulf Fw 190 179
Focke-Wulf Fw 190A 179
Fokker Dr.I 170
Fokker E series 166
Fokker E.II 166
Fokker E.III 166
Fonck, René 171
fording capabilities 67
Forrestal, USS 293
Franco-Prussian War (1870–71) 365
French forces
   Escadrille No3 ('The Storks') 168
   Escadrille SPA 48 171
   fighter aircraft 202
   Lafayett Escadrille 171
French aircraft carriers
   Charles de Gaulle 305
   Clemenceau 295
French armoured cars
   Autoblindé Peugeot 79
   Panhard EBR/FL-11 87
   Panhard et Levassor Type 178 80
French artillery
   Canon de 75 Mle 112
   Canon de 105mm mle 1913 Schneider 118
French fighters
   Dassault Mirage 2000 199
   Dassault Mirage III 191
   Dassault Rafale 202
   Nieuport 17 168
   SPAD XIII 171
French ground-attack aircraft
   Breguet XIX 206

French helicopters
    Lynx 239
French Indochina War (1945–54) 421, 423
French machine guns
    Hotchkiss Modèle 1914 421
French rifles
    Chassepot carbine 365
    FAMAS 387
French submachine guns
    MAS 38 405
French submarines
    Gustave Zédé 250
    Le Triomphant 270
    Surcouf 257
French surface warships
    Richelieu 332
French tanks
    AMX-13 56
    AMX-56 Leclerc 71
    Char B1 bis 22
    FT-17 14
    Leopard I 62
    Somua S-35 21
    FT-17 14
Furious, HMS 279
Fuso (battleship) 326
fuze systems 163
FV 101 Scorpion 70
FV 107 Scimitar 93
FV430 Bulldog Mk 3 109
FV432 APC 109
FV433 'Abbot' self-propelled gun 109
FV434 REME 109
FV438 Swingfire 109
FV510 Warrior 102
FV601 Saladin 89
FV603 Saracen 89

G

Galil 384
Gallipoli 114
Gatling gun 416
Gazelle helicopters 297
General Dynamics F-111 214
Gerald R. Ford, USS 311
German anti-aircraft artillery
    2cm (0.79in) Flakvierling 38 147
    2cm Flak 38 L/65 147
    3.7cm (1.46in) Flak 37 146
    3.7cm Flak 36 146

8.8cm Flak 18 144
    Flakpanzer Gepard 152
German anti-armour guns
    5cm Pak 38 L/60 153
    7.5cm Pak 40 L/46 154
German armoured cars
    SdKfz 232 81
    SdKfz 234/2 Puma 83
German armoured personnel carriers
    SdKfz 251 82
German artillery
    7.7cm FK 96 n.A. 115
    10.5cm leFH 18 light field howitzer 121
    15cm sFH 18 medium field howitzer 123
    15cm sIG 33 heavy infantry gun 122
    Big Bertha 119
    Paris Gun 120
    Wurfgranate 41 127
    Wurfkörper 42 127
German bombers
    Gotha bombers 218
German fighters
    Focke-Wulf Fw 190 179
    Fokker Dr.I 170
    Fokker E series 166
    Messerschmitt Bf 109 173
    Messerschmitt Me 262 185
German forces
    JG 1 170
    JG 2 'Richthofen' 173
    JG 3 173
    JG 7 185
    JG 26 179
    JG 300 179
German ground-attack aircraft
    Junkers Ju 87 Stuka 207
    Junkers Ju 88 208
    Messerschmitt Bf 110 209
German handguns
    Borchardt C/93 352
    Mauser C/96 353
    Pistole Parabellum P-08 354
    SIG P320 363
    Walther P38 359
German machine guns
    MG 08 418
    MG 34 425
    MG 42 427

German mortars
    sGrW 34 8cm Mortar 159
German rifles
    Dreyse Needle Gun 364
    FG 42 373
    Heckler & Koch G3 380
    Heckler & Koch G36 394
    Kar 98k 370
    MP44/StG44 374
    OICW/XM29 395
    PSG-1 390
German submachine guns
    Bergmann MP 18 402
    Heckler & Koch MP5 412
    MP 38/MP 40 404
German submarines
    Deutschland (U-155) 255
    Type XXI 261
    U-9 253
    U-47 (Type VIIB) 259
    U-459 (Type XIV) 260
    UC-25 256
German surface warships
    Bismarck 333
    Derfflinger 323
    Deutschland/Lützow 329
    Scharnhorst 331
    Tirpitz 336
German tanks
    Jagdpanzer VI Jagdtiger 49
    Leopard I 62
    Panzer 38(t) 24
    Panzer II Ausf F 20
    Panzer III Aus f 26
    Panzer IV Ausf F1 29
    Panzer V Panther Ausf D 39
    Panzer VI Tiger Ausf E 36
    Sturmgeschütz III 27
    Sturmmörser Tiger 44
    Sturmpanzerwagen A7V 15
    Tiger II 'King Tiger' 48
Gewehr 98 370
Gibson, Guy 223
Glock 17 362
Gloster Mars X Nightjar 279
Gloster Sea Gladiators 279, 280
Gotha bombers 218
Grabin, Vasiliy 157
Graf Spee (battleship) 329
Grenada 241
ground-attack aircraft 206–17
Grouper, USS 263

Grumman F-14 Tomcat 194
Grumman F6F Hellcat 184
Grumman SF-1 282
Guderian, Gen Heinz 35
Gulf War (1991)
    armoured personnel carriers 93
    artillery 137, 140
    fighter aircraft 196, 199, 201
    ground-attack aircraft 214, 215, 217
    helicopters 240, 241
    infantry fighting vehicle 98
    logistic and specialist aircraft 236
    tanks 54, 65, 68, 69
    see also Operation Iraqi Freedom
Gustave Zédé 250
Guynemer, Georges 168, 171

H

Haguenau, France 155
Haguro (cruiser) 330
Hahn, Hans von 173
Hakuryu 277
HAL-Dhruv helicopters 312
handguns 350–63
Handley Page Halifax 222
Harbin Z-9D SAR 307
Harrier GR7/9 planes 302
Hartmann, Erich 173
Hawker Hurricane 174
Hawker Hurricane Mk IID 174
Hawker Hurricane Mk IV 174
Hawker Siddeley Sea Harrier FRS Mk 1 294
Hawker Typhoon 213
Heckler & Koch G3 380
Heckler & Koch G36 394
Heckler & Koch MP5 412
Heckler & Koch MP5A3 412
helicopters 237–41, 297, 298, 302, 303, 304, 307
Helsingborg, HMS 345
Hermes, HMS 294
Higgins (destroyer) 299
Hiryu 283
Hogue (cruiser) 253
Holland, J.P. 251
Holland, USS 251
Hood, HMS 327, 333
Hornet, USS 220, 285

Hotchkiss Modèle 1914 421
Housatonic (sloop-of-war) 248
Hunley, CSS 248

I
I-400 262
I-401 262
IAV Stryker 106
Ilyushin Il-2 Shturmovik 210
IMI Desert Eagle 361
Immelmann, Max 166
Imperator Alexander II 315
Imphal 174
Indian aircraft carriers
    Vikrant, INS 312
    Viraat, INS 294
Indian forces 57
    Air Force 174, 199
Indian submarines
    Arihant, INS 278
Indian tanks
    Arjun Mk 2 76
Indiana, USS 337
Indomitable, HMS 320
Indonesia 58
Indonesian Air Force 190
infantry fighting vehicles 92,
    94, 96, 98, 104, 105
Intelligent Whale 249
Intrepid, USS 289
Invincible, HMS 302
Iowa, USS 338
Iran-Iraq War 194
Iranian Civil Militia 360
Iraq
    Iran-Iraq War 194
    Iraqi Army 431
    see also Gulf War (1991);
    Operation *Iraqi Freedom*
IS-3 52
Israel *see* Six Day War; Suez
Crisis; Yom Kippur War
Israeli Air Force 195
Israeli artillery
    Soltam M68 135
    Soltam K6 120mm (4.7in)
heavy field mortar 162
Israeli rifles
    Galil 384
Israeli submachine guns
    Uzi 411
Israeli tanks
    Merkava 66

Italian artillery
    OTO-Melara 105mm Mod
        56 131
Italian Campaign (WWII)
    artillery 156
    fighters 176, 183
    rifles 373
    surface warships 334
    tanks 38
Italian fighters
    Panavia Tornado 196
Italian handguns
    Beretta 92 & 93R 360
Italian surface warships
Vittorio Emanuele 319
Vittorio Veneto 334
Italian tank hunters
    B1 Centauro 103
Italian tanks
    Semovente DA 75/18 38
Italo-Turkish War (1911–12)
    319
Iwo Jima (1945) 85
Izumo 309

J
Jagdpanzer VI Jagdtiger 49
James E. Williams (destroyer)
    306
Japanese aircraft carriers
    Akagi 281
    Hiryu 283
    Izumo 309
    Jun'yo 288
    Shinano 290
Japanese battleships
    Yamamoto 290
Japanese fighters
    Mitsubishi A5M 'Claude'
        175
    Mitsubishi A6M Zero 178
Japanese forces 13
    2nd Sentai, 1st Koku Kentai
        178
    12th Naval Air Group 178
    Air Self-Defense Force, 8
    Hikotai 192
    Kwantung Army 18
Japanese infantry combat
    vehicles
    Type 89 105
Japanese submarines
    I-400 262

Soryu 277
Japanese surface warships
    Fuso 326
    Mikasa 317
    Yamato 335
Japanese tanks
    Type 95 Kyugo Light Tank 18
    Type 97 Chi-Ha 23
Java (cruiser) 330
Java Sea, Battle of (1942) 330
Junkers Ju 87 Stuka 207
Junkers Ju 88 208
Jun'yo 288
Jutland, battle of (1916) 320,
    323–4

K
K2 Black Panther 77
Ka-27 helicopter 303
Ka-27 'Helix' helicopter 339
Ka-28 ASW helicopters 312
Ka-31 303
Ka-31 AEW helicopter 312
Kaga 283, 284
Kamov Ka-25 'Hormone-A'
    helicopter 339
Kamov Ka-31 Helix AEW 307
Kar 98k 370
Katyusha rocket launcher 124
Kepford, Ira C. 'Ike' 182
Khalkhin Gol (1939) 17
Kiev 300
King George V, HMS 333
Kirov 339
Kirov Class 339
Korean War (1950–53)
    fighter aircraft 182, 187, 188,
        189
    logistic and specialist aircraft
        231
    surface warships 338
    tanks 41, 50
Kosovo 93, 394
Kursk Offensive (1943) 29, 51,
    210
Kursk (submarine) 271
Kuwait 100
KV-1A heavy tank 28
KV-2 28
KV-85 heavy tank 40

L
L7 A1 430
L85A2 rifle 391
L86 light support weapon
    435
L118 light gun 138
Lake Erie 342
Lancaster bombers 336
laser technology, tanks 74
LAV-25 99
Le Triomphant 270
Learoyd, P.D. 169
Lebanon 65, 241, 389
Leningrad front (WWII) 210
Leopard 1 62
Leopard 2 67
Leopard 2A1 67
Leopard 2A3 67
Leopard 2A4 67
Leopard AS1 10–11
Leroy Grumman, USNS 412
Lewis gun 419
Lexington, USS (CV-2) 282
Lexington, USS (CV-16) 287
Leyte Gulf, Battle of (1944)
    aircraft carriers 287
    fighters 184
    surface warships 326, 335
Leyte Gulf, USS 306
Liaoning 307
Libya
    armoured cars 84
    drones 245
    fighter aircraft 194, 200, 202
    ground-attack aircraft 214
    Operation *El Dorado Canyon*
        (1986) 200, 214
Littorio 334
Lockheed C-5 Galaxy 235
Lockheed C-130 Hercules 233
Lockheed F-80 Shooting Star
    187
Lockheed F-117 Nighthawk
    217
Lockheed P-38 Lightning 177
Lockheed P-38J 177
Lockheed SR-71 'Blackbird' 234
Lockheed Martin F-16 Fighting
Falcon 195
Lockheed Martin F-22 Raptor
    203
Lockheed Martin F-35
Lightning II 205

Lockheed-Martin F-35C 310
Löffler, Theodore 378
log carpet 42, 61
logistic and specialist aircraft 231–6
Los Angeles, USS 267
LT vz 38 light tank 24
Luger pistol 354
LVT-2 85
LVT-4 'Water Buffalo' 85
Lynx 239, 304, 340

M

M1 carbine 372
M1 garand 371
M1A1 Abrams 69
M1A2 Abrams 73
M1A2 SEPv2 tank 73
M2 Bradley 98
M2 Browning .50-cal 424
M3A1 'Grease Gun' 409
M3A3 General Lee 33
M3A3 Stuart 32
M4 carbine 393
M4A4 Sherman 37
M14 379
M16 381
M16A2 389, 393
M16A4 381
M21 383
M24 Chaffee 50
M26 Pershing 41
M27 IAR 398
M41 self-propelled gun 38
M41 Walker Bulldog 55
M43 105/25 38
M48 Patton 57
M50 Ontos 88
M60 (machine gun) 429
M60 Patton 59
M60A2 Patton (Starship) 59
M60E3 429
M109 howitzer 134
M109A1 howitzer 134
M110 Semi-Automatic Sniper System 399
M113 90
M120 mortar system 162
M163 Vulcan Air Defense System 150
M198 155mm howitzer 139
M198 medium howitzer 110–11

M224A1 Mortar 163
M270 MLRS 140
M551 Sheridan 63
M777 155mm howitzer 142
M1126 Stryker ICV 106
M1903 Springfield 369
M1917 14
M1919 Browning 423
M1938 120mm mortar 160
    machine guns 416–35
Madsen light machine gun 417
Maine, USS 316
Malan, Adolph 'Sailor' 176
Malayan Emergency 225
Mali, fighter aircraft 202
Malta 25, 176
Manchuria 18
Mannock, Edward 169
Marder 94
Marder III 24
Mark V Male 12
Marne, Battle of (1914) 112
Marseille, Hans-Joachim 173
Martini-Henry Rifle 366
MAS 38 405
Mauser C/96 353
Mauser M712 353
Maxim Gun/MG 08 418
Maxim, Hiram 418
Maxim Maschinengewehr 08 418
McCampbell, David 184
McCudden, James 169
McDonnell Douglas F-4 Phantom II 192
McDonnell Douglas F/A-18 Hornet 200
McFaul, USS 306
Mediterranean (WWII) 25, 209, 286
Merkava tank 66
Merlin HM.1 ASW 302
Messerschmitt Bf 109 173
Messerschmitt Bf 110 209
Messerschmitt Me 262 185
Messerschmitt Me 262B-1a/U1 185
MG 34 425
MG 42 427
Midway, Battle of (1942)
    aircraft carriers 281, 283–5
    fighters 178
    ground attack aircraft 212

Midway, USS 291
MiG 29K 303
Mikasa (battleship) 317
Mikoyan-Gurevich MiG-15 188
Mikoyan-Gurevich MiG-17 190
Mikoyan-Gurevich MiG-21 193
Mikoyan MiG-29 'Fulcrum' 198
Mikoyan MiG-29K 312
MiL Mi-24 'Hind' 238
Milius (destroyer) 299
mine-clearing tanks 45
mines 139
Mini Uzi 411
Minimi Mk Para 433
Missouri, USS 338
Mitsubishi A5M 'Claude' 175
Mitsubishi A5M4 175
Mitsubishi A6M Zero 178
Mitsubishi A6M2 178
Mitsubishi A6M5c 178
Mk III Valentine Infantry Tank 25
Mk VI Crusader I Cruiser Tank 30
Monadnock, USS 313
Mongolia 97
mortars 158–63
Mosin-Nagant M1891/30 Rifle 367
Moskva 298
MP 38/MP 40 404
MP44/StG44 374
MQ-1 Predator 242
MQ-8B Fire Scout 245
MQ-9 Reaper 244
multiple launch rocket system (MLRS) 140
Musashi (battleship) 287, 335
MV-22 Osprey 309
Mykhlik, V.I. 210

N

Nachi (cruiser) 330
Naradba, HMIS 148
Nasmith, Martin 254
Nautilus, USS (SSN571) 264
Nautilus, USS (V-6) 258
Nebelwerfer 42 127
Nefedovich, Georgii 181
Nelson, HMS 328
New Guinea 158, 161
New Zealand
    fighter aircraft 182

New Zealand forces 182, 419
Nicholas, USS 306
Nieuport 17 168
night-bombing/fighting 179, 185, 186, 208, 223, 224
Nimitz, USS 299
Normandy (1944)
    artillery 126, 148, 158
    tanks 31, 42–3, 45–7
North African campaign (WWII)
    armoured cars 84
    artillery 126, 156
    fighter aircraft 174, 176
    ground attack aircraft 209
    tanks 30, 32–3
North American B-25 Mitchell 220
North American F-86 Sabre 189
North American P-51 Mustang 180
North Korea, T-62 variant 60
North Vietnamese Army 58
Northrop B-2 Spirit 230
Northrop P-61 Black Widow 186
nuclear strike 199, 225

O

Ocean, HMS 304
Oerlikon 20mm 148
Ohio, USS 269
OICW/XM29 395
Oklahoma City, USS 267
Oklahoma, USS 281
Olds, Robin 190
Operation *Anaconda* (2002) 215
Operation *Desert Shield see* Gulf War (1991)
Operation *Desert Storm see* Gulf War (1991)
Operation *El Dorado Canyon* (1986) 200, 214
Operation *Frostbite* (1946) 291
Operation *Iraqi Freedom* (2003–)
    aircraft carriers 296, 299
    APC 93
    armoured personnel carriers 93
    artillery 110–11, 139
    bombers 225

drones 242, 244
fighters 164–5, 202
ground attack aircraft 216
helicopters 241
infantry fighting vehicles 106
logistic and specialist aircraft 236
machine guns 424
rifles 392, 393
tank hunters 103
tanks 65, 69
see also Gulf War (1991)
Operation *Jericho* (1944) 211
Operation *Lam Son* 719 (1971) 55
Operation *Prairie Fire* (1986) 200
Operation *Southern Watch* (1993) 299
Ordnance BL 60pdr 114
Ordnance ML 3in mortar 158
Ordnance QF 4.5in howitzer 116
Ordnance QF 13pdr 113
Ordnance QF 17pdr gun 156
Ordnance QF 25pdr Mk 2 126
Oscar II boats 271
OTO-Melara 105mm Mod 56 131

P
Pacific theatre (WWII)
aircraft carriers 281–5, 287–8
amphibious tractors 85
artillery 143, 158, 161
bombers 220, 224
fighter aircraft 174–5, 177–8, 182, 184, 186
ground-attack aircraft 212
rifles 372
surface warships 330, 335, 337
tanks 23, 32
Pakistani Army 57
Panavia Tornado 196
Panavia Tornado ADV 196
Pandur 100
Pandur Armoured Reconnaissance Fire Support Vehicle 100
Pandur Light Armoured Vehicle 100

Panhard EBR/FL-10 87
Panhard EBR/FL-11 87
Panhard et Levassor Type 178 80
Panther tanks 39
Panzer 38(t) 20, 24
Panzer II Ausf F 20
Panzer III Aus f 26
Panzer IV Ausf F1 8, 29
Panzer V Panther Ausf D 39
Panzer VI Tiger Ausf E 36
Panzerspähwagen P 204(f) 80
Paris Gun 120
Paris to New York, non-stop flight 206
Parrott, Enoch G. 313
Pearl Harbor 178, 263, 277, 281–2, 322
Philippine Sea, Battle of (1944) 184, 287
Pistole Parabellum P-08 354
PK machine gun 432
Poland campaign (WWII) 209
Polikarpov I-16 172
Polikarpov I-153 172
Polish Air Force 198, 238
Polish tanks
7TP Polish light tank 16
PPSh-41 407
Prince of Wales, HMS 310
Princeton, USS 184
Prinz Eugen 333
Project 705 Lira (Alfa Class) 268
PSG-1 390
PT-76 58

Q
QBZ-03 397
Queen Elizabeth, HMS 310

R
radar absorbent material (RAM) 217
RAF *see* British forces (RAF)
railway guns 119–20
Rainier (support ship) 299
Ratel 96
Red Baron 170
Reesman, Bill 190
Republic P-47 Thunderbolt 183
Repulse, HMS 327
resistance groups 406

Resolution, HMS 266
Rhine crossing 41
Richelieu 332
Richthofen, Manfred von 170
Rickenbacker, Eddie 171
rifles 364–401
rocket launchers 124, 127, 132, 140
Rodney, HMS 328, 333
Roma 334
Romanian Air Force 193
Romanian oil fields 221
Ronald R. Reagan, USS 246–7, 306
Royal Oak, HMS 259, 324, 331
RPD 428
RPK 431
RQ-4 Global Hawk 243
RS-82 air-launched rocket 124
Russian forces 58, 197
Russian Civil War (1917–22) 168
Russian-Japanese War (1905) 317, 417
Russian surface warships
Imperator Alexander II 315
see also Soviet surface warshsips
Russian tanks
T-14 Armata 78
T-90 72
see also Soviet tanks
Ryazanov, Vasily 210

S
SA80 391
Saint-Aignan-de-Cramesnil, France 46
Sakai, Saburo 178
Saladin 89
Santa Cruz Islands, Battle of (1942) 337
Saracen 89
Saudi Arabia 196
SB2C Helldivers 291
Scharnhorst 331
Schilling, David C. 183
Schneider, Walter 179
Schweinfurt factory raids (1943) 219
Scimitar 93
Sdkfz 7 144
SdKfz 232 81

SdKfz 234/2 Puma 83
SdKfz 251 82, 127
S.E.5a 169
Sea Devil, USS 263
Sea Harriers 302
Sea Hurricanes 280
Sea King ASaC Mk7 302
Sea King HC4 helicopters 297, 304
Seawolf, USS 272
Semovente DA 75/18 38
Seydlitz 324
sGrW 34 8cm Mortar 159
Shenyang J-15 fighter 307
Sherman Crab Mine-Clearing Tank 45
Sherman Firefly 156
Sherman VC Firefly 46
Shilka 151
Shinano 290
Shpagin, Georgi 407
SIG P320 363
Sino-Japanese Wars 17, 175
Six-Day War (1967) 53, 54, 56, 57, 191
Skate, USS 264
Skoda 30.5cm Howitzer 117
Smith, Paul Ray 424
SMLE 368
Soltam K6 120mm (4.7in) heavy field mortar 162
Soltam M68 135
Somalia 241
Somua S-35 21
Sonderanhänger 52 carriage 146
Sopwith Camel 167, 279, 325
Soryu 277, 283, 284
South African Air Force 176
South African infantry fighting vehicles
Ratel 96
South African rifles
Vektor R4 388
South African submachine guns
BXP 414
South Carolina, USS 321
South Dakota, USS 337
South Korean tanks
K2 Black Panther 77
Soviet aircraft carriers
Admiral Kuznetsov 303
Kiev 300

Moskva 298
Soviet anti-aircraft artillery
  ZSU-23-4 151
Soviet anti-armour guns
  76.2mm Divisional Gun M1942 (ZiS-3) 157
Soviet armoured personnel carriers
  BTR-60PA 91
  BTR-70 97
  BTR-80 101
  BTR-90 107
Soviet artillery
  2S19 Msta 141
  2S3 136
  122mm Howitzer D-30 133
  122mm Howitzer M1938 (M-30) 125
  152mm Howitzer M1943 (D-1) 129
  BM-21 Rocket Launcher 132
  Katyusha Rocket Launcher 124
Soviet bombers
  Tupolev Tu-22M 229
  Tupolev Tu-95 228
Soviet fighters
  Mikoyan-Gurevich MiG-15 188
  Mikoyan-Gurevich MiG-17 190
  Mikoyan-Gurevich MiG-21 193
  Mikoyan MiG-29 'Fulcrum' 198
  Polikarpov I-16 172
  Sukhoi Su-27 'Flanker' 197
  Yakovlev Yak-1/3/7/9 181
Soviet/Russian forces
  1st Attack Aviation Corps 210
  1st Guards IAP 172
  4th Air Army 197
  29th IAP 172
  130th Fighter Aviation Division 181
  277th Attack Aviation Division 210
  303rd Fighter Aviation Division 181
  840th Heavy Bomber Aviation Regiment 229
  924th Naval Missile Carrier Regiment 229

Soviet ground-attack aircraft
  Ilyushin Il-2 Shturmovik 210
Soviet helicopters
  MiL Mi-24 'Hind' 238
Soviet infantry fighting vehicles
  BMP-1 92
  BMP-3 104
Soviet machine guns
  PK machine gun 432
  RPD 428
  RPK 431
Soviet mortars
  M1938 120mm Mortar 160
Soviet rifles
  AN-94 401
  AK-12 401
  AK-47/AKM 375
  AK-74 385
  AK-101 & AK-103 396
  Mosin-Nagant M1891/30 Rifle 367
  SVD Dragunov 382
Soviet submachine guns
  PPSh-41 407
Soviet submarines
  Kursk (submarine) 271
  Project 705 Lira (Alfa Class) 268
Soviet surface warships
  Kirov Class 339
  Sovremennyy Class 341
Soviet tanks
  BT-5 17, 18
  IS-3 52
  KV-1A Heavy Tank 28
  KV-85 Heavy Tank 40
  PT-76 58
  T-26 16
  T-34/76 Model 1943 35
  T-34/85 51
  T-35 19
  T-54/55 54
  T-62 60
  T-64 60
  T-70 34
  T-72 65
Sovremennyy Class 341
SPAD XIII 171
Spanish-American War (1897) 316
Spanish Civil War (1936–39) 17, 20
Spanish forces 131

Spanish machine guns
  CETME Ameli 434
Spanish rifles
  CETME Model 58 378
Staghounds 86
Stahl, Peter 208
Stalingrad 160, 181, 404
Sten Mk 2 406
Sterling L2A1 410
Steyr AUG 386
Stingray 70
Stridsvagn 103B 64
Stryker 106
Studebaker trucks 124
StuG M42 38
Sturgeon Classs 265
Sturmgeschütz III 27
Sturmmörser Tiger 44
Sturmpanzerwagen A7V 15
SU-76 self-propelled gun. 34
SU-130 assault gun 60
submachine guns 402–15
submarines 248–78
Suez Crisis (1956) 56, 188, 225
Sukhoi Su-27 'Flanker' 197
Sukhoi Su-27K 303
Sukhoi Su-33 303
Super Etendard 295
Supermarine Spitfire 176
Supply, USNS 296, 306
Surcouf 257
surface warships 313–47
SVD Dragunov 382
Swedish all-terrain armoured vehicles
  BVS 10 Viking 108

Swedish anti-aircraft artillery
  40mm Bofors L/60 143
Swedish surface warships
  Visby 345
Swedish tanks
  Stridsvagn 103B 64
Sweeney, Brig Gen Thomas 249
Syria 65, 203, 303
  see also Yom Kippur War

T
T-14 Armata 78
T-26 16
T-34/76 Model 1943 35
T-34/85 51

T-35 19
T-54/55 54
T-62 60
T-64 tank 60
T-70 34
T-72 65
T-84 Oplot-M tank 70
T-90 34, 72
T17E1 Staghound Mk III 86
Talisman Saber 2005 exercise 10–11
Tamotsu, Lieutenant 175
Tarawa, USS 301
Taylor, USS 296
Tench, USS 263
Texas, USS 325
Thach (frigate) 299
Thai Army 70
Thompson, John T. 403
Thompson M1928 403
Ticonderoga Class 342
Tiger II 'King Tiger' 48
Tiger tank 36, 44, 48, 49
Tirpitz 336
Tokyo, bombing of 224
Trident, HMS 270
Tsushima, Battle of (1905) 317
Tupolev Tu-22M 229
Tupolev Tu-95 228
Type 22 340
Type 23 Frigate 343
Type 039 (Song) 273
Type 45 Destroyer 346
Type 56 rifle 375
Type 69 tank 60
Type 85 MBT 74
Type 89 105
Type 094 (Jin Class) 276
Type 95 Kyugo Light Tank 18
Type 97 Chi-Ha 23
Type 97 Shi-Ki 23
Type 97 Shinhoto Chi-Ha 23
Type 99 74
Type XXI 261

U
U-boats *see* German submarines
U-9 253
U-47 (Type VIIB) 259, 331
U-459 (Type XIV) 260
UAVs 242–5

UC-25 256
UC-74 256
UH-1 Iroquois 237
UH-60A Black Hawk 241, 304
unmanned aerial vehicles (UAVs) 242–5
US aircraft carriers
  Enterprise, USS (CV-6) 285
  Enterprise, USS (CVN-65) 296
  Forrestal, USS 293
  Gerald R. Ford, USS 311
  Intrepid, USS 289
  Lexington, USS (CV-2) 282
  Lexington, USS (CV-16) 287
  Midway, USS 291
  Nimitz, USS 299
  Ronald R. Reagan, USS 246–7, 306
  Tarawa, USS 301
  Yorktown, USS (CV-5) 284
US amphibious tractors
  LVT-4 'Water Buffalo' 85
US amphibious transport vehicles
  AAV-7 95
US anti-aircraft artillery
  90mm Gun M2 149
M163 Vulcan Air Defense System 150
US anti-armour guns
  3in Gun M5 155
US armoured cars
  T17E1 Staghound I 86
US armoured personnel carriers
  M113 90
US artillery
  105mm howitzer M2A1 128
  105mm howitzer M3 130
  M109 howitzer 134
  M109A1 howitzer 134
  M198 155mm howitzer 139
  M270 MLRS 140
  M777 155mm howitzer 142
US bombers
  B-24 Liberator 221
  Boeing B-17 Flying Fortress 219
  Boeing B-29 Superfortress 224
  Boeing B-52 Stratofortress 226

North American B-25 Mitchell 220
Northrop B-2 Spirit 230
US Civil War 248, 249, 313
US drones
  MQ-1 Predator 242
  MQ-8B Fire Scout 245
  MQ-9 Reaper 244
  RQ-4 Global Hawk 243
US fighter planes
  Boeing F-15E Strike Eagle 201
  Grumman F-14 Tomcat 194
  Grumman F6F Hellcat 184
  Lockheed F-80 Shooting Star 187
  Lockheed P-38 Lightning 177
  Lockheed Martin F-16 Fighting Falcon 195
  Lockheed Martin F-22 Raptor 203
  Lockheed Martin F-35 Lightning II 205
  McDonnell Douglas F-4 Phantom II 192
  McDonnell Douglas F/A-18 Hornet 200
  North American F-86 Sabre 189
  North American P-51 Mustang 180
  Northrop P-61 Black Widow 186
  Republic P-47 Thunderbolt 183
  Vought F4U Corsair 182
US forces
  1st Fighter Wing 203
  1st Marine Air Wing 212
  1st Marine Division 375
  3rd Armored Cavalry Regiment 9, 240
  3rd Law Enforcement Battalion 97
  3rd Marine Regiment 387, 398
  4th Fighter Wing 201
  5th Bomb Wing 226
  9th Strategic Reconnaissance Wing 234
  10th Mountain Division 240
  12th Marine Regiment 110–11

13th Bomb Squadron 230
14th Marines 139
17th Bombardment Group 220
18th Air Force/Air Forces Transportation 235
23rd Bomb Squadron 226
25th Fighter Interceptor Squadron 189
25th Infantry Division 162
26th Marine Expeditionary Unit 163
27th Fighter Squadron 203
35th Fighter-Bomber Squadron 187
36th Fighter-Bomber Squadron 187
37th Tactical Fighter Wing 217
51st Fighter Interceptor Wing 187
55th Fighter Squadron 177
56th Fighter Group 183
91st Bombardment Group 219
94th Aero Squadron 171
100th Infantry Battalion 161
103rd Aero Squadron 171
101st Airborne Division 155, 392
158th Aviation Regiment 240
227th Aviation Regiment 241
320th Air Expeditionary Wing 233
345th Bombardment Group (Medium) 220
354th Tactical Fighter Wing (Provisional) 215
357th Fighter Group 180
357th Fighter Squadron 180
361st Fighter Group 180
362nd Fighter Squadron 180
376th Bombardment Group 221
393rd Bomb Squadron 'Tigers' 230
394th Combat Training Squadron, 230
436th Military Airlift Wing 235
445th Airlift Wing 235
499th Bomb Squadron 220

509th Bomb Wing 230
520th Fighter Interceptor Squadron 189
527th Fighter Squadron 183
548th Night Fighter Squadron 186
706th Tactical Fighter Squadron 215
881st Bombardment Group 219
Marine Fighter Attack Squadron (VMFA) 314 200
Marine Medium Helicopter Squadron 166 (Reinforced) 301
Task Force 58 184
VC-3 182
VF-27 184
VF-84 184
US ground-attack aircraft
  AV-8B Harrier II 216
  Douglas SBD Dauntless 212
  Fairchild A-10 Thunderbolt II 215
  General Dynamics F-111 214
  Lockheed F-117 Nighthawk 217
US handguns
  Colt Detective Special 357
  Colt M1851 Navy & 1860 Army 351
  Colt M1911 355
US helicopters
  AH-64 Apache 240
  UH-1 Iroquois 237
  UH-60A Black Hawk 241
US infantry fighting vehicles
  IAV Stryker 106
  M2 Bradley 98
US logistic and specialist aircraft
  Consolidated PBY Catalina 232
  Douglas C-47 Skytrain 231
  E-3 Sentry 236
  Lockheed C-5 Galaxy 235
  Lockheed C-130 Hercules 233
  Lockheed SR-71 'Blackbird' 234
US machine guns
  BAR 422
  Lewis gun 419

M2 Browning .50-cal 424
M60 429
M1919 Browning 423
US mortars
60mm Mortar M2 161
M120 Mortar System 162
M224A1 Mortar 163
US rifles
Barrett M82A1 392
M1 carbine 372
M1 garand 371
M4 carbine 393
M14 379
M16 381
M16A2 389
M27 IAR 398
M110 Semi-Automatic
Sniper System 399
M1903 Springfield 369
OICW/XM29 395
US submachine guns
Calico M950 415
M3A1 'Grease Gun' 409
Thompson M1928 403
US submarines
Holland, USS 251
Hunley, CSS 248
Intelligent Whale 249
Los Angeles, USS 267
Nautilus, USS (SSN 571) 264
Nautilus, USS (V-6) 258
Ohio, USS 269
Seawolf, USS 272
Sturgeon Class 265
Tench, USS 263
Virginia, USS 274
US surface warships
Arleigh Burke Destroyer 344
DDX (Zumwalt Class) 347
Indiana, USS 337
Iowa, USS 338
Maine, USS 316
Monadnock, USS 313
South Carolina, USS 321
Texas, USS 325
Ticonderoga Class 342
Utah, USS 322
US tank destroyers
M50 Ontos 88
US tanks
M1A1 Abrams 69

M1A2 Abrams 73
M3A3 General Lee 33
M3A3 Stuart 32
M4A4 Sherman 37
M24 Chaffee 50
M26 Pershing 41
M41 Walker Bulldog 55
M48 Patton 57
M60 Patton 59
M551 Sheridan 63
M1917 14
Sherman Crab Mine-
Clearing Tank 45
Stingray 70
Utah, USS 322
Uzi 411

V
Valentine tanks 25
Valley Forge (cruiser) 299
Vektor R4 388
Venezuelan Army 396
Verdun, France 112, 168
Vickers 6-ton Light Tank 16
Vickers machine gun 420
Vietnam War (1955–75)
aircraft carriers 293
anti-aircraft artillery 150, 151
fighter aircraft 190
ground-attack aircraft 214
helicopters 237
logistic and specialist aircraft 233
rifles 381
submachine guns 409
tank destroyers 88
tanks 54, 55, 57, 58
Vikrant, INS 312
Villers-Bocage, France 36
Viraat, INS 294
Virginia, USS 274
Visby 345
Vittorio Emanuele 319
Vittorio Veneto 334
Vorgrimler, Ludwig 378
Vought F4U Corsair 182
Vought Multiple Launch Rocket
System 140
VT-4 tank 70
Vulcan Air Defense System
(VADS) 150

W
WAH-64 Apache 304
Walther P38 359
Warrior 102
Webley Mk V & Mk VI 356
Weddigen, Otto 253
West German artillery
FH-70 155mm Howitzer 137
West German fighters
Panavia Tornado 196
West German infantry fighting
vehicles
Marder 94
West German tanks
Leopard 2 67
West Virginia, USS 281
Westland Merlin HM2 343
Westland Sea King ASW
helicopters 294
Westland Walrus 279
Whippet 13
Whisner, William 189
Wilde Sau (Wild Boar) tactics 179
Willys MB Jeep 124, 160
Wittman, Michael 36, 46
World War I
aircraft carriers 279
armoured cars 79
artillery 112–20
bombers 218
field guns 112–15
fighter aircraft 166–71
handguns 354, 356
howitzers 116–17
machine guns 418–21
rifles 367–70
submarines 252–6
surface warships 319–25
tanks 12–15
World War II
aircraft carriers 279–89
anti-aircraft artillery 143–9
anti-armour guns 153–7
armoured cars 80–6
artillery 118, 121–30
bombers 219–24
fighter aircraft 172–86
ground-attack aircraft 207–13
handguns 354, 358–9
logistic and specialist aircraft 231–2

machine guns 418, 421–2, 425–7
mortars 158–61
rifles 367, 369–74
submachine guns 402, 404–9
submarines 259–63
surface warships 324–38
tanks 16–52
Wurfgranate 41 127
Wurfkörper 42 127

Y
Yakovlev Yak-1/3/7/9 181
Yakovlev Yak-41M 303
Yakovlev Yak-43 303
Yamamoto 290
Yamato 335
Yaremchoock, A.M. 367
Yom Kippur War (1973) 53, 54, 151
Yorktown, USS (CV-5) 284, 285
Ypres, Belgium 119

Z
Zemke, Hubert 183
Zeros 178
ZSU-23-4 151
Zuiho (light carrier) 287, 288
Zuikaku (carrier) 287
Zumwalt Class 347

Picture Credits

Alamy: 129 top (Interfoto), 141 top (eFesenko), 141 bottom (Alexey Zarubin), 250 bottom (Print Collector/Art Media), 271 (ITAR-TASS News Agency), 288 (PJF Military Collection), 307 top (Zeng Tao/Xinhua), 350 bottom (Interfoto), 352 both (Interfoto), 356 (Adam Greenslade), 361 bottom (Sunpix), 362 top (D Callcut), 363 top (dpa picture alliance), 363 bottom (Bob Daemmrich), 364 top (Artokoloro Quint Lox), 364 bottom (Bildagentur-online), 365 top (Antiqua Print Gallery), 366 top (Military Images), 395 top & bottom (PJF Military Collection), 405 top & bottom (UtCon Collection), 408 (Historic Collection), 413 (David Cole), 417 (Historic Collection), 431 top (Military Images), 431 bottom (PJF Military Collection)

Amber Books/Art-Tech: 8, 13 top, 14, 15, 17-22 all, 25, 26, 27, 29, 36, 39-42 all, 45, 47, 49, 55, 57, 64, 67, 68, 71, 79, 80 top, 81, 82, 83, 86, 91, 94, 112 top, 114 bottom, 121, 127, 128 top, 132 both, 133 top, 135 both, 137 top, 138, 143, 145 top, 146, 148 bottom, 149 both, 150, 152, 155 bottom, 166, 167, 168, 170, 172-186 all, 190, 207-213 all, 218-225 all, 228, 229, 231, 232, 250 top, 251, 252 top, 257, 264 both, 265, 266 bottom, 279, 281, 283, 286, 290, 292, 295 bottom, 298 both, 300, 328 top, 332 top, 333-335 all, 339 both, 340 top, 342 bottom, 343 top, 354, 359, 360, 361 top, 365 bottom, 366 bottom, 371, 377, 378 bottom, 381, 382 top, 385, 403, 404, 405 centre, 410, 416, 418, 419, 420, 422, 426

BAE Systems: 275 both, 346 top

Cody Images: 13 bottom, 16, 23, 30, 32, 33, 38, 43, 46, 50, 53, 56, 58, 61, 65, 66, 75, 80 bottom, 84, 85, 89, 93,102, 113, 114 top, 115-120 all, 122 top, 123 both , 126 top, 128 bottom, 136, 145 bottom, 147, 148 top, 153 top, 154 both, 155 top, 156, 157 bottom, 158 both, 159 both, 161 both, 248, 252 bottom, 253-256 all, 259-262 all, 266 top, 268 top, 270 bottom, 273 both, 278, 280, 282, 284, 285, 287 bottom, 289, 291, 293, 294, 295 top, 302, 313, 320 bottom, 321, 323 bottom, 324 both, 328-331 all, 332 bottom, 336, 337 bottom, 341 top, 343 bottom, 346 bottom, 368, 370, 373, 374 top, 384, 387 top, 390 both, 402, 409, 411, 414-415 all, 421, 423, 425, 427, 428 top, 433, 434, 435 both

Dassault: 199, 202

Defenceimagery.mod.uk: 109 (Cpl Andy Benson), 376 top (Owen Cooban), 376 bottom

Dreamstime: 70 top (Jukgrit Chaiwised), 129 bottom (Aleks49), 169 (I41coc12), 188 (Gary Blakeley), 305 (Drew Rawcliffe), 308 both (Colin Moore)

Mary Evans Picture Library: 317, 374 bottom (Sueddeutsche Zeitung)

Getty Images: 74 (AFP/Greg Baker), 76 top (AFP/Raveendran), 76 bottom (Hindustan Times), 77 (AFP/Jung Yeon-Je), 206 (Gamma-Keystone), 307 bottom (Visual China Group), 309 both (The Asahi Shimbun), 312 both (AFP/Manjunath Kiran), 396 (AFP/Juan Barreto)

Heckler & Koch: 395 centre

Huntington Ingalls: 311 both

Icollector.com: 357 top

Kockums: 345

Vitaly Kuzmin: 78, 107 top, 401

Library of Congress: 249, 316, 318, 320 top, 351, 369, 372

MONUSCO: 388 (Sylvain Liechti – CC BY-SA 2.0)

Photos.com: 356 top

Rock Island Auction: 357 bottom

Royal Navy: 310

Narayan Sengupta: 52

Shutterstock: 72 (Meoita)

Ukrainian State Archive: 24, 28, 34, 35, 51, 124, 125 both, 157 top, 160, 367, 407

U.S. Air National Guard: 107 bottom (Master Sgt. Andrew J. Moseley)

U.S. Army: 97 (Sgt. David Bedard), 100 top (Pfc. Caleb Foreman), 101 top (Sgt. 1st Class Walter E. van Ochten), 101 bottom (Sgt. Alexander Skripnichuk), 382 bottom (Jacob Kohrs)

U.S. Department of Defense: 9 both, 10/11, 37, 44, 54, 60, 63, 69, 73, 88, 90, 92, 95, 98, 99, 100 bottom, 103, 106 both, 110/111, 112 bottom, 130, 131, 133 bottom, 134, 137 bottom, 139 both, 140, 142 both, 151, 162-165 all, 171, 191, 196, 198, 200, 201, 203, 205, 214, 215, 217, 226, 227, 231, 233-247 all, 267, 268 bottom, 269, 272, 274 both, 287 top, 296 both, 297, 299, 301 both, 303, 304, 306, 338, 340 bottom, 341 bottom, 344 both, 347, 348/349, 355, 362 bottom, 375, 378 top, 379, 380, 383, 386, 387 bottom, 391-394 all, 399, 400, 406, 412, 424, 428 bottom, 429, 430, 432

U.S. Marine Corps: 108 (Sgt. Olivia G. Ortiz), 270 top (Sgt. David Bedard), 389 (Lance Cpl. Antonio J. Vega), 398 top (Lance Cpl. Levi Schultz), 398 bottom (Sgt. Anthony L. Ortiz)

U.S. Navy: 258 both, 263

All artworks are courtesy of Amber Books/Art-Tech except for those listed below:

BAE Systems: 275, 346

John Batchelor: 272

DBO Design: 74 bottom, 76, 77

Huntington Ingalls: 311

Kockums: 345

Military Visualizations Inc: 203-205 all, 300 both, 305-306 all, 347 all

Oliver Missing: 34-35 all